*Penguin Masterstudies*



# Biology

Clare Duggan was educated at St Joseph's College in Bradford. She went on to obtain an honours degree in microbiology from Imperial College and a Post-Graduate Certificate in Education from Chelsea College, University of London. After teaching in various tutorial colleges in London, she now produces science programmes for television.

Lesley Falconer was educated at Loreto College Grammar School in St Albans, Hertfordshire, and obtained a first-class honours degree in microbiology from Chelsea College, University of London. She carried out post-doctoral research into the microbiological degradation of cellulose at Queen Mary College, University of London, where she also held the post of temporary lecturer in microbiology for one year. She is at present Head of Science at Lansdowne Independent Sixth Form College, where she also teaches A-level biology. She has been teaching this subject for seven years.

Paul Haddlesey was educated at Bedford College, University of London, and received his Post-Graduate Certificate of Education from the Institute of Education at London University. He now teaches in a comprehensive school in north London.

*Penguin Masterstudies*
Advisory Editor: Stephen Coote

# Biology

**Clare Duggan and Lesley Falconer**
**with Paul Haddlesey**

Penguin Books

from Maria
Christmas 1989.

PENGUIN BOOKS

Published by the Penguin Group
27 Wrights Lane, London W8 5TZ, England
Viking Penguin Inc., 40 West 23rd Street, New York, New York 10010, USA
Penguin Books Australia Ltd, Ringwood, Victoria, Australia
Penguin Books Canada Ltd, 2801 John Street, Markham, Ontario, Canada L3R 1B4
Penguin Books (NZ) Ltd, 182–190 Wairau Road, Auckland 10, New Zealand

Penguin Books Ltd, Registered Offices: Harmondsworth, Middlesex, England

First published 1988



Made and printed in Great Britain by
Richard Clay Ltd, Bungay, Suffolk

Filmset in Monophoto Times

# Contents

# Introduction

## *Using this book*

This book contains the basic factual information required for the majority of A-level examination boards. It is in no way intended to take the place of a textbook. It is designed to be used as a supplement to the student's own notes, textbooks and general background reading.

At the end of each major section within the chapters there are subject-related questions selected from different examination boards. Rather than supplying direct answers, guidelines are given as to how to approach the questions and where to find the relevant information in the text. Students are reminded that there is no benefit to be gained from reading the questions *before* the information in the preceding chapter has been studied.

The biology syllabus at A-level encompasses an increasingly wide range of subject matter. In order to answer questions to a high standard, further information should be sought from textbooks such as those listed at the end of each chapter under 'Further reading'.

## *Assumed mathematical and physical knowledge*

Students are expected to have an understanding of the following subjects in order to cope with the A-level biology examination:

- mean, mode and median
- fractions and decimals
- ratios and proportions
- reciprocals
- percentages
- preparation of simple graphs using linear and logarithmic scales
- use of simple algebraic expressions, including substitution
- histograms, frequency diagrams and normal distribution curves
- standard deviation
- the electromagnetic spectrum
- laws of thermodynamics, activation energy, chemical bond energy and potential energy
- the colloidal state

- ions, molecules, acids, pH and buffers
- isotopes
- oxidation and reduction; electron and hydrogen transfer
- hydrolysis and condensation.

## *Differences between O- or GCSE and A-level study*

At A-level, students are expected to work more independently than they did at O-level or GCSE. Although a teacher will usually discuss the relevant points of a topic in the lesson, students will be expected to read around the topic at home. In order to write good essays it will often be essential to look up extra information and examples in addition to those given in the lesson.

The emphasis at A-level is on the understanding and application of knowledge rather than the recall of factual information. Students are expected to take more responsibility for their own understanding of the work, checking unclear points or facts for themselves.

Examination questions will not necessarily ask for information to be presented in the way it is found in a student's notes. It is important for students to write essay plans for a wide variety of questions on all parts of the syllabus. Essays on a particular topic will often vary in the general approach required or may require emphasis on different points.

## *Hints for successful A-level study*

### *Storage of notes*

The volume of notes taken at A-level will seem enormous compared with those at O-level or GCSE. It is therefore vitally important to keep them neatly in order. Ring-binders are probably the best type of file (much better than the envelope-type folders, in which notes easily become disorganized). It is worth getting into the habit of putting notes in order every evening. Failure to do so for even a couple of days may lead to confusion.

### *Taking notes*

The ability to take good, clear notes is a definite advantage in A-level study. It is an art worth mastering, since good notes are the key to efficient revision. No amount of revision from doodle-covered, badly written scraps of paper ever leads to good examination results. The following points may help.

(a) You should make yourself familiar with the basic outline of the lesson. It is often useful to read the relevant O-level notes for a topic the night before. This will give a good foundation on which to build the A-level lesson.
(b) Give your notes perspective by using a consistent style for main headings and subheadings and by underlining important words.
(c) When taking notes it is advisable to use abbreviations for unusually long words. This will enable you to get down all the relevant information. It is far better to get all the information down in an abbreviated form than to miss out important facts. In the actual examination, however, such abbreviations should not be used, although the use of chemical symbols is permitted if their meaning is explained on the first instance of use, e.g. carbon dioxide ($CO_2$). The rules for use of abbreviations vary with different examination boards, so it is advisable to check with your teacher first.
(d) It is always a good idea to highlight important facts or points in the syllabus using an asterisk (*) or other symbol. These may be points emphasized by the teacher which are likely to crop up in examinations. You can then easily find these points and ensure that you understand them fully.
(e) You should always make a note of any points which you have missed from lessons or points which require extra research, and add them as soon as possible. Failure to do so may leave vital gaps in the notes used for revision.
(f) It is important to go over the day's notes each evening with a textbook. This will enable you to fill in extra information and look up any points about which you were unclear.

### *Understanding the work*

One of the biggest mistakes made by students is to ignore points which they do not understand. It is vitally important to sort out any areas with which you have difficulty. This can be done by consulting the teacher at a convenient moment or by checking in a textbook. Since it is always likely that other members of the class will be unclear on these points also, students should not be reticent about asking questions. Sorting out problems early on will help you to understand subsequent work. The most difficult parts of the syllabus are always likely to be present in examinations, so putting in the effort to sort out such problems is likely to be worth while in the long run.

### *Being equipped*

Always have plenty of paper and writing materials at hand. Students who spend the crucial first ten minutes of a lesson looking for a pen, or who try to get the whole lesson's notes on to the back of a paper bag will never catch up with the workload.

### *Being awake*

A-level study is supposed to test mental ability. You should therefore ensure that your mental faculties are working efficiently by getting enough sleep.

## ***Preparing for examinations***

### *When and where to start*

It is very easy to spend weeks wondering where to begin to revise but to do nothing about it until it is too late. The best way for students to revise is to go through the day's lessons each evening while the material is still fresh in the mind. This will give a good grounding on which to build future revision.

### *Making a timetable*

It is a good idea to draw up a timetable, planning the subjects which are still to be revised in the time remaining. Sticking to the timetable is quite important, as it is very tempting to spend too long on one subject at the expense of other equally important ones. Most A-level biology examinations have at least one paper which covers the whole syllabus, so a basic understanding of each topic is essential.

### *Timing*

It is better to allocate a specific time to each subject than to open a huge file and attempt to wade through it all day. You can also make use of time which is normally wasted, e.g. while you are standing at a bus stop or walking down the road you can practise recalling information. Beware of wasting time by discussing how little you know with your friends – you could all put the time to good use!

### *Where to revise*

It is important to choose a place which is comfortable and practical and free from distraction. At home you may have to ask younger brothers and sisters to lower the noise level. If it is hard to work at home it may be worth going to the local library. If nothing is 'going in', and motivation is at an all-time low, it may be worth going for a refreshing walk and recalling information on the way rather than sitting at a desk staring blankly into space.

### *Length of time to revise*

Most people cannot concentrate and revise for longer than about an hour. After this nothing more will 'go in'. It is better to revise for periods of one hour and take short breaks between each period, than to try and stick it out for three or four hours.

### *Self-testing*

It is often useful to try to write down what has been learned. Simply reading a topic over and over does not guarantee that it has been learned properly. A good method of testing yourself is to write out all the major headings and subheadings for a topic and then fill in the main points for each heading without looking at the notes. For example, for part of Chapter 1 you might note:

CELLULAR ORGANIZATION
  Introduction
  Cell theory
  Cell structure
  – membranes (i) membrane composition
                       (ii) membrane structure
  – nucleus
  – mitochondria
  – endoplasmic reticulum
  – Golgi body
  – lysosome
  – centrioles
  – cilia and flagella
  – microvilli
  – microtubules

– cell wall
– chloroplast
Differences between plant and animal cells
Prokaryotic cells
Differentiation
Microscopy
– introduction
– optical (light microscope)
– phase contrast microscope
– fluorescent microscope
– dark ground microscope
– electron microscope
– comparison between optical and electron microscopes

You could do this for each chapter or topic to use as a reference test. After revising each topic it is essential to attempt all the questions provided on that topic and sort out any problems encountered.

### *Beware the excuses*

It is so easy to put off doing revision. Students are notorious for convincing themselves that it is more important to do something else, such as watching just one more programme on television or reading just one more magazine, before starting revision. The best thing to do in this situation is to make a plan of work for the day; one which is realistic and attainable. Never set unrealistic goals such as 'revise a whole year's work in one afternoon'. By attempting too much there will never be a sense of achievement. It is much better to get through a smaller amount of work thoroughly each day than to attempt a mountain of impossible tasks. Working in this planned way, you should feel confident about your progress, and this in turn should generate enthusiasm and improve revision skills.

## ***Taking the examination***

There are many clever people who are hopeless at taking exams. This is not because they are lacking in intelligence but simply because they have never mastered exam techniques. By following a few simple rules your chance of doing well in an exam can be greatly improved.

### *Adequate preparation*

You should familiarize yourself with the exam format – i.e. how many papers there are, what types of question are on each paper, and how many questions are to be answered. It is also a good idea to work out the time allocated to each question beforehand.

### *Timing*

It is inadvisable to spend longer than the allocated time on a question. A common mistake is for students to spend too long on one question, leaving insufficient time to finish the others. It is worth remembering that however much time is spent on one question, no more marks can be obtained than those allocated to it. The first 75 per cent of the marks for a question are fairly easy to obtain, while the remaining 25 per cent are more difficult to earn. It is therefore better to attempt the required number of questions, giving all the basic facts, than to try to write a perfect essay at the expense of missing out one question completely. In an exam where candidates are expected to answer four questions, 25 per cent of the marks will be given to each question. Missing one out therefore reduces the mark to 75 per cent before the paper has even been assessed, while missing out two whole questions means an initial reduction to 50 per cent. Correct timing is therefore crucial in exams. To ensure getting it right, it is useful to make a quick timetable for the exam, writing down the times allocated to each question and making an estimate of the time at which each new question should be started.

## ***Types of examination questions***

Different examination boards' questions tend to have slightly different formats. The main types of question are outlined below.

### *Multiple choice questions*

Multiple choice questions usually cover the whole syllabus. A few basic rules for answering them are listed below.

1. APPORTIONING TIME: You should never spend too long on one question. If a question is proving too difficult it is advisable to have an intelligent guess at the answer and come back to it later. Spending

too long on one question uses up valuable time needed to answer the other questions.

2. NEVER LEAVE AN ANSWER BLANK: Marks are only obtained for correct answers, they are not knocked off for those which are incorrect. If there are five alternatives in the question there will be a one in five chance of getting the answer correct from a totally random guess. It is therefore always worth a try.
3. THINK OF THE ANSWER FIRST: A good way of approaching multiple choice questions is to read the question and think of the answer before reading the choices. The correct answer can then be selected. This method saves time and often avoids the confusion of many similar answers. For example:
   In which organ is urea produced?
   Think of the answer 'liver'.
   (a) urine
   (b) liver
   (c) ureter
   (d) uterus
   (e) kidney
   This question illustrates the importance of selecting between apparently similar answers. Urea is found in the kidneys, ureters and urine but it is *produced* in the liver.
4. UNDERLINE IMPORTANT WORDS: Although speed is essential, it is more important to study the questions carefully in an unrushed manner. A key word in a question can alter its whole meaning. For instance:
   Bile is STORED in the . . .
   Bile is PRODUCED in the . . .
   Bile is SECRETED into the . . .
   (a) gall bladder
   (b) liver
   (c) pancreas
   (d) stomach
   (e) duodenum
   Bile is produced in the liver, stored in the gall bladder and secreted into the duodenum. Since the other alternatives are also structures concerned with digestion students could easily be confused unless they think carefully.
5. MAKING AN INTELLIGENT GUESS: An apparently difficult question can often be answered correctly using a process of elimination. To do this, answers which are unlikely to be correct are crossed

out, thus cutting down the range of possible choices. For example: Which is likely to be the correct sequence of events in the reproductive cycle of a newly discovered flowering plant?

(a) pollination
(b) development of the ovum
(c) development of the pollen grains
(d) differentiation of the zygote
(e) fertilization

(i) b c a e d
(ii) b c d e a
(iii) c e b a d
(iv) a e c b d

Suppose you are unsure whether b (development of the ovum) or c (development of the pollen grains) comes first. The correct answer can still be worked out by the process of elimination. Clearly the last letter in the series must be d (differentiation of the zygote), therefore only (i), (iii) or (iv) can be correct. The event occurring before d must be e (fertilization) therefore the correct answer is (i).

6. DON'T PANIC AT THE SIGHT OF UNFAMILIAR WORDS: You should never think a question is impossible simply because it contains names or words which you have not previously encountered. For example: *Branchiostoma virginiae* is a fish-like animal, commonly called amphioxus. It is a chordate, found in sea waters off the Florida coast. Which one of the following features will it definitely possess at some stage in its life cycle?

(a) a pair of jointed legs
(b) hard exoskeleton
(c) notochord
(d) cranium
(e) cartilaginous skeleton

The important fact is that the animal is a chordate and the only feature listed which all chordates have at some stage is the notochord (see p. 481). Although the animal may have some of the other features, the notochord is the only feature that it would definitely have, given the above information. It is therefore not essential to have encountered the name of the animal previously in order to answer the question correctly.

## *Structured questions*

Most examination boards include some type of structured question. This type of question is often designed to test the student's ability to interpret experimental data, work out simple problems and make logical deductions. As with all examination questions, it is important to read the question carefully – three or four times, if necessary – since a precise understanding of its meaning is essential if it is to be answered correctly and concisely. Usually a set number of lines are given on which to write the answer. Since the space allowed for answering the question is limited, it is important to answer fully and concisely in the space given. This means thinking carefully of how the answer is to be written before actually attempting it. Most questions only allow enough time and space to answer a question with the relevant facts, no marks are given for irrelevant information. A couple of minutes spent studying what the question actually requires is generally worth while.

Students should be familiar with the words used for examination instructions. Below are a number of instructive words frequently found in examination questions.

### 'Draw a diagram . . .'

Students should take note of the following guidelines:

- use a sharp pencil
- clear, thin lines must be used, with shading or colouring kept to a minimum
- labelling lines should be straight and should point clearly at the structure in question. Lines must never be crossed or arrowed
- all important features should be fully labelled
- a full title should be given, including details of the view or section being illustrated (e.g. transverse section (TS) or dorsal surface)

Annotated diagrams are diagrams which contain short explanations relating to the structure or function of the structure being illustrated. For example:

**Question:** Draw an annotated diagram of a TS of a young stem to show the function of the various parts.
**Answer:** TS of young stem of *Ranunculus*

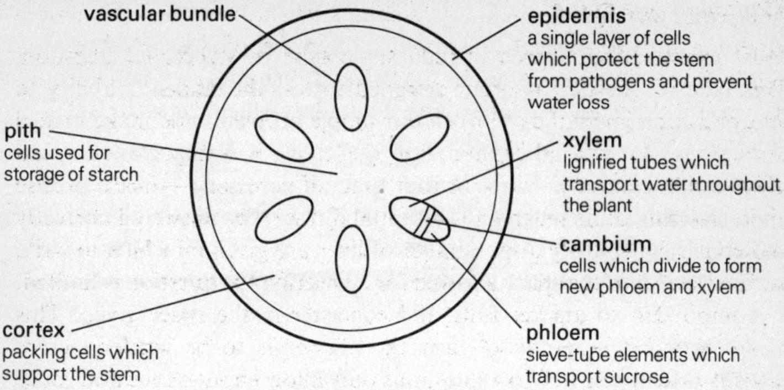
vascular bundle
epidermis
a single layer of cells which protect the stem from pathogens and prevent water loss
pith
cells used for storage of starch
xylem
lignified tubes which transport water throughout the plant
cambium
cells which divide to form new phloem and xylem
cortex
packing cells which support the stem
phloem
sieve-tube elements which transport sucrose

'List . . .'

A question which requires the candidate to list a number of items requires only that – a list with no other information. For example:

**Question:** List the five main features of insects.

**Answer:** One or two pairs of wings
Three pairs of jointed legs
Head, thorax and abdomen
Antennae
Tracheae

'Give the differences . . .'

A question which asks for the differences between two things can be answered either in prose or in the form of a table. It is often clearer and more concise to give a tabular answer. For example:

**Question:** Give two differences between wind- and insect-pollinated flowers.

**Answer:**

| *Wind-pollinated flowers* | *Insect-pollinated flowers* |
|---|---|
| Not brightly coloured | Brightly coloured |
| Not scented | Scented |

A common mistake made by students when answering this type of question is to be unclear about which feature applies to which subject. The answer 'One has coloured flowers and one does not' is inadequate because it does not indicate which flower has which characteristic.

## 'Compare . . .'

The instruction 'Compare' means that the candidate should list both differences and similarities. For example:

**Question:** Compare the tissues seen in a cross-section of a stem and a root.

**Answer:**

| *Root* | *Stem* |
|---|---|
| *Differences* | |
| 1 Xylem in centre of root, often in tetrarch formation | Xylem in vascular bundles, scattered in the stem |
| 2 No cuticle on piliferous layer, so water can enter | Cuticle present on epidermis confers waterproof protection |
| 3 Cambium not always present | Cambium present |
| 4 No pith | Contains pith |
| 5 Root hairs present | No root hairs |
| 6 Phloem in bundles between the arms of xylem | Phloem in vascular bundles |

*Similarities*

1 Both contain phloem and xylem
2 Cortex is present in both
3 In both there is a single layer of protective cells on outer surface – the exodermis (root) and epidermis (stem)

## Give named examples . . .

Whenever a named example is asked for in a question (e.g. 'Describe the life cycle of a *named* saprophytic fungus') marks will be given for actually naming it (e.g. *Mucor*). Note that the scientific notation should always be underlined in an examination.

## 'Distinguish between . . .'

'Distinguish between' means 'establish the differences between two or more processes'. For example, '*Distinguish* between meiosis and mitosis.' (See p. 383.)

'Define . . .'

A definition should be an accurate, concise description of a term. Lengthy descriptions or diagrams are not usually required. For example:

**Question:** Define one of the following terms: osmosis, enzyme, gene.

**Answer:** Osmosis is the passage of water or other solvent from a weak solution to a stronger one through a semi-permeable membrane.

'State . . .'

All that is required here is a list. For example:

**Question:** State three factors that affect the rate of enzyme activity.

**Answer:** Temperature, pH and substrate concentration.

'Significance'

'Biological significance' means biological importance: in other words, what important biological information can be obtained from a statement? For example:

**Question:** What is the biological *significance* of the following statement?

'Xerophytic plants have a thick waxy cuticle on their leaves.'

**Answer:** The statement is biologically significant because the cuticle confers waterproof properties on the leaves and reduces water loss at times of drought

### *Essay questions*

Most A-level boards set a choice of essay questions. A successful essay must be well planned, clearly written and contain all the relevant information.

1. It is essential to read the question carefully, examining each word for its significance. Many students lose marks by attempting an essay too hastily and hence giving the wrong information. It is a good idea to underline important words in the question. For example:

   **Question:** Give an illustrated account of the life cycle of a protozoan parasite which infects man.

   The question asks for an illustrated account, hence marks will be given for the relevant illustrations. The subject of the essay is the life cycle, so each stage should be mentioned clearly. Although other factors such as economic importance and methods of control could be mentioned in the final summary, they should not be the main point of the essay itself. Finally, it is particularly important to describe a suitable organism. It should be (i) a protozoan, (ii) a parasite and

(iii) infect man. Marks cannot be given for elaborate descriptions of organisms which do not fit the above requirements. Hence the life cycle of *Taenia* (tapeworm) or *Fasciola hepatica* (the liver fluke) are not suitable. An example which could be used is *Plasmodium vivax* (the malarial parasite); however the whole life cycle, including the mosquito stage, should be given.

2. Marks will be given for planning of the essay, and students should avoid presenting information in a jumbled manner with facts in the wrong places. It is always a good idea to write an essay plan, and even a very brief one will help with organization of the essay. For example, an essay plan for the above question could be written as follows:
   (a) Brief introduction – Names of parasite and hosts
   Brief mention of importance of disease
   (b) Illustration to show life cycle with relevant stages of parasite clearly labelled
   (c) Life cycle in mosquito
   (d) Infection of man and various stages of life cycle
   – sporozoite stage (liver)
   – merozoite stage (red blood cells)
   – symptoms
   (e) Summary – Drugs used to control disease
   – Methods of controlling mosquito population
   – Economic importance
3. In essay questions marks are often given for style and presentation. Students should therefore ensure that their writing is clear and legible, and that spellings (especially of biological names) are correct.

### *Points to remember in practical examinations*

1. Students should read all instructions carefully at least twice. Instructions may include the number of questions to be answered, which questions are compulsory, which questions refer to diagrams, photographs, etc.
2. If there is a choice of questions, the ones to be answered should be provisionally selected. The maximum number of questions allowed should always be attempted.
3. The content of the questions will often determine the order in which they should be attempted. For example, physiological experiments which require a range of readings over a period of time should be

attempted early on in the examination. Specimens or slides may have to be shared between candidates. Students should have a clear written reminder as to when it is their turn to use the specimen and should use it as soon as they receive it.

4. In classification questions, candidates should refer to visible features (not colour or size as these vary between individuals of the same species) and information should generally be tabulated. Marks are not usually awarded for a correct subgroup with an incorrect main group.
5. In dissection questions, marks are awarded for clear, tidy presentation. Tissue should not be cut away unnecessarily, but only to ensure that the required region is clearly displayed. Drawings should be an accurate record of the dissection; the drawing and the actual dissection will usually be compared after the examination. Students should ensure that they complete a fully labelled diagram of the dissection, as very few marks can be awarded for a dissection alone.
6. Time in experiments should be planned carefully. The answer should include:
   (i) An accurate description of the method (i.e. the exact times, temperatures and volumes used) as well as details of any controls or precautions used to minimize errors.
   (ii) Results, which must be clearly presented in tabular and graphical form. Details of the units used should always be labelled on axes.
   (iii) A discussion of the results. This is essential as a large proportion of the marks are allocated to this section. The discussion should include an explanation of the results obtained, with explanations for any results which appear unusual. Remember that if such results have been obtained in the experiment, they are not wrong: there must be some explanation for them.

## Examination boards

Information concerning the A-level examinations, including samples of past papers, may be obtained from the following addresses:

AEB — Associated Examining Board,
Wellington House,
Station Road,
Aldershot,
Hampshire GU11 1BQ

| | |
|---|---|
| Cambridge | University of Cambridge Local Examinations Syndicate,<br>Syndicate Buildings,<br>17 Harvey Road,<br>Cambridge CB1 2EU |
| JMB | Joint Matriculation Board,<br>(Agent) John Sherratt & Son Ltd,<br>78 Park Road,<br>Altrincham,<br>Cheshire WA14 5QQ |
| London | University of London School Examinations Board,<br>52 Gordon Square,<br>London WC1E 6EE |
| NIGCEEB | Northern Ireland Schools Examination Council,<br>Beechill House,<br>42 Beechill Road,<br>Belfast BT8 4RS |
| Oxford | Oxford Delegacy of Local Examinations,<br>Ewert Place,<br>Summertown,<br>Oxford OX2 7BZ |
| Oxford and Cambridge | Oxford and Cambridge Schools Examination Board,<br>10 Trumpington Street,<br>Cambridge CB2 1QB<br>*or*<br>Ellsfield Way,<br>Oxford OX2 8EP |
| SEB | Scottish Examinations Board,<br>(Agent) Robert Gibson & Sons Ltd,<br>17 Fitzroy Place,<br>Glasgow G3 7SF |
| SUJB | Southern Universities Joint Board,<br>Cotham Road,<br>Bristol BS6 6DD |
| WJEC | Welsh Joint Education Committee,<br>245 Western Avenue,<br>Cardiff CF5 2YX |

# 1. Cytology and histology

## *Cellular organization*

Living matter depends on the reactions and interactions of complex organic chemicals. These reactions require an aqueous medium in which to take place. The molecules involved must be 'held' together in an organized manner for the necessary reactions for 'life' to occur. It is the **cell** which contains and organizes the chemical reactions required for life.

Thus, living organisms are built up of microscopic structural units called cells. Some simple organisms consist of a single cell only and are termed **unicellular**, e.g. *Amoeba* spp. and *Chlamydomonas* spp. More complex animals and plants may contain hundreds, millions or even billions of cells. A typical cell consists of a nucleus, which contains the hereditary material, embedded in a mass of cytoplasm. Cytoplasm contains a variety of smaller components.

Robert Hooke used the word 'cell' in 1665 to describe the small compartments he saw in cork and other plant material. With improvements in the optical microscope, further types of cells were observed.

However, it was two German workers, Theodore Schwann and Matthias Schleiden, in 1838 who synthesized the concept of cellularity of organisms. This led to the **cell theory**. The cell theory may be summarized as follows:

1. Most organisms consist of microscopic bodies called cells.
2. Cells are units of essentially the same nature.
3. Cells always arise from pre-existing cells.
4. Cells are the living parts of the organism in which the metabolic reactions occur and to which the synthesis of new material is due.
5. Each cell of a many-celled organism corresponds in certain respects to the whole body of a simple protist (single-celled organism).

The cell theory gives a general definition of the cell but this can vary; for example, some cells are multinucleate (e.g. muscle cells) and others, such as phloem sieve tubes and mammalian erythrocytes, are anucleate (have no nucleus). However, these cells have still differentiated from a parent cell which contained a single nucleus.

## *Cell structure*

Cells are basically spherical in shape but, due to their varied functions, show remarkable diversity of structure. They generally range in size from 10 to 30 $\mu$m in diameter. Almost all cells possess an external limiting membrane, a nucleus (containing chromosomes), mitochondria, ribosomes and a system of internal membranes. There are also other widely distributed components, e.g. lysosomes, centrioles and cilia. Plant cells generally have additional structures, namely chloroplasts and well-developed cell walls.

### Membranes

The external membrane is less than 7 nm in thickness. Its existence was first discovered due to the behaviour of cells placed in various solutions. It was found that cells are permeable only to certain molecules (i.e. they are semi-permeable) and it was suggested that the surface was covered by a thin membrane containing fatty substances as an essential component. The membrane surrounding the cell may be referred to as the plasmalemma, or plasma or cell membrane.

The function of the plasma membrane is to control exchange of matter between the interior of the cell and the surrounding medium. It enables the cell to maintain concentrations of water, small ions and larger molecules different from those of the environment. Thus the plasma membrane is an essential component of living cells.

Bulk transport of fluid (pinocytosis), e.g. intake of liquid by *Amoeba*, or solids (phagocytosis), e.g. engulfing of bacteria by phagocytes, occurs across the cell border through infoldings of the membrane that enclose to form vesicles which are detached and move through the cytoplasm. The reverse of these processes is used for **secretion** of cell products.

Other membranes inside the cell display a similar structure to the plasma membrane and the term **unit membrane** is used to describe the basic structure of all of these.

#### *Membrane composition*

Cell membranes can be isolated through the techniques of cell fractionation. (This is the isolation of intracellular structures by differential centrifugation rerotating the samples of the cells at varying speed.) It has been found that all cell membranes contain lipids, generally about 35 per cent by weight, the remainder is mainly protein. Most of the lipids are phospholipids. These are rod-shaped molecules with hydrophilic groups making up one end of the molecule. The other part of the molecule consists of long, hydrophobic, hydrocarbon chains. Cholesterol occurs in substantial amounts in animal membranes. Very few of the membrane proteins have been purified well enough for detailed biochemical study.

*Membrane structure*

The Davson–Danielli model of the unit membrane proposed in the 1930s describes membranes as consisting of a bimolecular layer of lipids 4.0 to 5.0 nm wide covered with layers of protein on both surfaces to give a total width of 7.5 to 10.0 nm. The lipid molecules are orientated with their hydrophilic groups facing outwards. The hydrophobic hydrocarbon chains face each other in the centre. This model is now thought to describe some membranes, e.g. the myelin sheath of nerve fibres, but a variety of techniques, such as electron microscopy and X-ray diffraction, have shown that a large part of the protein is present in the hydrophobic core of the membrane.

Membrane proteins are largely hydrophobic and penetrate into the lipid layer. Some of these proteins span the entire thickness with their hydrophilic parts on both surfaces. (See Fig. 1.1.)

Hydrophobic bonds are present between the hydrocarbon chains of the lipids and hydrophobic amino acid residues on the surface of the proteins. These bonds stabilize the structure.

Recent studies (by Singer and Nicholson in 1972) suggest that the membrane is far less rigid than was originally supposed. It has been suggested that it has an oil-like consistency and that there is considerable sideways movement of lipid molecules within it. The protein molecules are considered to follow a mosaic arrangement, giving the structure the description the **fluid mosaic model** (Fig. 1.2).

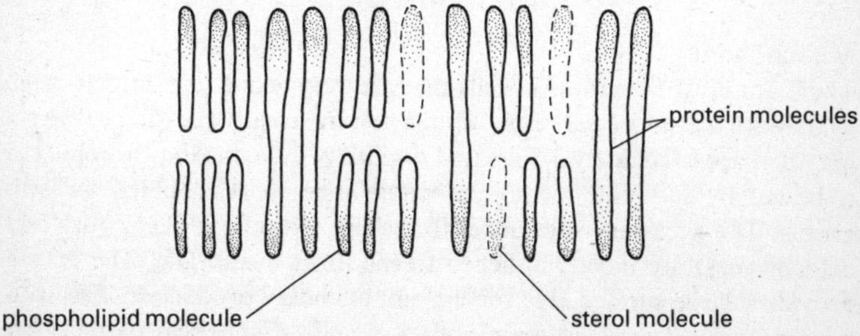
protein molecules
phospholipid molecule
sterol molecule

*Fig. 1.1* Arrangement of lipids and proteins in membranes. The shaded areas are the hydrophilic portions of the molecules

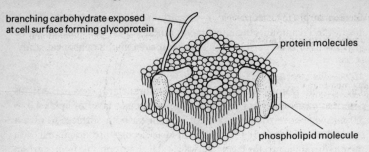

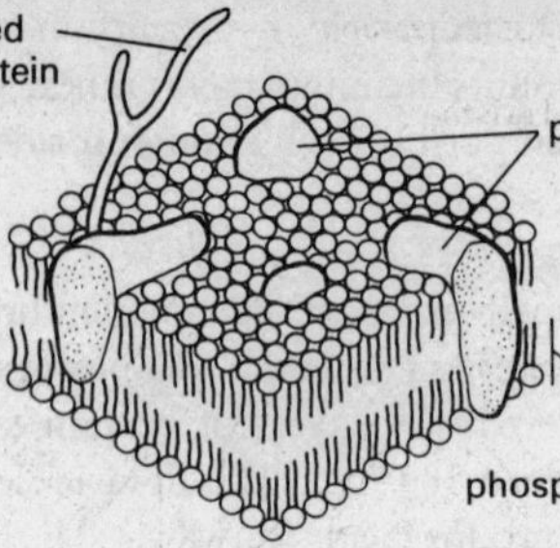
branching carbohydrate exposed at cell surface forming glycoprotein
protein molecules
phospholipid molecule

*Fig. 1.2* Fluid mosaic model of membrane structure (after Singer and Nicholson, 1972)

## Nucleus

The nucleus is bounded by the nuclear membrane. This comprises two unit membranes and is approximately 20 nm thick. The outer membrane appears rough under the electron microscope owing to the presence of ribosomes, and it may be continuous with the endoplasmic reticulum. The inner membrane is smooth and may provide a surface for the adhesion of chromatin strands. The nuclear membrane contains pores up to 100 nm across which allow the passage of large molecules between the nucleus and the cytoplasm.

Within the nuclear membrane is nucleoplasm containing DNA and nuclear ribosomes. The nucleus may contain one or more **nucleoli**. There is evidence to suggest that these are the sites of either the synthesis or the storage of ribosomal RNA (p. 408).

## Mitochondria

These are most numerous in cells that are very active (e.g. muscle cells) as they are the site of cell respiration. They are usually rod-shaped with a length of approximately 2.5 $\mu$m and a width of 1.0 $\mu$m. A mitochondrion is bound by a double membrane whose inner part is folded to form **cristae**. The necessary substances for cell respiration (e.g. enzymes and cytochromes) are mostly attached to the inner membrane. The cristae provide a large surface area for maximum energy production. Electron microscopy has revealed the presence of stalked spherical particles on the inner membrane (Fig. 1.3a). These particles are thought to be the site of oxidative phosphorylation.

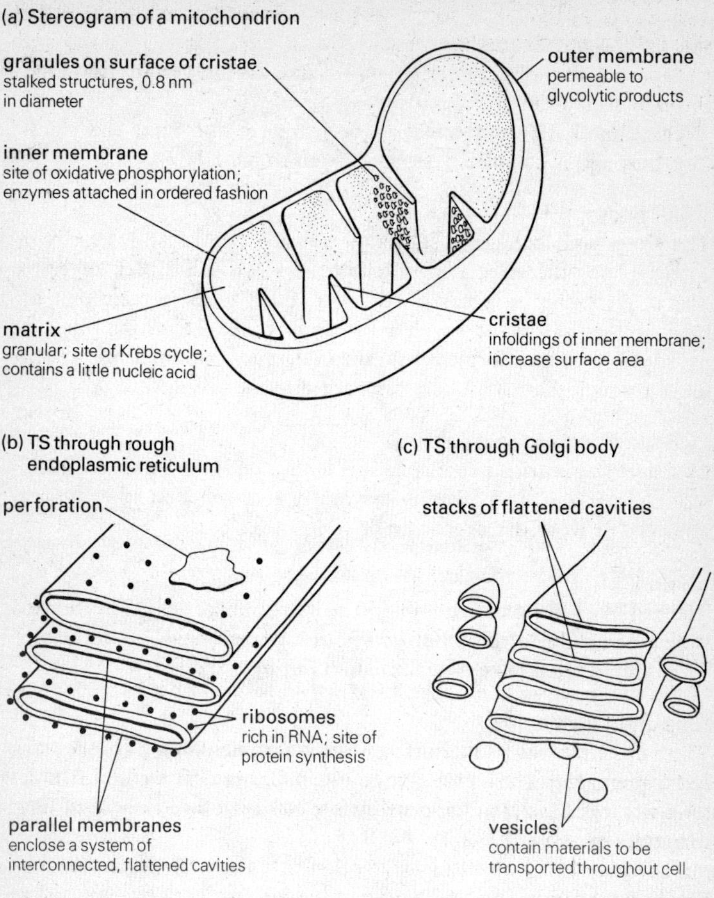
(a) Stereogram of a mitochondrion
granules on surface of cristae
stalked structures, 0.8 nm in diameter
outer membrane
permeable to glycolytic products
inner membrane
site of oxidative phosphorylation; enzymes attached in ordered fashion
matrix
granular; site of Krebs cycle; contains a little nucleic acid
cristae
infoldings of inner membrane; increase surface area
(b) TS through rough endoplasmic reticulum
perforation
ribosomes
rich in RNA; site of protein synthesis
parallel membranes
enclose a system of interconnected, flattened cavities
(c) TS through Golgi body
stacks of flattened cavities
vesicles
contain materials to be transported throughout cell

*Fig. 1.3* The major cell organelles as seen under the electron microscope. (a) stereogram of a mitochondrion; (b) TS through rough endoplasmic reticulum; (c) TS through Golgi body

## Endoplasmic reticulum

Within the cytoplasm is a system of membranes which make up the rough and smooth endoplasmic reticulum (ER). ER is essentially a series of interconnected sacs, frequently flattened and stacked in multiple layers and bounded by unit membranes.

The bulk of the ER is rough with ribosomes attached to the matrix side of the membranes (see Fig. 1.3b). Rough ER is involved with transporting the polypeptides, which are manufactured by the ribosomes, throughout the cell.

The smooth ER is thought to be involved with lipid and steroid transport and is completely separate from rough ER.

### Golgi body

The Golgi body comprises stacks of flattened cavities and is easily recognizable by the associated vesicles (Fig. 1.3c). It has been suggested that in the Golgi body carbohydrate is added to the protein that has been synthesized in the rough ER. These glycoproteins may then be packaged in vesicles formed from the Golgi membranes. These vesicles move through the cell and are discharged at the cell surface.

### Lysosome (suicide-bag)

Lysosomes appear as dense spherical bodies under the electron microscope. They contain powerful enzymes whose function is to destroy damaged or worn-out organelles or complete cells.

### Centrioles

The rod-like centrioles are found in pairs in animal cells. They have a similar structure to the basal bodies of cilia and flagella (see below). They are involved in spindle formation during cell division.

### Cilia and flagella

These are processes on the surfaces of certain cells. They have the same basic internal structure (9 + 2) (see Fig. 1.4), but cilia are up to 10 $\mu$m long whereas flagella are approximately 100 $\mu$m long. They both have diameters of about 0.3 $\mu$m.

They may be involved in locomotion in unicellular organisms (e.g. cilia in *Paramecium* spp. and flagella in certain species of bacteria and in *Euglena* spp.). Cilia are also found in higher animals (e.g. ciliated cells in the respiratory tracts of mammals). The lashing movement of cilia and flagella requires energy in the form of ATP.

At the base of both processes is a structure called the **basal body** which is necessary for movement. It is composed of the nine peripheral fibres only.

### Microvilli

These are hair-like projections formed from the folding of the cell membrane. They are approximately 1.0 $\mu$m long and 0.08 $\mu$m wide. They

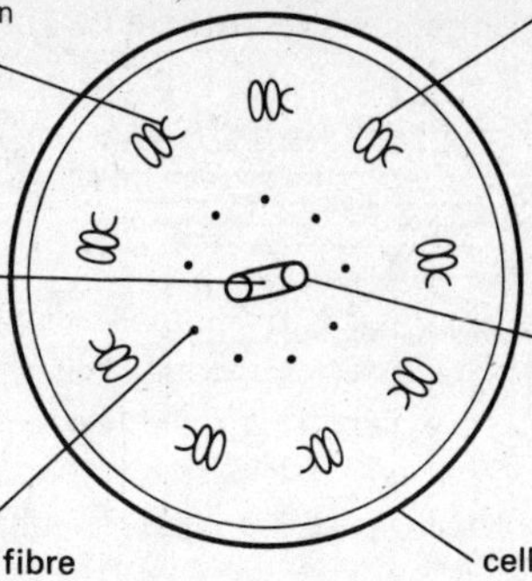
arm-like process
site of ATP breakdown
peripheral fibre
one of nine, paired, outer fibres
central sheath
central fibre
one of a single pair
secondary fibre
cell membrane

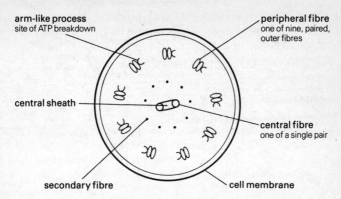

*Fig. 1.4* TS of a cilium, showing the 9 + 2 arrangement of the fibres

give the surface of the cell a fuzzy appearance under the optical microscope and serve to increase the surface area of the cell. Microvilli are very evident in the epithelial lining of the small intestine and in the convoluted tubules in the kidney (where they aid absorption of materials).

### Microtubules

These are made of protein and may occur singly or in bundles throughout the cell. They are thought to be involved in internal transport within cells.

### Cell wall

The cell membrane is not the outermost layer of plant cells. The cell wall (Fig. 1.5a) is prominent in plant tissues and has an important structural role. The major constituent in plant cell walls is cellulose, a carbohydrate. It is a polymer of glucose molecules (p. 52). Lignin may also be present to give additional structural support.

The plant cell wall contains perforations or **pits**. These allow lateral movement of materials in tissues such as xylem vessels and tracheids. In living tissues the pits frequently contain **plasmodesmata**. These are living strands of cytoplasm containing protein fibres which allow active transport of substances between cells.

A material is present between animal cells, the commonest component of which is hyaluronic acid. This a polymer of hexose, glucuronic acid and glucosamine.

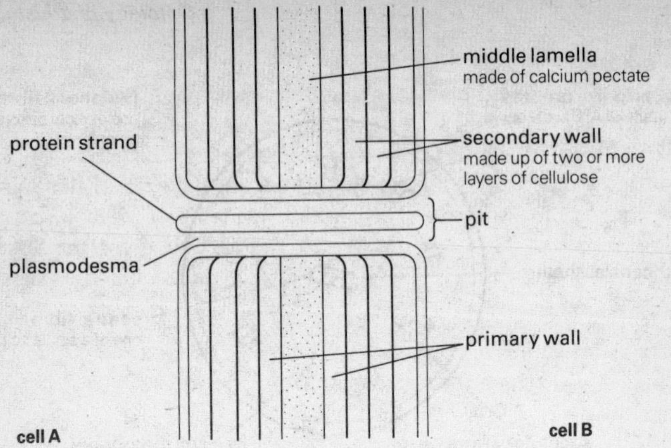
middle lamella
made of calcium pectate
protein strand
secondary wall
made up of two or more
layers of cellulose
pit
plasmodesma
primary wall
cell A
cell B

*Fig. 1.5*(a) Structure of the plant cell wall

*Fig. 1.5*(b) The structure of a chloroplast

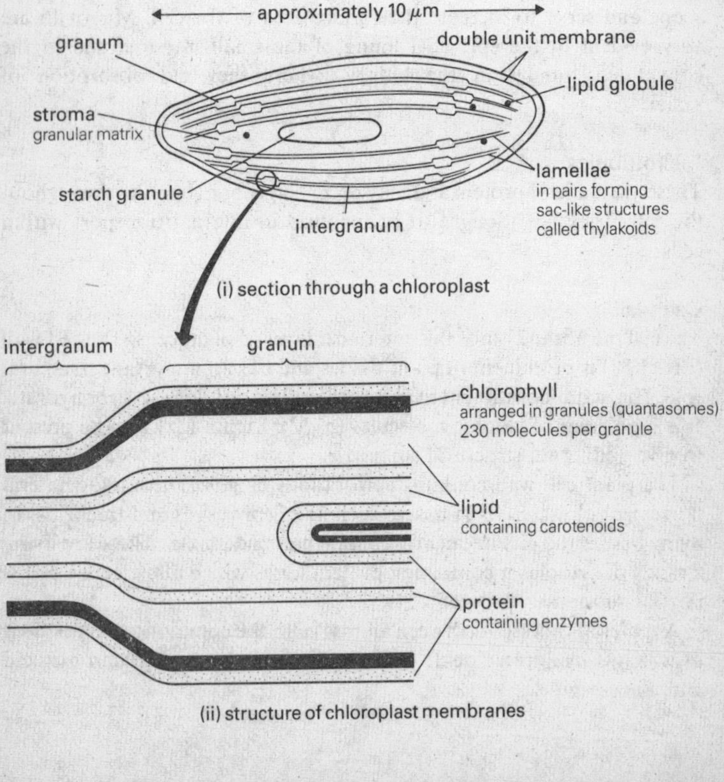
approximately 10 μm
granum
double unit membrane
lipid globule
stroma
granular matrix
starch granule
intergranum
lamellae
in pairs forming
sac-like structures
called thylakoids
(i) section through a chloroplast
intergranum
granum
chlorophyll
arranged in granules (quantasomes)
230 molecules per granule
lipid
containing carotenoids
protein
containing enzymes
(ii) structure of chloroplast membranes

### Chloroplast

Chloroplasts are ovoid bodies and are the site of photosynthesis. They are about 5 $\mu$m across the widest part and about 10 $\mu$m long (Fig. 1.5b). In section they are seen to consist of membranous lamellae which are thickened at intervals to form **grana**. These are the sites of the 'light' reactions of photosynthesis. The lamellae are embedded in a matrix called the **stroma**. This contains the enzymes required for the 'dark' reactions of photosynthesis. The stroma also contains numerous starch granules.

Further information on the organelles described above can be found in the chapters discussing their related metabolic processes.

## *Differences between plant and animal cells*

Plant and animal cells have the same basic plan but show obvious differences when they are mature (see Fig. 1.6).

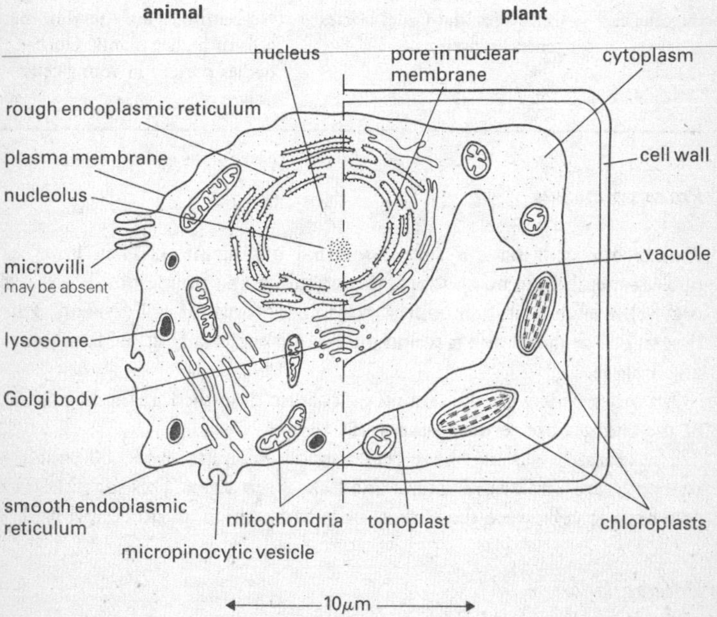
animal
plant
nucleus
pore in nuclear membrane
cytoplasm
rough endoplasmic reticulum
plasma membrane
cell wall
nucleolus
vacuole
microvilli may be absent
lysosome
Golgi body
smooth endoplasmic reticulum
mitochondria
tonoplast
chloroplasts
micropinocytic vesicle
10$\mu$m

*Fig. 1.6* Comparison of the ultrastructure of a generalized animal and a generalized plant cell

*Table 1.1.* Differences between plant and animal cells

| | *Animal* | *Plant* |
|---|---|---|
| Intercellular substance | May vary in animal cells, e.g. intercellular substance of bone, cartilage or blood | Universal cellulose cell wall conferring a more rigid shape |
| Vacuole | No structure comparable to sap vacuole. Food and contractile vacuoles may be present in unicellular animals | Large central sap vacuole. Contractile vacuoles may be found in unicellular plants |
| Pigmentation | Colour diffused through cytoplasm | Coloured plastids present |
| Storage | Generally store glycogen as granules or in solution in the cytoplasm | Starch is generally the storage compound. Storage is often in leucoplasts |
| Crystals | Not normally present | Often occur, e.g. calcium oxalate |
| Organelles | Centrioles and Golgi bodies generally present | No centrioles are found in the cells of higher plants. Golgi bodies present in young cells only |

### *Prokaryotic cells*

Prokaryotic cells have a simple internal organization. They have no nuclear membrane, no endoplasmic reticulum and no membrane-bound organelles such as mitochondria. No spindle forms at cell division. This type of cell organization is found only in the bacteria (Fig. 1.7) and blue-green algae.

All other cells with the complex structure described at the beginning of the chapter are termed **eukaryotic.**

The oldest fossils that have been found, which are over 3,000 million years old, are similar to bacteria and blue-green algae. This suggests that prokaryotic cells were the earliest cells from which all others evolved.

### *Differentiation*

Unicellular organisms reach a certain degree of **complexity** owing to their specialized organelles (e.g. organelles called myonemes perform

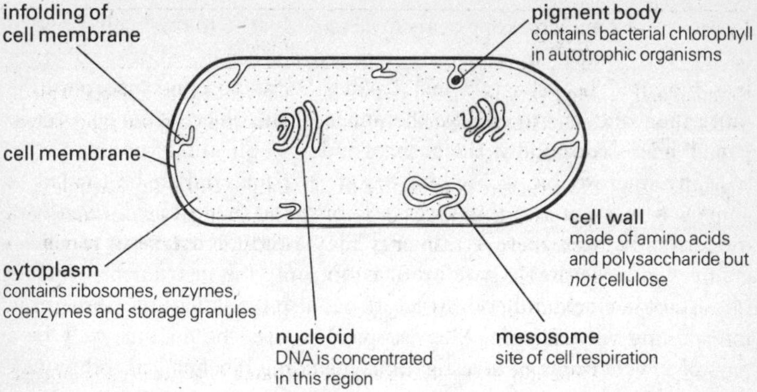
infolding of
cell membrane
pigment body
contains bacterial chlorophyll
in autotrophic organisms
cell membrane
cell wall
made of amino acids
and polysaccharide but
*not* cellulose
cytoplasm
contains ribosomes, enzymes,
coenzymes and storage granules
nucleoid
DNA is concentrated
in this region
mesosome
site of cell respiration

*Fig. 1.7* Generalized bacterium. (Some bacteria are motile – possessing simple flagella. These do not have the characteristic 9 + 2 structure (see Fig. 1.4), and they arise in the cytoplasm)

muscular functions and contractile vacuoles regulate water content). For further complexity many cells must exist together – this is known as the **multicellular condition.**

The simplest form of association is where cells clump together but still remain independent, e.g. *Gonium* – a collection of 100 or so *Chlamydomonas*-like cells. Taking the situation a step further, a ball of cells develops with the outer cells alone possessing flagella for locomotion, e.g. *Volvox* – a spherical colony of up to 20,000 *Chlamydomonas*-like cells. The inner cells become specialized for food manufacture and reproduction. Thus each cell in *Volvox* has become structurally adapted for a particular function (this is known as **differentiation**) although all cells still have to carry out the basic essential functions such as respiration. Differentiation is carried to its extreme in higher plants and animals. For example, nerve cells have become so specialized for transmission of electrical impulses that they have lost their ability to divide.

Obviously the more specialized a cell becomes for one particular function, the more efficiently it operates. This efficiency is increased if similar cells are grouped together to form a **tissue**. The working together of highly specialized cells is called **integration**. Tissues must function in co-operation with the other tissues in the body. When several tissues combine in a co-operative way they form an **organ**. An example is the heart, which is an organ made up of muscle and connective and epithelial tissues, regulated by nervous tissue.

## *Microscopy*

Leeuwenhoek's microscope bears little resemblance to the microscope of today. His **'simple' microscope** comprised one single, almost spherical lens mounted between two metal plates. A microscope incorporating more than one lens to enlarge the image of the object is called a **'compound' microscope** and is the basis of today's optical microscope.

Many microscopic techniques require the material to be treated in some way, e.g. cut into thin slices (sections) and then stained. Even with modern advances these treatments may produce **artefacts** (artificial changes in structure). Therefore it is not only the instrument which is important in elucidating cell structure but also the skill of the observer in interpreting what is seen. Microscopical studies should thus only be a part of a wide range of investigations including biochemical techniques.

### *Types of microscope*

#### Optical (light) microscope

The standard optical microscope is used for the majority of laboratory studies. It has a resolving power of 0.2 $\mu$m, which means that two points must be more than 0.2 $\mu$m apart for them to be perceived as separate. The optical microscope can only magnify up to a maximum of 1,500 times without loss of clarity. It uses an objective lens to magnify the image which is viewed and further magnified with the eyepiece or ocular. The final image is inverted, but compound microscopes may be adapted to produce a real image for drawing, projection or photography.

It is often necessary to study material without the aid of staining as this kills the tissue. Recent advances have made observations of unstained material much easier.

#### Phase contrast microscope

Invented by Zernike, this microscope makes use of the fact that transparent living cells contain structures which have different refractive indices by converting these differences into a visible form. Thus organelles, as well as biological processes such as pinocytosis and phagocytosis, may be studied.

#### Fluorescent microscope

Certain compounds have the ability to absorb short-wavelength radiation and re-emit the energy as light of a longer wavelength. This phenomenon is known as fluorescence. The fluorescent microscope induces fluorescence in the specimen, which appears as a luminous object upon a dark background.

### Dark ground microscope

This system produces a brilliant image against a completely dark background, in contrast to most other methods. This aids detection of fine structure and is particularly useful in observing the structural detail of aquatic organisms such as *Paramecium*, *Hydra* and *Daphnia*. It is possible to observe ciliary activity using this type of microscopy. High-power dark ground microscopy is very useful for detecting the presence of the parasites such as *Trypanosomes* in fresh blood samples.

For further details of these and other types of microscopes consult the references at the end of this section.

### Electron microscope

The properties of light set a limit on the amount of detail that can be resolved in optical microscopes. At magnifications above $\times 1{,}500$ no further detail would be revealed. Thus another form of radiation, other than visible light, is required to improve the resolving power.

In the electron microscope an electron gun takes the place of the lamp and acts as the source of illumination. Electron lenses perform similar functions to the glass lenses. The final image is projected on to a viewing screen or on to a photographic plate, as our eyes are not sensitive to electrons. The maximum magnification of an electron microscope is approximately $\times 200{,}000$.

One limitation of the electron microscope is that the specimens have to be examined under a vacuum as electrons only travel a short distance in air. As cells contain approximately 70 per cent water the vacuum would cause dehydration of living cells resulting in their collapsing and thus destroying their intricate structure. Cells are also too thick for a clear image to be produced using electrons. These problems are overcome by producing thin-sections (no more than 0.1 $\mu$m) and **fixing** them with chemicals such as osmium tetroxide to stabilize their structure. Even so, these treatments may result in the production of artefacts. Electron microscopists attempt to overcome this problem by varying the methods of preparation (e.g. varying the fixative).

Despite these problems the electron microscope has become invaluable in elucidating the **ultrastructure** of cells and hence in determining cell function.

*Table 1.2.* Comparison of the optical and electron microscopes

| *Optical* | *Electron* |
|---|---|
| Magnification up to ×1,500 | Magnification up to ×200,000 |
| Resolving power of 0.2 μm | Resolving power of 1 nm |
| Small depth of field | Large depth of field |
| Coloured image produced | Black and white image produced |
| Specimen viewed in air | Specimen must be viewed under vacuum |
| Specimen may be living or dead | Specimen is always dead |
| Preparation of specimen may be simple and quick | Preparation of specimen is lengthy and complex |
| Unaffected by magnetic fields | Affected by magnetic fields |
| Relatively cheap to buy and maintain | Expensive to buy and run, requiring a specialized technician |
| Portable | Requires a large, separate room |

## Further reading

D. W. Fawcett, *An Atlas of Fine Structure* (Saunders, 1966)

S. W. Hurry, *The Microstructure of Cells*, 4th edition (Murray, 1972)

A. P. M. Lockwood, *The Membranes of Animal Cells*, Studies in Biology No. 27, 2nd edition (Arnold, 1979)

J. A. Lucy, *The Plasma Membrane*, Oxford/Carolina Biology Reader No. 81 (Packard, 1975)

## Related questions

**Question:**
Give an account of the distribution and functions of the membranes of cells. [London, June 1981, Paper 2]

**Comments:**
This type of question is typical of the broad-based essay question. An important point to realize is that the question requires a knowledge of a wide range of structures in which membranes occur. Although the question obviously requires a discussion of the cell membrane, it must be noted that the question states 'the membranes of cells' which includes the membranes of the organelles within the cell.

A short, illustrated description of the unit membrane (p. 19) would be a good introduction, but the question does *not* require a lengthy discussion. Throughout the answer the two words 'distribution' and 'function' must be kept in mind. First describe the location of the membrane (e.g. surrounding the mitochondrion and also forming the cristae within it), and then discuss the function (e.g. the limiting membrane permits the inward diffusion of pyruvic acid and other suitable substrates for the Krebs cycle, the inner membrane and cristae hold the optimum amount of enzymes and electron carriers in an ordered position for oxidative phosphorylation). The description of the function must be specific, e.g. just saying the membrane surrounds the nucleus is not enough.

Although most organelles are common to both plant and animal cells, specialized plant organelles (e.g. chloroplasts) must be included. It must also be remembered that the cell membrane has many structural modifications (e.g. it is drawn into microvilli to increase the surface for absorption as in the kidney tubule).

In summary, it is important to use a wide range of examples with brief discussion on each rather than give lengthy explanations for a few.

**Question:**
The diagram below is of a generalized bacterial cell.

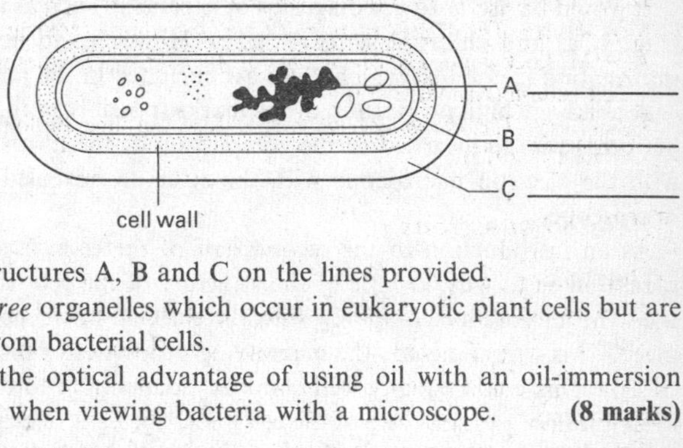
A
B
C
cell wall

(a) Label structures A, B and C on the lines provided.
(b) Name *three* organelles which occur in eukaryotic plant cells but are absent from bacterial cells.
(c) Explain the optical advantage of using oil with an oil-immersion objective when viewing bacteria with a microscope. **(8 marks)**

**Comments:**
(a) See Fig. 1.7. C is the capsule or slime layer. It is variable (even within one species) in chemical composition, e.g. it may consist of polypeptides, polysaccharides, or hyaluronic acid. Many bacteria do not possess such a surface layer.
(b) See p. 26. Remember prokaryotic cells have *no* membrane-bound organelles.

(c) This system allows the finer details of cellular structure of bacteria to become easily visible. The oil, which has a refractive index equal to that of glass, allows the light rays to travel in an optically homogeneous system so there is no refraction of light rays on leaving the coverslip. The lens thus has a magnification of × 100.

**Question**:
Describe the structure of cells as revealed by an electron microscope. How does this differ from the structure revealed by the light microscope?

**(20 marks)**

[London, Jan. 1982, Paper 2]

**Comments:**
This essay calls for a description of the *ultrastructure* of cells. Note that the title does not specify plant or animal, therefore both must be considered. The ultrastructure of plant and animal cells is described on pp. 17 to 25. It is important to include all the main organelles and briefly describe the structure of each rather than give one or two examples in a lot of detail. Try to include the size of the organelles. The cell membrane and cell wall should also be included.

It would be useful to use diagrams of organelles such as mitochondria (Fig. 1.3a) and chloroplasts (Fig. 1.5b). However, do not repeat any information in the text which you have included in the annotations.

A relatively high proportion of the marks (possibly in the region of 30 per cent) will be awarded to the comparison of the ultrastructure seen with the electron microscope with the structure revealed by the light microscope.

As an introduction to the second half of the essay a *very brief* explanation as to why so little of the structure of the cell is visible under the light microscope compared with the electron microscope should be given. This would include the magnifying properties of the microscopes (p. 30). This could equally well come as a conclusion to the essay. The description of the structure of the cell under the light microscope should emphasize the lack of detail visible, i.e. the cell membrane appears as a 'line' surrounding the cytoplasm, and mitochondria are only visible as rod-shaped structures under the highest magnification.

## *Tissue organization*

A collection of cells which are similar both morphologically and functionally and are joined by intercellular substances is called a **tissue**. The process of differentiation and maturation of tissues is called **histogenesis**. A **tissue culture** is formed when tissues or cells of animals and plants are grown artificially in a controlled environment. **Histology** is the study of the structure and chemical composition of plant and animal tissues related to their function.

The animal body is composed of four primary tissues:

1. **Epithelium** – cells are closely packed together and separated by very little intercellular substance.
2. **Connective tissue** – the intercellular substance may form the bulk of the tissue.
3. **Muscle** – primarily concerned with contraction.
4. **Nervous tissue** – concerned with rapid conduction of impulses.

Plant tissues are primary or secondary in origin. The primary tissues arise from **apical meristems** and the main types are:

1. **Xylem** – concerned with conduction of water and mineral salts.
2. **Phloem** – concerned with transport of food substances.
3. **Parenchyma** – chiefly concerned with the manufacture and storage of food.
4. **Collenchyma** – } supporting tissue.
5. **Sclerenchyma** – }

The secondary tissues arise from **lateral meristems** and they are mainly responsible for the growth in thickness of stems and roots. Secondary tissues include secondary phloem and xylem, and bark.

Plant tissue can also be classified into ground tissue, protective tissue, vascular tissue and mechanical tissue (see below).

## *Animal tissues*

### Epithelial tissue

This type of tissue forms the epidermis and the lining of respiratory, digestive and urinogenital passages. The cells are separated by a very small amount of intercellular substance. Epithelium may be derived from any of the three primary germ layers of the embryo – ectoderm, endoderm or mesoderm (p. 375). Epithelium is generally free from blood vessels. Nutrients reach the epithelium and waste products leave it after passing through the ground substance of adjacent connective tissue.

The main functions of the epithelium are:

1. Protective – epithelium completely covers the external surface (including the surface of the intestinal and respiratory tracts).
2. Secretory – epithelia secrete fluids and chemicals necessary for

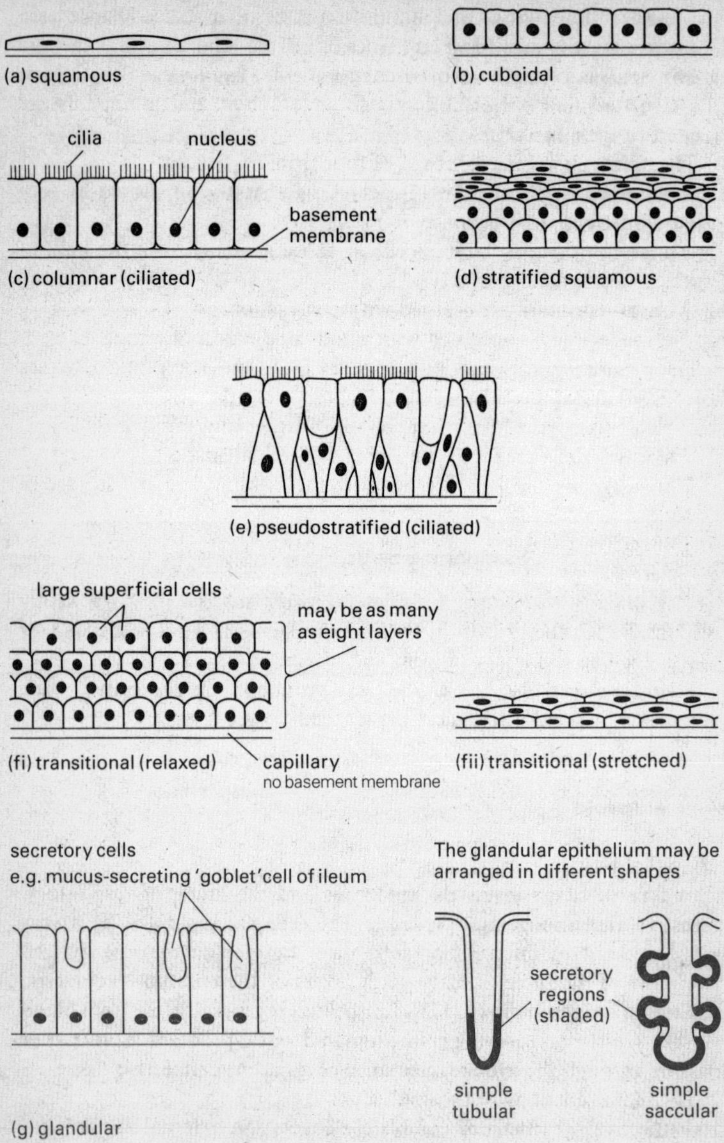
(a) squamous
(b) cuboidal
cilia
nucleus
basement
membrane
(c) columnar (ciliated)
(d) stratified squamous
(e) pseudostratified (ciliated)
large superficial cells
may be as many
as eight layers
(fi) transitional (relaxed)
capillary
no basement membrane
(fii) transitional (stretched)
secretory cells
e.g. mucus-secreting 'goblet' cell of ileum
The glandular epithelium may be
arranged in different shapes
secretory
regions
(shaded)
simple
tubular
simple
saccular
(g) glandular

*Fig. 1.8* Cellular arrangement in epithelial tissues

digestion, lubrication, protection, excretion of waste products, reproduction and metabolic regulation.

3. Absorptive – epithelia absorb food substances and preserve the water and salt content of the body.
4. Sensory – epithelia constitute important parts of sense organs, especially of smell and taste.
5. Lubricatory – epithelia line all the internal cavities of the body, e.g. the peritoneum and heart.

*Table 1.3.* Classification of epithelia

| *Type* | *Properties* | *Location* |
|---|---|---|
| Single-layered | | |
| Squamous | Thin, flat | Mesothelium, descending loop of Henlé |
| Cuboidal | Cube-like | Ducts, thyroid, choroid plexus |
| Columnar | Tall | Intestine, gall bladder |
| | Sometimes ciliated | Oviduct |
| Stratified (many-layered) | | |
| Stratified squamous | Superficial cells are thin and flat, deeper cells cuboidal and columnar | Skin, oesophagus, vagina |
| Columnar | Two or more layers of tall cells | Pharynx, large ducts of salivary glands |
| | Sometimes ciliated | Larynx |
| Pseudostratified | Cells attached to basement membrane but some extend to the surface and others only part of the way | Male urethra |
| | Sometimes ciliated | Respiratory passages |
| Transitional | Like stratified squamous in the fully distended bladder; in the empty bladder the superficial cells are rounded, almost spherical | Bladder |
| Glandular | May be simple tubular or saccular | Ileum |

Surface specialization is present in many epithelia, e.g. microvilli which increase the surface area, and cilia which may trap and propel substances along the surface of the epithelium. Epithelial cells also have the ability to glide over surfaces. This property is important in covering wounds to allow repair and in structures that must temporarily enlarge (e.g. transitional epithelium in the bladder).

The main types of epithelial tissue are classified and illustrated in Table 1.3 and Fig. 1.8.

## Connective tissue

This is one of the primary tissues of the animal body. It is different from the others in that the intercellular components are abundant. The cellular and intercellular components of connective tissue are listed below.

*Cellular components*

1. Fibroblasts – variable in shape, frequently with fine processes.
2. Mast cells – large and amoeboid with a central nucleus and granular cytoplasm.
3. Plasma cells – generally ovoid, some amoeboid movement.
4. Macrophages – variable in shape, highly phagocytic.
5. Fat cells – may be large, 80 nm or more.

*Intercellular components*

1. Reticular fibres – made up of fibrils, only seen using special silver techniques.
2. Collagen fibres – made up of fibrils; they are colourless and therefore are known as white fibres.
3. Elastin fibres – appear slightly yellowish with the light microscope.
4. Matrix – contains molecules secreted from the connective tissue cells, e.g. glycoproteins and antibodies, and also substances from the blood plasma, e.g. water, albumin and globulin.

All connective tissue has the same basic structure as in Fig. 1.9, but may differ owing to the presence of other cell types or the chemical composition of the matrix, etc. The main types of connective tissue are described below.

*Connective tissue proper*

1. Areolar tissue – This is found throughout the body, as packing in all organs. It connects the skin to the underlying structures, surrounds blood vessels and nerves. It can stretch and recover well.

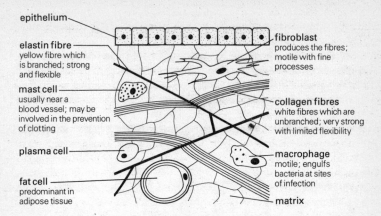

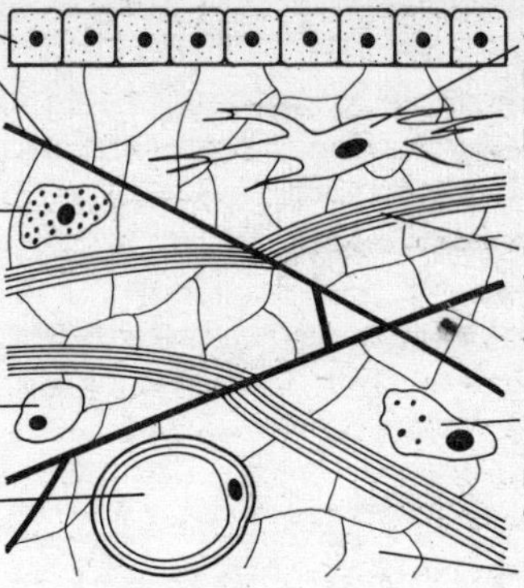
epithelium
elastin fibre
yellow fibre which is branched; strong and flexible
mast cell
usually near a blood vessel; may be involved in the prevention of clotting
plasma cell
fat cell
predominant in adipose tissue
fibroblast
produces the fibres; motile with fine processes
collagen fibres
white fibres which are unbranched; very strong with limited flexibility
macrophage
motile; engulfs bacteria at sites of infection
matrix

*Fig. 1.9* Components of connective tissue

2. Elastic tissue – the yellow elastic fibres predominate. This tissue combines strength and elasticity. It is largely responsible for the recovery of the lung after distension.
3. Adipose tissue – this results when the matrix of areolar tissue becomes filled with fat cells. In mammals it is mainly located in the dermis of the skin.

*Skeletal connective tissue*

1. Cartilage – There are three types of cartilage, classified according to the presence or absence of different types of fibres in the matrix.
   (i) Hyaline cartilage (Fig. 1.10) – contains no bundles of large fibres. Found in joints or in skeletons of elasmobranchs such as dogfish.
   (ii) Fibrocartilage – contains bundles of collagen fibres. Found in the patella and between vertebrae.
   (iii) Elastic cartilage – contains elastic fibres. Found in the epiglottis and the external ear.
2. Bone (Fig. 1.11) – cells are predominantly osteocytes arranged concentrically around an Haversian canal which contains the blood vessels and nerve fibres serving the osteocytes. This arrangement is known as an Haversian system. The fibres are almost entirely collagen. The hardness of bone is due to the mineral salts (85 per cent calcium phosphate, 10 per cent calcium carbonate, 4 per cent magnesium chloride and 1 per cent calcium fluoride).

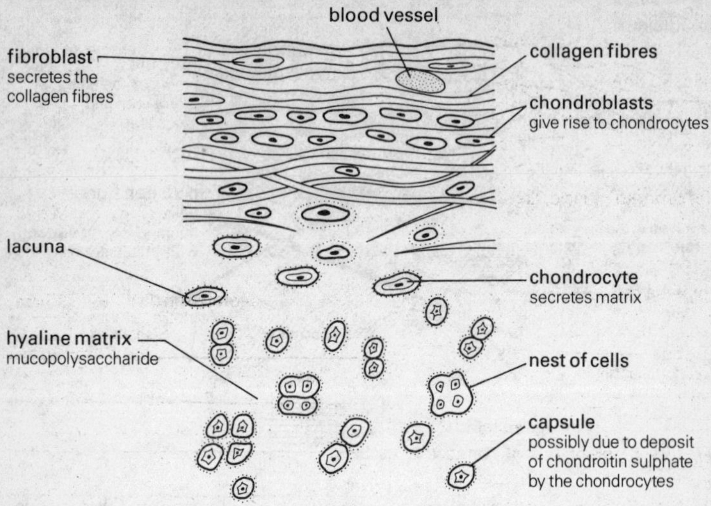
blood vessel
fibroblast
secretes the collagen fibres
collagen fibres
chondroblasts
give rise to chondrocytes
lacuna
chondrocyte
secretes matrix
hyaline matrix
mucopolysaccharide
nest of cells
capsule
possibly due to deposit of chondroitin sulphate by the chondrocytes

*Fig. 1.10* TS of hyaline cartilage (e.g. trachea)

*Fig. 1.11* TS of compact bone, showing Haversian system (e.g. femur)

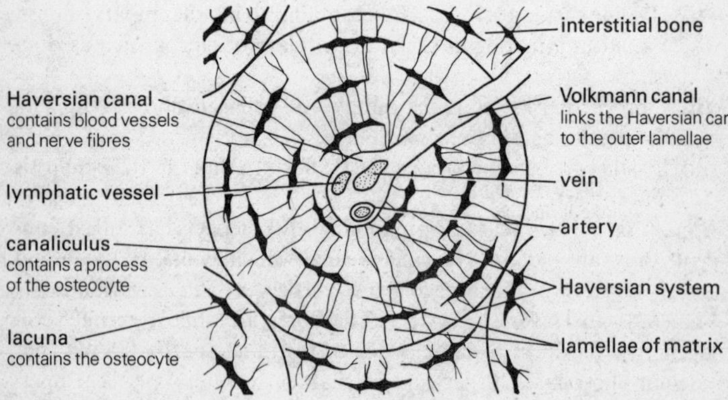
interstitial bone
Haversian canal
contains blood vessels and nerve fibres
Volkmann canal
links the Haversian canal to the outer lamellae
lymphatic vessel
vein
artery
canaliculus
contains a process of the osteocyte
Haversian system
lacuna
contains the osteocyte
lamellae of matrix

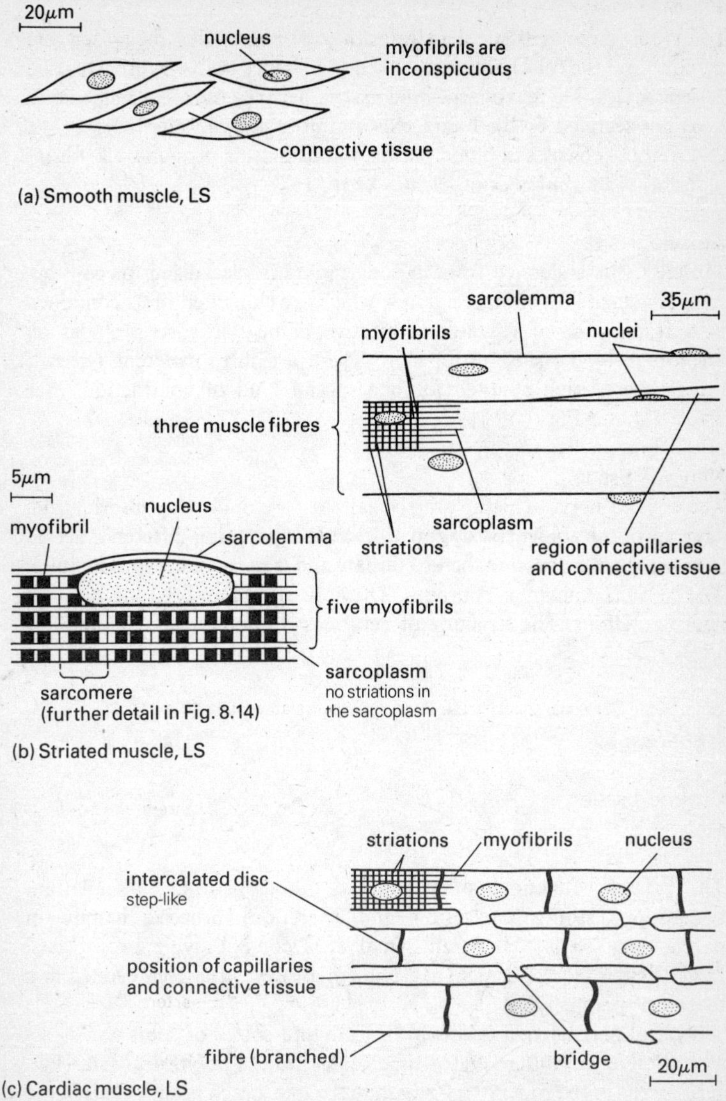
20μm
nucleus
myofibrils are inconspicuous
connective tissue
(a) Smooth muscle, LS
sarcolemma
35μm
myofibrils
nuclei
three muscle fibres
5μm
nucleus
myofibril
sarcolemma
sarcoplasm
striations
region of capillaries and connective tissue
five myofibrils
sarcoplasm
no striations in the sarcoplasm
sarcomere
(further detail in Fig. 8.14)
(b) Striated muscle, LS
striations
myofibrils
nucleus
intercalated disc
step-like
position of capillaries and connective tissue
fibre (branched)
bridge
20μm
(c) Cardiac muscle, LS

*Fig. 1.12* Three muscle tissue types

*Vascular connective tissue*

1. Blood – areolar tissue penetrates into structures like the spleen and bone and the cells become modified to produce both erythrocytes and leucocytes. There is a large fluid matrix between the cells. This matrix is not secreted by the blood cells and does not contain fibres.
2. Lymph – consists of blood plasma minus plasma proteins (e.g. fibrinogen) with a number of leucocytes (p. 162).

### Muscle tissue

Muscle tissue is derived from mesoderm and is specialized for contraction. It is made up of muscle fibres, which are elongated units contained in a framework of vascular connective tissue that also provides an anchorage to the skeleton or skin. There are three different types of muscle fibre, each adapted for one special kind of contraction. (See Table 1.4 and Fig. 1.12.)

### Nervous tissue

The cells in nervous tissue are specialized for conducting information. They have the ability to develop an electrical potential difference across their cell membranes and thereby initiate and transmit a nervous impulse. The cells are known as neurones. They are also secretory, and produce neurosecretions. The structure of neurones is discussed in Chapter 7.

## *Plant tissues*

### Ground tissue

*Parenchyma*

The primary functions of plants (i.e. photosynthesis, assimilation, respiration, storage, secretion and excretion) proceed mainly in parenchymal cells. All parenchymal cells contain living protoplasts. Other tissues (e.g. sclerenchyma, phloem and xylem) are embedded in a matrix of parenchyma.

Typical parenchyma occurs in the pith and cortex of roots and stems as a relatively undifferentiated tissue consisting of polyhedral cells (Fig. 1.13). Cells in the root cortex generally contain starch grains. Cells in the pith and cortex of stems contain starch grains and crystals (usually calcium oxalate). Parenchyma in flower parts or fruits may have yellow or red plastids in the cytoplasm, or purple or blue anthocyanin pigments

*Table 1.4.* Comparison of the three types of muscle tissue

| | *Smooth muscle, or non-striated involuntary* | *Striated muscle or skeletal voluntary* | *Cardiac muscle, or heart* |
|---|---|---|---|
| Location | Alimentary, respiratory and urinogenital tracts. Blood and lymph vessels. Ducts of glands. Ciliary muscle. Erector pili muscles of skin | Locomotory muscles, diaphragm, middle ear, sheets of muscle of abdominal wall | Heart only |
| Contraction | Slow, rhythmic and sustained. Impulses from the central nervous system (CNS) not essential for contraction | Rapid, powerful and not sustained. Contracts only in response to impulses from CNS transmitted via motor neurones | Fairly rapid. Rests between contractions. Not sustained. Myogenic but the rate is controlled by autonomic nervous system |
| Structure | | | |
| Fibre | Single cell | Multinucleate cell | Single branching cell |
| Sarcolemma | Absent | Present | Present |
| Nucleus | Central | Many at periphery of fibre | Central |
| Myofibrils | Inconspicuous | Conspicuous | Conspicuous |
| Cross striations | Absent | Present | Present |
| Branching | None | None | Frequent |
| Intercalated discs | Absent | Absent | Present |
| Size of fibre: | | | |
| length | 0.02 to 0.5 mm | 1 to 40 mm | 0.08 mm or less |
| diameter | 10 to 40 $\mu m$ | 8 to 10 $\mu m$ | 15 $\mu m$ |

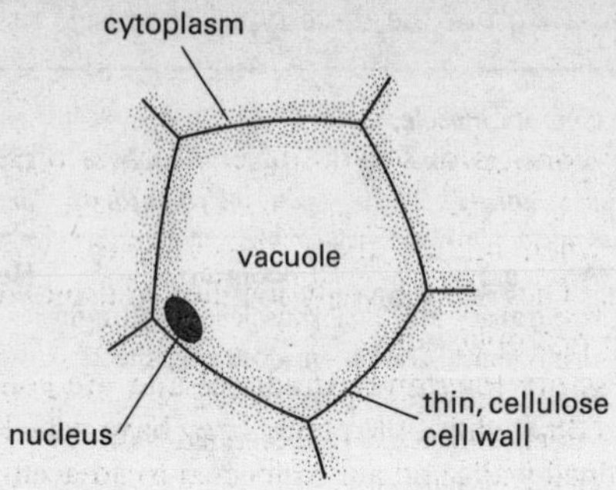
cytoplasm
vacuole
thin, cellulose
cell wall
nucleus

*Fig. 1.13* Parenchyma cells

in the vacuole. The mesophyll (tissue located between the upper and lower epidermis of leaves) is specially differentiated parenchyma called **chlorenchyma** (because its cells contain chlorophyll in distinct chloroplasts). Other specialized parenchymal cells form the endodermis and the companion cells.

## Protective tissue

### *Epidermis*

This is the outer layer of cells which covers the whole structure of the plant. It protects against injury, infection and desiccation.

Typical epidermal cells are flat, thin and closely packed with no intercellular spaces excepting stomatal pores. The outer wall is generally convex and thick. Epidermal cell walls are impregnated with a waxy substance (cutin), which forms an outer layer (the cuticle). Epidermal cells contain living protoplasts.

### *Periderm*

This is a layer of protective tissue which replaces the epidermis when it is sloughed off through secondary growth or abrasion. Suberin is generally deposited in the layers of the periderm. Lenticels may perforate the periderm at intervals. These are areas of loosely packed cells which are not suberized. They allow exchange of gases.

## Vascular tissue

### *Xylem*

Xylem generally consists of several different types of cells, both living and non-living.

1. Tracheids – when mature these are elongated vessels with finely tapering ends. They have heavily lignified and pitted secondary cell walls with no protoplasts.
2. Vessels – these are long and cylindrical and are connected to form long cylinders throughout the plant. They have wide lumens with less heavily thickened walls and are connected to adjacent cells via paired pits.

The type of thickening of the xylem elements may vary depending on their state of maturity (Fig. 1.14).

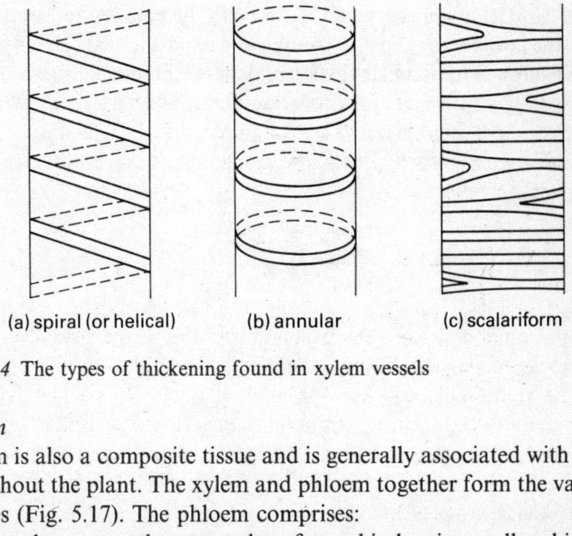
(a) spiral (or helical)
(b) annular
(c) scalariform

*Fig. 1.14* The types of thickening found in xylem vessels

### *Phloem*

Phloem is also a composite tissue and is generally associated with xylem throughout the plant. The xylem and phloem together form the vascular bundles (Fig. 5.17). The phloem comprises:

1. Sieve elements – these may be of two kinds: sieve cells which are found independently throughout the tissue and sieve-tube elements which form a long sieve-tube. The tube is interrupted at intervals by perforated sieve plates.
2. Companion cells – these are associated with the sieve-tube elements in angiosperms only. They are probably specialized parenchyma cells. A companion cell originates from the same meristematic cell as a

sieve-tube element by longitudinal division. They contain dense nucleated cytoplasm which is in communication with the cytoplasm of the sieve-tube by plasmodesmata through the pitted areas.

3. Parenchyma – these contain stored starch and fatty substances. The parenchyma cells are usually in communication with sieve-tube elements and companion cells by pitted areas.
4. Phloem fibres and sclereids – these occur in both primary and secondary phloem. In some species (e.g. *Tilia* (lime)) the fibres develop early and function mechanically throughout their lives.

## Mechanical tissue

### *Collenchyma*

This is a supporting tissue particularly of young shoot parts (Fig. 1.15). It is a simple tissue consisting of one cell type only. It is located near the surface, usually just under the epidermis. The cells are thickened at the corners. Collenchyma is typically formed in the petioles and vein ribs of leaves, the elongating zone of young stems and the pedicels of flowers. The cells may contain chloroplasts and starch grains.

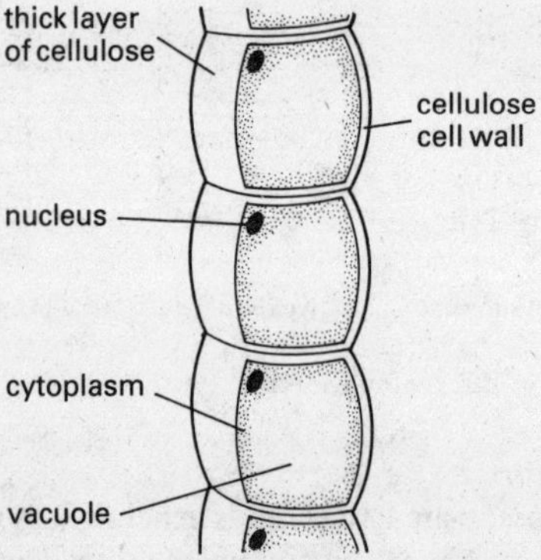
thick layer
of cellulose
cellulose
cell wall
nucleus
cytoplasm
vacuole

*Fig. 1.15* Collenchyma cells

### *Sclerenchyma*

Sclerenchyma's principal function is mechanical support of plants and plant parts and it has a widespread occurrence in vascular plants. The cells have thick secondary walls and are usually dead when mature. The cells vary in form with two general types:

1. Sclereids – these may vary in shape. They are found in the seed coats

(testa) and shells of nuts, in the bark of trees, in the flesh of fruits such as pears and in the xylem and pith of some plants.

2. Fibres – these are typically long (from a few millimetres to more than 0.5 m) with tapering ends. Their thick walls may be sparsely pitted. They are widely distributed, e.g. with vascular bundles in the stems and leaves of monocotyledons and in the xylem, phloem and cortex of dicotyledons. (See Fig. 1.16.)

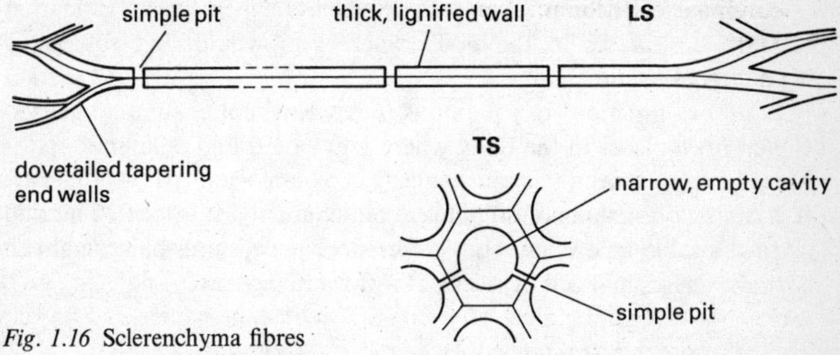
simple pit
thick, lignified wall
LS
dovetailed tapering end walls
TS
narrow, empty cavity
simple pit

*Fig. 1.16* Sclerenchyma fibres

## Further reading

B. Bracegirdle and P. H. Miles, *An Atlas of Plant Structure*, 2 volumes (Heinemann, 1971 and 1973)

W. H. Freeman and B. Bracegirdle, *An Atlas of Histology*, 2nd edition (Heinemann, 1967)

A. W. Ham and T. S. Leeson, *Histology* (Pitman Medical, 1961)

## Related questions

**Questions:**

An elongate cell with cellulose walls, tapering cross walls and thickening of the cellulose in the corners would be found in

(a) parenchyma
(b) collenchyma
(c) sclerenchyma
(d) xylem
(e) phloem

[Cambridge, Nov./Dec. 1981, Paper 3]

**Comment:**
This is a typical multiple choice question based on a detailed knowledge of the structure of tissues. The distinctive feature of the cells making up this tissue is the thickening of the cellulose in the corners of the cell. (See p. 44.)

**Questions:**
(a) Distinguish between the structure of squamous (pavement) and columnar epithelium. **(2 marks)**
(b) State *two* places in the body where you would find squamous (pavement) epithelium. **(2 marks)**
(c) State *two* functions of squamous (pavement) epithelium. **(2 marks)**
(d) State *two* places in the body where you would find columnar epithelium. **(2 marks)**
(e) State *two* functions of columnar epithelium. **(2 marks)**
(f) In the table below, give *two* differences between an epidermal cell and a mesophyll cell of a leaf of a flowering plant.

| | *Epidermal cell* | *Mesophyll cell* |
|---|---|---|
| (i) | | |
| (ii) | | |

**(2 marks)**

(g) In the table below, give *four* differences between the epidermis of a mammal and the epidermis of a leaf of a flowering plant.

| | *Mammal* | *Leaf of a flowering plant* |
|---|---|---|
| (i) | | |

| | *Mammal* | *Leaf of a flowering plant* |
|---|---|---|
| (ii) | | |
| (iii) | | |
| (iv) | | |

**(4 marks)**
**(Total 16 marks)**
[London, Jan. 1985, Paper 1]

**Comments:**
This is a detailed question concerning the structure and location of both plant and animal tissues.

(a) See p. 35. Apart from the obvious structural differences it should be noted that columnar cells may be ciliated.

(b) and (d) See p. 35.

(c) and (e) The functions of the tissues are obviously directly related to their structure:
Squamous epithelium – thin therefore useful in regions where rapid diffusion required. In common with all epithelia it forms a protective layer (e.g. lining the mouth).
Columnar epithelium – as it is very often ciliated it functions to expel unwanted particles from nasal cavities, trachea, etc. It also forms the lining of the intestine where it possesses microvilli to aid absorption of soluble products.

(f) This question compares two types of plant cell. The differences stem from the differences in function (i.e. an epidermal cell is protective whereas a mesophyll cell is photosynthetic). See pp. 124.

(g) This question requires a detailed knowledge of the differences between the two types of epidermis. Note that the question does not stipulate structural differences although these will probably be the first to come to mind.

| *Mammal* | *Leaf of a flowering plant* |
|---|---|
| (i) Epidermal cells have no cell wall | Epidermal cells have a cellulose cell wall |
| (ii) Mechanical protection provided by keratin | Waterproofing provided by cutin |
| (iii) Opaque, to protect the underlying cells from ultraviolet rays | Transparent to allow light to enter for photosynthesis which is carried out in underlying cells |
| (iv) Multiple layer of cells to allow abrasion of the surface to occur | One cell thick |

These are just four differences; others could be used (e.g. plant/animal differences such as presence and absence of cell vacuole).

# 2. Molecular biology

Most of the bulk of a living organism consists of water and dissolved salts. However, the relatively small proportion of organic matter is vital, both structurally and chemically. The organic matter is mainly composed of **carbohydrates**, **proteins** and **lipids**, either in the pure state, or more commonly combined with other substances.

**Biochemistry** is concerned with the study of the reactions involving these substances in living organisms.

## *Carbohydrates*

Carbohydrate is a term applied to a group of compounds which include the sugars, starch and cellulose. All carbohydrates contain the elements carbon, hydrogen and oxygen. The general formula for a carbohydrate is often represented as $C_x(H_2O)_y$. However, it is now evident that there are many substances with properties characteristic of sugars which deviate from the required hydrogen to oxygen ratio. An example is deoxyribose ($C_5H_{10}O_4$).

The carbohydrates may be separated into three major groups according to complexity: monosaccharides, oligosaccharides and polysaccharides.

### *Monosaccharides*

These are simple sugars consisting of a single carbohydrate unit which cannot be hydrolysed into simpler substances. They have the general formula $C_nH_{2n}O_n$ and are all reducing sugars, i.e. they have either an active aldehyde (–CHO) or ketone (–C=) group. They are all soluble in water. Monosaccharides are characterized by the length of their carbon chains, e.g. trioses ($C_3H_6O_3$), pentoses ($C_5H_{10}O_5$), hexoses ($C_6H_{12}O_6$), etc. Approximately 20 monosaccharides occur naturally and some examples are given in Table 2.1.

*Table 2.1.* Examples of some important monosaccharides and monosaccharide derivatives

| *Example* | *Location and function* |
|---|---|
| Monosaccharides | |
| Trioses | |
| Glyceric aldehyde | Intermediate product in photosynthesis and respiration |
| Pentoses<br>Ribose | Ribose and 2-deoxyribose make up the carbohydrate constituent of the nucleic acids – RNA and DNA, respectively (pp. 405 and 408). Ribose is also found in several vitamins and coenzymes |
| Ribulose | See under the derivatives, ribulose, ribulose diphosphate and ribulose phosphate, later in the table |
| Hexoses<br>Glucose | The most common sugar. Found in the free state in all higher plants and in particularly high concentrations in fruits such as grapes and figs. Found in lesser concentrations in animal body fluids, e.g. blood (0.08%). The principal carbohydrate metabolite. Absorbed from the alimentary canal in greater amounts than any other monosaccharide. (The chemistry of glucose is discussed in the text.) |
| Galactose | Found in agar and in a variety of gums and mucilages. It may be used as a respiratory substrate on conversion to glucose phosphate. Found in several polysaccharides |
| Fructose | Sweetest of all sugars. Found in fruit juices and the nectar of plants. The principal sugar in seminal fluid |
| Monosaccharide derivatives | |
| Phosphorylated sugars<br>Glucose-1-phosphate | Intermediate in the phosphorolytic breakdown and synthesis of polysaccharides in plants and animals (see p. 52) |

| *Example* | *Location and function* |
|---|---|
| Glucose-6-phosphate | Key intermediate in carbohydrate metabolism (see p. 103) |
| Ribulose diphosphate | The carbon dioxide acceptor in photosynthesis of higher plants |
| Ribulose phosphate | Intermediate in carbohydrate metabolism (see p. 103) |
| Sugar alcohols<br>Mannitol | Widespread in plants and plant exudates. Very sweet |

## The chemistry of glucose

Glucose is a typical monosaccharide. It exists in two forms (α and β), and a fresh solution is an equilibrium mixture of both the α and β **isomers**. (Isomers contain the same number and type of atoms but these are arranged in a different manner (see Fig. 2.1).) Glucose has an active aldehyde group.

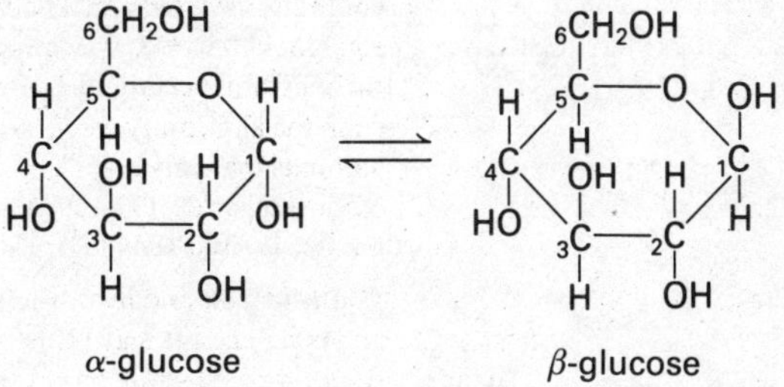

$_6CH_2OH$
H
$_5C$
O
H
H
$_4C$
OH
H
$_1C$
HO
$_3C$
$_2C$
OH
H
OH
α-glucose
$_6CH_2OH$
H
$_5C$
O
OH
H
$_4C$
OH
H
$_1C$
HO
$_3C$
$_2C$
H
H
OH
β-glucose


*Fig. 2.1* The two isomers of glucose. (There is a reversal of the –H and –OH groups at carbon atom number 1)

### *Oligosaccharides*

These are sugars composed of two or more monosaccharide units. Oligosaccharides have the same properties as their constituent monosaccharides, although these properties may be modified by the linking of the units together. For example, if the linkage leaves a reducing group from one of the monosaccharides free the resulting oligosaccharide is reducing.

The hydroxyl (–OH) group of one monosaccharide is condensed with the reducing (–H) group of another with the elimination of water and the formation of a glycosidic bond (see Fig. 2.2). If two sugars are joined a disaccharide results (see Table 2.2); three sugars result in a trisaccharide, and so on. All disaccharides are soluble. There is no sharp distinction between oligosaccharides and polysaccharides.

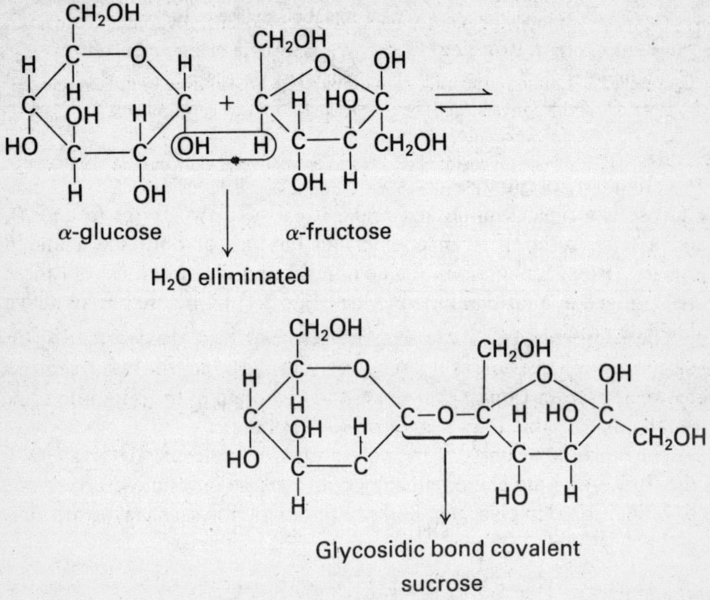
α-glucose
α-fructose
$H_2O$ eliminated
Glycosidic bond covalent
sucrose

*Fig. 2.2* Formation of the disaccharide sucrose

## *Polysaccharides*

Polysaccharides are formed by the condensation of large numbers of monosaccharides, and therefore have high molecular weights. Polysaccharides such as starch and glycogen consist of several thousand glucose units. Polysaccharides are insoluble in water or form colloidal solutions, and are non-reducing.

Polysaccharides act as reserve nutrients, e.g. glycogen and insulin, or as 'skeletal' material, e.g. cellulose and chitin.

*Table 2.2.* Examples of some important disaccharides

| *Example* | *Location and function* |
|---|---|
| Sucrose | Also known as cane or beet sugar. Occurs universally throughout the plant kingdom in fruits, seeds, roots and flowers. Non-reducing. Very soluble in water. Transports sugar |
| Maltose | Composed of two molecules of α-glucose. Main end-product of animal and plant amylase action. Not generally found in the pure state. Reducing |
| Lactose | Found in the milk of mammals (2.8%). Souring of milk is due to the conversion of lactose to lactic acid by certain bacteria, e.g. *Lactobacillus acidophilus*. The glycosidic bond is formed between C-atom 1 of α-galactose and C-atom 4 of α-glucose. Reducing |
| Cellobiose | Formed during the hydrolysis of cellulose. Reducing |
| Trehalose | Found in yeasts and other fungi. Non-reducing |

The properties of a polysaccharide depend to a great extent on the nature of the glycosidic bond. A 1→6 glycosidic bond (the bond is formed between C-atom 1 on one molecule and C-atom 6 of the other molecule) is far more flexible than a 1→4 or 1→3 bond.

The constituent units of the polysaccharide molecule are arranged in the form of a long chain, either unbranched, as in cellulose and starch, or branched, as in glycogen. Some examples of polysaccharides are given in Table 2.3.

## Proteins

A protein is a compound made up of various amino acids. Proteins are of importance in all biological systems, playing a wide variety of structural and functional roles. They form the organic basis of structures such as hair, tendons, muscles, skin and cartilage. All enzymes are types of proteins. Many hormones, e.g. insulin and somatotrophin or growth hormone, are also proteins. The substances responsible for oxygen and electron transport (haemoglobin and cytochromes, respectively) are conjugated proteins, i.e. protein attached to another molecule, in these cases a metallic ion. Chromosomes are complex nucleoproteins – proteins conjugated with nucleic acids. Viruses are also made up of nucleoproteins.

*Table 2.3.* Examples of important polysaccharides

| *Example* | *Location and function* |
|---|---|
| Storage polysaccharides | |
| Starch | Straight-chained starch molecules are known as amylose (1→4 glycosidic bonds). Branched starch molecules are known as amylopectin (1→4 glycosidic bonds with →6 branches). Most starch granules contain 20–30% amylose, the rest being amylopectin. Starch is the reserve carbohydrate stored in seeds, roots or stems of plants. It is a natural polymer of glucose. |
| Glycogen | Primary reserve compound in animals. Found in muscles and liver of all higher animals as well as the cells of lower animals. Also found in some lower plants, e.g. fungi. Biochemical reactions are similar to starch, e.g. hydrolysed by the same amylase to yield maltose and dextrins. Branched structure similar to amylopectin, i.e. 1→4 glycosidic bonds with 1→6 branches. |
| Insulin | Reserve polysaccharide in some plants, particularly in the family Compositae where it is found in the tubers and roots of the dahlia and dandelion. Composed of fructose units. |
| Skeletal polysaccharides | |
| Cellulose | Main polysaccharide in living plants. Forms the skeletal structure of the cell wall. Occurs together with other polysaccharides called hemi-celluloses. These are derived from other sugars, e.g. xylose, arabinose, and mannose. In the woody parts of plants it is mixed and sometimes covalently linked with lignin. Chain of 1→4 linked glucose molecules (2,000–4,000 molecules long). Cellulose is in the form of fibrils which are visible under the optical microscope. These are found in the primary and secondary cell walls and are arranged to form layers. The electron microscope reveals microfibrils inside the fibrils. |

| *Example* | *Location and function* |
|---|---|
| Chitin | Forms the basis of the exoskeletons of arthropods and the cell walls of fungi.<br>Long, unbranched molecule consisting of acetyl glucosamine units linked by 1→4 bonds. It is similar to cellulose but the hydroxyl group on C-atom 2 is replaced with an $NHCOH_3$ group (acetamido). |
| Pectin | Group of polysaccharides occurring in the cell walls and intercellular layers of all land plants. Gel-forming, therefore used commercially in jams and jellies. Has a high molecular weight (30,000→300,000). |
| Other biologically important carbohydrates | |
| Mucilage (gum) | Naturally occurring, high molecular weight (200,000), organic plant product. The detailed structure is unknown. Considered to help in water storage, aid in germination and seed dispersal, and act as a food reserve.<br>Most mucilages are cellulose-based polysaccharides. |
| Mucin (mucus) | Found covering the cavities which communicate with the environment in vertebrates (i.e. digestive, respiratory and genital tracts).<br>Is a glycoprotein with a molecular weight of 2 million.<br>Contains a high proportion of carbohydrate (70%) relative to protein. |

Amino acids are organic compounds having one or more basic amino groups (–$NH_2$), and one or more acidic carboxyl groups (–COOH). More than 80 amino acids have been found in living organisms. Approximately 20 serve as the building blocks for proteins.

All the amino acids of proteins, and most of those that occur naturally, are α-amino acids – an amino group and a carboxyl group are attached to the same carbon atom (the α-carbon). This carbon atom also carries a hydrogen atom. Its fourth bond is satisfied by any of a wide variety of groups, represented by the letter R in Fig. 2.3. In the simplest amino acid, glycine, R is a hydrogen atom. In all other amino acids R is an organic radicle. For example, in alanine it is a methyl group (–$CH_3$).

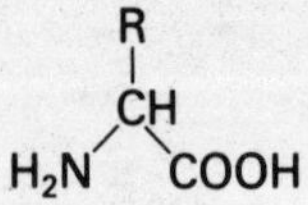

*Fig 2.3* Structural formula for an amino acid

All of the amino acids (with the exception of glycine) possess a centre of symmetry at the carbon atom, and they can therefore exist in either of two mirror image forms (isomers).

Amino acids generally occur linked together (i.e. as peptides) in living tissues. The amino group of one amino acid is linked to the carboxyl group of another via a **peptide bond** that is formed by a condensation reaction which produces water (see Fig. 2.4). Consequently, a molecule of water must be added when a peptide bond is broken.

Amino acids are capable of linking together, via peptide bonds, to form chains of varying lengths. These are called **polypeptides.** Proteins are polypeptides ranging in size from about 50 to many thousand amino acid residues.

The linear arrangement of the amino acid residues in a protein is termed its sequence or **primary structure.** This specificity of sequence is remarkable considering the possible permutations of sequence in even as small a protein as insulin. Insulin has a molecular weight of 5,732 and contains 51 amino acids, giving a possible $10^{51}$ variations. However, the pancreatic cells produce the correct sequence each time. (See 'Protein synthesis', p. 409.)

Scientists have been preoccupied with sequencing proteins since the mid-1940s. F. Sanger determined the primary sequence of insulin and S. Moore and W. H. Stein sequenced the enzyme ribonuclease (which has 124 amino acid residues).

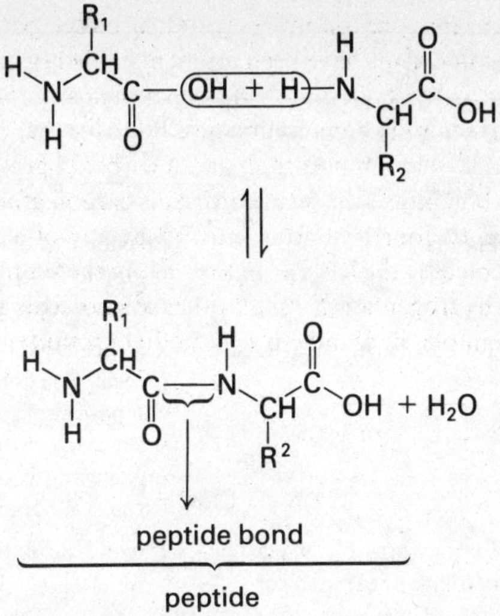
R1
H
O
H
CH
N
C
OH + H
N
C
CH
OH
H
O
R2
R1
H
O
H
CH
N
C
N
C
CH
OH + H2O
H
O
R2
peptide bond
peptide

*Fig. 2.4* Formation of a peptide bond

The polypeptide backbone of a protein can fold in several ways by using the hydrogen bonds between the oxygen of the carboxyl group and the nitrogen of the amino group. The folding of each protein is determined by its particular sequence of amino acids.

There are two main classes of protein molecules – **fibrous** and **globular**. They are separated by their differences in structure.

### *Fibrous proteins*

In fibrous proteins, the backbone of amino acids is coiled to form a helix, with stability being achieved by hydrogen bonds forming between adjacent peptide bonds. The fibrous proteins can form a network through a small number of covalent bonds between fibres.

Fibrous proteins are generally insoluble in water, and are highly resistant to proteolytic enzymes. Examples are listed in Table 2.4.

### *Globular proteins*

These generally have a more spherical shape than fibrous proteins, which gives them a high degree of solubility in water. The $NH_4^+$ and

*Table 2.4.* Examples of fibrous proteins

| *Example* | *Occurrence* | *Role* |
|---|---|---|
| Keratin | Hair, wool, horn, feathers | Protective |
| Myosin<br>Actin | Muscle | Contractile |
| Fibrinogen | Plasma | Precursor of **fibrin**, which is the insoluble fibrous protein formed during blood-clotting |
| Collagen | Tendon, cartilage, fish scales | The most abundant animal protein. The fibrillar component of soft connective tissue. Major component of organic matrix of calcified tissue, e.g. bone, dentine |
| Elastin | Elastic fibres, e.g. in elastic cartilage of external ear | Provides flexibility |

*Table 2.5.* Examples of globular proteins

| *Example* | *Occurrence* | *Role* |
|---|---|---|
| Haemoglobin | Erythrocytes in vertebrates<br>Plasma of some annelids and molluscs | Oxygen-carrying pigment |
| Albumin | Mammalian tissues<br>Bacteria, fungi, plants<br>Some foods | Responsible for about 80% of the total osmotic regulation in blood. Transports fatty acids between adipose tissues |
| Casein | Milk | Makes up 80% of milk protein |
| $\beta$-globulin | Serum | Associated with antibody activity |

$COO^-$ groups along the polypeptide backbone link together in many different areas forming hydrogen bonds. These bonds, together with Van der Waals forces (hydrophobic interactions) knit the molecule together into its globular shape.

If a globular protein is heated or treated with strong acids or alkalis the hydrogen bonds are broken and it reverts to a more fibrous form.

All enzymes and protein hormones are globular proteins, and examples of some common globular proteins are listed in Table 2.5.

### *The properties of proteins*

The properties of proteins are determined by their amino acid composition. For example, the net charge on a protein depends on the relative numbers of basic (e.g. lysine and arginine) and dicarboxylic (e.g. aspartic and glutamic acids) amino acids. The net charge strongly influences the solubility of the protein at different pH values.

Proteins may contain many side branches that can release or take up protons ($H^+$), and they may therefore act as excellent buffers. The fact that the pH of blood varies only very slightly is due to the buffering capacity of the blood proteins.

The interaction of the side chains of amino acids provides some proteins (enzymes) with the ability to catalyse essential reactions in metabolism.

The specific binding of small ions to the side chains of proteins allows the transport of essential metal ions in and out of cells, as in the action of the sodium pump within certain cells (e.g. nerve cells and the loop of Henlé).

## *Lipids*

The term 'lipid' covers a wide range of substances. However, all lipids are insoluble in water and insoluble in alcohol.

For convenience the lipids may be divided into three categories:

1. Neutral fats
2. Phospholipids
3. Steroids, e.g. cholesterol

Lipids always contain **glycerol**, a three-carbon chain with three –OH groups. In **neutral fats** each –OH group may condense with a **fatty acid** (general formula RCOOH) to form a **triglyceride** (Fig. 2.5). In the fatty acids the R group is usually a simple unbranched chain of $CH_2$ residues.

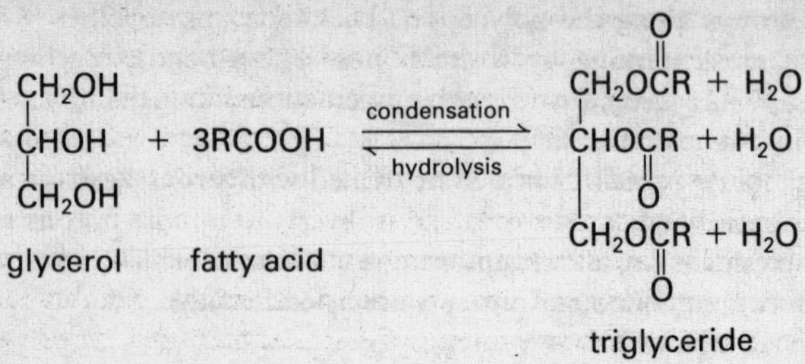
CH₂OH
CHOH
CH₂OH
+ 3RCOOH
condensation
hydrolysis
CH₂OCR + H₂O
CHOCR + H₂O
CH₂OCR + H₂O
O
glycerol
fatty acid
triglyceride

*Fig. 2.5* Formation of a lipid

Fatty acids may be **saturated** or **unsaturated**.

Saturated fatty acids are chemically inert and stable. An example is palmitic acid (Fig. 2.6). This is one of the commonest components of both plant and animal fats.

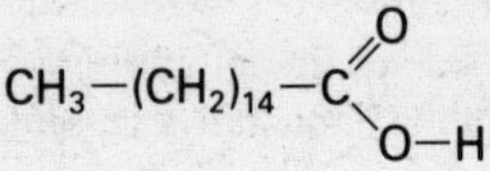
CH₃–(CH₂)₁₄–C
O
O–H

*Fig. 2.6* Structure of palmitic acid (in which 14 $CH_2$ groups make up the hydrocarbon chain)

Unsaturated fatty acids contain a double bond between the central carbon atoms; they therefore do not contain their full complement of hydrogen atoms. Oleic acid (Fig. 2.7) is an example of an unsaturated fatty acid.

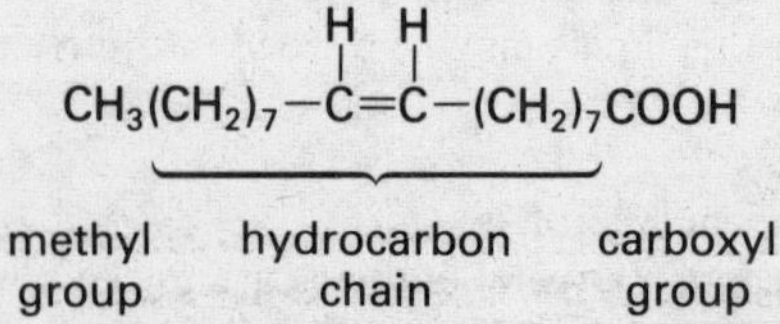
H H
CH₃(CH₂)₇–C=C–(CH₂)₇COOH
methyl group
hydrocarbon chain
carboxyl group

*Fig. 2.7* Structure of oleic acid (which has a double bond in the centre of the hydrocarbon chain)

In the **phospholipids** one of the three OH groups of the glycerol condenses with a phosphoric acid derivative, with a general formula ($HPO_3X$). The phosphoric acid derivative confers polarity on the phospholipid molecule. The glycerol and phosphoric acid end of the molecule is polar, and therefore water-soluble; the fatty acid portion is water-insoluble and non-polar.

Phospholipids are an important constituent of all membranes. Membranes vary widely in lipid composition. Animal membranes generally have less lipid than protein, with protein to lipid ratios ranging from 1:1 in the erythrocyte membrane to 2:1 in the nuclear membrane, to 3.6:1 in the inner mitochondrial membrane, to 10.3:1 in the myelin sheath. Plant chloroplast membranes are 50 per cent lipid.

**Steroids** are very complex and have certain properties in common with lipids. Cholesterol is an example of a steroid. It is essentially a long fatty acid side chain folded into four flat rings (Fig. 2.8). In other steroids, e.g. vitamin D and sex hormones, the position of the OH group and the nature of the side chains may vary.

Some biologically important lipids are listed in Table 2.6.

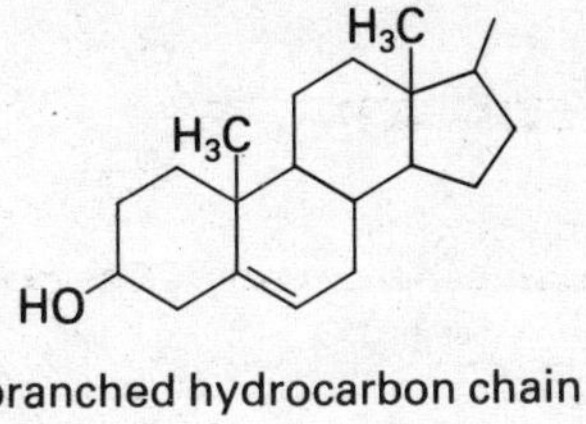
H3C
H3C
HO
branched hydrocarbon chain

*Fig. 2.8* Structure of cholesterol

### *Tests for carbohydrates, proteins and lipids*

See Table 2.7.

### *Further reading*

J. Edelman and J. M. Chapman, *Basic Biochemistry* (Heinemann, 1978)

C. F. Phelips, *Polysaccharides*, Oxford/Carolina Biology Reader No. 27 (Packard)

D. C. Phillips and A. C. T. North, *Protein Structure*, Oxford/Carolina Biology Reader No. 34, 2nd edition (Packard, 1978)

*Table 2.6.* Examples of some biologically important lipids

| *Example* | *Function* |
|---|---|
| Neutral fats | |
| Saturated fats | Accumulated in the fat deposits of the body and act as an energy store and insulatory layer |
| Unsaturated fats | Reactive; take part in metabolism |
| Phospholipids | |
| Cardiolipin (diphosphatidyl glycerol) | A polar lipid. Main component of plant membranes; generally absent from animal membranes |
| Steroids | |
| Cholesterol | The main non-polar membrane lipid. Lacking in bacterial membranes, but is the main component in erythrocyte membranes and myelin. |
| Vitamin D | Involved in uptake of calcium and phosphorus (see p. 142) |
| Sex hormones, e.g. oestrogen, progesterone, testosterone | See p. 279 |
| Adrenal cortex hormones, e.g. cortisol, corticosterone hormones, aldosterone | See p. 279 |
| Bile acids | See p. 153 |

### *Related questions*

**Question:**

(a) Give the general formula for a carbohydrate. **(1 mark)**

(b) The carbohydrate illustrated has been formed from two hexose sugars.

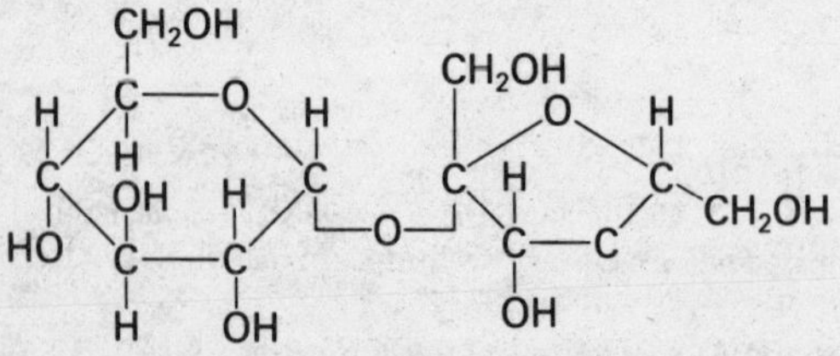
CH₂OH
H
C
O
H
H
C
OH
H
C
HO
C
C
H
OH
O
CH₂OH
O
H
C
H
C
CH₂OH
C
C
OH

What type of carbohydrate is this? **(1 mark)**

(c) Name the type of chemical bond which joins the two hexose units together in the molecule. **(1 mark)**
(d) What is the name given to the chemical reaction in which two or more hexose sugars combine to form larger units? **(1 mark)**
(e) Give one function of the carbohydrate illustrated in living organisms.
(f) Name a storage polysaccharide commonly found in mammals. **(1 mark)**
  (i) In which organ of the body would you expect it to occur in relatively large amounts? **(1 mark)**
  (ii) Where is it deposited in the cells of this organ? **(1 mark)**
  (iii) In what physical form is this substance found in cells? **(1 mark)**

[Oxford, July 1982, Paper 1]

**Comments:**
(a) See p. 49.
(b) See p. 52. Joining of two monosaccharide units results in a disaccharide. The answer requires the type of carbohydrate, not the name of it.
(c) See p. 52. It is the covalent glycosidic bond.
(d) See p. 52. A condensation reaction, i.e. one in which a molecule of water is removed.
(e) See p. 53.
(f) See p. 52.
  (i) See p. 54.
  (ii) In the cytoplasm in granules.
  (iii) A branched structure with 1→4 glycosidic bonds with 1→6 branches

**Question:**
Discuss the role of carbohydrates in the lives of organisms. **(20 marks)**

[London, June 1980, Paper 2]

**Comments:**
This general essay tests your ability to *plan* carefully. It is the *role* of carbohydrates that must be discussed, not the structure. However, a *brief* description of the general structure of carbohydrates could be included as an introduction (see p. 49). Note that the title specifies *organisms*; therefore both animals and plants should have approximately equal coverage.

*Table 2.7.* Tests for carbohydrates, proteins and lipids

| *Substance* | *Test* | *Comments* |
|---|---|---|
| Carbohydrates | | |
| Reducing sugars (e.g. glucose, fructose) | (i) Equal quantities of Fehling's solutions A (copper sulphate) and B (sodium potassium tartrate and sodium hydroxide) are added to the sugar solution. The mixture is boiled. The reducing sugar reduces the blue copper II oxide to red copper I oxide, which is precipitated.<br>(ii) Benedict's solution (copper sulphate, sodium citrate and sodium carbonate) is boiled with sugar solution. A positive result is shown by the production of a red precipitate, indicating the presence of reducing sugars | The Benedict's test is more sensitive |
| Non-reducing sugars (e.g. sucrose) | A negative result is obtained with the Fehling's and Benedict's solutions unless the disaccharide is first hydrolysed by boiling with dilute acid | The Fehling's or Benedict's reactions will only occur in neutral alkaline solution so the acid must be neutralized before testing |
| Polysaccharides | | |
| Starch | Addition of iodine solution to a cold solution of starch results in a blue/black coloration. This colour will disappear on heating | The colour is due to a complex formed between the iodine and starch. The iodine is positioned in the centre of the helical starch molecule |
| Cellulose | Cellulose will give a blue colour with Schultze's solution (chlor-zinc-iodide) | |

| | | |
|---|---|---|
| Proteins | (i) The test solution is heated with a few drops of Millon's reagent (mercuric nitrate and nitrite). Presence of a protein is indicated by a deep red colour.<br>(ii) Biuret test – a little sodium hydroxide is added to the test solution. 1% copper sulphate solution is then added dropwise. A positive test is indicated by a violet colour. | The deep red coloration is due to the presence of a phenolic group in the amino acid tyrosine. It is therefore only a test for proteins containing tyrosine. All proteins give a positive result with the biuret test. This is due to the presence of –NH–CO– groups in the molecule |
| Lipids | (i) A little of the test material is added to approximately 2 $cm^3$ of ethyl alcohol and shaken well. An equal quantity of cold water is then added and mixed. Cloudiness indicates the presence of a lipid.<br>(ii) All lipids form a 'grease spot' on filter paper.<br>(iii) If the red dye, Sudan III, is added to a mixture of lipid and water only the lipid will retain the dye. | The cloudiness is due to the lipid forming an emulsion with the water |

One approach to the essay is to take the seven characteristics of life and discuss how carbohydrates are necessary for each. Do not ignore the compounds which are a carbohydrate chemically linked to another molecule, for example the nucleotides where the carbohydrate is a pentose sugar, or derivatives such as ribulose diphosphate. All the information required is in Tables 2.1, 2.2 and 2.3 (pp. 50–55). All classes of carbohydrates should be considered, i.e. monosaccharides, disaccharides and polysaccharides.

Select examples related to each of the vital processes. In certain cases it will be difficult to find a large number of detailed examples, but do not be tempted to leave them out altogether. For example, for reproduction you should mention that fructose is the principal sugar found in seminal fluid (providing an energy source for the sperm) and mucin (glycoprotein) is a common component of cell secretions (acting as a lubricant and protecting underlying cells in vaginal secretions).

In some cases repetition will occur, e.g. the use of glucose as a universal energy source. Just discuss this in some detail under respiration and then refer to this during the remainder of the essay.

Round off the essay by emphasizing the versatility of carbohydrates, both in their range of functions and their ability to link with other molecules to further increase their roles.

## *Metabolism*

**Metabolism** is the name given to all the chemical reactions taking place within a living organism.

**Anabolism** refers to the manufacture of large organic molecules from small molecules, e.g. the formation from glucose of starch (in plants) or glycogen (in animals), which can then be stored until required for energy. Anabolic reactions are responsible for the manufacture of all cell components, e.g. production of proteins from amino acids, cellulose from sugars and fats from fatty acids and glycerol.

**Catabolism** is the breakdown of large organic molecules into their smaller constituent molecules, e.g. breakdown of starch or glycogen to glucose, or of fats to fatty acids. This ensures a readily available source of food molecules for energy or for building new cell components.

The anabolic and catabolic reactions to an organism must work in a balanced manner in order to provide the body with the correct amounts of stored and available food.

## *Enzymes*

Enzymes are globular proteins which act as catalysts, i.e. they regulate the rate of chemical reactions but themselves remain unchanged. The main groups of enzymes are listed in Table 2.8.

*Table 2.8.* Range of enzyme activities

| *Enzyme group* | *Reactions catalysed* | *Examples* |
|---|---|---|
| Transferases | Transfer atoms or groups of atoms from one substrate to another | Phosphorylases<br>Transaminases |
| Oxidoreductases | All oxidation–reduction reactions | Dehydrogenases – removal of hydrogen<br>Oxidases – addition of oxygen |
| Isomerases | Transfer of atoms from one part of a molecule to another (i.e. rearrangement of the molecule) | Glucose phosphate isomerase converts glucose-6-phosphate to fructose-6-phosphate |
| Hydrolases | Hydrolytic reactions – addition of water across a bond causing cleavage | Peptidases<br>Lipases<br>Dehydrases |
| Lyases | Removal of a group of atoms to yield a double bond | Decarboxylases remove COOH groups |
| Ligases | Formation of a bond between two substrate molecules using energy from the splitting of ATP | Glucose + ATP to glucose-6-phosphate + ADP using the enzyme hexokinase |

### *Characteristics of enzymes*

1. Enzymes are specific – each enzyme catalyses a specific reaction.
2. Enzyme-controlled reactions are reversible – enzymes will catalyse reactions in either direction, the direction depending on other factors such as pH, or substrate concentration.
3. The shape of an enzyme may be changed during a reaction, but is resumed upon completion of the reaction.
4. During a reaction enzymes may be used over and over again, so only very small quantities are required.

### *How enzymes work*

Enzymes usually speed up the rate of a reaction by reducing the activation energy of the reaction (i.e. the amount of energy required for the reaction to occur). (See Fig. 2.9.)

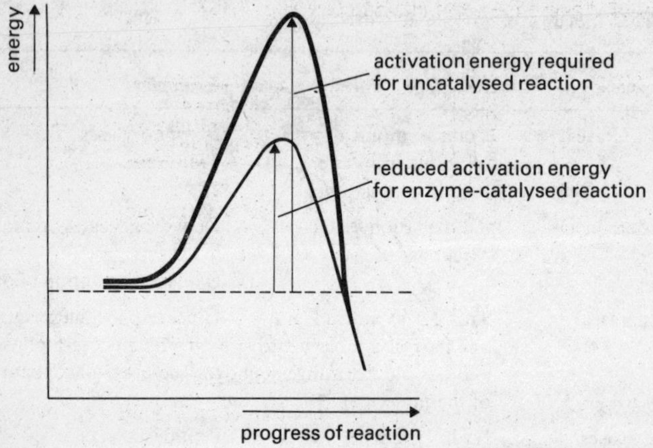
energy
activation energy required for uncatalysed reaction
reduced activation energy for enzyme-catalysed reaction
progress of reaction

*Fig. 2.9* Energy requirements for catalysed and uncatalysed reactions

Although it is not fully understood how enzymes work, it is known that the enzyme contains an active site. This is a place on to which the reacting chemical or chemicals (i.e. the substrates) adhere in order for reactions to occur. The active site has a very precise shape, so that only specific substrate molecules can fit into it, like a key fitting into a lock (Fig. 2.10).

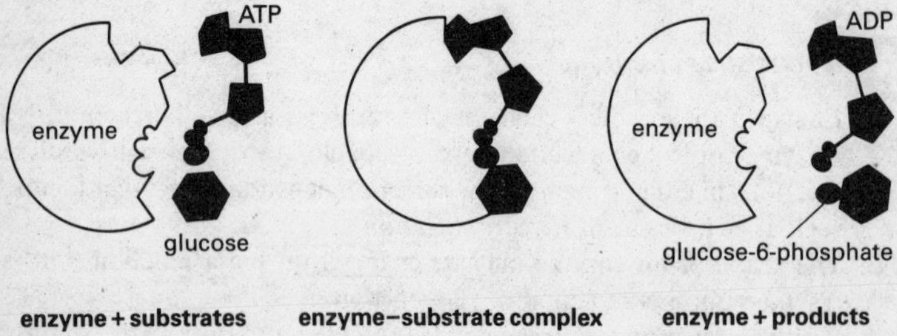
ATP
enzyme
glucose
ADP
enzyme
glucose-6-phosphate
enzyme + substrates
enzyme–substrate complex
enzyme + products

*Fig. 2.10* Formation of glucose-6-phosphate, using the enzyme hexokinase

### *Factors affecting the rate of enzyme activity*

#### Substrate concentration

The rate of reaction increases with an increase in substrate concentration, provided there is excess enzyme (see Fig. 2.11)

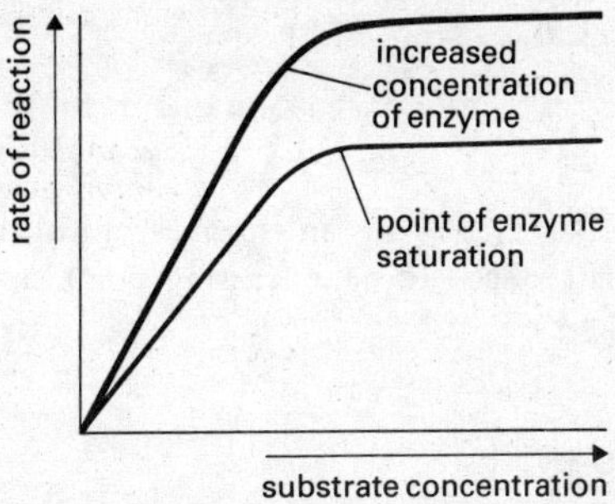
rate of reaction
increased concentration of enzyme
point of enzyme saturation
substrate concentration

*Fig. 2.11* Relationship between the rate of an enzyme-controlled reaction and substrate concentration

#### Enzyme concentration

If the enzyme concentration is increased, the rate of reaction also increases (see Fig. 2.12).

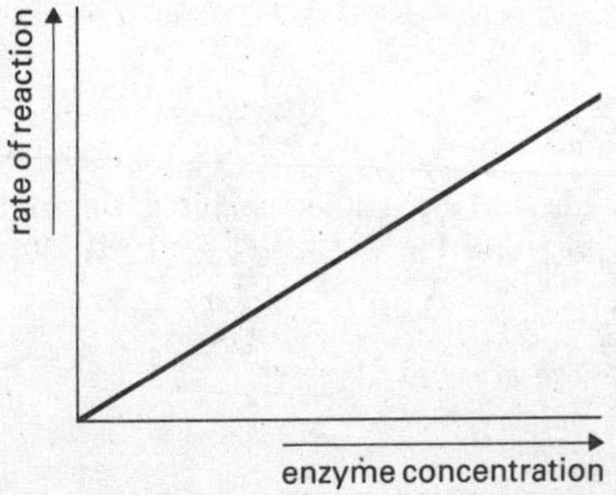
rate of reaction
enzyme concentration

*Fig. 2.12* Relationship between the rate of an enzyme-controlled reaction and enzyme concentration

### Temperature

All enzymes work best at an optimum temperature. The rate of reaction generally increases with an increase in temperature due to an increase in the kinetic energy of the molecules making enzyme/substrate collisions more frequent. This increase in reaction rate occurs up to an optimum temperature; above this the enzyme is denatured which alters the shape of the active site preventing substrate attachment. The term temperature coefficient is used to express the effect of a 10 °C rise in temperature on the rate of a chemical reaction

$$Q_{10} = \frac{\text{rate of reaction at } t + 10\ ^{\circ}\text{C}}{\text{rate of reaction at } t\ ^{\circ}\text{C}}$$

Over a range of 0–40 °C, $Q_{10}$ for an enzyme-controlled reaction is 2. If the temperature is reduced to near freezing point enzymes are inactivated. (See Fig. 2.13.)

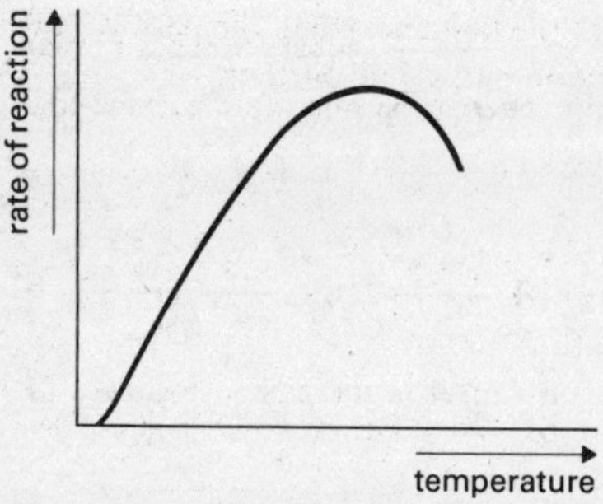
rate of reaction
temperature

*Fig. 2.13* Relationship between the rate of an enzyme-controlled reaction and temperature

### pH

Most enzymes work best at a particular pH, e.g. pepsin at pH 2, salivary amylase at pH 7 and trypsin at pH 8.5 (Fig. 2.14).

## *Regulation of enzyme activity*

### Feedback inhibition

Metabolic pathways consist of a number of steps, each step being controlled by a different enzyme. During the pathway shown in Fig. 2.15a,

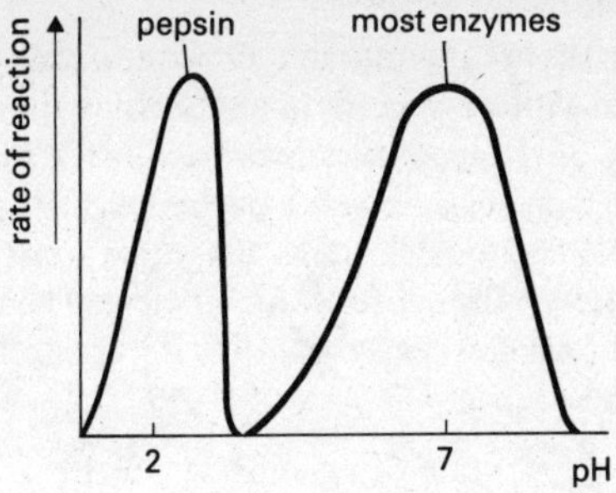

rate of reaction
pepsin
most enzymes
2
7
pH


*Fig. 2.14* Relationship between the rate of an enzyme-controlled reaction and pH

molecule A is converted to molecule B, and subsequently to molecule F via a series of steps, each of which is controlled by a different enzyme. In feedback inhibition (Fig. 2.15b), an accumulation of the end-product (F) causes inhibition of the first enzyme in the pathway (which converts A to B), hence the reaction can go no further.

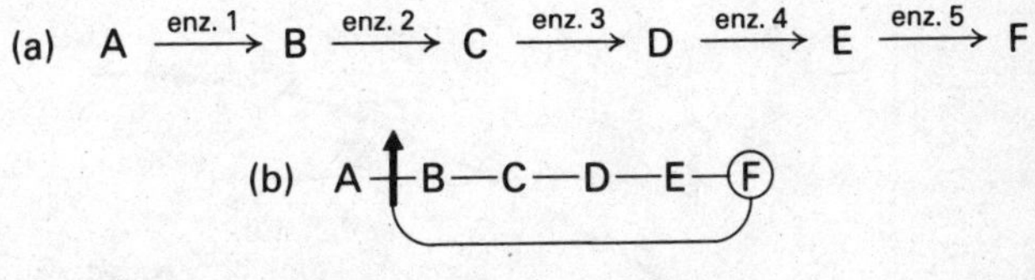

(a) A enz. 1 B enz. 2 C enz. 3 D enz. 4 E enz. 5 F
(b) A—B—C—D—E—F


*Fig. 2.15* Metabolic pathways and feedback inhibition

Inhibition is brought about by binding of the product molecules (called effectors) on to the first enzyme. This alters the shape of the active site, so that substrate molecules can no longer bind to it. As the amount of product decreases, the effectors dissociate from the enzyme molecules and the enzyme regains its normal shape. The substrate can then bind to the active site, allowing the series of reactions to continue. The pathway is therefore self-regulating.

Sometimes the effector is not the end-product of a pathway, but is a different molecule. For example, in the Krebs cycle (see p. 103), the enzyme succinate dehydrogenase is inhibited by NADH and also by

ATP. Enzymes which are regulated in such a way are called allosteric enzymes (Fig. 2.16). They contain two sites: an active site for substrate binding and a second site for binding of the effector.

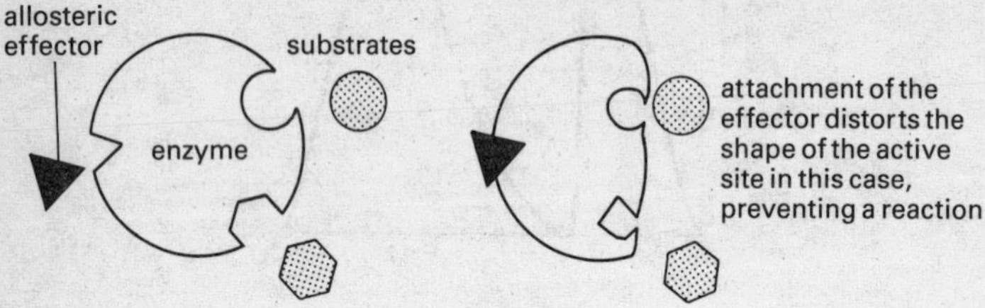
allosteric
effector
substrates
enzyme
attachment of the
effector distorts the
shape of the active
site in this case,
preventing a reaction

*Fig. 2.16* Functioning of allosteric enzymes

## Competitive inhibition

Molecules similar in shape to the substrate molecule may compete for the active site (see Fig. 2.17). For example, during the Krebs cycle, oxidation of succinic acid by succinate dehydrogenase is inhibited by the introduction of malic acid, as both molecules can bind to the active site. If many of the active sites are occupied by malic acid, then the overall oxidation of succinic acid will be slower.

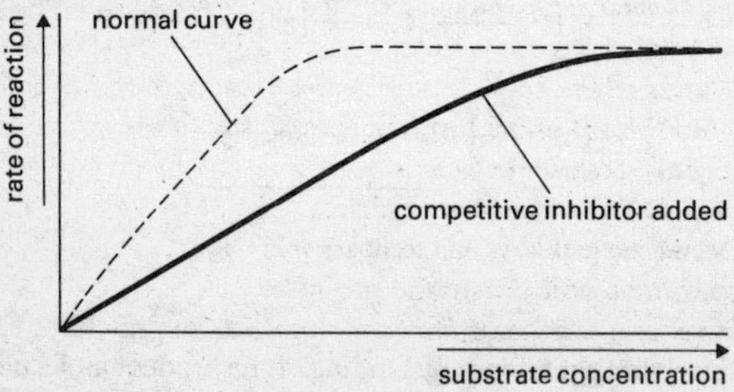
normal curve
rate of reaction
competitive inhibitor added
substrate concentration

*Fig. 2.17* Graph to show the effect of a competitive inhibitor

## Non-competitive inhibition

In this type of inhibition a foreign particle competes with the substrate for the active site and binds irreversibly to it, preventing any further enzyme action (see Fig. 2.18). Many such foreign molecules are well-known poisons, such as cyanide which combines with cytochrome

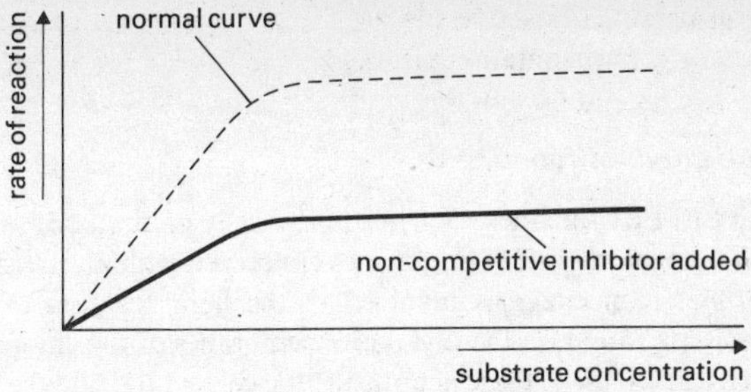
normal curve
rate of reaction
non-competitive inhibitor added
substrate concentration

*Fig. 2.18* Graph to show the effect of a non-competitive inhibitor

enzymes during electron transport, so preventing respiration and causing death). Nerve gases contain molecules that attack the enzyme cholinesterase which plays a vital role in the transmission of nerve impulses.

### Activation of zymogens

The other type of regulatory enzyme (apart from allosteric enzymes) is covalently modulated enzymes. These exist as inactive precursor molecules called zymogens (e.g. pepsinogen and chymotrypsinogen which are digestive enzymes). When such molecules are released into the gut they undergo selective hydrolytic cleavage to release the active form. For example, pepsinogen is converted to pepsin. Zymogen molecules are stored in the glands where they are made and exert no enzyme activity until released into the gut and converted irreversibly to the active form. Zymogens are only released when food is present for digestion, so production is regulated to suit requirements.

### Cofactors, coenzymes and prosthetic groups

Many enzymes require another atom or molecule to be present in order for them to function properly.

(a) COFACTORS: these are inorganic substances required for certain enzymes to function correctly, e.g. $Fe^{2+}$ ions are required for action of the enzyme catalase.

(b) COENZYMES: these are non-protein, organic substances usually required to transfer substrates to the active site, e.g. nicotinamide adenine dinucleotide (NAD) works in conjunction with dehydrogenase enzymes.

(c) PROSTHETIC GROUPS: these are non-protein, organic substances which are permanently bound to the enzyme and may form an integral part of the active site itself, e.g. cytochrome oxidase has a prosthetic group containing iron.

### *Where are enzymes found?*

1. INTRACELLULAR: these act inside the cells of the body and may be *in solution in the cell* (e.g. enzymes concerned with glycolysis) or *on membranes* (e.g. enzymes involved in the light reaction of photosynthesis are found on the thylakoid membranes of the chloroplasts).
2. EXTRACELLULAR: these act outside the cells of the body, e.g. those secreted on to food by fungi or house-flies or the enzymes released into the gut for digestion.

## *Further reading*

P. Cohen, *Control of Enzyme Activity*, 2nd edition (Chapman and Hall, 1983)
Paul C. Engel, *Enzyme Kinetics*, 2nd edition (Chapman and Hall, 1981)
C. H. Wynn, *The Structure and Function of Enzymes*, Studies in Biology No. 42, 2nd edition (Arnold, 1979)

## *Related questions*

**Question:**

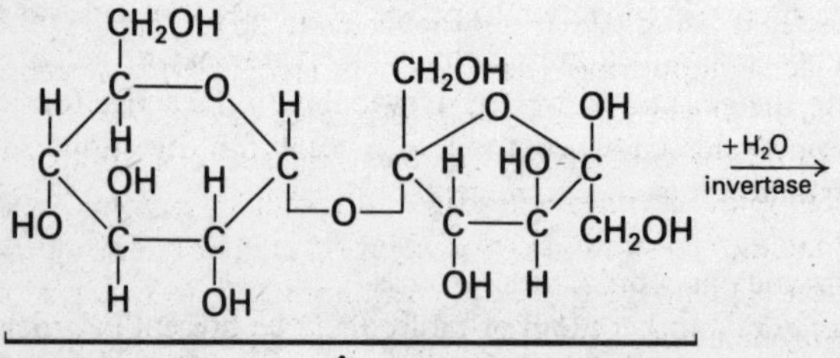
+H₂O
invertase

A

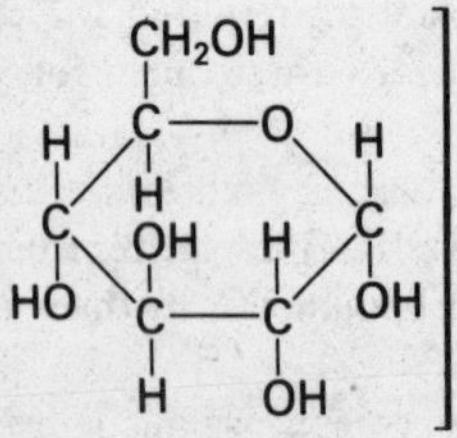

B

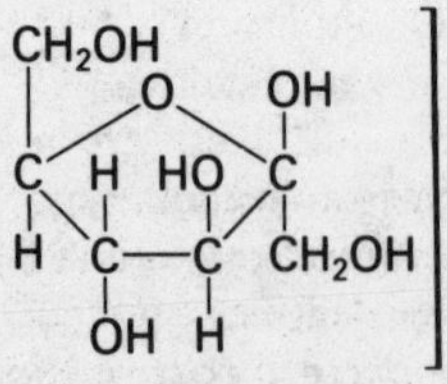

C

(a) State the name given to the reaction outlined above.

(b) Identify the components

A ______________________________________

B ______________________________________

C ______________________________________

(c) State *four* factors which affect the activity of intracellular enzymes.

(i) ______________________________________

(ii) ______________________________________

(iii) ______________________________________

(iv) ______________________________________

**(8 marks)**

[AEB, June 1981, Paper 1]

**Comments:**

(a) Note that water is being added to a molecule to split a bond.

(b) To identify each component it is necessary to recognize that glucose is a hexose sugar and fructose is a pentose sugar (see p. 50).

(c) See p. 59. Do not be confused by the term 'intracellular enzymes'; factors affecting all enzymes will affect intracellular ones as well. Also note that the question asks for 'factors' affecting the rate of enzyme action. Do not get these factors confused with ways of regulating enzyme activity such as feedback inhibition.

**Question:**

In the following diagram, each of the curves P, Q and R represents an enzyme-controlled reaction in one of the following situations:

(i) with the enzyme uninhibited

(ii) with a non-competitive inhibitor added to the enzyme

(iii) with a competitive inhibitor added to the enzyme

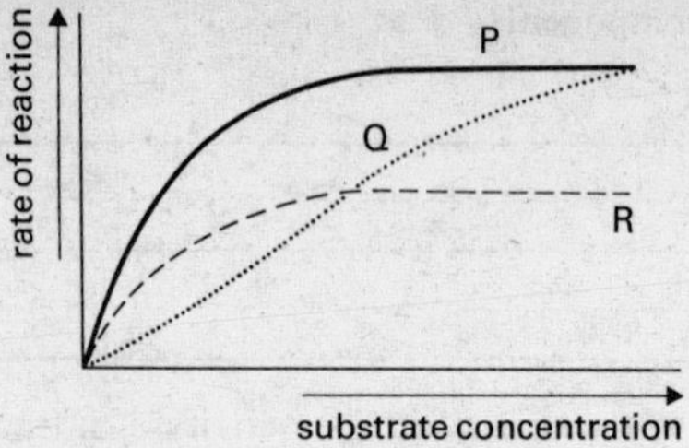
rate of reaction
P
Q
R
substrate concentration

Which curve represents each situation?

| | *Uninhibited enzyme* | *Competitive inhibitor added* | *Non-competitive inhibitor added* |
|---|---|---|---|
| A | P | Q | R |
| B | P | R | Q |
| C | Q | R | P |
| D | R | P | Q |
| E | R | Q | P |

[Cambridge, Nov. 1981]

**Comments:**
See p. 72. First establish the curve which represents the normal situation for the rate of reaction of an uninhibited enzyme; from experimental work you should recognize this as P. Then it is necessary to decide which curve, Q or R, represents addition of each of the different types of inhibitors. Remember that non-competitive inhibitors bind irreversibly to the enzyme, preventing any subsequent enzyme action. This causes the final rate of reaction to be lower than normal. Therefore R must represent the non-competitive inhibitor. This leaves Q as the curve for competitive inhibition. Characteristically, the rate of reaction is slower for this curve since inhibitors are competing for the active sites. However, the final rate of reaction is the same as for the normal situation since all the substrate is eventually used up. Therefore the correct answer would be A.

**Question:**

(a) What is an enzyme?

________________________________________

________________________________________

**(2 marks)**

(b) List *four* factors that affect the rate of enzyme activity.

(i) ____________________________________

(ii) ____________________________________

(iii) ____________________________________

(iv) ____________________________________

**(4 marks)**

(c) (i) Give an example of *one* plant and *one* animal enzyme that act *intracellularly* and state their functions.

plant enzyme ______________________________

function __________________________________

________________________________________

animal enzyme _____________________________

function __________________________________

________________________________________

**(4 marks)**

(ii) Give an example of *one* plant and *one* animal enzyme that act *extracellularly* and state their functions.

plant enzyme ______________________________

function ______________________________

______________________________

animal enzyme ______________________________

function ______________________________

______________________________

**(4 marks)**

(d) (i) Define the term coenzyme.

______________________________

______________________________

**(1 mark)**

(ii) Explain the role of a *named* coenzyme in enzyme activity.

______________________________

______________________________

**(2 marks)**

(Total 17 marks)

[London, Jan. 1983, Paper 1]

**Comments:**

(a) There are only two marks for this question, and long, detailed answers are not required. You should mention that enzymes are globular proteins and that they are biological catalysts. See p. 67.

(b) See p. 69. Note that you are only asked to list the factors. Any further explanation will waste time and not gain any extra marks.

(c) (i) Intracellular enzymes act within the cell. You can therefore choose any of the enzymes involved in respiration (animals) or in photosynthesis (plants), but remember to choose an enzyme for which you know the function. The function must be stated clearly. For

example, 'hexokinase, converts glucose to glucose-6-phosphate' is a better answer than 'something to do with respiration'. See p. 103.
(ii) Extracellular enzymes act outside the cell. Examples could include any of those involved in extracellular digestion, e.g. in man or housefly (see p. 148). Plant extracellular enzymes are harder to think of; look up those involved in saprophytic nutrition such as in *Mucor* (see p. 157).

(d) (i) and (ii) See p. 73. Remember that 'define' requires you to state clearly what a coenzyme actually is, whereas 'the role' requires you to state the function. Note that you are asked to state the function of a *named* coenzyme, so there will be a mark for naming one.

**Question:**
Explain briefly the meaning of the following terms in relation to enzyme structure and activity:

(i) prosthetic group; ______________________________

______________________________

**(2 marks)**

(ii) coenzyme; ______________________________

______________________________

**(2 marks)**

(iii) non-competitive inhibition; ______________________________

______________________________

**(2 marks)**

(iv) active site. ______________________________

______________________________

**(2 marks)**

**Comments:**
(i) See p. 73.
(ii) See p. 73.
(iii) See p. 72.
(iv) See p. 68.
The key words are 'in relation to enzyme structure and activity'. It is therefore important to stress how each factor affects the enzyme's structure or function.

**Question:**
Discuss the role of enzymes in living organisms.

[London, Jan. 1982, Paper 2]

**Comments:**
This is an essay which could be tackled in a number of ways: there is obviously no absolutely correct way. It is important to avoid hurriedly writing down everything you know about enzymes, which would be missing the point of the question and would gain very few marks. Perhaps the most obvious way to tackle the question is to look at the emphasis on 'living' organisms, and discuss why enzymes are necessary for life.

**Suggested essay plan:**

Introduction: Give a simple definition of enzymes and their function as catalysts. Stress the importance of enzymes in all aspects of life: no living organism exists without enzymes.

Main part: Briefly go through each of the characteristics of life, mentioning the importance of enzymes in each process and any special condition or disease resulting from their absence.

(i) Nutrition – enzymes in photosynthesis, digestion, chemosynthesis.

(ii) Reproduction – enzymes involved in reproductive cycles and in replication of DNA during mitosis.

(iii) Growth – protein synthesis, interpretation of the DNA code.

(iv) Excretion – production of non-toxic excretory substances, functioning of excretory organs.

(v) Locomotion – enzymes involved in muscular action.

(vi) Sensitivity – enzymes involved in transmission of nerve impulses and various brain functions.

(vii) Respiration – enzyme-controlled pathways, generation of ATP, e.g. cytochrome oxidase.

Concluding section: Essential and non-essential enzymes.

Give examples of enzymes whose absence would cause death or disease (e.g. an absence of photosynthetic enzymes would prevent photosynthesis and therefore drastically alter life as we know it since there would be no food). Other enzymes are not so essential (e.g. the absence of a minor digestive enzyme would not cause undue harm in an animal if it could derive sufficient nourishment from other sources).

Special adaptations of enzymes to different modes of life (e.g. organisms living at extremes of temperature – thermophilic bacteria have enzymes which function at high temperatures).

The special case of viruses – where enzymes are required to lyse the cell after replication.

Mutations – the basis of evolution – are often expressed as an alteration in enzyme production, thus enabling an organism to become different in some way.

Wherever possible, name the enzymes involved. However, do not exclude examples merely because you cannot remember the name of the enzyme: the ideas are more important than remembering names accurately.

# 3. Respiration

There are two parts to the respiration process: external respiration (gaseous exchange), which is the method by which an organism obtains oxygen and removes carbon dioxide; and internal respiration (cellular or tissue respiration), which is the breakdown of food, usually in the presence of oxygen, to release energy which is stored in ATP.

## *External respiration – gaseous exchange*

Oxygen is present in the surrounding air or water and enters the organism by diffusion.

### General types of surfaces for gaseous exchange

In simple organisms with only one or a few cells, oxygen ($O_2$) enters directly by diffusion and carbon dioxide ($CO_2$) and water vapour are removed (see Fig. 3.1).

As organisms evolved and became multicellular, their shapes adapted to give a relatively large surface area for gaseous exchange. A large surface area/volume ratio ensures that enough oxygen reaches the internal cells which are not exposed to the oxygen-containing medium. Such shape adaptations include flatness (e.g. flatworm; see Fig. 3.2). Hollow centres also provide a large surface area for gaseous exchange. Examples include coelenterates such as *Hydra* (Fig. 3.3).

Larger animals cannot obtain sufficient oxygen by means of shape adaptations, and they have therefore developed special structures for obtaining oxygen:

1. External gills (e.g. polychaete worms). These have the disadvantage of being easily damaged. See Fig. 3.4.
2. Internal gills (e.g. fish). Water is drawn over the gills and oxygen extracted. See Fig. 3.5.
3. Tracheae (e.g. insects). A system of fine tubes branches throughout the body and supplies the tissues with oxygen.
4. Lungs (e.g. all air-breathing vertebrates). Tracheal and bronchial tubes lead to many sack-like alveoli, which provide a large surface area for diffusion. Associated muscles and the skeleton provide an effective mechanism for ventilating the lungs (i.e. moving the air in and out).

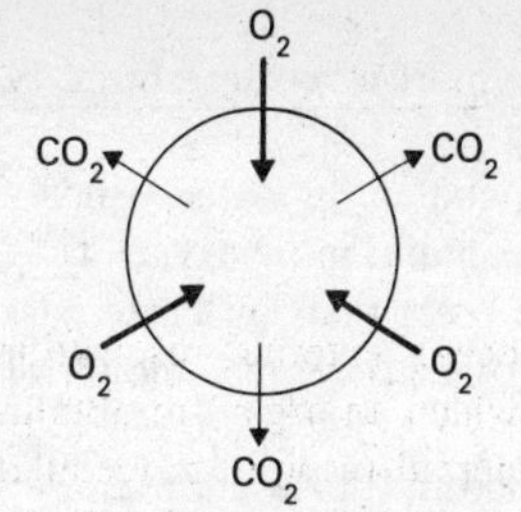
$O_2$
$CO_2$

*Fig. 3.1* Gaseous exchange in a unicellular organism

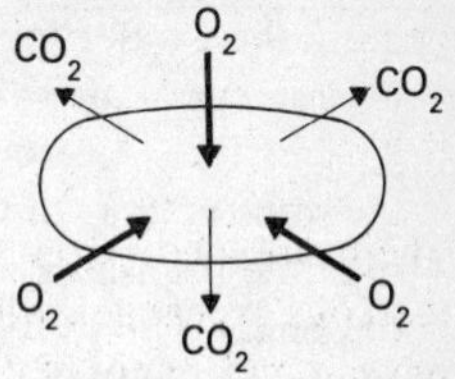
$O_2$
$CO_2$

*Fig. 3.2* Gaseous exchange in a flattened organism

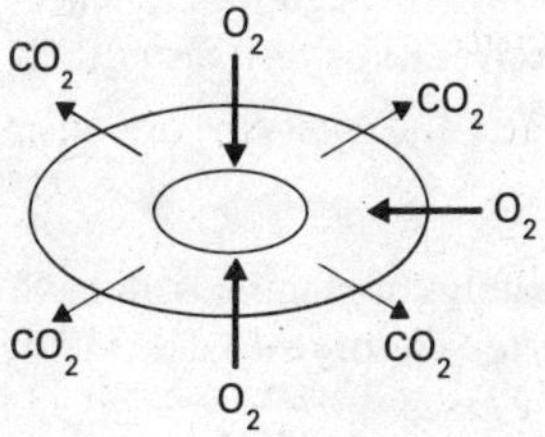
$O_2$
$CO_2$

*Fig. 3.3* Gaseous exchange in a hollow-centred organism

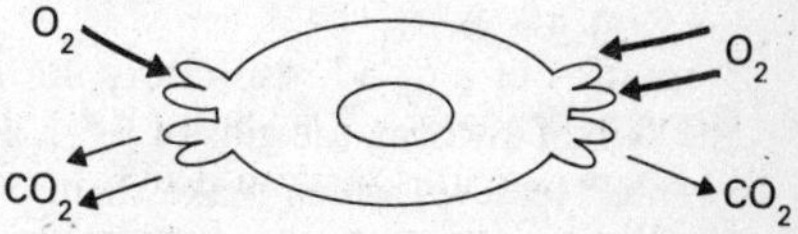
$O_2$
$CO_2$

*Fig. 3.4* Diffusion in an external-gilled organism

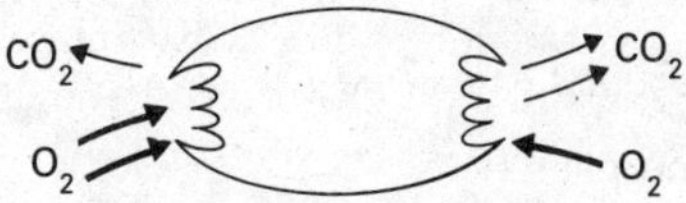
$CO_2$
$O_2$

*Fig. 3.5* Diffusion in an internal-gilled organism

## Concentration gradients

Oxygen will only enter cells by diffusion along a concentration gradient, i.e. if there is more oxygen outside the cell than inside it. In simple organisms, oxygen is used up in respiration within the cells, so fresh oxygen constantly enters. In large animals, with special breathing structures, oxygen has to be removed from the respiratory surface (lungs, gills, etc.) by a circulatory system. This ensures a constant intake of oxygen since the concentration gradient is maintained.

### Respiratory media

Air and water both contain oxygen, but air is a more efficient respiratory medium than water for a number of reasons:

1. $O_2$ content of air = 105–130 $cm^3$/litre; $O_2$ content of water = 0.04–9.0 $cm^3$/litre. A certain volume of air thus contains more oxygen than the same volume of water. Therefore more water than air has to pass over the respiratory surface in order to provide the same amount of oxygen.
2. Water is heavier than air, and also more viscous. It takes more energy to move water than to move air. For example, a fish spends approximately 20 per cent of its energy in breathing movements, whereas a land animal only spends 1–2 per cent of its energy in ventilation.
3. Oxygen diffuses quickly through air but slowly through water; hence, a respiratory surface in contact with air receives its oxygen faster than a respiratory surface in contact with water.

### Properties of a good respiratory surface

The skin of a worm, the gills of a fish and the lungs of mammals all have common features which make them efficient respiratory surfaces:

1. A large surface area for rapid diffusion of gases.
2. Moist, to enable gases to dissolve in solution.
3. Thin, to enable rapid exchange of gases across the surface.
4. A vascular or circulatory system to remove oxygen from the respiratory surface, in order to maintain the concentration gradient.

## *Mechanisms of gaseous exchange*

### Terrestrial flowering plants

During the day, plants are photosynthesizing, and carbon dioxide is taken in and oxygen produced. This oxygen is utilized by the cells for respiration and any excess is released to the environment. At night there is no photosynthesis, so the plants take in oxygen and release carbon dioxide.

The various parts of the plant have special structures to facilitate gaseous exchange:

(a) Leaves and green stems – contain stomata, which are small pores allowing movement of gases into and out of the leaf or stem.
(b) Woody stems – obtain their oxygen through lenticels.
(c) Roots – have many tiny root hairs which increase the surface area and allow diffusion of gases into and out of the root. A plant will die in waterlogged soils because the roots cannot obtain oxygen.

## Insects

*Structure and functioning of tracheae*

In insects, the body wall of the thorax and abdomen have small pores or spiracles, which are connected to all organs of the body by fine tubes called tracheae (Fig. 3.6a). The tracheae develop as ingrowths of the body wall, and are lined with chitin. Each trachea ends in microscopic tracheal cells that extend as intracellular tracheoles. The end of a tracheole is filled with fluid through which oxygen and carbon dioxide diffuse to reach adjacent tissuc cells. The walls of the tracheoles are thin and moist to aid rapid diffusion. As the cells respire, they use oxygen and produce carbon dioxide, which maintains the concentration gradient for diffusion of oxygen from tracheoles to cells and the flow of carbon dioxide in the opposite direction.

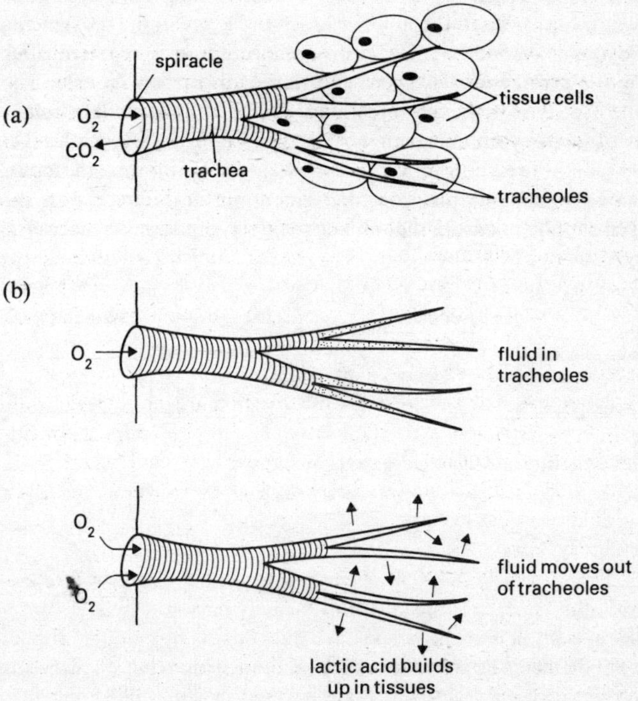
(a)
spiracle
$O_2$
$CO_2$
trachea
tissue cells
tracheoles
(b)
$O_2$
fluid in tracheoles
$O_2$
$O_2$
fluid moves out of tracheoles
lactic acid builds up in tissues

*Fig. 3.6*(a) An insect trachea; (b) Control of breathing in an insect

The efficiency of this system depends on the rapid diffusion rate of oxygen in air as compared with that in water, and on the relatively small size of tracheate animals. Some insects have valves (lids) to cover the spiracles, and these prevent loss of water.

*Control of breathing in insects*

1. The tracheoles contain varying amounts of watery fluid. During muscular activity, e.g. flying, the cells do not have enough oxygen to respire properly, so lactic acid is produced and accumulates in the tissue fluid. This increases the osmotic pressure of tissue fluid, and has the effect of drawing water out of the tracheoles, enabling more oxygen to pass to the cells (Fig. 3.6b).
2. Some insects, e.g. locusts, have muscles which control breathing by bringing about rhythmic movements of the thorax and abdomen.

   An experiment can be performed to demonstrate the variation in breathing movement rate in locusts. A locust is placed in a syringe as shown in Fig. 3.7, and the number of rhythmic breathing movements or beats per second is calculated. The procedure is repeated after filling the syringe with oxygen, and then with carbon dioxide. The results usually indicate that breathing movements are rapid in conditions of low oxygen and high carbon dioxide. If the oxygen level is increased, the breathing movements slow down. In this way, the locust appears to adapt its breathing movements in accordance with the oxygen supply, to ensure that an adequate oxygen supply reaches the body.

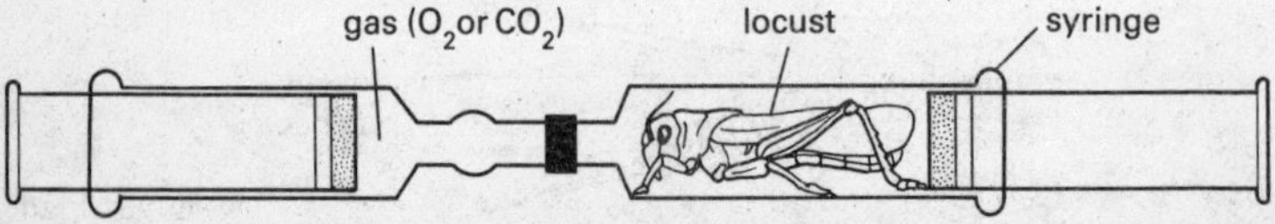
gas ($O_2$ or $CO_2$)
locust
syringe

*Fig. 3.7* Monitoring breathing movements in a locust

## Fish

The respiratory surface is the gills. Fish usually have four sets of comb-like gills on each side of the head. Each gill consists of a double row of slender gill filaments attached to a skeletal branchial arch. Gill filaments bear many transverse plates which are covered in thin, folded lamellae. The lamellae increase the surface area for gaseous exchange, and are well supplied with capillaries to remove oxygenated blood and maintain the concentration gradient. Bony and cartilaginous fishes have slightly different gill structures. They also have differing modes of ventilation (inhalation and exhalation) and gaseous exchange. (See Figs. 3.8–3.15.)

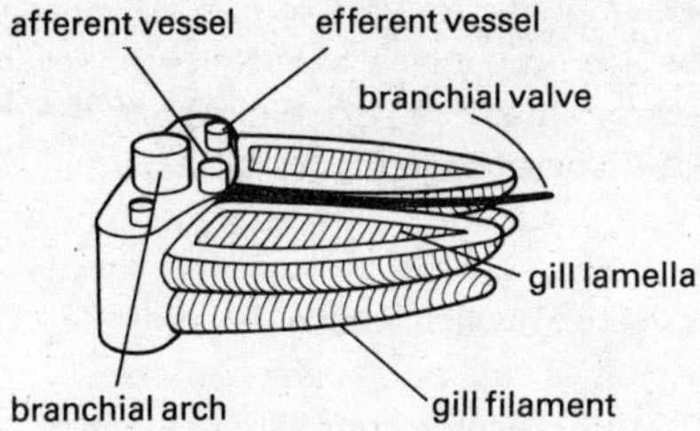
afferent vessel
efferent vessel
branchial valve
gill lamella
branchial arch
gill filament

*Fig. 3.8* Section through a gill of a cartilaginous fish

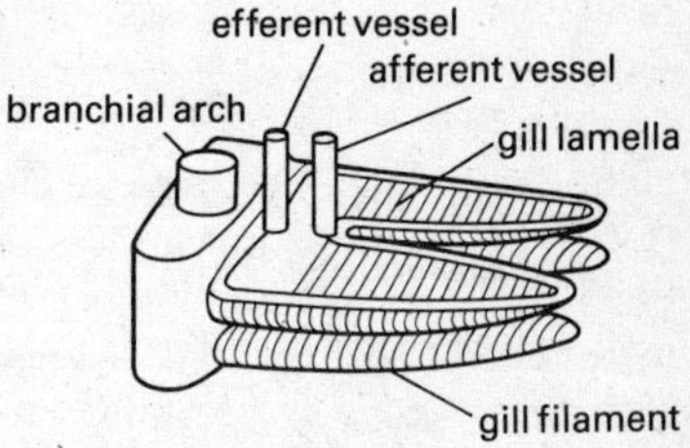
efferent vessel
afferent vessel
branchial arch
gill lamella
gill filament

*Fig. 3.9* Section through a gill of a bony fish

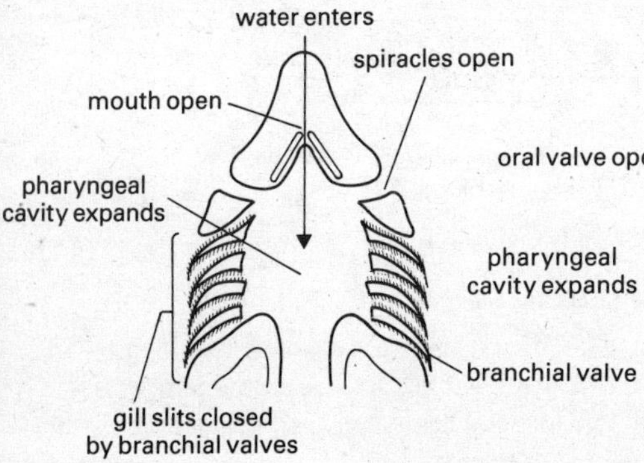
water enters
spiracles open
mouth open
pharyngeal cavity expands
branchial valve
gill slits closed by branchial valves

*Fig. 3.10* Inhalation in a cartilaginous fish

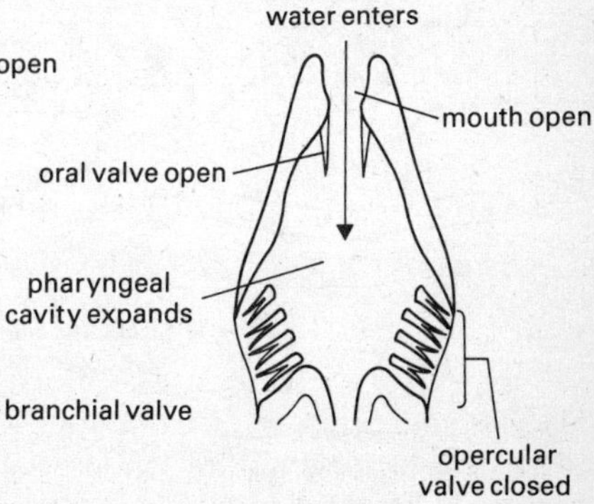
water enters
mouth open
oral valve open
pharyngeal cavity expands
opercular valve closed

*Fig. 3.11* Inhalation in a bony fish

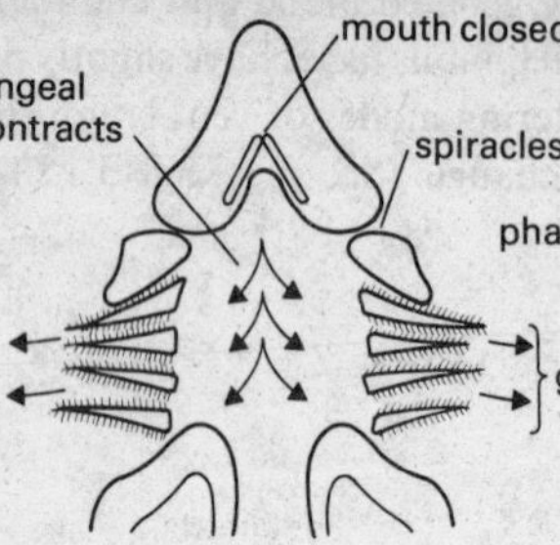
mouth closed
pharyngeal cavity contracts
spiracles closed
gill slits open
water leaves

*Fig. 3.12* Exhalation in a cartilaginous fish

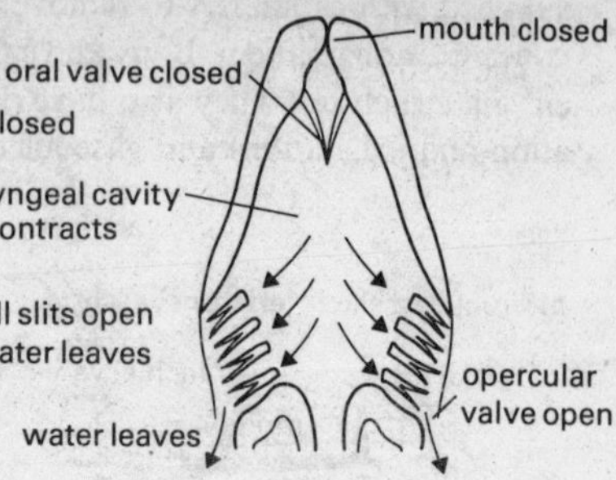
mouth closed
oral valve closed
pharyngeal cavity contracts
opercular valve open
water leaves

*Fig. 3.13* Exhalation in a bony fish

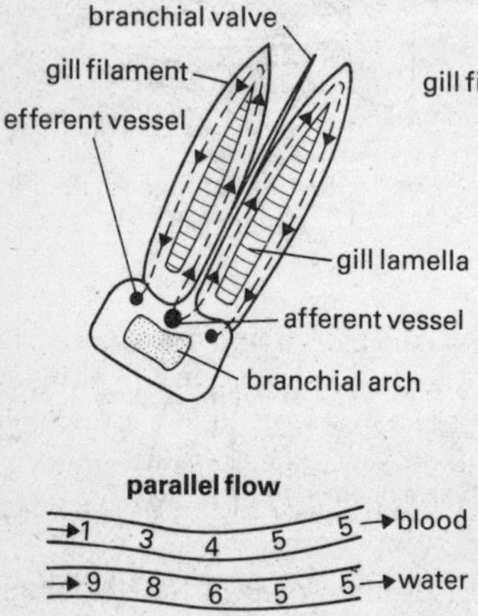
branchial valve
gill filament
efferent vessel
gill lamella
afferent vessel
branchial arch
parallel flow
1 3 4 5 5 blood
9 8 6 5 5 water

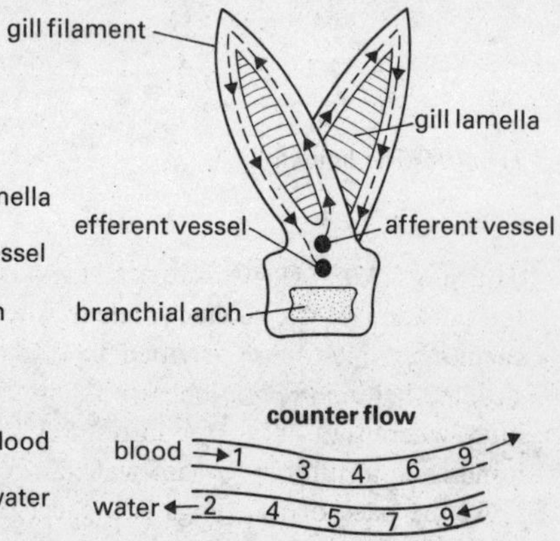
gill filament
gill lamella
efferent vessel
afferent vessel
branchial arch
counter flow
blood 1 3 4 6 9
water 2 4 5 7 9

numbers indicate relative $O_2$ concentrations

*Fig. 3.14* Gaseous exchange in a cartilaginous fish

*Fig. 3.15* Gaseous exchange in a bony fish

## Mammals (e.g. man)

The respiratory surface is the lungs.

*Structure of lungs*

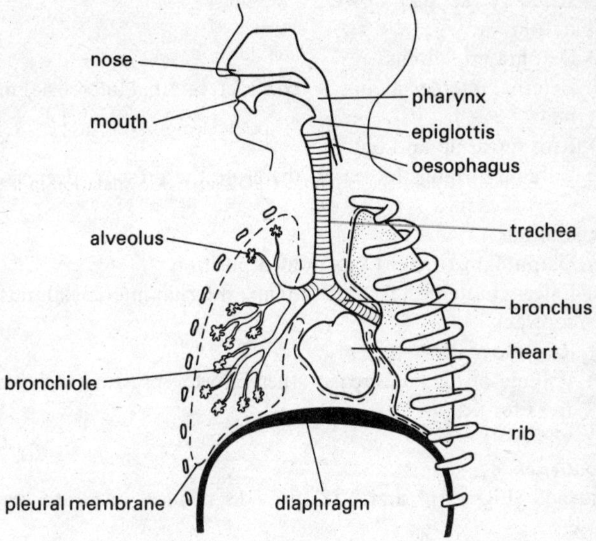
nose
mouth
pharynx
epiglottis
oesophagus
trachea
alveolus
bronchus
heart
bronchiole
rib
pleural membrane
diaphragm

*Fig. 3.16* The human lungs

The lungs (Fig. 3.16) are situated inside the thorax, and are connected to the outside by a tube – the trachea. The trachea is kept open by rings of cartilage, which are C-shaped to allow movement in the oesophagus situated behind. The trachea splits into two bronchii, one going to each lung, where they subdivide into many bronchioles. Each bronchiole terminates in a number of thin-walled, sac-like alveoli.

At the base of the lungs is a sheet of muscle called the diaphragm, which is attached at the edges to the thoracic wall. Surrounding the lungs are the pleural membranes, which secrete pleural fluid. This lubricates and 'cushions' the lungs against the ribs during ventilation movements.

The lungs are lined internally with a mucus lining, and the tubes contain ciliated epithelium to aid movement of dust particles or bacteria up into the pharynx where they can be swallowed.

### *Ventilation movements*

Ventilation of the lungs is brought about by movements of the diaphragm, ribs and sternum (breastbone), together with the internal and external intercostal muscles, which act antagonistically.

The sequences are as follows:

1. Inhalation
   (a) Diaphragm flattens
   (b) External intercostal muscles contract, internal intercostal muscles relax
   (c) Ribs move up and out
   (d) Volume of lungs increases, therefore the pressure decreases and air rushes in.
2. Exhalation
   (a) Diaphragm relaxes to its domed position
   (b) External intercostal muscles relax, internal intercostal muscles contract
   (c) Ribs move down and in
   (d) Volume of lungs decreases, therefore the pressure increases and air is forced out

*Gaseous exchange*

The alveoli (Figs. 3.17 and 3.18) provide an ideal respiratory surface because:

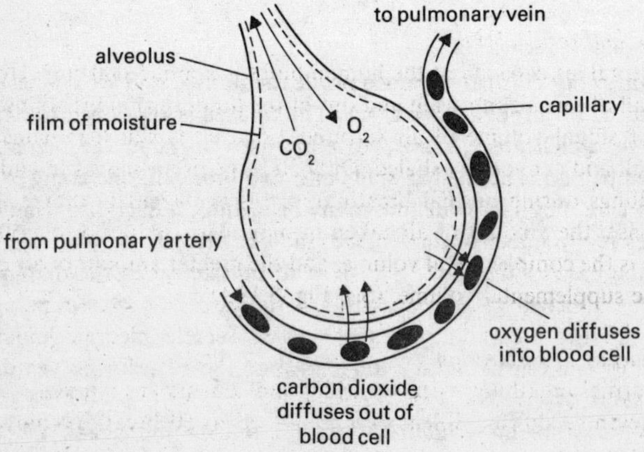
to pulmonary vein
alveolus
capillary
film of moisture
$O_2$
$CO_2$
from pulmonary artery
oxygen diffuses into blood cell
carbon dioxide diffuses out of blood cell

*Fig. 3.17* Exchange of gases in the alveolus

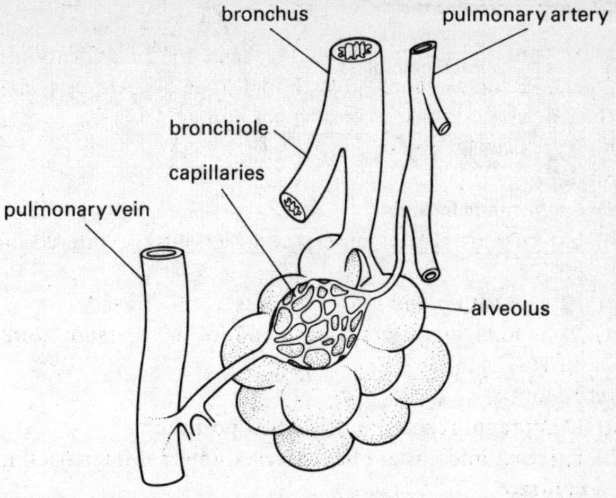
bronchus
pulmonary artery
bronchiole
capillaries
pulmonary vein
alveolus

*Fig. 3.18* Section through a mammalian lung

1. They provide a large surface area for gaseous exchange.
2. They are moist.
3. They are thin-walled – 50 $\mu$m thick.
4. They are well supplied with capillaries to remove oxygenated blood and thus maintain the concentration gradient.

*Tidal and residual air*

The total air capacity of the human lungs is about 5,000 cm$^3$. However, not all of this air moves in and out of the lungs during breathing. There is a residual volume of air (around 1,500 cm$^3$) which remains in the alveoli and cannot be exhaled. Only 500 cm$^3$ of air moves in and out of the lungs during normal breathing – this is the tidal volume. During exercise, the amount of air taken in may increase by up to 1,500 cm$^3$. This is the complemental volume, and the greater amount of air exhaled is the supplemental volume. (See Fig. 3.19.)

*Frequency of inspiration*

Normal breathing = 16 breathing movements per minute.

Breathing during violent exercise = up to 50 breathing movements per minute.

Ventilation rate = tidal volume × frequency of inspiration

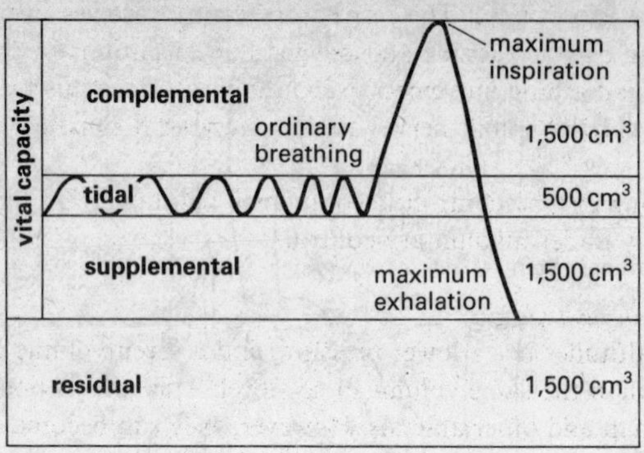
maximum
inspiration
complemental
ordinary
breathing
1,500 cm³
vital capacity
tidal
500 cm³
supplemental
maximum
exhalation
1,500 cm³
residual
1,500 cm³

*Fig. 3.19* Lung capacity and breathing in man

*The composition of inspired and expired air*
See Table 3.1.

*Table 3.1.* Composition of inspired and expired air

| | *Inspired* (%) | *Expired* (%) |
|---|---|---|
| $O_2$ | 20* | 16 |
| $CO_2$ | 0.04 | 4 |
| N | 79 | 79 |
| Other gases (pollutants) | 0.06 | 0.06 |
| Water vapour | Variable | Saturated |

* Air actually reaching the alveoli only contains 14% $O_2$, since $O_2$ must diffuse through the residual air before it reaches the walls of the alveoli.

*Control of respiration*

1. CHEMICAL CONTROL: The medulla oblongata at the base of the brain contains a respiratory centre which is extremely sensitive to carbon dioxide concentration in the blood. A slight increase in carbon dioxide concentration causes deeper, faster, breathing movements, until the carbon dioxide concentration returns to normal. Chemoreceptor cells in the aorta and carotid artery (the aortid and carotid glomi) detect changes in the oxygen concentration of the blood and send impulses to the respiratory centre which alters the breathing rate accordingly.

2. Nervous control: The respiratory centre receives information concerning carbon dioxide and oxygen concentrations in the blood and alters breathing movements accordingly. It does this by sending impulses via the spinal nerves to the intercostal muscles and diaphragm.

   Breathing can be controlled voluntarily within certain limits, but it is mostly under involuntary control.

*Effects of high altitude*

Air at high altitudes has a lower pressure, and a given volume contains less oxygen than the same volume at sea-level. This affects normal respiration in man and other animals. However, they can become acclimatized to such conditions, and living at high altitudes for a length of time causes the following changes to occur:

1. Increase in the number of red blood cells (erythrocytes) and therefore a greater amount of haemoglobin in the blood.
2. Increase in the normal ventilation rate.
3. Faster heart beat.

*Adaptations to diving*

Mammals whose lifestyle involves deep-sea diving have adapted to cope with difficulties in respiration in the following ways:

1. Larger blood volumes compared to land animals of the same size.
2. Larger blood vessels, to act as reservoirs of oxygenated blood.
3. Slower heart beat.
4. During diving, blood is diverted from the digestive system and other organs to the vital organs (e.g. heart and brain).
5. Organs containing air spaces, such as the lungs, are adapted to cope with the air compression incurred at such depths.
6. Respiratory centres do not work automatically during diving, so there is more tolerance to variations in carbon dioxide and oxygen levels in the blood.
7. There are greater concentrations of myoglobin to store oxygen for muscle activity.
8. Greater lung capacity.

Man may become slightly adapted to deep-sea diving (e.g. in lung capacity and blood volume) but for long-term submergence, equipment is necessary. Divers carry tanks of compressed air and face masks, and the air provides oxygen and ensures that the lungs remain inflated (at such pressures they would normally collapse). The increased pressure causes nitrogen to enter the lungs and dissolve in the bloodstream. At depths greater than 200 ft the nitrogen concentration becomes excessive and may cause divers to lose conciousness. If a diver returns to the surface too quickly, the bubbles of nitrogen expand causing painful cramps called 'the bends'. For this reason deep-water divers must spend time in decompression chambers after surfacing.

### The respirometer

There are many types of respirometers, which measure respiratory quotients (see p. 106), but they all work on the same general principles. See Fig. 3.20.

During aerobic respiration the volume of oxygen consumed is usually equal to the volume of carbon dioxide evolved; therefore there will be no overall change in volume in a closed vessel which contains a respiring animal. However, if a substance which absorbs carbon dioxide is present (e.g. sodium or potassium hydroxide), there will be a decrease in volume equal to the amount of carbon dioxide given out and this can be measured. In the case of aerobic respiration, this volume is also equal to the amount of oxygen consumed.

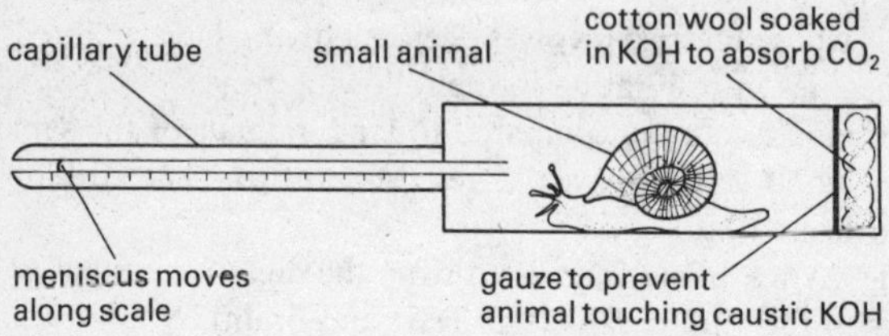
capillary tube
small animal
cotton wool soaked in KOH to absorb $CO_2$
meniscus moves along scale
gauze to prevent animal touching caustic KOH

*Fig. 3.20* A simple respirometer

The two main errors with this apparatus are:

1. Temperature changes causing expansion or contraction of the air.
2. Failure of the sodium or potassium hydroxide to absorb all the carbon dioxide.

## *Further reading*

D. Heath and D. R. Williams, *Life at High Altitude*, Studies in Biology No. 112 (Arnold, 1979)

H. V. Hempleman and A. P. M. Lockwood, *Physiology of Diving in Man and Other Animals*, Studies in Biology No. 99 (Arnold, 1978)

G. M. Hughes, *Vertebrate Respiration* (Heinemann, 1963)

G. M. Hughes, *The Vertebrate Lung*, Oxford/Carolina Biology Reader No. 59, 2nd edition (Packard, 1979)

R. M. G. Wells, *Invertebrate Respiration*, Studies in Biology No. 127 (Arnold, 1980)

V. Wigglesworth, *Insect Respiration*, Oxford/Carolina Biology Reader No. 48 (Packard, 1972)

## *Related questions*

**Question:**

(a) State *three* features of respiratory surfaces which are common to all vertebrate animals, and briefly explain why each is important.

first feature ______________________________

importance ______________________________

______________________________

second feature ______________________________

importance ______________________________

______________________________

third feature ______________________________

importance ______________________________

______________________________

**(6 marks)**

(b) Explain the possible effects of a decrease in environmental temperature on the rate of gas exchange in

(i) a well-illuminated foliage leaf

**(2 marks)**

(ii) a small mammal

**(2 marks)**

(c) Explain the possible effects of a decrease in light intensity on gas exchange in a previously well-illuminated foliage leaf.

**(4 marks)**

**(Total 14 marks)**

[London, Jan. 1982, Paper 1]

**Comments:**

(a) See p. 84.

(b) (i) As the leaf is well illuminated, the stomata are open and free diffusion of gases can occur. Diffusion is a physical process, directly affected by temperature. A decrease in temperature decreases the kinetic energy of the gas molecules which in turn decreases diffusion.

(b) (ii) A reduction in temperature leads to an increase in metabolic rate in order to maintain the internal body temperature at a constant value. Since an increase in metabolic rate increases the demand for oxygen, the breathing rate and hence the amount of gaseous exchange increases accordingly.

(c) A decrease in light intensity reduces the rate of photosynthesis, which in turn has the effect of closing stomata. If stomata are closed, gaseous diffusion is reduced.

**Questions:**

Insects breathe by means of a tracheal system which opens to the exterior of the body via spiracles. The opening and closing of the spiracles can be regulated by muscles. The following traces indicate the opening and closing of the spiracles of a flea under different experimental conditions.

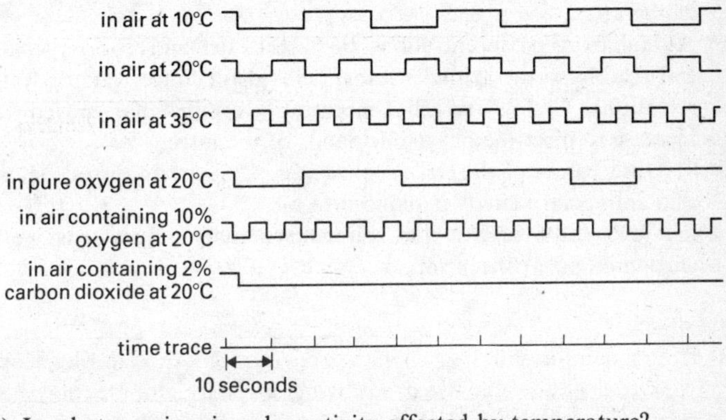
in air at 10°C
in air at 20°C
in air at 35°C
in pure oxygen at 20°C
in air containing 10% oxygen at 20°C
in air containing 2% carbon dioxide at 20°C
time trace
10 seconds

(a) In what way is spiracular activity affected by temperature?

_______________________________________________

_______________________________________________

_______________________________________________

(b) Suggest why changes in the oxygen concentration result in different spiracular activity.

(c) (i) What is the main effect on spiracular activity of increasing carbon dioxide concentration to 2%?

(ii) What does this suggest about the control of the spiracles?

[In the style of AEB]

**Comments:**

This is a question which tests your ability to interpret experimental data.

(a) Observation of the first three tests, with increasingly higher temperatures, shows that the frequency of spiracular activity increases with temperature. See p. 85.

(b) At high oxygen concentrations, the insect's demands for oxygen are met readily so the spiracles remain closed for longer (aiding water retention). At low oxygen concentrations, spiracular movements increase to meet the oxygen demands of the insect.

(c) (i) Observation of the trace representing 2% carbon dioxide shows that spiracular activity is reduced to nil.

(ii) The results suggest that spiracular activity is very sensitive to carbon dioxide concentration.

**Question:**

(a) (i) Using information given in the above graphs, explain why people who are not acclimatized to living at high altitude may lose consciousness at altitudes between 6,000 and 9,000 metres above sea-level.

(ii) In mountainous areas of the world, small populations exist at altitudes exceeding 6,000 metres. Suggest three physiological ways in which people become acclimatized to such conditions.

(b) (i) In 1968 the Olympic Games were held in Mexico at a relatively high altitude of 2,242 metres above sea-level. Given this information,

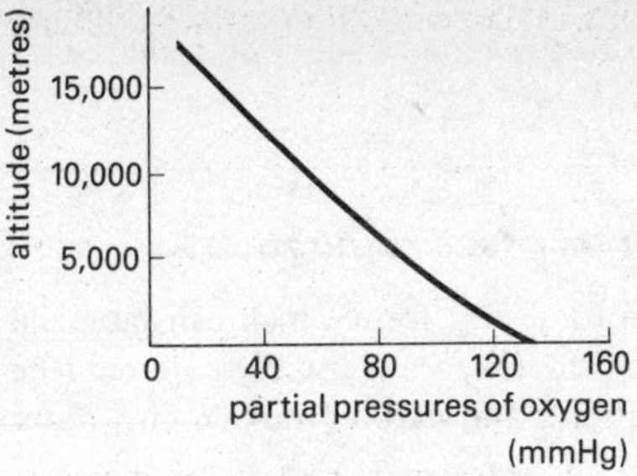
altitude (metres)
15,000
10,000
5,000
0
40
80
120
160
partial pressures of oxygen
(mmHg)

**graph A**

Demonstrates the relationship between altitude and partial pressures of oxygen

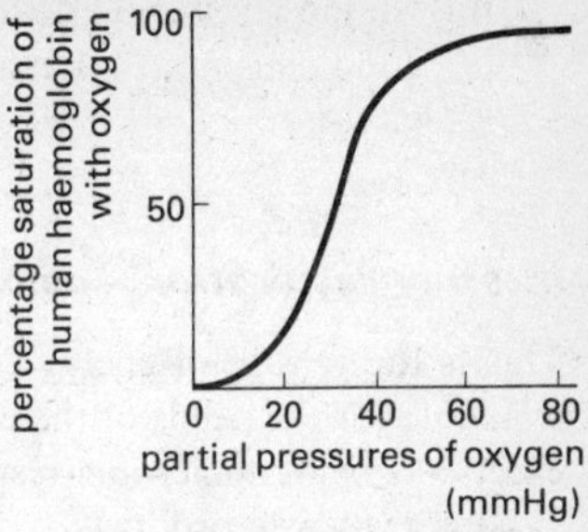
percentage saturation of human haemoglobin with oxygen
100
50
0
20
40
60
80
partial pressures of oxygen
(mmHg)

**graph B**

Demonstrates the percentage of haemoglobin associated with oxygen to form oxyhaemoglobin over a range of partial pressures of oxygen

suggest why some athletes would have a distinct advantage over others.

(ii) What activity could the disadvantaged athletes incorporate into their training programme to improve their chances at high altitude?

(iii) What test could be done to check whether an athlete had become acclimatized to high altitude?

[In the style of AEB]

**Comments:**

(a) (i) This is a question which tests your ability to interpret graphical data. It is also the type of question which requires careful thought if the conclusions drawn are to be expressed clearly and concisely.

Unconsciousness is likely to occur if the brain receives insufficient oxygen. Above 6,000 metres, partial pressures of oxygen in the atmosphere are low (see graph A). Because of the low partial pressures, haemoglobin does not carry enough oxygen to satisfy the needs of the brain (graph B), so people may become unconscious as a result.

(ii) See p. 93.

(b) (i) Athletes who have lived most of their lives at high altitudes will be acclimatized to low oxygen levels, whereas those who normally live at low altitudes will not be acclimatized.

(ii) Athletes who are not acclimatized should undertake high-altitude training in order to improve their chances.

(iii) Blood tests could be taken to give an indication of the number of blood cells/mm³ compared to the blood counts of acclimatized athletes.

## *Internal respiration – cellular or tissue respiration*

This is the release of energy from food in a form which can be made available for the needs of the organism. Oxygen is usually required (the exception being anaerobic respiration), and carbon dioxide and water vapour are waste products.

For a carbohydrate the process can be expressed simply as:

$$C_6H_{12}O_6 + 6O_2 \rightarrow 6CO_2 + 6H_2O + \text{energy}$$

However, this equation is only a summary of the long chain of reactions which actually occur.

### *Storage of energy*

When energy is released from food, it is stored in a compound called adenosine triphosphate (ATP). This compound is a basic nucleotide consisting of a nitrogen-containing group (adenine) and a ribose sugar

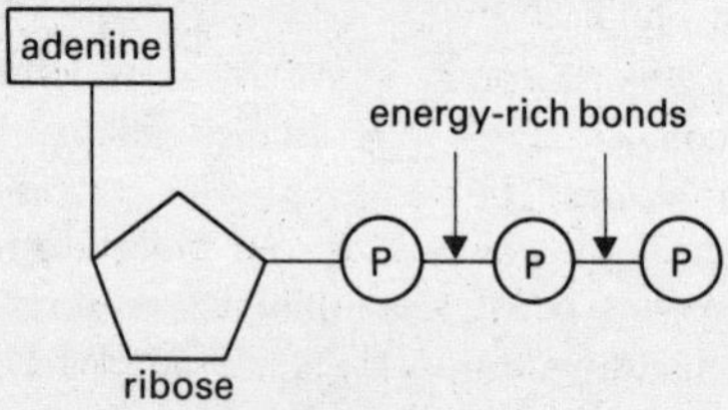
adenine
energy-rich bonds
P
P
P
ribose

*Fig. 3.21* The structure of ATP (simplified)

with three phosphate groups attached to it (see Fig. 3.21). Two of these phosphate groups are held on to the molecule by energy-rich bonds, i.e. if these bonds are removed by hydrolysis then large amounts of energy are released (Fig. 3.22). If a phosphate group is removed from ATP, the molecule becomes adenosine diphosphate (ADP), and if two phosphate groups are removed it becomes adenosine monophosphate (AMP). The phosphate group of AMP is not held by an energy-rich bond and removal of this group does not result in release of large quantities of energy.

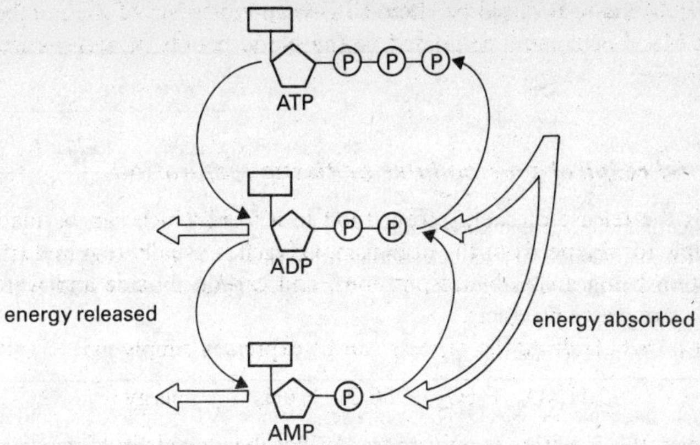
ATP
ADP
energy released
energy absorbed
AMP

*Fig. 3.22* Absorption and release of energy by ATP

When energy is released in the cell, it is used to convert ADP to ATP, and ATP then acts as a temporary store for this energy until it is required by the body.

### *Electron (hydrogen) carriers*

Many reactions in cellular respiration involve the release of high-energy electrons, which become attached to molecules called electron carriers or electron acceptor molecules. The electrons are subsequently passed down to acceptor molecules of lower energy, and the energy released in the process is used to produce ATP. Sometimes the electrons are released in conjunction with a hydrogen ion ($H^+$). They are then in the combined form of a hydrogen atom, and are passed to carriers called hydrogen acceptors. At a later stage, the hydrogen atom splits into an electron and a hydrogen ion, and only the electron is transferred further.

### *Glycolysis*

This is the first stage of the respiratory process. It takes place in the cytoplasm and oxygen is not required. The stages are listed below, and summarized in Fig. 3.23.

1. Glucose is 'energized', or phosphorylated, to form glucose-6-phosphate by converting a molecule of ATP to ADP using the enzyme hexokinase.

*Table 3.2.* Common metabolic electron (hydrogen) carriers

| | Oxidation state | |
|---|---|---|
| *Type of carrier* | *Oxidized* | *Reduced* |
| Hydrogen carriers | | |
| Nicotinamide adenine dinucleotide | NAD | $NADH_2$* |
| Nicotinamide adenine dinucleotide phosphate | NADP | $NADPH_2$ |
| Flavine adenine dinucleotide | FAD | $FADH_2$* |
| Electron carriers | | |
| Cytochromes (contain iron) | $Fe^{3+}$ | $Fe^{2+}$ |

* Each molecule of $NADH_2$ gives rise to three ATP molecules, and each molecule of $FADH_2$ gives rise to two ATP molecules, via the electron transfer chain.

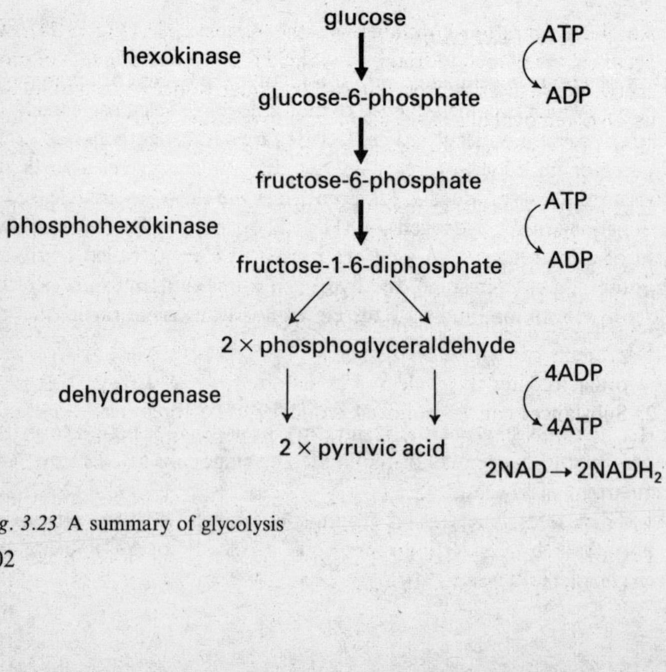
glucose
hexokinase
ATP
ADP
glucose-6-phosphate
fructose-6-phosphate
phosphohexokinase
ATP
ADP
fructose-1-6-diphosphate
2 × phosphoglyceraldehyde
dehydrogenase
4ADP
4ATP
2 × pyruvic acid
2NAD → 2NADH2

*Fig. 3.23* A summary of glycolysis

2. Glucose-6-phosphate is converted to fructose-6-phosphate, which is further phosphorylated to fructose-1-6-diphosphate by converting another ATP molecule to ADP and using the enzyme phosphohexokinase.
3. Fructose-1-6-diphosphate is then split to form two molecules of phosphoglyceraldehyde, which are then converted by a series of reactions to two molecules of pyruvic acid. During these reactions, four molecules of ATP are formed per glucose molecule (giving an overall yield of two ATP molecules). Hydrogen removed from the molecules as phosphoglyceraldehyde is converted to pyruvic acid using enzymes called dehydrogenases. The hydrogen is used to convert molecules of nicotinamide adenine dinucleotide (NAD) to the reduced form ($NADH_2$). Two molecules of $NADH_2$ are formed per glucose molecule, and each can give rise to three ATP molecules via the electron transport chain, later on in respiration. This means a *total energy gain* from glycolysis of eight ATP molecules.

### *The Krebs cycle (tricarboxylic acid cycle)*

Aerobic respiration continues via the Krebs cycle (Fig. 3.24), which occurs in the mitochondria. Pyruvic acid is converted to a $C_2$ compound, acetyl COA, by a process known as oxidative decarboxylation, which involves removal of a molecule of carbon dioxide. Acetyl COA combines with a $C_4$ compound, oxaloacetic acid, to form a $C_6$ compound, citric acid. Citric acid is converted by a number of stages to form oxaloacetic acid again. This cycle involves removal of two molecules of carbon dioxide (decarboxylation), and also removal of hydrogen using dehydrogenase enzymes which pass on the hydrogen to acceptor molecules NAD and FAD. The advantages of the cyclic process are:

1. The cycle unifies the metabolic processes: carbohydrates, fats and proteins can all be broken down to acetyl COA or pyruvic acid in order to enter the cycle and be oxidized.
2. Substances can be removed from the cycle for other purposes, e.g. acetyl COA for the formation of fats, and succinyl COA for the formation of haemoglobin or chlorophyll.
3. Products from the breakdown of amino acids, α-ketoglutaric acid and oxaloacetic acid can enter the cycle at the relevant points.
4. Fifteen molecules of ATP are formed as a result of the Krebs cycle, i.e. 30 per glucose molecule.

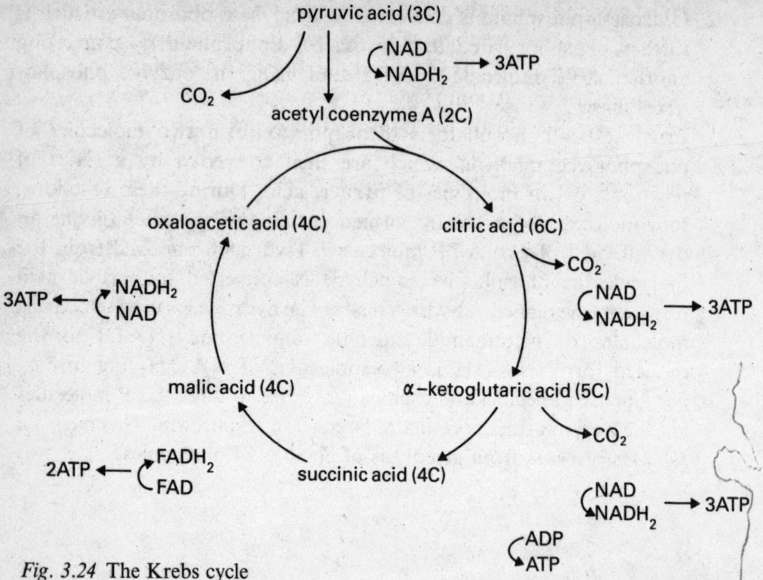
pyruvic acid (3C)
NAD
NADH2
3ATP
CO2
acetyl coenzyme A (2C)
oxaloacetic acid (4C)
citric acid (6C)
CO2
NAD
NADH2
3ATP
3ATP
NADH2
NAD
malic acid (4C)
α-ketoglutaric acid (5C)
CO2
2ATP
FADH2
FAD
succinic acid (4C)
NAD
NADH2
3ATP
ADP
ATP

*Fig. 3.24* The Krebs cycle

### *Oxidation (release of energy)*

Each molecule of $NADH_2$ is used to generate three molecules of ATP via the electron transport chain. As electrons are passed down the chain to carriers at progressively lower energy levels, energy is released and used to generate ATP from ADP. The process occurs in the mitochondria, and is described below and in Fig. 3.25.

1. $H^+$ ions from $NADH_2$ are passed to a secondary acceptor, FAD, to form $FADH_2$, and one ATP molecule results from the process.
2. $H^+$ ions are then released from $FADH_2$, and the electrons from the hydrogen atoms are passed along a series of cytochromes. (Cytochromes are chromoproteins containing iron. The iron can be in the reduced state ($Fe^{2+}$) or the oxidized state ($Fe^{3+}$), depending on whether electrons have been added to or taken away from the molecule.)
3. As the electrons are passed along the chain of cytochromes, two molecules of ATP are formed.

4. The cytochrome at the end of the chain, cytochrome oxidase, enables the $H^+$ ions to combine with oxygen to form water. Cytochrome oxidase is inhibited by the metabolic poison cyanide.

Although oxygen is only required to remove excess hydrogen ions as water, it is essential for the process of aerobic respiration. The name given to the process by which oxygen enables ATP to be formed from ADP is oxidative phosphorylation.

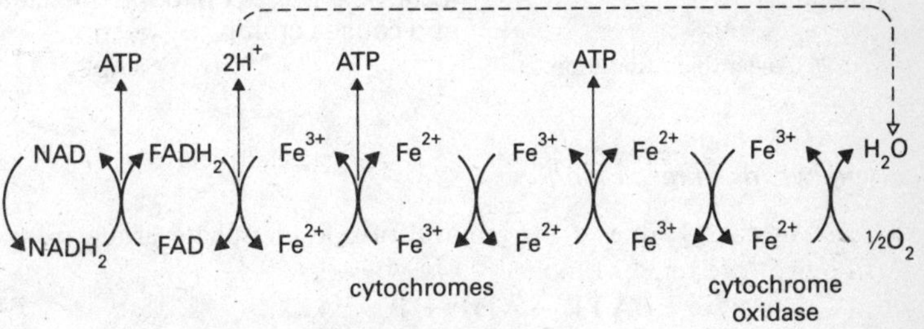
ATP
2H+
ATP
ATP
NAD
NADH2
FADH2
FAD
Fe3+
Fe2+
Fe2+
Fe3+
Fe3+
Fe2+
Fe2+
Fe3+
Fe3+
Fe2+
H2O
½O2
cytochromes
cytochrome oxidase

*Fig. 3.25* The electron transfer chain

## *Requirements for respiration*

Oxygen – required to remove hydrogen ions as water: without it the Krebs cycle cannot operate.

Suitable temperature – required for the correct functioning of enzymes. The rate of respiration rises steadily between 0 and 40 °C, but slows down above this temperature, owing to denaturing of protoplasm.

Moisture – enzymes must be in solution to work properly; below 15% moisture respiration is very slow, e.g. as in dry seeds.

## *Anaerobic respiration*

In the absence of oxygen, pyruvic acid cannot enter the Krebs cycle. Instead it undergoes anaerobic respiration (in plants called fermentation) (see Fig. 3.26). $NADH_2$, produced in glycolysis, is used to donate hydrogen atoms during the reaction. Hence the net energy gain is only two molecules of ATP per glucose molecule. The regeneration of oxidized NAD enables glycolysis to continue.

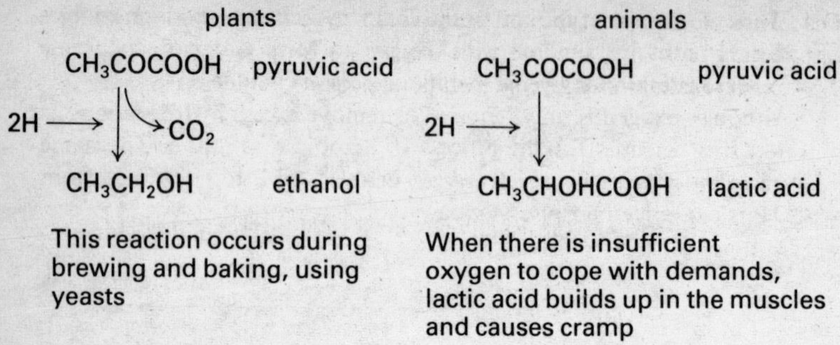
plants
CH3COCOOH pyruvic acid
2H
CO2
CH3CH2OH ethanol
This reaction occurs during brewing and baking, using yeasts
animals
CH3COCOOH pyruvic acid
2H
CH3CHOHCOOH lactic acid
When there is insufficient oxygen to cope with demands, lactic acid builds up in the muscles and causes cramp

*Fig. 3.26* Anaerobic respiration

### *Energy yields in respiration*

Release of energy, due to the removal of one phosphate group from ATP, gives rise to 34 kJ/mole:

$$\text{ATP} \rightarrow \text{ADP} + \text{P} + 34\text{ kJ}$$

1. In aerobic respiration the yield per glucose molecule is:

| | | |
|---|---|---|
| Glycolysis | 8 ATP | 2 ATP produced directly |
| | | 2 molecules of $NADH_2$ yield 6 ATP |
| Krebs cycle | 30 ATP | 2 ATP produced directly |
| | | 8 molecules of $NADH_2$ yield 3 ATP each = 24 ATP |
| | | 2 molecules of $FADH_2$ yield 2 ADP each = 4 ATP |

   Therefore the total yield of ATP per glucose molecule = 38 ATP. Energy yield = 38 × 34 kJ = 1,292 kJ/mole glucose. (This is approximately 45 per cent efficiency.)

2. In anaerobic respiration the energy yield is 2 molecules of ATP per glucose molecule.

   This gives rise to an energy yield of 2 × 34 kJ = 68 kJ/mole glucose (approximately 2 per cent efficiency).

### *Respiratory quotient*

The respiratory quotient (RQ) is the ratio of the carbon dioxide released to the oxygen consumed.

$$\text{RQ} = \frac{CO_2 \text{ evolved}}{O_2 \text{ consumed}}$$

Oxidation of different types of food gives rise to different respiratory quotients.

1. Aerobic oxidation of glucose usually has an RQ of 1.0.

$$C_6H_{12}O_6 + 6O_2 \longrightarrow 6CO_2 + 6H_2O$$

$$RQ = \frac{6}{6} = 1$$

2. Aerobic oxidation of fat usually has an RQ of approximately 0.7. For example,

$$\underset{\text{(stearic acid)}}{C_{18}H_{36}O_2} + 26O_2 \longrightarrow 18CO_2 + 18H_2O$$

$$RQ = \frac{18}{26} = 0.7$$

The respiratory quotient when measured in man is approximately 0.85, indicating the oxidation of both fat and carbohydrate. Protein is not usually oxidized except in extreme circumstances such as starvation.

The respiratory quotient can also tell us about the metabolism of an organism.

1. A high RQ (greater than 1) indicates a shortage of oxygen and the occurrence of anaerobic respiration. High RQs also result from the conversion of carbohydrate to fat; during the process oxygen is released. This oxygen is used immediately for respiration in the liver, and hence is not detected although the carbon dioxide output is. The process is most pronounced in mammals preparing to hibernate, which are laying down fat reserves.
2. A low RQ (less than 0.7) results from a low carbon dioxide output. It occurs in photosynthesizing plants, as the carbon dioxide produced in respiration is diverted to be used in photosynthesis. At night photosynthesis does not occur, $CO_2$ is released, and the RQ rises accordingly.

## Further reading

C. Bryant, *The Biology of Respiration*, Studies in Biology No. 28, 2nd edition (Arnold, 1980)

J. B. Chappell, *The Energetics of Mitochondria*, Oxford/Carolina Biology Reader No. 19, revised edition (Packard, 1978)

G. M. Hughs, *Vertebrate Respiration* (Heinemann, 1963)

P. Nichols, *Cytochromes and Biological Oxidation*, Oxford/Carolina Biology Reader No. 66 (Packard, 1975)

H. Opik, *Respiration of Higher Plants*, Studies in Biology No. 120 (Arnold, 1980)

***Related questions***

**Question:**
(multiple choice)

1. Respiratory Quotient, RQ, is calculated in terms of the volumes of oxygen taken up and carbon dioxide evolved, as follows:

   (a) $\frac{CO_2}{O_2}$ (b) $\frac{O_2}{CO_2}$ (c) $\frac{O_2 - CO_2}{O_2}$ (d) $\frac{O^2 - CO_2}{CO_2}$

2. Where in the cell does glycolysis occur?
   (a) mitochondria
   (b) endoplasmic reticulum
   (c) cytoplasm
   (d) lysosomes
3. How many moles of ATP does one mole of $NADH_2$ give rise to via the electron transport chain?
   (a) 1
   (b) 2
   (c) 3
   (d) 4
4. Which of the following statements regarding oxygen is incorrect?
   (a) It is required for the Krebs cycle to operate
   (b) It is required for glycolysis to operate
   (c) Anaerobic respiration occurs in its absence
   (d) It is only combined with hydrogen in the last stages of respiration
5. Aerobic respiration of malic acid can be represented as

   $$C_4H_6O_5 + 3O_2 \longrightarrow 4CO_2 + 3H_2O + \text{energy}$$

   The respiratory quotient of this reaction is
   (a) 0.7
   (b) 0.75
   (c) 1.0
   (d) 1.3
   (e) 1.5

**Comments:**

1. See p. 106.
2. See p. 101.
3. See p. 104.
4. See p. 105.
5. This question is simply testing the ability to work out a respiratory quotient (see p. 106). Candidates should not be alarmed if they have not previously encountered the formula for malic acid, only the amounts of oxygen consumed and carbon dioxide released are required to answer the question.

**Question:**

The diagram below is an outline of the Krebs cycle, also known as the tricarboxylic acid cycle and the citric acid cycle.

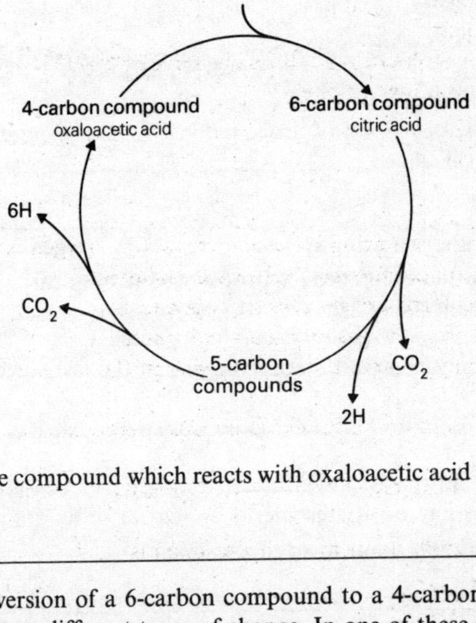
4-carbon compound
oxaloacetic acid
6-carbon compound
citric acid
6H
$CO_2$
5-carbon compounds
$CO_2$
2H

(a) Name the compound which reacts with oxaloacetic acid to give citric acid.

________________________________________

(b) The conversion of a 6-carbon compound to a 4-carbon compound involves two different types of change. In one of these changes, so-called *hydrogen acceptors* are involved.

(i) Name a hydrogen acceptor which is used in this process.

________________________________________

(ii) Explain why the term *hydrogen acceptor* is not strictly correct.

(c) Explain why the Krebs cycle can only take place under aerobic conditions.

[AEB, Nov. 1981, Paper 1]

**Comments:**

(a) See Fig. 3.24.

(b) See p. 101.

(c) See p. 105.

**Question:**

(a) Explain with the aid of an equation how the respiratory quotient (RQ) is calculated.

**(2 marks)**

(b) Calculate the theoretical RQ of a seed if only carbohydrate such as glucose is being metabolized and completely oxidized.

**(2 marks)**

(c) How would the RQ of a hibernating animal such as a dormouse living entirely on its reserve of stored fat differ from the above? Give a reason.

**(2 marks)**

The RQ for a resting human adult is approximately 0.85. A person undertook violent exercise for 30 seconds and the RQ was measured at regular intervals afterwards. The results are shown on the graph below.

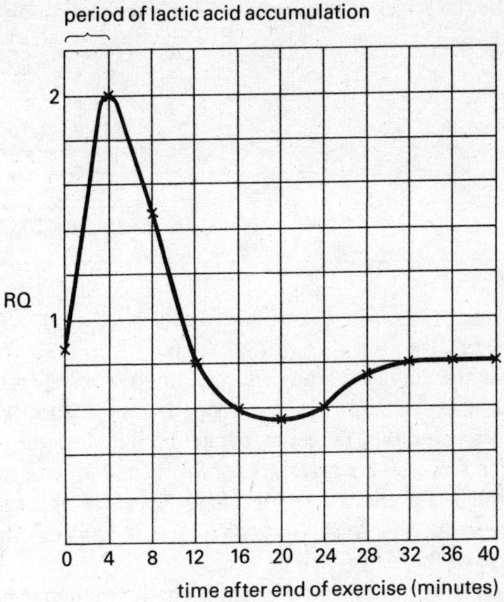
period of lactic acid accumulation
RQ
2
1
0 4 8 12 16 20 24 28 32 36 40
time after end of exercise (minutes)

(d) (i) How long does the RQ remain below the normal level?

_______________________________________________

**(1 mark)**

(ii) Explain the rise in RQ during the four-minute period following violent exercise.

_______________________________________________

_______________________________________________

**(1 mark)**

(iii) Explain the reasons for the subsequent fall in RQ.

_______________________________________________

_______________________________________________

**(2 marks)**

(iv) In the period immediately following exercise, lactic acid accumulates in the muscles and lowers the pH of the blood. The change in pH stimulates the respiratory centres and increases the rate of ventilation.

Describe the effect of the increased lung ventilation on the pH of the blood.

---

**(1 mark)**

[Oxford, July 1982, Paper 2]

**Comments:**

(a) and (b) See p. 106.

(c) In this case the animal is living entirely on fat, consequently the RQ value will be lower than for the carbohydrate, i.e. approx. 0.7. (It is important to note that the animal is actually hibernating and living on its fat reserves. This gives a very different RQ from that of an animal which is preparing to hibernate. Such animals convert carbohydrate to fat, releasing carbon dioxide in the process, and causing an increase in the RQ.)

(d) (i) This is the length of time for which the RQ remains below 0.85. It can easily be found from the graph by calculating the length of time for which the curve is below 0.85 on the horizontal axis.

(ii) The rise in RQ on the graph corresponds to the period during which lactic acid is being accumulated. At this time, the muscles are still respiring anaerobically, producing lactic acid and carbon dioxide in the absence of oxygen. This causes a rise in the RQ.

(iii) After violent exercise, normal breathing resumes, and the oxygen debt incurred during anaerobic respiration is paid back. The increase in oxygen consumption causes a lowering of the RQ.

(iv) Increased lung ventilation means there will be increased supplies of oxygen to the blood. The oxygen can be used to oxidize lactic acid to carbon dioxide and water. The reduction in acid concentration causes the pH of the blood to rise, i.e. to become less acid.

**Question:**

(a) Give an equation that summarizes (i) aerobic respiration and (ii) anaerobic respiration.

(i) aerobic respiration

(ii) anaerobic respiration

**(2 marks)**

(b) What might induce anaerobic respiration in (i) parenchyma cells in a plant root and (ii) mammalian striated muscle fibres?

(i) parenchyma cells in a plant root

(ii) mammalian striated (skeletal) muscle fibres

**(2 marks)**

(c) What is meant by the term 'respiratory quotient'?

**(4 marks)**

(d) For each of the following respiratory quotient values in a green plant, state the type of respiratory substrate being used and the conditions in which the process occurs.

| Respiratory quotient | Respiratory substrate | Conditions in which process occurs |
|---|---|---|
| 1.0 | | |
| 0.7 | | |
| 0.5 | | |

**(6 marks)**

(e) Why are high respiratory quotient values obtained from tissues involved with conversion of carbohydrate to fat?

---

---

**(3 marks)**

**(Total 17 marks)**

[London, Jan. 1983, Paper 1]

**Comments:**

(a) (i) See p. 100.

(ii) See p. 106. The question does not specify whether the equation should be for plants or animals, therefore either could be given.

(b) Anaerobic respiration occurs when the supply of oxygen is insufficient to meet the demands of the organism. You are required to give a situation where this is likely to occur for the examples given. Roots are likely to be short of oxygen in times of flooding. Waterlogged soils do not contain oxygen, therefore cells in the root would be forced to respire anaerobically. Muscle fibres are likely to be deprived of oxygen during violent exertion.

(c) See p. 106.

(d) The respiratory quotient of a green plant will be affected by the occurrence of photosynthesis. Photosynthesis has the effect of lowering the RQ since it consumes carbon dioxide and produces oxygen. For the RQ values given, a number of combinations of substrates and conditions are possible. For example, an RQ of 1.0 is likely to represent oxidation of carbohydrate in the dark (no photosynthesis). An RQ of 0.7 could represent either oxidation of fat in the dark, or oxidation of carbohydrate in shaded light (i.e. only a small amount of photosynthesis occurring). An RQ of 0.5 is characteristic of carbohydrate oxidation in sunlight when carbon dioxide is being used in photosynthesis and oxygen is being released.

(e) See p. 107.

**Question:**

Describe the processes by which a flowering plant acquires and uses energy.

(London, Jan. 1982, Paper 2)

**Comments:**

This is an essay which encompasses a large amount of information. The question is testing your ability to condense this information into a coherent organized essay which contains the relevant points without attempting to give details of biochemical pathways. Hence you should not simply draw cycles of each pathway involved.

*Suggested essay plan:*

How the plant *acquires* energy:

1. Cyclic photophosphorylation – production of ATP in the light stage of photosynthesis.
2. Aerobic respiration.
3. Anaerobic respiration in waterlogged soils.

How the plant *uses* energy:

Energy from (1) is used in the dark stage of photosynthesis for manufacture of 3C-sugars which are then used for other synthetic reactions producing (a) glucose and starch; (b) protein; and (c) fat.

Energy from (2) is used in (a) active transport; (b) cell division; and (c) hormone manufacture.

# 4. Nutrition

Plants and animals must synthesize, or be provided with, certain materials necessary for the maintenance of life. These materials are called **nutrients**, and the processes by which an organism acquires nutrients are defined as **nutrition**.

Green plants can synthesize all their complex compounds from simple organic materials – they are **autotrophic**. Animals must rely on the activities of plants for their organic food requirements – they are **heterotrophic** (see p. 138). Fungi and most bacteria are also heterotrophic. It is this fundamental difference that is the basis of most structural and physiological differences between plants and animals.

## *Autotrophic nutrition*

### *Photosynthesis*

This is the process by which green plants build up carbohydrates from organic materials ($CO_2$ + water), using energy from sunlight which is absorbed by the pigment chlorophyll. Oxygen is released as a by-product.

#### Requirements for photosynthesis

In order to demonstrate these requirements, starch production is usually taken to indicate the occurrence of photosynthesis.

1. CARBON DIOXIDE: A healthy potted plant is destarched by leaving it in a dark cupboard overnight. The plant is then set up as illustrated in Fig. 4.1. After 6 hours, the leaves from the flasks are detached and tested for starch by (i) boiling the leaf gently to soften it and melt the cuticle; (ii) placing the leaf in boiling 90 per cent alcohol to decolourize the leaf; (iii) adding iodine in potassium iodide solution, which turns the leaf blue-black if starch is present. The leaf in flask 1 which had no carbon dioxide available does not make starch, while the control leaf (in flask 2) does.
2. WATER: Since water is needed for many functions in the plant, it is difficult to demonstrate its necessity for photosynthesis. The best way to show that water is required is to use the heavy isotope of water

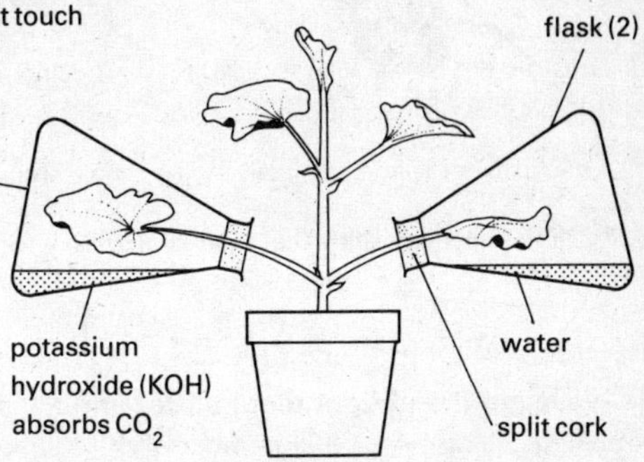
Notes
1. The flasks must be airtight to prevent exchange of gases. Therefore the split corks should be sealed with vaseline
2. Potassium hydroxide is caustic, therefore do not let it touch the leaf
flask (2)
flask (1)
potassium hydroxide (KOH) absorbs $CO_2$
water
split cork

*Fig. 4.1* Experiment to show that carbon dioxide is required for photosynthesis

$H_2{}^{18}O$ and demonstrate its assimilation into carbohydrates (see p. 126).

3. SUITABLE TEMPERATURE: Photosynthesis has an optimum temperature of 30 °C. Since it is an enzyme-controlled process, a reduction in temperature will reduce the amount of photosynthesis, and an increase above 40 °C will stop the process altogether, owing to denaturing of the enzymes. Generally, the rate of reaction doubles for every 10 °C increase in temperature. (See temperature coefficient, p. 70.)
4. CHLOROPHYLL: The necessity for chlorophyll in photosynthesis can be shown by using a variegated leaf, e.g. ivy. Starch is only found in the green parts of the leaf, which contain chlorophyll. The absence of chlorophyll in the white areas shows that chlorophyll is required for photosynthesis.
5. LIGHT: A plant is destarched by placing it in a dark cupboard overnight. A thin piece of black paper is then placed over part of a leaf and secured in place on both sides. The leaf is illuminated for 6 hours, and is then removed from the plant and tested for starch as detailed under the carbon dioxide experiment. Starch is found to be absent in the covered part of the leaf, but present in the uncovered part (Fig. 4.2). This demonstrates that leaves can only photosynthesize in the presence of light.

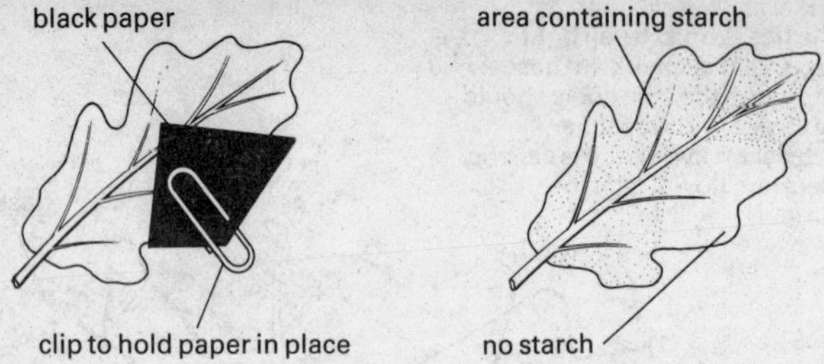
black paper
area containing starch
clip to hold paper in place
no starch

*Fig. 4.2* Experiment to show that light is necessary for photosynthesis

## The wavelengths of light required for and used in photosynthesis

White light is composed of a number of different colours or wavelengths, ranging from 400 nm (blue) to 760 nm (red). Some of these wavelengths are more suitable for photosynthesis than others. The following experiment, illustrated in Fig. 4.3, demonstrates the use made of different wavelengths of light in photosynthesis.

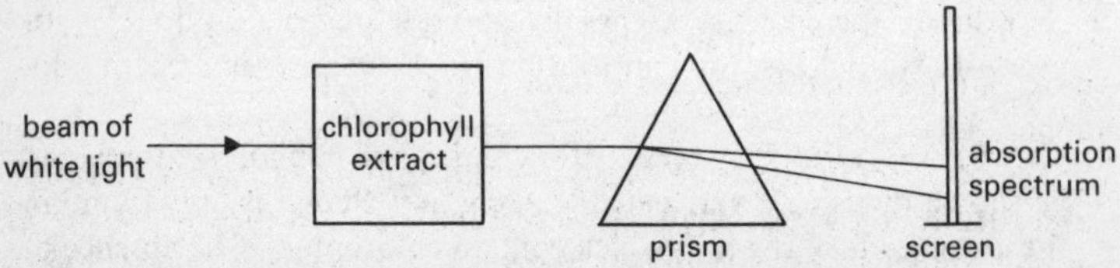
beam of
white light
chlorophyll
extract
prism
absorption
spectrum
screen

*Fig. 4.3* Experiment to determine the wavelengths of light absorbed by chlorophyll

A solution of chlorophyll extract is illuminated by a single beam of white light. The light emerging from the solution is split into its separate colours using a prism. The spectrum formed on the screen is deficient in certain colours which have been absorbed by the solution, hence it is called an **absorption spectrum**. The amount of each colour which has

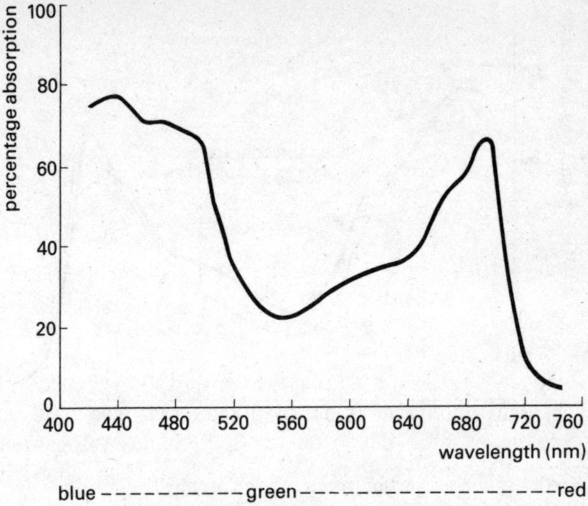
percentage absorption
100
80
60
40
20
0
400
440
480
520
560
600
640
680
720
760
wavelength (nm)
blue ----------green------------------red

*Fig. 4.4* The absorption spectrum for chlorophyll

been absorbed by the chlorophyll can be found by comparing the absorption spectrum to a normal spectrum (Fig. 4.4). The colours most absorbed by the chlorophyll are red and blue. Green is absorbed least, most of it passing through – that is why chlorophyll and therefore leaves appear green.

The absorption spectrum illustrates the amount of each wavelength absorbed by the chlorophyll. However, the fact that these wavelengths are all absorbed by chlorophyll extract does not mean they are used exclusively in photosynthesis – some may be used for other purposes.

To demonstrate which wavelengths are actually used in photosynthesis, leaves are illuminated with different coloured lights, and the amount of photosynthesis at each wavelength is estimated by either (i) the percentage carbohydrate or (ii) the percentage oxygen produced. The resulting spectrum is called the action spectrum, and it closely resembles the absorption spectrum (see Fig. 4.5). At point X on the graph (approx. 490 nm), blue wavelengths are absorbed by carotenes in the chlorophyll extract, but are not used in photosynthesis; this accounts for the difference in shape of the two curves.

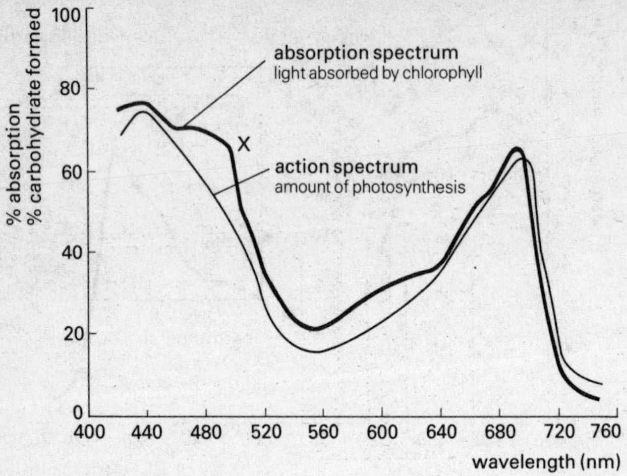
% absorption
% carbohydrate formed
100
80
60
40
20
0
absorption spectrum
light absorbed by chlorophyll
X
action spectrum
amount of photosynthesis
400
440
480
520
560
600
640
680
720
760
wavelength (nm)

*Fig. 4.5* Absorption and action spectra for chlorophyll

### Experiments to show the effects on photosynthesis of varying light intensity and wavelength

The apparatus is set up as shown in Fig. 4.6, using the pond weed, *Elodea*. The *Elodea* is placed in pond water in a test-tube, which is then immersed in a constant temperature water bath.

As the *Elodea* photosynthesizes, bubbles of oxygen are given off, and collect in the fluted end of the capillary tube. The oxygen bubble is then drawn over the scale, using the syringe. The volume of oxygen given off per unit time can be estimated by reading off the length of the air column in the capillary tube after a fixed length of time (usually 5 minutes). This volume can be used to estimate the rate of photosynthesis.

*1. To show the effect of light intensity on photosynthesis*

The experiment is set up in a darkened room and a light source (lamp or slide projector) is used to illuminate the test-tube. Starting wth the light source 10 cm from the test-tube, the volume of oxygen evolved over a standard length of time is found. After allowing the *Elodea* time to adjust to new lighting conditions, the experiment is then repeated with the light source at different distances from the test-tube. The light intensity = $1/d^2$, where $d$ is the distance of the light source from the test-tube.

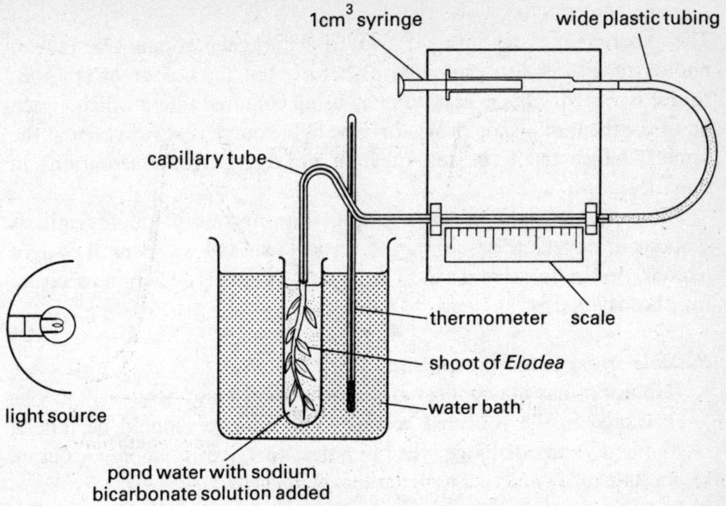
1cm³ syringe
wide plastic tubing
capillary tube
thermometer
scale
shoot of *Elodea*
water bath
light source
pond water with sodium bicarbonate solution added

*Fig. 4.6* Experiment to demonstrate the effect of light on photosynthesis

The results are then plotted on a graph, showing light intensity on the horizontal axis, and the rate of photosynthesis (volume of oxygen) on the vertical axis, as in Fig. 4.7.

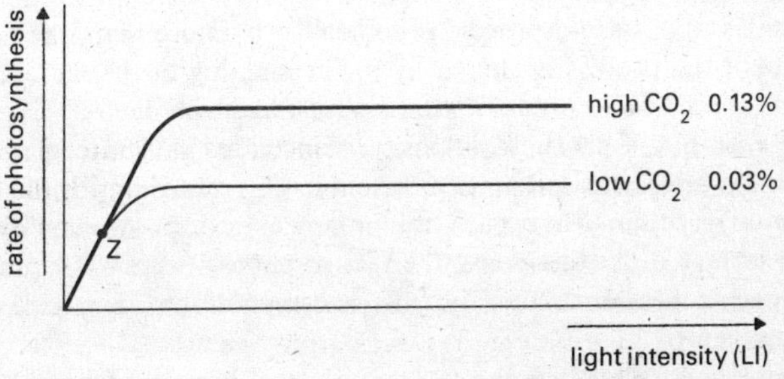
rate of photosynthesis
high $CO_2$ 0.13%
low $CO_2$ 0.03%
Z
light intensity (LI)

*Fig. 4.7* Graph to show the rate of photosynthesis at varying light intensities

*2. To show the effect of different colour (wavelength) of light on photosynthesis*

The experiment is set up as above, in a darkened room. The rate of photosynthesis is also estimated as before, but the colour of the light source is varied. This is best done by using coloured filters which attach on to the front of a slide projector. The light source is always kept at the same distance from the test-tube, in order to avoid fluctuations in intensity.

The results are plotted on a graph, showing rate of photosynthesis (volume of oxygen released) on the vertical axis and wavelength of light (colour) on the horizontal axis. The resulting graph is an action spectrum for photosynthesis.

*Possible errors in the experiments*

1. Bubbles of gas may collect around the leaves, and hence will not be registered in the collected volume. The test-tube should be tapped frequently to dislodge the bubbles to give a more accurate reading.
2. Increases in temperature cause expansion of the gas bubbles and give inaccurately high readings. However, the constant-temperature water bath, together with regular thermometer readings to check the temperature, can be used to control such errors.
3. A low carbon dioxide concentration can be a limiting factor in photosynthesis (see below), and can result in artificially low readings. Therefore, sodium bicarbonate (sodium hydrogencarbonate) must be added to the pond water to ensure an excess of carbon dioxide.

## The interaction of the factors controlling photosynthesis

*The law of limiting factors*

This states that when a process is controlled by more than one factor, the rate of the process is altered by the availability of the factors, and will be reduced in accordance with the least available factor.

For example, if the light intensity is increased, the rate of photosynthesis is also increased up to a certain level (point Z on Fig. 4.7). No further increase can then occur until the concentration of carbon dioxide is also increased. At this point, the rate of photosynthesis is limited by the concentration of carbon dioxide, and carbon dioxide is called the limiting factor.

Any of the factors necessary for photosynthesis – carbon dioxide concentration, light intensity, and temperature – can be limiting factors.

The effects of carbon dioxide as a limiting factor can be shown using the apparatus in Fig. 4.6. As before, the light intensity can be altered using light sources at different distances from the test tube and the rate of photosynthesis can be seen to increase with increase in light intensity up to a certain level. There is then no more increase until extra sodium bicarbonate is added to provide a higher concentration of carbon dioxide.

*The compensation point*

During the day, plants respire and photosynthesize simultaneously. Respiration breaks down carbohydrates, while photosynthesis builds them up. When respiration and photosynthesis proceed at the same rate, there is no net gain or loss of carbohydrate and this is known as the compensation point. The compensation period is the time taken for a plant to reach its compensation point after being placed in darkness. Shade plants usually reach this point faster than those which like bright sunlight owing to the former's ability to utilize dim light.

## Adaptations of plants to maximize photosynthesis

Increase in photosynthetic efficiency usually involves some adaptation for obtaining the maximum amount of light.

(a) Height – forest trees grow tall and form a canopy over the forest to ensure a good light supply (e.g. oak, sycamore, horse chestnut).

(b) Climbing plants – these obtain more light by 'creeping' towards a source of light (e.g. ivy).

(c) Leaf mosaics – plants with many leaves often arrange them in a mosaic pattern. This prevents overlapping, and ensures maximum exposure to light (e.g. rhododendron).

(d) Leaf structure – leaves (see Fig. 4.8) are adapted for efficient photosynthesis in a number of ways:

 (i) They are thin and flat with a large surface area. This ensures that light can reach all cells.

 (ii) The upper epidermis has no chloroplasts, so that more light can pass through to the palisade layer.

 (iii) They are well supplied with veins composed of xylem and phloem. Xylem brings water to the leaves and ensures a layer of moisture around the cells so that carbon dioxide can dissolve and pass into the cells by diffusion.

 (iv) Air spaces between cells of the spongy layer (mesophyll) allow diffusion of gases into and out of cells.

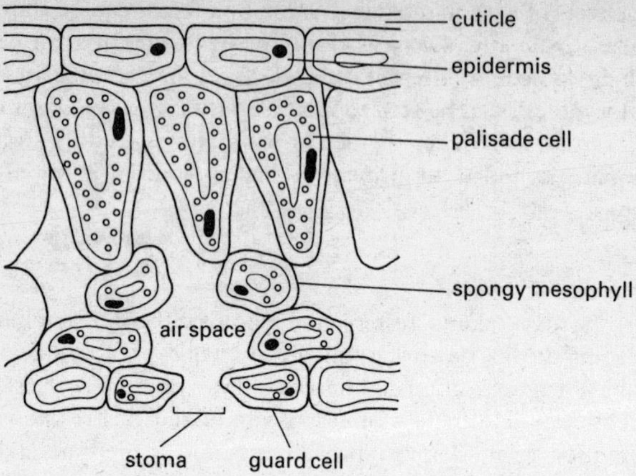
cuticle
epidermis
palisade cell
spongy mesophyll
air space
stoma
guard cell

*Fig. 4.8* TS of a leaf

(v) The lower epidermis contains many pores or stomata, which allow exchange of gases.
(vi) The palisade layer is well packed with chloroplasts.
(vii) Chloroplasts (see p. 25) are oval structures containing stacks of membranes or lamellae, called grana, which are embedded in a watery fluid called stroma. Chlorophyll molecules are found in 'packs' of 230, called quantosomes. The lamellae hold the quantosomes in a position where they will absorb the maximum amount of sunlight.

## The pigments used in photosynthesis

Chlorophyll extract (obtained from chloroplasts) actually contains a mixture of five pigments. These can be separated by acetone chromatography (see Fig. 4.9). A spot of chlorophyll extract is placed on chromatography paper, and the tip of the paper is immersed in acetone. The five different pigments in the extract are separated out as the acetone is absorbed up the paper.

Chlorophyll is the most abundant pigment, and its function is to absorb light energy. Other pigments absorb light energy and pass it on to chlorophyll a. Chlorophyll a belongs to a series of chemicals called porphyrins (synthesized from succinic acid – see Krebs or TCA cycle). It has a similar structure to haemoglobin, but has a magnesium atom instead of iron, and this is thought to enhance its light-absorbing properties.

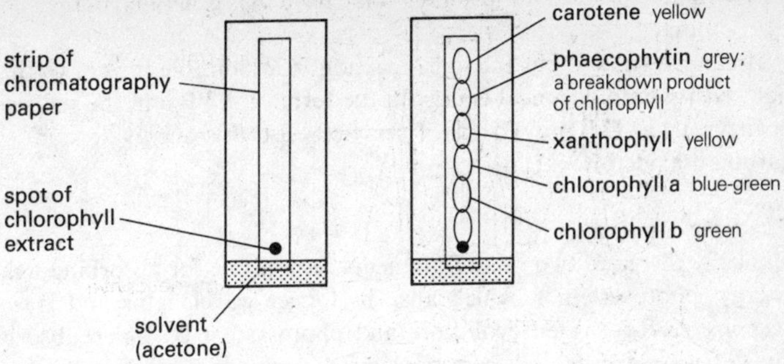
strip of chromatography paper
spot of chlorophyll extract
solvent (acetone)
carotene yellow
phaecophytin grey; a breakdown product of chlorophyll
xanthophyll yellow
chlorophyll a blue-green
chlorophyll b green

*Fig. 4.9* Separation of pigments from chlorophyll extract by chromatography

## The chemistry of photosynthesis

Photosynthesis can be represented by the following equation:

$$\underset{\text{Carbon dioxide}}{6CO_2} + \underset{\text{Water}}{6H_2O} \xrightarrow[\text{sunlight}]{} \underset{\text{Glucose}}{C_6H_{12}O_6} + \underset{\text{Oxygen}}{6O_2}$$

However, this is not only an oversimplification of what actually happens, but it is also misleading since it gives the impression that the oxygen released comes from carbon dioxide. Labelling experiments have shown that this is not so. It has been shown by a number of experiments that photosynthesis actually consists of two stages. The first phase, called the **light reaction**, is dependent om the presence of light, but the second phase, called the **dark reaction**, is enzyme-controlled and does not require light. Both reactions take place in the chloroplasts – the light reaction in the grana and the dark reaction in the stroma.

*Evidence for the existence of the light and dark reactions*

The two reactions were identified in an experiment in 1958 by Arron and colleagues as follows:

1. Chloroplasts were illuminated in the absence of carbon dioxide so that light energy could be trapped and converted into a chemical form.
2. The chloroplasts were disrupted and the grana in which the light reaction took place were removed.
3. The remaining stroma were then exposed to radioactive carbon dioxide in the dark.
4. The carbon dioxide was seen to be converted in the dark to sugars.

To do this the energy must have come from that generated in the light reaction.

It is now known that the light reaction is responsible for converting light energy into chemical energy in the form of ATP and the reduced coenzyme $NADPH_2$. The dark reactions use this energy to convert carbon dioxide into sugars.

*The light reaction*

Basically there are two sets of pigments responsible for absorbing light energy: photosystem I, which absorbs longer wavelengths and is *not* responsible for oxygen evolution; and photosystem II, which absorbs shorter wavelengths and is responsible for oxygen evolution. In most living plants, photosystems I and II work together in the following way:

1. Light is absorbed by the pigments in both photosystems I and II, causing two electrons to be emitted from the pigment molecules of each system.
2. At the same time, a water molecule is split into hydrogen ions and oxygen in photosystem II ($H_2O \rightarrow 2H^+ + 2e^- + \frac{1}{2}O_2$). The electrons released from this reaction replace those lost earlier from the pigment molecule of photosystem II.
3. The electrons released from the pigment of photosystem II are passed along a series of electron acceptors to photosystem I and at the same time two molecules of ADP are converted to two molecules of ATP. Production of ATP from photoinduced electron transport is called photophosphorylation.
4. The two electrons from photosystem I combine with a molecule of NADP and with two hydrogen ions to form $NADPH_2$. Since electrons have been added, $NADPH_2$ is said to be reduced.
5. Oxygen is released and $NADPH_2$ and ATP are subsequently used in the dark reactions.

When both photosystems I and II proceed simultaneously, as shown in Fig. 4.10, the process is called non-cyclic photophosphorylation.

It is thought that the two systems evolved separately, photosystem I first, and then photosystem II. Many bacteria possess only photosystem I and are incapable of producing oxygen. When this occurs (Fig. 4.11) no $NADPH_2$ is formed and the process is called cyclic photophosphorylation. The electrons released from the pigment molecules eventually return via a series of electron acceptors.

*The dark reaction*

In these reactions, hydrogen from $NADPH_2$ is combined with carbon,

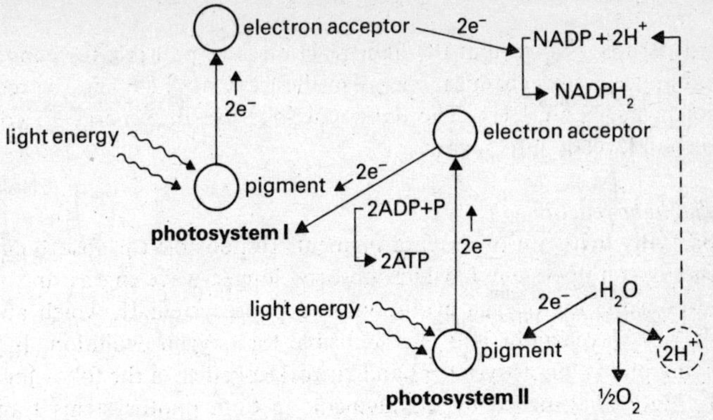
electron acceptor
2e⁻
NADP + 2H⁺
NADPH₂
2e⁻
light energy
pigment
2e⁻
electron acceptor
photosystem I
2ADP+P
2ATP
2e⁻
light energy
2e⁻
H₂O
pigment
2H⁺
photosystem II
½O₂

*Fig. 4.10* Non-cyclic photophosphorylation

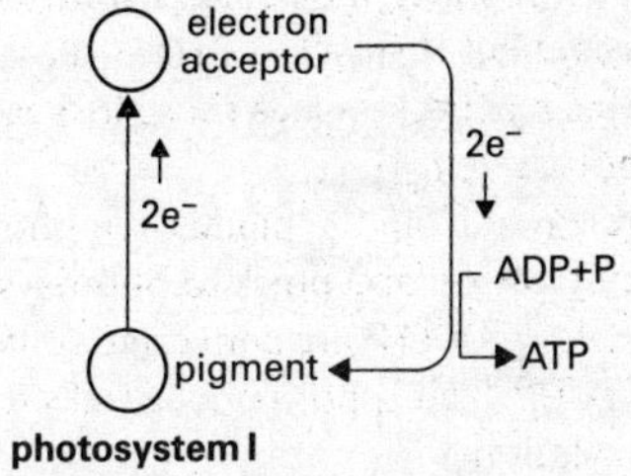
electron
acceptor
2e⁻
2e⁻
ADP+P
ATP
pigment
photosystem I

*Fig. 4.11* Cyclic photophosphorylation

using energy from ATP to form hexose sugars. This process is called **carbon fixation**. The reactions (which can proceed in the dark or the light) take place in a cycle called the Benson–Calvin cycle, each step being controlled by a specific enzyme. In this cycle, carbon dioxide is not directly combined with hydrogen to form a carbohydrate. Instead both elements are gradually incorporated into existing organic molecules as follows, and illustrated in Fig. 4.12.

1. The starting molecule contains five carbon atoms and is called ribulose diphosphate.
2. Three molecules of carbon dioxide are combined with three molecules of ribulose diphosphate forming three 6C molecules. These three 6C molecules split in two to form six molecules of phosphoglycerate, each containing three carbon atoms (see Fig. 4.12b).

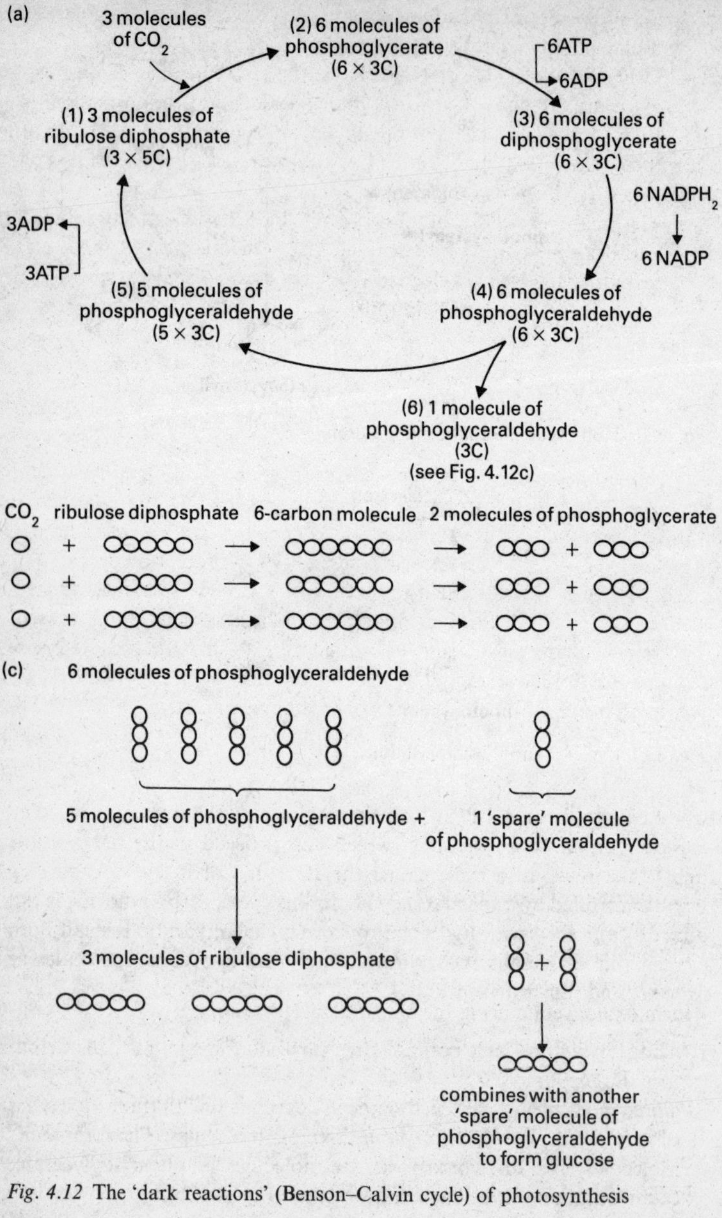
(a)
3 molecules of $CO_2$
(2) 6 molecules of phosphoglycerate (6 × 3C)
6ATP
6ADP
(1) 3 molecules of ribulose diphosphate (3 × 5C)
(3) 6 molecules of diphosphoglycerate (6 × 3C)
6 $NADPH_2$
6 NADP
3ADP
3ATP
(5) 5 molecules of phosphoglyceraldehyde (5 × 3C)
(4) 6 molecules of phosphoglyceraldehyde (6 × 3C)
(6) 1 molecule of phosphoglyceraldehyde (3C) (see Fig. 4.12c)
(b) $CO_2$ ribulose diphosphate 6-carbon molecule 2 molecules of phosphoglycerate
(c) 6 molecules of phosphoglyceraldehyde
5 molecules of phosphoglyceraldehyde +
1 'spare' molecule of phosphoglyceraldehyde
3 molecules of ribulose diphosphate
combines with another 'spare' molecule of phosphoglyceraldehyde to form glucose

*Fig. 4.12* The 'dark reactions' (Benson–Calvin cycle) of photosynthesis

3. Six molecules of phosphoglycerate are converted to six molecules of diphosphoglycerate using six molecules of ATP.
4. Using six molecules of $NADPH_2$, the six molecules of diphosphoglycerate are converted to six molecules of phosphoglyceraldehyde.
5. Five of the phosphoglyceraldehyde molecules are converted, using three ATP molecules, into three molecules of ribulose diphosphate which can regenerate the cycle.
6. The spare molecule of phosphoglyceraldehyde can combine with another similar molecule (formed in a previous turn of the cycle) to form a hexose sugar, glucose. To form one molecule of glucose, two turns of the cycle are required.

The overall reaction is:

$$6\text{RuDP} + 6\text{CO}_2 + 18\text{ATP} + 12\text{NADPH}_2 \rightarrow 6\text{RuDP} + \text{glucose} + 12\text{NADP}$$

Numerous experiments have led to an understanding of how photosynthesis occurs. For example, an experiment to show the intermediates in the Benson–Calvin cycle was performed by Calvin. He illuminated green algae in the presence of radioactive carbon dioxide for a few seconds, then quickly killed the cells and obtained an extract from the chloroplasts. Using chromatographic techniques, the different molecules present in the extract could be isolated and tested for the presence of radioactivity. The radioactive carbon dioxide was found to be incorporated into a $C_3$ molecule called phosphoglyceraldehyde, which showed that this was one of the molecules involved in the dark reactions of photosynthesis in green algae. By stopping the reaction at various times after the initial fixation of carbon dioxide, the pathway through which the radioactive carbon compounds were made was established.

*Fixation of carbon dioxide by $C_4$ plants*

In some plants, such as sugar cane and maize, phosphoglycerate is not the first compound into which carbon dioxide is incorporated. Instead, it is incorporated into a molecule called phosphoenol pyruvic acid to form oxaloacetate using the enzyme phosphoenol pyruvate carboxylase. The first detectable radioactive compound in the cycle is oxaloacetate, which is a $C_4$ compound. This gives rise to the name $C_4$ plants (normal plants are called $C_3$ plants since they form a $C_3$ compound).

Phosphoenol pyruvate carboxylase has a very high affinity for carbon dioxide, unlike ribulose diphosphate carboxylase, which has a much lower affinity. $C_4$ fixation is therefore more efficient than $C_3$ fixation. $C_4$

plants require more ATP than $C_3$ plants and can maintain a high rate of photosynthesis in conditions of low carbon dioxide concentration (e.g. dense tropical vegetation).

### *Chemosynthesis*

Some bacteria can synthesize organic substances from inorganic materials using energy from chemical reactions instead of sunlight. Carbon dioxide is the principal carbon source, and energy is obtained from the oxidation of reduced inorganic compounds (e.g. $NH_3$, $H_2$, $NO_2$, $Fe^{2+}$).

1. IRON BACTERIA: These bacteria live in streams with a high iron ore content. They obtain energy from oxidation of iron II salts to iron III salts, i.e. $Fe^{2+} \rightarrow Fe^{3+}$.
2. COLOURLESS SULPHUR BACTERIA: These bacteria oxidize hydrogen sulphide to sulphur and water, i.e. $2H_2S + O_2 \rightarrow 2S + 2H_2O$.
3. NITRIFYING BACTERIA: These bacteria, which are found in soil, obtain energy by oxidation of ammonia to nitrites. Examples include *Nitrosomonas* and *Nitrococcus*.

## Further reading

D. Hall and K. K. Rao, *Photosynthesis*, Studies in Biology No. 37, 2nd edition (Arnold, 1981)

C. P. Whittingham *Photosynthesis*, Oxford/Carolina Biology Reader No. 9, 3rd edition (Packard, 1981)

## Related questions

**Question:**

(a) With reference to the light and dark reactions of photosynthesis, explain why the simple equation $6CO_2 + 6H_2O$ + light energy $\rightarrow C_6H_{12}O_6 + 6O_2$ is an oversimplification and could even be misleading. **(12 marks)**

(b) Briefly explain how each of any *three* environmental factors, *other than light intensity*, may affect the rate of photosynthesis. **(6 marks)**

(c) With reference to light as a limiting factor, explain the existence of different compensation points in sun and shade plants. **(2 marks)**

[London, Jan. 1983, Paper 2]

**Comments:**

(a) See p. 125.
(b) See experiments described on pages 117–122.
(c) See p. 123.

**Question:**

Which one of the following substances is formed during the dark stage of photosynthesis?

A ATP
B oxygen
C pyruvic acid
D reduced NADP
E ribulose diphosphate

[Cambridge, Nov. 1981, Paper 3]

**Comments:**

Note that the question asks for the substance which is *formed* during the *dark* reaction of photosynthesis. See p. 126. Certain substances may be present for the reaction to occur, but they are not necessarily *made* during the reaction.

**Question:**

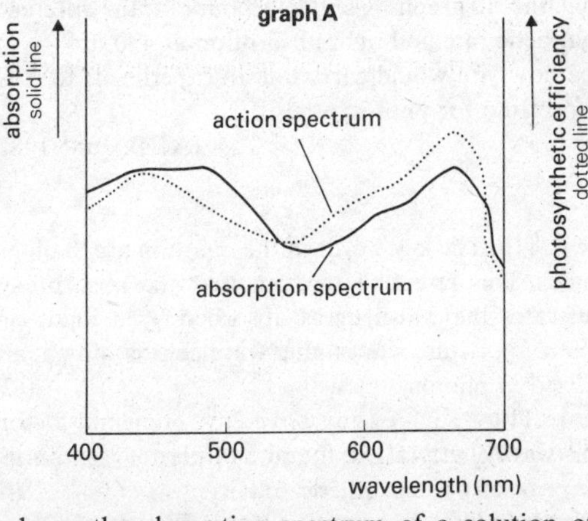
graph A
absorption
solid line
photosynthetic efficiency
dotted line
action spectrum
absorption spectrum
400
500
600
700
wavelength (nm)

Graph A shows the absorption spectrum of a solution of pigments extracted from bean leaves and the action spectrum of a bean plant determined by measurement of the rate of photosynthesis when illuminated by different wavelengths of light.

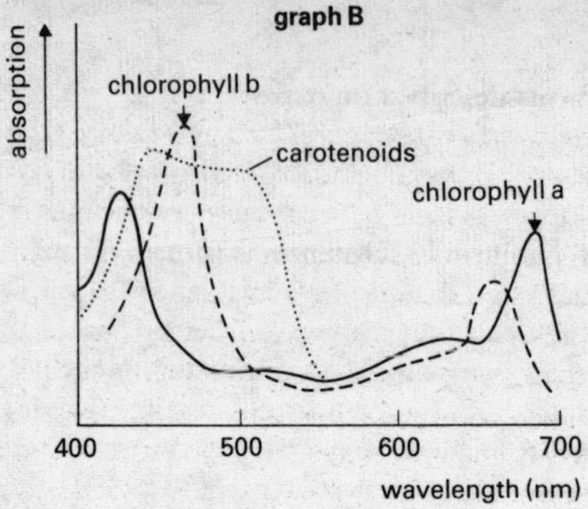
graph B
absorption
chlorophyll b
carotenoids
chlorophyll a
400
500
600
700
wavelength (nm)

Graph B shows the absorption spectra of thrce pigments which have been extracted from bean leaves and examined individually.

(a) With reference to graph A
- (i) comment on the biological significance of the relationship between the action spectrum and the absorption spectrum,
- (ii) relate the visible colour of a leaf to the absorption spectrum,
- (iii) state the approximate wavelength at which photosynthesis is most efficient. **(4 marks)**

(b) With reference to graphs A and B, account for the difference between photosynthetic rate and light absorption at 490 nm. **(2 marks)**

(c) Describe how you would carry out an experiment to determine the action spectrum for photosynthesis. **(6 marks)**

[AEB, June 1982, Paper 2]

**Comments:**

(a) (i) See p. 118. The key words in the question are 'biological significance'. This refers to the fact that the absorption spectrum illustrates the wavelengths absorbed by a plant whereas the action spectrum shows the wavelengths which are actually utilized in photosynthesis.
- (ii) See p. 119.
- (iii) This wavelength can be found by interpolation on the graph at the peak of photosynthetic activity.

(b) See p. 120 (Fig. 4.5).

(c) See p. 122. To obtain all the marks for this question it is necessary to draw a diagram and give full experimental details, including how the results would be recorded and used to produce an action spectrum.

**Question:**

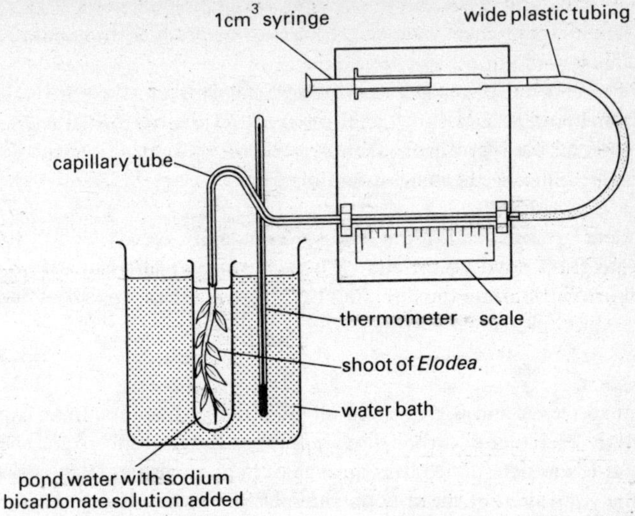

1cm³ syringe
wide plastic tubing
capillary tube
thermometer
scale
shoot of *Elodea*.
water bath
pond water with sodium bicarbonate solution added


The apparatus shown above can be used to indicate the rate of photosynthesis of an aquatic plant.

(a) What data can be obtained with this apparatus? **(2 marks)**

(b) Explain how you would use the apparatus to investigate the effect of changes in light intensity on the rate of photosynthesis. **(7 marks)**

(c) What relationship between light intensity and rate of photosynthesis would you expect the apparatus to show? Explain your answer. **(4 marks)**

(d) Describe *two* possible sources of inaccuracy in the experiment and explain how you might overcome them. **(4 marks)**

(e) When the gas given off by an aquatic plant is collected and analysed the percentage of oxygen present is frequently as low as 40 per cent even under optimum photosynthesizing conditions. Give reasons for this phenomenon. **(3 marks)**

**(Total 20 marks)**

[AEB, Nov. 1980, Paper 2]

**Comments:**

(a) See p. 120. 'Data' means the actual results you record, i.e. volume of oxygen given off per unit time.

(b) See p. 120. To obtain full marks for this question a full account of the experiment must be given, including how the results for light intensity and rate of photosynthesis are obtained and the graph you would draw. There is no need to draw a diagram of the apparatus as this is given in the question.

(c) This is best explained by drawing a graph, with rate of photosynthesis on the vertical axis and light intensity on the horizontal axis. The rate of photosynthesis should increase with light intensity until carbon dioxide becomes a limiting factor (see p. 121, Fig. 4.7).

(d) See p. 122.

(e) Other gases found in the bubbles include nitrogen, which dissolves out from pond water, and carbon dioxide, which results from respiration. Carbon dioxide can also be given off as a result of adding sodium bicarbonate to the water.

**Question:**
Plant species A and B grow naturally in different habitats. In an experiment the exchange of carbon dioxide between the atmosphere and species A and B was determined over a range of light intensities from darkness to the equivalent of mean noon sunlight. A constant temperature was maintained throughout the experiment. The amount of carbon dioxide absorbed or released was determined by measuring the carbon dioxide concentration in a stream of air before and after it had passed over the plants. The data obtained are given below.

| *Light intensity as a percentage of mean noon sunlight* | *Net carbon dioxide absorption in arbitrary units* | |
|---|---|---|
| | *Species A* | *Species B* |
| 0 | − 0.1 | − 0.8 |
| 10 | + 3.0 | + 0.5 |
| 20 | + 5.3 | + 3.5 |
| 30 | + 6.5 | + 7.0 |
| 40 | + 6.5 | + 9.3 |
| 50 | + 6.7 | + 11.5 |
| 60 | + 6.8 | + 13.2 |
| 70 | + 7.0 | + 15.0 |
| 80 | + 6.5 | + 17.0 |
| 90 | + 6.8 | + 18.0 |
| 100 | + 6.7 | + 19.0 |

(a) Plot these data on a single set of axes. **(5 marks)**

(b) Discuss the extent to which species A and species B might be able to grow in the same habitat. **(4 marks)**

(c) (i) What is meant by the term 'compensation point'?
(ii) Clearly indicate on your graph the compensation point for species B. **(2 marks)**

(d) (i) What is meant by the term 'limiting factor'?
(ii) From your knowledge of photosynthetic pathways, explain precisely how *three* named factors can be limiting in photosynthesis. **(7 marks)**

(e) Distinguish between $C_3$ and $C_4$ plants. **(2 marks)**

[AEB, Nov. 1982, Paper 2]

**Comments:**

(a) Since the graph is to have both curves drawn on the same set of axes, a scale must be chosen on the vertical axis which will accommodate the results for both species A and species B, i.e. ranging from − 0.8 to + 19.0. Remember to include the following: labelled axes, an indication of which curve is A and which is B, and a title for the graph.

(b) Carbon dioxide absorption is taken to indicate the amount of photosynthesis occurring at each different light intensity. Species A has a higher rate of photosynthesis at low light intensities than species B. At high light intensities the situation is reversed, and species B has a higher rate of photosynthesis than species A. It would seem, therefore, that species A is most successful in low light intensity and species B is more successful at higher intensities. It is possible that the two species could grow in the same habitat if species B was a tall plant with access to direct sunlight and species B was a shorter plant which grew in the shade.

(c) (i) See p. 123.
(ii) This is the point at which net carbon dioxide absorption is zero.

(d) (i) See p. 122.
(ii) 1. Temperature – the rate of reaction doubles for every 10 °C rise in temperature, the optimum temperature being 30 °C. Only the dark reaction is limited by temperature, since it is enzyme-controlled. If there is an excess of carbon dioxide and light, photosynthesis could be limited by low temperatures.

2. Carbon dioxide – $CO_2$ is combined with ribulose diphosphate and converted into sugars during the dark reaction. $CO_2$ is therefore a substrate in an enzyme-controlled reaction, so

the rate of reaction will be proportional to its concentration. If there is an excess of light at the optimum temperature, photosynthesis will be limited by the concentration of $CO_2$.

3. Light intensity – light is necessary to release electrons from pigment molecules during the light reaction. Coupled with the electron transfer is synthesis of ATP and $NADPH_2$, which are subsequently used in the dark reaction. If the light intensity is low, the supply of ATP and $NADPH_2$ to the dark reaction is reduced and the rate of photosynthesis reduced accordingly.

(e) See p. 129.

**Question:**

Read through the following account of photosynthesis and then write on the lines the most appropriate word or words to complete the account.

There are four pigments found in the chloroplasts of higher plants; chlorophyll a, chlorophyll b, ____________ and ____________. Chlorophyll a absorbs mainly red and ____________ light. The absorption of light causes the displacement of an electron from the chlorophyll a molecule. This electron may be passed back to the chlorophyll via a series of ____________ which are at a progressively lower energy level. Coupled with this electron transfer is the synthesis of ____________. This compound may be subsequently used in the dark reaction of photosynthesis which occurs in the ____________ region of the chloroplast. During non-cyclic photophosphorylation, the electron is combined with ____________ ions resulting from the photolysis of ____________ to form the reduced coenzyme called ____________. This reduced coenzyme is used in the ____________ cycle to convert ____________ acid to phosphoglyceraldehyde, which can be converted to ____________ which is the acceptor molecule for the carbon dioxide used in photosynthesis. The electron emitted from the chlorophyll molecule is replaced by electrons from the ____________ ions produced by the photolysis reaction. As a result ____________ gas is given off. **(Total 14 marks)**

[London, June 1981, Paper 2]

**Comments:**

See p. 124 (Pigments used in photosynthesis), p. 126 (The light reaction), and p. 126 (The dark reaction).

**Question:**

(a) In the space below, make a labelled diagram of a chloroplast to show its structure as seen under an electron microscope.

**(6 marks)**

(b) Name, and give the colour of, the *four* pigments that usually make up the 'chlorophyll' in a leaf.

| *Name of pigment* | *Colour* |
| --- | --- |
| (i) | |
| (ii) | |
| (iii) | |
| (iv) | |

**(4 marks)**

(c) What do you understand by the term 'action spectrum'?

**(2 marks)**

(d) Draw a graph, on the axes provided, to show the action spectrum of typical green leaves. **(2 marks)**

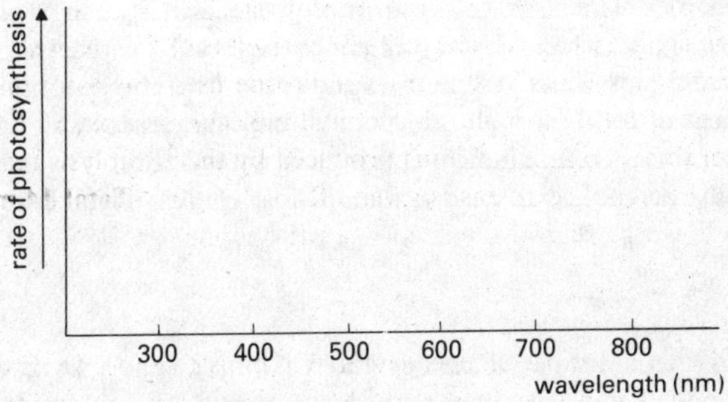
rate of photosynthesis
300
400
500
600
700
800
wavelength (nm)

(e) Describe the part played by 'chlorophyll' in the light stage of photosynthesis.

______________________________________________

______________________________________________

______________________________________________

______________________________________________

______________________________________________

**(5 marks)**
**(Total 19 marks)**
[London, June 1982, Paper 1]

**Comments:**
(a) See p. 24.
(b) See p. 124.
(c) See p. 119.
(d) See p. 120.
(e) See p. 126.

## *Heterotrophic nutrition*

### *Nutrients that must be provided in the diet of man*

#### Carbohydrates

These are the usual source of energy. In a natural diet only small quantities of monosaccharides and disaccharides would occur (e.g. glucose in fruits and lactose in milk). However, sucrose is a common additive to the 'modern' diet. The large, indigestible polysaccharides, such as cellulose, act as roughage, which aids movement of the food by peristalsis, satisfies hunger and aids water retention in the colon (thereby speeding up the movement of food through the gut). Polysaccharides such as starch are insoluble and therefore indigestible in their natural form. For this reason they must be cooked to release the amylose chains, which can then be broken down by digestive enzymes.

#### Fats

Fats provide a source of energy and vitamins (e.g. A, D, E and K). Most animals can survive with little or no dietary fat, as fat can be synthesized from carbohydrates or the intermediates of protein metabolism. The unsaturated fats linoleic and linolenic acids cannot be synthesized in man – they must be supplied in the diet. They are therefore termed '**essential fatty acids**'.

### Proteins

Proteins supply the organic nitrogen required by animals. They provide the raw materials for growth and repair of body tissues and for the manufacture of enzymes and hormones. Proteins from plant sources do not provide the whole range of 'essential amino acids' required by man, animal proteins do. From these essential amino acids the full range of necessary amino acids can be synthesized.

In general animals require up to twelve essential amino acids. Some Protozoa only require one type of amino acid in their diet to supply the amino group, and from this they can synthesize all the amino acids they need.

Proteins may be used as an energy source if carbohydrates and fats are in short supply. They are the main energy source in carnivorous animals.

A daily intake of 1 g protein per kg of body weight per day is recommended; however, infants and pregnant and lactating women require more protein in their diet because of growth, supplies for the developing foetus and milk production, respectively.

### Minerals

These comprise inorganic chemical elements and ions. They are required in small amounts but are essential for the healthy functioning of the body. The main mineral requirements and functions in man are listed in Table 4.1.

### Vitamins

Vitamins (see Table 4.2) are organic compounds essential for the normal functioning of the body. They are present in the food in minute quantities (usually less than 0.15 per cent of man's daily food intake).

Vitamins have different site preferences for absorption; for example, ascorbic acid is absorbed in the duodenum and vitamin $B_{12}$ in the ileum.

Vitamins function as coenzymes (see p. 73) and are therefore generally concentrated in tissues which are the most metabolically active. Thus animal liver and kidneys are useful sources of vitamins.

*Table 4.1.* Mineral requirements and functions

| *Mineral and main sources* | *Average adult daily requirement* | *Function* |
|---|---|---|
| Macronutrients (required in relatively large amounts) | | |
| Calcium (dairy products, bread) | 1.1 g | Component of bones and teeth. Vital for normal functioning of cell membranes and neuromuscular system. Essential for blood clotting and muscle contraction. |
| Chloride (meats, salt) | 5.2 g | Important in osmoregulation, regulation of acid–base balance. Acid (HCl) is a component of gastric juice. |
| Magnesium (cheese, vegetables) | 0.34 g | Like calcium, it is necessary for the normal functioning of the neuromuscular system. Vital for a variety of enzyme systems. |
| Phosphorus (cheese, yeast extract) | 1.4 g | Necessary for formation of bones and teeth. Component of DNA, RNA and ATP. Involved in nerve impulse transmission. |
| Potassium (meat, potatoes) | 3.3 g | Important in osmoregulation, regulation of acid–base balance, and nerve impulse transmission. |
| Sodium (cheese, salt) | 4.4 g | Is the most osmotically active ion in body fluids. Necessary for acid–base balance (most abundant cation (positive ion) in body fluids). Necessary for nerve impulse transmission. |

*Table 4.1.* (*contd*) Mineral requirements and functions

| *Mineral and main sources* | *Average adult daily requirement* | *Function* |
|---|---|---|
| Micronutrients (required in relatively small amounts) | | |
| Cobalt (meat, yeast) | 0.3 mg | Components of vitamin $B_{12}$, which is important in protein metabolism. |
| Copper (liver, legumes) | 3.5 mg | Necessary for formation of haemoglobin, melanin and certain enzymes. Involved in energy-release reactions. |
| Fluoride (seafood, water) | 1.8 mg | Necessary for bone and teeth formation and for prevention of decay. |
| Iodine (fish, iodized salt) | 0.2 mg | Component of the hormone thyroxine. |
| Iron (liver) | 16.0 mg | Component of haemoglobin and myoglobin, and cytochromes. |
| Manganese (cereals) | 3.7 mg | Required for bone development and amino acid metabolism. |
| Zinc (meats, legumes) | 13.0 mg | Component of various enzymes (e.g. dehydrogenases and carbonic anhydrase). Essential for amino acid metabolism. |

*Table 4.2.* Vitamin requirements and functions in man

| Vitamin and sources | Average adult daily requirement | Role | Deficiency symptoms |
|---|---|---|---|
| Fat-soluble | | | |
| A: retinol (halibut and cod-liver oils, dairy produce) | 0.75 mg | Essential constituent of rhodopsin (opsin and vitamin A, see p. 264). Necessary for normal glycoprotein synthesis | Night-blindness (nyctalopia). Bone abnormalities. Nerve degeneration |
| D: cholecalciferol (fish oils). Vitamin D (dehydrocholesterol) precursor is secreted at the skin surface and is activated by radiation | 0.0025 mg | Increases intestinal absorption of calcium. Mobilizes bone material to maintain blood calcium and phosphate levels | Rickets (poor bone growth) accompanied by bone malformation |
| K: phylloquinone (green plants). Synthesized by bacteria in the rectum | Not known | Necessary for manufacture of prothrombin | Failure of clotting mechanism, leading to haemorrhaging |
| E: tocopherol (wheat germ, milk, egg yolk) | Not known | It conserves vitamins A, C, D and K by acting as an antioxidant as it is easily oxidized | Sterility in rats. No symptoms observed in man |

| | | | |
|---|---|---|---|
| Water-soluble | | | |
| $B_1$: thiamine (whole grains, liver) | 1.2 mg | Functions in enzyme systems as a component of the coenzyme co-carboxylase | Beri-beri (nervous and muscle tissue affected resulting in poor growth) |
| $B_2$: riboflavin (leafy vegetables, liver, milk) | 1.7 mg | Functions biochemically in two coenzymes, flavin mononucleotide (FMN) and flavin adenine dinucleotide (FAD), which participate in oxidation–reduction reactions | Poor growth. Deterioration of skin, eyes, liver and nerves |
| $B_3$: nicotinic acid (yeast, cereal, grains) | 18 mg | Functions biochemically in two coenzymes: nicotinamide adenine dinucleotide (NAD) and its phosphate (NADP). Also forms part of acetyl coenzyme A | Pellagra (blotchy, scaly skin). Nervous disorders, e.g. memory loss and depression. Digestive disorders |
| C: ascorbic acid (citrus fruits, fresh vegetables) | 30 mg | Necessary for the formation of an amino acid found in structural proteins, particularly collagen. Promotes use of calcium in bones and teeth | Scurvy (fragile bones, sore and swollen joints and gums) |

*Table 4.3.* Recommended daily intake of some nutrients

| Age (years) | Energy (kJ) | Protein (g) | Calcium (mg) | Iron (mg) | Vit. A (mg) | Vit. $B_1$ (mg) | Vit. $B_2$ (mg) | Vit. $B_3$ (mg) | Vit. C (mg) | Vit. D (mg) |
|---|---|---|---|---|---|---|---|---|---|---|
| < 1 | 3.3 | 20 | 600 | 6 | 0.450 | 0.3 | 0.4 | 5 | 15 | 0.01 |
| 3–4 | 6.7 | 40 | 500 | 8 | 0.300 | 0.6 | 0.8 | 9 | 20 | 0.01 |
| 12–14 | 11.7 | 70 | 700 | 14 | 0.725 | 1.1 | 1.4 | 16 | 25 | 0.0025 |
| Males | | | | | | | | | | |
| 18–64 | | | | | | | | | | |
| sedentary | 11.3 | 68 | 500 | 10 | 0.750 | 1.1 | 1.7 | 18 | 30 | 0.0025 |
| very active | 15.1 | 90 | 500 | 10 | 0.750 | 1.4 | 1.7 | 18 | 30 | 0.0025 |
| 65–74 | 9.8 | 59 | 500 | 10 | 0.750 | 0.9 | 1.7 | 18 | 30 | 0.0025 |
| Females | | | | | | | | | | |
| 18–54 | | | | | | | | | | |
| general | 9.2 | 55 | 500 | 12 | 0.750 | 0.9 | 1.3 | 15 | 30 | 0.0025 |
| very active | 10.5 | 63 | 500 | 12 | 0.750 | 1.0 | 1.3 | 15 | 30 | 0.0025 |
| 55–74 | 8.6 | 51 | 500 | 10 | 0.750 | 0.8 | 1.3 | 15 | 30 | 0.0025 |
| pregnant | | | | | | | | | | |
| (3–9 months) | 10.0 | 60 | 1,200 | 15 | 0.750 | 1.0 | 1.6 | 18 | 60 | 0.01 |
| lactating | 11.3 | 68 | 1,200 | 15 | 1.200 | 1.1 | 1.8 | 21 | 60 | 0.01 |

*Source*: Department of Health and Social Security, 1969.

### A balanced diet

The diet must contain enough energy for the body's needs. This energy is expressed in joules (J). The number of joules required depends upon the age, activity, sex and size of the body. In a balanced diet, the energy sources should be distributed between carbohydrates, proteins and fats. The diet must also supply sufficient mineral salts, vitamins and water for the body's needs. Table 4.3 gives examples of recommended daily nutrient intake in man.

## *Feeding mechanisms*

Heterotrophs have developed various mechanisms for obtaining their food material. These feeding mechanisms are understandably diverse, and depend largely on habitat. For convenience animals may be separated on the basis of food-particle size.

### Macrophagous feeders

These animals feed on relatively large food particles, and so feed only occasionally. The large particles are broken up by chemical and physical means. Examples of macrophagous feeders are given in Table 4.4.

### Microphagous feeders

These are aquatic animals that feed on relatively small food particles. This necessitates continuous feeding. Some examples are given in Table 4.5.

### Fluid feeders

These animals may actively suck up fluids or may absorb fluids across their body surface (wallowers). Examples are given in Table 4.6.

## *Digestion*

This is the process by which the complex organic molecules in foods are broken down into simpler units which can be utilized by cells for energy or incorporated into living protoplasm.

*Table 4.4.* Macrophagous feeders

| *Example* | *Description of method of feeding* |
|---|---|
| *Amoeba* | The locomotory pseudopodia flow around a suitable food source (e.g. *Chilomonas,* a flagellate) and enclose it in a food vacuole with a drop of water in a process known as phagocytosis. |
| Coelenterates (e.g. *Obelia, Hydra*) | Carnivorous. The prey, e.g. *Daphnia*, are caught and paralysed by the nematocysts of the tentacles, and are swallowed whole. Digestion follows swallowing. |
| *Lumbricus* (earthworm) | Collects leaves, either by gripping between the prostomium and peristomium or by suction due to retraction of the pharynx, and returns to burrow. The material is sucked into the alimentary canal by contraction of the muscle strand connected to the pharynx. |
| *Astacus* (crayfish) | Omnivorous. Food is seized by the chelae and pushed towards the mouth where it is shredded into smaller pieces by the mandibles. The finer particles are ingested. (Mastication before swallowing occurs in many mammals, including man.) |
| Gastropod molluscs (e.g. *Helix, Littorina*) | Herbivorous. Food material, e.g. leaf-matter and algae, is removed by the scraping action of the radula. The radula is manipulated by a complex system of muscles, and it is also used for conveying food to the buccal cavity. |
| *Asterias* (starfish) | Carnivorous with a preferred diet of bivalve molluscs. The arms of the starfish enclose the prey with the opening of the bivalve facing the predator's mouth. Pressure from the tube-feet opens the shell. The starfish's gut is everted and surrounds the soft part of the mollusc which it digests. The resultant fluid is wafted into the gut by ciliary currents. |

*Table 4.5.* Microphagous feeders

| *Example* | *Description of method of feeding* |
|---|---|
| *Paramecium* | Feeds on bacteria or minute organic particles. These are taken into the body as the organism moves through the water with the oral groove and gullet pointing in the direction of the movement. The oral groove and gullet are ciliated, and the cilia of the gullet are specialized for wafting particles along. Food particles and drops of water are enveloped in food vacuoles at the bottom of the gullet. The food vacuoles circulate through the cytoplasm. |
| *Peranema* | Flagella direct food particles, e.g. protozoa, towards the cytostome (cell mouth), which operates separately from the reservoir. There are two supporting rods near the cytostome to puncture and hold the prey. |
| Many crustacea, (e.g. *Daphnia, Balanus,* the acorn barnacle) | Feathery structures on the limb, known as setae, are used to strain particles from the water and direct them to the mouth. |
| Sea cucumber (an echinoderm) | Feeds on detritus which adheres to and is taken into the mouth by the large, modified, mucus-covered, tube feet which surround it. |
| *Chaetopterus* (an annelid) | Spins nets of mucus from the mouth. When these are full due to water currents, both the nets and their contents are ingested. |
| 'Whalebone' whales (e.g. *Balaeria*) | The upper jaws have plates of fused hairs or 'whalebone' which act as a sieve trapping small crustaceans. |

*Table 4.6.* Fluid feeders

| *Example* | *Description of method of feeding* |
|---|---|
| *Anopheles* (malarial mosquito) | The labrum and second maxillae form a tube. Within this tube are five fine stylets formed from the mandibles, the first maxillae and the hypopharynx. These pierce the skin of the prey and blood is sucked up by the crop aided by the production of an anticoagulant in the saliva. |
| *Hirudo* (leech) | A short muscular pharynx sucks blood from the wound in the prey's skin made by three jaws. An anticoagulant and vasodilator is present in the saliva. |

*continued*

*Table 4.6. (contd)*

| *Example* | *Description of method of feeding* |
|---|---|
| *Musca* (house-fly) | Stylets are absent and the labium terminates in a bilobed 'labellum' over which saliva flows on to the food. The fluid food material is then sucked up into the alimentary canal for absorption. |
| *Taenia* (tapeworm) | Small food particles are readily available as a result of the action of the host's digestive system. These are absorbed through the cuticle of the tapeworm. No real feeding mechanism is present. The lack of feeding mechanism is generally a feature of **endoparasites**; other examples include *Trypanosoma* and *Monocystis*. |

## Physical digestion

The food generally requires mechanical treatment (mastication) before or after it has been taken into the body. Mastication is especially needed in herbivorous animals, that utilize cellulose and other plant materials, or where the prey has a hard exoskeleton. Mechanical breakdown involves the teeth, tongue, cheeks and lower jaw. It increases the surface area of the food for chemical digestion.

### *Dentition*

Mammals are generally **diphyodont** (have two sets of teeth, the milk and permanent sets) and **heterodont** (have different types of teeth). A typical mammalian tooth is shown in Fig. 4.13. The **polyphyodont** (teeth replaced many times) and **homodont** (teeth are all of the same type) condition is found in most vertebrates other than mammals.

The numbers and kind of teeth may be expressed by a formula, for example:

$$\text{Rabbit}\ \frac{2\ 0\ 3\ 3}{1\ 0\ 2\ 3} = 28$$

$$\text{i c pm m}$$

$$\text{Dog}\ \frac{3\ 1\ 4\ 2}{3\ 1\ 4\ 3} = 42$$

In these formulae, i = incisors, c = canines, pm = premolars and m = molars. Half the upper jaw is described above the line and half the lower jaw below it. Note that there are no canines present in the rabbit.

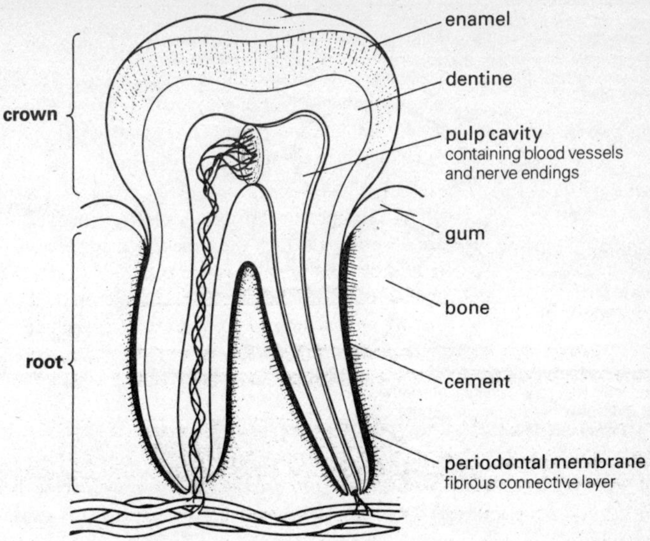
enamel
dentine
crown
pulp cavity
containing blood vessels
and nerve endings
gum
bone
root
cement
periodontal membrane
fibrous connective layer

*Fig. 4.13* Vertical section through a mammalian tooth

Dentition, jaw structure, jaw muscles, jaw articulation and skull structure are related to the specific diet of the animal and they therefore differ in carnivores, herbivores and omnivores (Fig. 4.14).

## Chemical digestion

The final processes of digestion are always chemical, commonly involving hydrolysis.

Where chemical digestion takes place inside a chamber inside the cell, as in a cytoplasmic vacuole in *Amoeba*, it is termed **intracellular**. When this digestion takes place outside the cell, as in higher animals and saprophytes, it is termed **extracellular**.

A summary of the stages in chemical digestion in the alimentary canal of man is given in Table 4.7, and sections through the stomach and ileum walls in Figs 4.15 and 4.16.

There are variations in the alimentary canal of animals, depending on diet. For example, a herbivore tends to have a much longer alimentary canal than a carnivore to cope with the large volumes of relatively indigestible vegetation. The modified stomach of a ruminant is illustrated in Fig. 4.17.

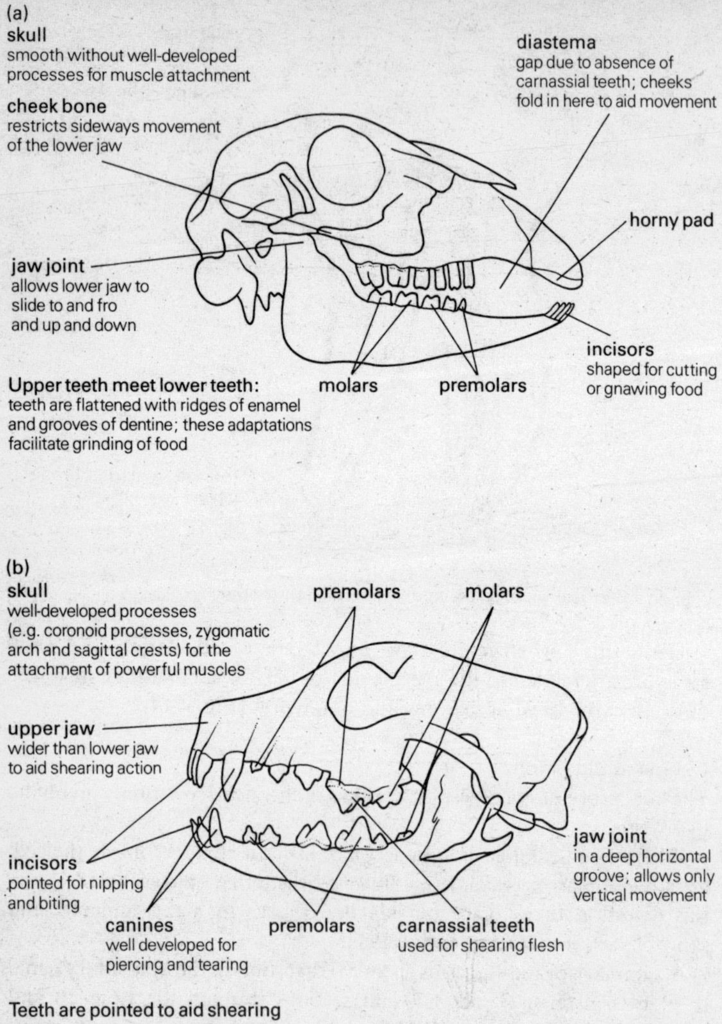
(a)
skull
smooth without well-developed processes for muscle attachment
cheek bone
restricts sideways movement of the lower jaw
diastema
gap due to absence of carnassial teeth; cheeks fold in here to aid movement
horny pad
jaw joint
allows lower jaw to slide to and fro and up and down
incisors
shaped for cutting or gnawing food
molars
premolars
Upper teeth meet lower teeth:
teeth are flattened with ridges of enamel and grooves of dentine; these adaptations facilitate grinding of food
(b)
skull
well-developed processes (e.g. coronoid processes, zygomatic arch and sagittal crests) for the attachment of powerful muscles
premolars
molars
upper jaw
wider than lower jaw to aid shearing action
jaw joint
in a deep horizontal groove; allows only vertical movement
incisors
pointed for nipping and biting
canines
well developed for piercing and tearing
premolars
carnassial teeth
used for shearing flesh
Teeth are pointed to aid shearing

*Fig 4.14* Comparison of the dentition and jaw structure of (a) a herbivore (sheep) and (b) a carnivore (dog)

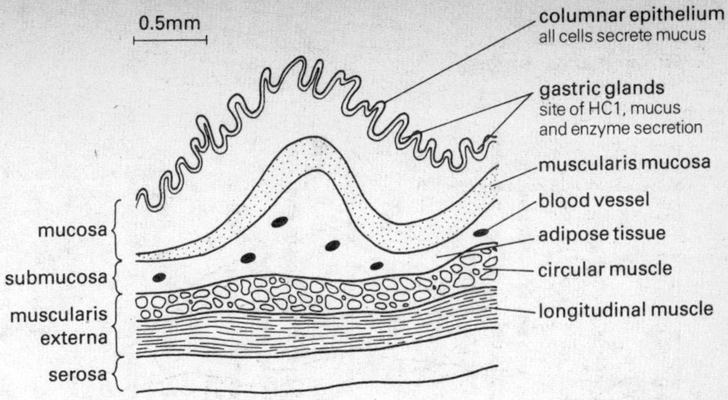
0.5mm
columnar epithelium
all cells secrete mucus
gastric glands
site of HC1, mucus
and enzyme secretion
muscularis mucosa
blood vessel
adipose tissue
circular muscle
longitudinal muscle
mucosa
submucosa
muscularis
externa
serosa

*Fig. 4.15* LS of the stomach wall

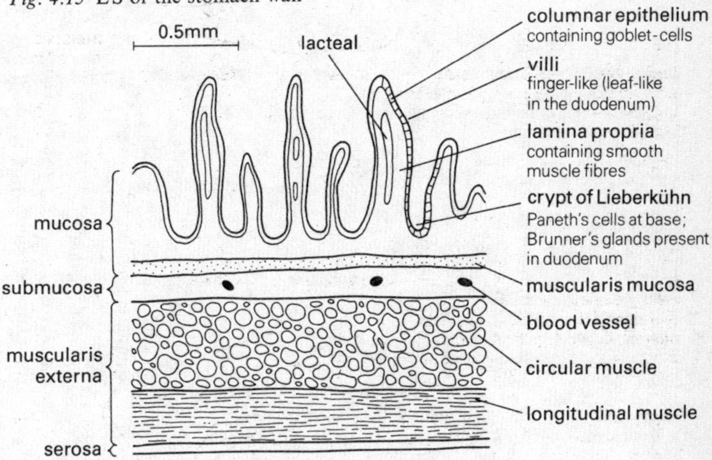
0.5mm
lacteal
columnar epithelium
containing goblet-cells
villi
finger-like (leaf-like
in the duodenum)
lamina propria
containing smooth
muscle fibres
crypt of Lieberkühn
Paneth's cells at base;
Brunner's glands present
in duodenum
muscularis mucosa
blood vessel
circular muscle
longitudinal muscle
mucosa
submucosa
muscularis
externa
serosa

*Fig. 4.16* LS of the ileum

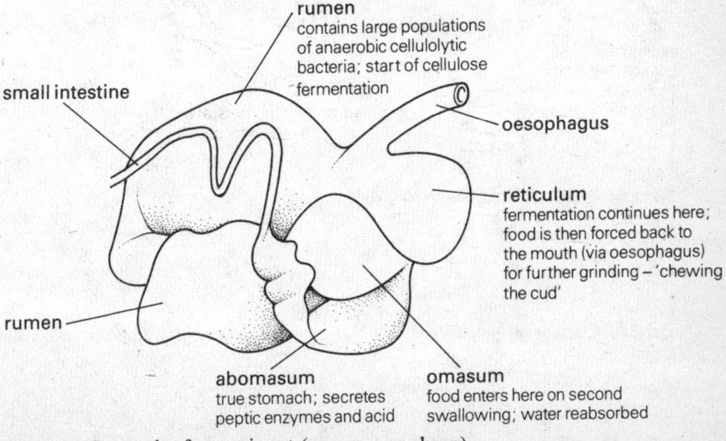
rumen
contains large populations
of anaerobic cellulolytic
bacteria; start of cellulose
fermentation
small intestine
oesophagus
reticulum
fermentation continues here;
food is then forced back to
the mouth (via oesophagus)
for further grinding – 'chewing
the cud'
rumen
abomasum
true stomach; secretes
peptic enzymes and acid
omasum
food enters here on second
swallowing; water reabsorbed

*Fig. 4.17* Stomach of a ruminant (e.g. cow or sheep)

*Table 4.7.* Summary of chemical digestion in man

| *Secretion and optimum pH* | *Secreted by* | *Site of action* | *Factors stimulating production* | *Components of secretion* | *Action* |
|---|---|---|---|---|---|
| Saliva (pH 6–7) | Salivary gland | Buccal cavity | Reflex stimulation on sight and smell of food | Salivary amylase | Cooked starch → dextrins → maltose |
| | | | | Salts | Maintains correct pH |
| | | | | Mucin | Binds food into a bolus |
| Gastric juice (pH 2) | Gastric glands in stomach wall (Fig. 4.15) | Stomach | Reflex stimulation on presence of food. Gastrin (hormone) stimulates oxyntic cells to produce HCl | Rennin (in young) | Converts soluble caseinogen to an insoluble form for breakdown by pepsin |
| | | | | Pepsinogen, activated to pepsin by HCl | Proteins → polypeptides |
| | | | | Lipase | Fats → fatty acids and glycerol |
| | | | | Hydrochloric acid | Provides pH 1–2. Kills bacteria and prepares calcium and iron salts for absorption |
| | | | | Mucus | Protects stomach wall from autolysis |
| Pancreatic juice | Pancreas | Duodenum | Secretion of the alkaline fluid is stimulated by the hormone secretin. Another hormone, pancreozymin, stimulates enzyme secretion | Amylase | Starch → dextrins → maltose |
| | | | | Trypsin | Proteins → polypeptides and amino acids |
| | | | | Peptidases | Polypeptides → amino acids |
| | | | | Chymotrypsin | Casein → polypeptides |
| | | | | Lipase | Fats → fatty acids and glycerol |
| | | | | Nucleases | Nucleic acids → nucleotides |

| | | | | | |
|---|---|---|---|---|---|
| Bile | Liver | Duodenum | Reflex action. Secretin stimulates production of bile and cholecystokinin (hormone) stimulates bile release | Bile pigments (bilirubin and biliverdin) | Excretory products |
| | | | | Bile salts | Emulsify fats, activate pancreatic lipase, increase the efficiency of carbohydrate- and protein-digesting enzymes. Also increase the uptake of vitamins A, D and K |
| | | | | Sodium bicarbonate | Adjusts pH |
| | | | | Cholesterol | Excretory product |
| Intestinal juice | Wall of ileum (Fig. 4.17) | Small intestine | Presence of food material causes mechanical stimulation of intestinal lining | Amylase | Starch → dextrins → maltose |
| | | | | Maltase | Maltose → glucose* |
| | | | | Sucrase | Sucrose → glucose* and fructose* |
| | | | | Lactase | Lactose → glucose* and galactose* |
| | | | | Enterokinase | Trypsinogen → trypsin |
| | | | | Peptidases | Peptides → amino acids* |
| | | | | Nucleotidases | Nucleotides → nitrogen bases,* pentose sugars* and phosphoric acid |
| | | | | Lipase | Fats → fatty acids* and glycerol* |

* These are the soluble products of digestion and they are absorbed across the villi of the small intestine by diffusion and active transport. Monosaccharides are generally absorbed as complexes (e.g. sugar phosphate); fatty acids and glycerol may be absorbed as chloromicrons (droplets of neutral fats).

### *Assimilation*

This is the building up of the simple products of digestion into the complex constitutents of the organism.

The products of digestion generally pass to the liver via the hepatic portal vein prior to 'processing'. An exception is the fatty acids and glycerol, which are resynthesized into lipids and transported as emulsions in the lymphatic system.

### *Egestion*

This is the elimination of undigested food material (mainly cellulose in omnivores and herbivores) plus gut secretions, bacteria and water. The colon (large intestine) and the rectum of land vertebrates including man are the main areas of the intestine where water reabsorption occurs (Fig. 4.18). On reaching the rectum the waste material (faeces) is solid, and is expelled by muscular contraction of the rectal walls via the anus. The constituents of the faecal matter vary greatly with the animal and its diet.

## *Types of heterotrophic nutrition*

Modes of heterotrophic nutrition include parasitism and saprophytism in addition to the carnivorous, herbivorous and omnivorous forms.

### Parasitism

Parasitism is a relationship between two organisms in which one, the parasite, obtains advantages from its association with the other, the host. The host usually suffers injury from the parasite. The parasite and host are usually of different species.

A parasite has to adjust from the free-living condition, and therefore (i) the host must provide all the nutritional requirements of the parasite; (ii) the parasite has to form a very close attachment to the host; and (iii) the offspring of the parasite must be able to find new hosts. Parasites have evolved many modifications to enable them to satisfy the above three requirements.

1. *Structural modifications*
   Loss or reduction of locomotory structures, e.g. *Fasciola*, *Taenia*.
   Loss or reduction of feeding apparatus or alimentary canal, e.g. *Taenia*, *Plasmodium*.

(a)

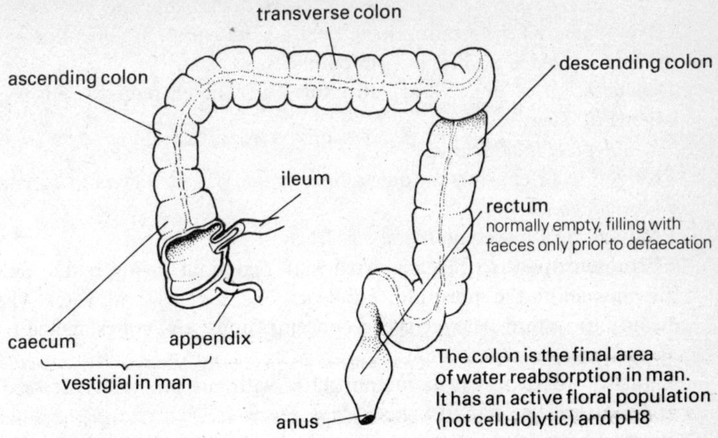
transverse colon
ascending colon
descending colon
ileum
rectum
normally empty, filling with faeces only prior to defaecation
caecum
appendix
vestigial in man
The colon is the final area of water reabsorption in man. It has an active floral population (not cellulolytic) and pH8
anus

(b)

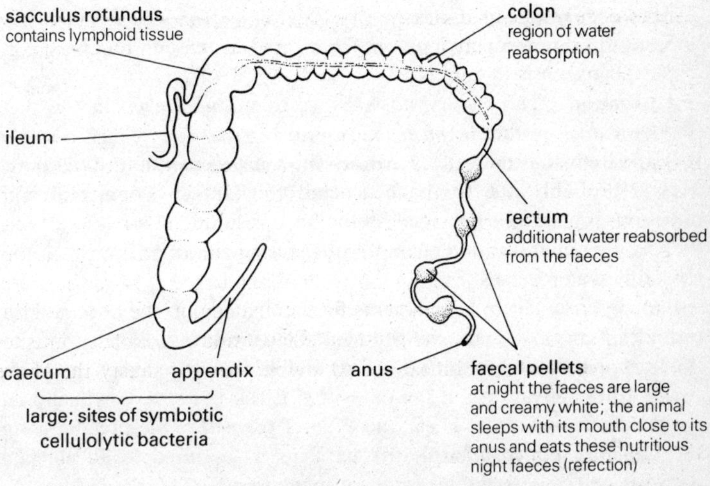
sacculus rotundus
contains lymphoid tissue
colon
region of water reabsorption
ileum
rectum
additional water reabsorbed from the faeces
caecum
appendix
anus
faecal pellets
at night the faeces are large and creamy white; the animal sleeps with its mouth close to its anus and eats these nutritious night faeces (refection)
large; sites of symbiotic cellulolytic bacteria

*Fig. 4.18* Comparison of the large intestines of (a) an omnivore (man) and (b) a herbivore (rabbit). (Drawings not to scale.)

Development of specialized structures for attachment to host, e.g. the hooks and suckers of *Taenia*, and suckers of *Fasciola* and leeches.

Development of penetrating structures, e.g. haustoria in fungi, boring devices in aphids and tapeworm embryos.

Degeneration of unnecessary structures, e.g. much reduced sensory organs of *Taenia*.

2. *Physiological modifications*

   Production of enzymes to digest host tissue, e.g. cellulases of fungi, *Plasmodium*.

   Production of anticoagulants, e.g. leech.

   Chemosensitivity to reach a particular region of host's body, e.g. *Plasmodium* in the mosquito, *Fasciola*.

   Ability to respire at low oxygen concentrations, e.g. gut parasites.

3. *Reproductive modifications*

   Parasites are generally hermaphroditic with the possibility of self-fertilization, e.g. many fungi, *Taenia*, *Fasciola*.

   Production of vast numbers of reproductive structures, e.g. cysts, spores. A single tapeworm may produce over 70 million fertile eggs per day.

   Highly resistant reproductive structures for overcoming adverse conditions outside the host or within certain regions of the host's body, e.g. spores of *Phytophthora* (potato blight fungus), cysts of *Monocystis*, eggs in *Ascaris*.

   Specialized reproductive phases for a rapid increase in numbers, e.g. parthenogenesis in aphids.

   Utilization of secondary hosts as vectors, e.g. *Taenia* in the pig, *Plasmodium* in the *Anopheles* mosquito.

It is apparent that parasites generally show a degeneration of features. This is probably due to the beneficial, constant environmental and nutritional conditions provided by the host, resulting in a reduced need for feeding apparatus and sense organs. Energy is concentrated on the reproductive processes.

Parasites are generally **endoparasitic** (i.e. live within the host) as this provides a more constant environment. **Ectoparasites** use the surface of the host as a habitat, e.g. *Pulex* (flea) and *Viscum* (mistletoe).

It is to the advantage of the parasite if it can live saprophytically on the dead remains of the host. This type of parasite, widespread among the fungi, is termed a **facultative parasite**, as opposed to an **obligate parasite** which can only live in or on living tissue.

### Saprophytism

Several species of fungi, e.g. *Mucor* and *Serpula lacrymans* (dry-rot fungus), and bacteria derive their nutritional requirements from the products of, or the dead remains of, other organisms. The remains must be soluble for absorption by the saprophyte. The saprophyte thus produces **extracellular** digestive enzymes which convert the complex organic material to a simple diffusible form in a process known as **putrefaction** or decay. Saprophytes are therefore ecologically important in the recycling of nutrients (see p. 439).

Animals which feed on dead and decaying material, e.g. *Peranema* (a flagellate), are generally known as *saprozoites*.

## Further reading

W. H. Homer Andrews, *Liver*, Studies in Biology No. 105 (Arnold, 1979)

J. B. Jennings, *Feeding, Digestion and Assimilation in Animals*, 2nd edition (Macmillan, 1972)

J. Morton, *Guts*, Studies in Biology No. 7, 2nd edition (Arnold, 1979)

C. H. Wynn, *The Structure and Function of Enzymes*, Studies in Biology No. 42 (Arnold, 1972)

## Related questions

**Question:**

The table below sets out the average minimum daily diet requirements for protein and calcium based on data provided by the World Health Organization.

| *Age group in years* | *Protein in g* | *Calcium in mg* |
|---|---|---|
| 1–3 boys | 23 | 800 |
| 12–15 boys | 45 | 1,200 |
| 23–50 males | 45 | 750 |

(a) Suggest a reason for:

(i) the difference in protein requirement between 1–3-year-old boys and 12–15-year-old boys;

(ii) the similarity in protein requirements between 12–15-year-old boys and 23–50-year-old males.

(b) Suggest a reason for the difference in calcium requirement between 12–15-year-old boys and 23–50-year-old males.
(c) Explain why rickets occurred more frequently in children in industrial areas than in children from rural areas. Your explanation should include a reference to the calcium data given above.

[AEB, June 1979, Paper 2]

**Comments:**

This type of question is testing your ability to relate the data provided to your knowledge of dietary requirements. Each section requires only short answers – two lines in most cases.

(a) (i) Protein is necessary for the production of enzymes, cell membranes and certain hormones. It is essential for metabolism, growth and repair. Boys in the 12–15 age group are entering a very rapid growth phase, including puberty, in which new cell material is being laid down.

(ii) As protein is required for repair, etc., as outlined above and on p. 58, a large amount of protein will still be required for maintenance of the bodies of the 23–50-year-old males.

(b) See p. 140. Boys aged 12–15 years are growing rapidly and will need calcium for bone formation.
(c) This question tests your knowledge of the relationship between calcium and vitamin D. Children in rural areas would have access to dairy produce containing calcium and the clearer atmosphere would increase the chance of vitamin D production in skin due to sunlight.

**Question:**

(a) Make a labelled diagram of a vertical section through a mammalian tooth to illustrate its structure. **(6 marks)**
(b) Relate dentition to diet in (i) a *named* herbivore and (ii) a *named* carnivore. **(6 marks)**
(c) Outline *two* different methods of feeding in named multicellular invertebrates. **(8 marks)**

[London, June 1984, Paper 2]

**Comments:**

The marks are fairly evenly spread throughout this question, therefore spend approximately equal time on each section (about 10 minutes).

(a) This question does not specify which type of tooth should be drawn – a molar would be a suitable choice. See Fig. 4.13. The question only asks for the structure to be illustrated. Do not waste time on lengthy annotations describing the function.

(b) The information required for this section can be found in Fig. 4.14. Remember to name your two animals. Emphasize the tough fibrous nature of vegetation containing cellulose and the need to catch and hold struggling prey in carnivores.

(c) See pp. 146–148. Remember the question stresses two *named multicellular invertebrates*. Therefore *Amoeba* will *not* do. You must choose *two different* methods (e.g. *Daphnia* – filter feeding – and *Helix* (garden snail) – scraping action of radula). It is obviously better to use examples you have studied in some detail, as you will be able to write more confidently and in greater detail.

**Question:**

Give a full account of any four proteolytic (protein digesting) enzymes of the human digestive system. For each state:

(i) its site of production (be as precise as you can in locating this),

(ii) the form in which it is secreted (actual chemical formulae are not required),

(iii) its effect on the substrate molecule on which it acts,

(iv) the particular event or condition which stimulates its production and release.

[JMB, June 1977]

**Comments:**

The information required is found in Table 4.7. Take each proteolytic enzyme in turn and answer, where possible, in the order that the question is asked. Do take into account the extra information in the brackets, i.e. 'be as precise as you can in locating this'. Taking pepsin as an example, do not simply state that it is produced in the cells lining the stomach. More accurately it is produced in the chief (or peptic) cells found in the wall at the base of the gastric glands (see Fig. 4.15), located in the epithelium of the stomach.

Remember that many proteolytic enzymes are secreted as inactive precursors to prevent autolysis of the intestinal lining. For example, pepsin is secreted as pepsinogen, which is activated by hydrochloric acid. Pepsin is a component of the gastric juice. The gastric juice is produced as a result of the sight, smell, taste or expectation of food (reflex action). In addition, the presence of food in the stomach provides chemical and mechanical stimulation of the stomach lining; this causes production of the gastric juice and the hormone gastrin, which circulates in the blood and causes the gastric glands to secrete hydrochloric acid.

When answering section (iii) do be accurate, e.g. pepsin hydrolyses proteins to polypeptides whereas trypsin hydrolyses proteins to polypeptides *and* amino acids.

# 5. Transport

## *Circulation in animals*

In small organisms with only one or a few cells, food and oxygen can reach all the cells by simple diffusion, waste products being removed similarly. As organisms became more complex, circulatory systems evolved with the following components:

(a) blood
(b) a pump – the heart } the blood system
(c) blood vessels } the blood system
(d) a lymphatic system

### *Blood*

#### The composition of blood

Blood is made up of 60 per cent plasma and 40 per cent white and red blood cells.

*Plasma*

Plasma is a watery fluid in which the blood cells are carried. It has the following composition:

Water – 92%
Inorganic salts (e.g. NaCl) – 0.9%
Dissolved food
Proteins (e.g. fibrinogen, prothrombin)
Urea
$CO_2$, $O_2$
Hormones
(Dissolved food to Hormones: 7%)

*Blood cells or corpuscles*

See Table 5.1.

#### Functions of blood

Blood has two main functions: transport and defence.

*Transport of oxygen*

Oxygen has to be carried from the respiratory organs (lungs or gills) to

*Table 5.1.* Structures and functions of mammalian blood cells

| *Type of blood cell* | *Structure* | *Site of production* | *Function* |
|---|---|---|---|
| Erythrocytes (red blood cells – 5,000,000/mm³) | Biconcave; circular; no nucleus | Red bone marrow | Carry oxygen; remain in blood vessels. |
| Leucocytes (white blood cells – 5,000–9,000/mm³) | | | |
| Granulocytes (polymorphonuclear leucocytes) or phagocytes | All have lobed nuclei which stain purple with Wright's stain. Granular cytoplasm. | Bone marrow | Amoeboid, can leave blood and enter tissues to engulf invading micro-organisms. |
| Neutrophils (75%) | Granules stain weakly with Wright's stain. | | Protect against bacterial infection. |
| Eosinophils (2–5%) | Granules stain red with eosin. | | Respond to inflammation. |
| Basophils (0.5%) | Granules stain dark blue with Wright's stain. | | Function unknown. |
| Lymphocytes (20–25%) | Single large nucleus, stains blue with Wright's stain. | | |
| B cells | | Lymph nodes | Produce antibodies. |
| T cells | | Cells that originate in thymus gland. | Involved in graft rejection and other immune responses. |
| Monocytes (2–6%) | Single large nucleus, stains blue with Wright's stain. | Spleen; bone marrow | Motile; phagocytic. |
| Platelets (250,000/mm³) | Fragments of broken down red blood cells. | Bone marrow | Used in clotting. |

all tissues in the body. Since it is not very soluble in water, it is carried by specialized respiratory pigments. Examples of respiratory pigments include:

Chlorocruorin – green due to iron; found in plasma of polychaete worms.
Haemocyanin – blue due to copper: found in plasma of molluscs and crustaceans.
Haemoerythrin – red due to iron: found in corpuscles of nematodes.
Haemoglobin – red due to iron: found in corpuscles of vertebrates and in plasma of some annelids.

Respiratory pigments must be able to carry sufficient oxygen and also must be able to release it rapidly to respiring tissues. The location of the respiratory pigment in the blood cells prevents it from being removed during excretion.

*Haemoglobin*

STRUCTURE: Haemoglobin is composed of a protein (globin) and an iron-containing porphyrin (haem). Four protein and four haem units are found in each haemoglobin molecule. Each haemoglobin molecule can therefore combine with four molecules of oxygen. There is only a loose association between each oxygen molecule and the haem unit to which it is attached. For this reason the oxygen can dissociate easily from the haemoglobin molecule.

FUNCTION: The amount of oxygen carried by haemoglobin in the blood is related to the amount of oxygen available. The amount of oxygen available is usually measured as the partial pressure of oxygen [$PO_2$]; the units used being any of the following: mm Hg, cm Hg, pascals, $KN/m^2$ or atmospheres.

At the lungs, blood is saturated with oxygen. [$PO_2$] = 100 mm Hg and haemoglobin becomes 100 per cent saturated with oxygen. In respiring tissues, oxygen is being consumed continuously and [$PO_2$] is often as low as 40 mm Hg. Thus, as haemoglobin travels around the body from the lungs to respiring tissues, the [$PO_2$] of the blood decreases. As [$PO_2$] of the blood drops from 100 mm Hg to 60 mm Hg, not much oxygen is released, but when it drops below 60 mm Hg, oxygen is released rapidly. This ensures that haemoglobin releases oxygen to the tissues which most require it.

*Dissociation curves*

These graphs show how the amount of oxygen carried by haemoglobin is related to the concentration of oxygen in the surrounding medium. Different animals have different dissociation curves, often relating to their lifestyle or environment (see Figs 5.1 to 5.6).

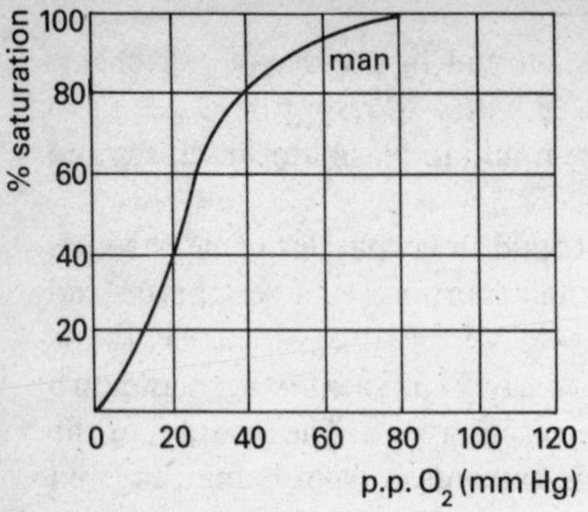
% saturation
100
80
60
40
20
man
0
20
40
60
80
100
120
p.p. $O_2$ (mm Hg)

*Fig.* 5.1 Oxygen–haemoglobin dissociation curve for normal adult human male

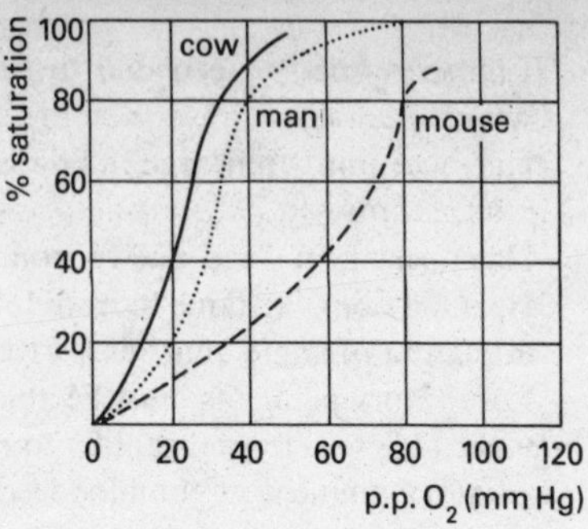
% saturation
100
80
60
40
20
cow
man
mouse
0
20
40
60
80
100
120
p.p. $O_2$ (mm Hg)

*Fig.* 5.2 Oxygen–haemoglobin dissociation curves for cow, man and mouse showing effect of animal size

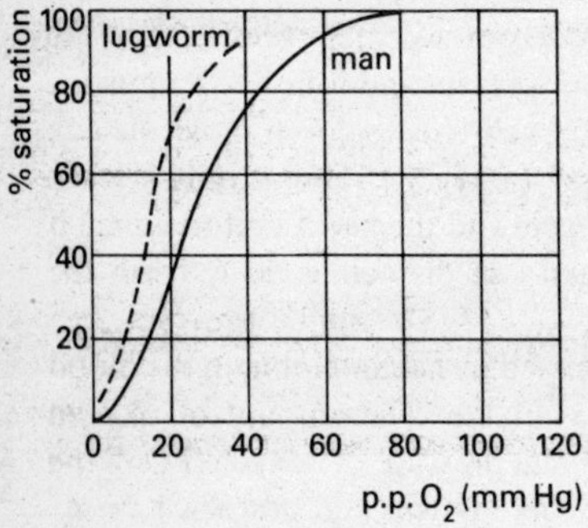
% saturation
100
80
60
40
20
lugworm
man
0
20
40
60
80
100
120
p.p. $O_2$ (mm Hg)

*Fig.* 5.3 Oxygen–haemoglobin dissociation curves for lugworm and man showing effect of habitat

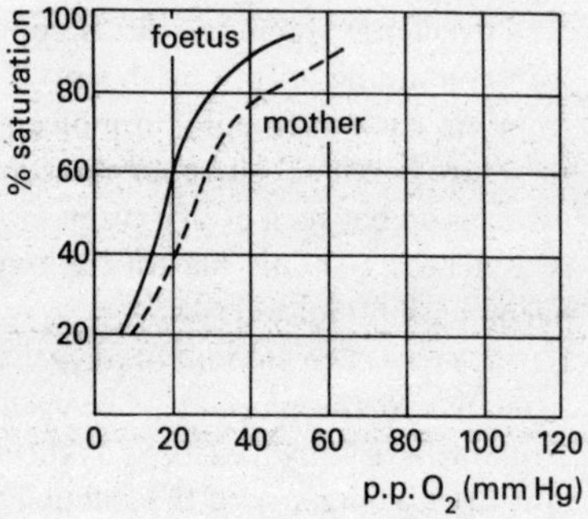
% saturation
100
80
60
40
20
foetus
mother
0
20
40
60
80
100
120
p.p. $O_2$ (mm Hg)

*Fig.* 5.4 Oxygen–haemoglobin dissociation curves for mother and foetus

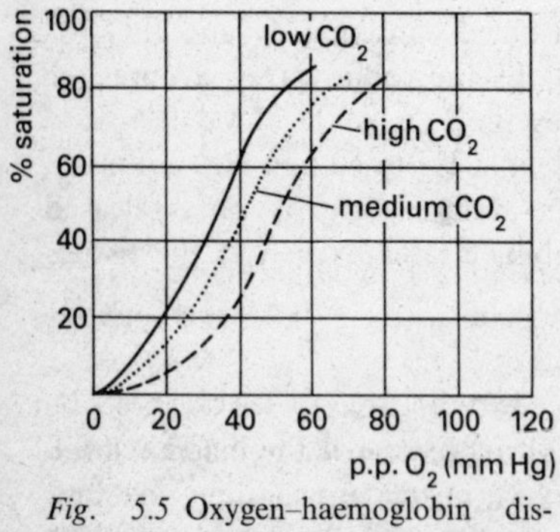
% saturation
100
80
60
40
20
low $CO_2$
high $CO_2$
medium $CO_2$
0
20
40
60
80
100
120
p.p. $O_2$ (mm Hg)

*Fig.* 5.5 Oxygen–haemoglobin dissociation curves at different blood carbon dioxide concentrations showing Bohr effect

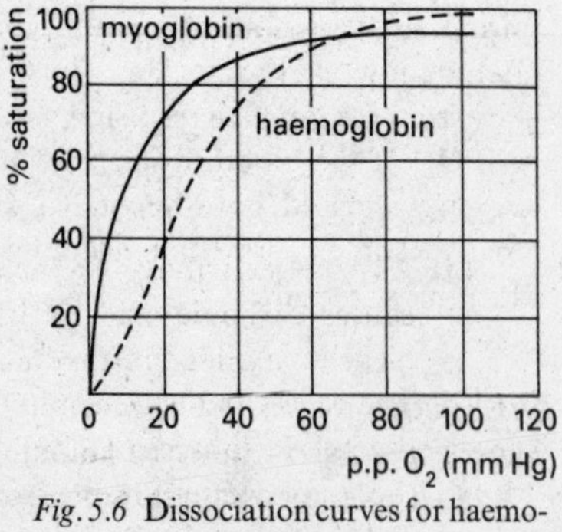
% saturation
100
80
60
40
20
myoglobin
haemoglobin
0
20
40
60
80
100
120
p.p. $O_2$ (mm Hg)

*Fig.* 5.6 Dissociation curves for haemoglobin and myoglobin

*Transport of carbon dioxide*

Carbon dioxide is transported in the blood from respiring tissues to the lungs, where it is removed. Carbon dioxide is carried in three ways:

1. As bicarbonate ions in the plasma (5%).

$$\underset{\text{carbon dioxide}}{CO_2} + \underset{\text{water}}{H_2O} \rightleftharpoons \underset{\text{carbonic acid}}{H_2CO_3} \rightleftharpoons \underset{\text{hydrogen ion}}{H^+} + \underset{\text{bicarbonate ion}}{HCO_3^-}$$

2. As carbamino compounds (10–20%). Carbon dioxide may combine with the amino acid groups of the haemoglobin molecule.

$$CO_2 + \underset{\text{Haemoglobin}}{H_6NH_2} \rightleftharpoons \underset{\text{Carbamino compound}}{H_6\text{–}NHCOO^-} + \underset{\text{Hydrogen ion}}{H^+}$$

3. As bicarbonate in the red blood cells (85%).
   (a) Carbon dioxide enters the red blood cells and combines with water to produce carbonic acid. The reaction is accelerated by the enzyme carbonic anhydrase.

$$CO_2 + H_2O \underset{\text{Carbonic anhydrase}}{\rightleftharpoons} H_2CO_3$$

   (b) Carbonic acid dissociates to form hydrogen and bicarbonate ions.

$$H_2CO_3 \rightleftharpoons H^+ + HCO_3^-$$

   (c) As more carbon dioxide enters the blood, the blood becomes more acid. An increase in acidity causes haemoglobin to give up more oxygen. This is called the Bohr effect (see Fig. 5.5); it ensures that oxygen is supplied readily to respiring tissues which are themselves producing carbon dioxide.

Chloride shift

(a) As explained above, an increase in carbon dioxide concentration causes carbonic acid to dissociate to form hydrogen ions and bicarbonate ions in the blood cell.

(b) The red blood cell membrane is permeable to $HCO_3^-$ ions but not to $H^+$ ions. So $HCO_3^-$ ions pass out of the blood cell into the surrounding plasma.

(c) This causes an increase in the acidity of the red blood cell which, if allowed to rise unchecked, would kill the cell.

(d) To neutralize the pH of the blood cell, chloride ions ($Cl^-$) enter from the plasma. This is called the chloride shift.

*Defence mechanisms*

Foreign bodies (bacteria and other microscopic invaders) may enter the body through a cut, or through the mouth and respiratory tracts. When this happens the blood's defence mechanisms are called into action.

1. *Clotting*

When a blood vessel is cut or injured, a thick clot is formed which acts as a plug, preventing blood loss and entry of bacteria at the cut. This occurs as follows:

(a) Damaged platelets and tissues in the area of the cut release an enzyme thrombokinase.

(b) In the presence of $Ca^{2+}$ ions, thrombokinase acts upon prothrombin (a plasma protein) to produce thrombin.

(c) Thrombin converts the soluble blood protein fibrinogen to a tangled mesh of fibres called fibrin.

(d) Blood corpuscles become entangled in fibrin around the cut to form a clot:

platelets ⟶ thrombokinase

↓ $Ca^{2+}$

prothrombin (produced in liver in presence of vitamin K) ⟶ thrombin

↓

fibrinogen ⟶ fibrin

↓

clot

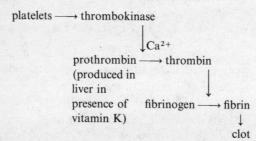

Clotting of blood is normally prevented by the presence of a substance called heparin which inhibits the conversion of prothrombin to thrombin.

2. *The inflammatory response*

This refers to a series of reactions which occur when the skin is cut or injured.

(a) Clotting occurs and the open wound is plugged to prevent further entry of micro-organisms.

(b) Cells adjacent to the cut produce histamines and other chemicals which make the capillaries expand to accommodate the masses of white blood cells which flood into the area.

(c) Histamines also produce a rise in temperature, creating an environment which is unfavourable for many bacteria.
(d) Large numbers of white blood cells enter the injured area and form pus. Neutrophils digest bacteria by phagocytosis, while lymphocytes produce antibodies.

If the localized inflammatory response fails to destroy the infection, the immune system comes into action.

3. *The immune response*

Organisms which have had previous contact with a particular pathogen may be resistant to reinfection by it, and are said to be immune to that pathogen.

Immunity arises from production of globular proteins called antibodies. These chemicals are highly specific and recognize sites on the invading pathogen on to which they can attach. The sites on the pathogens are called antigens, and may be a particular sequence of amino acids or polysaccharides. The antibody will combine with the correct antigen in a lock and key manner, similar to that of an enzyme and substrate.

(a) Production of antibodies (see Fig. 5.7).
 (i) Immature B cell lymphocyte has contact with the invading antigen.
 (ii) Immature lymphocyte develops into mature lymphocyte called a plasma cell. This produces large numbers of antibodies in response to the particular antigen.
 (iii) The mature lymphocyte divides, producing numerous replicas, all of which are capable of antibody production.
 (iv) After 3 to 6 days, antibody production has reached a level where the invading pathogens have been destroyed.
 (v) Even after the pathogen has been eliminated, mature lymphocytes remain in the blood and will produce antibodies upon reinfection by the same pathogen. Such lymphocytes are called memory cells, since they are sensitive to that particular antigen. The body is then said to be immune to that particular disease-causing microorganism.
 (vi) Upon reinfection, immediate antibody production occurs and the pathogens are destroyed before they can multiply and create an infection.
(b) Action of antibodies
 (i) Agglutinins – cause pathogens to stick together so that they are more easily engulfed by phagocytes.

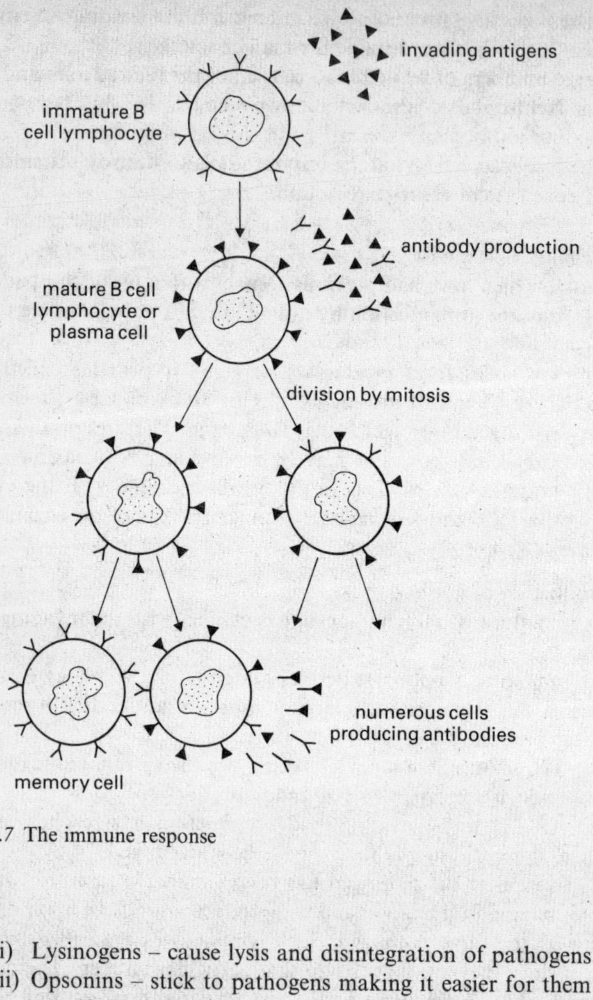
invading antigens
immature B
cell lymphocyte
antibody production
mature B cell
lymphocyte or
plasma cell
division by mitosis
numerous cells
producing antibodies
memory cell

*Fig. 5.7* The immune response

(ii) Lysinogens – cause lysis and disintegration of pathogens.
(iii) Opsonins – stick to pathogens making it easier for them to be engulfed by phagocytes.
(iv) Antitoxins – neutralize the toxins produced by pathogens.
(v) Precipitins – cause aggregation of antigens and precipitate them.

(c) Artificial immunization
(i) Long-term immunization is achieved by introducing a small amount of antigen into the blood (vaccination). The appropriate

antibodies are formed by lymphocytes, and memory cells remain in the blood ready to fight that pathogen if infection should occur. For example, immunity to polio virus is obtained by introducing a small amount of heat-killed virus into the blood.

(ii) Short-term immunization. Short-term immunization is sometimes necessary as, for various reasons, heat-killed pathogens cannot always be used for vaccination. For some infections, large quantities of antibodies are given instead. This provides an immediate immunity which is only short-lived, since antibodies are eventually broken down by the body. This is why some vaccinations, e.g. hepatitis, cholera and tetanus, only provide a short-term immunity. Another type of short-term immunity is that given to a baby by the mother. Antibodies leak across the placenta from the mother to the baby. A few weeks after birth these antibodies are destroyed and the baby has to start building its own immunity.

(d) Disorders of the immune system

Allergies are caused by over-reaction of the immune system. Particles of dust or pollen are weak antigens, i.e. most people do not respond to them. Sometimes the immune system produces antibodies which not only stick to the dust and pollen grains, but also to the surrounding tissue cells. The antibodies produce inflammation of these tissues causing rashes and hay fever.

(e) Transplants

The immune system can distinguish between 'self' and 'not self'. Substances which are present in embryonic life, while the immune system is developing, are recognized as belonging to oneself and will not be attacked in later life. Conversely, the body will usually reject any foreign invaders which enter the body. Unfortunately, this includes rejection of organs such as hearts, kidneys, skin and other tissues which may be used for transplants. Rejection is initiated largely by the T cell lymphocytes (see Table 5.1) which aggregate around transplants and attack the foreign cells. This means that donors have to be chosen extremely carefully if the operation is to be successful.

Autoimmune diseases are rare, but they occur when the body's recognition system breaks down and the individual produces antibodies against his or her own proteins.

## Human blood groups

The red blood cells of some humans contain chemicals on their surface which act as antigens. These may be either of two types of antigen A or B, both or neither. There are also antibodies *a* and *b* in the plasma:

antibody *a* attacks antigen A
antibody *b* attacks antigen B

However, plasma does not contain antibodies which would attack the antigens of its own blood cells (see Table 5.2)

*Table 5.2.* Human blood groups

| *Blood group* | *Antigens on red blood cells* | *Antibodies in plasma* |
|---|---|---|
| A | A | b |
| B | B | a |
| AB | A + B | none |
| O | none | a + b |

Blood grouping is of great importance when blood from a donor is used for transfusion to a sick person (see Table 5.3). If the two blood types are incompatible, clumping or agglutination of blood cells occurs. If antigens are present in the donor's blood which are absent from the recipient's blood, antibodies will attack them as if they were 'foreign bodies'. Group O is called the universal donor and group AB is the universal recipient.

*Table 5.3.* Compatibility of blood groups

| *Blood group of recipient* | *Blood groups that can be safely donated* |
|---|---|
| A | A, O |
| B | B, O |
| AB | A, B, AB, O |
| O | O |

### *Rhesus (Rh) factor*

As well as the A and B type antigens, 85 per cent of the population have another antigen in their red blood cells. They are said to be $Rh^+$ or

Rhesus positive; the remaining 15 per cent of people whose blood does not contain the antigen are $Rh^-$ (Rhesus negative).

Transfusion of $Rh^-$ blood to an $Rh^+$ recipient is safe, but $Rh^+$ to $Rh^-$ can be harmful.

If an $Rh^-$ mother bears an $Rh^+$ foetus (in such a case $Rh^+$ is inherited from the father), $Rh^+$ cells may accidentally enter the maternal circulation. This causes the mother to produce antibodies against $Rh^+$, but these do not harm the pregnancy. However, if she becomes pregnant again with another $Rh^+$ foetus, antibodies cross the placenta and destroy the foetal red blood cells, with fatal results for the baby. To prevent this happening, the mother can be injected with $Rh^+$ antibodies after her first pregnancy, and these kill off the stray foetal erythrocytes before her natural immunity builds up against them.

### *Blood systems*

These can be categorized as follows:

1. Open systems – e.g. arthropods and molluscs. In many small animals, blood is supplied to the organs by arteries and drained away through veins, but there are no capillaries connecting the two. Instead, the organs lie in a reservoir of blood, often called a haemocoel.
2. Closed systems – e.g. annelids and vertebrates. The blood is completely enclosed in blood vessels which branch throughout the body. To get into the surrounding tissues, food and oxygen has to pass out of the blood through the capillary walls. Closed systems may be of two types (see Fig. 5.8):

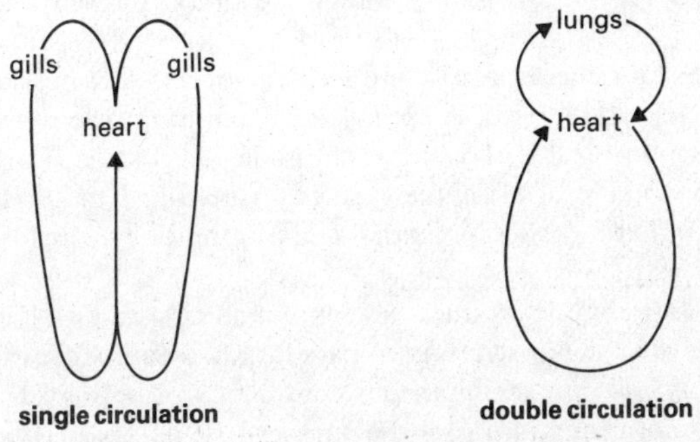
gills
gills
heart
single circulation
lungs
heart
double circulation

*Fig. 5.8* Single and double circulatory systems

(a) Single circulatory systems – e.g. fish. Blood passes the heart only once for every circuit round the body.
(b) Double circulatory systems – e.g. mammals. Blood goes to the heart twice for every circuit round the body. Blood is first pumped to the lungs whereupon it returns to the heart for an extra boost before circulating round the body. If blood did not return for this extra boost it would move very slowly round the body.

## The heart

The heart pumps blood around the body. It has an essential role, to keep the blood moving and to maintain blood pressure.

The simplest heart (e.g. annelids) is merely a thickened blood vessel capable of muscular contraction. However, in more highly evolved animals the heart is more complex. In fish the heart is divided into two chambers – an atrium (auricle) and a ventricle. Birds and mammals have four chambers – two atria and two ventricles. The right ventricle pumps deoxygenated blood to the lungs and the left ventricle pumps oxygenated blood around the body. The structure and functions of the human heart are shown in Figs 5.9. and 5.10.

### *Heartbeat (cardiac rhythm)*

Blood enters the right atrium through two large veins, the venae cavae, and enters the left atrium through the pulmonary veins. As the auricles swell with blood, they contract simultaneously, forcing blood into the ventricles, through the tricuspid and bicuspid valves. As the ventricles fill with blood they also contract simultaneously, the right ventricle pumping blood into the pulmonary artery and the left ventricle pumping blood to the aorta. During ventricular contraction the tricuspid and bicuspid valves are held tightly shut by tendons attached to papillary muscles.

The signal for the atria to contract is myogenic, i.e. it arises in the muscle of the atrium itself. A specialized patch of muscle in the wall of the right atrium, called the sino-atrial node, acts as the heart's 'pacemaker'. It is made of a unique type of tissue called the nodal tissue, capable of initiating action potentials and transmitting them, like a nerve, across the heart.

The sino-atrial node produces an action potential and itself contracts. This causes a wave of excitation to pass instantaneously over to the left atrium. This sets up a simultaneous contraction of both atria.

The wave of excitation from the auricles stimulates a second area of nodal tissue called the atrio-ventricular node. This branches throughout

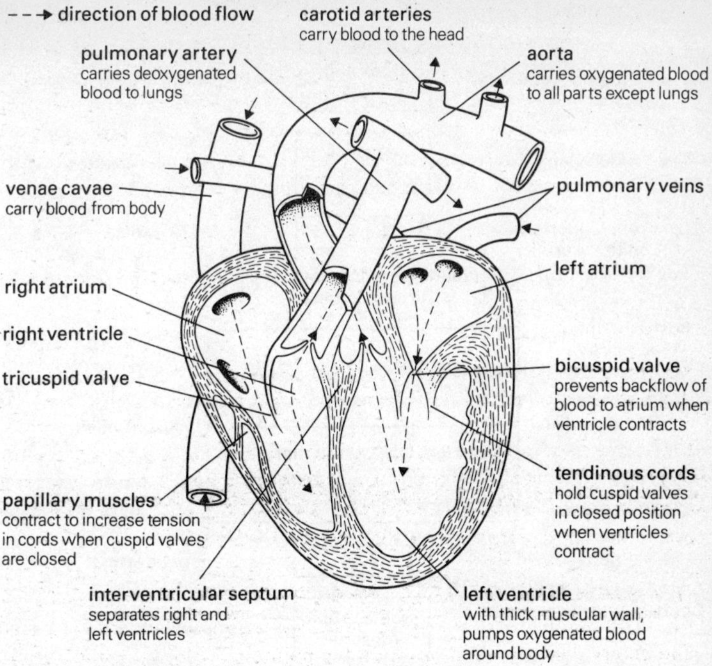

--→ direction of blood flow
carotid arteries
carry blood to the head
pulmonary artery
carries deoxygenated
blood to lungs
aorta
carries oxygenated blood
to all parts except lungs
venae cavae
carry blood from body
pulmonary veins
left atrium
right atrium
right ventricle
tricuspid valve
bicuspid valve
prevents backflow of
blood to atrium when
ventricle contracts
tendinous cords
hold cuspid valves
in closed position
when ventricles
contract
papillary muscles
contract to increase tension
in cords when cuspid valves
are closed
interventricular septum
separates right and
left ventricles
left ventricle
with thick muscular wall;
pumps oxygenated blood
around body


*Fig. 5.9* LS of the human heart

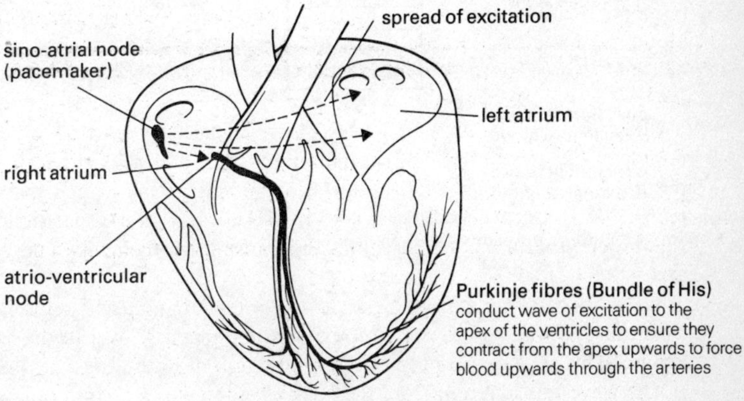

spread of excitation
sino-atrial node
(pacemaker)
left atrium
right atrium
atrio-ventricular
node
Purkinje fibres (Bundle of His)
conduct wave of excitation to the
apex of the ventricles to ensure they
contract from the apex upwards to force
blood upwards through the arteries


*Fig. 5.10* Diagram illustrating the specialized muscle tissue in the human heart

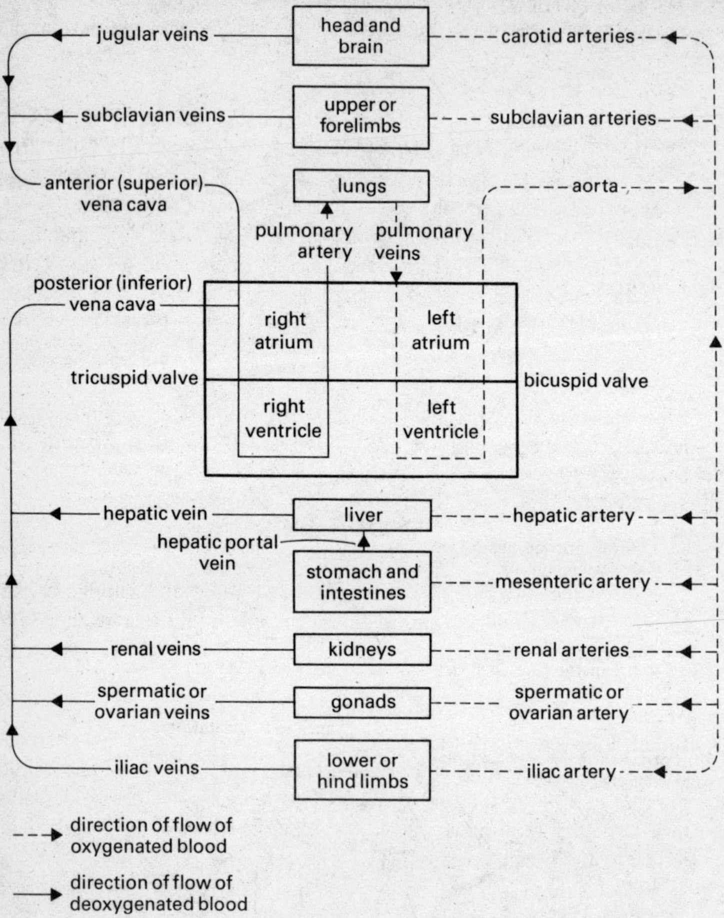

jugular veins
head and brain
carotid arteries
subclavian veins
upper or forelimbs
subclavian arteries
anterior (superior) vena cava
lungs
aorta
pulmonary artery
pulmonary veins
posterior (inferior) vena cava
right atrium
left atrium
tricuspid valve
bicuspid valve
right ventricle
left ventricle
hepatic vein
liver
hepatic artery
hepatic portal vein
stomach and intestines
mesenteric artery
renal veins
kidneys
renal arteries
spermatic or ovarian veins
gonads
spermatic or ovarian artery
iliac veins
lower or hind limbs
iliac artery
direction of flow of oxygenated blood
direction of flow of deoxygenated blood


*Fig. 5.11* Outline diagram of mammalian circulation

the ventricles, forming a network called the Purkinje fibres (Bundle of His). The atrio-ventricular node contains fibres which transmit impulses slowly, causing a delay between the auricular and ventricular contractions.

*Control of heartbeat*

Heartbeat is affected by the autonomic nervous system, see p. 245.

1. NERVOUS CONTROL: Sympathetic nerves stimulate the sino-atrial node and increase heartbeat. Parasympathetic nerves (via the vagus nerve) have the opposite effect and slow down the heartbeat.
2. CHEMICAL CONTROL: Hormones, such as adrenaline and nora-drenaline, as well as certain drugs, e.g. amphetamines, have the effect of increasing heartbeat. An increase in carbon dioxide in the blood also increases heartbeat.

*Cardiac output*

This is the amount of blood pumped per minute. It depends on the number of beats per minute and the amount of blood pumped at each beat.

cardiac output = no. beats/min. × no. of litres of blood/beat

## Blood vessels

The three types of blood vessels, arteries, veins and capillaries, are summarized in Table 5.4, and the main vessels and the organs they serve are shown in Fig. 5.11.

*Maintenance of peripheral flow*

Blood flows initially by pressure from the heart. To maintain a good circulation, however, the muscles in the artery walls constrict and help to pump blood along into capillaries. Veins do not have muscular walls, but they have semi-lunar valves to prevent back-flow of blood on its return to the heart.

### *The lymphatic system*

This consists of a number of swellings called the lymph nodes, which are connected by a network of lymph vessels. The vessels contain a fluid called lymph, which is similar to blood plasma but does not contain red blood cells.

The lymphatic system is composed of a branching network of vessels present in every part of the body. It often runs parallel to the blood circulation but is in contact with it at only one or two points.

*Table 5.4.* Comparison of arteries, veins and capillaries

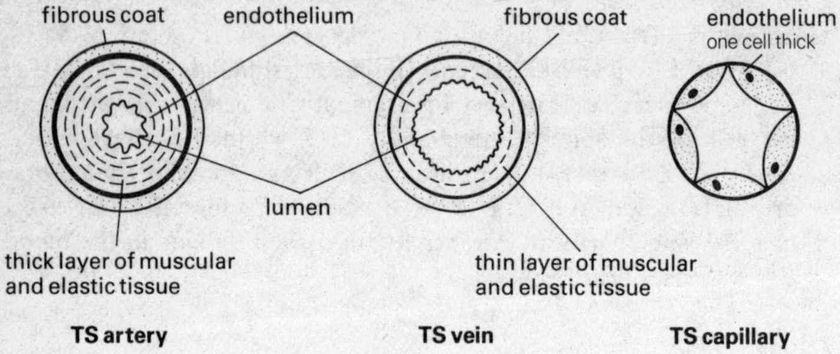
fibrous coat
endothelium
fibrous coat
endothelium
one cell thick
lumen
thick layer of muscular
and elastic tissue
thin layer of muscular
and elastic tissue
TS artery
TS vein
TS capillary

| *Artery* | *Vein* | *Capillary* |
|---|---|---|
| Contains endothelium lining | Contains endothelium lining | Contains endothelium lining |
| Tubular | Tubular | Tubular |
| Carries $O_2$ blood, except pulmonary artery | Carries de$O_2$ blood, except pulmonary veins | Carries both $O_2$ and de$O_2$ blood |
| Thick walls containing muscular and elastic tissue | Thin walls, less muscular and elastic tissue | Very thin walls (one cell thick), no muscular or elastic tissues |
| Carries blood away from the heart | Carries blood to heart | Carries blood to and from the heart |
| Not permeable | Not permeable | Permeable; fluids pass in and out of walls |
| No valves (except aorta and pulmonary artery) | Semi-lunar valves present | No valves |
| Contains blood under high pressure | Contains blood at low pressure | Contains blood at intermediate pressure |

Lymph is moved along by contraction of the surrounding muscles and is prevented from flowing backwards by valves in the lymph nodes.

Functions of the lymphatic system

1. The lymph nodes produce white blood cells which are used to defend the body against pathogens.
2. Pathogens are transported via the lymph to the lymph nodes where they are destroyed.
3. The lymphatic system acts as a drainage system for excess tissue fluid containing waste materials. This is returned to the blood via two main lymph vessels, the right lymphatic duct and the thoracic duct which empties into the vena cava just before it reaches the heart.
4. It transports fat droplets from the intestine and deposits them in the blood. The fat gives lymph its characteristic milky colour.

## *Further reading*

C. Chapman, *The Body Fluids and their Functions*, Studies in Biology No. 8, 2nd edition (Arnold, 1980)

C. J. Inchley, *Immunobiology*, Studies in Biology No. 128 (Arnold, 1981)

N. Maclean, *Haemoglobin*, Studies in Biology No. 93 (Arnold, 1978)

E. Neil, *The Human Circulation*, Oxford/Carolina Biology Reader No. 82, 2nd edition (Packard, 1979)

F. K. Sanders, *Interferons: An Example of Communication*, Oxford/Carolina Biology Reader No. 88 (Packard, 1981)

M. Vassalle, *The Human Heart*, Oxford/Carolina Biology Reader No. 82, 2nd edition (Packard, 1979)

## *Related questions*

**Question:**

(a) Describe the structure and the functions of the cells in the blood of a mammal. **(14 marks)**

(b) What part does the lymphatic system play in the life of a mammal? **(6 marks)**

[London, Jan. 1982, Paper 2]

**Comments:**

(a) This part of the question has 14 marks (out of 20), therefore just over two-thirds of the time should be spent on it (i.e. 25 minutes). The key words are 'structure' and 'function'. Candidates should ensure that both are given for each type of blood cell.

For the structures of all blood cells see Table 5.1. The brief description of the functions given in the table should be supplemented with more detailed descriptions from the rest of the text. However, it is important to avoid including unnecessary material and you should concentrate on the actual functions of blood cells themselves. For example, a full description of the inflammatory response is unnecessary – only the part played by phagocytes is important in answering this question.

*Suggested essay plan:*

Red blood cells – Erythrocytes

(i) structure

(ii) function – transport of oxygen, including a brief description of the role of haemoglobin. (Note: no discussion of respiratory pigments in other animals is required, since the question asks for a mammal. There is also no need to discuss dissociation curves.)

White blood cells – Leucocytes

1. Granulocytes – structure of neutrophils, eosinophils and basophils; function of granulocytes in the inflammatory response (see p. 166).
2. Monocytes – structure and function in inflammatory response.
3. Lymphocytes – structure; function of B cells in immune response and antibody production (see p. 167) and function of T cells in transplant rejection (see p. 169).
4. Platelets – fragments of broken-down blood cells involved in clotting. (Note: an explanation of clotting is not required since platelets are not really blood cells.)

(b) This part of the question has 6 marks, so you should spend approximately one-third of the allocated time (12 minutes) on it. The main facts are covered in the text (see p. 175).

The lymphatic system is concerned basically with draining waste fluids from the tissues and returning them to the bloodstream, where they can be filtered out in the kidneys.

**Question:**

The diagram below illustrates the nervous conducting system of a mammalian heart.

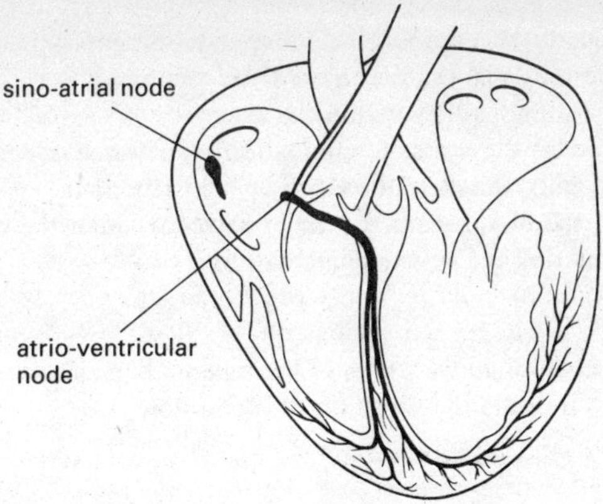
sino-atrial node
atrio-ventricular
node

(a) Describe how this conducting system initiates and transmits the impulses which bring about contraction of heart muscle. **(5 marks)**

(b) During exercise the volume of venous blood returning to the heart increases and this results in stronger contraction. What causes the initial increase in the volume of venous blood? **(2 marks)**

(c) Give a detailed account of how heart rate is regulated by the nervous system and by the endocrine system during periods of prolonged physical activity. **(6 marks)**

(d) Explain how an almost continuous flow of blood is maintained through the arteries even though blood flow from the ventricles is discontinuous. **(4 marks)**

(e) Explain why the pressure of blood in the systematic circulation of a fish is lower than the pressure of blood in the systemic circulation of a mammal. **(3 marks)**

[AEB, June 1982, Paper 2]

**Comments:**

(a) See p. 172.

(b) During exercise adrenaline is produced, and this redirects blood from the outer limbs to the vital organs including the heart. This causes an increase in the volume of venous blood.

(c) See p. 175. During prolonged physical activity blood passing through the hypothalamus contains a high concentration of carbon dioxide. This affects heartbeat via the autonomic nervous system and also induces adrenaline production.

(d) The arteries have a very thick muscular wall and narrow lumen. Consequently, when a large volume of blood enters from the ventricle, the muscular walls constrict and the blood is forced into an almost continuous flow within the artery.

(e) The blood in the systemic circulation of a fish has come directly from the gills and it is therefore at a low pressure, whereas in a mammal the blood from the lungs passes through the heart again before entering the systemic circulation.

**Question:**

The diagram below shows a plan of the mammalian circulatory system. Small arrows indicate the direction of blood flow.

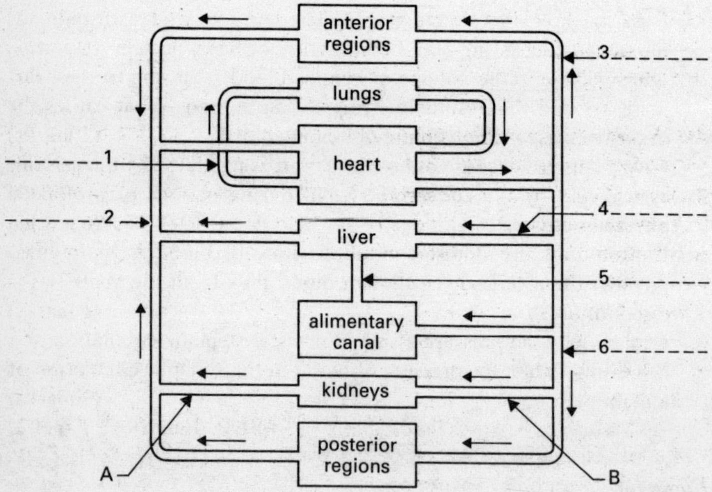
anterior regions
lungs
heart
liver
alimentary canal
kidneys
posterior regions
1
2
3
4
5
6
A
B

(a) Identify the *six* numbered vessels by writing their names on the lines provided.
(b) Name *two* substances which would always be present in substantial quantities in vessel B and considerably reduced in A.

(i) ____________________

(ii) ____________________

(c) State *four* differences between the circulatory system shown in the diagram and the circulatory system of a fish.

(i) ____________________

(ii) ____________________

(iii) ____________________

(iv) ____________________

[AEB, June 1980, Paper 1]

**Comments**

(a) See Fig. 5.11, 'Outline diagram of mammalian circulation'
(b) Two substances in high concentration in vessel B but low in vessel A could be any of the substances removed by the kidneys, see p. 221.
(c) Four differences between the circulatory system of a mammal and a fish.

| *Fish* | *Mammal* |
|---|---|
| 1. Single circulatory system | Double circulatory system |
| 2. Two-chambered heart | Four-chambered heart |
| 3. Gaseous exchange at gills | Gaseous exchange at lungs |
| 4. Mixing of oxygenated and deoxygenated blood | *No* mixing of oxygenated and deoxygenated blood |

**Question:**
The graph below shows the dissociation curves for human oxy-haemoglobin at three partial pressures of carbon dioxide.

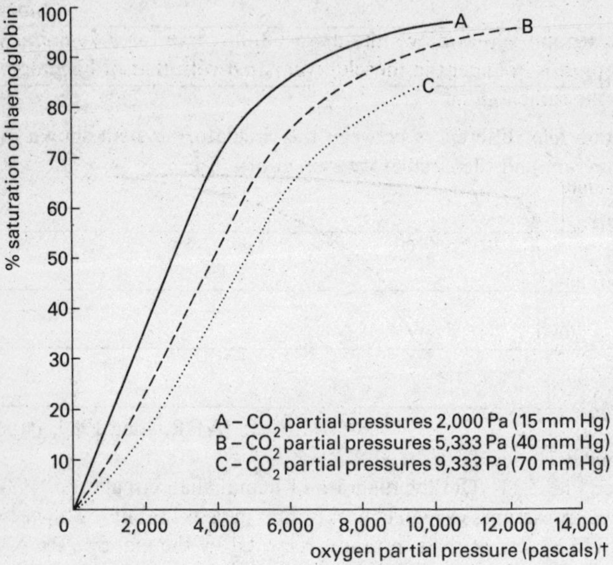
% saturation of haemoglobin
100
90
80
70
60
50
40
30
20
10
0
2,000
4,000
6,000
8,000
10,000
12,000
14,000
oxygen partial pressure (pascals)†
A
B
C
A – $CO_2$ partial pressures 2,000 Pa (15 mm Hg)
B – $CO_2$ partial pressures 5,333 Pa (40 mm Hg)
C – $CO_2$ partial pressures 9,333 Pa (70 mm Hg)

†A pascal (Pa) is a unit of pressure. A pressure of 100,000 pascals is approximately equal to atmospheric pressure (760 mm Hg)

(a) What effect does an increase in the carbon dioxide pressure have on the oxygen-carrying capacity of haemoglobin?

________________________________________

**(2 marks)**

(b) State where in the mammalian body the partial pressure of carbon dioxide is likely to be

(i) low ____________________________________

(ii) high ____________________________________

**(2 marks)**

(c) What effect will variations in the partial pressure of carbon dioxide in different parts of the mammalian body have on the transport of oxygen?

---

**(2 marks)**

(d) The graph below shows the dissociation curve for myoglobin (the respiratory pigment in muscle) compared with that of haemoglobin in the same animal.

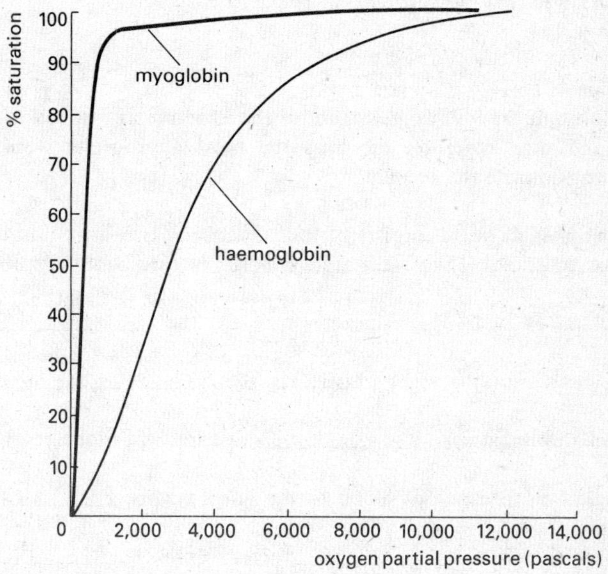
% saturation
100
90
80
70
60
50
40
30
20
10
0
2,000
4,000
6,000
8,000
10,000
12,000
14,000
oxygen partial pressure (pascals)
myoglobin
haemoglobin

State the physiological significance of the relationship between these two pigments.

---

**(4 marks)**

[London, June 1980, Paper 1]

**Comments:**

(a) This is testing your knowledge of the 'Bohr effect' (see p. 163).

(b) 'Partial pressure' in this context is equivalent to concentration. Areas of *low* carbon dioxide concentration can include the lungs, pulmonary vein, etc. Areas of *high* carbon dioxide concentration can include very metabolically active organs such as the liver, or regions such as the pulmonary artery. Give *one* example for each.

(c) See p. 163. Variations in the partial pressure of carbon dioxide in different parts of the body will ensure haemoglobin releases oxygen in the areas where it is needed most, i.e. in areas of high carbon dioxide partial pressure such as respiring tissues.

(d) See p. 164.

**Question:**

Read through the following account of the structure and action of the heart and then write on the lines the most appropriate word or words to complete the account.

The mammalian heart consists of four chambers; two atria (auricles) and two ventricles. Their walls are composed of cardiac muscle fibres.

The chamber with the thickest wall is the ______________.

Blood flows into the right auricle via the ______________ and is pumped through the ______________ valve into the right ventricle.

The right ventricle pumps blood to the lungs via the ____________ artery which contains ____________ valves to prevent ____________ of blood into the ______________. The pacemaker of the heart is termed the ____________ and lies in the wall of the ____________.

Special impulse-conducting tissue runs from the pacemaker. It is termed ______________ tissue, and stimulates the contraction of the chambers. **(Total 10 marks)**

[London, Jan. 1983, Paper 1]

**Comments:**
See p. 172.

**Question:**
(a) What is meant by 'myogenic' in relation to cardiac muscle?

**(1 mark)**

(b) How is the contraction of the two atria (auricles) kept separate from that of the two ventricles?

**(2 marks)**

(c) What role is played by the papillary muscles during the contraction of the ventricles?

**(2 marks)**

(d) How is a heartbeat of a mammal initiated?

**(3 marks)**

[London, Jan. 1982, Paper 1]

**Comments:**
See p. 172.

## ***Transport in plants***

### *Transport of water*

This is summarized in Fig. 5.12.

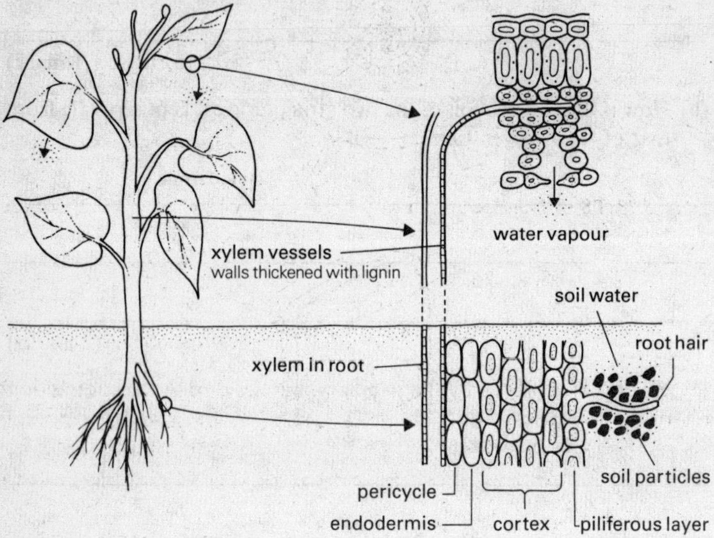
water vapour
xylem vessels
walls thickened with lignin
soil water
root hair
xylem in root
soil particles
pericycle
endodermis
cortex
piliferous layer

*Fig. 5.12* Water movement in a bean plant

#### Uptake of water by roots

Roots have the following adaptations to aid water uptake (see Fig. 5.13):

1. The absorption area of the root has numerous root hairs to increase the surface area through which water can be absorbed.
2. The exodermis has no cuticle.
3. The phloem does not form a continuous ring around the xylem as it does in mature stems. Instead it is found in bundles, between outstretched arms of xylem, enabling water to move into the xylem easily.
4. The layers of cells around the pericycle, called the endodermis, are thickened with a waterproof layer of suberin on their horizontal and radial walls forming short 'pipes' for channelling water into the xylem vessels (see Fig. 5.14 and below). These cells may also be involved in active pumping of water and mineral salts into xylem vessels.

The mechanism of water uptake is as follows (see Fig. 5.15):

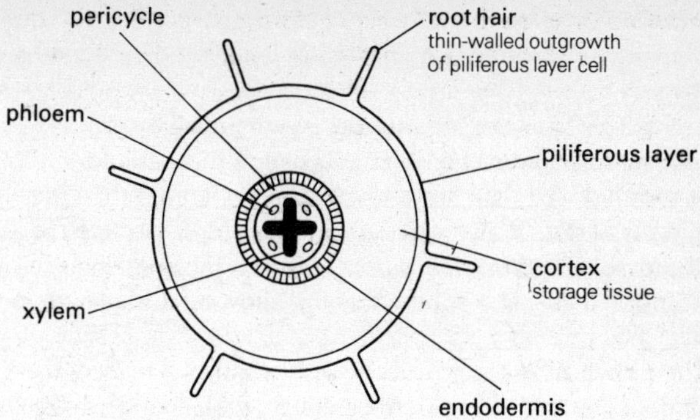
pericycle
root hair
thin-walled outgrowth
of piliferous layer cell
phloem
piliferous layer
cortex
storage tissue
xylem
endodermis

*Fig. 5.13* TS of *Ranunculus* root

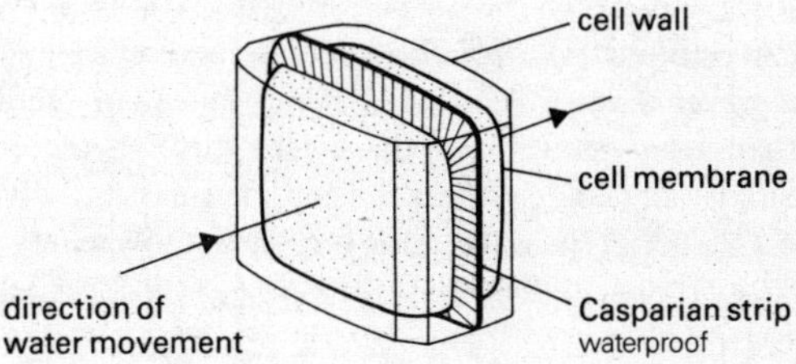
cell wall
cell membrane
direction of
water movement
Casparian strip
waterproof

*Fig. 5.14* Endodermal cell

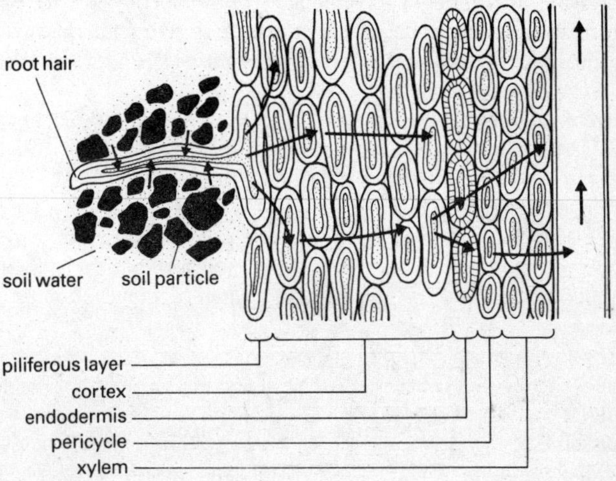
root hair
soil water
soil particle
piliferous layer
cortex
endodermis
pericycle
xylem

*Fig. 5.15* Uptake of water by roots

1. The vacuoles of root hair cells contain a concentrated solution of salts and therefore have a higher water potential than the surrounding soil water.
2. Water passes from the soil into the root hair cell by osmosis, and as a result the solution in the vacuole becomes more dilute.
3. The root hair cell then has a lower water potential than the adjacent cell in the cortex. Water passes from the root hair cell to the adjacent cell and so on across the cortex, leaving the root hair cell with a concentrated vacuolar solution again, allowing it to absorb more soil water.
4. Water moves across the cortex by osmosis until it reaches the cylinder of endodermal cells. As described above, each endodermal cell has its horizontal and radial walls thickened with suberin. This thickened waterproof layer is called the Casparian strip. To enter a xylem vessel, water has to be funnelled through an endodermal cell. The endodermis therefore prevents vertical and radial movement in the cortex and ensures that water passes into the xylem through the endodermal protoplasm. In some older plants the endodermis is heavily thickened and there are special 'passage' cells for water movement.

*Root pressure*

If the stem of a plant is removed, water still exudes from the cut end for some time (see Fig. 5.16). The pressure causing this to happen is called root pressure. It is thought to originate from the pericycle cells, which are normally adjacent to the xylem vessels, actively pumping salts into the xylem, resulting in water entering by osmosis.

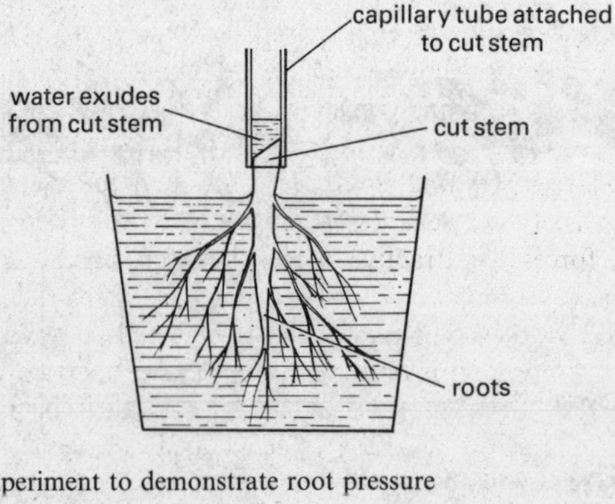
capillary tube attached to cut stem
water exudes from cut stem
cut stem
roots

*Fig. 5.16* Experiment to demonstrate root pressure

## Transport of water up the stem

Water moves up a stem in the xylem vessels (see Fig. 5.17). This can be shown by immersing a cut stem in a beaker containing water and a red dye, eosin. After several hours sections are taken from the stem and examined under a microscope. Invariably, the dye is concentrated in the xylem vessels, indicating that they are responsible for transport of water up the stem.

Xylem vessels are well suited to their function. They are long cylindrical cells which are dead and have lost their contents, and their walls are thickened with lignin to resist the pressure of water in them.

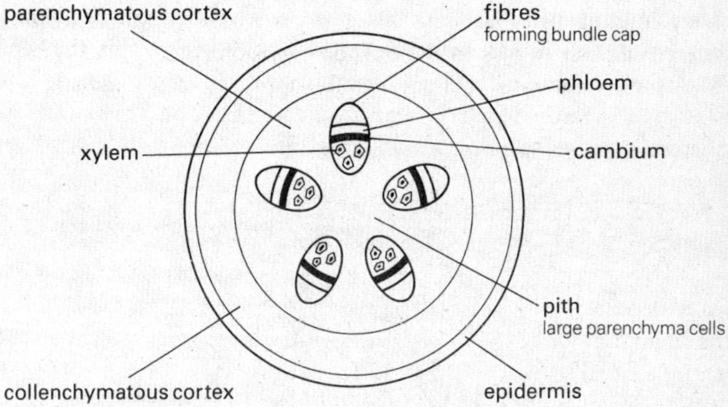
parenchymatous cortex
fibres
forming bundle cap
phloem
xylem
cambium
pith
large parenchyma cells
collenchymatous cortex
epidermis

*Fig. 5.17* TS of young *Helianthus* stem

### *Mechanism of water movement in xylem*

As water evaporates from the leaves, water is drawn up the xylem vessels as long, unbroken columns of water. This is possible because of two types of forces:

1. Adhesive forces – strong attractive forces between water molecules and the walls of the xylem vessels causing water to stick to the vessels.
2. Cohesive forces – attractive forces between neighbouring water molecules.

These forces give the column of water a high tensile strength, so the columns do not break. It is only because of this property of water, and the narrow size of the xylem vessels, that water is able to be pulled up the plant in this manner. It is often referred to as the cohesion–tension theory of water movement.

### Transpiration

Transpiration is the evaporation of water from the leaves and is a purely physical process. As water evaporates from the leaf surface, water is drawn up the xylem vessels to replace it. This force is called the transpiration pull and it is responsible for 'sucking' the majority of water up the plant.

Leaves are adapted to transpiration in the following ways:

1. They are usually wide and flat to provide a large surface area for evaporation.
2. They contain many air spaces among their cells, enabling diffusion of water from all cells into the intercellular air spaces.
3. They contain many stomata which allow water to diffuse from the outside environment.
4. They have numerous vein endings to supply water to the leaf.

*The mechanism of transpiration* (*Fig. 5.18*)

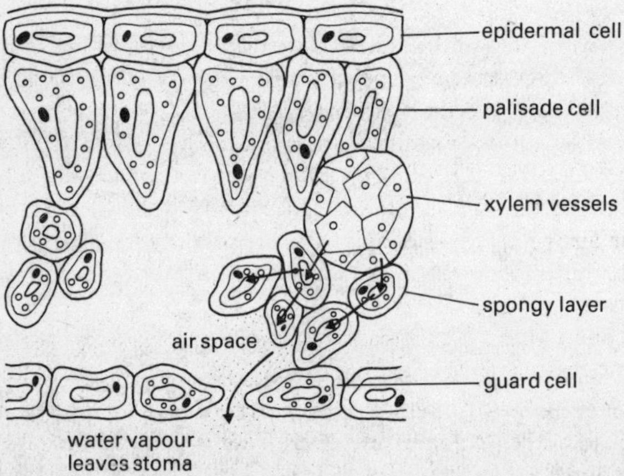
epidermal cell
palisade cell
xylem vessels
spongy layer
air space
guard cell
water vapour
leaves stoma

*Fig. 5.18* Movement of water through a leaf

1. Cells adjacent to the xylem vessels in the leaf become full of water. This water may:
   (a) diffuse into neighbouring cells via strands of cytoplasm called plasmodesmata,
   (b) move into adjacent cells by osmosis, or
   (c) evaporate into intercellular spaces until the air spaces are saturated with water.

2. There exists an osmotic gradient between the saturated air in the leaf and the relatively dry air outside. Water vapour molecules diffuse from the saturated air in the leaf, through the stomata, into the less saturated outer air where the vapour pressure and hence the water potential is lower.
3. The loss in water causes a slight drying of the air in the intercellular spaces. Water molecules then evaporate from the cells bordering the air spaces. As these cells lose water they draw on water reserves from adjacent cells, which in turn draw water from the xylem vessels by osmosis.

*Evapotranspiration*

This term is used for the water lost in transpiration of plants plus the water lost in evaporation from the soil itself. It is a useful term, used in calculating the amount of water required for irrigation purposes on a particular area of land.

*Environmental factors affecting transpiration rate*

1. HUMIDITY: The air inside a leaf is saturated with water, so the drier the air outside, the steeper the diffusion gradient will be, and hence the more rapid the transpiration rate.
2. AIR MOVEMENTS: In still air there is a tendency for a layer of moist air to collect over the leaf. This reduces the diffusion gradient between the leaf and the atmosphere and consequently decreases transpiration. If the air is moving, the moist air is constantly replaced by dry air, so the diffusion gradient remains steep and transpiration does not decrease.
3. TEMPERATURE: An increase in temperature increases transpiration for two reasons: (i) The air in the intercellular spaces becomes warmer and consequently is able to hold more water vapour. This has the effect of increasing the diffusion gradient and hence increasing transpiration. (ii) The extra heat provides energy for latent heat of vaporization so more water will evaporate from the leaf surface.
4. LIGHT INTENSITY: Increased light intensity will increase transpiration owing to: (i) the heating effect (see above), and (ii) opening of stomata. If stomata are closed, transpiration effectively stops. Usually stomata open during the daytime and close at night. The effect of light on stomatal opening is thought to occur in the following way. During the daytime, carbon dioxide is used in photosynthesis, so the pH of the guard cells becomes more alkaline (carbon dioxide combines with water to form carbonic acid). Alkaline conditions favour the

enzymatic breakdown of starch to glucose which increases the glucose concentration of the guard cell vacuole. As the water potential of the guard cell increases, water enters by osmosis, and the guard cell swells and becomes turgid. When guard cells swell, they form two kidney-bean shaped cells with an open pore in the centre. Stomata are therefore open in daylight. During the night-time, carbon dioxide accumulates in the guard cells and is converted to carbonic acid. Acidic conditions favour the conversion of glucose to starch, and the water potential of the guard cells is reduced. As a result, the guard cells lose water and become flaccid. Loss in turgidity causes the guard cells to lose their shape, they flatten and the pore closes. Hence at night stomata are closed. (See Fig. 5.19.)

Recent observations have shown that there are fluctuations in the concentration of certain mineral ions in the guard cells during the opening and closing of stomata. For example, an increase in potassium ions ($K^+$) accompanies stomatal opening; the ions accumulate and lead to an increase in turgidity. Simultaneous increases in concentrations of other substances, such as malate ions, have been detected. These may lead to an accumulation of hydrogen ions in the

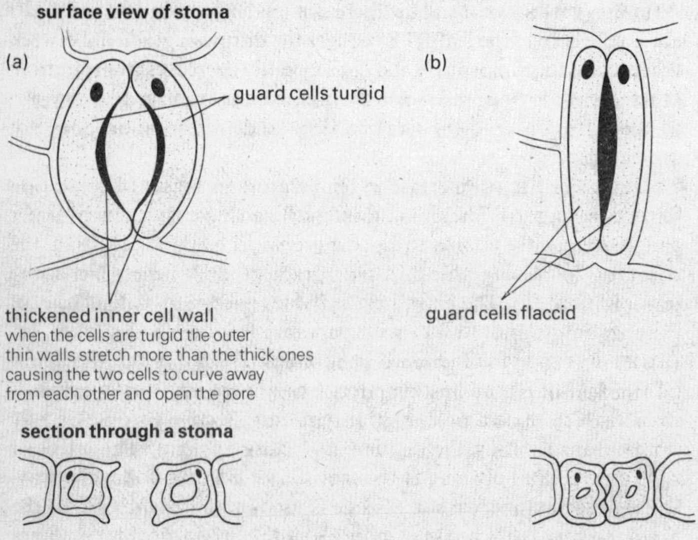
surface view of stoma
(a)
guard cells turgid
(b)
thickened inner cell wall
when the cells are turgid the outer thin walls stretch more than the thick ones causing the two cells to curve away from each other and open the pore
guard cells flaccid
section through a stoma

*Fig. 5.19* Opening and closing of stomata: (a) during the day, (b) at night

guard cells, which are thought to be exchanged for $K^+$ ions from surrounding epidermal cells. The malate ions help to raise the water potential of the guard cells, leading to stomatal opening.

5. SOIL CONDITIONS: If water cannot be absorbed properly, transpiration will be reduced. Absorption of water will be retarded by lack of soil water, cold temperatures, poor aeration and an increase in the concentration of ions in the soil solution.

*Morphological factors affecting transpiration rate*

Plants can be classified as one of three types, depending on water requirements. These are:

1. xerophytes – able to live in very dry places
2. hydrophytes – live in water or wet soil
3. mesophytes – best in habitats with moderate water supply.

Each type of plant has features which make it adapted for growth in particular conditions.

1. *Adaptations in xerophytes*

Xerophytes live in dry conditions and must therefore:

(a) absorb the maximum amount of water;
(b) store water;
(c) reduce water loss (transpiration);
(d) have morphological features to cope with drought.

These four types of adaptation are described in more detail below.

(a) Most xerophytes have extensive root systems. These may be either shallow and wide to make the most of light rainfall, or long and deep to reach underground water supplies.
(b) The stem and sometimes the leaves may contain tissues adapted for water storage (succulents).
(c) There are a number of features which help to reduce water loss:
    (i) Thick waterproof cuticles. The cuticle is also often shiny so that it reflects heat away from the leaf with subsequent reduction in transpiration.
    (ii) Sunken stomata (e.g. some pines, holly). Stomata are sunk into the leaf in pits. Water evaporates from the pore and collects in the pit where it cannot be blown away by air currents. This reduces the diffusion gradient, and hence reduces transpiration.
    (iii) Leaves may have a comparatively small surface area to reduce transpiration (e.g. pine needles). Leaves may even be absent (e.g. in *Opuntia* only the stem photosynthesizes).
    (iv) Rolled leaves (e.g. marram grass). Moist air is trapped inside

the roll which reduces transpiration by decreasing the diffusion gradient. Sometimes tiny hairs are present inside the rolled surface to capture moisture.

(v) High osmotic potential of cell sap. Leaf cells of many xerophytes are capable of holding more water than normal leaves. This reduces evaporation from cell walls into the intercellular air spaces.

(vi) Diurnal closing of stomata. Many xerophytes have stomata closed in the evenings which practically stops transpiration.

(d) Morphological features to cope with drought include:

(i) Reduced cell size. Most xerophytes have small cells, which are less likely to wilt than large cells.

(ii) Resistance to desiccation. Often extensive lignification is present to support the plant if wilting occurs.

(iii) Highly developed vegetative propagation (e.g. prickly pear). This cuts out the need for sexual reproduction which often requires water.

2. *Adaptations in hydrophytes*

Hydrophytes live in water or wet soil and often suffer from water loss because the osmotic potential of the surrounding medium is higher than that in the plant cells. They therefore have adaptations:

(a) to increase water uptake: cells of the root exert a higher osmotic potential than normal roots, enabling them to take in water by osmosis;

(b) for water storage: water-conserving tissues store water to ensure supplies for the plant if the external osmotic potential exceeds that in the cells of the root (e.g. when plants are left submerged in mud at low tides).

3. *Adaptations in mesophytes*

Mesophytes live in areas of adequate rainfall and therefore have no special features for water conservation. They typically have broad, flat leaves with numerous stomata, and no water storage tissues or specially adapted root systems. The rate of transpiration is typically high compared to that of xerophytes and hydrophytes.

*Measuring transpiration*

There are many types of apparatus which measure transpiration. The most common is the potometer.

In potometer experiments the apparatus is set up as shown in Fig. 5.20, ensuring that the following precautions are taken:

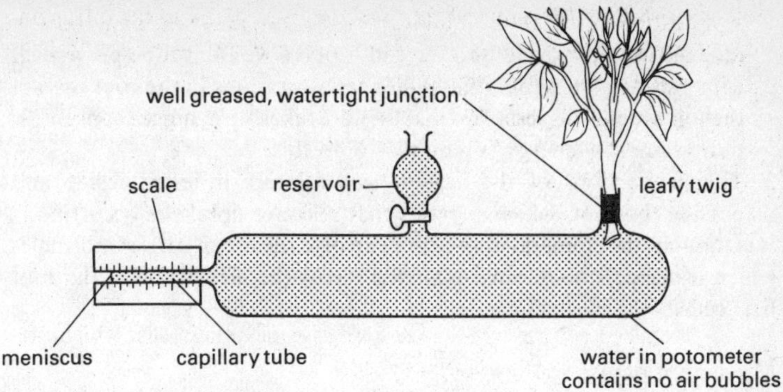
well greased, watertight junction
scale
reservoir
leafy twig
meniscus
capillary tube
water in potometer contains no air bubbles

*Fig. 5.20* A simple potometer

1. The leafy twig is initially cut under water to prevent air entering the xylem vessels and introducing an air lock, which would prevent movement of water. The twig is fastened into the potometer while under water for the same reasons.
2. There must be no air bubbles (which could enter the twig) in the potometer.
3. All openings (e.g. the reservoir tap and twig holder) must be well greased to prevent loss of water by evaporation.

Transpiration is measured by timing movement of the water meniscus over a set distance (e.g. 1 cm). The potometer is placed in different conditions: cold still air, warm still air, cold moving air, warm moving air (hair dryer) and humid air (kettle). The meniscus is returned to its original position between each experiment by adding water from the reservoir.

The major assumption with this apparatus is that water lost at the leaves (transpiration) is equal to water uptake. It is water uptake which directly affects movement of the meniscus.

### *Uptake and transport of mineral salts*

Plants require a number of minerals in order to remain healthy. Mineral ions are usually found in solution in the soil. See p. 449.

#### Uptake of minerals

Like water, minerals enter the plant through the root hairs. However, they do not appear to simply diffuse passively into the root. Uptake of minerals is thought to be an active (energy-requiring) process since:

1. Application of metabolic inhibitors to the root prevents ion uptake: if ions diffused passively into the root uptake would not be prevented.
2. Minerals are often found in higher concentrations in the root than in the soil water. This indicates that they are taken up against a concentration gradient – energy is required to do this.
3. The proportions of the various minerals are different inside and outside the root, which suggests that selective uptake is occurring.

It is thought that mineral uptake may involve the use of carrier molecules which transport the selected minerals across the membrane of the root hair cells.

## Movement across the cortex

Minerals may move across the cortex in two ways (see Fig. 5.21)

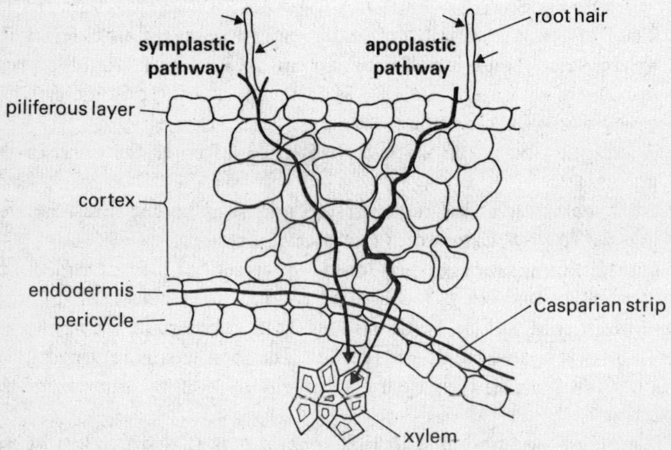
root hair
symplastic pathway
apoplastic pathway
piliferous layer
cortex
endodermis
pericycle
Casparian strip
xylem

*Fig. 5.21* Movement of water and minerals across the root

1. Symplastic pathway. Water passes by osmosis, and minerals by active transport, through the membranes and cytoplasm of the cells in the cortex. This may also include some movement through plasmodesmata.
2. Apoplastic pathway. Water and minerals diffuse through the cell walls and intercellular spaces between cells. When they reach the endodermis they can no longer travel in this manner owing to the Casparian strip. Water is then taken into the endodermal cells by osmosis and the minerals are actively transported into the endodermal cells.

### Movement in the xylem

The Casparian strip prevents leakage of minerals back into the cortex. Experiments using radioactive minerals have shown that they are moved up the xylem in the flow of water. Cells in the leaves and stem may then take minerals from the xylem vessels as they require them.

## *Translocation (transport of sugars)*

Translocation is the movement of food from the site of manufacture (leaves) to either a storage organ (roots, fruits, seeds) or a place of growth (buds, cambium). Food is transported as sucrose in the phloem tissues (Fig. 5.22), and may move up or down the plant.

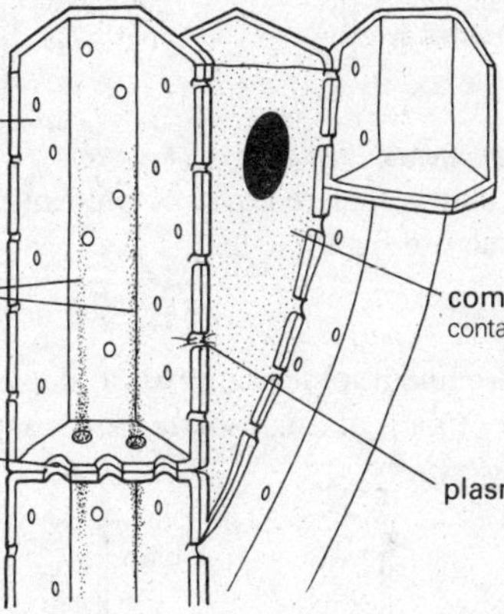
sieve-tube element
transcellular strands
sieve plate
companion cell
containing dense cytoplasm
plasmodesma

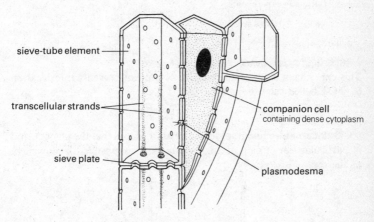

*Fig. 5.22* Structure of phloem

### Evidence that translocation is in the phloem

This evidence is provided by a series of experiments.

1. *Ringing experiments (Fig. 5.23)*

A ring of bark, including the phloem, is stripped from a healthy plant. After several hours the cells above and below the cut are examined. The sugar content above the cut is found to increase, while that below the cut decreases considerably. This indicates that sugar is transported in the phloem.

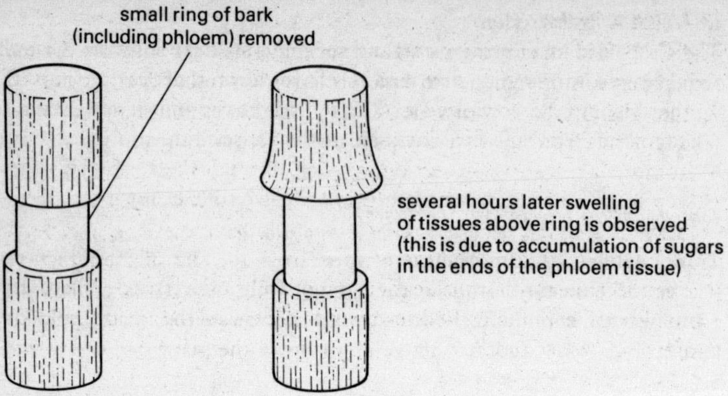
small ring of bark
(including phloem) removed
several hours later swelling
of tissues above ring is observed
(this is due to accumulation of sugars
in the ends of the phloem tissue)

*Fig. 5.23* Ringing experiments

2. *Labelling experiments (see Fig. 5.24)*
This experiment shows that removal of phloem prevents translocation of $^{14}C$-labelled sucrose from the leaf.

3. *Autoradiographic experiments*
$^{14}CO_2$ micro-autoradiographic examination shows that the phloem, and in particular sieve tubes, of angiosperms are responsible for movement of sucrose.

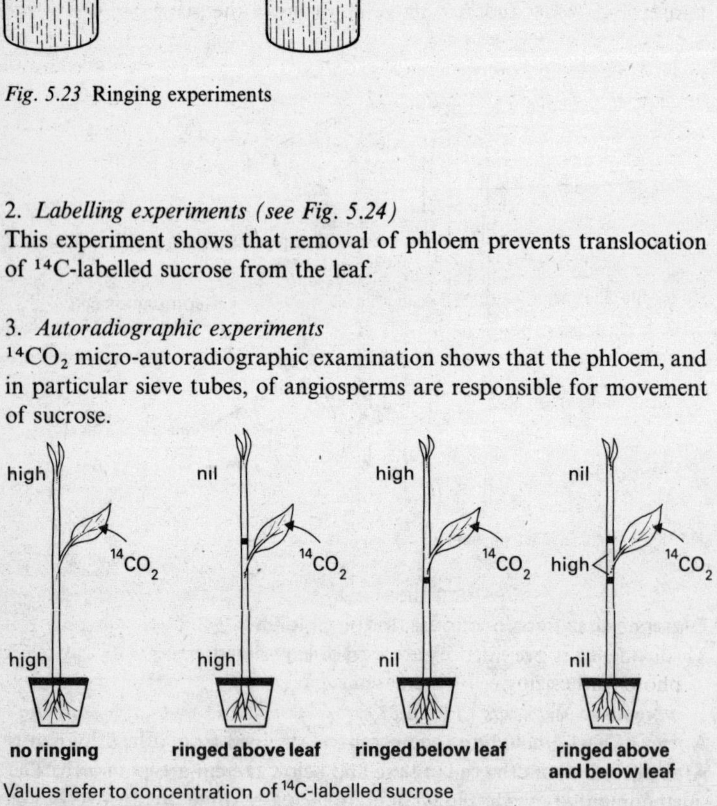
high
high
$^{14}CO_2$
no ringing
nil
high
$^{14}CO_2$
ringed above leaf
high
nil
$^{14}CO_2$
ringed below leaf
nil
high
nil
$^{14}CO_2$
ringed above and below leaf
Values refer to concentration of $^{14}C$-labelled sucrose

*Fig. 5.24* Effect of ringing the phloem on the translocation of $^{14}C$-labelled sucrose from the leaf of a bean plant

4. *Use of aphids*

Aphids feed by piercing stems and sucking out sugar solution. An aphid is allowed to pierce a stem and is left for approximately 2 hours. The aphid is then anaesthetized and its stylet is cut so that it remains in the stem. The stylet acts as a tiny pipe, and sugar solution continues to pour from it. If a transverse section is taken through the stem, the stylet is seen to gain its sugar solution from the sieve-tube elements.

## Mechanism of translocation

The mechanism of translocation is not fully understood. There are a number of hypotheses which attempt to explain the action, and these are:

1. *Mass flow (Münch) (see Fig. 5.25)*

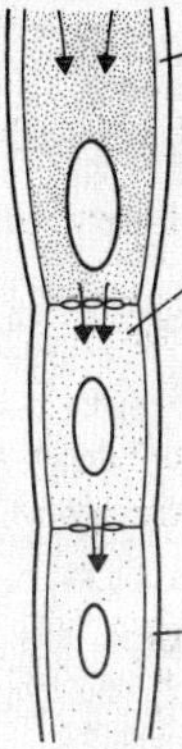
site of sugar production
sieve-tube element containing high concentration of sugar solution
hydrostatic pressure forces sugar solution through sieve plate
low sugar concentration

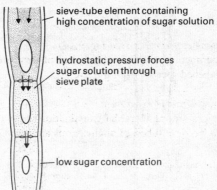

*Fig. 5.25* Mass-flow theory of translocation

This theory assumes that the sugar solution as a whole rather than just the sugar molecules moves. It is suggested that phloem cells near to the site of sugar production are constantly fed quantities of sugar from photosynthesizing cells. Increased sugar concentration in a cell causes an increase in the water potential, so water enters by osmosis and the cell swells. The contents of the cell are thus under pressure. Phloem cells nearer the storage area contain little sugar since all sugar is converted to starch in that area, so sugar solution is forced along the sieve tubes from an area of high concentration (site of production) to an area of low concentration (storage or growth tissue).

However, there are criticisms of this theory:

(a) A huge turgor pressure would be required to force such quantities of sugar solution through the sieve plates. Scientists are not sure whether such pressures exist.

(b) Not a physiological answer – phloem cells have high metabolic activity. Translocation is stopped if oxygen is absent or metabolic inhibitors are present, suggesting some type of active transport.

(c) Sugars may move in both directions and often move from areas of low sugar concentration to areas of high concentration.

2. *Transcellular strand theory (Thaine) (see Fig. 5.26)*
This theory proposes that sugars are transported by a streaming effect along strands of cytoplasm. There are claims to have seen such strands, however, other workers refute this.

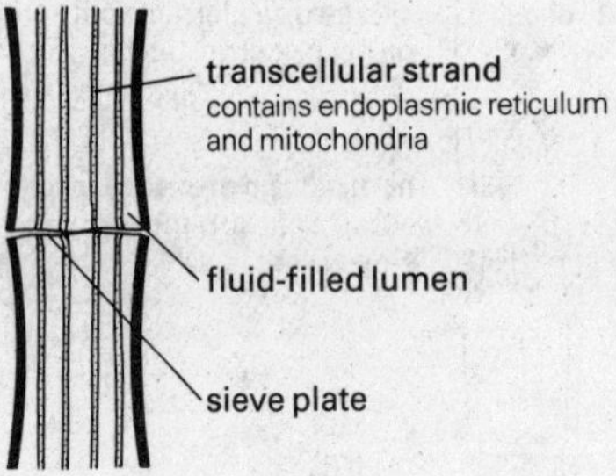
transcellular strand
contains endoplasmic reticulum
and mitochondria
fluid-filled lumen
sieve plate

*Fig. 5.26* Transcellular strand theory of translocation

3. *Electro-osmosis (Spanner)*
This theory suggests that sugar solution flows through sieve plates in response to an electro-osmotic gradient created by potassium ($K^+$) ions. Few workers accept this theory.

4. *Protoplasmic streaming (De Vries) (see Fig. 5.27).*
This theory suggests that a circular movement of protoplasm occurs in the sieve elements. This would account for bidirectional movement in the same sieve element. Sugars are moved across the sieve plate by active transport. However, this theory has been criticized since translocation does not stop under conditions such as cold temperatures which prevent protoplasmic streaming.

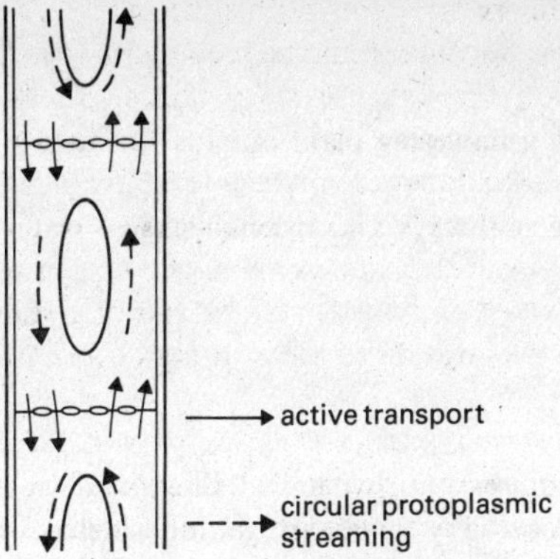
active transport
circular protoplasmic streaming

*Fig. 5.27* Protoplasmic streaming theory of translocation

## *Further reading*

O. V. S. Heath, *Stomata*, Oxford/Carolina Biology Reader No. 37 (Packard, 1975)

R. O. Knight, *The Plant in Relation to Water*, 2nd edition (Heinemann, 1967)

E. S. Martin, M. E. Donkin and R. A. Stevens, *Stomata*, Studies in Biology No. 155 (Arnold, 1983)

M. Richardson, *Translocation in Plants*, Studies in Biology No. 10 (Arnold, 1975)

A. J. Rutter, *Transpiration*, Oxford/Carolina Biology Reader No. 24 (Packard, 1972)

J. Sutcliffe, *Plants and Water*, Studies in Biology No. 14, 2nd edition (Arnold, 1979)

J. Sutcliffe and D. A. Baker, *Plants and Mineral Salts*, Studies in Biology No. 48, 2nd edition (Arnold, 1981)

S. R. J. Woodell, *Xerophytes*, Oxford/Carolina Biology Reader No. 39 (Packard, 1973)

F. B. P. Wooding, *Phloem*, Oxford/Carolina Biology Reader No. 15 (Packard, 1971)

## *Related questions*

**Question:**

(a) Explain how a flowering plant obtains (i) water and (ii) ions.

**(10 marks)**

(b) Describe the pathways and mechanisms of water transport in the plant. **(10 marks)**

[London, June 1981]

**Comments:**

This question requires a fairly detailed, illustrated account of the uptake of water and ions. Try to avoid getting sidetracked and including information which is not really requested, such as adaptations of roots to water and ion uptake.

(a) (i) See p. 188 and Fig. 5.15.

(ii) See p. 195 and Fig. 5.21. Include both the symplastic and the apoplastic pathways.

(b) Uptake of water has already been described in (a); there is therefore no need to repeat it. This part of the question should deal with movement of water up the stem and with transpiration. Do not include adaptations of xylem vessels or leaves to water transport as this is not necessary.

*Suggested plan:*

Diagram of water movement in a bean plant (see Fig. 5.12).
Brief mention of root pressure, see p. 188.
Transport of water up the stem, see p. 189.
Mechanism of water movement in the xylem, see p. 189.
Transpiration, see p. 190.

**Question:**

(a) State *three* factors that *directly* influence the rate of transpiration from the leaves of a flowering plant.

first factor ______________________________

second factor ______________________________

third factor ______________________________

**(3 marks)**

(b) Using the axes below, draw a curve to indicate the changes you would expect in the rate of transpiration of a herbaceous flowering plant over a 24-hour period during hot, dry, sunny weather.

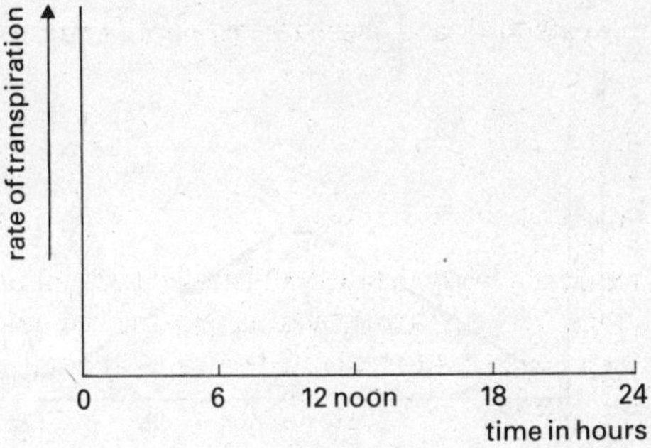
rate of transpiration
0
6
12 noon
18
24
time in hours

**(4 marks)**

(c) Explain the significance of the shape of the curve you have drawn in (b).

______________________________________________

______________________________________________

______________________________________________

______________________________________________

______________________________________________

______________________________________________

**(4 marks)**
**(Total 11 marks)**
[London, July 1982, Paper 1]

**Comments:**

(a) See p. 191. The key word in the question is 'directly'. Factors which affect transpiration indirectly, such as light intensity, are not required.

(b) Transpiration increases gradually with light intensity which reaches a peak at midday. In the dark, transpiration stops altogether. Hence a graph which relates transpiration to light intensity would look like that drawn below.

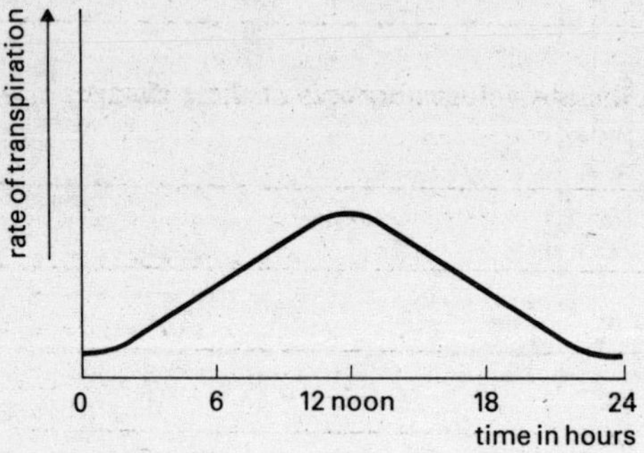
rate of transpiration
0
6
12 noon
18
24
time in hours

(c) The key word is 'significance', i.e. what is important about the curve. The rate of transpiration is proportional to the light intensity and therefore has a peak at midday. After this transpiration declines slowly and it remains low during periods of darkness. Since light intensity affects transpiration, via its effect on the photosynthesis of guard cells and hence the opening and closing of stomata, the curve also represents the rate of photosynthesis.

**Question:**

The graph below shows variation in the diameter of an herbaceous stem growing in natural conditions.

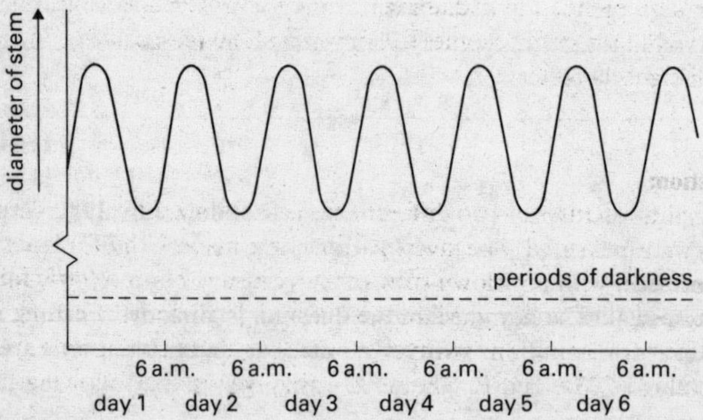
diameter of stem
periods of darkness
6 a.m.
6 a.m.
6 a.m.
6 a.m.
6 a.m.
6 a.m.
day 1
day 2
day 3
day 4
day 5
day 6

(a) Summarize the changes which are occurring in the diameter of the stem.

______________________________________________

______________________________________________

(b) Explain the physiological causes of these changes.

______________________________________________

______________________________________________

______________________________________________

______________________________________________

[AEB, June 1981, Paper 1]

**Comments:**

(a) 'Summarize' is the key word; it means state the important facts concisely.

Since the periods of darkness are drawn in on the graph, it is likely that they are significant. By drawing vertical lines at the beginnings and ends of these periods, it is possible to see what happens at the corresponding areas of the curve. It is then clear that during periods of darkness the stem diameter increases and during periods of light the diameter decreases.

(b) Transpiration has an effect on stem diameter. As transpiration increases during daylight there is a 'sucking effect' on the stem which causes a reduction in diameter. Conversely, when transpiration stops at night the stem becomes full of water and swells, causing an increase in stem diameter.

**Question:**

Transpiration rates of two different species of flowering plants (grown in pots) were measured. The investigations were made with the plants in still air and then with air blown over them by means of an electric fan. The fan was switched on immediately after taking the fourth reading in still air, i.e. at B. Then it was switched to successively higher speeds at hourly intervals at C, D, and E. The results are given in the following table.

| *Time (h)* | *Transpiration rate (g m⁻² h⁻¹)* | |
|---|---|---|
| | *Plant X* | *Plant Y* |
| A. Still air, fan stationary | | |
| 0.25 | 250 | 70 |
| 0.50 | 230 | 60 |
| 0.75 | 260 | 60 |
| 1.00 | 260 | 60 |
| B. Fan switched on | | |
| 1.25 | 340 | 80 |
| 1.50 | 350 | 90 |
| 1.75 | 340 | 90 |
| 2.00 | 350 | 90 |
| C. Fan speed increased | | |
| 2.25 | 420 | 110 |
| 2.50 | 440 | 120 |
| 2.75 | 420 | 110 |
| 3.00 | 430 | 120 |
| D. Fan speed increased | | |
| 3.25 | 550 | 140 |
| 3.50 | 530 | 140 |
| 3.75 | 530 | 140 |
| 4.00 | 480 | 150 |
| E. Fan speed increased | | |
| 4.25 | 430 | 170 |
| 4.50 | 320 | 180 |
| 4.75 | 250 | 180 |
| 5.00 | 160 | 190 |

(a) Using a single set of axes, plot the transpiration rate of each plant to show any changes occurring during the period of the experiment. **(7 marks)**

(b) What does your graph show about the transpiration rate of the two plants during the first three hours of the experiment? **(5 marks)**

(c) Account for the differences in the shapes of the two curves during the final two hours. **(4 marks)**

(d) Suggest an ecological group to which each plant might belong. **(2 marks)**

(e) Describe *four* structural differences which these plants are likely to possess. **(4 marks)**

(f) (i) These results have been obtained by determining changes in mass. What apparatus could be used to compare the rate of water uptake in X and Y?
(ii) Suggest *three* problems which are encountered in setting up this apparatus and explain how they can be overcome. **(8 marks)**

**(Total 30 marks)**

[AEB, June 1980, Paper 2]

**Comments:**

(a) This question tests your ability to plot a graph. The question asks for the graph to be plotted on a single set of axes. This is no problem for the horizontal axis (time in hours), but the vertical axis, which represents the variable characteristic (transpiration rate), needs to cover the smallest and largest values for each plant. A useful scale would probably be 0 to 550.

(b) Note that the question only relates to the first three hours. What happens after then is irrelevant to this answer. It should be obvious from the graph whether the transpiration rate increases in the first three hours or not. The steepness of each curve represents the rate of increase in the transpiration rate over a period of time. It should also be apparent, therefore, if one plant has a higher rate of transpiration than the other. During the three-hour period, the wind speed increases. The steepness of each curve therefore represents the increase in the rate of transpiration with increase in wind speed.

(c) Similar rules for interpretation of the curve apply as in (b) above. However, note that it is the final two hours in question.

(d) See p. 193. Y appears to conserve water, even in the presence of high wind speeds. It is therefore likely to be a xerophyte. X loses water by transpiration more easily and is therefore probably a mesophyte.

(e) Note that the question asks for 'structural features'. You should avoid answers like 'reduce water loss' or 'store water', since these are not structural features. Actual structures like 'water storage tissues' or 'broad leaves' should be given. For clarity of presentation it is a good idea to list the four features in a table.

(f) (i) and (ii) See p. 194. Since there are 8 marks available for this question it is probably a good idea to draw a diagram of the potometer with a brief explanation of how it works.

**Question:**

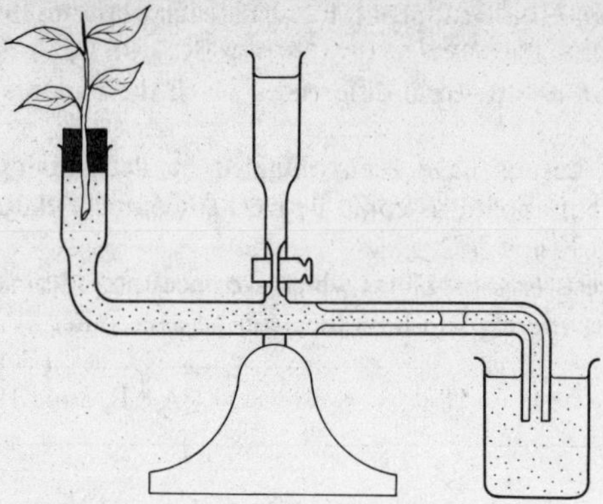

(a) What is the name given to the apparatus illustrated? **(1 mark)**

(b) In measuring the water vapour loss from the leaves using this apparatus, what major assumption has to be made? **(1 mark)**

(c) Why is it advisable to immerse the whole apparatus in water and also to cut the end of the shoot under water before it is placed in the apparatus? **(1 mark)**

(d) What measurements must be made in order to determine the *rate* of transpiration of the shoot? **(2 marks)**

(e) Suggest one method by which you might measure the *rate* at which sap rises up the xylem of a tall forest tree. **(2 marks)**

[Oxford, June 1980, Paper 1A]

**Comments:**

(a) The apparatus is a potometer. There are many variations in the design of potometers and you should not be confused by diagrams of apparatus which are different from those with which you are familiar. All potometers work on the same basic principles.

(b) The rate of transpiration is strictly the volume of water lost in a given period of time. However, the distance moved by the water meniscus is taken to represent the volume of water lost when using a potometer.

(c) See p. 195.

(d) The measurements taken are:

| Time (minutes) | Distance moved by meniscus in the given time (mm) | Distance/time (mm per minute) |
|---|---|---|
| e.g. 5 min. | 10 mm | 2 mm/min. |

(e) A tall forest tree can be fed with radioactive water, and the rate of transpiration measured as the rate of water rises up the tree, detected by a Geiger counter.

**Question:**
The sieve tube is an important cell element in the phloem of flowering plants.

(a) List two structural features characteristic of sieve tubes:

(i) ____________________

(ii) ____________________

**(2 marks)**

(b) Name one other type of cell which occurs in phloem tissue.

____________________

**(1 mark)**

(c) How does this cell differ from a sieve tube?

____________________

**(1 mark)**

(d) Carbohydrates formed in the leaves may be transported to the roots of a plant through the phloem.

Describe one simple experiment which you could perform to demonstrate this.

____________________

____________________

____________________

**(3 marks)**

(e) Although several theories have been advanced to explain the transport of solutes in the phloem there is still general lack of agreement among plant physiologists on how this transport is achieved.

Give *two* reasons for this disagreement.

(i) ____________________

(ii) ____________________

**(2 marks)**

**Comments**

(a), (b) and (c) See Fig. 5.22.

(d) Only a very brief account of the experiment is required since only three lines are given for the answer. The experiment has to show two factors: (i) that carbohydrate is transported from the leaves to the roots, and (ii) that this occurs in the phloem. A very simplified version of the experiment shown in Fig. 5.24 would be adequate. E.g. 'Feed radioactive $CO_2$ to the leaves of a plant. Two days later examine roots and cut section through the stem. Examine for presence of radioactive sucrose in the root and in the phloem tissues of the stem.'

(e) There are many reasons why plant physiologists disagree on the exact method of translocation. However, they can be summarized as (i) difficulty in testing hypotheses on living tissues (translocation needs to be studied in the whole living plant), (ii) different workers appear to have widely differing observations which are often contradictory.

**Question:**

Various processes determine the amount of water held by soil and the water relationships of plants.

(a) State *two* physical processes by which water is retained in soil.

(i) ________________________ (ii) ________________________

(b) State *one* physical process by which water molecules enter roots.

__________________________________________________

(c) Name *three* processes by which water is carried up through the stem of a flowering plant and briefly explain how each operates.

(i) ______________________________________________

______________________________________________

______________________________________________

(ii) ______________________________________________

______________________________________________

______________________________________________

(iii) ______________________________________________

______________________________________________

______________________________________________

(d) Name *two* physical processes which are involved in the removal of water molecules from the mesophyll cells of a leaf into the atmosphere and briefly describe the role of each process.

(i) ______________________________________________

______________________________________________

(ii) ______________________________________________

______________________________________________

**(13 marks)**

**Comments:**

(a) See p. 449.
(b) See p. 188.
(c) See p. 189.
(d) See p. 190.

# 6. Homeostasis

Cells require a steady state of optimum conditions for their correct functioning. Thus the composition of the tissue fluid surrounding every cell must remain within certain critical limits.

The maintenance of these constant internal conditions, despite fluctuations in the external environment, is known as **homeostasis**. Homeostatic mechanisms also occur within cells.

Homeostasis is a dynamic process, as it is continually responding to changes both internal and external to the organism.

The endothermic animals have the most well-developed homeostatic mechanism, involving all the body systems.

The principles of homeostasis are particularly evident in the processes of osmoregulation, temperature regulation and blood sugar regulation (see p. 282).

Many homeostatic processes are controlled by feedback mechanisms in which the response to a stimulus itself affects that stimulus. **Negative feedback** is particularly important in homeostatic regulation. Being self-regulating, it is especially useful for regulating hormones, as in the example given in Fig. 6.1. See also p. 277. **Positive feedback** mechanisms where both stimulus and response are intensified are rare. An example of a positive feedback mechanism is the stimulation of uterus contraction by oxytocin (p. 282).

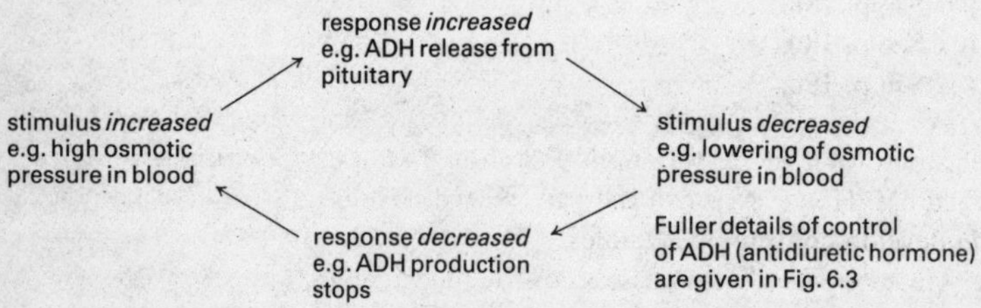

response *increased*
e.g. ADH release from pituitary
stimulus *increased*
e.g. high osmotic pressure in blood
stimulus *decreased*
e.g. lowering of osmotic pressure in blood
response *decreased*
e.g. ADH production stops
Fuller details of control of ADH (antidiuretic hormone) are given in Fig. 6.3


*Fig. 6.1* Negative feedback

## Osmoregulation and excretion

Movement of water in a living system is due to **osmosis**. Osmosis is the diffusion of water from a dilute (**hypotonic**) solution to a more concentrated (**hypertonic**) solution through a semi-permeable membrane. Osmosis will continue until the concentrations of the solutions on either side of the membrane are equal, i.e. until an equilibrium is reached in which the solutions are **isotonic**.

Osmoregulation is the maintenance of an **osmotic balance** within the organism. It is the control of the amount of water and dissolved substances in the cell and in the organism as a whole.

Organisms will have different osmoregulatory problems depending on their environment.

### Problems of osmoregulation in various groups of animals

#### Marine organisms

Primitive organisms were probably marine, and the tissue fluids of animals are essentially dilute saline solutions. However, marine organisms still have osmotic problems because the results of metabolism cause fluctuations in the concentration of their tissue fluids.

In general marine organisms have the problems of (a) losing water by osmosis, and (b) gaining mineral salts by diffusion.

These problems are overcome in different ways as detailed below.

*Invertebrates*

Invertebrates generally have tissue fluid isotonic to sea-water, their surfaces are permeable, they are unable to osmoregulate and their tissues are not tolerant to wide fluctuations in concentration. Invertebrates therefore adjust by equilibrating their body fluids with the external environment.

For example, marine protozoa, such as marine *Amoeba*, have cytoplasm isotonic to sea-water and therefore do not usually form contractile vacuoles. However, when they are placed in dilutions of sea-water they *do* develop contractile vacuoles.

Most marine ciliates possess contractile vacuoles, indicating that their cytoplasm is hypertonic.

*Vertebrates*

The concentration of mineral salts in the cytoplasm of marine vertebrates is much lower than that of sea-water. All vertebrates can osmoregulate.

Both elasmobranchs and teleosts have waterproof skin and scales which help reduce the overall salt and water exchanges. However, they differ in other methods of osmoregulation.

1. MARINE ELASMOBRANCHS (e.g. *Scyliorhinus* (dogfish)) have body fluids *hypotonic* to sea-water. They therefore *lose* water and *gain* salts over the membranes of the gills, buccal cavity and pharynx.

   However, the blood plasma is maintained at a level *slightly hypertonic* to sea-water, owing to the retention of nitrogenous wastes, urea and trimethylamine oxide. These filtered nitrogenous wastes are reabsorbed by specialized regions of the kidney tubules. The tissues of the elasmobranchs can tolerate high levels of nitrogenous waste. These levels would be lethal to other vertebrates, as urea breaks the hydrogen bonds in protein molecules, thus disrupting their enzymatic properties.

   A little water enters by osmosis and excess is removed by a constant flow of hypotonic urine. Any excess salts are eliminated by the rectal gland.

2. MARINE TELEOSTS (e.g. *Gadus* (cod)) have fluids *hypotonic* to sea-water and tend to *lose* water by osmosis and *gain* salts by diffusion over the large surface area of the gills.

   To overcome these problems they:

   (a) Drink sea-water.
   (b) Actively take up salts in the gut wall. This produces localized hypertonic areas and causes water to enter by osmosis. The absorbed excess salts are then actively removed via chloride-secreting cells of the gills.
   (c) Produce small volumes of urine as a result of kidneys which have relatively few, small glomeruli.

### Brackish water organisms

The salt concentration in brackish water is between that of sea-water and fresh-water. It can range from 0.5 to 30 parts per thousand. Estuarine waters are classed as brackish because of salt concentration fluctuations resulting from the interactions of tidal and river flow. Intertidal zones, in contrast, have narrow fluctuations which are mainly due to rainfall on shallow water. Thus the main osmoregulation problems in brackish water are due to the variable osmotic conditions in estuarine waters.

Motile animals can migrate up and down with the tide keeping themselves in favourable osmotic conditions. In general estuarine animals can live in a wide range of osmotic environments (euryhaline) either because of tissue tolerance or because of homeostatic regulation.

Animals in intertidal regions have an additional problem of water loss between tides owing to evaporation from their permeable body surfaces. However, some have adaptations, and the shore crab (*Carcinus maenus*) can survive for up to eight days in air by tolerating a blood concentration increase of 33 per cent.

### Freshwater organisms

Fresh water generally has a salinity of less than 0.5 per cent. The osmoregulation problems of organisms in this environment are:

(a) Water gain by osmosis.
(b) Salt loss by diffusion.

The inhabitants of fresh water may overcome these problems by:

1. Having a low permeability to water.
2. Having the ability to eliminate water efficiently.
3. Conserving salts efficiently.
4. Being able to absorb salts from the environment.

More details of methods of osmoregulation are given below.

#### *Invertebrates*

Protozoa (e.g. *Amoeba*) are permeable to water, have a large surface area to volume ratio, and have a cytoplasm hypertonic to fresh water. The result is a continuous entry of water by osmosis. If this influx of water remained unchecked, it would result in a dilution of the cytoplasm and an increase in cell volume leading to disruption. Therefore, the excess water is eliminated by the contractile vacuole. This is an active process requiring energy.

The rate of contractile vacuole formation is proportional to:

(a) the concentration of the external medium;
(b) the temperature;
(c) the available energy (thus any factors affecting respiration, e.g. metabolic poisons, also affect the rate of contractile vacuole formation).

Salts have to be taken up by active transport to replace those expelled with the water.

#### *Vertebrates*

The body fluids of teleosts (e.g. trout) are hypertonic to fresh water and water enters over the large surface area of the gills, buccal cavity and pharynx. Such organisms overcome this problem by:

1. Possessing well-developed kidneys with many large glomeruli. These produce large volumes of urine.

2. Producing very *dilute* urine by extensive reabsorption of salts from the renal fluid into the bloodstream.
3. Actively taking up salts from the environment via chloride-secreting cells in the gills.

Amphibians (e.g. frogs) are similar to teleosts in their osmoregulation, producing large volumes of dilute urine and actively taking up salts across their skin.

### Terrestrial organisms

The main osmoregulation problem for terrestrial organisms is water loss by evaporation. A balance must be achieved between (a) water lost by evaporation from the skin and respiratory surfaces and also in the urine and faeces, and (b) water gained in the diet and as a by-product of metabolism.

Salts are usually readily available in the diet.

Methods of osmoregulation, with the exception of mammalian kidneys which are dealt with in a separate section, are described below.

#### *Invertebrates*

In insects, the waxy epicuticle is impermeable to water. However, water is lost through the spiracles (p. 85) and from areas such as the joints of the limbs where the cuticle is thin to allow movement.

The Malpighian tubules in insects are the site of osmoregulation. They conserve water by:

(a) Producing a very hypertonic urine.
(b) Forming uric acid, which is a non-toxic, insoluble, nitrogenous waste and can therefore be eliminated without loss of water.

#### *Vertebrates*

1. REPTILES reduce water loss by:
   (a) possessing keratinized skin and scales;
   (b) possessing kidneys with reduced glomeruli;
   (c) producing insoluble uric acid;
   (d) reabsorbing water from the faeces in the cloaca.
2. BIRDS show the same adaptations to reduce water loss as reptiles, but they still have a large water loss via the respiratory surfaces owing to their high metabolic rate and temperature.
3. MAMMALS
   Mammals reduce water loss due to evaporation by:
   (a) possessing a keratinized skin;
   (b) trapping a still layer of saturated air in the body hair.

However, substantial losses still occur owing to:
(a) the need for evaporation to lower the body temperature;
(b) the respiratory ventilation movements.

Mammals found in desert conditions show remarkable adaptations for water conservation. For example, the camel can survive for 60 days on green food and 17 days on dry food. It can do this because:
(a) The hump is a store of subcutaneous fat which can provide metabolic water. The hump allows efficient temperature regulation to occur throughout the rest of the body.
(b) Camels can tolerate a loss of 40 per cent of their body water (20 per cent is fatal to other mammals).
(c) When water is available camels are capable of rapid water intake (as much as 40 litres in 10 minutes).

### *The mammalian kidney*

The mammalian kidneys maintain the normal compositions and volume of the body fluids by performing the following functions:
1. Excretion of metabolic wastes such as urea.
2. Osmoregulation.
3. Maintenance of the ion balance for ions such as $Na^+$, $K^+$, $Ca^{2+}$, $Mg^{2+}$, $H^+$, $Cl^-$, $HCO_3^-$.
4. Maintenance of the pH balance by the selective excretion of $H^+$ and $HCO_3^-$.

The functional unit of the kidney is the **nephron**. A human kidney has in excess of 1 million nephrons, and these filter approximately 120 $cm^3$ blood per minute. Urine is produced as the end-product from the nephron by selective reabsorption from the glomerular filtrate in specialized regions (see Table 6.1).

#### The loop of Henlé

Mammals can conserve water by producing concentrated urine. Their abilities in this area vary, and desert animals such as the kangaroo rat can produce a urine which is ten times more concentrated than the urine of an animal such as the beaver. The kangaroo rat owes this ability to the fact that its kidneys have deep medullas with long loops of Henlé. (In contrast, kidneys of amphibians have no loops of Henlé and these animals are unable to produce a concentrated urine.)

Thus the role of the loop of Henlé (Fig. 6.2) is to produce a concentrated urine by acting as a countercurrent multiplier. The basis of this mechanism is the sodium pump located in the ascending limb of the loop

*Table 6.1.* Summary of activities of the various regions of the nephron and the collecting duct. A nephron consists of a Bowman's capsule, glomerulus, proximal tubule, loop of Henlé and distal tubule

| *Region* | *Role* | *Adaptations* | *Microstructure* |
|---|---|---|---|
| Bowman's capsule (cortex) | Filters the renal blood under high pressure in the knot of capillaries known as the glomerulus (ultra filtration), resulting in glomerular filtrate which contains no plasma proteins or corpuscles. Only 1% of the glomerular filtrate becomes urine. | The visceral wall of the Bowman's capsule consists of podocytes. Thus, essentially, only the basement membrane separates blood from the cavity of the Bowman's capsule. The endothelium of the glomerular capillary has pores which act as a filter. The parietal (outside) wall of the Bowman's capsule is composed of squamous epithelium. | 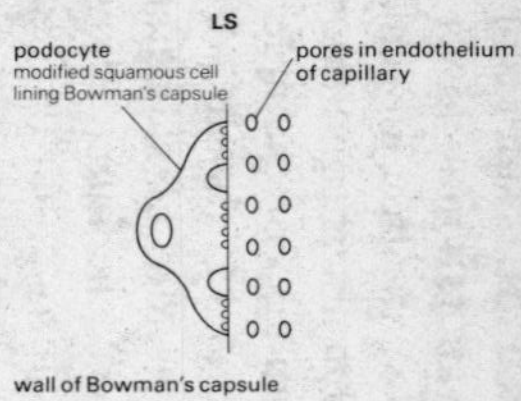 LS<br>podocyte<br>modified squamous cell lining Bowman's capsule<br>pores in endothelium of capillary<br>wall of Bowman's capsule |
| Proximal tubule (cortex but projects into medulla) | Site of reabsorption of 100% glucose, 80% water and 80% salts. | To increase the surface area for reabsorption the proximal tubule is (a) very convoluted, and (b) composed of cells with a brush border. The cells contain many mitochondria to provide energy for the active reabsorption of glucose and mineral salts. | 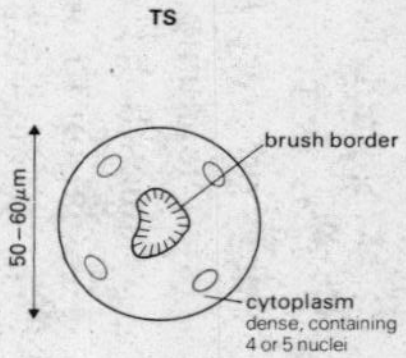 TS<br>50–60μm<br>brush border<br>cytoplasm dense, containing 4 or 5 nuclei |

| | | | |
|---|---|---|---|
| Loop of Henlé (medulla but projects into cortex) | Acts as a countercurrent multiplier (see Fig. 6.2). | The cells are impermeable to water and are not convoluted. Cells contain many mitochondria, to provide energy for the sodium-pump mechanism. | 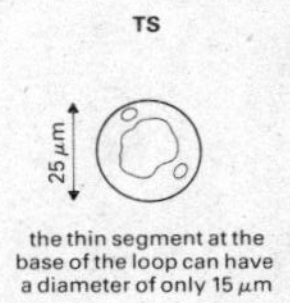 TS 25 μm the thin segment at the base of the loop can have a diameter of only 15 μm |
| Distal tubule (cortex) | Site of reabsorption of water and remaining salts. | This region is shorter than the proximal tubule and cells do not have a brush border as less reabsorption is undertaken. | 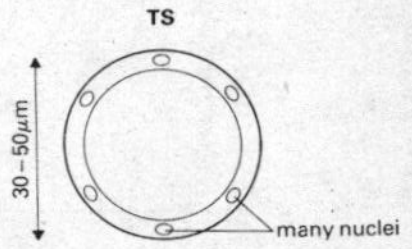 TS 30 – 50μm many nuclei |
| Collecting duct (cortex and medulla) | Reabsorption of water, resulting in the production of a hypertonic urine. The collecting ducts empty urine into the renal pelvis. | It has a large lumen as many nephrons are connected to one collecting duct. | 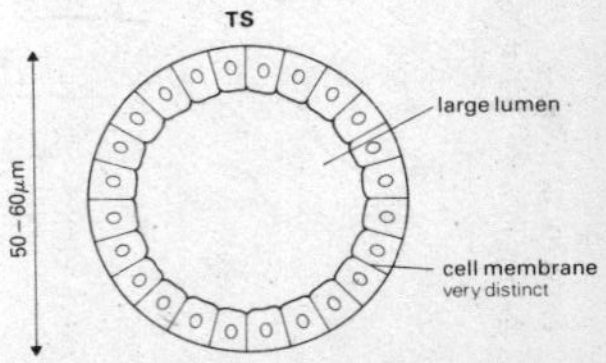 TS 50 – 60μm large lumen cell membrane very distinct |

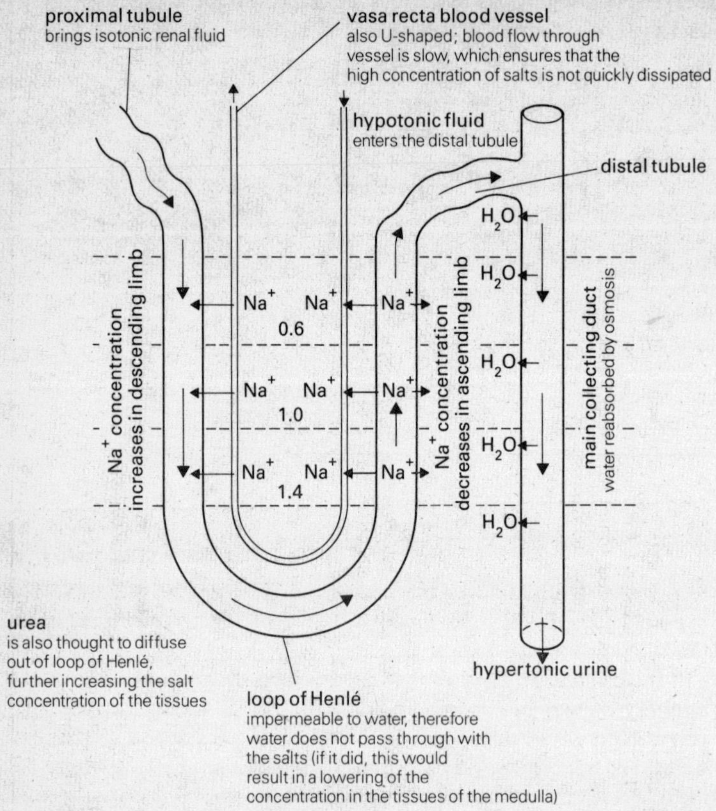
proximal tubule
brings isotonic renal fluid
vasa recta blood vessel
also U-shaped; blood flow through vessel is slow, which ensures that the high concentration of salts is not quickly dissipated
hypotonic fluid
enters the distal tubule
distal tubule
Na+ concentration increases in descending limb
Na+ Na+ Na+
0.6
Na+ Na+ Na+
1.0
Na+ Na+ Na+
1.4
Na+ concentration decreases in ascending limb
H2O
main collecting duct
water reabsorbed by osmosis
urea
is also thought to diffuse out of loop of Henlé, further increasing the salt concentration of the tissues
loop of Henlé
impermeable to water, therefore water does not pass through with the salts (if it did, this would result in a lowering of the concentration in the tissues of the medulla)
hypertonic urine

*Fig. 6.2* Function of the loop of Henlé (figures for $Na^+$ concentration in osmoles per litre)

of Henlé. This pump mechanism actively extrudes sodium ions from the renal fluid in the ascending limb into the descending limb via the tissues of the medulla, raising the concentration in the descending limb slightly above that in the ascending limb (unit effect), and producing a region of high salt concentration in the deep part of the medulla. In this region the thin-walled collecting ducts open into the renal pelvis. The high concentration of sodium in the tissues causes water to be drawn out of the collecting duct by osmosis. This raises the concentration of the fluid in the collecting duct resulting in the production of hypertonic urine. A comparison between concentrations of various substances in the glomerular filtrate and the urine is given in Table 6.2.

*Table 6.2.* Comparison of glomerular filtrate and urine (percentage compositions)

| | *Glomerular filtrate* | *Urine* |
|---|---|---|
| Water | 98 | 96 |
| Urea | 0.03 | 2 |
| Ammonia | 0.0004 | 0.04 |
| Glucose | 0.10 | 0 |
| Protein | 0 | 0 |
| Sodium ions | 0.32 | 0.32 |
| Chloride ions | 0.30 | 0.60 |
| Potassium ions | 0.02 | 0.15 |
| Sulphate ions | 0.003 | 0.18 |

## Control of water reabsorption

The osmotic pressure of the blood is monitored by osmoreceptors in the carotid bodies of the neck. These send information to the brain which then sends information to the neurohypophysis of the pituitary. The hypothalamus can also be directly affected by the osmotic pressure of the blood flowing through it.

If the osmotic pressure of the blood is high the posterior lobe of the pituitary secretes antidiuretic hormone (ADH) which increases the permeability of the distal convoluted tubule and the collecting ducts to water. The opposite will occur if the blood concentration is lowered, i.e. the ADH secretion decreases; less water is reabsorbed, the urine becomes hypotonic and increases in volume, and blood concentration is increased. This process, which is an example of a negative feedback mechanism, is summarized in Fig. 6.3.

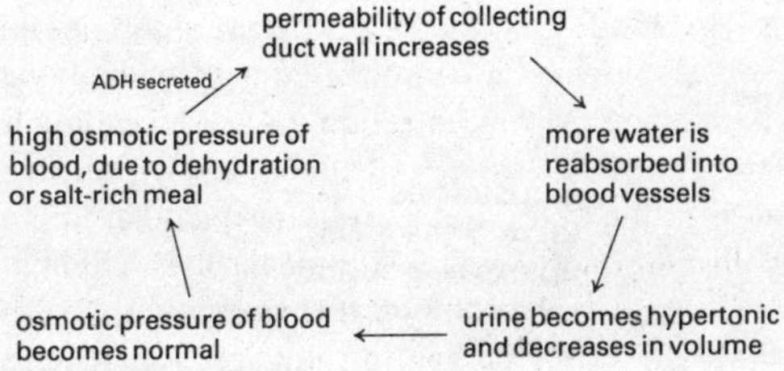
permeability of collecting duct wall increases
ADH secreted
high osmotic pressure of blood, due to dehydration or salt-rich meal
more water is reabsorbed into blood vessels
osmotic pressure of blood becomes normal
urine becomes hypertonic and decreases in volume

*Fig. 6.3* Control of water-absorption: a summary

If ADH is not produced (owing to a faulty pituitary) large volumes of dilute urine are continually lost (diabetes insipidus) leading to very rapid dehydration. Alcohol inhibits ADH production and thus produces similar effects.

### Control of ions

It is important that mammals should control the concentration of ions relative to each other as well as their total quantity, in order to maintain a constant ionic composition of the blood and tissue fluids.

*Regulation of sodium and potassium ions*

The relative concentration of these ions in the human body is controlled by aldosterone. This substance is a steroid, and is produced by the cortex of the adrenal glands. It (a) increases the uptake of sodium ions by the gut, and (b) promotes the reabsorption of sodium ions in the kidney while eliminating potassium ions. Thus the level of sodium ions in the blood rises and the level of potassium ions falls.

The production of aldosterone is regulated by sodium ions as summarized in Fig. 6.4.

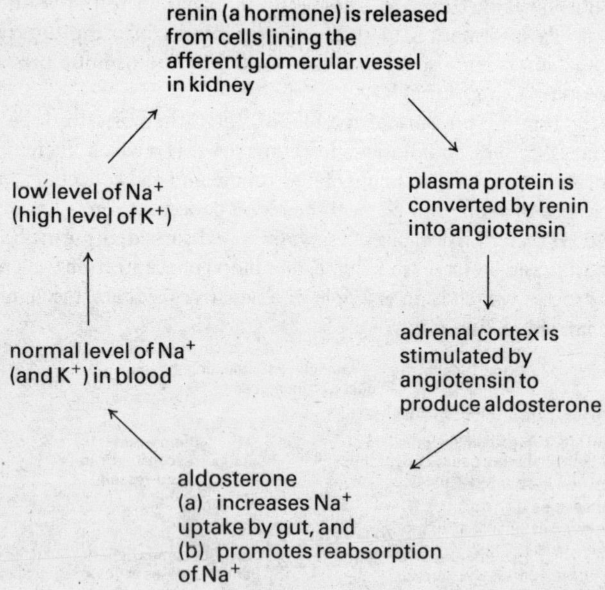
renin (a hormone) is released from cells lining the afferent glomerular vessel in kidney
plasma protein is converted by renin into angiotensin
adrenal cortex is stimulated by angiotensin to produce aldosterone
aldosterone (a) increases Na⁺ uptake by gut, and (b) promotes reabsorption of Na⁺
normal level of Na⁺ (and K⁺) in blood
low level of Na⁺ (high level of K⁺)

*Fig. 6.4* The control of sodium and potassium ions: a summary

Water reabsorption accompanies sodium ion reabsorption in the kidney, thus causing an increase in blood volume and therefore blood pressure, i.e. aldosterone raises blood pressure.

A fall in blood pressure results in the production of aldosterone as the renin-producing cells in the kidney are also stimulated directly by a fall in blood pressure.

*Regulating calcium and phosphate ions*

The concentrations of these ions are controlled by the hormone parathormone, which is secreted by the parathyroids.

The functions of parathormone are:

(a) To increase the uptake of calcium ions by the gut.
(b) To increase the reabsorption of calcium ions by the kidneys.
(c) To effect the release into the bloodsteam of calcium and phosphate ions from the bones.
(d) To increase the elimination of phosphate ions by the kidneys.

Therefore, its overall effect is to raise the concentration of calcium ions relative to phosphate ions.

The concentration of calcium ions in the blood controls parathormone production, as summarized in Fig. 6.5.

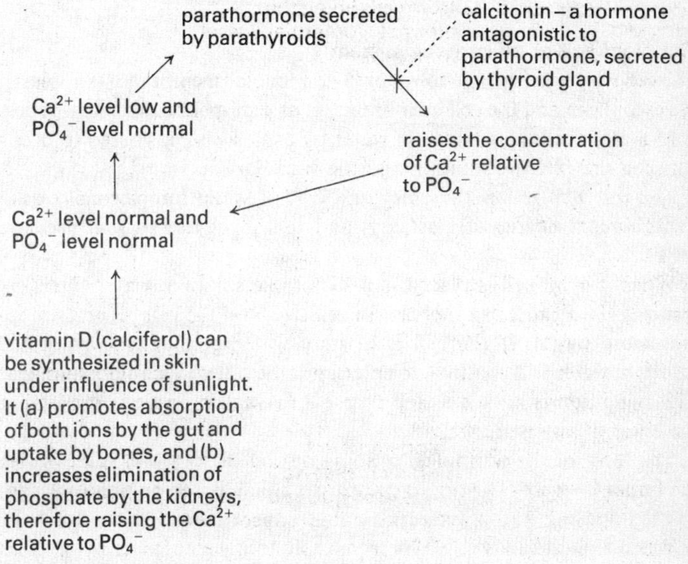
parathormone secreted by parathyroids
calcitonin – a hormone antagonistic to parathormone, secreted by thyroid gland
$Ca^{2+}$ level low and $PO_4^-$ level normal
raises the concentration of $Ca^{2+}$ relative to $PO_4^-$
$Ca^{2+}$ level normal and $PO_4^-$ level normal
vitamin D (calciferol) can be synthesized in skin under influence of sunlight. It (a) promotes absorption of both ions by the gut and uptake by bones, and (b) increases elimination of phosphate by the kidneys, therefore raising the $Ca^{2+}$ relative to $PO_4^-$

*Fig. 6.5* The control of calcium and phosphate ions: a summary

### *Ion regulation in plants*

Ions are *selectively* absorbed from the soil, i.e. there is a preferential uptake of potassium ions from the soil. Ions are also selectively secreted into the xylem from surrounding cells in a process which is thought to involve the pericycle (p. 187).

Most of the regulation occurs at cell level, where each cell absorbs the ions it needs and passes the unwanted ions into the sap vacuole.

### *Excretion in animals*

This is summarized in Table 6.3.

### *Osmoregulation in plants*

Plant cells have a strong cellulose cell wall which prevents the over-expansion and lysis that would be experienced by an animal cell if water entered from a hypotonic solution by osmosis. Thus plant cells do not need to osmoregulate as actively as animal cells and they can tolerate a wider range of water content.

#### The plant cell as an osmotic system

The cell wall is permeable to water. The vacuolar membrane (tonoplast), the cytoplasm and the cell membrane act as semi-permeable membranes.

In a plant cell the passage of water by osmosis is considered to occur between the external solution and the vacuolar sap.

The cell wall resists the entry and exit of water into the cell owing to its limited degree of elasticity, and this gives rise to **wall pressure** (WP).

When a plant cell is placed in a hypotonic solution, water enters by osmosis. This causes an increase in cell size, and the cell becomes more and more **turgid**. If the cell is in pure water or a highly hypotonic solution, water will continue to enter until the cell wall is fully expanded. This condition is known as **full turgor** – the wall pressure is preventing the entry of any more water.

The force of the protoplast pushing out on the cell wall is known as the **turgor pressure**. The turgor pressure is equal, but of an opposite sign, to the opposing wall pressure.

When a plant cell is in a hypertonic solution, water leaves by osmosis and the cell decreases in size, becoming less and less turgid (i.e. more

*Table 6.3.* Summary of common animal excretory products

| *Excretory product* | *Source* | *Animal* |
|---|---|---|
| NITROGENOUS COMPOUNDS | | |
| Ammonia (highly soluble in water; very toxic) | 1. Deamination of amino acids<br>2. Breakdown of urea by urease | Ammonotelic animals (e.g. freshwater teleosts, and some gastropod molluscs and crustaceans) |
| Urea (highly soluble in water; Non-toxic | Deamination of amino acids to form ammonia which is converted to urea in the ornithine cycle | Ureotelic animals<br>1. Aquatic animals (e.g. elasmobranch and teleost fishes, amphibians)<br>2. Mammals |
| Uric acid (highly insoluble) | Thought to be synthesized from ammonia | Uricotelic animals. Terrestrial animals adapted for water conservation (e.g. insects, birds and reptiles) |
| Trimethylamine oxide (fairly soluble) | Methylation of ammonia followed by oxidation | Marine fish (e.g. elasmobranchs such as sharks and dogfish) |
| Creatine | From phosphates in muscle (p. 312) | Some mammals (e.g. man) |
| INORGANIC COMPOUNDS | | |
| Carbon dioxide | 1. Respiratory metabolism | All animals |
| | 2. Breakdown of urea | Animals with urease (e.g. some snails and crustaceans) |
| Water | 1. Osmoregulation | Most animals |
| | 2. Hydrolytic metabolism | Most animals |
| Mineral salts | Osmoregulatory processes | Most animals |

**flaccid**). Provided the external solution is sufficiently hypertonic, water continues to leave until the protoplast shrinks so much that it draws away from the cell wall. This shrinkage is known as **plasmolysis**. The point at which the cytoplasm just begins to pull away from the cell wall is known as **incipient plasmolysis**. At incipient plasmolysis there is no wall pressure.

The water relations in a plant cell can be summarized by the following equation.

$$\underset{\text{Water potential}}{\psi} = \underset{\text{Osmotic potential}}{OP} + \underset{\text{Wall pressure}}{WP}$$

1. Water potential: The force with which water enters a cell used to be called suction pressure (SP) or diffusion pressure deficit (DPD). This implied that the cell sucks water in, and is misleading; thus the term water potential is now used. Water potential is given a negative sign and has the same value as SP or DPD.
2. Osmotic potential: The osmotic potential is a solution's capacity to take in water across a semi-permeable membrane. The osmotic potential is a negative pressure and is given a negative sign.

At plasmolysis $\psi$ = OP. When two solutions have the same OP they are said to be **isotonic**.

At full turgor OP = WP, i.e. the osmotic potential is exactly counterbalanced by the wall pressure, and the cell can take in no more water.

Plants have no specific osmoregulatory organs, but in conditions of extreme water deprivation their structural modifications decrease the rate of water loss.

Plants with modifications for water conservation are known as **xeromorphic** and they can be divided into xerophytes and halophytes (see p. 193).

## Plants modified for water conservation

**Xerophytes** are found where there is a water shortage coupled with high transpiration rates. Their modifications are outlined on p. 193.

**Halophytes** are found in apparently water-rich areas, such as salt-marshes and estuaries, where **physiological drought** conditions exist owing to the high salt content. They have the following adaptations.

1. Their root cells have a higher osmotic potential than other plants, enabling them to take in water by osmosis.
2. They are able to store water in specialized tissues.

Some plants may have active osmoregulatory mechanisms. For example, *Atriplex* (the Australian saltbush) has specialized epidermal bladder cells in which excess salt is actively deposited. These bladder cells then either burst or drop off.

## Plants modified to deal with excess water

Some plants have the problem of excess water, because more water is taken into the plant than can be removed by evaporation. This occurs particularly in tropical rain forests where the humidity is high. Water oozes out of *hydathodes* at the ends of the veins of the leaves in a process known as **guttation**.

Water must continually move in the transpiration stream to supply mineral salts and to aid cooling.

## *Temperature regulation*

The physical processes of heat gain and loss are as follows:

1. RADIATION: Diffusion of heat from a warm object to a cooler one via the air. A man in a room heated to 21 °C can lose up to 60 per cent of his own heat this way.
2. CONDUCTION: Transfer of heat from a warm object to a cool object in contact with each other. For example, a person sitting on a chair in a cold room will lose heat to the chair and floor.
3. CONVECTION: Cooling due to warm air pockets being replaced by cooler air. These air movements speed up cooling by radiation and evaporation.
4. EVAPORATION: The change of a liquid to a vapour is always accompanied by cooling (latent heat of vaporization). A man in a room heated to 21 °C can lose 25 per cent of his own heat by the evaporation of sweat.

### *Temperature regulation in animals*

#### Ectotherms (poikilotherms)

These comprise all animals except mammals and birds. Ectotherms cannot control their internal temperature. Therefore, their body temperature equilibrates with the environmental temperature. They produce little internal heat and have little insulation.

Terrestrial ectotherms use behavioural adaptations to keep their body temperature stable. These include:

1. Burrowing (e.g. desert lizards burrow at night to create a warm atmosphere from their body heat).
2. Being nocturnal and thereby avoiding the heat of the day.
3. Basking in the sun to raise their body temperature by radiation from the sun, convection currents in the air, reflection from nearby surfaces and conduction from rocks, sand, etc. (e.g. snakes and many lizards).

By relying on behavioural means these animals manage to maintain their body temperature at approximately 36 °C.

Aquatic ectotherms do not have the same problems as terrestrial ectotherms as water has a high specific heat capacity, providing a fairly stable environment.

### Endotherms (homoiotherms)

Mammals and birds can maintain their body temperature within certain limits independently of the external environment.

This provides the advantages of:

1. Optimum conditions for enzyme-controlled processes.
2. The ability to survive in a wide range of habitats.

Endotherms produce much internal heat and they are well insulated.

To maintain a constant body temperature the amount of heat lost must equal the amount of heat gained.

The homeostatic control of body temperature is summarized in Fig. 6.6 and methods of control are detailed below.

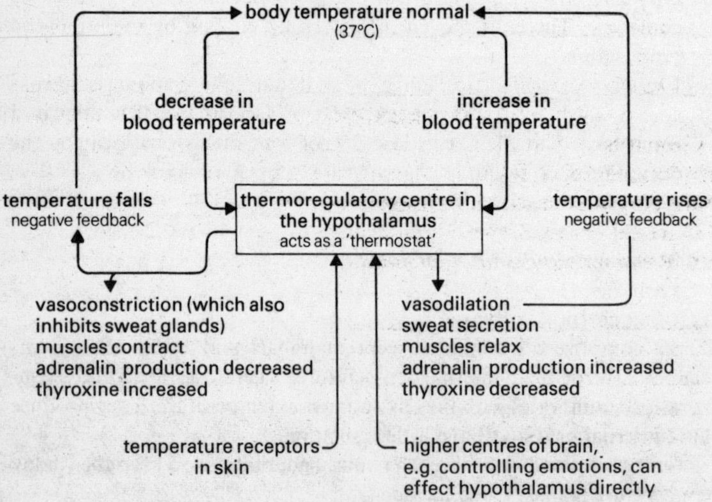
body temperature normal
(37°C)
decrease in
blood temperature
increase in
blood temperature
temperature falls
negative feedback
thermoregulatory centre in
the hypothalamus
acts as a 'thermostat'
temperature rises
negative feedback
vasoconstriction (which also
inhibits sweat glands)
muscles contract
adrenalin production decreased
thyroxine increased
vasodilation
sweat secretion
muscles relax
adrenalin production increased
thyroxine decreased
temperature receptors
in skin
higher centres of brain,
e.g. controlling emotions, can
effect hypothalamus directly

*Fig. 6.6* Homeostatic control of body temperature in man: a summary

*Methods of conserving heat in an endotherm*

1. SUBCUTANEOUS FAT: This is an insulating layer of fat which is very thick in mammals such as the polar bear, seal, whale, etc.
2. RAISING OF HAIR OR FEATHERS: These may be raised by erector pili-muscles in order to provide a thicker insulatory layer of air.

3. VASOCONSTRICTION of the superficial blood vessels in the dermis of the skin. This reduces heat loss by radiation, convection and conduction. Vasoconstriction of the blood vessels supplying the sweat glands stops sweat secretion and prevents loss of heat due to evaporation. Exposed areas such as ears possess **shunt vessels** which operate in prolonged cold conditions, causing blood to bypass the surface of the skin. However, if the cold continues for too long the cells die and frost-bite results.
4. INCREASE IN METABOLIC RATE: This is promoted by hormones from the adrenal cortex and medulla and the thyroid gland (p. 281). The greatest amount of heat is produced by the liver.
   Reflex muscle twitches lead to shivering to generate more heat. There is also a general increase in muscle tone (slight sustained contraction).

*Methods of dissipating heat in an endotherm*

1. LIMITED AND LOCALIZED SUBCUTANEOUS FAT (e.g. localized in hump of camel and neck of buffalo and bison). This allows loss of heat from body surface.
2. HAIR AND FEATHERS LOWERED by the relaxation of the erector pili-muscles, thus reducing insulation.
3. VASODILATION of superficial blood vessels, in order to increase heat loss due to radiation, convection and conduction. The supply of blood to sweat glands is also increased by vasodilation (see below).
4. SWEATING OR PANTING: One litre of sweat removes about 2,424.4 kJ from the human body.

   Man has approximately 2 million sweat glands which are present at birth. The ecrine sweat glands are involved in temperature regulation.

   Sweat is composed of approximately 99 per cent water and 0.1 to 0.4 per cent sodium chloride. It also contains traces of urea, ammonia, lactic acid (the excretory function is secondary to that of temperature control) and traces of a large number of other substances (e.g. urocanic acid which is thought to protect cells from ultraviolet light).

   There are no sweat glands in the dog and cat families except in the pads of the paws. Therefore cats and dogs lose heat by panting, which speeds up evaporation from the lungs and dissipates heat from the pulmonary capillaries.
5. DECREASE IN METABOLIC RATE generates less body heat. Animals are therefore less active in hot conditions.

### *Temperature regulation in plants*

Plants produce much less heat than animals because of their lower metabolic rates. They can be considered as ectotherms as they cannot maintain a constant internal temperature. Plant tissues can tolerate fairly wide fluctuations in temperature, and plants in different geographical regions are adapted to different temperature ranges.

They keep cool by:

1. TRANSPIRATION (see p. 190): However, the maximum effect rarely reduces the temperature by more than 5 °C.
2. WILTING: This decreases the surface area of the leaves exposed to the sun. (Direct sunlight can raise the temperature of leaves up to 80 °C.)
3. Having LOBED LEAVES (e.g. oak leaves lose heat more quickly than less-lobed leaves).
4. STOMATA: These may open fully to increase cooling by transpiration, but there must be a good water supply.

## *Further reading*

R. N. Hardy, *Homeostasis,* Studies in Biology No. 63 (Arnold, 1976)

D. B. Moffat, *The Control of Water Balance by the Kidney,* Oxford/Carolina Biology Reader No. 14, 2nd edition (Packard, 1978)

## *Related questions*

**Question:**

Read through the following account and then write on the lines the most appropriate word or words to complete the account.

An increase in the external temperature of a mammal is detected by ____1____ in the skin. From these, ____2____ are sent along the ____3____ neurones to the ____4____ brain. Increased blood temperature is detected by the ____5____ which is the section of the brain lying just above the pituitary gland. Reactions which cause heat to be lost are initiated. The hair ____6____ muscles ____7____, also the blood flow to the sweat glands is ____8____ so that ____9____ sweat is released. As sweat ____10____ from the skin surface ____11____ heat of vaporization is lost and the skin is cooled. Mammals with a constant body temperature are known as ____12____, while animals which are unable to regulate body temperature by physiological means are known as ____13____.

**(Total 13 marks)**

[London, Jan. 1985, Paper1]

**Comments:**

It is important with this type of question to read the paragraph very carefully in order that the nature of the subject is understood and undue repetition does not occur. Note that the answers may be more than one word long.

This paragraph is concerned with temperature control in a mammal, or more accurately with the responses undergone by a mammal (endotherm) to a rise in environmental temperature. Words 1 to 5 are concerned with the detection of the change in temperature (see Chapter 7).

1 = temperature receptors or thermoreceptors
2 = impulses
3 = sensor (or afferent) neurones (i.e. neurones directing impulses to the central nervous system)
4 = fore
5 = hypothalamus

For words 6 to 13 see pp. 228–230.

**Question:**

The data below show the osmolality (osmotic concentration of fluid) of the glomerular filtrate as it passes down the tubule of the human kidney under conditions of water shortage and water excess.

| | | Osmolality (mOsm/l) | |
|---|---|---|---|
| Region of tubule | Distance along tubule (mm) | when water in short supply | when water available in excess |
| Proximal convoluted tubule | 0 | 300 | 300 |
| | 3 | 301 | 301 |
| | 6 | 300 | 300 |
| | 9 | 302 | 302 |
| | 12 | 300 | 300 |

| Region of tubule | Distance along tubule (mm) | Osmolality (mOsm/l) when water in short supply | Osmolality (mOsm/l) when water available in excess |
|---|---|---|---|
| Loop of Henlé | 15 | 328 | 328 |
| | 18 | 1,000 | 1,000 |
| | 21 | 1,200 | 1,200 |
| | 24 | 800 | 800 |
| | 27 | 180 | 180 |
| | 30 | 100 | 100 |
| Distal convoluted tubule | 33 | 108 | 95 |
| | 36 | 122 | 90 |
| | 39 | 158 | 85 |
| | 42 | 255 | 81 |
| Collecting tubule | 45 | 305 | 77 |
| | 48 | 470 | 73 |
| | 51 | 1,200 | 70 |

(a) Plot (on a single graph) the data to show the changes in concentration as the fluid passes down the tubule. **(7 marks)**
(b) Explain the change in concentration that occurs as the filtrate passes through the loop of Henlé. **(7 marks)**
(c) With reference to the control mechanisms, explain how water is absorbed in the distal tubule and the collecting tubule. **(7 marks)**
(d) The kidneys of African rats, which eat vegetation with a high salt content, and desert rats have much longer loops of Henlé than have laboratory rats.
Explain the significance of this observation. **(4 marks)**

**(Total 25 marks)**

[AEB, Nov. 1980, Paper 2]

**Comments:**

(a) Note that the graph must include the information for both conditions. If using one axis ensure the two lines are clearly distinguished and labelled. Do not forget to give the graph a title.
(b) See Fig. 6.2 and p. 217. Stress that the changes in the filtrate concentration are the same for both conditions. Remember that the function of the loop of Henlé is to concentrate sodium ions in the medulla of

the kidney by actively pumping them out of the ascending limb. The sodium ions accumulate in the descending limb and, because of the flow of the filtrate, a greater concentration accumulates in the U-bend. Thus the first three concentrations (328, 1,000 and 1,200) are found in the descending limb, and the last three concentrations (800, 180 and 100) in the ascending limb owing to the sodium pump mechanism.

Seven marks are available for this section of the question, so the answer should be fairly detailed (i.e. more than one or two sentences are required).

(c) See p. 221. Again the seven marks available require detail of the hormonal mechanism and its direct effect.

(d) Both these animals need to conserve water: this need has to be related to the role of the loop of Henlé.

**Question:**

(a) Define the term homoiothermy **(1 mark)**

The diagram below shows the relationship between resting metabolic rate and ambient (environmental) temperature in a mammal.

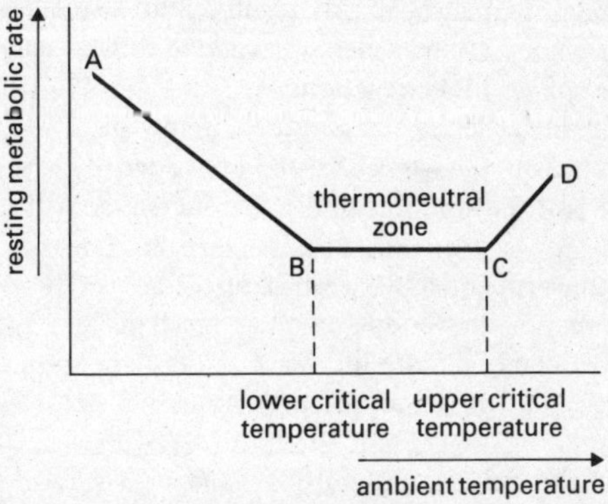

resting metabolic rate
A
D
thermoneutral zone
B
C
lower critical temperature
upper critical temperature
ambient temperature


(b) (i) Explain the significance of the thermoneutral zone between points B and C. **(4 marks)**

(ii) What initial effect does a rise in metabolic rate have upon internal body temperature? **(1 mark)**

(c) Suggest why the resting metabolic rate rises when a mammal is subjected to environmental temperatures between

(i) points B and A;

(ii) points C and D. **(2 marks)**

(d) Describe and explain *one* type of physiological mechanism by which mammals dissipate body heat. **(2 marks)**

(e) Describe *one* type of behavioural mechanism by which a *named* mammal escapes the effects of excessive environmental heat. **(2 marks)**

(f) Explain why a small mammal is liable to lose heat to the environment more rapidly than a larger one. **(2 marks)**

(g) When a mammal is in hibernation, what happens to its
 (i) body temperature;
 (ii) metabolic rate. **(2 marks)**

(h) Why is hibernation a useful mechanism? **(2 marks)**

**(Total 18 marks)**

[London, Jan. 1984, Paper 1]

**Comments:**

(a) See p. 228.

(b) (i) In the thermoneutral zone the resting metabolic rate remains constant despite an increase in the environmental temperature. In this temperature range the mammal's physical processes are maintaining a constant internal temperature and therefore metabolic rate.
(ii) A rise in the metabolic rate results in an immediate increase in the internal body temperature. This is due to heat energy being the by-product of catabolic reactions.

(c) (i) A is the lower lethal temperature. Below the lower critical temperature (B), physical mechanisms are aided by chemical means, with the result that the metabolic rate increases as the temperature falls.
(ii) D is the upper lethal temperature. Above the upper critical temperature (C), the body's cooling mechanisms fail, and consequently the metabolic rate increases as the temperature rises.

(d) See p. 229. Note that the question states physiological means *not* behavioural.

(e) Note that the behavioural mechanisms in a *named mammal* are required. Examples could include burrowing by mammals such as the kangaroo rat, or man moving into shade or removing excess layers of clothing.

(f) A small mammal has a larger surface area to volume ratio than a larger mammal. It can therefore lose heat over a relatively larger surface by the processes outlined on p. 229.

(g) (i) The body temperature falls, and is generally maintained at a lower point.

(ii) The metabolic rate falls to the minimum required for maintaining life.

(h) Hibernation takes place when the environmental temperature is low and food is scarce. When animals hibernate they essentially enter a deep sleep. The lowering of the metabolic rate that occurs is one way of conserving energy and therefore food reserves. Hibernation is particularly useful in small mammals as they have to have a plentiful food supply to sustain their very high metabolic rates. The high metabolic rate is necessary to generate the heat required to maintain their body temperature as they lose heat rapidly.

**Question:**

Discs were cut from two areas of an old, sprouting potato tuber (see diagram).

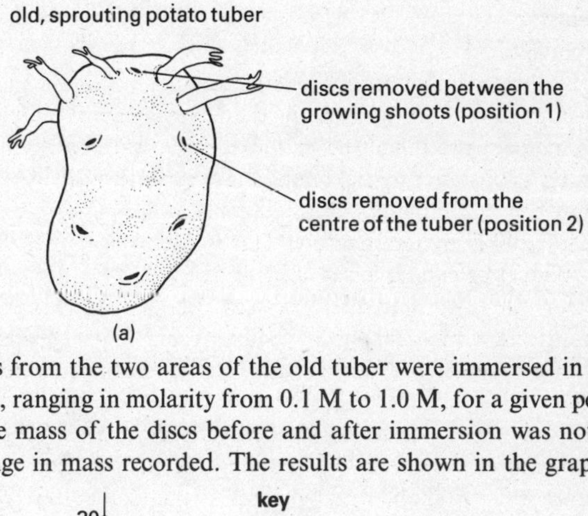
old, sprouting potato tuber
discs removed between the growing shoots (position 1)
discs removed from the centre of the tuber (position 2)

(a)

The discs from the two areas of the old tuber were immersed in sucrose solutions, ranging in molarity from 0.1 M to 1.0 M, for a given period of time. The mass of the discs before and after immersion was noted and any change in mass recorded. The results are shown in the graph.

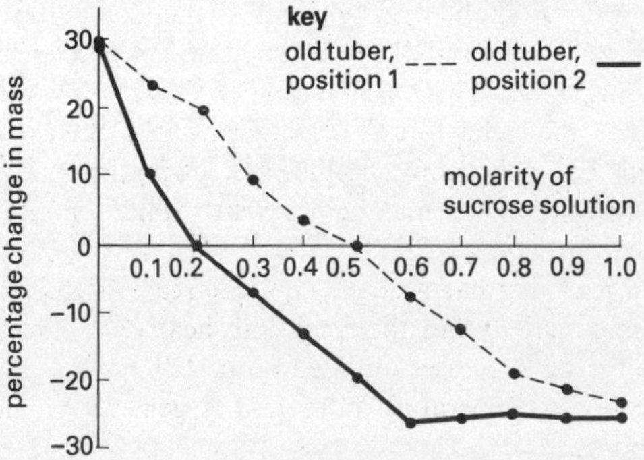
key
old tuber, position 1
old tuber, position 2
percentage change in mass
30
20
10
0
−10
−20
−30
0.1 0.2 0.3 0.4 0.5 0.6 0.7 0.8 0.9 1.0
molarity of sucrose solution

(b)

(a) (i) What is meant by a '1.0 M solution of sucrose'?
(ii) What precautions should be taken when weighing the discs before and after immersion.
(iii) When discs from position 1 were immersed in 0.5 M sucrose solution there was no change in the mass of the discs. Give a reason for this observation.

(b) (i) Give an explanation for the differences in water potential between the two sets of discs.
(ii) How would you experimentally support your explanation?

[in the style of JMB]

**Comments:**

This question is based on an investigation into the water potential of potato tubers.

(a) (i) A 1.0 M solution of sucrose is equivalent to 1.0 mole of sucrose made up to 1.0 litre in a volumetric flask using distilled water. 1.0 mole of sucrose = 342 g sucrose.
(ii) As a change in mass is being used as the criterion for determining the water potential of potato tubers, only the mass of the potato discs should be obtained. Thus blotting of the discs with filter paper, or equivalent, should be carried out.
(iii) The important point here is to stress that there was no *net* loss or gain of water by the cells of the tuber as the water potential of the tissue of the potato tuber and the water potential of the external solution are equal. Thus the water potential of 0.5 M sucrose solution is equal to the water potential of the tuber tissue.

(b) (i) The water potential is higher (more negative) in the discs from position 1 near the growing shoots, i.e. there is a greater concentration of solutes here. This is due to the immobilization of insoluble storage compounds to soluble products required to provide energy and new cell material for growing shoots. The tissue from position 2 will have a high concentration of insoluble storage material, principally starch, and therefore has a lower water potential (i.e. is less negative). Remember water potential has a negative value.
(ii) Testing with quantitative Benedict's solution (Table 2.7) would give an indication of the relative concentrations of reducing sugars (which are soluble) in the two areas. However this does not take into account the relatively small amount of soluble non-reducing sugars, mineral salts, etc.

# 7. Co-ordination

Co-ordination is the ability of living organisms to be aware of, and respond to, changes in the environment. Complex, multicellular organisms must also possess a mechanism for controlling and co-ordinating the various bodily activities. Two systems are concerned with this: the **nervous system**, which controls rapid events, and the **endocrine** (hormone) system, which controls longer-lasting events.

## *The nervous system*

### *Nerve tissues*

Nerve tissue is composed of nerve cells (neurones), and there are three types (see Fig. 7.1):

1. SENSORY NEURONES (afferent neurones): Sensory neurones carry information from the sense organs to the brain and spinal cord. Impulses pass from cells in the sense organs, along a long thread of cytoplasm called a **dendron** to the cell body of the neurone, and from the cell body to the central nervous system (CNS) along a cytoplasmic thread called the **axon**.
2. MOTOR NEURONES (efferent neurones): These carry information from the CNS to the muscles and glands (the effectors). Impulses pass from the CNS to the cell body of the neurone along short threads of cytoplasm called **dendrites**, and from the cell body via a long cytoplasmic thread, the **axon**, to a muscle or gland.
3. INTERMEDIATE NEURONES (multipolar neurones): Intermediate neurones pass information from sensory neurones either to another intermediate neurone or to a motor neurone. They are abundant in the brain and spinal cord.

### Nerve fibres

These are the axons and dendrons surrounded by fatty protective sheaths. The myelin sheaths are formed by growth of Schwann calls (see Fig. 7.2); they provide electrical insulation and speed up the transmission of impulses. Speed of transmission also increases with increased axon diameter. In large animals axons may be over a metre in length.

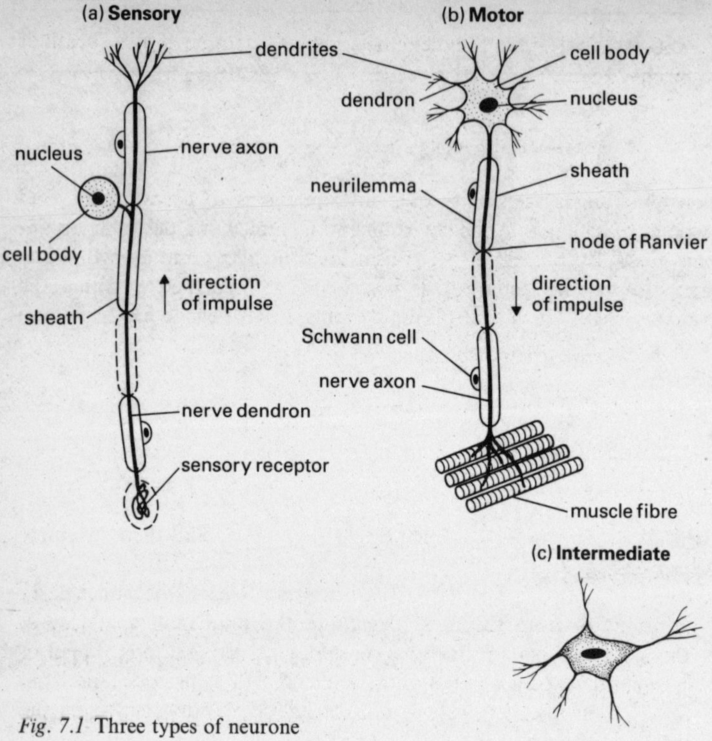
(a) **Sensory**
dendrites
nucleus
nerve axon
cell body
direction of impulse
sheath
nerve dendron
sensory receptor
(b) **Motor**
cell body
dendron
nucleus
sheath
neurilemma
node of Ranvier
direction of impulse
Schwann cell
nerve axon
muscle fibre
(c) **Intermediate**

*Fig. 7.1* Three types of neurone

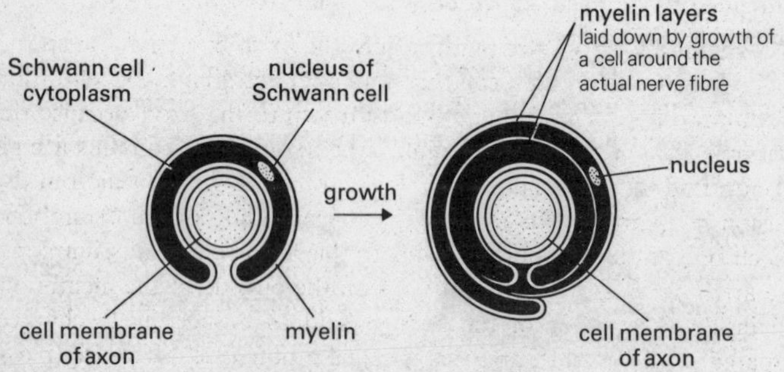
Schwann cell cytoplasm
nucleus of Schwann cell
growth
cell membrane of axon
myelin
myelin layers
laid down by growth of a cell around the actual nerve fibre
nucleus
cell membrane of axon

*Fig. 7.2* Growth of Schwann cell and associated myelin layers around axon

A **nerve** (Fig. 7.3) is a bundle of nerve fibres surrounded by a sheath of connective tissue.

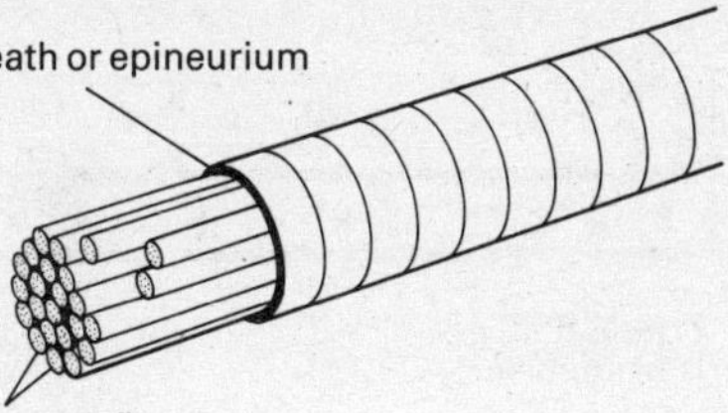
nerve sheath or epineurium
bundle of nerve fibres
axons and dendrons

*Fig. 7.3* Structure of a nerve

## *Nerve impulses*

Nerve impulses are electrical in nature. The electric current in an axon or dendron consists of a stream of positively charged sodium ions. (This is unlike electric current in a wire which is a stream of electrons.)

The passage of an impulse down an axon depends on the following properties of an axon:

1. The membrane around the axon is impermeable to sodium ($Na^+$) ions.
2. $Na^+$ ions are pumped out of the axon by active transport – a process involving large amounts of ATP.
3. Potassium ($K^+$) ions are pumped into the axon by active transport.

The fluid surrounding the axon therefore contains a high concentration of sodium ions which are unable to diffuse into the axon because the membrane is impermeable to sodium. The axon, itself, contains a high concentration of potassium ($K^+$) ions, some of which leak out by diffusion in an attempt to equalize the concentration of potassium ions on each side of the membrane. Owing to this leakage of potassium ions, there are more positively charged ions on the outside of the membrane than inside. The inside of the axon is said to be negatively charged compared to the outside, and this is called a potential difference (p.d.). When no impulse is passing down the nerve, this potential difference measures − 60 millivolts and is called the **resting potential** (see Fig. 7.4).

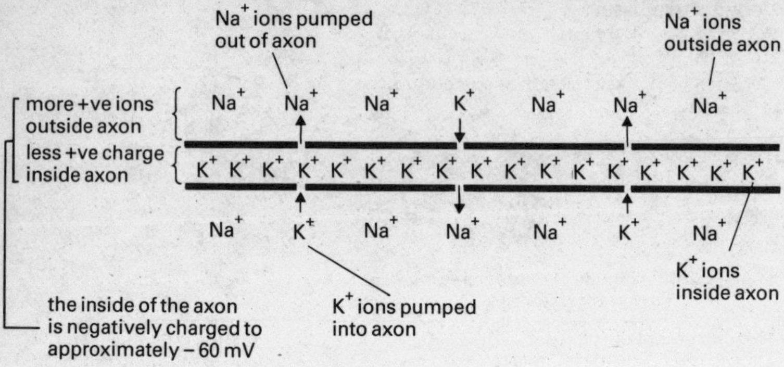
Na⁺ ions pumped out of axon
Na⁺ ions outside axon
more +ve ions outside axon
less +ve charge inside axon
Na⁺ Na⁺ Na⁺ K⁺ Na⁺ Na⁺ Na⁺
K⁺ K⁺ K⁺ K⁺ K⁺ K⁺ K⁺ K⁺ K⁺ K⁺ K⁺ K⁺ K⁺ K⁺ K⁺ K⁺ K⁺
Na⁺ K⁺ Na⁺ Na⁺ Na⁺ K⁺ Na⁺
K⁺ ions inside axon
the inside of the axon is negatively charged to approximately – 60 mV
K⁺ ions pumped into axon

*Fig. 7.4* An axon in its resting stage

### Generation of a nerve impulse

1. At the tip of the axon, a stimulus is given by making a tiny part of the membrane permeable to sodium ions.
2. The sodium ions rush into the axon by diffusion until the concentration of positive ions on each side of the membrane is equal. At this point, the p.d. between the outside and inside of the axon is zero (i.e. the membrane is depolarized).
3. Sodium ions may carry on entering until the inside becomes more positively charged than the outside. This sudden alteration in the distribution of charge (and therefore p.d.) is called an **action potential** (see Fig. 7.5).
4. The action potential lasts for about 120 milliseconds, and after that the membrane regains impermeability to sodium ions. Sodium ions are pumped out again, and the resting potential is restored.

### Transmission of a nerve impulse down the axon

An impulse passes down the axon as a travelling action potential.

1. As a result of the initial action potential, the inside of the axon becomes positively charged by the influx of sodium ions at that point.
2. The active area contains a high concentration of sodium ions which are attracted to the negatively charged area adjacent to it, so there is a flow of sodium ions down the axon.
3. The flow of sodium ions reduces the p.d. across the adjacent membrane (i.e. depolarizes it by reducing the difference in charge), thus

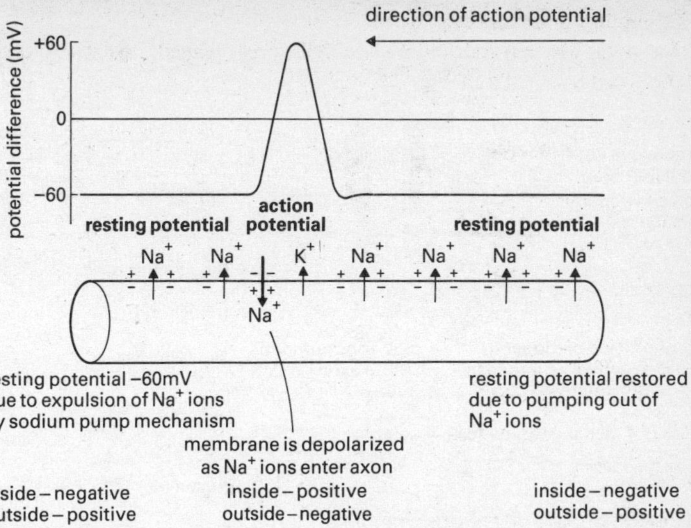

direction of action potential
potential difference (mV)
+60
0
−60
resting potential
action potential
resting potential
Na⁺ Na⁺ K⁺ Na⁺ Na⁺ Na⁺ Na⁺
Na⁺
resting potential −60mV due to expulsion of Na⁺ ions by sodium pump mechanism
membrane is depolarized as Na⁺ ions enter axon
resting potential restored due to pumping out of Na⁺ ions
inside – negative outside – positive
inside – positive outside – negative
inside – negative outside – positive


*Fig. 7.5* Passage of an action potential down the axon

facilitating the passage of the action potential along the axon. In this way, the impulse travels the length of the axon as a chain reaction, until it reaches its destination.

In vertebrates the myelin sheath increases conduction velocity. When an action potential arrives at one node of Ranvier (a point where myelin sheath is absent), an electric current is set up between this node and an adjacent node, and this generates an action potential at the second node. This effect is virtually instantaneous, so that the action potential appears to jump from one node to the next. This type of conduction can lead to velocities of about 100 m per second in some vertebrate axons.

### Characteristics of nerve impulses

(a) Action potentials are all-or-nothing responses – either they occur or they do not. There is no difference in their size, since this depends on the number of sodium and potassium ions, and these do not vary.

(b) The frequency of action potentials can alter with the intensity of the original signal. Since there has to be a refractory (resting) period between each impulse, there can be no more than 1,000 action potentials per second.

## Synaptic transmission

The point where two or more nerve cells meet is called a **synapse** and has the structure shown in Fig. 7.6.

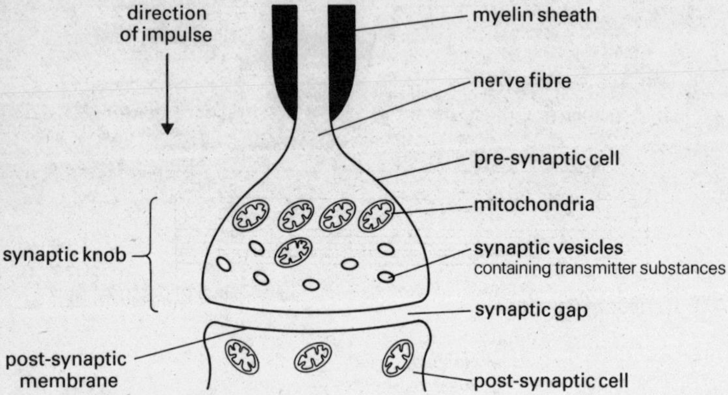
direction of impulse
myelin sheath
nerve fibre
pre-synaptic cell
mitochondria
synaptic knob
synaptic vesicles
containing transmitter substances
synaptic gap
post-synaptic membrane
post-synaptic cell

*Fig. 7.6* Synapse between two neurones

The nerve impulse can only pass across the synapse in one direction, and does so by chemical means as follows:

1. A swelling at the end of the axon, the **synaptic knob**, contains a number of small vesicles (only visible under an electron microscope). These vesicles contain **transmitter substances**, e.g. acetyl choline, adrenaline, noradrenaline or serotonin. On arrival of the nerve impulse, the vesicles release their contents into the synaptic gap and the transmitter substance passes across the gap by diffusion.
2. The transmitter substances combine with receptor sites on the swelling of the post-synaptic cell. This causes a change in membrane permeability, and the nerve impulse passes down the next cell as described previously.
3. When the impulse has passed across the synapse the transmitter substance is either destroyed by enzymes (e.g. the enzyme cholinesterase destroys acetyl choline) or is recaptured by the pre-synaptic cell to be re-used (e.g. noradrenaline).

## Neuro-muscular junctions

Eventually the impulse reaches its destination, usually a muscle. To make the muscle contract, the impulse must pass across a junction between the end of the motor axon and a membrane called the sarcolemma which surrounds the muscle fibres. (See Fig. 7.7.)

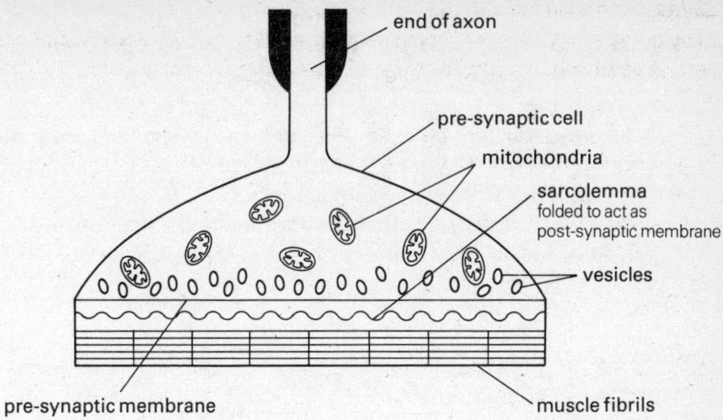
end of axon
pre-synaptic cell
mitochondria
sarcolemma
folded to act as
post-synaptic membrane
vesicles
pre-synaptic membrane
muscle fibrils

*Fig. 7.7 A neuro-muscular junction*

1. Arrival of an impulse at a synaptic knob causes release of a transmitter substance.
2. The transmitter diffuses across the gap to the muscle fibre membrane where it affects the permeability of the sarcolemma to ions, and sets off an action potential down the muscle fibre.
3. This causes the endoplasmic reticulum (in muscle called the sarcoplasmic reticulum) in the muscle fibres to release calcium ions, and the interaction of actin with myosin which converts ATP to ADP.
4. As a result, the muscle fibres shorten and the muscle contracts.

Interference with the transmission of nerve impulses

Some anaesthetics work by decreasing the permeability of the axon membranes to the sodium ions, with the result that impulses from pain receptors cannot reach the brain.

Nerve gases act by inhibiting cholinesterase, and the continued presence of acetyl choline in the synapse then causes repeated nerve impulses or spasms and can eventually lead to death. Chemicals like strychnine and eserine act in a similar manner.

### *Parts of the nervous system*

The nervous system has two main parts: the **central nervous system** (CNS), which comprises the brain and spinal cord, and the **peripheral nervous system**, which includes all the nerves outside the CNS. These include the sensory nerves, which take information from the sense organs (receptors) to the CNS, and the motor nerves, which take messages from the CNS to the muscles and glands (effectors). There are two types of peripheral nerves:

1. Spinal nerves, which originate in the spine, each containing a dorsal and ventral root into the spine. They are mixed nerves, i.e. one nerve may contain both sensory and motor fibres.
2. Cranial nerves, which originate in the head and neck. Some are mixed nerves; some only contain sensory or motor fibres.

*Table 7.1.* Comparison between the sympathetic and the parasympathetic systems

| *Sympathetic* | *Parasympathetic* |
|---|---|
| Originates in the thoracic and lumbar areas of the spinal cord | Originates from the vagus nerve, which in turn originates in the medulla of the brain. Has branches going to all major organs of the body. Also includes the cranial nerves and nerves originating in the sacral area of the spinal cord. |
| Points of synapse are in ganglia near the spinal cord called the sympathetic chain and the coeliac ganglion. Hence, pre-synaptic fibres are short and post-synaptic fibres are long | Points of synapse are in or near the target organ. Hence, pre-synaptic fibres are long and post-synaptic fibres short |
| Post-synaptic nerve endings release adrenaline or noradrenaline | Post-synaptic nerve endings release acetyl choline |
| Has the same effects as the hormone adrenaline, i.e. causes muscle contraction and mobilizes the body's resources in times of stress or danger | Has opposite effects to adrenalin, i.e. causes muscle relaxation, and conserves and stores the body's resources |
| The system acts diffusely, i.e. has a more general effect | More capable of independent activity in each of its parts |
| Some areas have sympathetic connections only (e.g. skin, liver, spleen, visceral arteries and adrenal medulla) | All other areas have both parasympathetic and sympathetic connections |

### The peripheral nervous system

There are two parts to the peripheral nervous system:

1. The **somatic nervous system**, which controls conscious actions including reflex actions. It has myelinated nerve fibres.
2. The **autonomic nervous system**, which controls unconscious or involuntary actions (e.g. heartbeat, breathing, peristalsis, secretion of glands). The nerve fibres may be unmyelinated. The autonomic system has two main divisions, the **sympathetic** and **parasympathetic**. These are anatomically distinct, and each system opposes the other in its function. Tables 7.1 and 7.2 compare the structures and functions of the sympathetic and the parasympathetic systems, and they are shown diagrammatically in Fig. 7.8.

### The central nervous system (CNS)

*The brain*

This is the enlarged and specialized front part of the spinal cord. Throughout evolution, the brain has become larger and more complex, and many animals have relatively simple brains compared to the human brain, which is very specialized.

The brain has two kinds of tissues: **white matter**, which is the myelinated nerve fibres, and **grey matter**, which includes the nerve cell bodies and the unmyelinated nerve fibres. There are also **glial cells** which support and nourish the neurones and affect electrical potentials by altering ionic balance.

A *simple brain* is composed of three sensory areas and two motor areas (see Fig. 7.9).

*Table 7.2.* Functions of the autonomic nervous system

| *Sympathetic* | *Parasympathetic* |
|---|---|
| Prepares body for action (causes adrenal medulla to secrete adrenaline) | Prepares body for relaxation |
| Increases heartbeat | Slows heartbeat |
| Dilates arteries of skeletal muscles | Dilates arteries in gut |
| Dilates pupil | Contracts pupil |
| Contracts bladder and anal sphincters | Relaxes bladder and anal sphincters |
| Increases sweating | Increases production of saliva and tears |
| Slows peristalsis | Increases peristalsis |
| Dilates bronchioles | Constricts bronchioles |
| Makes hairs stand on end | – |

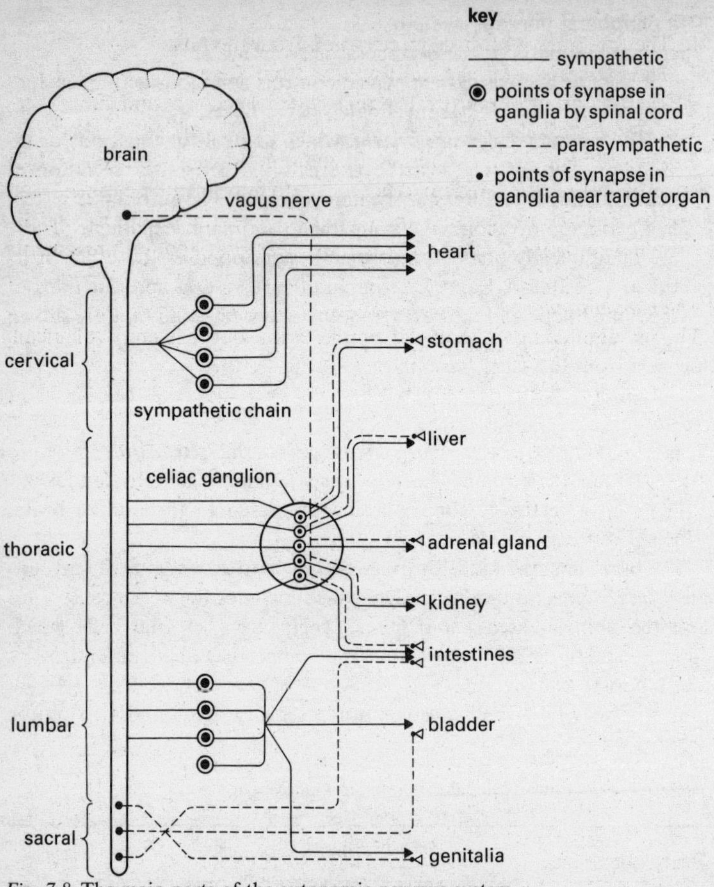
key
sympathetic
points of synapse in ganglia by spinal cord
parasympathetic
points of synapse in ganglia near target organ
brain
vagus nerve
heart
cervical
sympathetic chain
stomach
liver
celiac ganglion
thoracic
adrenal gland
kidney
intestines
lumbar
bladder
sacral
genitalia

*Fig. 7.8* The main parts of the autonomic nervous system

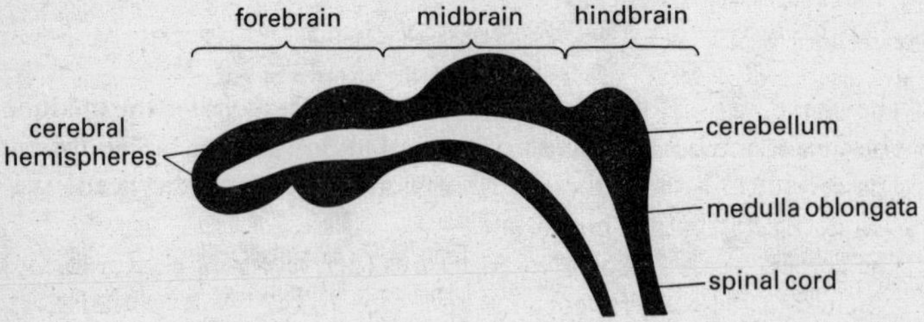
forebrain
midbrain
hindbrain
cerebral hemispheres
cerebellum
medulla oblongata
spinal cord

*Fig. 7.9 The simple brain*

The sensory areas are:

1. The forebrain – receives information from the nose.
2. The midbrain – receives information from the eyes.
3. The hindbrain – receives information from the ears and sk

The motor areas are:

1. The cerebellum – a swelling in the hindbrain which controls and co-ordinates muscles, thus making accurate movements possible.
2. The medulla oblongata – the region between the hindbrain and the spinal cord which controls breathing, heartbeat and gut movements.

*The human brain*

This is more complex than the simple brain, but it is embryologically derived from the same basic parts (see Fig. 7.10).

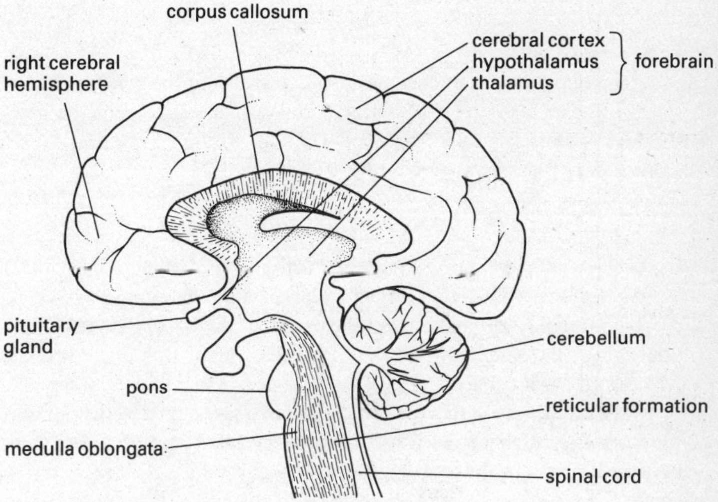
corpus callosum
cerebral cortex
hypothalamus
thalamus
forebrain
right cerebral hemisphere
pituitary gland
cerebellum
pons
reticular formation
medulla oblongata
spinal cord

*Fig. 7.10* LS through the human brain

1. The brainstem – at the top of the spinal cord. It includes the medulla oblongata, the pons (derived from the hindbrain) and the midbrain.
2. The cerebellum – a bulbous structure at the back of the head. It is also derived from the hindbrain.
3. The cerebrum and associated structures (derived from the forebrain) – including the cerebral cortex, the thalamus and the hypothalamus. The cerebrum is divided into two large cerebral hemispheres which

envelope the rest of the brain, with the brainstem and cerebellum beneath them.

*1. The brainstem*

Many fibres pass through the brainstem from the brain to the spinal cord and vice versa. The **medulla oblongata** contains nerve fibres and cell bodies concerned with heartbeat, respiration and gut movements. The **pons** contains a bridge of fibres connecting the brainstem with the cerebellum. The **midbrain** functions as a relay centre and performs some reflex actions concerned with sight and hearing. The **reticulum** is a network of fibres in the central core of the brainstem; it is connected to all the sensory input of the brain and 'decides' whether the incoming information is important and warrants extra attention or whether it is unimportant and can be ignored.

*2. The cerebellum*

The cerebellum is connected to the spinal cord and to the cerebral cortex by nerve fibres. It controls voluntary movements initiated in the cerebrum and is concerned with balance. Damage to the cerebellum causes unco-ordinated, jerky movement.

*3. The cerebrum*

This consists of two large **cerebral hemispheres** connected by three bundles of fibres called the **corpus callosum** and the **commisures**. The interior contains white matter and the exterior part is composed of grey matter which is folded to increase the surface area; this outer layer is called the **cerebral cortex**.

It is essentially the cerebrum which has increased in size throughout evolution. The cerebrum of a fish is still very small and is mostly concerned with smell. In the reptiles, the cerebrum is relatively larger, and in man the cerebrum represents 80 per cent of the brain. It is this increase in size which accounts for the increased capacity for learning, intelligence and memory. In particular, these abilities are associated with the development of an area in the cerebrum called the **association cortex**, which is not known in lower animals. This is an area not associated with definite sensory or motor activity. Experiments have shown that damage to this area can cause loss of learning ability, will, intention, planning, etc.; in fact most of the attributes considered part of man's 'mind'.

Experiments have shown that different areas of the cortex are asso-

ciated with particular functions (see Fig. 7.11). There is a speci
area and a corresponding motor area which, respectively, recei
and initiate somatic muscle movements. There are also areas c
with visual and auditory information.

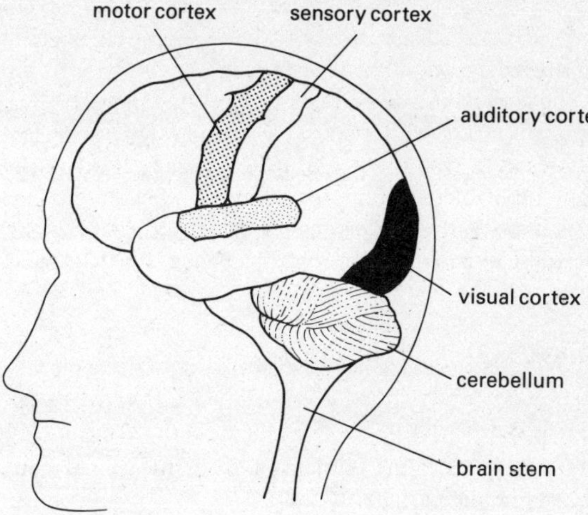
motor cortex
sensory cortex
auditory cortex
visual cortex
cerebellum
brain stem

*Fig. 7.11* Mapping the cerebral cortex

*4. The thalamus*

The thalamus consists of a pair of oval-shaped bundles of grey matter which act as a relay system for sensory information going to the cerebrum. It also connects to the reticular formation.

*5. The hypothalamus*

Situated below the cerebrum, the hypothalamus controls the secretion of tropic hormones from the anterior pituitary and thus controls and co-ordinates the endocrine system. It is also the pleasure centre of the brain; there are areas which stimulate sexual activity, hunger, thirst, anger and pleasure.

*The spinal cord*

This is a hollow tube filled with cerebro-spinal fluid. The walls of the tube have three layers: the outer layer is connected to the vertebrae of the spinal column and is tough. The outer layer is called the dura mater, the middle layer is the arachnoid mater and the innermost layer is the pia mater. In transverse section (see Fig. 7.12) the spinal cord appears as two kinds of material, a thick, white, outer layer composed of myelinated nerve fibres and an inner, grey area of nerve cell bodies. The spinal cord has two rows of nerves down its whole length.

## Further reading

R. H. Adrian, *The Nerve Impulse*, Oxford/Carolina Biology Reader No. 67 (Packard, 1980)
E. G. Gray, *The Synapse*, Oxford/Carolina Biology Reader No. 35 (Packard, 1977)
D. G. Jones, *Neurones and Synapses*, Studies in Biology No. 135 (Arnold, 1981)
P. N. R. Usherwood, *Nervous Systems*, Studies in Biology No. 36 (Arnold, 1973)

## Related questions

**Question:**

(a) The diagram shows a motor neuron from the spinal cord of a mammal. Name the parts A, B and C.

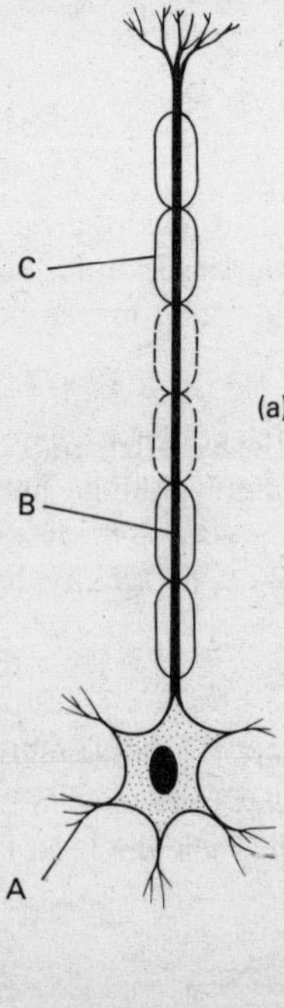
C
(a)
B
A

(b) Graph Y shows the change in membrane potential and graph Z the permeability of the axon membrane to sodium ($Na^+$) and potassium ($K^+$) ions during a nerve impulse.

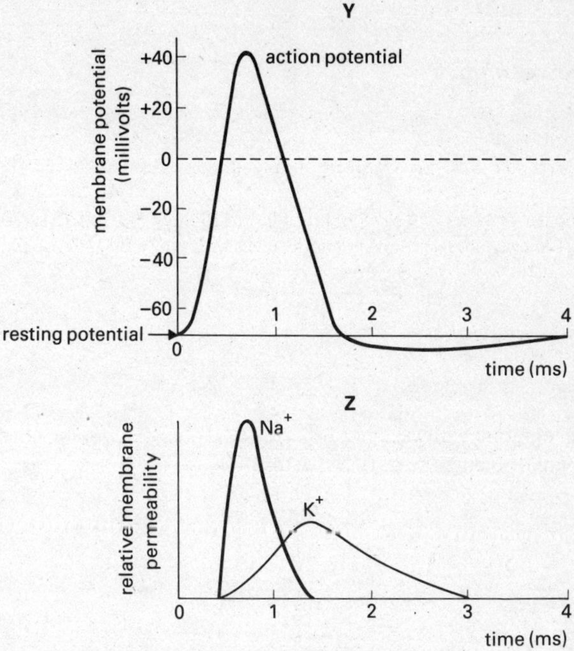
Y
membrane potential (millivolts)
+40
+20
0
-20
-40
-60
action potential
resting potential
0
1
2
3
4
time (ms)
Z
relative membrane permeability
Na⁺
K⁺
0
1
2
3
4
time (ms)
(b)

Using information from the graphs, explain the processes occurring during the passage of an impulse along the neuron. **(7 marks)**

[AEB, June 1984, Paper 1]

**Comments:**

(a) See Fig. 7.1b.

(b) See p. 240. Note that the question asks for an explanation 'using information from the graphs'. You should therefore relate the sequence of events to the changes in membrane permeability and membrane as shown in the graphs.

**Question:**

The diagram below represents the relationship between parts of two nerve cells (neurones).

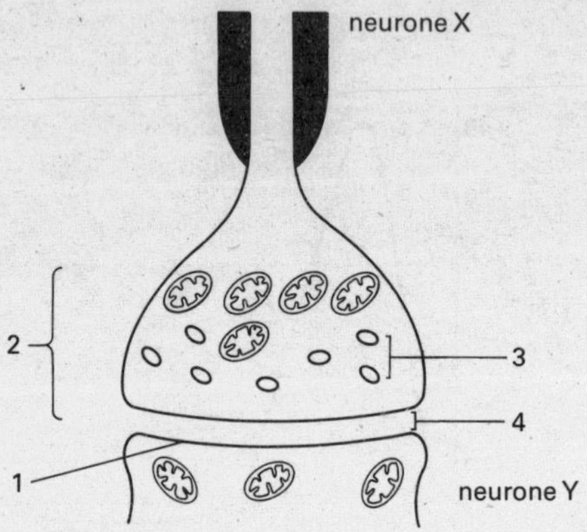
neurone X
2
3
4
1
neurone Y

(a) Name the parts numbered 1–4. **(4 marks)**

(b) How does a nerve impulse pass across the gap numbered 4?

**(4 marks)**

**(Total 8 marks)**

[London, June 1982, Paper 1]

**Comments:**

(a) See p. 242.
(b) See p. 242.

### *Nervous actions*

Actions in response to stimuli may be conscious or unconscious.

1. UNCONSCIOUS ACTIONS: These are actions of which we are not aware, e.g. peristalsis or gland secretion.
2. CONSCIOUS ACTIONS: These are actions of which we are aware. Conscious actions may be **controlled** (i.e. directed by the brain, as with walking, talking, etc.) or they may be **uncontrolled** and therefore not directed by the brain. The uncontrolled actions are called **reflex actions** and are the simplest of all nervous actions. One example of a reflex action is the knee-jerk reflex arc (Fig. 7.12), and other examples are given in Table 7.3.

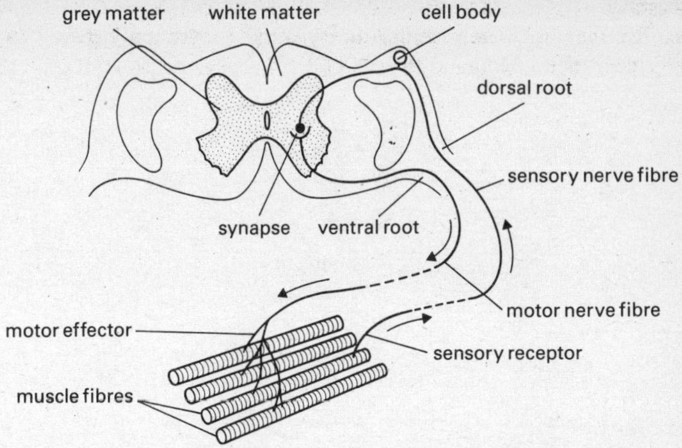
grey matter
white matter
cell body
dorsal root
sensory nerve fibre
synapse
ventral root
motor nerve fibre
motor effector
sensory receptor
muscle fibres

*Fig. 7.12* The knee-jerk reflex arc

Reflex actions have the following characteristics:

(a) They are rapid, automatic responses to set stimuli.
(b) They are inborn (i.e. do not need to be learned).
(c) The same stimulus always gives the same response.

*Table 7.3.* Examples of reflex actions

| *Reflex* | *Stimulus* | *Response* |
|---|---|---|
| Coughing | Particles in respiratory tract | Contraction of abdominal and intercostal muscles; relaxation of diaphragm |
| Blinking | Particles in the eye | Closing eyelids by contraction of eye muscles |
| Pupil reflex | Increased light intensity | Circular muscles of eye contract, thus reducing diameter of pupil |
| Swallowing | Food touching back of mouth | The soft palate and larynx are raised, the epiglottis covers the glottis and a peristalsis wave passed down the oesophagus |

**Question:**

(a) The diagram below shows the synaptic connection between two neurones P and Q and the cell body of a third neurone, R.

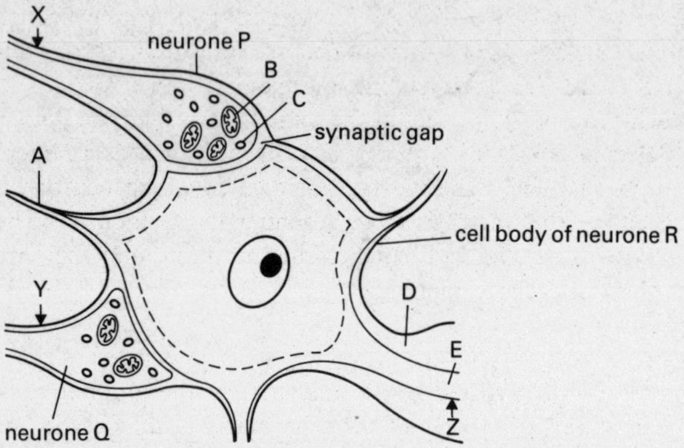
X
neurone P
B
C
synaptic gap
A
cell body of neurone R
Y
D
E
Z
neurone Q

State the names of the five parts labelled A, B, C, D and E.

**(5 marks)**

(b) An electric impulse applied at X causes depolarization of the membrane at that point and an action potential can subsequently be recorded at Z.

(i) Explain what is meant by depolarization.

(ii) Explain how the impulse is transmitted across the synaptic gap.

(iii) Describe what happens at the synapse following the transmission of a single impulse.

(iv) Explain why the impulse from neurone P cannot pass to neurone Q.

(v) State the effect of any *one* named drug on synaptic transmission. **(13 marks)**

(c) If an electric stimulus is applied to Y at the same time as one is applied to X so that the action potentials arrive at the synapses simultaneously, *no* action potential can subsequently be recorded at Z. What does this indicate about the function of neurone Q? Suggest how neurone Q operates. **(2 marks)**

**(Total 20 marks)**

[AEB, June 1980, Paper 2]

**Comments:**

(a) See p. 242, Fig. 7.6.

(b) (i) See p. 240.

(ii) and (iii) See p. 242.

(iv) Since the nerve impulse can only pass in one direction along the nerve and across the synapse, it could not pass from neurone P back into the synapse at Q as it would be travelling in the wrong direction.

(v) See p. 243 (e.g. strychnine, eserine).

(c) When neurone Q operates at the same time as neurone P no impulse is detected at Z. This implies that neurone Q acts as an intercepting neurone: it blocks the message being sent along neurone P, thus preventing this message from reaching its destination. There are many of these types of synapses in the brain, and they are often involved in decision-making.

**Question:**

(a) State *two* ways in which the functions of the autonomic nervous system differ from those of the other parts of the nervous system.

(i) ______________________________

(ii) ______________________________

(b) The roles of the sympathetic and parasympathetic systems within the autonomic nervous system are often antagonistic. Give *one* example of this type of antagonistic control and explain the precise roles of the sympathetic and parasympathetic systems in your example.

______________________________

______________________________

______________________________

(c) Name the transmitter substances which are produced by the autonomic nervous system.

______________________________

**(7 marks)**

[AEB, Nov. 1982, Paper 1]

**Comments:**

(a) (i) and (ii) See p. 245.

(b) See Table 7.2.

(c) See Table 7.1.

**Question:**
The diagram shows a lateral view of the human brain.

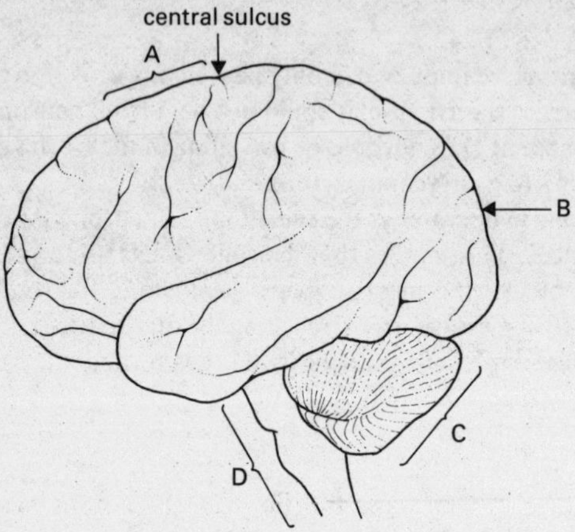
central sulcus
A
B
C
D

(a) (i) Name the surface regions labelled A and B.

A ______________________________

B ______________________________

(ii) State *one* probable effect on human behaviour of a malfunctioning of

region A ______________________________

region B ______________________________

(b) (i) Name the part labelled C.

______________________________

(ii) State the main function of part C.

______________________________

(c) (i) Name the part labelled D.

______________________________

(ii) State *one* function of part D.

______________________________________________

**(8 marks)**

[AEB, Nov. 1982, Paper 1]

**Comments:**

You should note that the diagram is a surface view of the brain, not a section through it.

(a) (i) See Fig. 7.11.

(ii) See p. 249. It can be assumed that damage to a particular area of the brain will cause malfunctioning of the response under its control.

(b) See p. 248.

(c) (i) See p. 249, Fig. 7.11.

(ii) See p. 248.

## Behaviour

Broadly speaking there are two types of behaviour, instinctive and learned, although in many cases it is difficult to distinguish between the two.

### *Instinctive behaviour*

This refers to behaviour which does not have to be learned and which is often characteristic of a particular species. Instinctive behaviour is thought to be genetically controlled, but is also subject to environmental influence. For example, birds that are reared in isolation from their parents still know how to make a nest, and how to sing like other birds of their species. This knowledge could not have been learned and therefore must have been inherited. Courtship and feeding behaviour are also instinctive, but are more subject to environmental influence.

#### Releasing stimuli

These are environmental factors which evoke a behavioural response. Often these features are possessed by other animals. Examples include:

1. Colour – the red colour of a robin's breast is used to threaten other males, whereas the red belly of the male stickleback is used to attract females.
2. Posture – an aggressive dog will threaten another dog by standing erect, baring its teeth and snarling.

### Motivational stimuli

These are internal factors which determine an animal's responsiveness to outside stimuli. Animals are often motivated towards certain behaviour patterns as a result of their internal physiological state. Examples include:

1. Hunger – large predators (e.g. lions and wolves) instinctively kill smaller prey to eat. However, they will only do so if they are hungry. The extent of the animal's hunger determines its motivation to kill.
2. Courtship and mating behaviour – this behaviour is brought about in birds by the presence of sex hormones, which in turn are controlled by day length. The eyes detect light and messages are sent to the brain. When the days become sufficiently long (in spring), the pituitary gland produces gonadotrophic hormones, and these induce reproductive behaviour.

## *Learned behaviour*

This is behaviour which is learned in an animal's lifetime and can therefore not be inherited. For example, man cannot inherit the ability to ride a bicycle; each individual must learn for himself. There are five types of learned behaviour.

### 1. Habituation

When an organism is subjected constantly to a stimulus, it may cease responding in the normal way. For example, the fan worm, *Sabella*, usually responds to touch by retracing its fan of tentacles, but after constant touching the worm learns not to move its tentacles and is said to have become habituated.

### 2. Associative learning

This is when an animal learns to associate a particular action with a reward or punishment. For example, a puppy is house-trained by being punished each time it urinates in the house, and it soon learns to go outside.

Associative learning usually involves conditioned reflexes. It was first demonstrated by Pavlov, a Russian scientist who worked with dogs. Pavlov rang a bell each time he was about to feed the dogs. Eventually he reached a stage where the dogs produced saliva merely at the ringing of a bell, even if no food was supplied. The production of saliva in response to the bell was called a conditional reflex.

### 3. Exploratory learning

This is the ability of animals to remember landmarks in the environment. Experiments with mice have shown that they will find their way out of a maze, especially if food is placed at the exit and they are hungry. If a mouse is repeatedly placed in the maze, it soon learns the way out, and each time it is replaced it makes fewer and fewer wrong turnings. This is an important learning process for animals in the wild, since it enables them to learn the landmarks of their environment.

### 4. Imprinting

This is how an animal learns its identity – usually by noting the characteristics of its parents and following them around. For example, if a young mallard is raised by foster-parents of a different species, it will subsequently try to mate with a bird of the foster-parent species.

### 5. Insight learning

This is the most complex form of learning. It involves reasoning and intelligence, and provides the ability for abstract thought and problem solving. Insight learning is usually associated with a well-developed memory. In humans this ability is also linked to development of the cerebral hemispheres, which contain thousands of multijunction synapses.

## *Further reading*

J. Archer, *Animals under Stress*, Studies in Biology No. 108 (Arnold, 1979)

D. Attenborough, *Life on Earth* (Collins, 1979)

J. C. Bowman, *Animals for Man*, Studies in Biology No. 78 (Arnold, 1977)

J. Brady, *Biological Clocks*, Studies in Biology No. 104 (Arnold, 1978)

J. D. Carthy, *The Study of Behaviour*, Studies in Biology No. 3, 2nd edition (Arnold, 1979)

J. Deag, *Social Behaviour of Animals*, Studies in Biology No. 118 (Arnold, 1980)

J. B. Free, *The Social Organization of Honeybees*, Studies in Biology No. 81 (Arnold, 1977)

M. A. Jeeves, *Experimental Psychology: An Introduction for Biologists*, Studies in Biology No. 47 (Arnold, 1974)

B. Lofts, *Animal Photoperiodism*, Studies in Biology No. 25 (Arnold, 1970)

J. B. Messenger, *Nerves, Brains and Behaviour*, Studies in Biology No. 114 (Arnold, 1979)

P. J. B. Slater, *Sex Hormones and Behaviour*, Studies in Biology No. 103 (Arnold, 1978)

D. M. Stoddart, *Mammalian Odours and Pheromones*, Studies in Biology No. 73 (Arnold, 1976)

## *Related questions*

**Question:**

(a) Distinguish clearly between
  (i) tropic and reflex responses
  (ii) instinctive and learned behaviour. **(8 marks)**

(b) Describe *one* example of a tropism and *one* example of a reflex response. **(8 marks)**

(c) Describe the significance of the examples that you have described to the life of the organism concerned. **(4 marks)**

**Comments:**

(a) This type of question is often best answered in the form of a table. Below is given a basic answer plan: you should expand this with your own additional information.

*Table 7.4.* Differences between tropic and reflex responses

| *Tropic response* (see p. 303) | *Reflex response* |
|---|---|
| Hormonal reaction | Nervous reaction |
| Growth response | Muscular response |
| Longer time to take effect | Very short time to take effect |

*Table 7.5.* Differences between instinctive and learned behaviour

| *Instinctive behaviour* | *Learned behaviour* |
|---|---|
| Inborn, does not have to be learned during an animal's lifetime | Not inborn, must be acquired during an animal's lifetime |
| Characteristic for each separate species | May vary within a species |
| Usually behaviour which is necessary for the success of the organism | Not necessarily essential for the success of the organism, although it can be |
| Not usually altered during the animal's lifetime, although slight changes may be made | Can be altered frequently to suit changing circumstances |
| Not intelligent or reasoned behaviour | Behaviour may be reasoned and intelligent |

(b) See p. 303 and p. 353. A simple account of each action, accompanied by annotated diagrams, should be adequate to answer this question. Detailed explanations of nervous or hormonal mechanisms are not required. The arm-jerk reflex arc, which is almost identical to the knee-jerk reflex arc, would be an alternative example of a reflex response.

(c) The key word is 'significance', i.e. why is the action important in the organism's life? It is important to note that the answers to this question must correspond to the examples given in (b); for example if the tropism described was phototropism then the importance is that it enables plants to grow towards a source of light. The arm-jerk reflex arc could prevent a serious burn or injury, by causing a jerking movement of the arm and hand away from a hot or painful stimulus.

## The sense organs

The sense organs detect changes in the environment and inform the brain via a system of sensory nerves. Different sense organs are responsible for detecting different types of stimuli.

| *Sense organ* | *Stimulus* |
|---|---|
| Eyes | Light |
| Ears | Sound and gravity |
| Skin | Mechanical pressure, temperature |
| Tongue | Chemicals |
| Nose | Chemicals |

Each sense organ contains clusters of sensory cells called receptors. **Receptors** convert a particular stimulus, e.g. light, sound, chemical, mechanical or heat energy into electrical energy in the form of action potentials in a neurone. Any system which converts another type of energy into electrical signals is called a **transducer**. Common mechanical examples are video cameras or microphones. There are several general features common to all sensory receptors:

1. Each receptor is specialized to receive one type of energy only (e.g. light, sound, pressure, etc.), but whatever the stimulus, it is transformed into electrical energy in the form of action potentials.
2. All receptors, when stimulated, produce a generator potential which is caused by depolarization of the membrane of the receptor cell. (The

size of the generator potential is proportional to the size of the stimulus.)
3. Receptors have a threshold value of stimulation; below this value no impulse is created in the neurones.
4. Receptors may become adapted to a particular stimulus, i.e. they cease to produce nerve impulses if the stimulus continues. For example, we may 'get used' to certain smells. However, the time for each receptor to become adapted to a stimulus is variable.
5. All receptors contain sensory cells which often have an extended thread of cytoplasm to detect the stimulus.

### *The eye*

O-level (or GCSE) understanding of the general structure and functions of the human eye (see Fig. 7.13) is assumed in this section.

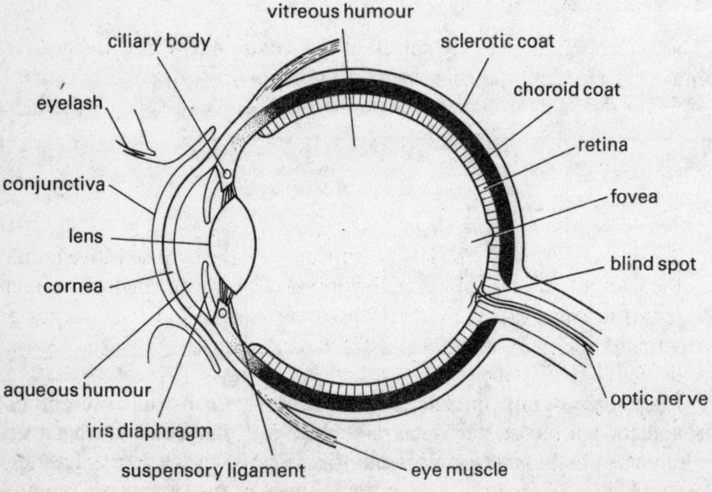
vitreous humour
ciliary body
sclerotic coat
eyelash
choroid coat
retina
conjunctiva
fovea
lens
blind spot
cornea
aqueous humour
optic nerve
iris diaphragm
suspensory ligament
eye muscle

*Fig. 7.13* LS through the human eye

### Entry of light into the eye

This is through a hole called the pupil, which alters in size depending on the light intensity. Pupil size is altered by two sets of muscles in the iris – the circular muscles and the radial muscles which act antagonistically (see Fig. 7.14).

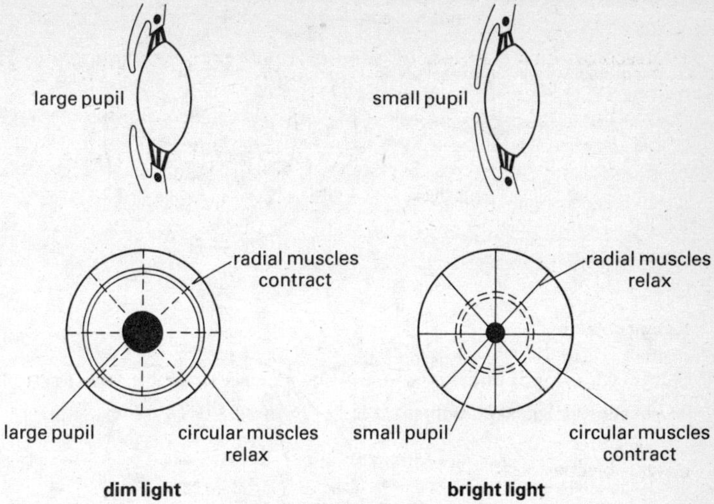
large pupil
small pupil
radial muscles contract
radial muscles relax
large pupil
circular muscles relax
small pupil
circular muscles contract
dim light
bright light

*Fig. 7.14* Alteration of pupil size by the iris diaphragm

## Accommodation of the eye

This is the means by which light is focused on the light-sensitive retina at the back of the eye, in order to form a clear image. Light is refracted (bent) to some extent by the transparent cornea and the aqueous and vitreous humours, but most refraction is due to the elastic lens just behind the iris. Depending on the angle at which light enters the eye, the lens changes shape in order to bend the light by just the right amount and form a focused image. The thickness of the lens is altered by the circular muscles and the suspensory ligaments, which act antagonistically (see Fig. 7.15).

The black choroid layer absorbs any stray light in the eye, preventing reflection.

## Image formation

The retina is composed of two types of cells (see Fig. 7.16):

(a) Rods – which are sensitive to dim light.

(b) Cones – which are sensitive to bright light and colour.

These are compared in Table 7.6.

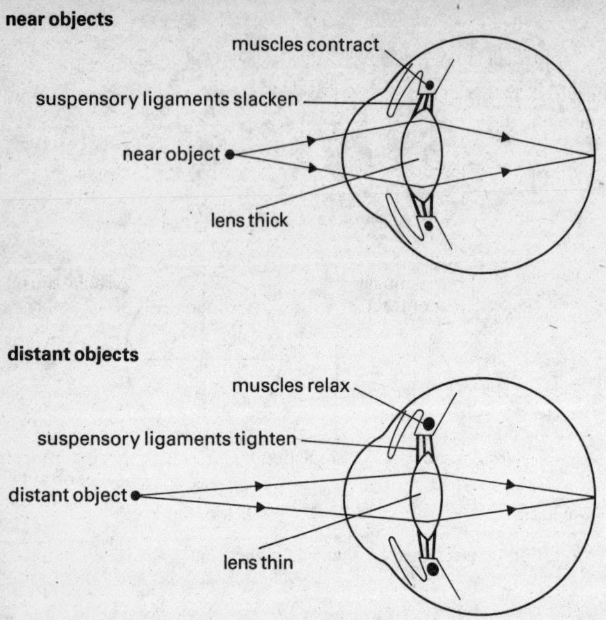
near objects
muscles contract
suspensory ligaments slacken
near object
lens thick
distant objects
muscles relax
suspensory ligaments tighten
distant object
lens thin

*Fig. 7.15* Accommodation of the eye

The process of image formation occurs as follows:

1. Light passes through the network of neurones on the inner layer of the retina until it reaches the pigmented area of the rods and cones.
2. If sufficient light is present, the pigment molecule rhodopsin temporarily splits in two. This causes an alteration in the membrane of the rod or cone cell, and an action potential is set up in the adjacent bipolar cell.
3. Nerve impulses then pass through a series of elaborate interconnections to the ganglion cells, whose axons join to form the optic nerve. (The point where the optic nerve leaves the eye is called the blind spot. As there are no rods or cones present, an image focused here would not be seen.)

### Activity of the visual cortex in the brain

Neurones from the retina join to form the optic nerve. Fibres from each eye come together at the visual relay centre of the thalamus, where they

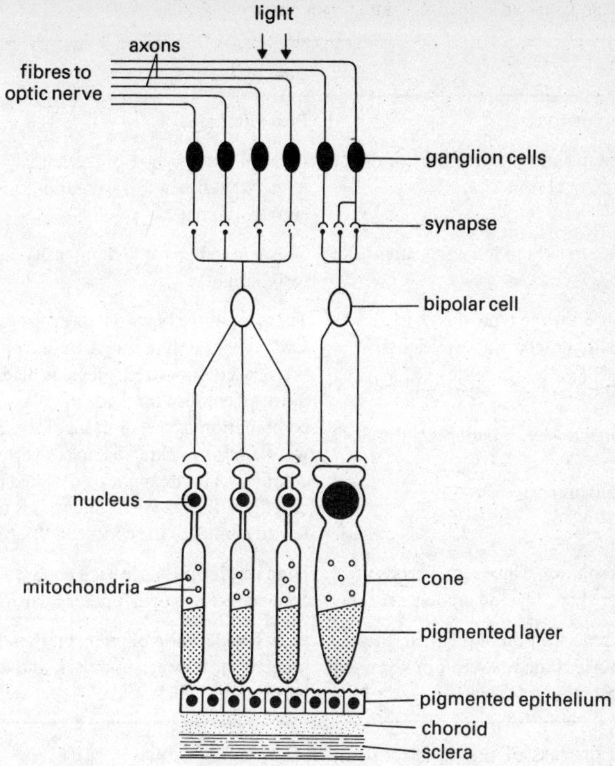
light
axons
fibres to
optic nerve
ganglion cells
synapse
bipolar cell
nucleus
mitochondria
cone
pigmented layer
pigmented epithelium
choroid
sclera

*Fig. 7.16* The retina of the vertebrate eye

synapse with fibres leading to the visual cortex in the cerebrum. The visual cortex is thought to consist of a 'map' of neurones corresponding to those in the retina, so that the image formed on the retina is rebuilt in electrical form in the visual cortex. There are also neurones which appear to be stimulated by different types of movement, e.g. horizontal or vertical movement. The result is a complex visual processing system which integrates the incoming information and gives man an informed visual sense.

### Adaptations of the eyes of vertebrates

1. BINOCULAR VISION (stereoscopic vision): When the eyes are placed such that their two fields of vision overlap, the brain condenses the

*Table 7.6.* Comparison of rods and cones in man

| *Rods* | *Cones* |
|---|---|
| More numerous | Less numerous |
| Located around the periphery of the retina | Located in the centre of the retina – the fovea, or yellow spot, is composed entirely of cones |
| Sensitive to light at low intensities (dim light) | Sensitive to light of high intensity (bright light) |
| There is only one type of rod cell, and this is stimulated by all wavelengths except red | There are three types of cone cells. Each type is only sensitive to one of the primary colours – red, green or blue. Since all colours are made up of a combination of one or more of these wavelengths, we are able to see various colours. Colour cannot be detected in dim light since the light intensity is too low to stimulate the cones |
| Low resolution, since several rods are connected to only one bipolar neurone | High resolution, since each cone is connected to its own bipolar neurone |
| Rapid regeneration of pigment, therefore shorter time between impulses, and good perception of flicker | Slow regeneration of pigment, therefore longer time between impulses, and less perception of flicker |

two images to form a single image and can then judge distances between objects. Animals which need to judge distances accurately for hunting tend to have binocular vision, e.g. eagles, lions, wolves.

2. WIDE-FIELD VISION: Grazing animals (e.g. sheep, horses and cows) tend to have one eye on each side of the head, and therefore the fields of vision do not overlap. Although they have little perception of distances, the eyes are set high and provide a wide field of view to watch for predators.
3. NOCTURNAL VISION: Animals such as lemurs, hedgehogs and owls tend to have large eyes to allow maximum entry of light. They also possess only rod cells, which are more light-sensitive than cone cells, and they therefore do not see in colour.
4. HIGH RESOLUTION VISION: Eagles and other bird predators often have two foveas in each retina and have strong powers of accommodation, enabling them to see small animals from very great distances.

They also have a high concentration of cone cells, e.g. a hawk has 1 million cones per $mm^2$ compared to man with 160,000 cones per $mm^2$.

### The ear

Knowledge of the structure and functions of the ear to O-level (or GCSE) standard is assumed. The structure of the human ear is shown in Fig. 7.17.

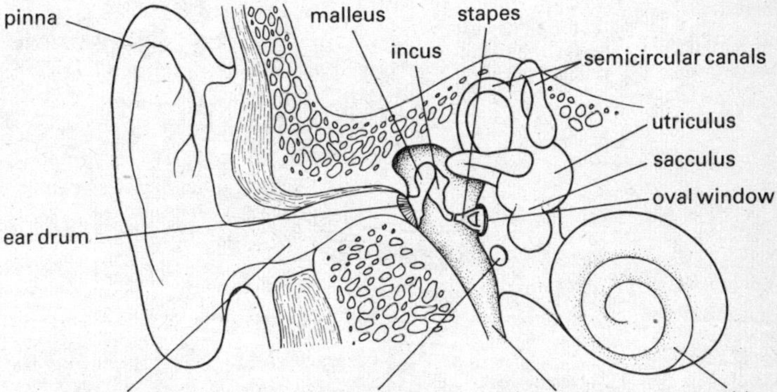
pinna
malleus
stapes
incus
semicircular canals
utriculus
sacculus
oval window
ear drum
external auditory meatus
round window
eustachian tube
cochlea

*Fig. 7.17* Structure of the human ear

The ear contains two types of receptor: those detecting sound vibrations (hearing) and those responding to gravity (balance).

#### Hearing

Sound vibrations in the air enter the ear via the pinna, and travel down a bony tube called the external auditory meatus until they reach the ear drum. Vibrations are transferred to the inner ear by the ossicles – three small bones which act as an amplifying system. Muscles attached to the bones prevent excessive vibrations from very loud noises. The eustachian tube, which connects the middle ear with the back of the throat, helps to equalize pressure in the middle ear with atmospheric pressure.

Each time the oval window vibrates, the round window also vibrates in the opposite direction to prevent a pressure build-up of fluid in the cochlea. The coiled cochlea is a fluid-filled tube containing receptors in the form of hair cells. The receptors are located in a central canal of the cochlea called the organ of Corti, which is surrounded by fluid (see Fig. 7.18). As sound vibrations pass through the fluid, the basilar membrane vibrates, causing hair cells to press against the tectorial membrane above them, and an impulse is generated in the auditory nerve. It is thought that different areas of the organ of Corti are sensitive to different frequency vibrations: those nearer the oval window detect high-pitched sounds and those further away detect vibrations of lower pitch.

The human auditory range is approximately 16 Hz to 20 kHz, although this may be reduced with age owing to loss in elasticity of the ear drum.

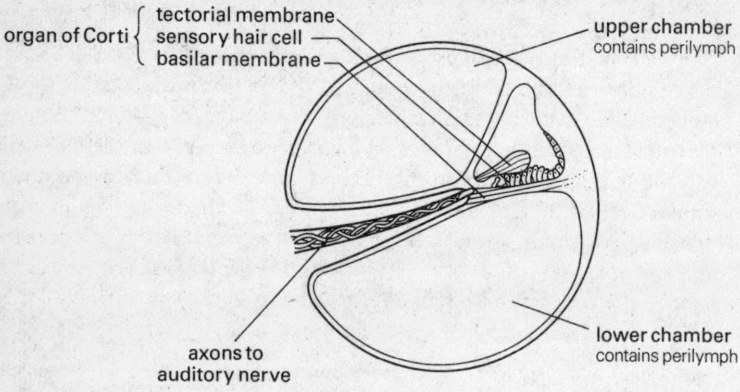
organ of Corti
tectorial membrane
sensory hair cell
basilar membrane
upper chamber
contains perilymph
axons to
auditory nerve
lower chamber
contains perilymph

*Fig. 7.18* Section through the cochlea

## Balance

Receptors concerned with balance and posture are located in the semicircular canals and in the utriculus and sacculus.

The semicircular canals are three fluid-filled canals located at right angles to each other. At the end of each canal is a swelling called the ampulla (Fig. 7.19), which contains a receptor called the cupula, capable of detecting movements of the fluid. Movement of the head causes fluid to move in one of the canals. The fluid presses against the jelly of the cupula, causing the hair cells to bend, and an impulse to be sent along nerve fibres to inform the brain. If a person spins in one direction for a period of time and then suddenly stops, the fluid continues to move, stimulating the receptors in the ampulla and giving the impression of movement or dizziness.

The utriculus and sacculus are filled with endolymph, have walls which

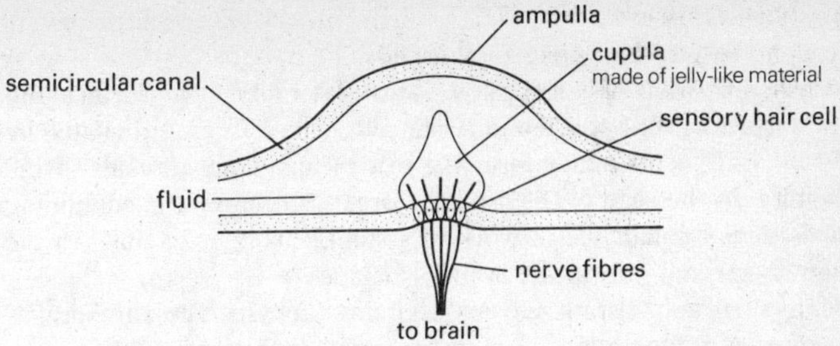
ampulla
cupula
made of jelly-like material
semicircular canal
sensory hair cell
fluid
nerve fibres
to brain

*Fig. 7.19* Section through the ampulla

are thickened in places and contain sensory hair cells. Each cell has a nerve fibre running from the base and a hair-like projection at the tip embedded in jelly containing crystals of calcium carbonate. When a person is upright, the calcium carbonate crystals press on the hair cells, causing impulses to pass to the brain. Conversely, when upside down, the crystals do not press on the hair cells and the nerve impulses are reduced. The brain is thus constantly informed of the person's position and can send information to correct it. The regions of the walls containing the sensory hair cells are called maculae (sing. macula) (Fig. 7.20).

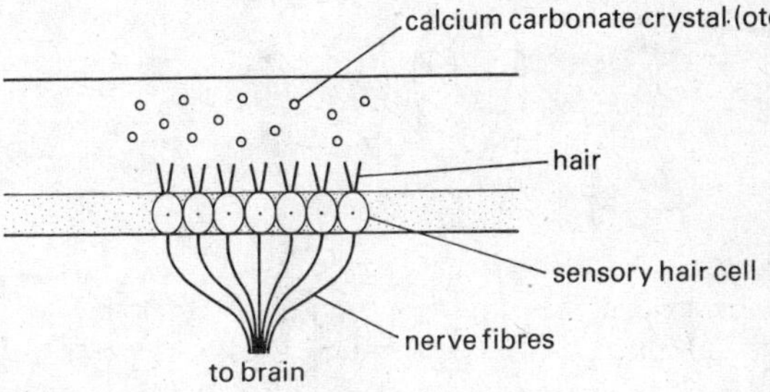
calcium carbonate crystal (otolith)
hair
sensory hair cell
nerve fibres
to brain

*Fig. 7.20* Section through a macula

## Adaptations of the ear in other animals

1. Some animals are able to use muscles in the pinna to move the ears towards a source of sound. Humans appear to have lost the ability to move their ears.
2. Animals hear different ranges of frequencies to suit their varying

lifestyles. Dogs can hear whistles which humans cannot hear. Insects respond to very high-frequency sounds.

3. In fish, a network of canals known as the lateral line, which run along the surface of the body, contain hair cells. The cells are stimulated by water movements and inform the fish of any other animals in the vicinity. In the head of the fish is an organ, the labyrinth, containing semicircular canals which work in a similar manner to those in the human ear and inform the brain of balance.
4. Many small animals (e.g. jellyfish) contain statocysts. These are specialized receptors containing calcium carbonate, which inform the organism of its orientation towards gravity (balance).

### *Sensory receptors in the skin*

Specialized receptors are found all over the skin; these include receptors for pain, heat/cold, touch and pressure (see Figs 7.21 and 7.22). Certain

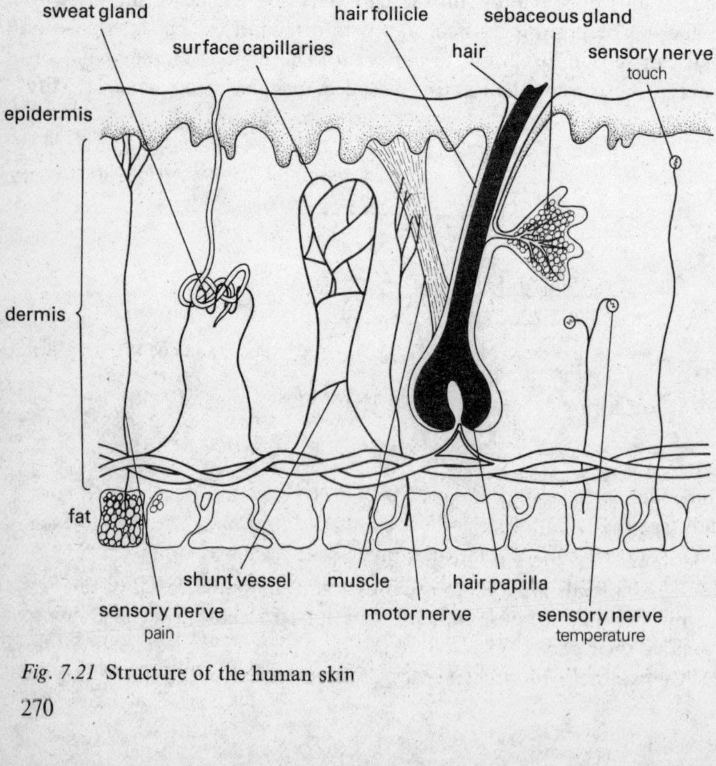
sweat gland
hair follicle
sebaceous gland
surface capillaries
hair
sensory nerve
touch
epidermis
dermis
fat
shunt vessel
muscle
hair papilla
sensory nerve
pain
motor nerve
sensory nerve
temperature

*Fig. 7.21* Structure of the human skin

areas of the skin are more sensitive to particular stimuli owing to the presence of a higher concentration of receptors. For example, the backs of the knees contain a high concentration of touch receptors.

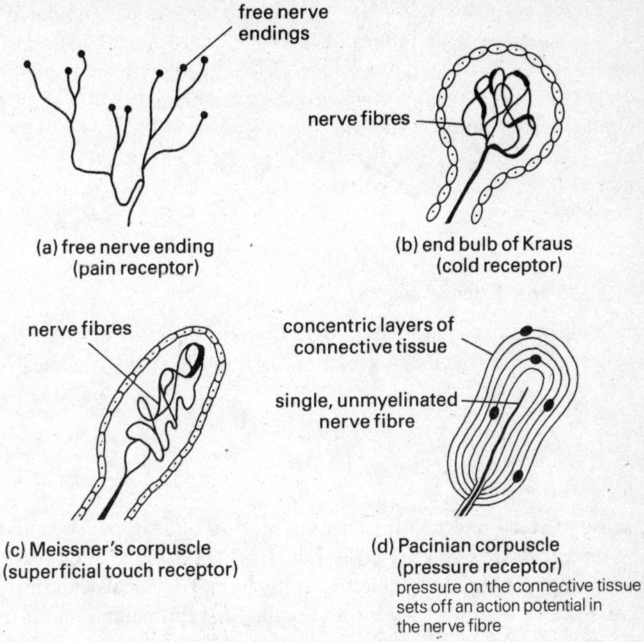
free nerve endings
(a) free nerve ending (pain receptor)
nerve fibres
(b) end bulb of Kraus (cold receptor)
nerve fibres
(c) Meissner's corpuscle (superficial touch receptor)
concentric layers of connective tissue
single, unmyelinated nerve fibre
(d) Pacinian corpuscle (pressure receptor)
pressure on the connective tissue sets off an action potential in the nerve fibre

*Fig. 7.22* Receptors found in the skin

## *Chemoreception*

### *Taste*

Embedded in the tongue are groups of sensory receptor cells called taste buds (see Fig. 7.23). These cells are sensitive to certain chemicals which dissolve in the moisture on the tongue. If a chemical is present in sufficient concentration, the cells are stimulated and nerve impulses pass along fibres from the base of the cells to the brain. There are four kinds of specialized taste buds, which detect sweet, sour, salt and bitter chemicals, and these are located on specific areas of the tongue.

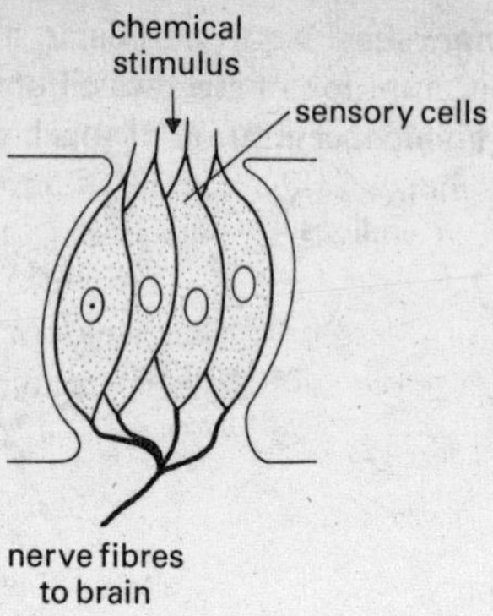
chemical
stimulus
sensory cells
nerve fibres
to brain

*Fig. 7.23* Section through a taste bud

*Smell*

The sense of smell refers to the chemoreception of airborne substances.

The receptors are olfactory cells (Fig. 7.24), which are found high up in the nasal passages in the olfactory epithelium. Chemicals entering the nose dissolve in the moist layer on the olfactory epithelium, and if they are present in sufficient quantities, nerve impulses pass from the olfactory cells to the brain.

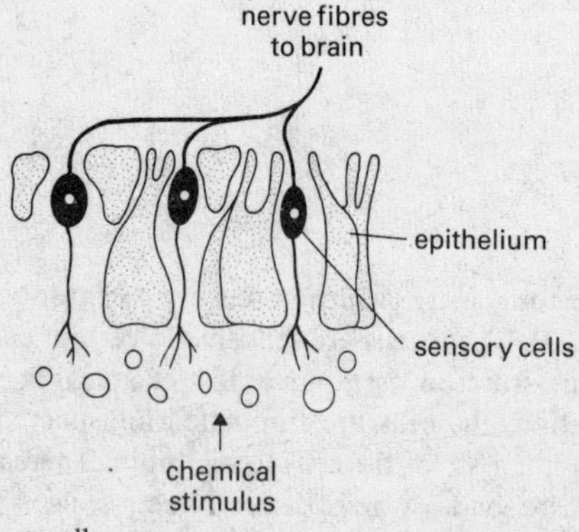
nerve fibres
to brain
epithelium
sensory cells
chemical
stimulus

*Fig. 7.24* Olfactory cells

*Smell and taste in animals other than man*

The senses of taste and smell appear to play a much larger role in the lives of some animals than they do in man. Some animals produce chemical messengers (pheromones), which are synthesized in special glands and released into the environment. For example, the female gypsy moth produces small amounts of a pheromone which attracts male moths, the males being able to detect the chemical from several miles away. Animals such as cats and dogs spray urine to outline their territory and warn off other males.

## Further reading

I. Friedman, *The Human Ear*, Oxford/Carolina Biology Reader No. 73, 2nd edition (Packard, 1979)

R. L. Gregory, *Visual Perception*, Oxford/Carolina Biology Reader No. 40 (Packard, 1973)

M. E. Rosenberg, *Sound and Hearing*, Studies in Biology No. 145 (Arnold, 1982)

R. A. Weale, *The Vertebrate Eye*, Oxford/Carolina Biology Reader No. 71, 2nd edition (Packard, 1978)

## Related questions

**Question:**

The diagram below shows the structure of an ampulla and part of a semicircular canal of the ear of a mammal.

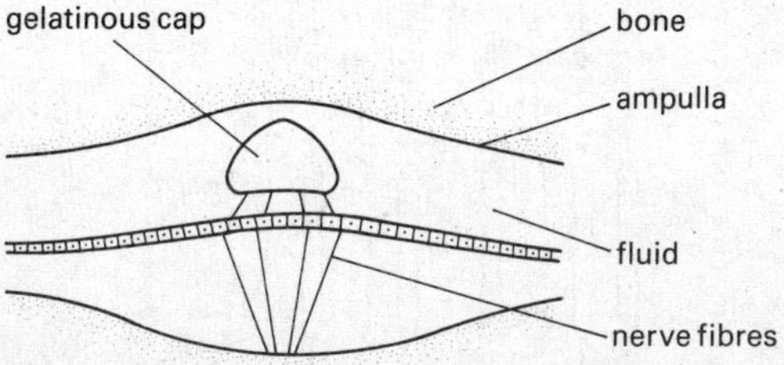
gelatinous cap
bone
ampulla
fluid
nerve fibres

Describe a reflex arc which will result from stimulation of this sense organ. Include details of the stimulation.

**Comments:**

The reflex arc in question is concerned with balance.

A reflex arc involves three stages:

1. Stimulation, see p. 261.
2. Passage of nerve impulses, see p. 240.
3. The effect.

A reflex arc has the same basic stages, irrespective of the type of reflex action being undertaken.

A stimulus causes an impulse to pass via a sensory nerve to the brain or spinal cord (for the part of the brain controlling balance see p. 248). A return impulse is automatically sent to the effector organ (muscles in the head and neck) via a motor nerve in order to initiate a response.

Details of both the stimulation and the effect should be included in the answer.

**Question:**

The diagram below represents the retina of the human eye as seen in section.

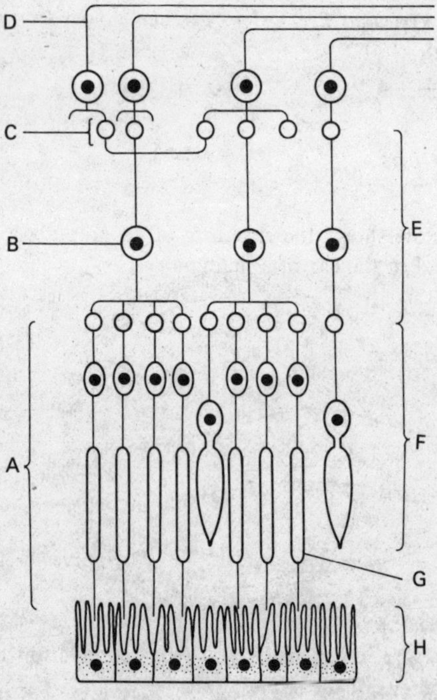
D
C
B
E
A
F
G
H

(a) Name the parts A to H: **(8 marks)**
(b) Account for the following.
  (i) Rod cells produce an indistinct image. **(2 marks)**
  (ii) Rod cells are concerned with night vision. **(2 marks)**
  (iii) Cone cells are capable of colour perception. **(2 marks)**
  (iv) Visual acuteness is greatest at the region of the fovea. **(2 marks)**
  (v) When a person enters a dimly lit room from bright sunlight, the room at first seems dark but gradually objects become visible. **(2 marks)**

**(Total 18 marks)**

[London, Jan. 1983, Paper 1]

**Comments:**
(a) See p. 265, Fig. 7.16.
(b) (i), (ii), (iii) and (iv) See p. 266, Table 7.6.
Note that an indistinct image is produced owing to low resolution.
(v) In bright sunlight the pupil contracts to reduce the amount of light entering the eye. On entering a dark room, the pupil is initially small, but soon dilates to cope with the new lighting conditions, enabling clearer vision.

**Question:**
The diagram below represents a section through the eye of a mammal.

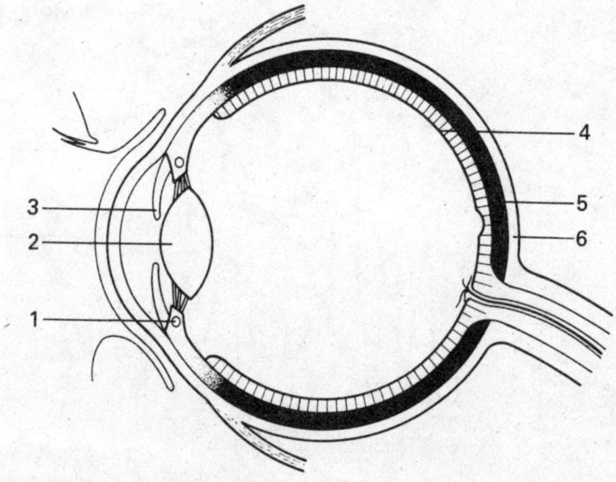
4
3
5
2
6
1

(a) Name the parts labelled 1 to 6 on the diagram. **(4 marks)**

(b) Describe the parts played by 1, 2, 3 and 4 when a distant object is viewed in poor light. **(12 marks)**
**(Total 16 marks)**
[London, Jan. 1982, Paper 1]

**Comments:**

(a) See p. 262, Fig. 7.13, 'LS through the human eye'.
(b) The key words are 'distant' and 'poor light'. For 1 and 2 see p. 264 'Accommodation of the eye' (distant objects); for 3 see p. 263 'Entry of light into the eye' (dim light); and for 4 see p. 264 'Image formation'. Note that only one type of cell is stimulated in dim light.

## *The endocrine system*

The endocrine system involves the production of potent chemical messengers called **hormones**, which are produced in ductless **endocrine glands** and secreted into the bloodstream. Hormones are circulated around the body but exert an effect only on particular **target organs**. The endocrine glands in man are shown in Fig. 7.25, and the principal hormones,

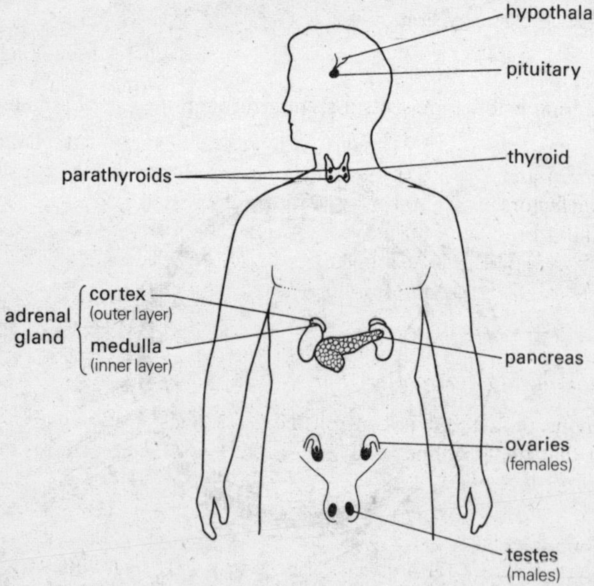
hypothalamus
pituitary
thyroid
parathyroids
adrenal gland
cortex
(outer layer)
medulla
(inner layer)
pancreas
ovaries
(females)
testes
(males)

*Fig. 7.25* Endocrine glands in man

together with the gland producing them, the target tissues and the hormones' effects are listed in Table 7.8. The nervous and endocrine systems are compared in Table 7.7.

*Table 7.7.* Differences between the nervous and endocrine systems

| *Nervous system* | *Endocrine system* |
|---|---|
| Messages are sent by electrical nerve impulses | Messages sent by chemical means |
| Rapid transmission of impulse | Slow transmission |
| Brief duration | Longer duration |
| Very localized effects | Widespread general effects |
| Transmitted in nerve fibres | Transmitted in bloodstream |
| Each stimulus only reaches one part of the body | Each stimulus reaches all body parts |
| Stimulus originates in sense receptor | Stimulus originates from gland |

## The pituitary gland and the hypothalamus

The pituitary gland is situated below the hypothalamus in the brain, and it produces a number of hormones, including tropic hormones which themselves regulate hormone production in other endocrine glands.

The pituitary gland is under the influence of the hypothalamus (see Figs 7.26 and 7.27). The hypothalamus produces chemicals called releasing factors, which travel down the pituitary stalk and either stimulate or inhibit production of hormones from the anterior pituitary lobe.

The hypothalamus also produces two hormones which pass into the posterior lobe of the pituitary for secretion.

### *Control of hormone production*

Hormone production is controlled by feedback, i.e. by assessing the effect that the hormone is having on the body. There are two types of feedback:

#### 1. Negative feedback

As the effect of the hormone increases, less hormone is required, therefore production decreases. The opposite also applies – if the hormone is

*Table 7.8.* The principal hormones in man and other higher animals

| *Hormone* | *Endocrine gland* | *Target tissue(s)* | *Principal effects* |
|---|---|---|---|
| *Protein and polypeptide hormones* | | | |
| Growth hormone (GH) (somatotropin) | Anterior pituitary | Liver, kidney | Increased protein synthesis |
| Adrenocorticotropic hormone (ACTH) | Anterior pituitary | Adrenal cortex<br>Corpus luteum | Formation of adrenocorticosteroids<br>Secretion of progesterone |
| Thyroid-stimulating hormone (TSH) or thyrotropin | Anterior pituitary | Thyroid gland | Production of thyroxine |
| Follicle-stimulating hormone (FSH)<br>Luteinizing hormone (LH) } Gonadotropins | Anterior pituitary | Reproductive organs | Development and functioning of gonads |
| Prolactin | Anterior pituitary | Mammary glands | Milk production |
| Melanocyte-stimulating hormone | Anterior pituitary | Skin | Changes colour and camouflage in frog<br>Function in man unknown |
| Oxytocin | Posterior pituitary | Uterine muscle, mammary glands | Stimulates uterine muscle contraction in pregnant females and release of milk during suckling |
| Antidiuretic hormone (ADH) (vasopressin) | Posterior pituitary | Kidney tubules | Increased water reabsorption in kidney tubule |
| Insulin | Pancreas | Liver, muscles, adipose tissues | Increased anabolic reactions (especially conversion of glucose to glycogen) |
| Glucagon | Pancreas | Liver, adipose tissues | Glucogenesis (i.e. conversion of glycogen to glucose) |

| | | | |
|---|---|---|---|
| Parathyroid hormone | Parathyroids | Skeleton, kidney, intestines | Increased metabolism of calcium, promotes bone growth |
| Calcitonin | Thyroid and parathyroid | Bone | Increased absorption of $Ca^{2+}$ ions from tissue fluid |
| Gastrin | Endocrine cells of gastro-intestinal tract | Stomach | Acid secretion |
| Secretin | | Duodenum | Production of bile and pancreatic fluid |
| Pancreozymin | | Pancreas | Secretion of enzymes into pancreatic fluid |
| *Hormones derived from amino acids* | | | |
| Adrenaline (epinephrine) | Adrenal medulla | Liver, muscle, adipose tissues | Catabolic reactions of carbohydrate (especially glycogen to glucose) |
| Noradrenaline (norepinephrine) | | | |
| Thyroxine | Thyroid | General | Increased metabolic activity, controls growth and development |
| *Steroid hormones* | | | |
| Androgens (testosterone) | Testes | Prostate gland, seminal vesicles | Development and normal functioning of reproductive organs |
| Oestrogens (progesterone) | Ovaries | Breasts, uterus, vagina | |
| Adrenocorticosteroids (aldosterone) | Adrenal cortex | Kidney | Controls reabsorption of sodium from kidney tubules |
| Glucocorticostereoids (corticosterone) | Adrenal cortex | Liver | Promotes breakdown of glycogen and proteins to glucose |
| *Hormones derived from fatty acids* | | | |
| Prostaglandins | Ubiquitous distribution in mammalian tissues | General | Many effects including contraction and relaxation of smooth muscle. Associated with fertility in uterus. Thought to bring about effects by altering the permeability of membranes |

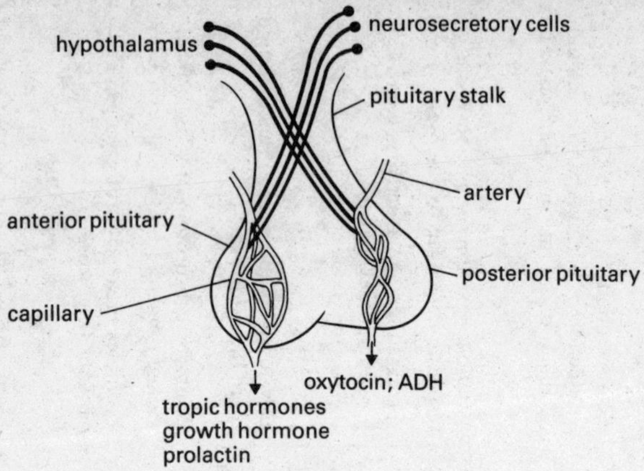
neurosecretory cells
hypothalamus
pituitary stalk
artery
anterior pituitary
posterior pituitary
capillary
oxytocin; ADH
tropic hormones
growth hormone
prolactin

*Fig. 7.26* The relationship between the hypothalamus and the pituitary

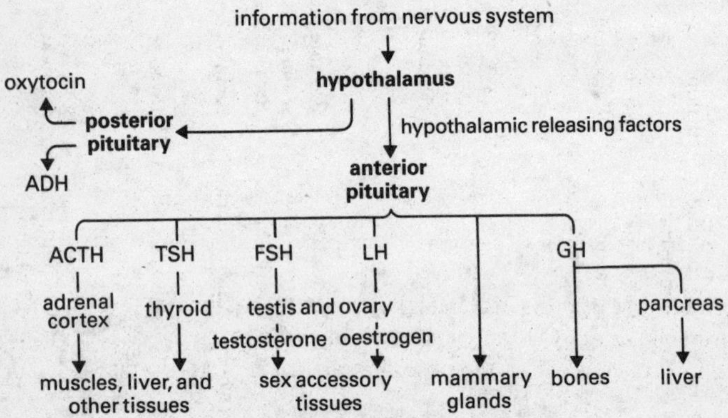
information from nervous system
hypothalamus
oxytocin
posterior pituitary
hypothalamic releasing factors
ADH
anterior pituitary
ACTH
TSH
FSH
LH
GH
adrenal cortex
thyroid
testis and ovary
pancreas
testosterone
oestrogen
muscles, liver, and other tissues
sex accessory tissues
mammary glands
bones
liver

*Fig. 7.27* Hormones under the control of the hypothalamus

having little effect on the body, more is produced. Examples A, B and C are examples of negative feedback.

*Example A*

If the blood passing through the hypothalamus has a high osmotic pressure, ADH production is increased, and the kidney tubules reabsorb more water until the osmotic pressure of the blood is lowered (see Fig. 6.1, p. 212). The hypothalamus also receives information from the brain about the external environment, and alters the hormone balance accordingly.

*Example B*
Hormones under the control of the hypothalamus are regulated via the appropriate releasing factors. If a hormone such as thyroxine is in excess, the pituitary ceases production of thyrotropin, which in turn reduces production of thyroxine in the thyroid gland (see Fig. 7.28).

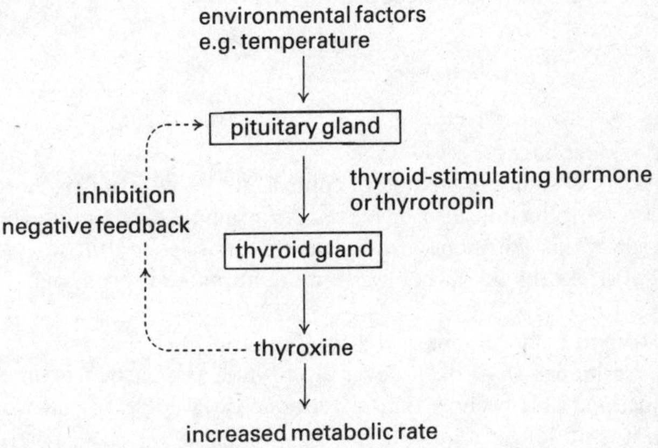
environmental factors
e.g. temperature
pituitary gland
thyroid-stimulating hormone
or thyrotropin
inhibition
negative feedback
thyroid gland
thyroxine
increased metabolic rate

*Fig. 7.28* Regulation of the hormone thyroxine

In the case of prolactin, the releasing factor inhibits production of the hormone, since it is only required in pregnant females. When milk production is required, the releasing factor is not produced.

*Example C: Control of blood sugar level*
Three hormones affect blood sugar level: adrenaline, glucagon and insulin. Adrenaline and glucagon increase blood sugar levels by encouraging conversion of glycogen to glucose. Insulin has the opposite effect, it decreases the blood sugar level by converting glucose to glycogen.

If the blood sugar level is low, adrenaline and glucagon are produced. If the blood sugar level is high, insulin is produced (see Fig. 7.29).

If the body is incapable of producing insulin, glucose will not be converted to glycogen and the disease diabetes (diabetes mellitus) results.

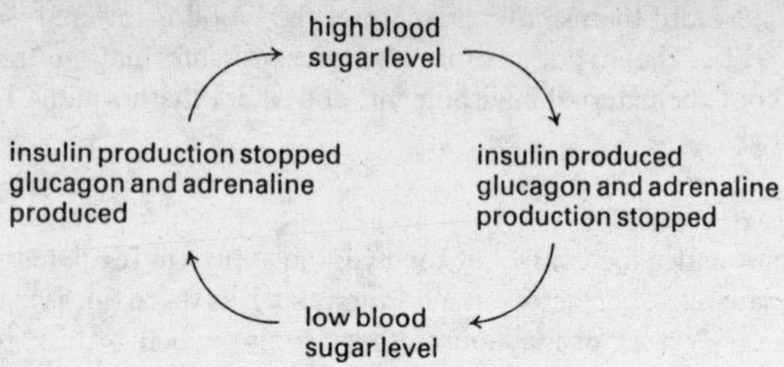
high blood
sugar level
insulin produced
glucagon and adrenaline
production stopped
low blood
sugar level
insulin production stopped
glucagon and adrenaline
produced

*Fig. 7.29* Regulation of the blood sugar level

### Positive feedback

This is a less common method of control. As the effect of the hormone increases, production also increases. An example is the production of oxytocin. This hormone causes uterine muscle contraction during childbirth. As the uterus contracts, more hormone is produced.

### Breakdown of hormones

Most hormones are broken down by enzymes at a particular time after production. This ensures that a hormone does not carry on working when it is no longer required.

## *Mechanism of hormone action*

Although hormones circulate around the body in the bloodstream, they only produce effects on certain target organs. It is thought that cells on the target organ contain receptor molecules on their surfaces. The hormone which affects a particular target organ 'recognizes' the receptors, and binds on to them like a key fitting into a lock. Each hormone only 'locks' into the receptor of its particular target organ. This ensures that hormone action is extremely specific.

Examples of hormone action are given below:

### Example 1: A hormone causing an increase in cyclic AMP (see Fig. 7.30)

Many hormones, e.g. adrenaline, glucagon, ACTH, ADH, TSH, LH and the prostaglandins, trigger the production of an enzyme called adenyl

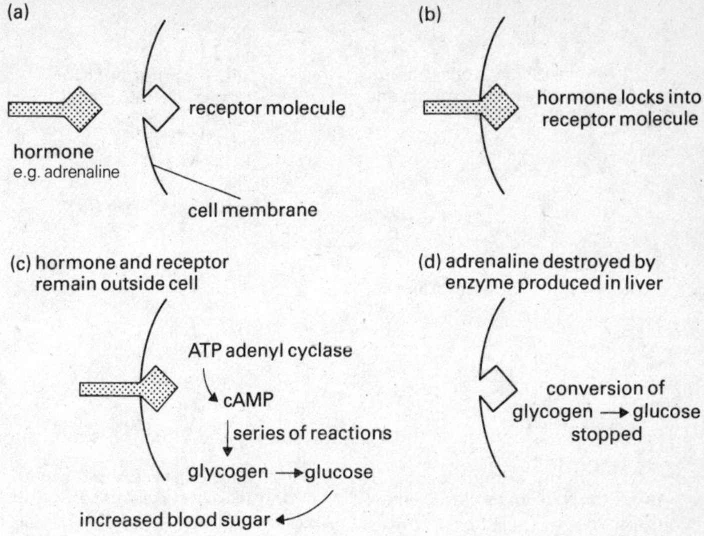

(a)
receptor molecule
hormone
e.g. adrenaline
cell membrane
(b)
hormone locks into receptor molecule
(c) hormone and receptor remain outside cell
ATP adenyl cyclase
cAMP
series of reactions
glycogen → glucose
increased blood sugar
(d) adrenaline destroyed by enzyme produced in liver
conversion of glycogen → glucose stopped


*Fig. 7.30* Mechanism of action of hormones that increase the production of cyclic AMP

cyclase. This enzyme converts ATP to cyclic AMP (cAMP). (cAMP is similar to normal AMP (p. 100), but the phosphate molecule is linked to the main part of the molecule in a cyclic manner.) An increase in the concentration of cAMP initiates further reactions in the cell (e.g. activation of the enzymes which break down glycogen in response to adrenaline).

### Example 2: A hormone causing a decrease in cAMP

Insulin causes a reduction in the cellular concentration of cAMP. This has the opposite effect to that of adrenaline.

### Example 3: Action of steroid hormones (see Fig. 7.31)

Unlike the hormones described above, steroid hormones do not remain bound to the membrane. Instead, the hormone and its receptor both move into the cell where they initiate changes in DNA function and may act by altering the rate of protein synthesis by specific genes (see p. 409).

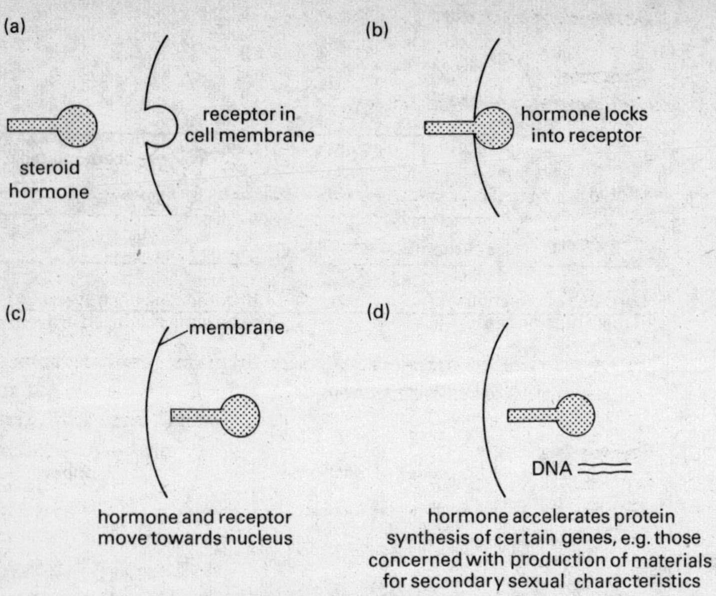
(a)
(b)
receptor in cell membrane
hormone locks into receptor
steroid hormone
(c)
(d)
membrane
DNA
hormone and receptor move towards nucleus
hormone accelerates protein synthesis of certain genes, e.g. those concerned with production of materials for secondary sexual characteristics

*Fig. 7.31* Action of steroid hormones at a target cell

## Further reading

R. A. L. Batt, *Influences on Animal Growth and Development*, Studies in Biology No. 116 (Arnold, 1980)

J. Buckle, *Animal Hormones*, Studies in Biology No. 158 (Arnold, 1983)

P. C. Clegg and A. G. Clegg, *Hormones, Cells and Organisms* (Heinemann, 1969)

F. J. Ebling and K. C. Highman, *Chemical Communication*, Studies in Biology No. 19 (Arnold, 1969)

P. J. Randle and R. M. Denton, *Hormones and Cell Metabolism*, Oxford/Carolina Biology Reader No. 79 (Packard, 1979)

## *Related questions*

**Question:**
(a) Complete the table below.

| *Hormone* | *Stimulus causing secretion* | *Site of secretion* | *Effect of increasing hormone concentration* |
|---|---|---|---|
| adrenaline | | | |
| thyroxine | | | |

(b) By referring to *either* adrenaline *or* thyroxine, explain the meaning of the term 'negative feedback'. **(10 marks)**
[AEB, June 1981, Paper 1]

**Comments:**
(a) See p. 278, Table 7.8.
(b) See p. 277.

## *Plant hormones*

There are three main hormones which control growth and development in plants:
Auxins – produced in stem apex and young leaves
Gibberellins – produced in mature leaves
Cytokinins – produced in roots
The hormones move from the site of production to other parts of the plant where they initiate changes in development.

In plants it appears to be the balance of hormones that is important rather than the amount of an individual hormone. For example, in a culture of dividing cells in a test-tube, a high cytokinin/auxin ratio produces a large number of small cells, whereas a low cytokinin/auxin ratio causes only a few giant cells to be made. For normal growth the correct ratio of the two hormones is required.

### *Auxins*

These were the first plant hormones to be discovered, when the presence of auxin in the tips of oat stems (coleoptiles) was seen to increase growth (see p. 286). Auxins are now known to have a number of functions:

1. control cell elongation;
2. initiate roots in cuttings;
3. prevent leaf abscission and fruit drop;
4. role in fruit development;
5. control of bud growth;
6. role in phototropic and geotropic responses.

### 1. Control of elongation

Auxins have been shown to increase growth in plants (both higher plants and algae). Evidence for this was obtained from experiments using indole acetic acid (IAA), the most abundant auxin. Oat coleoptiles were decapitated and growth stopped. Growth was restored by application of IAA.

To explain this, it was proposed that auxin is produced in the shoot tip and passes down to the region of elongation where it enhances growth. Growth of the coleoptile stem is in proportion to the amount of IAA present, up to an optimum value (Fig. 7.32). At very high concentrations of IAA, growth is inhibited. This explains why high concentrations of auxins can be used as herbicides.

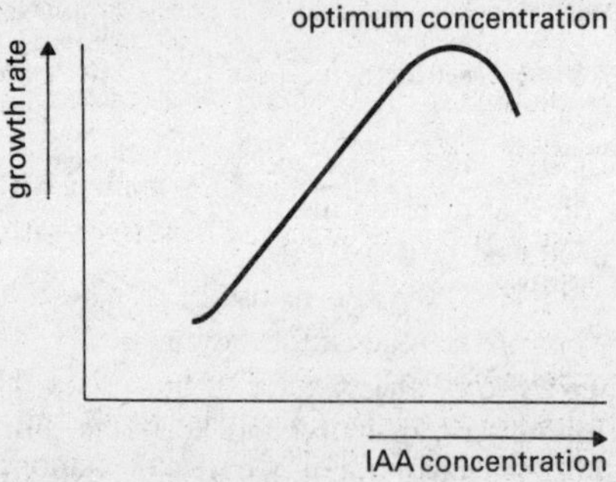
optimum concentration
growth rate
IAA concentration

*Fig. 7.32* Graph to show growth rate of a shoot against IAA concentration

Growth of a cell depends on extension of the cell walls – the cell contents simply expand to fill the extra space. In order to extend, the cell wall must become more plastic so that it can be stretched. Auxin is thought to encourage cell growth in the following ways:

(a) It causes an increase in the concentration of hydrogen ($H^+$) ions.

This provides a more favourably acidic environment for the action of enzymes which break down the cell wall (e.g. cellulase and pectin methyl esterase which break down cellulose and pectin, respectively).

(b) Auxin increases glucose uptake, so that the cell will have sufficient turgor to take up water, expand the cell contents and stretch the cell wall.

(c) It increases synthesis of new cell wall components to fill in the 'gaps' in the newly enlarged cell wall.

(d) There is also some evidence that auxins may induce particular genes to produce the enzymes required for cell growth.

### 2. Initiation of roots in cuttings

In small concentrations, auxins induce root formation in cut stems. This is thought to be related to the cytokinin/IAA ratio. See below.

### 3. Prevention of leaf abscission and fruit drop

Auxin is present in young leaves, but does not appear to affect their growth. Before a leaf or fruit can drop, an abscission layer of parenchyma cells forms across the stalk, and a layer of cork is deposited across the scar. The cells of the abscission layer become drier and lose their contents. This continues until the cells are dead, and the leaf or fruit then drops. Pectin in the middle lamella is broken down, possibly by auxin-induced activity of the enzyme pectin methyl esterase.

Abscission and fruit drop have been correlated with decreased concentration of auxin. Farmers often spray fruit trees with auxin to prevent all the fruit dropping.

### 4. Role in fruit development

The seeds of fruits are known to produce auxin, and many fruits (e.g. strawberries) will not develop if their seeds are removed.

Auxins may be responsible for the ripening of fruit by increasing the activity of enzymes which digest pectin in the middle lamella and weaken the cells, making the fruit softer. Auxin also appears to increase ethene production, which helps to ripen fruit.

### 5. Control of bud growth

Apical buds produce high concentrations of auxin, which inhibit growth of lateral buds. If the apical bud is removed, the lateral buds grow, making the plant bushier (see Fig. 7.33).

tip removed
no auxin
produced in tip
lateral branches
develop

*Fig. 7.33* Development of lateral branches on removal of the shoot tip

## 6. Role in phototropic and geotropic responses

*Phototropism*

Experiments on oat coleoptiles have shown that shoots are generally positively phototropic (bend towards light) and roots are negatively phototropic (bend away from light). It is thought that auxin encourages growth in shoots, but retards growth in roots.

In shoots, light appears to cause a redistribution of auxin, such that auxin moves away from the illuminated side of a coleoptile. Clearly, if more auxin is present on the shaded side of the coleoptile, these cells will grow more than those on the illuminated side, causing bending towards the light (see Fig. 7.34).

The opposite effect is apparent in roots, since the side with most auxin grows least (see Fig. 7.35).

*Geotropism*

If seedlings are kept in the dark, the shoot grows up and the root grows down. Since no light is present to influence the direction of growth, it is thought that the directional growth is due to gravity. Shoots grow away from gravity (negative geotropism) and roots grow towards gravity (positive geotropism).

(a) GEOTROPISM IN SHOOTS: It is known that certain cells in the shoot contain large starch grains called amyloplasts or statocysts. These are heavy, and fall to the base of the cells which they occupy (see Fig. 7.36). Treatment which destroys starch grains (e.g. heating) prevents the geotropic response of a seedling.

It is thought possible that contact of starch grains with the cell membrane 'tells' the shoot which way up it is, by inducing auxin

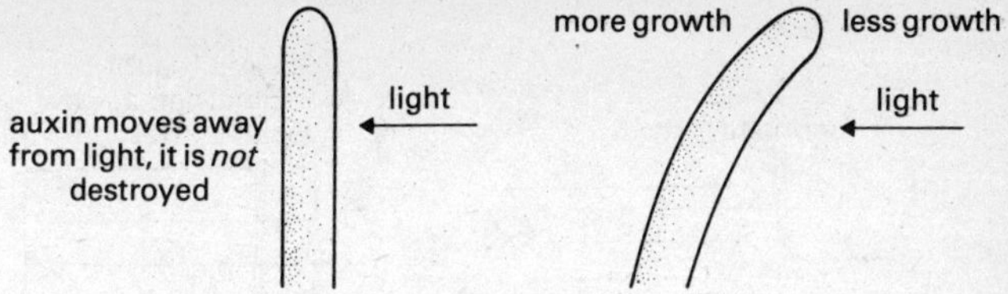
auxin moves away from light, it is *not* destroyed
light
more growth
less growth
light

*Fig. 7.34* Phototropic response of a shoot

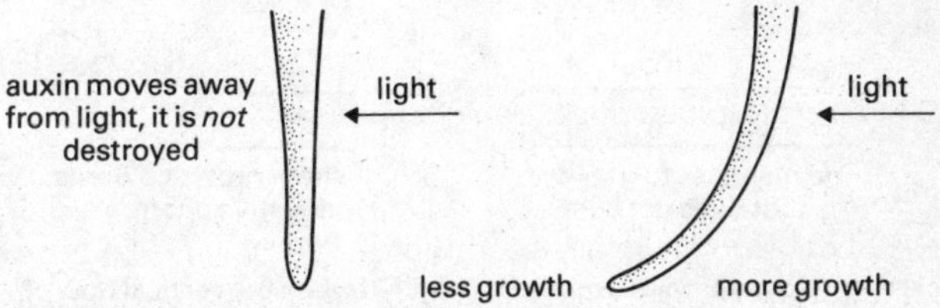
auxin moves away from light, it is *not* destroyed
light
less growth
light
more growth

*Fig. 7.35* Phototropic response of a root

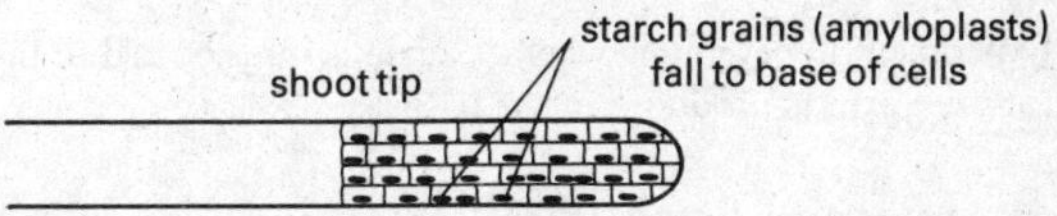
starch grains (amyloplasts) fall to base of cells
shoot tip

*Fig. 7.36* Amyloplasts of shoot cells and their response to gravity

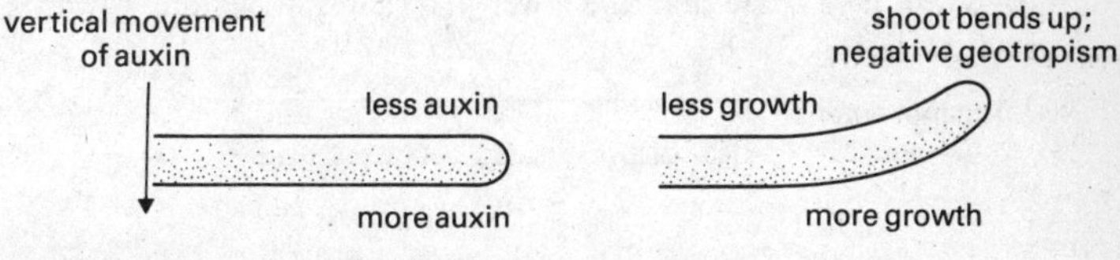
vertical movement of auxin
less auxin
more auxin
shoot bends up; negative geotropism
less growth
more growth

*Fig. 7.37* Distribution of auxin in a horizontal shoot

production. If the auxin diffused to the base of a horizontally placed shoot, the upper side would grow more than the lower side causing bending upwards (away from gravity). (See Fig. 7.37.)

An experiment to see whether auxin is translocated to the base of a horizontal shoot, or whether it is actually produced in the base, is shown in Fig. 7.38.

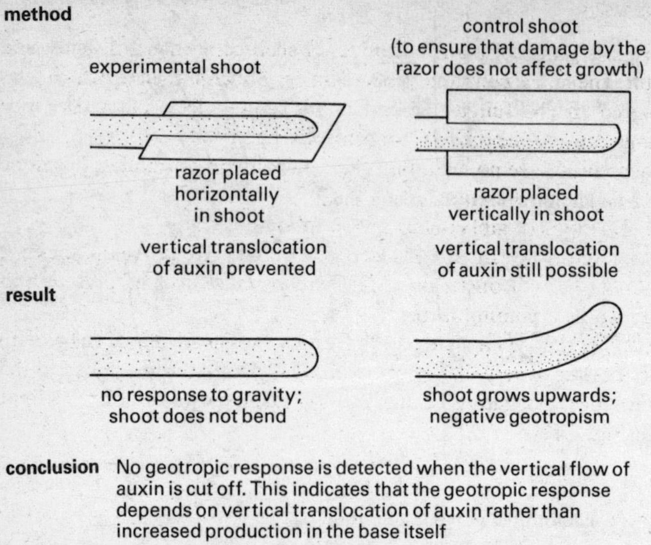
method
experimental shoot
control shoot
(to ensure that damage by the
razor does not affect growth)
razor placed
horizontally
in shoot
razor placed
vertically in shoot
vertical translocation
of auxin prevented
vertical translocation
of auxin still possible
result
no response to gravity;
shoot does not bend
shoot grows upwards;
negative geotropism
conclusion
No geotropic response is detected when the vertical flow of
auxin is cut off. This indicates that the geotropic response
depends on vertical translocation of auxin rather than
increased production in the base itself

*Fig. 7.38* Experiment to determine whether auxin is translocated to the base of a shoot or if more auxin is produced in the base

(b) GEOTROPISM IN ROOTS: Roots are extremely sensitive to auxin, and their growth is inhibited by its presence. Horizontally placed shoots tend to accumulate auxin at the base, in a manner similar to that in shoots. Since auxin inhibits growth in roots, the upper part grows at a faster rate than the lower part, causing bending towards gravity (see Fig. 7.39).

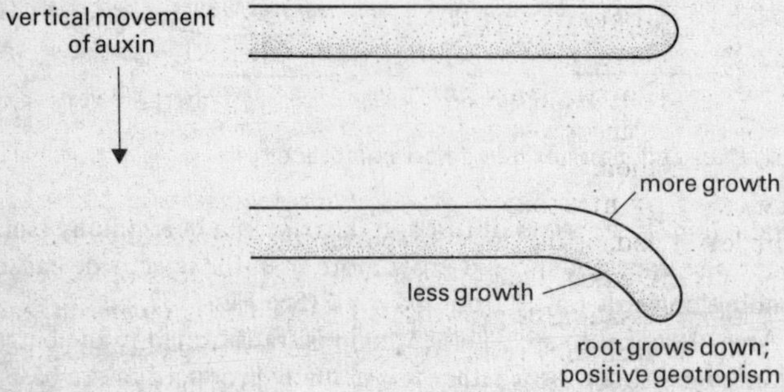
vertical movement
of auxin
more growth
less growth
root grows down;
positive geotropism

*Fig. 7.39* Geotropism in roots

### *Gibberellins*

These are a group of plant hormones concerned with cell division and growth. The most common gibberellin is gibberellic acid, which was discovered in the fungus *Gibberella fujikuroi*, which parasitizes rice seedlings causing the disease 'foolish seedling'.

Gibberellins have no action on their own: auxin or another hormone usually has to be present.

The functions of gibberellins are as follows:

1. CONTROL OF CELL ELONGATION AND GROWTH: Auxin does not promote growth on its own. Gibberellin must also be present and may act as a limiting factor.
2. ROLE IN GROWTH OF ROSETTE PLANTS: Dwarf plants (or rosette varieties) have very little gibberellin. If a gibberellin is applied to the internodes, elongation occurs and the plant grows to normal height (see Fig. 7.40).

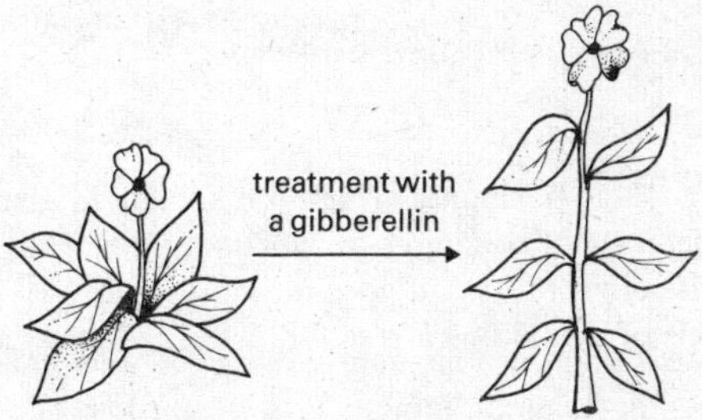
treatment with
a gibberellin

*Fig. 7.40* Treatment of a rosette plant with a gibberellin

3. PROMOTION OF SEED GERMINATION: When seeds begin to imbibe water, the embryo produces gibberellin. Gibberellin induces the aleurone layer to synthesize enzymes. These break down the food reserves, starch and protein, to a soluble form which can be used during germination.
4. DORMANCY OF BUDS AND SEEDS: Gibberellins are produced in mature leaves and, as the days get shorter, the amount of gibberellin produced is decreased. Lack of gibberellins at the apex of the plant brings about cessation of growth, and dormancy is incurred. Dormancy can be artificially reversed by application of gibberellins, and is naturally reversed when the synthesis of gibberellins in the leaves increases in spring.

5. FLOWERING: Some plants only flower after periods of cold, or after exposure to a certain number of hours of daylight. Such plants (e.g. cabbage, carrots) can be made to flower without this exposure if they are treated with gibberellic acid.
6. DIFFERENTIATION: The auxin/gibberellin ratio appears to control the rate of differentiation of cambium to xylem and phloem.

*Abscissic acid*

This is a chemical found in high concentration in dormant buds and seeds. It acts as an antagonist to gibberellin and auxin.

It has been postulated that the onset of dormancy depends on the balance of gibberellic acid and abscissic acid.

*Ethene*

This is a chemical that accelerates fruit ripening and inhibits bud growth. Low concentration of auxins induces ethene formation.

### *Cytokinins*

Cytokinins are plant hormones which are similar in structure to the DNA base adenine and contain, e.g., kinetin, zeatin. They are found in immature seeds, plant roots and coconut milk.

The functions of cytokinins are as follows:

#### 1. Interact with auxins to producc cell division and differentiation in cell cultures

If callus cells are grown on agar with a constant cytokinin/auxin ratio, cell division occurs, but there is no differentiation. Alteration of the cytokinin/auxin ratio induces differentiation. If the ratio is increased, buds and shoots develop. If the ratio is decreased, roots develop.

This ratio is thought to affect development in the plant in the following way. Normally the shoot is saturated with auxin, which is produced in the shoot apex, and the root is saturated with cytokinin (since this is produced in the roots). It is thought, therefore, that upward movement of cytokinin to the shoot increases the cytokinin/auxin ratio, causing bud and shoot development. In a similar manner auxin moves down to the roots, decreasing the ratio of cytokinin/auxin, causing root development. (See Figs 7.41 and 7.42.)

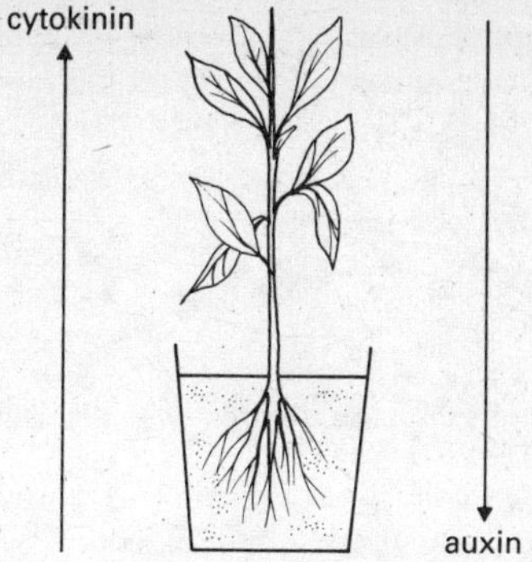
cytokinin
auxin

*Fig. 7.41* Translocation of cytokinin and auxin in plants

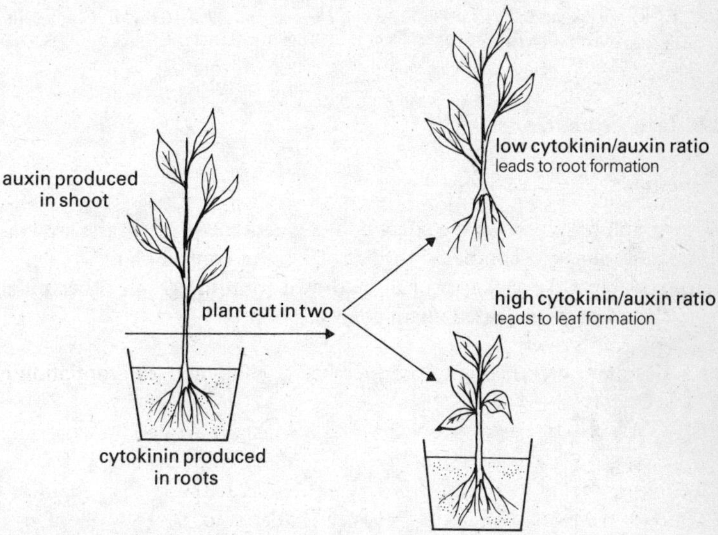
auxin produced
in shoot
plant cut in two
cytokinin produced
in roots
low cytokinin/auxin ratio
leads to root formation
high cytokinin/auxin ratio
leads to leaf formation

*Fig. 7.42* Effects of altering the cytokinin/auxin ratio in plants

## 2. Translocation of substances in leaves

If a spot of cytokinin is placed on a leaf, substances in the leaf move towards the spot (Fig. 7.43). Eventually, the rest of the leaf turns brown and dies while the spot remains healthy and green. It has been postulated that certain plant parasitic fungi and bacteria produce cytokinin-like substances, enabling them to drain the leaf of its resources.

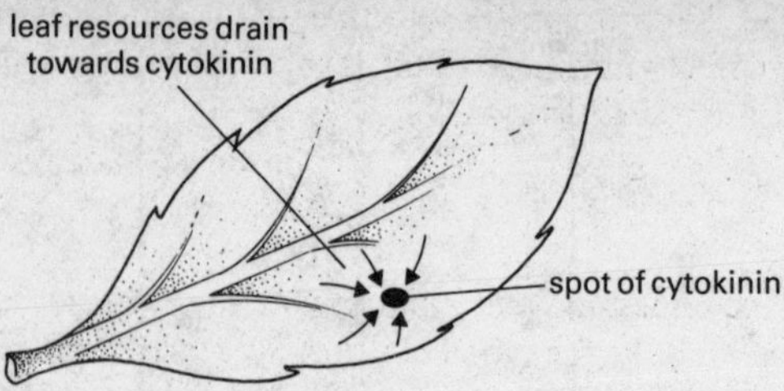
leaf resources drain towards cytokinin
spot of cytokinin

*Fig. 7.43* Movement of substances towards cytokinin in a leaf

## *Further reading*

T. A. Hill, *Endogenous Plant Growth Substances*, Studies in Biology No. 46, 2nd edition (Arnold, 1980)

R. E. Kendrick and B. Frankland, *Phytochrome and Plant Growth*, Studies in Biology No. 68 (Arnold, 1976)

## *Related questions*

### Question:

The graph below shows the effect of auxin concentration on the growth of oat seedlings as compared to that of a set of control plants.

(a) What broad conclusions can be drawn from the graph concerning the effect of increased auxin concentration on
  (i) root growth;
  (ii) shoot growth.

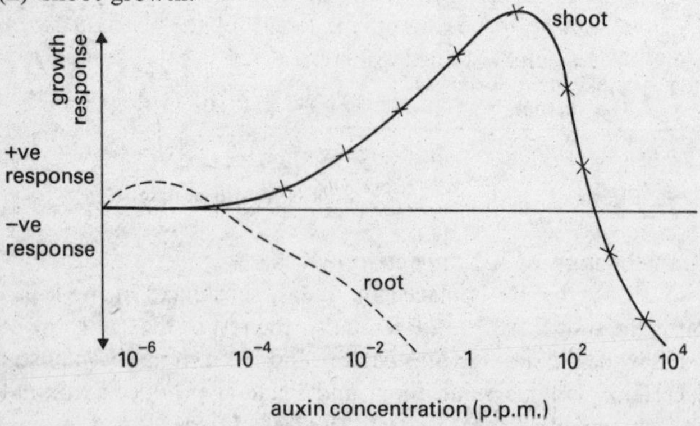
shoot
growth response
+ve response
−ve response
root
$10^{-6}$
$10^{-4}$
$10^{-2}$
1
$10^{2}$
$10^{4}$
auxin concentration (p.p.m.)

(b) From the graph it can be seen that shoot growth is substantially reduced at concentrations of 100 p.p.m. Explain how artificial auxins can be of use in agriculture.

[in the style of AEB, Paper 1]

**Comments:**

This is a question testing your ability to interpret graphical data.

(a) The question asks for broad conclusions regarding the relationship between auxin concentration and shoot and root growth. At first sight the graph may appear confusing, since the effect of auxin varies at different concentrations. In order to give a general conclusion about auxin and root and shoot growth the general trend of the graph must be given, i.e. what happens over the majority of the curve. It can therefore be said that auxin 'generally' increases growth in shoots but inhibits growth in roots.

(b) See p. 287. Auxin is more readily absorbed by broad-leaved plants than by cereals. Broad-leaved plants are also less resistant to auxin than cereals. This is of use in agriculture where the main crops are cereals and the weeds are broad-leaved plants such as plantains and dandelions. Artificial (synthetic) auxins can therefore be used as herbicides to kill weeds but not crops.

**Question:**

Segments 10 mm long were cut from just behind the apex of a batch of oat coleoptiles and equal numbers then placed in each of six petri dishes. Five dishes contained equal volumes of an auxin solution, indoleacetic acid (IAA), at different concentrations while the sixth contained an equal volume of distilled water. The six dishes were placed in a light-proof cupboard for 24 hours and the length of the segments then re-measured. The results obtained are given below:

| *IAA solution concentration (parts per million)* | *Average length (mm) after 24 hours* |
|---|---|
| $10^{-3}$ | 11.0 |
| $10^{-4}$ | 19.0 |
| $10^{-5}$ | 24.5 |
| $10^{-6}$ | 22.0 |
| $10^{-6}$ | 18.0 |
| Distilled water | 17.5 |

(a) Plot a graph to show the relationship between the change in length of the coleoptiles and IAA concentration. **(4 marks)**

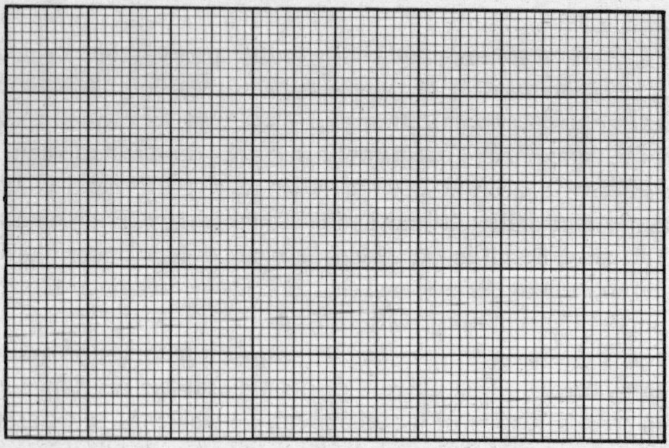

(b) From a study of your graph state two facts which you can deduce about the effect of IAA on the growth of oat coleoptiles. **(2 marks)**

(c) Why are some segments placed in distilled water in the experiment? **(1 mark)**

(d) Give one reason for selecting the segments from immediately behind the apex of the coleoptile. **(1 mark)**

(e) Explain what you think would happen to the segments if they were placed in even higher concentrations of IAA. Also show this on your graph. **(2 marks)**

(f) IAA is a plant hormone. Which of the following is also a plant hormone? Underline your choice.
chlorophyll;
cytochrome;
ethene (ethylene);
oxytocin;
riboflavin.

(g) State *one* function of this hormone. **(2 marks)**

[Oxford, June 1981, Paper 1]

**Comments:**

(a) This is a question which tests your ability to plot a graph. IAA concentration should be on the horizontal axis and the variable factor (length) on the vertical axis. Distilled water represents an IAA concentration of zero.

(b) You should have observed that IAA has different effects on growth depending on its concentration. Above $10^{-5}$ p.p.m. growth is inhibited, while below this value growth is increased.

(c) The segments which were immersed in distilled water provide a set of control results since they show how much growth occurs in the absence of applied IAA.

(d) The tissue immediately below the plant apex is the region of elongation and growth and is therefore the type of tissue most likely to respond to growth hormones such as IAA.

(e) See Fig. 7.32.

(f) and (g) See p. 292.

**Question:**

In the table below, state *three differences* between plant hormones and animal hormones.

| *Plant hormones* | *Animal hormones* |
|---|---|
| (i) | |
| (ii) | |
| (iii) | |

**(3 marks)**

[London, June 1982, Paper 2 – part question]

**Comments:**

Table of differences between plant and animal hormones.

| *Plant hormones* | *Animal hormones* |
|---|---|
| General distribution and effect on whole plant | Specific distribution and effect on various target organs |
| Hormones not produced in glands | Hormones produced in glands |
| Constant production | Production regulated by feedback mechanisms |

## *Plant responses to stimuli*

### *Responses to light*

#### Photoperiodism

This is the ability of plants to detect and respond to the changing periods of light and darkness in the 24-hour day. Investigations have shown that daylength (hours of light in each day) controls flowering in many plants. There are three kinds:

1. SHORT-DAY PLANTS: These flower when the daylength is less than a critical value. For example, ragweed produces flowers when there are fewer than 14½ hours of light per day. Short-day plants usually flower in spring (e.g. cocklebur, strawberries, primroses).
2. LONG-DAY PLANTS: These flower when the daylength is greater than a critical value. For example, spinach requires at least 14 hours of light per day before it will flower. Long-day plants usually flower in summer (e.g. clover, lettuce, potatoes).
3. DAY-NEUTRAL PLANTS: Flowering is unaffected by daylength in these plants (e.g. carrot, begonia).

The requirement for daylength to be greater or less than a critical value explains why certain plants are never found in unsuitable areas, e.g. spinach is never found in the tropics because daylength never exceeds 14 hours.

Experiments using the short-day plant cocklebur, which requires less than 15½ hours light, showed that the photoperiod is detected by the leaves. A plant stripped of all its leaves could not be induced to flower, but if only a very small portion of one leaf was left on the plant, flowering occurred. Further experiments revealed that if the light period was interrupted by short bursts of darkness, flowering was unaffected. However, if the dark period was interrupted by even a one-minute flash of light, flowering did not occur. This indicated that it was the dark period rather than the light period which controlled flowering, and that the length of uninterrupted darkness was the critical factor. (See Fig. 7.44.)

#### Germination

Lettuce seeds will only germinate if exposed to light. This is true of many seeds, and is a useful phenomenon since it 'tells' the seed how near to the soil surface it is and ensures that germination only occurs when there is sufficient light for the plant to grow successfully. It has been found that the wavelength of light responsible for inducing germination corresponds to red light, i.e. 660 nm. It has also been discovered that light of 730 nm wavelength (infra-red light) has the effect of inhibiting germination.

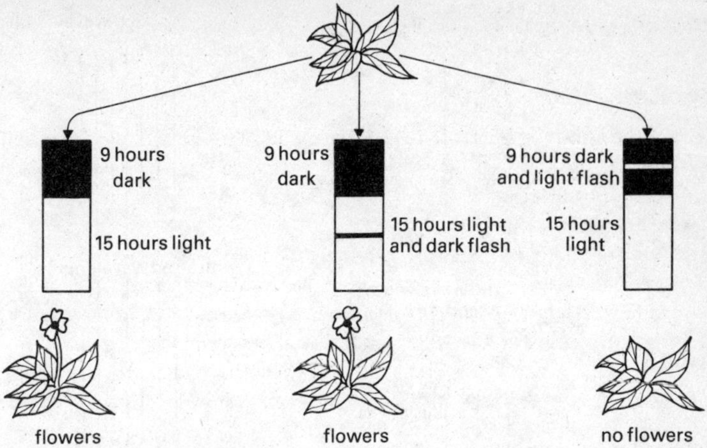
9 hours dark
15 hours light
9 hours dark
15 hours light and dark flash
9 hours dark and light flash
15 hours light
flowers
flowers
no flowers

*Fig. 7.44* Effect of light and dark periods on a short-day plant

If seeds are exposed to alternate flashes of red and infra-red light, the occurrence of germination depends on the type of light used in the last flash. If the last flash is red, germination occurs; if the last flash is infra-red, then germination is inhibited.

It has been found that seeds contain a chemical called phytochrome, which exists in two forms: $P_{660}$ and $P_{730}$. $P_{730}$ is the active form. When $P_{660}$ absorbs red light it is converted to $P_{730}$, and when $P_{730}$ absorbs infra-red light it is converted back to $P_{660}$. The other way in which $P_{730}$ is converted back to $P_{660}$ is by exposure to long periods of darkness. These relationships are summarized in Fig. 7.45.

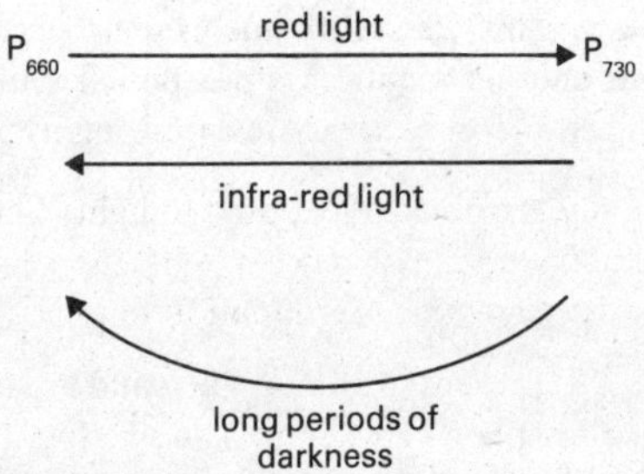
red light
P660
P730
infra-red light
long periods of darkness

*Fig. 7.45* Phytochrome

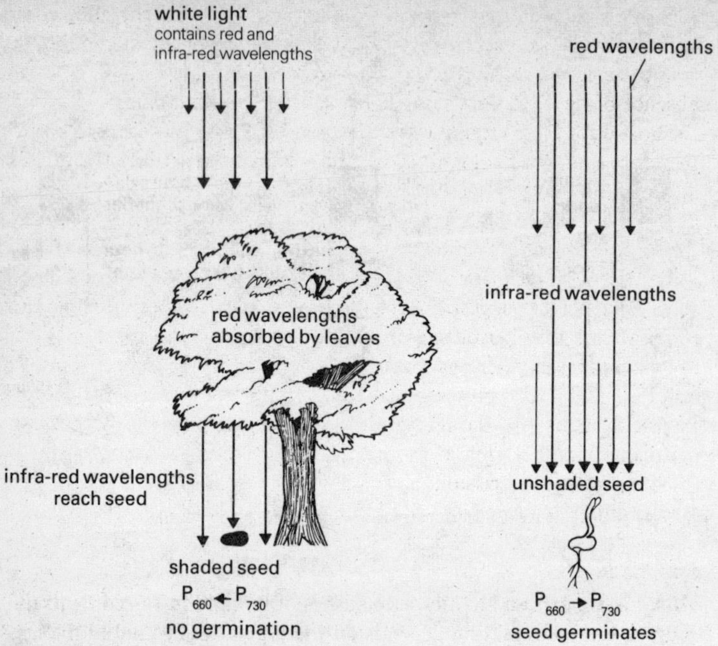
white light
contains red and
infra-red wavelengths
red wavelengths
red wavelengths
absorbed by leaves
infra-red wavelengths
infra-red wavelengths
reach seed
unshaded seed
shaded seed
P660 ← P730
no germination
P660 → P730
seed germinates

*Fig. 7.46* Effect of red/infra-red light on seed germination

The presence of $P_{730}$ appears to promote germination, therefore the ratio of red/infra-red light reaching the seedling determines whether germination will occur or not.

On the forest floor, the type of light reaching the seed depends on the amount of leaf cover in the tree growth above it. Red light is absorbed by pigments in the leaves, but infra-red light is not. The balance of red/infra-red light is then altered such that the light reaching the seed contains more infra-red light. This causes phytochrome to be converted to the inactive $P_{660}$ form and germination is postponed until the light conditions improve. When a forest area is cleared, many seedlings develop with the production of active $P_{730}$ by red light (see Fig. 7.46).

### Phytochrome and flowering

$P_{660}$ and $P_{730}$ are also present in adult plants, and are thought to control flowering. In short-day plants $P_{730}$ inhibits flowering. In long-day plants $P_{730}$ promotes flowering.

White light contains more red light than far red light and, consequently, during the day, plants will have phytochrome mostly in the $P_{730}$ active state. At night, $P_{730}$ is converted slowly back to $P_{660}$ in the absence of light. In darkness, therefore, $P_{660}$ predominates.

Short-day plants require low exposure to $P_{730}$ for flowering to occur – therefore a minimum of light. They also require long periods of unbroken darkness, so that $P_{660}$ predominates and is not converted to $P_{730}$. Long-day plants require high exposure to $P_{730}$ for flowering to occur, and therefore a maximum amount of daylight.

The exact mechanism of phytochrome action is not known. There is some evidence to suggest that phytochrome acts by altering membrane permeability, thus permitting or inhibiting movement of hormones such as gibberellin. Another hypothesis is that phytochrome is an enzyme and that $P_{730}$ and $P_{660}$ represent the active and inactive forms of the enzyme. Phytochrome is also thought to play a role in other plant responses:
(a) opening and closing of flowers and leaves at night (photonasty);
(b) onset of leaf abscission; and
(c) dormancy.

### Stratification

Many plants require a period of cold weather before they will flower. This is called stratification, and is often followed by a requirement for a period of long days to prevent the seedling from flowering too early in spring. Stratification is an important consideration in timing the planting of cereal crops. Usually, cereals must be planted before winter in order for them to flower in summer. If cereals are planted in spring, after the necessary cold period, flowering will not occur until the plants have been through a winter. Seeds can be put through an artificial form of stratification by moistening them and reducing the temperature to 1 °C for a number of weeks (vernalization).

## *Other responses*

### Touch responses in plants (thigmonasty)

Some plants respond rapidly to touch, by closing their leaves. Examples include *Mimosa*, Venus flytrap and sundew.

The Venus flytrap catches crawling insects. The leaves are hinged in the centre and are covered in tiny hairs. If the hairs are stimulated by touch, the base of the hair cell is depolarized, setting up an action potential which propagates throughout the leaf. By changing the turgor of certain cells, the leaves shut in approximately one second, trapping the insect inside. As the insect struggles, more action potentials are triggered and the trap shuts tighter. The insect is then digested.

### Circadian rhythms

Throughout the plant and animal kingdom, organisms show 'daily' movements which are called circadian rhythms. Examples include the opening and closing of flowers, and sleeping and many behavioural patterns of animals. Such rhythms are controlled by the mysterious 'biological clock'. It is not known whether the mechanism which controls these rhythms is endogenous, i.e. comes from within the organism, or whether it is controlled by some external factor, e.g. the earth's magnetic field, cosmic rays or the earth's rotation.

### Chemotropism

This is a growth movement of part of a plant in response to a chemical stimulus. Examples include growth of a pollen tube towards chemicals released through the micropyle, or growth of fungal hyphae away from the products of their metabolism.

### Chemotaxis

This is movement of a motile organism in response to a chemical stimulus. Examples include the swarming of motile fungal zoospores towards chemicals produced by the roots they infect, the swimming of antherozooids (sperms) of mosses, liverworts and ferns towards the archegonium (eggs) which produce malic acid, and movement of slime-mould amoebae in response to the chemical acrasin.

## *Further reading*

R. E. Kendrick and B. Frankland, *Phytochrome and Plant Growth*, Studies in Biology No. 68, 2nd edition (Arnold, 1983)

T. A. Villiers, *Dormancy and the Survival of Plants*, Studies in Biology No. 57 (Arnold, 1975)

S. William, *Photoperiodism in Plants* (Hillman, 1975)

*Table 7.9*. Plant responses to stimuli

| *Type of response* | *Stimulus* | *Name of response* | *Examples* |
|---|---|---|---|
| Tropic | | | |
| This is a growth movement of part of a plant in reponse to a directional stimulus.* | Light | Phototropism | Growth of plant shoots towards light (+ve phototropism) |
| | | | Growth of plant roots away from light (−ve phototropism) |
| | Gravity | Geotropism | Growth of plant shoots away from gravity (−ve geotropism) |
| | | | Growth of plant roots towards gravity (+ve geotropism) |
| | Water | Hydrotropism | Growth of roots towards water. (Shoots show no response) |
| | Chemicals | Chemotropism | Growth of pollen tube down the style in response to chemicals produced by the embryo sac (+ve chemotropism) |
| | | | Growth of fungal hyphae away from the products of their metabolism (−ve chemotropism) |
| | | | Growth of roots towards areas of high mineral concentration in soil water (+ve chemotropism) |
| | Touch | Thigmotropism | Twining of pea and vine tendrils around supporting structures |
| Tactic | | | |
| Movement of a freely motile organism or part of an organism in response to a directional stimulus. | Light | Phototaxis | Movement of the fruiting bodies of the fungus *Pilobolus* towards light |

*Table 7.9* (cont.)

| *Type of response* | *Stimulus* | *Name of response* | *Examples* |
|---|---|---|---|
| Movement towards the stimulus is +vely tactic. Movement away from the stimulus is −vely tactic. | | | Movement of unicellular algae towards a light source |
| | Temperature | Thermotaxis | Movement of unicellular green algae (e.g. *Chlamydomonas*) towards areas of optimum temperature |
| | Chemicals | Chemotaxis | Movement of fungal zoospores in response to chemical produced by the roots which they infect (e.g. zoospores of *Phytophthera palmivora* which infect fruit trees) |
| | | | Movement of slime-mould amoebae in response to the chemical acrasin |
| | | | Movement of the male gametes of mosses, liverworts and ferns in response to malic acid produced by the female gametes |
| Nastic | | | |
| Movement of part of a plant in response to a stimulus. The direction of the response is unrelated to that of the stimulus | Light | Photonasty | Closing of flower petals at night and opening in the daytime (e.g. daisies) |
| | Temperature | Thermonasty | Opening of flowers at high temperatures and closing at low temperatures (e.g. tulips) |
| | Touch | Thigmonasty | Insectivorous plants, e.g. Venus flytrap (*Dionaea*) and *Mimosa*, close rapidly when touched – a mechanism brought about by a series of action potentials |

* +ve tropism = growth towards the stimulus; −ve tropism = growth away from stimulus.

## *Related questions*

**Question:**
When a young pea seedling is placed horizontally in a dark chamber and allowed to grow for a few days, it is found that the shoot curves upwards and the root downwards. Investigations have shown that in such situations there is a higher concentration of an auxin (indole acetic acid) on the lower side of both the shoot and the root.

(a) (i) Auxins are known to influence cell elongation. Suggest how the increased concentration of auxin brings about the upward curvature of a shoot but the downward curvature of a root.
(ii) Describe how you would carry out an investigation to determine whether the increased auxin concentration in the shoot is a result of auxin synthesis on the lower side of the shoot or of a redistribution of auxin in the shoot. **(10 marks)**

(b) The diagram shows enlargements of two cells, one from each side of the root cap of a cress seedling (*Lepidium sativum*).

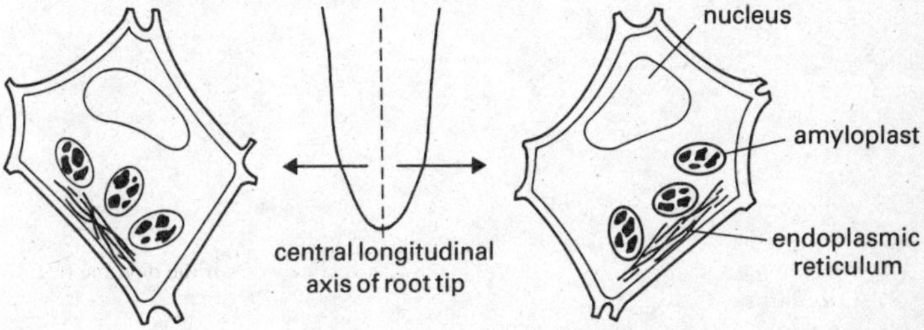
nucleus
amyloplast
endoplasmic reticulum
central longitudinal axis of root tip

Suggest the mechanism by which these cells respond to gravity. **(3 marks)**

(c) In addition to gravity, light can influence plants in a number of ways.
(i) State *four* different ways in which plants respond to light, other than phototropic or photosynthetic responses.
(ii) Explain how any *one* of these responses is brought about. **(7 marks)**

**Comments:**

(a) (i) See p. 288. This question can be adequately answered using a brief explanation and annotated diagrams.
(ii) See the experiment described on p. 290.

(b) Although the question concerns roots, the mechanism of action of the amyloplasts (starch grains) is the same as that explained for shoots (see p. 288). The effect of increased auxin concentration in shoots is the opposite to that in roots. Therefore roots grow towards gravity while shoots grow away from it.

(c) (i) See p. 303, Table 7.9.
(ii) Since there are 7 marks for this part of the question, candidates are advised to choose a response which they know a reasonable amount about, for example 'phytochrome and flowering' (p. 298) or 'phytochrome and germination' (p. 298).

# 8. Support and locomotion

## *Support*

Land organisms evolved from aquatic organisms. Aquatic vertebrates are supported by the water while their skeletons provide protection and the rigid framework for muscle attachment required for locomotion.

The subsequent exploitation of a terrestrial environment necessitated the use of the skeleton for support.

### *Support in plants*

In a terrestrial environment, the competition for light has led to the evolution of plants over 100 metres in height.

Support in plants is provided by two means.

#### 1. Mechanical strengthening

Plant cells possess a firm cellulose cell wall. Additional strength may be provided by lignin in collenchyma and the stronger sclerenchyma.

Woody plants are supported by their xylem. As xylem is dead, and therefore does not make any energy demands, trees can grow to enormous heights. The 'wood' of woody plants is essentially sclerenchyma.

In dicotyledonous stems the mechanical tissues are located close to the perimeter (see Fig. 5.17) as the main forces to which the stem is exposed are the bending forces due to the action of the wind. In contrast, the root undergoes 'pulling' stresses and compression as it pushes through the soil. In order to deal with these forces the mechanical tissues form a central core.

#### 2. Turgor

In herbaceous plants, support is achieved by the turgidity of parenchyma in the pith and cortex. Turgor is the hydrostatic pressure created by water entering cells by osmosis (p. 224).

## *Support and locomotion in animals*

There are three main types of animal skeleton.

### 1. Hydrostatic skeletons

Animals such as earthworms utilize hydrostatic pressure for support. The coelemic fluid is virtually incompressible, thus allowing the segmentally arranged muscles to act on it and bring about locomotion. The circular and longitudinal muscles co-ordinate to produce peristaltic waves along the length of the animal from the head backwards. These waves of contraction are accompanied by protraction of the chaetae, and the combined effect results in an effective propulsion.

### 2. Exoskeletons

Arthropods possess a chitinous exoskeleton which in some cases (e.g. lobster, crab and crayfish) is impregnated with calcium carbonate for added protection.

The exoskeleton acts as a supporting structure and an area for muscle attachment (Fig. 8.1). As a completely rigid exoskeleton would prevent movement, segments of exoskeletons are attached to each other by thin flexible cuticle. The exoskeleton is also interrupted by the openings of various glands, the digestive, respiratory and reproductive systems, and sensory hairs.

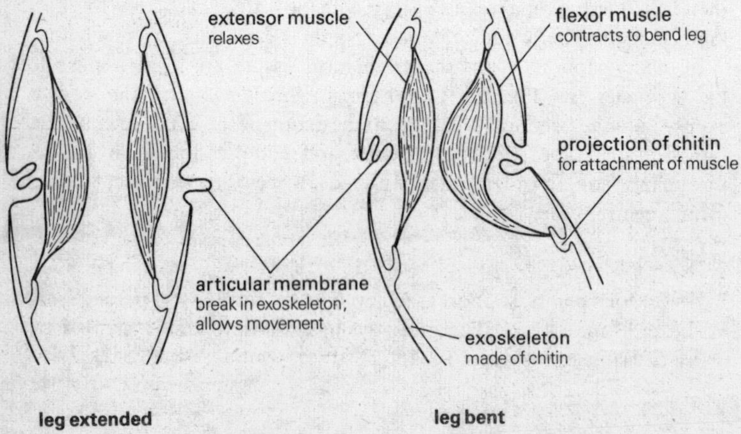
extensor muscle
relaxes
flexor muscle
contracts to bend leg
projection of chitin
for attachment of muscle
articular membrane
break in exoskeleton;
allows movement
exoskeleton
made of chitin
leg extended
leg bent

*Fig. 8.1* Muscle attachment in an insect (antagonistic muscles responsible for leg movement)

The exoskeleton is secreted by the underlying epidermal cells and is essentially a cuticle composed of three layers:

(a) Epicuticle – outer layer, which is thin, waxy and waterproof.

(b) Exocuticle – the middle layer, which is rigid, being made of chitin (p. 55) impregnated with tanned proteins.

(c) Endocuticle – the layer adjacent to the epidermal cells and consisting of flexible chitin.

Chitin is a dead material, so the cuticle must be shed at intervals to permit growth. This moulting process is known as **ecdysis**.

### 3. Endoskeletons

Endoskeletons are found in vertebrates. They are mesodermal, comprising bone or cartilage or both.

Cartilage forms the entire skeleton of elasmobranch fishes (e.g. shark and dogfish) and the first skeleton of mammalian embryos. Most vertebrates are supported by a bony skeleton.

The arrangement of an endoskeleton, whether of bone or cartilage, follows a uniform plan:

An **axial skeleton** runs the length of the body near the dorsal surface. In the trunk and tail this consists of separate **vertebrae**. In the head it consists of the **skull**, which is made up of the **cranium**, surrounding the brain, and the **jaws**. The upper jaw is fused to the cranium and the lower jaw is connected to the upper jaw by a movable joint.

Attached to the skeleton in the trunk of vertebrates are the **ribs**. In land vertebrates there is a central axial skeleton or **sternum**.

The remainder of the skeleton is known as the **appendicular skeleton** and is made up of the limbs. Limbs are not present in the simplest vertebrates, however, and some other vertebrates have lost their limbs in the course of evolution. The appendicular skeleton, therefore, cannot be regarded as a classifying feature of the vertebrates.

In most mammals the complete vertebral column is arched and resembles the arch of a bridge. The limbs can be compared to the bridge pillar supports. The shapes of the bones in the skeletons relate to their use for muscle attachment, leverage and jointing.

Joints are present throughout the skeleton to provide flexibility for movement. Synovial joints allow the greatest degree of movement. Examples can be seen in the jaw, between the atlas and axis (where the skull meets the vertebral column) and between bones in the fingers and toes. The ball and socket joint of the hip is also a typical synovial joint (Fig. 8.2).

The bones of the skeleton must be strong and light, with a certain

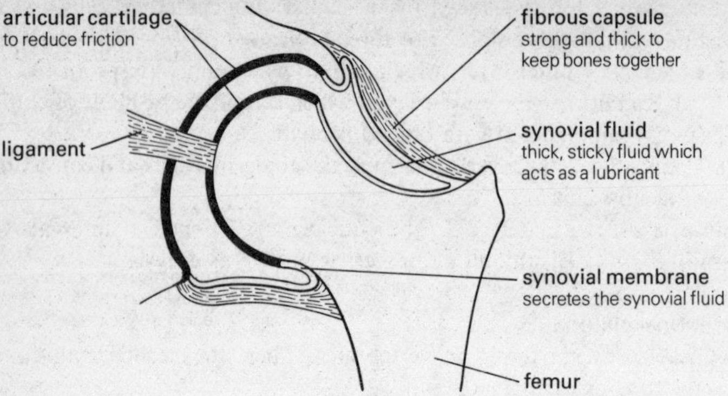
articular cartilage
to reduce friction
ligament
fibrous capsule
strong and thick to keep bones together
synovial fluid
thick, sticky fluid which acts as a lubricant
synovial membrane
secretes the synovial fluid
femur

*Fig. 8.2* Synovial joint, typified by the ball-and-socket joint of the hip

degree of flexibility. A main supportive bone in mammals is the **femur** (Fig. 8.3). It supports much of the body weight, particularly in humans which are bipedal, and is thus under compression. It thus experiences most stress around the outside with very slight strain in the centre. The femur is adapted for coping with this strain by having compact bone on the outside with a central hollow marrow cavity. The hollow centre confers a reduction in weight. This type of structure is also advantageous for resisting the bending and torsion forces to which the femur is subjected.

There are a number of similarities between the supportive structure of a long bone (such as the femur) and a herbaceous stem.

(a) Their overall shape is the same, i.e. long, thin cylinders.
(b) The supporting tissue is located around the outside, i.e. compact bone and the vascular bundles in the long bone and herbaceous stem, respectively.
(c) They have relatively light, non-supporting tissue in the centre. Like the long bone, some herbaceous stems, e.g. dandelions, are hollow. Pith may be present in some other stems, and this could act as a secondary supporting tissue owing to turgor.

## Types of locomotion

### Amoeboid movement

This is the means of locomotion in amoeboid protozoans, slime fungi, nematode spermatozoa and vertebrate cells such as lymphocytes.

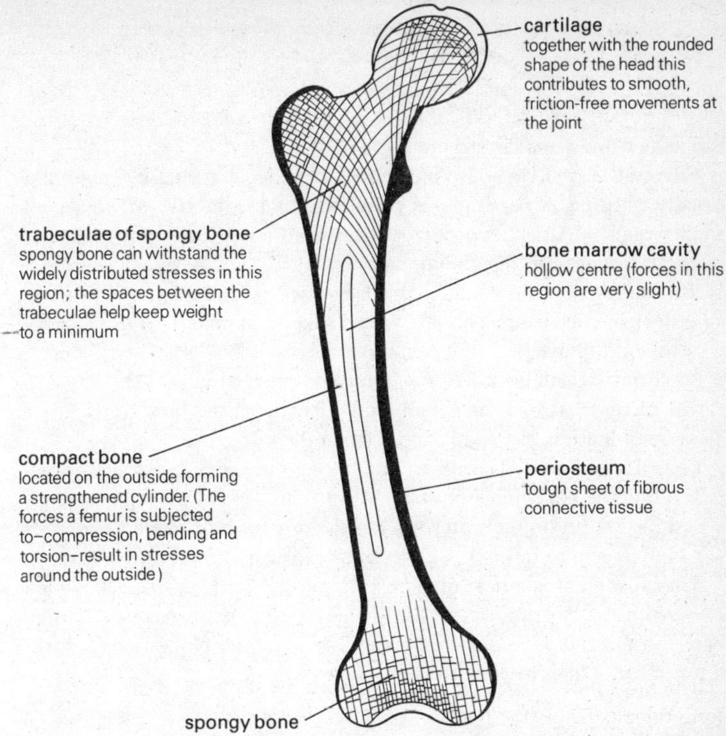
cartilage
together with the rounded shape of the head this contributes to smooth, friction-free movements at the joint
trabeculae of spongy bone
spongy bone can withstand the widely distributed stresses in this region; the spaces between the trabeculae help keep weight to a minimum
bone marrow cavity
hollow centre (forces in this region are very slight)
compact bone
located on the outside forming a strengthened cylinder. (The forces a femur is subjected to–compression, bending and torsion–result in stresses around the outside)
periosteum
tough sheet of fibrous connective tissue
spongy bone

*Fig. 8.3* LS of mammalian femur, showing structural adaptations to the forces to which it is subjected

Movement is due to protoplasmic streaming, without active propulsion by any specialized part.

Cytoplasm is thixotropic, i.e. can undergo gel-sol-gel changes. At the point where the pseudopodium is to be formed, the cytoplasm (plasmagel) liquefies, thus creating a weakness in this region. The liquid endoplasm (plasmasol) is forced into this region causing streaming. It then solidifies, forming plasmagel on either side of the weakened region.

The three main theories to explain the force that maintains the flow of cytoplasm are:

1. The endoplasm is *pushed* forwards when the posterior end contracts.
2. The core of endoplasm is *pulled* forwards as the anterior gel contracts.

3. The endoplasm is pushed forwards by sliding filament ratchets. This theory has features in common with muscular contraction (see below).

### *Ciliary and flagellar movement*

See ciliary and flagellar structure (p. 22).

Cilia and flagella produce movement in aqueous media by rapid and usually rhythmical beating. They are used as locomotive organelles in small organisms such as protozoa, in ciliated larvae and in gametes.

The movement of the cilium may be:

1. Pendular – the straight cilium beats backwards and forwards, bending only from its base. The effective stroke is similar to the recovery stroke only faster.
2. Flexural – bending starts at the tip and passes towards the base. In the recovery stroke the cilium straightens from the base to the tip.
3. A combination of pendular and flexural.

Flagella commonly beat in an undulating movement, in which waves pass along the flagellum from base to tip. This type of movement exerts a pushing action on the water, and so the organism or gamete proceeds with the flagellum trailing (e.g. vertebrate sperm).

The movement is more complex in organisms such as *Euglena*, which swim with the flagellum in front. In this case the wave passes from the base to tip *around* the flagellum as well as along it. This causes a cork-screw effect which propels the body forward.

### *Muscular movement*

Specialized muscle tissue is common in invertebrates and vertebrates. Contractile *threads* (e.g. myonemes) are found in some protozoa and are used for locomotion in some parasites (e.g. *Monocystis*). Musculo-epithelial cells are found in coelenterates, where most of the ectoderm and endoderm cells possess 'muscle-tails' which are contractile fibres.

The muscle tissue involved in locomotion is striated (skeletal) muscle (see p. 40) which characteristically contracts, and also tires, rapidly.

#### The theory of muscle contraction

Observations of the ultrastructure, and selective chemical treatment of the myofibrils of striated muscle, have shown thick filaments of the protein myosin and thin filaments of the protein actin which overlap each other. The ultrastructure shows dark and light banding. The dark bands correspond to areas where actin and myosin overlap, and the light bands to actin only (Fig. 1.12b).

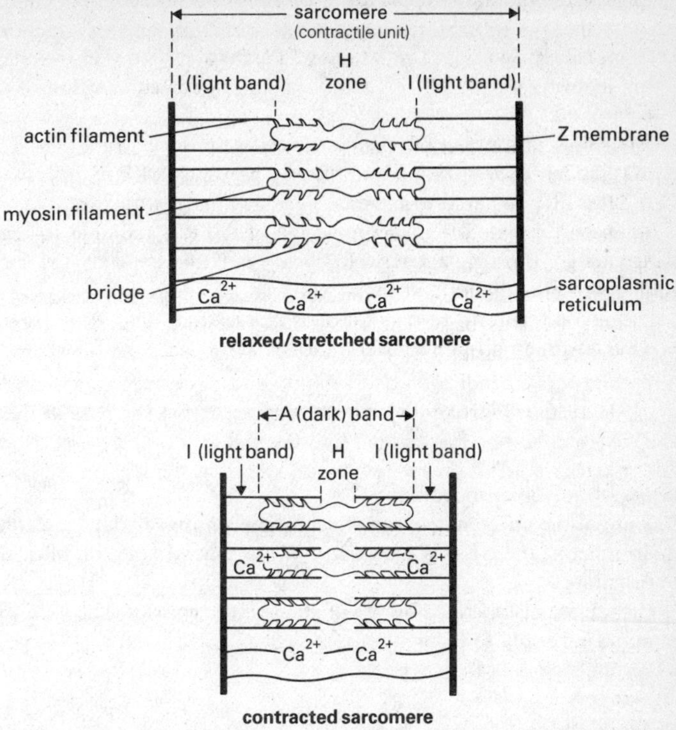
sarcomere
(contractile unit)
H
I (light band)
zone
I (light band)
actin filament
Z membrane
myosin filament
bridge
Ca2+
Ca2+
Ca2+
Ca2+
sarcoplasmic
reticulum
relaxed/stretched sarcomere
A (dark) band
I (light band)
H
zone
I (light band)
Ca2+
Ca2+
Ca2+
Ca2+
contracted sarcomere

*Fig. 8.4* Diagrammatic representation of the sliding filament hypothesis

When contracted, the myofibrils showed wider dark bands and narrower light bands. However, there was no actual *shortening* of the actin and myosin filaments.

These observations indicated that the actin and myosin filaments were sliding over each other, and this led to the **sliding filament hypothesis** (Fig. 8.4), which supposes the following conditions necessary for the sliding of the filaments:

1. Resting potential present on sarcolemma.
2. Depolarization due to action potential set up at neuro-muscular junction.
3. Passage of action potential sarcoplasmic reticulum vesicles which pump calcium ions into the sarcoplasm.
4. Calcium ions activate troponin (protein) which displaces tropomyosin

(protein) at the site of the myosin bridge formation, allowing binding to occur.

5. Immediately on bridge formation ATPase is activated. This results in the hydrolysis of ATP to supply the energy for contraction of the bridge.
6. After muscle contraction, the vesicles take up the calcium ions. This lowers their concentration and thereby prevents ATP hydrolysis.
7. ATP is also required to break the bridge after contraction.

It has been estimated that one molecule of ATP is required for *each* bridge to go through a complete cycle, and this explains the large numbers of mitochondria in the sarcoplasm.

The second energy reserve is phosphocreatine. This requires the enzyme creatine phosphotransferase to split it:

$$\text{ADP} + \text{phosphocreatine} \xrightarrow{\text{creatine phosphotransferase}} \text{ATP} + \text{creatine}$$

## Types of muscular movement

Because of the different ways in which organisms have adapted to their environments, there is a great variety of movement based on muscular contraction.

The skeleton is operated by sets of **antagonistic muscles**. The following components apply to locomotion:

(a) propulsion
(b) support
(c) stability

Some of the main types of muscular locomotion are described below.

### *Swimming*

In the fish there is a metameric arrangement of skeletal muscle in the body wall. This allows contractions to pass posteriorly in a wave form. The muscles of the right and left sides of the fish act antagonistically about the relatively incompressible spinal column. The waves pass down each side alternately.

The vertebrae are joined in such a way as to allow movement in only one plane. Therefore muscular contraction brings about a movement of the body from side to side. As the wave of contraction proceeds posteriorly, the thrust increases owing to the greater degree of flexibility towards the tail. It reaches a maximum at the caudal fin.

The bulk of the skeletal muscle in fishes lies in **myotomes** corresponding to the vertebrae. The myotomes are separated from each other by connective tissue. There are also skeletal muscles between the pelvic and pectoral girdles and related fins, and these control stability.

Yawing is regulated by the dorsal and anal fins. In teleosts the lateral flattening of the body also helps regulate yawing. Rolling is prevented by all the fins (vertical and horizontal) offering resistance to the water. Pitching is regulated by the pectoral and pelvic fins (i.e. the horizontal fins).

In elasmobranchs, such as the dogfish, there is *no* swim bladder and the net specific gravity is slightly greater than the sea water. A particular depth or rise is maintained by swimming forwards. Lift is provided by the heterocercal tail, pectoral fins and the shape of the head.

In teleosts, buoyancy is provided by the swim bladder and the pectoral fins. The swim bladder is a gas-filled sac that lies under the vertebral column and functions as a hydrostatic organ.

Speed in teleosts is proportional to the length of the body and the frequency of tail beats. A maximum speed is soon reached as the frequency of tail beats decreases with length.

The streamlined shape improves efficiency. In animals such as the whale and dolphin which have horizontal tail flukes, the stroke is up and down rather than the side-to-side movement in fishes.

### *Insect flight*

The movement of the wings in insects provides both forward thrust and lifting power. The wings are controlled by two sets of muscles: direct and indirect.

1. *Direct muscles.* These are attached to the wing bases and they control the wing setting.
2. *Indirect muscles.* These are attached to the walls of the thorax and *not* to the wings. (NB. The attachment of the wings to the thorax is a good example of a lever.)

Contraction of the indirect muscles alters the shape of the thorax and results in movement of the wings. The rate of beating can be several hundred times per second.

In the Diptera the hind-wings have become modified to form halteres. These have special muscles, are freely movable and are capable of vibration. They perceive stimuli related to balance and enable the insect to co-ordinate flight movements.

### *Bird flight*

Flight is the main method of locomotion in birds. The structure of the bird has the following adaptations for flight.

1. The body is very light – most of the long bones are hollow and many of the cavities are filled with air sacs which communicate with the lungs.
2. There is a large wing-span.
3. The feathers form a smooth large surface.
4. There are powerful pectoral muscles for rapid wing movement (eight beats per second in some cases).

When a current of air moves against the surface of a wing with its front edge tilted upwards, the air will encounter less resistance over the upper surface and will have greater velocity. Thus a negative pressure is created above the wing. Air under the wing has to overcome a greater resistance, and thus exerts a positive pressure upwards against the wing. The combination of these two forces lifts the wing. The force of the air also tends to sweep the wing backwards horizontally (Fig. 8.5). The wing of the bird acts as an aerofoil.

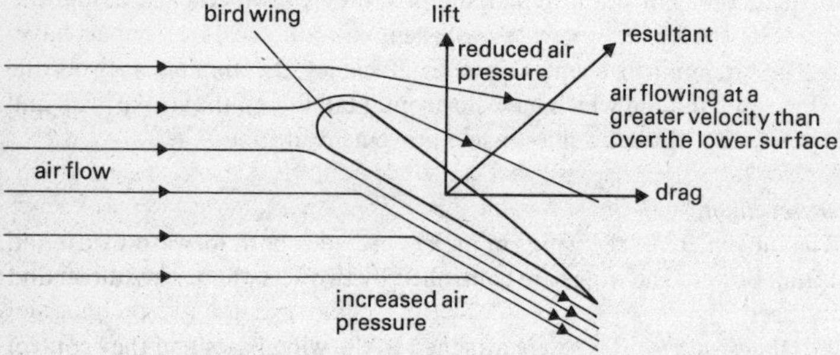
bird wing
lift
resultant
reduced air pressure
air flowing at a greater velocity than over the lower surface
air flow
drag
increased air pressure

*Fig. 8.5* The bird wing acting as an aerofoil

When the wings are flapping, the downstroke is vertical and gives lift. The upstroke is upwards and backwards and gives forward thrust. Feathers interlock on the downstroke, increasing air resistance and therefore upward thrust. On the upstroke the feathers open, lessening the air resistance and therefore decreasing any down thrust.

Soaring is achieved by making use of rising air currents. It is only possible for birds with a large wing span, e.g. eagles and vultures.

Steering is affected by the tail and unequal beating of the wings. The tail and wings can also be used as brakes.

*Flight in mammals*

Bats are the only mammals capable of true flight. The wings are made up of a thin layer of skin which is stretched between the fore and hind limbs and attached to the sides of the body. The bones of the forearm are elongated to provide a framework for the wing. The index and middle fingers of the hand support the leading edge of the wing while the other two fingers extend back to the trailing edge. The trailing edge is also supported at the ankle. The wrist bones are fused to give the wings strength.

The movements of the wings used to produce flight are similar to those used by birds.

Gliding has become effective in a few vertebrates where a horizontal membrane confers upthrust on the body from the air. Examples of gliding mammals include the flying squirrels of Africa and the flying lemurs of the Philippines.

*Walking and running*

These methods of locomotion are achieved by special appendages which act as levers against a firm support. They are principally an adaptation to a terrestrial habit. In order to be able to walk and run, animals have had to solve the problems of balance, support and shock absorption.

*Insects*

Each of the six legs of an insect is a tube of chitinous exoskeleton. Along the length of each leg are flexible joints. Pairs of antagonistic muscles are found *inside* each limb (see Fig. 8.1).

A walking insect will have three legs in contact with the ground at any one time. The arrangement of legs touching the ground, two on one side and one on the other, forms a tripod and confers stability.

*Mammals*

The various muscles used by mammals in walking are classified according to the effects they produce:

(a) *flexors* bend a limb at a joint
(b) *extensors* straighten a limb at a joint
(c) *abductors* move a limb away from the body
(d) *adductors* move a limb towards the body.

In tetrapods the triceps extensor muscles of the forelimbs serve to straighten the limbs and hold the body up. The forelimbs also dissipate the upthrust on impact with the ground when landing, etc. In bipedal organisms the forelimbs are used for lifting weights (see Fig. 8.7).

In all mammals the hind limbs provide thrust (which moves the body forwards) from the pressure of the foot against the ground. (Fig. 8.6 illustrates the forces about the tetrapod vertebral column). The

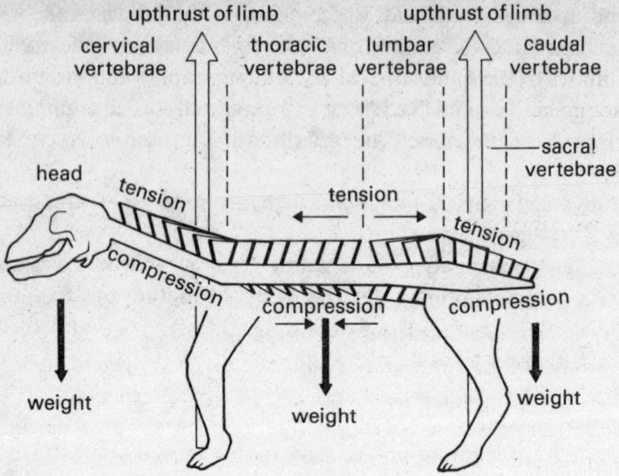
upthrust of limb
upthrust of limb
cervical vertebrae
thoracic vertebrae
lumbar vertebrae
caudal vertebrae
sacral vertebrae
head
tension
tension
tension
compression
compression
compression
weight
weight
weight

*Fig. 8.6* Forces about the vertebral column of a tetrapod

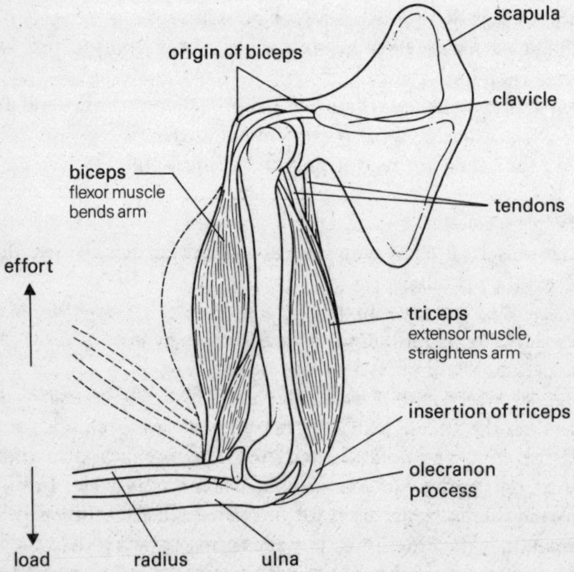
scapula
origin of biceps
clavicle
biceps
flexor muscle
bends arm
tendons
effort
triceps
extensor muscle,
straightens arm
insertion of triceps
olecranon
process
load
radius
ulna

*Fig. 8.7* Muscles associated with movement in the fore-limb of a bipedal animal

propulsive or power stroke is provided by the contraction of extensor muscles straightening the limb. The recovery stroke is made by bending the limb with flexor muscles. Thus in locomotion the bones of the limbs are acting as levers. The limbs are operated by sets of antagonistic muscles acting across well-lubricated joints.

### *Movement in plants*

It is essential for animals to move in order to find food and to find a mate in sexual reproduction. Plants can fulfil these requirements by remaining in a fixed position.

However, certain unicellular algae, e.g. *Chlamydomonas* and some bacteria, possess flagella and undergo tactic movements.

Motile reproductive structures (e.g. zoospores) are common in the lower groups and motile gametes are present in phyla up to and including the gymnosperms.

These movements are restricted to water or water-films.

Slime fungi 'creep' over wet surfaces in a form of amoeboid movement.

Growth movements such as tropisms (see p. 288) and mechanical movements such as the opening of fern sporangia are also found. The mechanical movements are hygroscopic, i.e. due to water absorption.

Only in the most highly evolved terrestrial plants, the angiosperms, are all signs of locomotion lost.

## *Further reading*

J. Currey, *Animal Skeletons*, Studies in Biology No. 22 (Arnold, 1970)
J. Gray, *Animal Locomotion* (Weidenfeld & Nicolson)
C. J. Pennycuick, *Animal Flight*, Studies in Biology No. 33 (Arnold, 1972)
J. W. S. Pringle, *Insect Flight*, Oxford/Carolina Biology Reader No. 47 (Packard, 1974)
D. R. Wilkie, *Muscle*, Studies in Biology No. 11, 2nd edition (Arnold, 1976)

## *Related questions*

**Question:**
Muscles achieve movement by reacting against each other and against a skeleton.

(a) What type of skeleton occurs in (i) a mammal, (ii) an earthworm and (iii) an insect? **(3 marks)**

(b) In the table below state (i) where in the limb of a mammal you would expect to find tendons and ligaments, and (ii) whether or not the tendon and ligament are elastic.

| | (i) Site | (ii) Elasticity |
|---|---|---|
| TENDONS | | |
| LIGAMENTS | | |

**(4 marks)**

(c) What properties of muscle tissue require that muscles work in antagonistic pairs? **(2 marks)**

(d) On the diagrams below, draw in the muscles and their attachments that cause the following movements.
(i) The movement of the human arm at the elbow. (Label the muscles you have drawn.)

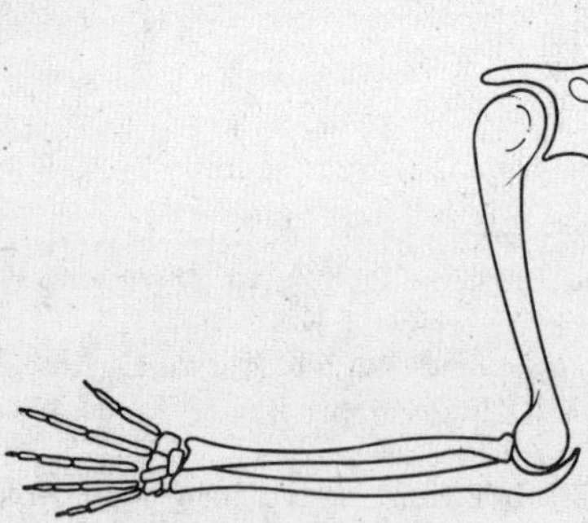

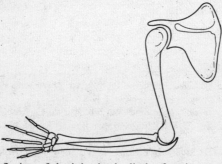

(ii) The flexing of the joint in the limb of an insect.

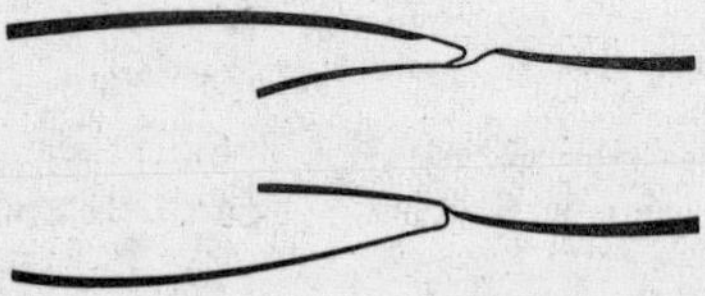

**(6 marks)**

(e) Describe how the skeleton of an earthworm is used, together with muscles and chaetae, to achieve locomotion. **(4 marks)**

**(Total 19 marks)**

[London, Jan. 1985, Paper 1]

**Comments:**

(a) (i) endoskeleton
(ii) hydrostatic skeleton
(iii) exoskeleton

(b) Tendons – attaching skeletal muscle to bone, non-elastic
Ligaments – attaching bones to bones across joints, elastic

(c) In answering this part of the question it must be remembered that muscles are only effective during contraction. There must therefore be a pair working together in which the contraction of one stretches the other.

(d) (i) The question asks for the muscles and *their attachments* to be drawn, and therefore the origin and insertion of each muscle must be illustrated accurately. Do not forget to name the muscles.
For diagram and labels see Fig. 8.7. Remember the biceps contracts to bend the arm, i.e. it is a flexor muscle.
(ii) See Fig. 8.1. Note the absence of chitin projections on the figure in question. Therefore attach the muscles directly to the exoskeleton either side of the joint.

(e) See p. 308.

**Question:**

(a) The figure below is a diagrammatic representation of a longitudinal section through the head of a human femur.

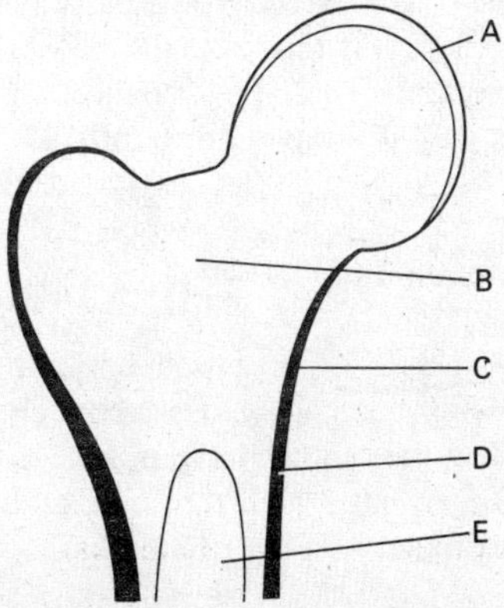
A
B
C
D
E

State the names of the *five* parts labelled A, B, C, D and E. **(5 marks)**

(b) Explain how the bone structure represented in the diagram assists in:
(i) reducing the overall weight of the skeleton without reducing its strength
(ii) allowing smooth friction-free movement at joints
(iii) distributing the weight of the animal from bone to bone when the limb bones are in different relative positions. **(8 marks)**

(c) (i) State *three* ways in which the structure of a long bone such as a femur and the stem of a herbaceous plant are similar. **(3 marks)**
(ii) Name *two* different types of stress which operate both on long bones and on plant stems. **(2 marks)**

(d) The tensile strength of tendon is much greater than that of muscle. What is the significance of this difference in tensile strengths? **(2 marks)**

**(Total 20 marks)**

**Comments:**

(a) See Fig. 8.3.

(b) (i) The spongy bone combines strength with lightness owing to the distribution of trabeculae in the lines of stress and the air spaces between them. The outer layer of compact bone provides a rigid cylinder to withstand stresses around the outside, but has a lightweight interior (bone marrow).
(ii) The cartilage together with the rounded shape of the head of the bone helps smooth, friction-free movements at the joint. Do *not* mention synovial fluid, as the synovial membrane and related structures are not shown in the diagram.
(iii) The shape of the head of the bone is such that it forms a ball and socket joint with the neighbouring bone (in this case the pelvis) allowing limb movement in many directions. This type of connection channels the downward force, due to weight, straight down the shaft of the bone.

(c) (i) See p. 310.
(ii) Compression – due to pressure.
Tension – due to bending.

(d) As the tendon has a higher tensile strength it prevents the muscle contracting too powerfully and possibly damaging itself. Stretch receptors, which discharge impulses to the central nervous system, are found in tendons. The tendon organ has a high threshold and only responds when the tension is extreme.

## 9. Reproduction and development

### *Reproduction*

Reproduction is the ability of living organisms to produce new organisms which are like themselves. There are two types: sexual and asexual reproduction. Plants and lower animals often reproduce asexually and/or sexually, but higher animals only reproduce sexually. The differences between sexual and asexual reproduction are summarized in Table 9.1.

*Table 9.1.* Differences between sexual and asexual reproduction

| *Sexual* | *Asexual* (*non-sexual*) |
|---|---|
| Fusion of two haploid gametes to form a zygote | No fusion of gametes |
| Usually two parents (however, flowers may be self-pollinated, and some lower animals (e.g. tapeworms and annelids) have male and female sex organs) | One parent |
| Offspring usually have varied characteristics – some from each parent | Offspring identical to parent |
| Generally small numbers of offspring | Often large numbers of offspring |

#### *Asexual reproduction*

#### Examples of asexual reproduction

1. *Binary fission (e.g. bacteria, many protozoans)*
When the organism reaches a certain size it splits into two, forming two 'daughter' cells which are genetically identical to the parent (see Fig. 9.1).

2. *Budding (e.g. yeast)*
Young cells begin to grow as 'buds' on the parent cell. They enlarge and eventually separate from the parent, forming a new individual (Fig. 9.2).

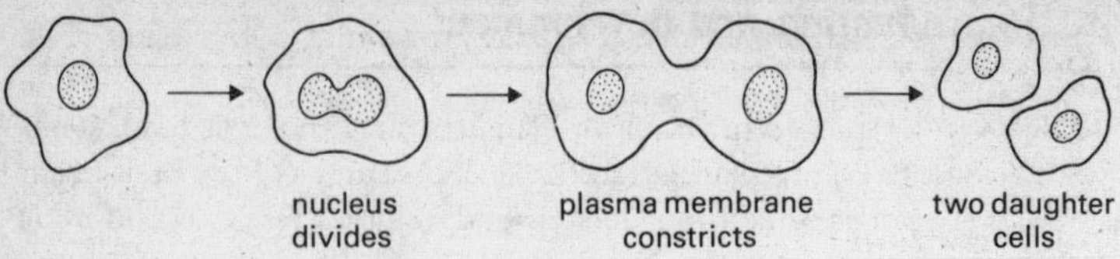
nucleus
divides
plasma membrane
constricts
two daughter
cells

*Fig. 9.1* Binary fission (e.g. *Amoeba*)

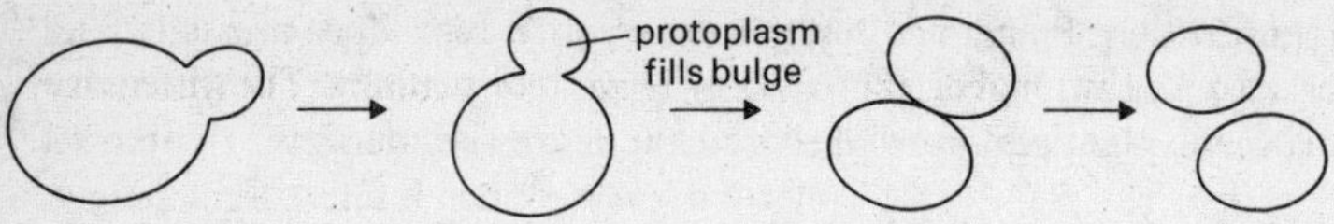
protoplasm
fills bulge

*Fig. 9.2* Budding in yeast

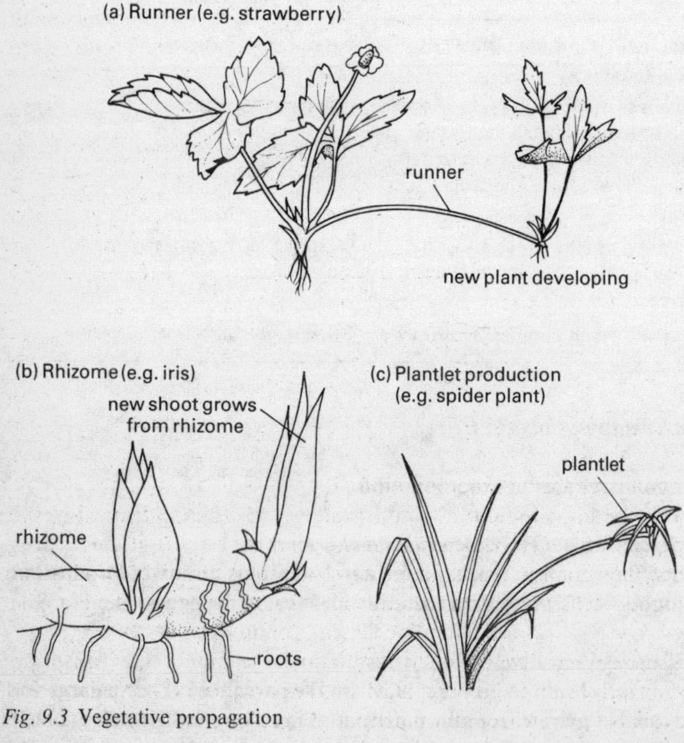
(a) Runner (e.g. strawberry)
runner
new plant developing
(b) Rhizome (e.g. iris)
new shoot grows
from rhizome
rhizome
roots
(c) Plantlet production
(e.g. spider plant)
plantlet

*Fig. 9.3* Vegetative propagation

3. *Vegetative propagation*
Part of the plant becomes detached and grows into a new plant (Fig. 9.3).

(a) RUNNERS (e.g. strawberries): Runners are above-ground stems which lie flat on the soil surface. Scale leaves and axillary buds occur at every node, while roots and stems develop at every second node and grow to form a new plant.
(b) RHIZOMES (e.g. irises): Rhizomes are underground stems which grow away from the parent and eventually develop roots and leaves to form a new plant.
(c) PLANTLET PRODUCTION (e.g. spider plant, mother of thousands): Small plantlets grow out from the leaves or stems of the parent plant. The plantlet has roots and leaves. When it falls off the parent, or reaches the soil, it will grow into a new individual.

4. *Sporulation* (*Fig. 9.4*)
Many fungi produce asexual spores. These are not to be confused with seeds, which are sexually produced. Spore production involves no fusion of gametes and therefore is asexual.

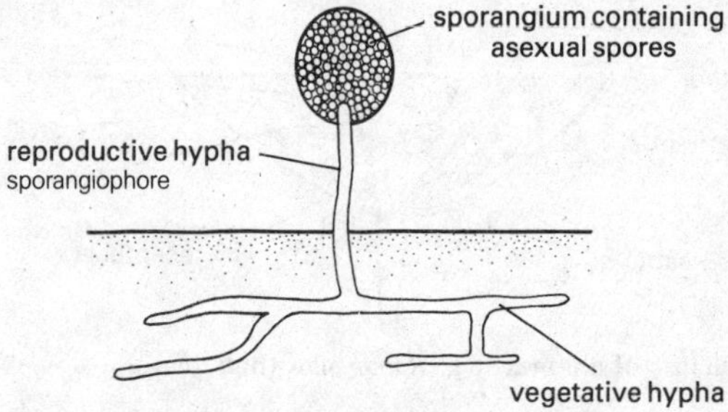
sporangium containing
asexual spores
reproductive hypha
sporangiophore
vegetative hypha

*Fig. 9.4* Sporulation (e.g. *Mucor*)

## Disadvantages of asexual reproduction

1. There is no variation in the offspring, which are all identical to the parent. This may be beneficial if the parent is successful, but it does not allow for any adaptation to new conditions. (Sexual reproduction produces offspring with variation and the offspring will therefore be more capable of adapting to changing conditions.)
2. Asexual reproduction often results in large numbers of offspring growing close to the parents where they will be in competition for available light, space and nutrients. (Overcrowding is often avoided

in sexual reproduction owing to seed dispersal and production of fewer offspring.)

Advantages of asexual reproduction

1. Asexual reproduction is a useful mechanism for colonizing available space. Large numbers of offspring are produced in a relatively short time, preventing growth of neighbouring species in that area.
2. Reproduction can occur asexually without the requirement for pollination and fertilization, which can be difficult if the parents are widely separated.

### *Sexual reproduction in flowering plants*

The reproductive part of a higher plant is the flower. Flowers may vary in size, shape and colour, but they all have the same basic components which are illustrated in Fig. 9.5.

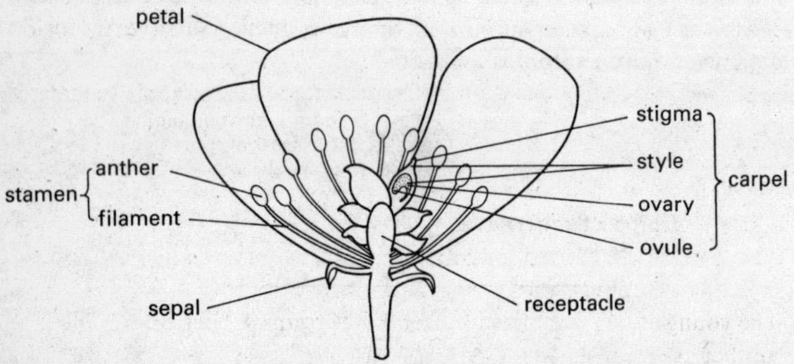
petal
stigma
style
carpel
ovary
ovule
anther
stamen
filament
sepal
receptacle

*Fig. 9.5* Structure of a flower (e.g. *Ranunculus* (buttercup))

The flower is composed of four sets or whorls of modified leaves, arranged in circles around a swollen part of the stem apex, called the receptacle. These four whorls are: (a) sepals, (b) petals, (c) stamens and (d) a carpel or carpels.

(a) SEPALS: These are small green leaves which surround the flower when it is a bud. As the flower grows the sepals are pushed to the outside and hang from the base of the receptacle. The whorl of sepals is known as the calyx.

(b) PETALS: These are the usually brightly coloured, conspicuous part of the flower. They are often scented, with a nectary at the base to attract insects. Petals are collectively known as the corolla.

(c) STAMENS: These form a whorl inside the corolla. Each stamen is composed of a stalk or filament, bearing a swollen part at the tip called the anther, which contains pollen grains (male gametes). Collectively, the stamens are known as the androecium.

(d) CARPEL OR CARPELS: These comprise the central whorl of the flower. Each carpel has three distinct parts. The swollen base, called the ovary, contains female gametes (ovules). Attached to the ovary is a short stalk, called the style, and this has a swollen, sticky apex, called the stigma, where pollen is deposited. The carpels are collectively known as the gynaecium.

The perianth is a term used to include both the calyx and the corolla. It is useful when describing flowers such as tulips, where the sepals and petals are almost indistinguishable from each other.

Flowering plants can be of two types:

1. Monoecious (hermaphrodite) plants are those which contain both male and female parts in the same flower. Most flowering plants are of this type.
2. Dioecious plants, e.g. corn and some varieties of apple trees. These have male and female parts on different flowers; hence there are male and female plants.

Development of the male gametes (Fig. 9.6)

(a) The anther is separated longitudinally into two lobes and each lobe contains two pollen sacs.

(b) The young anther contains four separate groups of cells called pollen mother cells.

(c) Each pollen mother cell undergoes meiosis by two successive divisions to form four haploid cells called microspores.

(d) Each haploid cell then divides by mitosis to form a pair of haploid cells which contain only half the normal number of chromosomes. One cell contains the generative nucleus and the other contains the tube nucleus.

(e) A thick wall forms around the pair of cells and may develop a spiky or sculptured surface. This is the pollen grain. When the pollen is ripe, a longitudinal slit develops in the anther lobe and the pollen is released.

(f) When a pollen grain lands on a stigma (pollination), it develops a pollen tube. The tube nucleus degenerates and the generative nucleus divides to form two sperm nuclei.

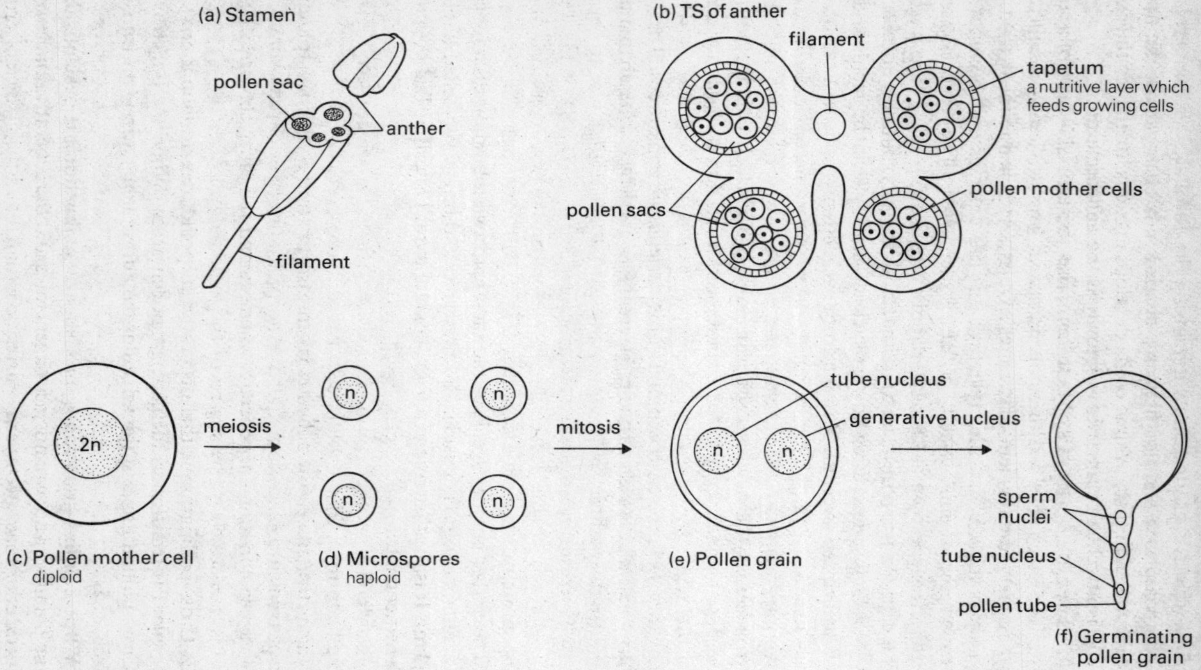
(a) Stamen
pollen sac
anther
filament
(b) TS of anther
filament
tapetum
a nutritive layer which feeds growing cells
pollen mother cells
pollen sacs
2n
meiosis
n
n
n
n
mitosis
tube nucleus
generative nucleus
n
n
sperm nuclei
tube nucleus
pollen tube
(c) Pollen mother cell
diploid
(d) Microspores
haploid
(e) Pollen grain
(f) Germinating pollen grain

*Fig. 9.6* Development of the pollen grain (male gametes)

### Development of the female gametes (Fig. 9.7)

The ovary is a hollow structure, divided into one or more chambers called locules. Usually, one ovule develops in each chamber of the ovary and is attached to the ovary walls by tissue called placenta.

(a) The ovule develops from a dome of meristematic cells in the placenta. The outer cells of this dome form two protective layers called the integuments, which are intact except for a small hole called the micropyle. Inside the structure one cell enlarges and becomes the megaspore mother cell.

(b) The megaspore mother cell divides by meiosis to yield four haploid cells (megaspores), each with only half the normal number of chromosomes. The rest of the tissue inside the integuments is then called the nucellus. The four haploid megaspores lie in a row in the nucellus. The three megaspores nearest the micropyle die and disintegrate, while the megaspore furthest away from the micropyle enlarges and develops into the embryo sac.

(c) The haploid nucleus in the embryo sac divides by mitosis to produce two nuclei. These migrate to opposite ends of the embryo sac where they themselves undergo two mitotic divisions, resulting in four haploid cells at each end of the sac. One nucleus from each end then migrates to the centre of the embryo sac where they fuse to form a binucleate endosperm mother cell. At the micropylar end of the embryo sac this leaves three nuclei called the egg apparatus: one is the egg cell or female gamete and the other two are called synergid cells. At the other end of the sac are three antipodal cells.

Some biologists consider the embryo sac to be a seven-celled haploid plant. It is then called the female gametophyte. This is important to note when comparing life cycles. See p. 340.

### Pollination

This is the transfer of pollen from the anthers to the stigmas. There are two types of pollination:

1. Self-pollination – this occurs when pollen from the anthers of a plant is transferred to the stigma of the same plant.
2. Cross-pollination – this occurs when pollen from the anthers of a plant is transferred to the stigma of another plant.

Cross-pollination has the advantage of introducing variation into the offspring, which will then adapt more easily to changing conditions. Self-pollination (inbreeding) produces offspring which are identical to the parents and show no variation. However, it can be advantageous if members of the species are sparsely populated and the chance of cross-

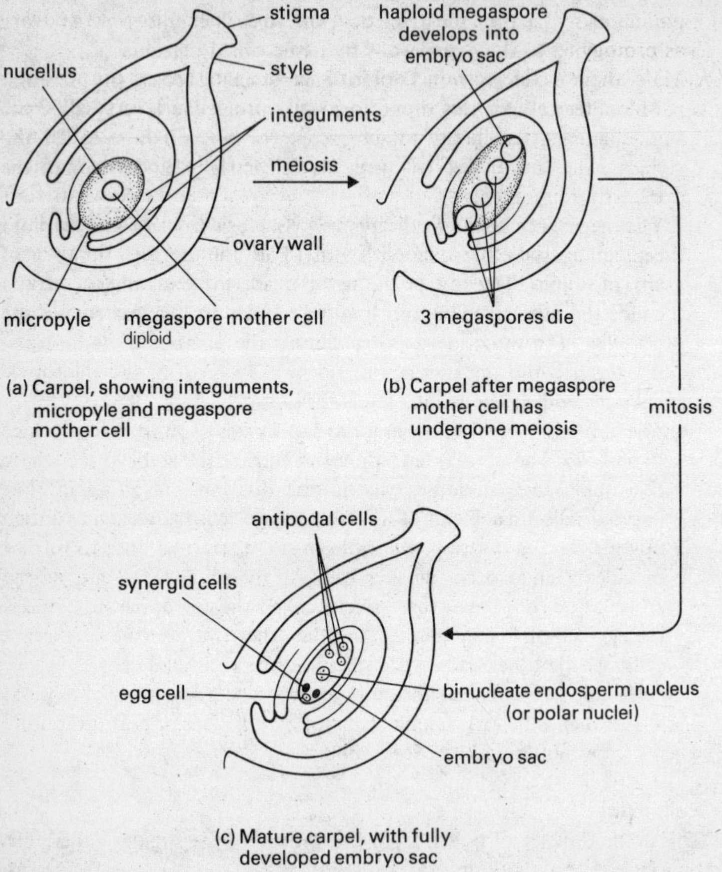
stigma
nucellus
style
integuments
meiosis
ovary wall
micropyle
megaspore mother cell
diploid
(a) Carpel, showing integuments, micropyle and megaspore mother cell
haploid megaspore develops into embryo sac
3 megaspores die
(b) Carpel after megaspore mother cell has undergone meiosis
mitosis
antipodal cells
synergid cells
egg cell
binucleate endosperm nucleus (or polar nuclei)
embryo sac
(c) Mature carpel, with fully developed embryo sac

*Fig. 9.7* Development of the egg cell (female gamete)

pollination occurring is low. Also, if the parent plant is a particularly successful variety, it would enable rapid colonization.

*Factors encouraging outbreeding* (*cross-pollination*)

1. Male and female reproductive parts ripen at different times. For example in white dead nettle (*Lamium album*) the anthers ripen before the stigmas, so pollen is dispersed before the stigmas become sticky.

This condition is known as protandry. In wild arum (*Arum maculatum*) the stigma ripens before the anthers, and will have already been pollinated by the time the anthers ripen. This type of flower is known as protogynous.

2. Male and female reproductive parts of the same plant are incompatible. Primrose flowers show this condition, called heterostyly (see Fig. 9.8). Primrose has two types of flowers: pin-eyed, with a long style and stamens placed half-way down the corolla tube, and thrum-eyed, with long stamens but a short style. When an insect visits the the flower, pollen sticks to the proboscis at a level corresponding to the stigma of the other type of flower. In addition to this, the pollen grains produced by each type of flower are of two sizes, and therefore the pollen grains of one flower are more suited to the stigmas of the other type of flower.

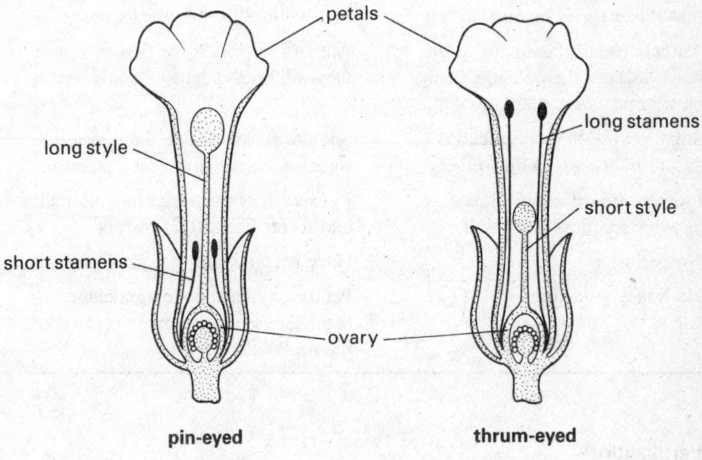
petals
long style
short stamens
ovary
long stamens
short style
pin-eyed
thrum-eyed

*Fig. 9.8* Structure of primrose flowers (*Primula vulgaris*)

3. In orchids there is only one stamen, containing two pollen sacs. When an insect feeds on the flower, the pollen sacs are brushed on to its head. The insect thus removes all the pollen to another flower, preventing self-pollination.
4. Dioecious plants (e.g. corn) have male and female parts on different plants; hence self-pollination is impossible.

*Wind and insect pollination*

Most flowers are adapted to a particular type of pollination. For example, sweet peas, orchids and irises are adapted to pollination by bees. They have a lip petal which acts as a landing-stage for the insect. The nectaries are also deep inside the flower, where only a long-tongued insect can reach. Flowers which have become adapted to either wind or insect pollination tend to show characteristic features. See Table 9.2.

*Table 9.2.* Comparison of wind- and insect-pollinated flowers

| *Wind-pollinated flowers* | *Insect-pollinated flowers* |
|---|---|
| Produce large quantities of pollen, since much of it will not reach the flowers which are to be pollinated | Produce smaller quantities of pollen, since there is a greater chance of it reaching a flower of the correct species |
| Pollen is small, light and smooth so that it can travel in weak air currents | Pollen is large and spiky to ensure that it sticks to the insect's body |
| Anthers usually hang out of the flower, where the pollen is easily blown away (e.g. plantains) | Anthers are inside the flower, where they will brush against visiting insects |
| Stigmas are often conspicuous to ensure pollen sticks on to them | Stigmas tucked inside the flower, since pollen is delivered by insects |
| Flowers are often dull (green or brown), scentless and small | Flowers are large, brightly coloured and scented to attract insects |
| No nectaries | Have nectaries for insects to feed on |
| No honey guidelines | Petals may have honey guidelines (e.g. *Ranunculus*) to guide insects to the nectar |

## Fertilization

Fertilization is the fusion of the male gamete with the female gamete to form a zygote. Each gamete is haploid, and therefore has only half the normal number of chromosomes. When they fuse together, the zygote nucleus is produced, and this has a full set of chromosomes (diploid).

A pollen tube grows out from the pollen grain on the surface of the stigma. The tube grows down the style and enters the embryo sac through the micropyle. It is thought that the tube grows in response to chemicals produced by the embryo sac (chemotropism).

One of the sperm nuclei fuses with the egg cell to form a zygote. The zygote has two sets of chromosomes (2n) and is diploid. The remaining sperm nucleus fuses with the binucleate endosperm cell. This produces a cell with three sets of chromosomes (3n) from which the endosperm develops.

## Fruit and seed formation

The zygote divides by mitosis and differentiates to form an embryo consisting of the young root (radicle), shoot (plumule) and the seed leaves (cotyledons). As the embryo develops, the petals and stamens of the flower fall off. The ovary develops into the fruit and the ovules develop into the seeds. Hence, the number of seeds in a fruit reflects the number of fertilized ovules in the ovary.

The ovary wall may become tough and thin (e.g. a pea pod) or it may become soft and fleshy (e.g. a peach, where the skin and flesh are both part of the ovary wall). The fruit wall (pericarp) has up to three layers – a firm endocarp, a fleshy mesocarp and a skin or exocarp. It is important to know which parts of the flower develop into the fruit and seed components and these are listed in Table 9.3.

*Table 9.3.* The development of fruit and seed parts

| *Flower structure* | *Fruit or seed component* |
|---|---|
| Ovary | Whole fruit |
| Ovary wall | Fruit wall |
| Ovule | Seed |
| Integuments | Seed coat |
| Zygote | Embryo (root, shoot and cotyledons) |
| Endosperm nucleus and sperm nucleus | Endosperm |
| Micropyle of embryo sac | Micropyle of seed coat |
| Placenta | Stalk attaching seed to ovary wall |

Not all seeds have an endosperm – some seeds store their food in the seed leaves (cotyledons).

Examples of the four main seed types:

- dicotyledon, non-endospermic (e.g. pea, broad bean)
- dicotyledon, endospermic (e.g. castor oil plant)
- monocotyledon, non-endospermic
- monocotyledon, endospermic (e.g. maize)

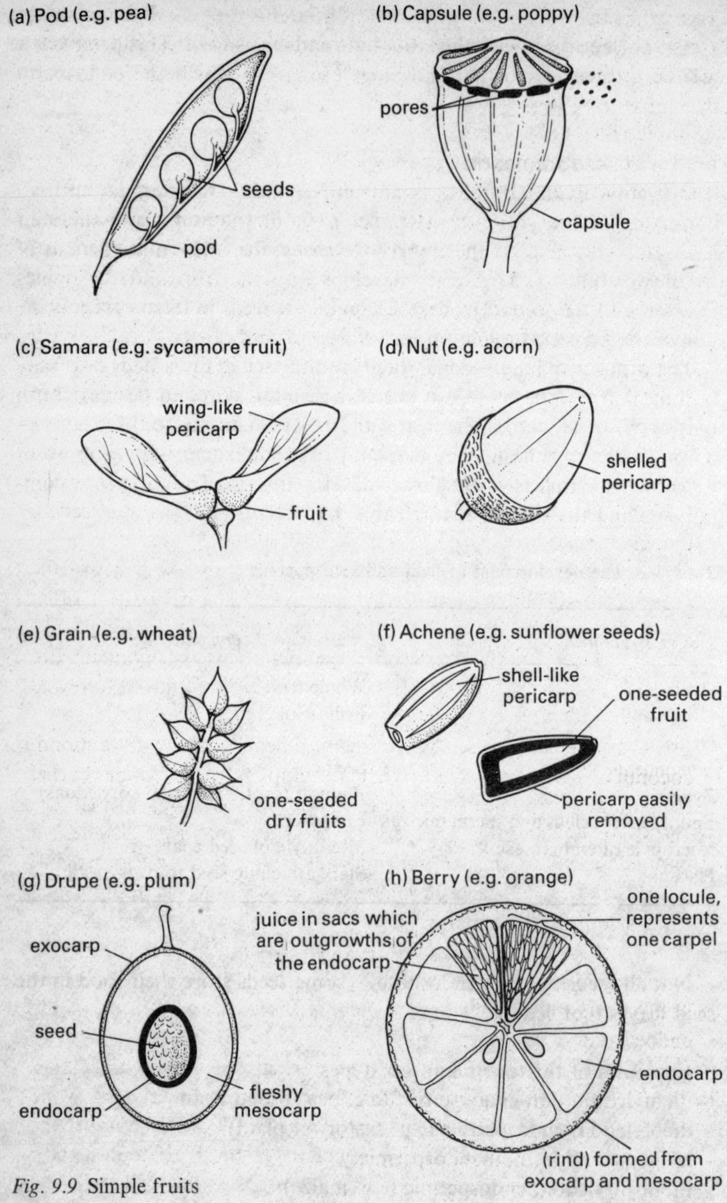
(a) Pod (e.g. pea)
seeds
pod
(b) Capsule (e.g. poppy)
pores
capsule
(c) Samara (e.g. sycamore fruit)
wing-like pericarp
fruit
(d) Nut (e.g. acorn)
shelled pericarp
(e) Grain (e.g. wheat)
one-seeded dry fruits
(f) Achene (e.g. sunflower seeds)
shell-like pericarp
one-seeded fruit
pericarp easily removed
(g) Drupe (e.g. plum)
exocarp
seed
endocarp
fleshy mesocarp
(h) Berry (e.g. orange)
juice in sacs which are outgrowths of the endocarp
one locule, represents one carpel
endocarp
(rind) formed from exocarp and mesocarp

*Fig. 9.9* Simple fruits

*Types of fruits*
Fruits are classified according to the number of ovaries and flowers required to make the fruit.

1. Simple fruits (Fig. 9.9)
These are derived from a single ovary:
(a) PODS AND LEGUMES (e.g. pea, bean, peanut): The ovary forms the pod and the ovules develop into the seeds. The pericarp is tough and thin. Legumes often split open (dehisce) along lines in the pericarp called sutures.
(b) CAPSULES (e.g. poppy, iris): Capsules are derived from compound ovaries, i.e. an ovary composed of two or more fused carpels. Each carpel produces many seeds which are enclosed in the tough, capsule-shaped pericarp. Seeds are released through pores in the pericarp (poppy) or opening lids (plantain) or by dehiscence (iris).
(c) SAMARAS (e.g. ash, elm, maple): These are fruits with wing-like pericarps to aid dispersal.
(d) NUTS (e.g. walnut, acorn, chestnut, hazelnut): A nut is a one-seeded, indehiscent, dry fruit with a hard pericarp (shell).
(e) GRAINS (e.g. wheat, rice, oats, barley): These are the fruits of the grass family. They are one-seeded dry fruits. The pericarp is often fused with the seed coat and can only be removed by milling.
(f) ACHENES (e.g. sunflower): These are single-seeded fruits with dry walls, but unlike grain fruits, the pericarp is easily removed to reveal the seed.
(g) DRUPES (e.g. olive, cherry, plum, peach, apricot, almond, coconut): These are fruits that develop from a single carpel containing two ovules – one develops into a seed, the other aborts and does not develop. The pericarp develops into three layers – a hard endocarp which surrounds the seed coat, a fleshy mesocarp and a thin, skin-like exocarp. In almonds and coconuts the fleshy mesocarp becomes dry at maturity.
(h) BERRIES: These are fleshy fruits which develop from a compound ovary containing several carpels. Many seeds are embedded in the fleshy part, which in examples such as tomato is composed of the endocarp and mesocarp.

Citrus fruits (e.g. oranges and lemons) are also classified as berries. The thick leathery rind is formed from the exocarp and mesocarp, while the fleshy part is the endocarp. Juice is contained in sacs or outgrowths of the endocarp wall. Each locule (segment) of the fruit represents a carpel and each carpel usually produces two seeds.

Other berry fruits include water-melons, cucumbers and pumpkins. The rind of the fruit is formed from receptacle tissues fused with the exocarp. The fleshy part is the mesocarp and endocarp.

2. Aggregate fruits (Fig. 9.10)
These are aggregates of simple fruits on a common receptacle. The whole aggregate is formed from many carpels. Examples include strawberry, raspberry and blackberry.

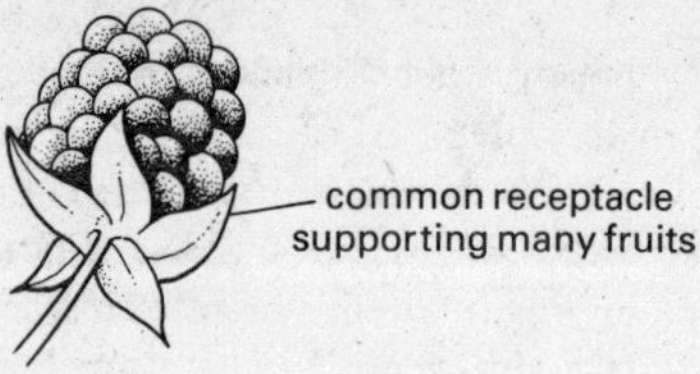
common receptacle
supporting many fruits

*Fig. 9.10* Aggregate fruit (e.g. blackberry)

3. Multiple fruits (Fig. 9.11)
These are formed from individual ovaries of several flowers. Examples include mulberry, pineapple and fig.

*Fig. 9.11* Multiple fruit (e.g. pineapple)

## Dispersal of fruits and seeds

To prevent overcrowding and encourage colonization of new ground, seeds must be dispersed, i.e. removed from the parents.

There are four main agents of dispersal: wind, water, animals and mechanical. Fruits and seeds usually have adaptations for dispersal by one of these mechanisms.

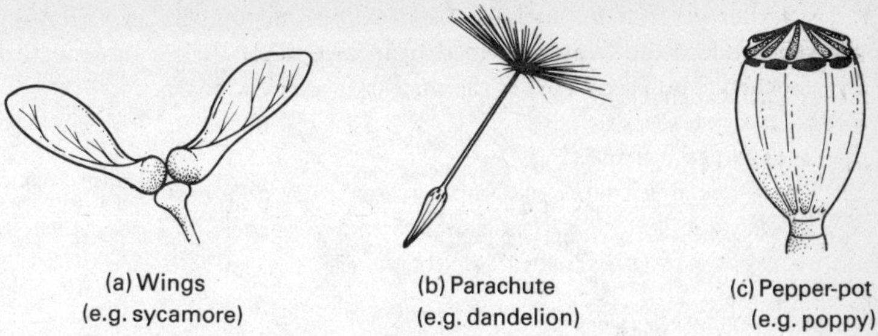
(a) Wings
(e.g. sycamore)
(b) Parachute
(e.g. dandelion)
(c) Pepper-pot
(e.g. poppy)

*Fig. 9.12* Three adaptations to wind dispersal

1. Wind dispersal (see Fig. 9.12).
2. Water dispersal. Fruits and seeds may have air sacs or a hollow interior to improve buoyancy (e.g. lily and coconut).
3. Animal dispersal. Many fruits and seeds have hooks or barbs which adhere to the fur, feathers or hair of animals, who then carry them away (see Fig. 9.13). Examples include thistle and cocklebur. Sticky seeds, such as mistletoe and some marsh plants, may be carried on the feet of birds. Other seeds are carried internally. Fleshy fruits are eaten by animals. The seeds pass through the digestive system and germinate from the discharged excrement. Often the seed coat is softened by digestive juices, and this aids seed germination. Birds, because of their wide migration, can carry seeds a long distance.
4. Mechanical dispersal – dehiscent fruits (see Fig. 9.14).

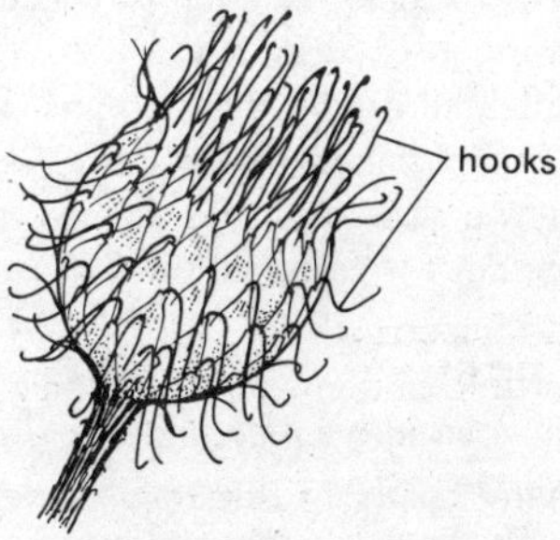
hooks

*Fig. 9.13* Fruit dispersed by animals (e.g. burdock)

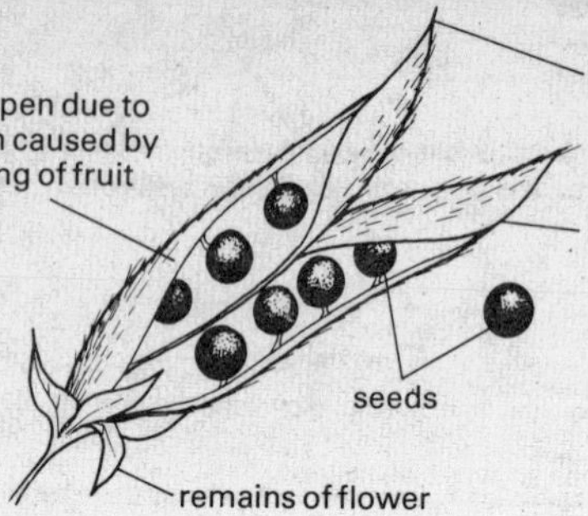
remains of stigma
split open due to
tension caused by
drying of fruit
pod derived from
ovary wall
seeds
remains of flower

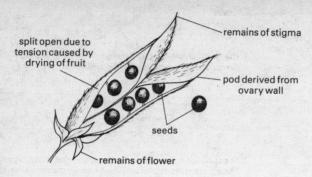

*Fig. 9.14* Dehiscent fruit (e.g. pea)

## Seed dormancy

Some seeds will not germinate, even when given water, oxygen and a suitable temperature. In these cases other factors are required to break the dormant period, and these include:

1. Mechanical damage – often the testa is impermeable to water and must be damaged before the seed can germinate (e.g. lotus seeds).
2. Light – some seeds (e.g. lettuce and grasses) require light for germination. See p. 298.
3. Need for further development – e.g. orchid seeds which are dispersed while the embryos are immature. Germination cannot occur until the embryo has developed.
4. Low temperature – some seeds require a period of low temperature before they will germinate (vernalization). See p. 301.
5. High temperature – this is a fairly rare requirement, but some seeds need a period of intense heat such as that provided by fires. This type of plant is seen growing after forest fires.
6. Removal of chemical inhibitors – desert plants often have natural chemical inhibitors impregnated in the testa. A heavy rainfall is required to leach out the chemicals, and thereby to ensure that there is sufficient water present for germination.

## Germination (see Fig. 9.15)

This is the growth of the seed into a seedling. For germination to occur three factors are necessary:

1. Water – enters through the micropyle and required to swell the seed and burst the tough outer coat, the testa. Also required for the

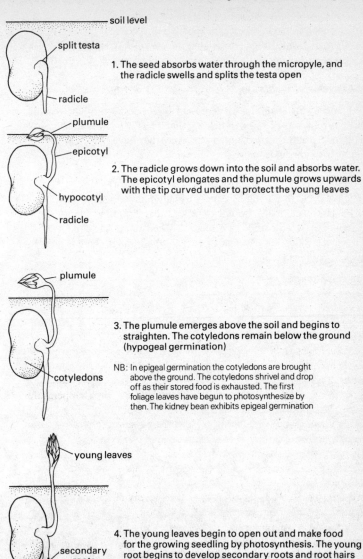

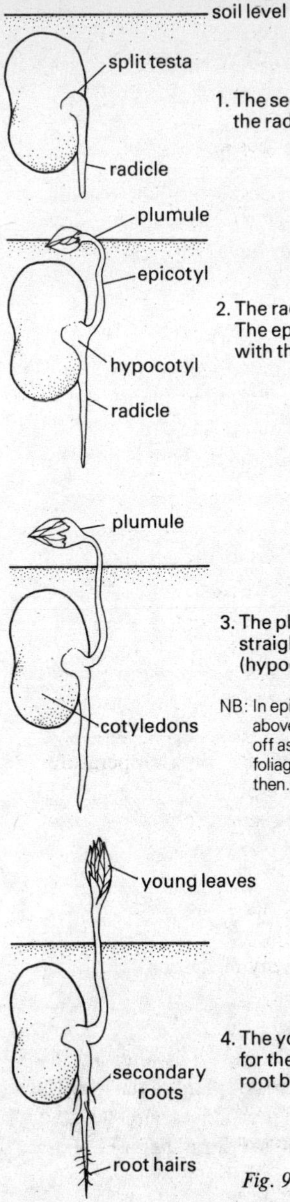
soil level
split testa
radicle
plumule
epicotyl
hypocotyl
radicle
plumule
cotyledons
young leaves
secondary roots
root hairs

1. The seed absorbs water through the micropyle, and the radicle swells and splits the testa open

2. The radicle grows down into the soil and absorbs water. The epicotyl elongates and the plumule grows upwards with the tip curved under to protect the young leaves

3. The plumule emerges above the soil and begins to straighten. The cotyledons remain below the ground (hypogeal germination)

NB: In epigeal germination the cotyledons are brought above the ground. The cotyledons shrivel and drop off as their stored food is exhausted. The first foliage leaves have begun to photosynthesize by then. The kidney bean exhibits epigeal germination

4. The young leaves begin to open out and make food for the growing seedling by photosynthesis. The young root begins to develop secondary roots and root hairs

*Fig. 9.15* Germination of the pea (*Pisum sativum*)

working of the enzymes. But most seeds will not germinate in waterlogged soils because of the lack of oxygen.

2. Correct temperature – to enable the enzymes to work.
3. Oxygen – required for respiration to obtain energy for growth.

### *Life cycles of plants*

When drawing diagrams to represent life cycles, a diploid structure is usually represented as 2n, indicating that it has two sets of chromosomes. Haploid structures are denoted as n, since they have only half the normal number of chromosomes.

#### The life cycle of an angiosperm (flowering plant)

The life cycle of an angiosperm is usually represented as shown in Fig. 9.16. However, many botanists believe that flowering plants show an alternation of generations (see below). The embryo sac can be classified as a seven-celled haploid plant (see p. 329), although there is no distinct gametophyte stage in the life cycle.

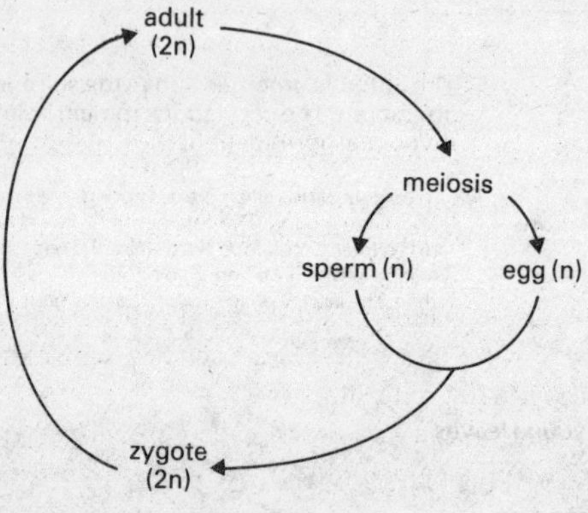
adult
(2n)
meiosis
sperm (n)
egg (n)
zygote
(2n)

*Fig. 9.16* Life cycle of an angiosperm

#### Alternation of generations

Mosses, liverworts and ferns have a life cycle known as alternation of generations. This means that there are two types of plant in the life cycle: a haploid plant called the gametophyte (since it produces gametes) and a diploid plant called the sporophyte, since it produces haploid spores. The life cycle is usually represented as shown in Fig. 9.17.

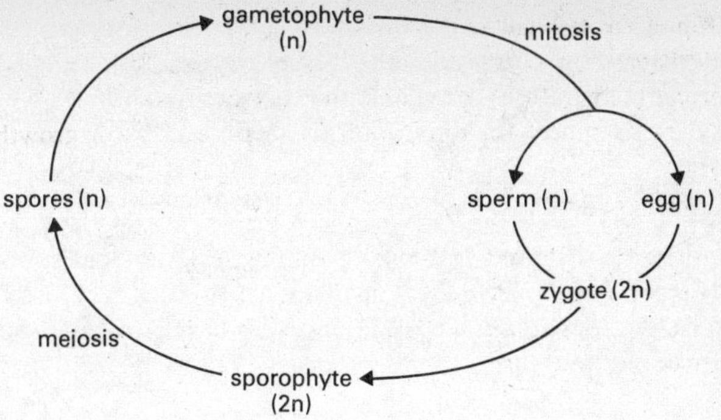
gametophyte
(n)
mitosis
spores (n)
sperm (n)
egg (n)
zygote (2n)
meiosis
sporophyte
(2n)

*Fig. 9.17* Alternation of generations

*The life cycle of a fern (Fig. 9.18)*

(a) The mature sporophyte produces clusters of sporangia, called sori, on its undersurface. The sori are often protected by a layer of tissue called the indusium.
(b) Each sporangium contains diploid spore mother cells which divide by meiosis to produce numerous haploid spores.
(c) The sporangium wall consists of a layer of unevenly thickened cells called the annulus. In dry weather the cells lose water by evaporation and the resulting tension ruptures the wall along a line of weak cells called the stomium. The sporangium is split open, and spores are released.
(d) Each spore develops into a haploid plant called a gametophyte. The gametophyte is flat, green and heart-shaped, with rhizoids growing from it. It is usually only short-lived.
(e) The male reproductive structures, called antheridia, develop on the undersurface of the gametophyte. Each antheridium contains many sperm cells.
(f) The female reproductive structures (archegonia) develop around the notch of of the gametophyte. Archegonia are flask-shaped and each contains only a single egg cell.
(g) Fertilization only occurs when moisture is present, since the sperm must swim from the antheridia to the archegonia.
(h) The resulting zygote develops into a diploid plant which produces roots and grows into a mature sporophyte. The gametophyte dies and disintegrates.

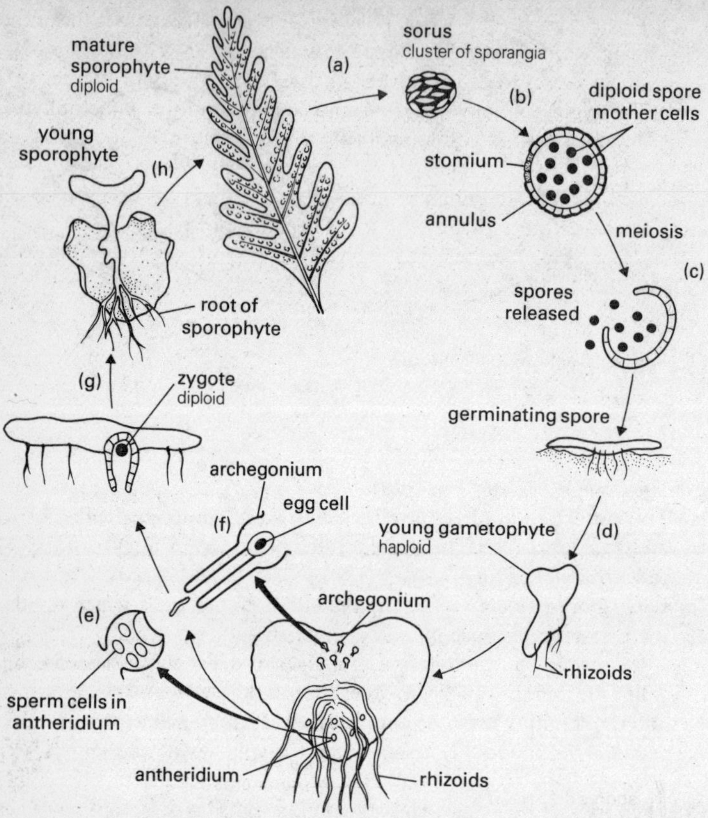

mature
sporophyte
diploid
young
sporophyte
(h)
root of
sporophyte
(a)
sorus
cluster of sporangia
(b)
diploid spore
mother cells
stomium
annulus
meiosis
(c)
spores
released
germinating spore
(d)
young gametophyte
haploid
rhizoids
archegonium
antheridium
rhizoids
(e)
sperm cells in
antheridium
(f)
archegonium
egg cell
(g)
zygote
diploid


*Fig. 9.18* Life cycle of a fern (e.g. *Polypodium vulgare*)

*The life cycle of a moss (Fig. 9.19)*

(a) The gametophyte consists of a branched, filamentous structure called a protonema. Leafy shoots also develop on the protonema – these consist of a stalk with spirally arranged leaves on it and rhizoids at the base. Every cell of the gametophyte is haploid.
(b) Antheridia (male reproductive structures) and archegonia (female reproductive structures) develop at the tips of the leafy shoots. The antheridia produce hundreds of haploid sperm, but each archegonium has only one egg cell.

(c) Fertilization occurs when moisture is present. This causes the antheridia to split open, releasing sperm which swim into the archegonia. A single sperm fuses with the egg cell to form a diploid zygote.
(d) The zygote initially absorbs nourishment from the gametophyte. It develops into a young sporophyte consisting of a foot, seta and sporangium.
(e) Cells in the sporangium develop into diploid spore mother cells which divide by meiosis to form haploid spores.
(f) When spores are released they germinate to form a haploid protonema.

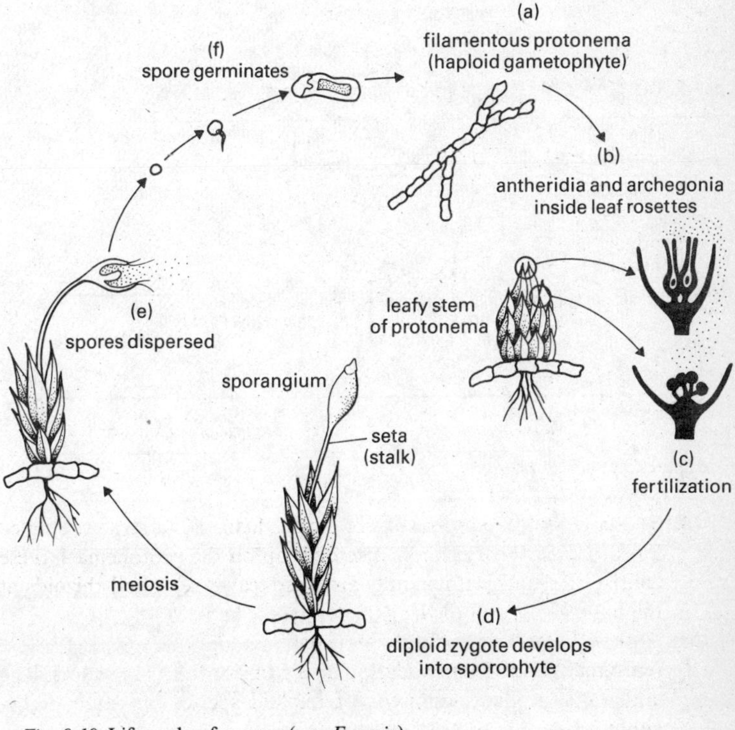
(a)
filamentous protonema
(haploid gametophyte)
(f)
spore germinates
(b)
antheridia and archegonia
inside leaf rosettes
leafy stem
of protonema
(e)
spores dispersed
sporangium
seta
(stalk)
(c)
fertilization
meiosis
(d)
diploid zygote develops
into sporophyte

*Fig. 9.19* Life cycle of a moss (e.g. *Funaria*)

### *Further reading*

M. Black, *Control Processes in Germination and Dormancy*, Oxford/Carolina Biology Reader No. 20 (Packard, 1972).

D. Lewis, *Sexual Incompatibility in Plants*, Studies in Biology No. 110 (Arnold, 1979).

T. E. Weier *et al.*, *Botany: An Introduction to Plant Biology* (Wiley, 1982)

### *Related questions*

**Question:**

(a) In the table below, name the structures labelled A–F in the diagram. In the table (in the right-hand column) name the structures which A–F develop into after fertilization has taken place.

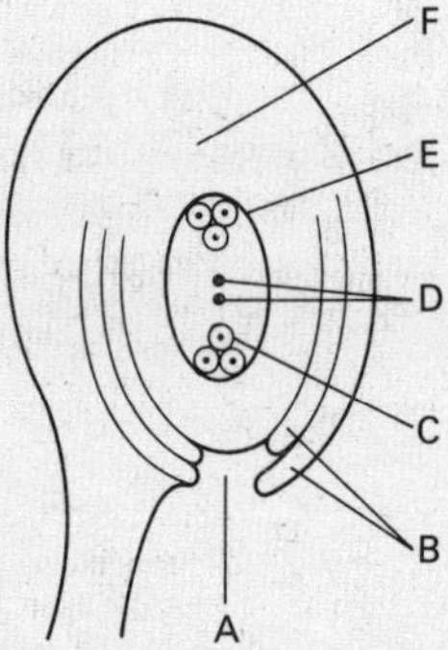
F
E
D
C
B
A

| | *Name of structure* | *Fate after fertilization* |
|---|---|---|
| *A* | | |
| *B* | | |
| *C* | | |
| *D* | | |
| *E* | | |
| *F* | | |

(b) What is the main problem with reproduction in a terrestrial environment?
(c) Name one way in which plants are adapted to overcome this problem.

[In the style of AEB]

**Comments:**
(a) See p. 330, Fig. 9.7, and p. 333, Table 9.3.
(b) Problems (for plants) involved in reproduction in a terrestrial as opposed to an aquatic environment include the transfer of gametes during pollination.
(c) Plants are adapted to terrestrial pollination in a number of ways. These include the possession of brightly coloured and scented flowers to attract insects, which then transfer the pollen as they visit other flowers.

**Question:**
(a) In many groups of plants the sporophyte generation is the dominant stage in the life cycle. Comment on the biological significance of this phenomenon.
(b) The diagram shows a vertical section through a fern sporangium.

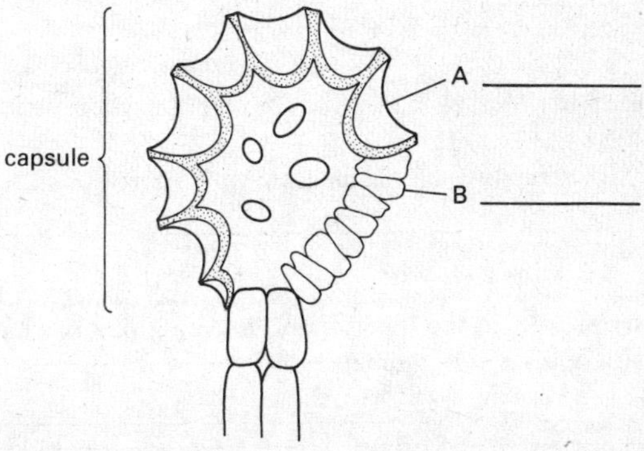
capsule
A
B

(i) Identify the parts labelled A and B on the lines next to the diagram.
(ii) Relate the structure of A and of B to the function each performs.

**(8 marks)**

[AEB, Nov. 1982, Paper 1]

**Comments:**

(a) The sporophyte is significant since it is the diploid stage of the plant. This is important in evolutionary terms because the gametophyte or haploid generation is often reduced to serving as a reproductive structure only, as in the angiosperms.

(b) (i) and (ii) See p. 341 and Fig. 9.18.

**Question:**

The diagram below represents the life cycle of a flowering plant.

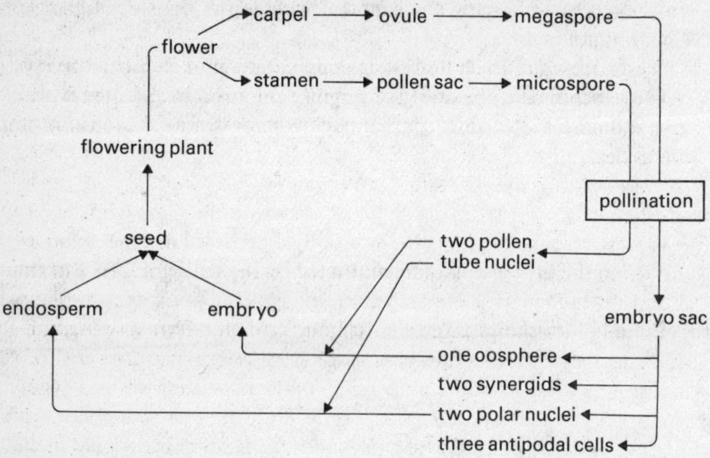
carpel
ovule
megaspore
flower
stamen
pollen sac
microspore
flowering plant
pollination
seed
two pollen
tube nuclei
endosperm
embryo
embryo sac
one oosphere
two synergids
two polar nuclei
three antipodal cells

(a) Write the letter M at each place on the diagram where meiosis occurs in the life cycle.

(b) Identify the structures on the diagram which correspond to sperm in animals.

______________________________

(c) State the process in the life cycle of flowering plants which corresponds to copulation in animals.

______________________________

(d) State *three* differences between the life cycle shown in the diagram and that of a moss.

(i) ______________________________

______________________________

(ii) ______________________________________________

______________________________________________

(iii) ______________________________________________

______________________________________________

**(8 marks)**

[AEB, Nov. 1981, Paper 1] (modified)

**Comments:**

This is a question which tests your understanding of reproductive cycles. You are expected to be able to recognize the main stages of a life cycle, and compare the various components to analogous structures in other life cycles.

(a) See pp. 327 and 329 and Figs 9.6 and 9.7.

(b) The sperm are the male gametes, therefore the male gametes in the diagram must be identified.

(c) Copulation is the mechanism by which the male gametes are transferred to the female gametes. Hence the equivalent process in plants is pollination. It is important to note that copulation is merely the transfer of the gametes and does not necessarily lead to fertilization. Fertilization is the actual fusion of the male and female gametes to form a zygote.

(d) In this type of question it is always important to make clear which characteristics belong to which organism. The differences could include:

(i) The life cycle of a moss contains an independent haploid stage whereas that of the flowering plant does not.

(ii) The sporophyte stage of the moss produces asexual haploid spores while that of the flowering plant does not.

(iii) In the moss, gametes are produced in a leafy protonema, whereas in the flowering plant they are produced in a flower.

## *Reproduction in humans*

### *The male reproductive system*

The male gametes (spermatozoa – usually shortened to sperm) are produced in the testes, which are enclosed in an external sac called the scrotum or scrotal sac. The testes lie outside the body, where a cooler temperature provides the ideal conditions for sperm development.

## Spermatogenesis

Each testis is packed with coiled seminiferous tubules which produce sperm. Between the tubules are interstitial cells responsible for male hormone production. There are two types of cells in the tubules – spermatogenic (sperm-producing) cells and Sertoli cells which provide nutrients for the developing sperm. Spermatogenic cells are found at various stages of development in the tubules. (See Figs 9.20 and 9.21.)

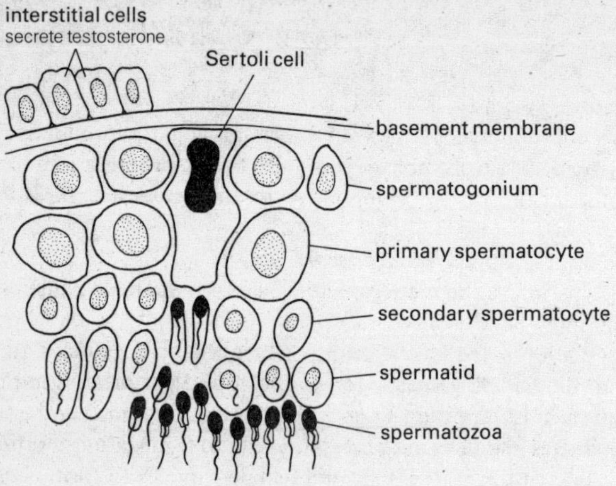
interstitial cells
secrete testosterone
Sertoli cell
basement membrane
spermatogonium
primary spermatocyte
secondary spermatocyte
spermatid
spermatozoa

*Fig. 9.20* Wall of seminiferous tubule to show spermatozoa development

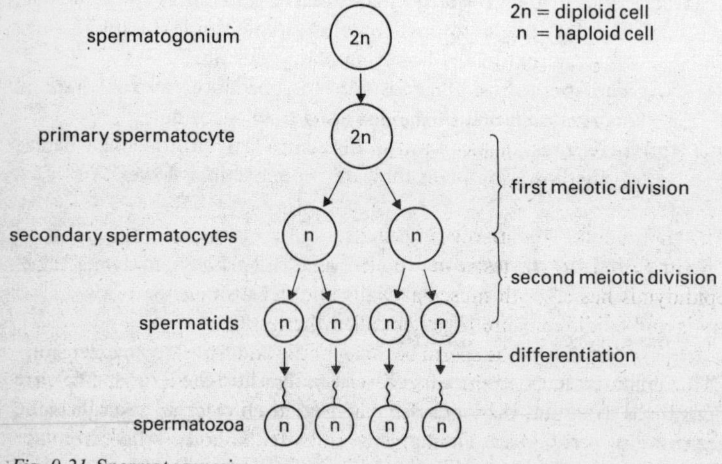
2n = diploid cell
n = haploid cell
spermatogonium
2n
primary spermatocyte
2n
first meiotic division
secondary spermatocytes
n
n
second meiotic division
spermatids
n
n
n
n
differentiation
spermatozoa
n
n
n
n

*Fig. 9.21* Spermatogenesis

## The structure of the sperm (Fig. 9.22)

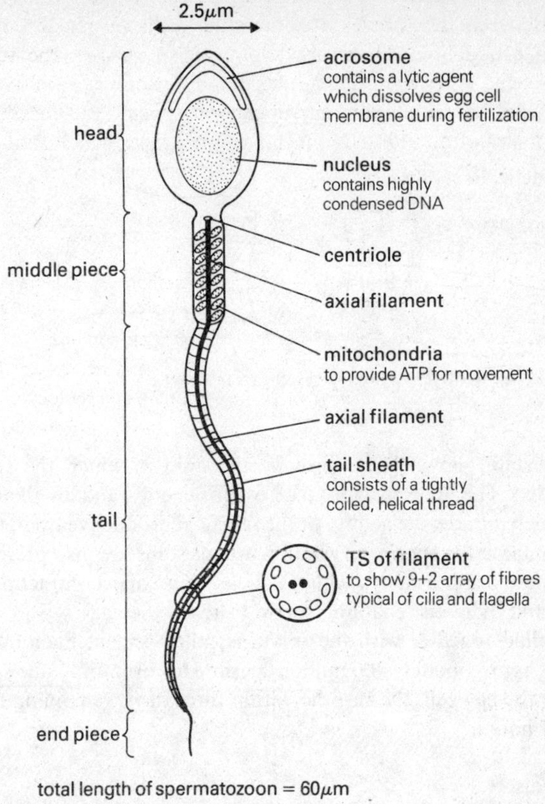
2.5μm
head
middle piece
tail
end piece
acrosome
contains a lytic agent
which dissolves egg cell
membrane during fertilization
nucleus
contains highly
condensed DNA
centriole
axial filament
mitochondria
to provide ATP for movement
axial filament
tail sheath
consists of a tightly
coiled, helical thread
TS of filament
to show 9+2 array of fibres
typical of cilia and flagella
total length of spermatozoon = 60μm

*Fig. 9.22* Structure of a human spermatozoon

## The pathway of the sperm (Fig. 9.23)

Sperm pass from the testis to a coiled tube called the epididymis. The epididymis has smooth muscular walls and lies around the testis. (The testis and epididymis are together called the testicle.)

After several hours the sperm become motile and travel to an extension of the epididymis called the vas deferens, where they are stored. The vas deferens is surrounded by arteries, nerves and connective tissue, which are collectively called the spermatic chord. After storage in the lower vas deferens, sperm pass up into the abdominal cavity, to the seminal vesicles

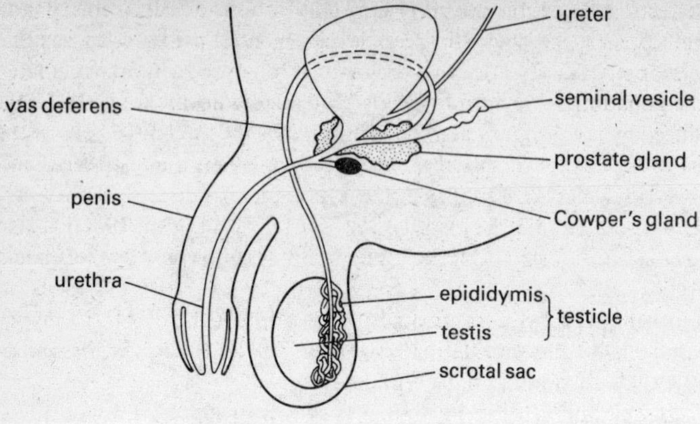
ureter
seminal vesicle
vas deferens
prostate gland
penis
Cowper's gland
urethra
epididymis
testicle
testis
scrotal sac

*Fig. 9.23* The male reproductive system (side view)

and prostate gland. These provide the fluid in which the sperm are suspended. The fluid provides fructose for energy, and an alkaline solution which reduces the acidity of the female reproductive tract, making it more suitable for sperm survival. Prostaglandins are also present in the fluid; these are hormones which increase muscular contractions in the uterus and oviducts, enabling sperm to reach the egg.

The fluid together with the sperm is called semen. Each ejaculation releases approximately 400 million sperm. However, only one sperm can fertilize the egg cell, the rest die within three days, remaining fertile for only 24 hours.

### The penis

The function of the penis is to deposit sperm cells in the reproductive tract of the female. It is composed of three cylindrical masses of spongy tissue which are capable of filling with blood and making the penis erect. Down the centre of the penis is a tube called the urethra which is connected to both the vas deferens and the bladder. It therefore serves as a joint opening for semen and urine. As the penis moves in and out of the vagina, muscles in the scrotum, epididymis and vas deferens contract, causing semen to move into the urethra and out of the penis.

### Male sex hormones

Testosterone is the principal male hormone. It is one of a group of hormones called androgens, which all have similar effects to testosterone.

Its effects include production and maturation of all primary and secondary male characteristics, e.g. development of penis, testes, seminal vesicles, body hair and deep voice. Testosterone production is regulated by the gonadotrophic hormone called luteinizing hormone (LH). LH is produced by the pituitary gland and stimulates the interstitial cells of the testes to increase production of testosterone. When the testosterone of the blood reaches a certain level, the hypothalamus directs the pituitary to cease production of LH, so the testosterone level of the blood is also reduced accordingly. This type of regulation is called negative feedback. See p. 277.

Another pituitary hormone, also under the control of the hypothalamus, is follicle-stimulating hormone (FSH). It acts on the seminiferous tubules, stimulating sperm development.

The regulation of these hormones is shown in Fig. 9.24.

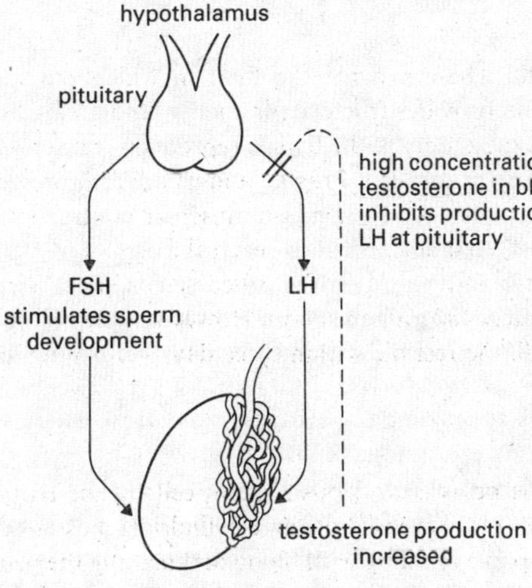
hypothalamus
pituitary
high concentration of testosterone in blood inhibits production of LH at pituitary
FSH
stimulates sperm development
LH
testosterone production increased

*Fig. 9.24* Regulation of male reproductive hormones

### *The female reproductive system*

The structure of the female reproductive system is shown in Fig. 9.25.

#### The production and development of ova

The female gametes (ova) are produced in the ovaries. These are two oval-shaped bodies suspended in the abdominal cavity and held in place

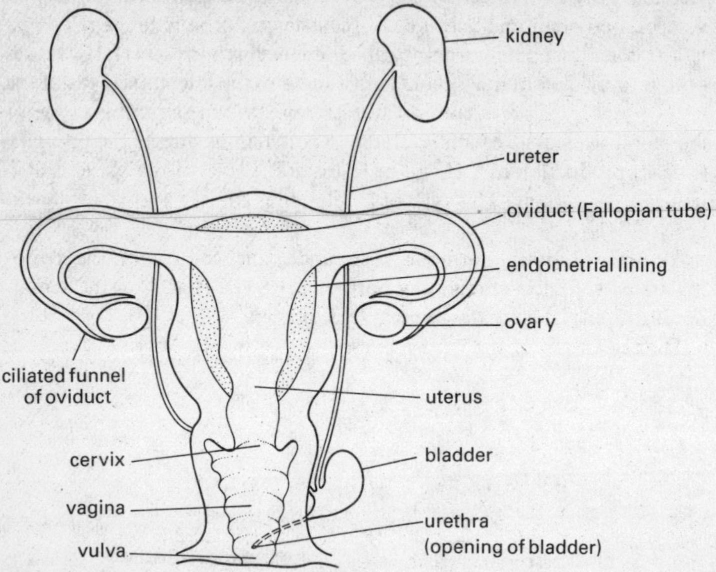
kidney
ureter
oviduct (Fallopian tube)
endometrial lining
ovary
ciliated funnel
of oviduct
uterus
cervix
bladder
vagina
urethra
(opening of bladder)
vulva

*Fig. 9.25* The female reproductive system

by ligaments. When a female is born, the ovaries contain 400,000 primary oocytes which have reached the prophase I stage of meiosis (see p. 382) but which do not develop further until puberty. At the onset of puberty, one egg matures approximately every 28 days from alternate ovaries. This process is under hormonal control.

In the development of ova, or oogenesis (see Fig. 9.26), the primary oocyte undergoes a first meiotic division to produce a secondary oocyte and a smaller polar cell. This unequal division ensures that all the reserves are passed on to the one secondary oocyte; the polar cell eventually dies. Similarly, the secondary oocyte undergoes the second meiotic division to produce a single ovum and another polar cell (which also dies). Thus, all the reserves from the original oogonium are channelled into one ovum (Fig. 9.27a). The oocyte develops near to the surface of the ovary and is surrounded by specialized cells which supply it with nutrients (Fig. 9.27b). This oocyte and these cells are collectively called an ovarian (or Graafian) follicle. In the final stages of ovum development, the follicle protrudes from the ovary like a blister. Eventually the

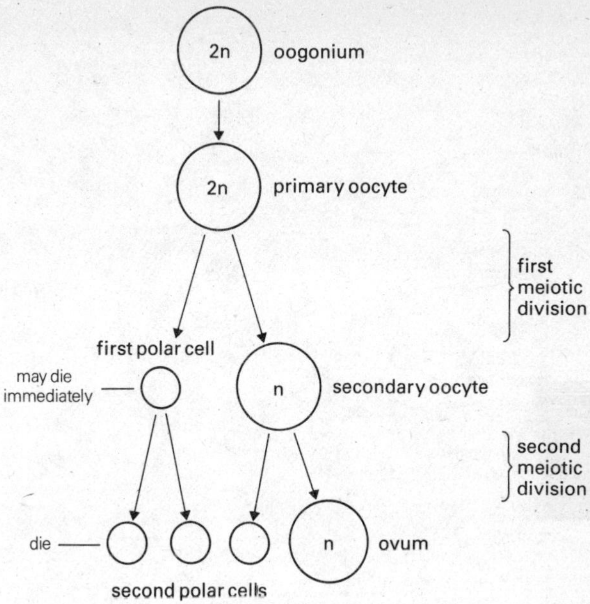
2n
oogonium
2n
primary oocyte
first
meiotic
division
first polar cell
may die
immediately
n
secondary oocyte
second
meiotic
division
die
n
ovum
second polar cells

*Fig. 9.26* Oogenesis

follicle bursts, releasing the ovum into the ciliated opening of the oviduct; this is **ovulation**. The ovum travels along the oviduct towards the uterus, while the remaining cells form a structure called the corpus luteum. If the egg is fertilized, the corpus luteum remains and produces progesterone. If not, the corpus luteum disintegrates.

### The vagina and uterus

The vagina is a muscular tube which connects the uterus with the outside. The uterus is at right angles to the vagina, and lies on top of the bladder. It is a hollow structure with a lining called the endometrium. The endometrium has two layers: an outer layer which is shed during menstruation and an inner layer which remains. The opening of the uterus is called the cervix, and the sperm must swim through the cervix in order to reach the ovum.

### Fertilization and implantation

The ovum only lives for 24 hours, so if fertilization is to be successful, it

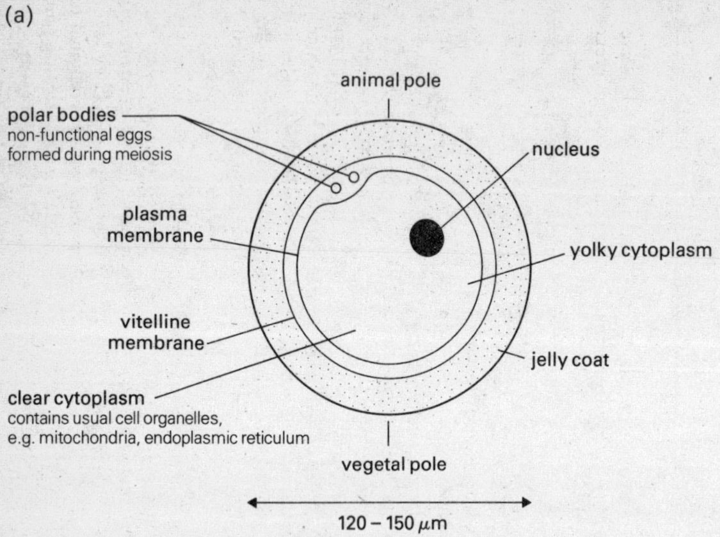
(a)
animal pole
polar bodies
non-functional eggs
formed during meiosis
nucleus
plasma
membrane
yolky cytoplasm
vitelline
membrane
jelly coat
clear cytoplasm
contains usual cell organelles,
e.g. mitochondria, endoplasmic reticulum
vegetal pole
120 – 150 μm

*Fig. 9.27* (a) A generalized animal ovum; (b) Section through an ovary

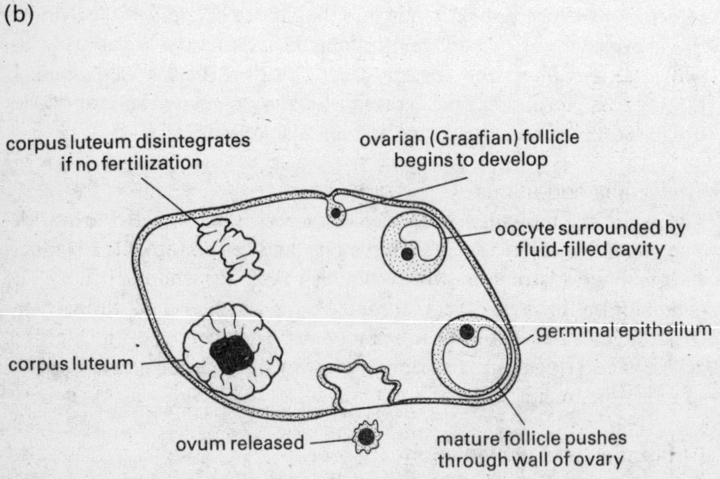
(b)
corpus luteum disintegrates
if no fertilization
ovarian (Graafian) follicle
begins to develop
oocyte surrounded by
fluid-filled cavity
germinal epithelium
corpus luteum
ovum released
mature follicle pushes
through wall of ovary

*Table 9.4.* Female sex hormones

| | *Site of production* | *Effects* | *Regulation* |
|---|---|---|---|
| Gonadotrophins | | | |
| Luteinizing hormone (LH) | Pituitary gland, under control of hypothalamus | (i) Causes ovulation<br>(ii) Increases progesterone synthesis | Production of LH decreases in response to a high progesterone concentration |
| Follicle-stimulating hormone (FSH) | Pituitary gland, under control of hypothalamus | (i) Production and development of ovarian follicles<br>(ii) Increases oestrogen production | Production of FSH decreases in response to high oestrogen concentration |
| Oestrogen | Produced by the ovarian follicles in response to the presence of FSH | (i) Development of female sexual characteristics, e.g. external genitalia, breasts, fat deposits<br>(ii) Together with progesterone, thickens the endometrial lining | As the concentration of oestrogen increases, the hypothalamus prevents further production of FSH by the pituitary. FSH no longer stimulates the follicles to produce oestrogen, so the concentration is reduced (negative feedback) |
| Progesterone | Produced by the corpus luteum in response to the presence of LH | Thickens the endometrium, preparing it for embryo implantation | As the concentration of progesterone increases, the hypothalamus prevents further production of LH by the pituitary. LH is required to stimulate progesterone synthesis, so the latter's concentration is reduced as well (negative feedback) |

must occur in the oviduct. The fertilized egg then takes 2–3 days to reach the uterus where, 3–4 days later, it becomes embedded in the endometrium. If the ovum is not fertilized, it is shed in the menstrual flow.

### Female sex hormones

See Table 9.4.

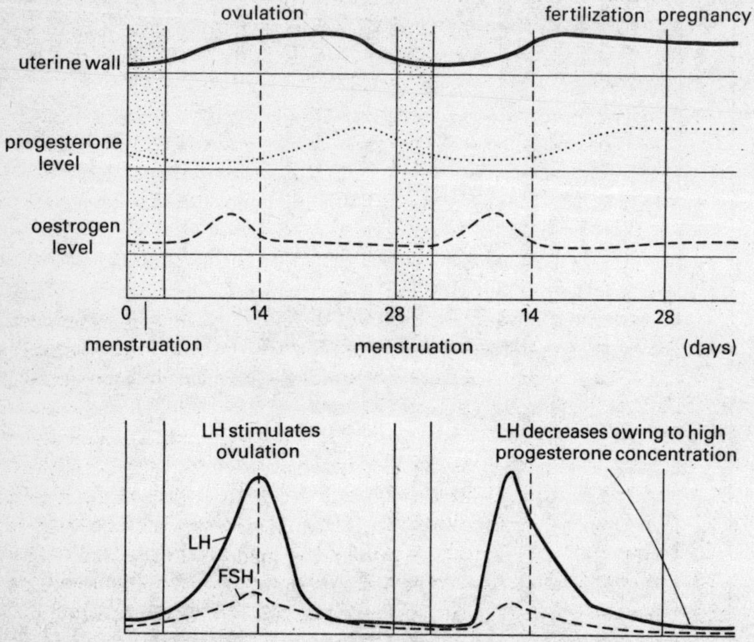
ovulation
fertilization
pregnancy
uterine wall
progesterone level
oestrogen level
0
14
28
14
28
menstruation
menstruation
(days)
LH stimulates ovulation
LH decreases owing to high progesterone concentration
LH
FSH

*Fig. 9.28* Hormones involved in the human oestrus cycle

### The menstrual cycle (Fig. 9.28)

1. Menstruation involves the shedding of the endometrial lining – this constitutes the beginning of the menstrual cycle.
2. FSH is produced by the pituitary, and causes an ovarian follicle to develop.
3. As the follicle develops, it produces an increasing amount of oestrogen which has two effects: (i) it regenerates the endometrial lining, and (ii)

as the concentration of oestrogen in the blood increases, the hypothalamus directs the pituitary to step up production of LH (positive feedback).
4. Increasing amounts of LH induce ovulation and also stimulate production of progesterone by the corpus luteum.
5. As the concentration of progesterone and oestrogen increases, production of LH and FSH stops.
6. A reduction in the gonadotrophins (FSH and LH) causes the endometrial lining to be released (menstruation).

*Fertility and contraceptive pills*

Fertility pills contain large doses of gonadotrophins. These have the effect of inducing multiple ovulation, and therefore often lead to multiple births.

Contraceptive pills (commonly known as the Pill) contain a combination of oestrogen and progesterone. If taken daily, the concentration of oestrogen and progesterone in the blood is high enough to prevent FSH and LH from being produced. In the absence of LH there is no ovulation, so pregnancy never occurs. When a female stops taking the pill at the end of the menstrual cycle, the endometrium is shed, even though ovulation has not occurred.

### Pregnancy and hormones

When an embryo implants in the uterus, the placenta is formed. The placenta begins to produce gonadotrophic hormones of its own, which stimulate the corpus luteum to produce oestrogen and progesterone in large quantities. In the later stages of pregnancy the placenta produces oestrogen and progesterone itself.

### *Contraception*

See Table 9.5.

### *Fertilization*

Fertilization proceeds as follows:
1. The egg which is released from the ovary is a secondary oocyte and has not yet undergone its second meiotic division.
2. When the head of a sperm reaches the egg, the acrosome releases chemicals which soften the outer egg membrane (the vitelline membrane).

*Table 9.5.* The effectiveness of various contraceptive methods

| *Method* | *Pregnancies expected in one year (%)* | *Adverse side-effects* | *Comments* | *Causes of failure* |
|---|---|---|---|---|
| Sterilization of man or woman | 0.003 | None if decision is made carefully | Operation needed | Sperm still in men's upper reproductive tracts: two sperm-free ejaculations indicate that intercourse without contraceptives may begin |
| The Pill | 0.003 | Varies from person to person and Pill to Pill | Medical supervision essential; menstrual bleeding less than normal | Forgetfulness: failure rates higher in poorly educated communities |
| Intra-uterine device (IUD) | 1–5 | Some people have increased menstrual bleeding | Medical insertion and supervision essential | Some people still become pregnant, others cannot tolerate an IUD; greater failure rates in first year of use |
| Diaphragm plus spermicide | 7–12 | None: some complain of loss of sexual pleasure | Diaphragm must be fitted by trained person and its use understood | Failure rate depends on level of user's education/affluence/degree of privacy; diaphragm can be displaced by constipation |
| Condom alone | 7–14 | None; several complain of loss of sexual pleasure | Easily available, needs no supervision | Putting on after contact with vagina; sperm escaping on removal |

| | | | | |
|---|---|---|---|---|
| Spermicide alone | 18–23 | None unless individual suffers allergy | Aerosols best, as they cover area more completely | Leaving one very small place untreated |
| Withdrawal | 20 | Less sexual satisfaction | | Only one healthy sperm on the edge of a healthy vagina is enough for pregnancy |
| 'Safe' period | 18–24 ('Temperature method' with no intercourse before ovulation, 6) | Worry | Time of ovulation may vary from month to month | Variations in life of egg and sperm |

*Source:* Nuffield Biology.

3. The acrosome membranes then form a structure which pierces the egg membranes and the head and middle piece of the sperm enter the egg.
4. Thickening of the egg membranes prevents further entry of sperm.
5. The egg cell undergoes its second meiotic division to form a true haploid ovum.
6. Fusion of the egg and sperm nuclei then produces a diploid zygote which travels to the uterus.

## *Gestation*

### *Development of the zygote*

As the fertilized egg travels to the uterus it divides mitotically to form a ball of cells called the blastocyst. This is known as cleavage. This is followed by gastrulation, when the cells arrange themselves in distinct layers (Fig. 9.29).

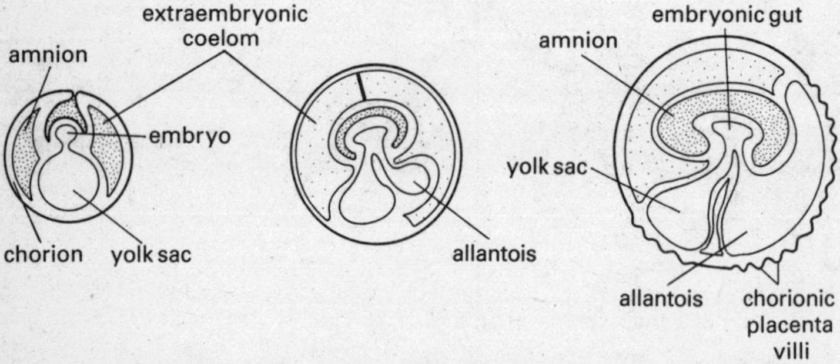
extraembryonic
coelom
amnion
embryo
chorion
yolk sac
allantois
embryonic gut
amnion
yolk sac
allantois
chorionic
placenta
villi

*Fig. 9.29* Development of the embryonic membranes in a mammal

1. FORMATION OF EXTRAEMBRYONIC MEMBRANES. Two membranes grow around the embryo. The inner membrane, the amnion, encloses the embryo in amniotic fluid, which protects it. The outer membrane is called the chorion, and the space between the two is the extraembryonic coelom, which is connected to the coelom of the embryo.
2. FORMATION OF THE PLACENTA. An outgrowth from the embryonic gut, the allantois, grows between the two membranes in the extraembryonic coelom. The chorion and the allantois develop into the placenta. Villi, containing blood capillaries, grow out into the material tissues of the uterus, where they absorb nourishment. The

allantois develops into the umbilical cord, which connects the embryo to the placenta. It contains an umbilical artery, which transfers food and oxygen from the mother to the embryo, and an umbilical vein, which returns waste materials to the maternal circulation.

Features of the placenta (Fig. 9.30)

1. Oxygen, food, water and salts pass from the mother to the foetus.
2. Waste products, carbon dioxide and urea pass from the foetus to the mother for removal.

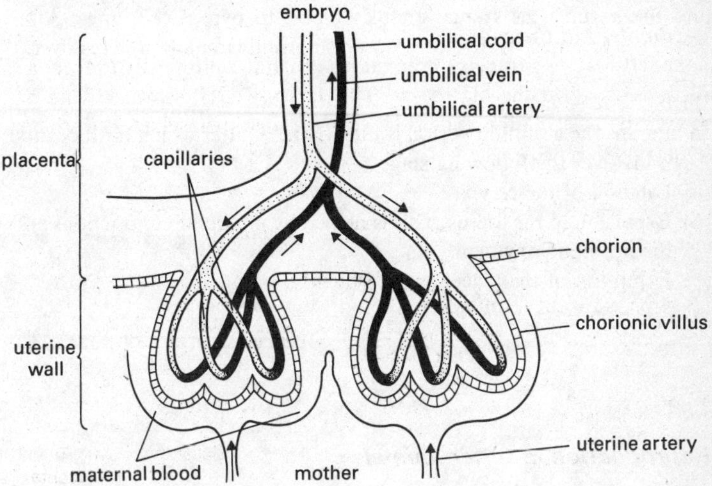
embryo
umbilical cord
umbilical vein
umbilical artery
placenta
capillaries
chorion
chorionic villus
uterine wall
uterine artery
maternal blood
mother

*Fig. 9.30* Blood flow in the placenta

3. The blood of the foetus and the mother do not mix. This is important for two reasons:
   (a) The foetus may have the father's blood group, which could be incompatible with the mother's blood.
   (b) The pressure of the mother's blood is much higher than that of the growing foetus. Mixing would therefore cause serious damage.
4. As the foetus grows, the placenta produces increasing amounts of hormones to prevent ovulation and menstruation.
5. The placenta allows the passage of certain hormones (not sex hormones) which will not damage the foetus.
6. It prevents passage of some pathogens – although many can still pass.

7. The placenta allows passage of antibodies which confer a certain amount of immunity to the foetus.
8. It attaches the foetus to the wall of the uterus.

#### Organogenesis

This is the development of the organ systems from specific layers of cells in the embryo. Circulatory systems, nervous systems, etc., are all formed. The lungs of the embryo are not used during gestation. Blood is shunted through a hole between the auricles, called the foramen ovale, and also through a duct, the ductum arteriosus, which links the pulmonary artery and the aorta. This system enables blood to bypass the lungs. After birth, the foramen ovale closes up and normal circulation takes over.

#### Birth

In humans the gestation period is nine months, after which birth occurs. Birth involves the following stages:

(a) Dilation of the cervix.
(b) Expulsion of the foetus. This is helped by muscular contractions and the hormone oxytocin.
(c) Expulsion of the placenta (afterbirth).

## ***Reproduction in other animals***

### *Reproductive cycles*

Females of most animal species (except humans) will only mate during the time when they are fertile; this period is known as oestrus or heat. Depending on the animal species, this period may vary from a few hours (e.g. mice) to a few weeks. Similarly, the frequency of these periods varies in different species: rabbits and mice have an oestrus period every few weeks, elephants only once every two years.

In some animals (e.g. cats and rabbits) copulation is the stimulus for ovulation to occur. This is a very efficient system, since the egg stands a high chance of being fertilized.

In birds, mating often depends on seasonal changes. Increase in day-length causes hormonal production in the pituitary, which leads to maturation of the gonads (sex organs).

*Courtship in mammals*

Courtship in mammals is extremely complex. Most mammals have a very good sense of smell and scent is therefore an important part of their sexual behaviour. For example, the scent produced by a bitch in season will attract dogs from a wide area.

Once a male has been attracted to a female he will usually have to woo her. The way this is done is unique to each species and there is therefore considerable variation.

In the rabbit the male stimulates the female by displaying his white underside when jumping over her, at the same time squirting a jet of urine over her.

Touch may also play an important role in some mammals. Many ungulates stimulate the female by touching her flanks several times with their outstretched forelimbs. Many male insectivores and rodents nuzzle the female's hindquarters and lift them up.

In mammals whose vision is the dominant sense, visual displays play a greater role in courtship. This is especially so in humans. Humans are unique among mammals in that society has developed to a stage where courting and mating may occur without the production of children. This brings into question the necessity of a lifelong mate to help in caring for the offspring. Thus in humans the purpose of courtship is becoming quite different from that in other animals.

## Further reading

B. Dale, *Fertilization in Animals*, Studies in Biology No. 157 (Arnold, 1983)

W. H. Freeman and B. Bracegirdle, *An Atlas of Embryology*, 2nd edition (Heinemann, 1967)

G. Hart, *Human Sexual Behaviour*, Oxford/Carolina Biology Reader No. 94 (Packard, 1977)

P. J. Hogarth, *Viviparity*, Studies in Biology No. 75 (Arnold, 1976)

P. Rhodes, *Birth Control*, Oxford/Carolina Biology Reader No. 4, 2nd edition (Packard, 1976)

## Related questions

**Question:**

The following graph illustrates the levels of oestrogen and progesterone during the human menstrual cycle.

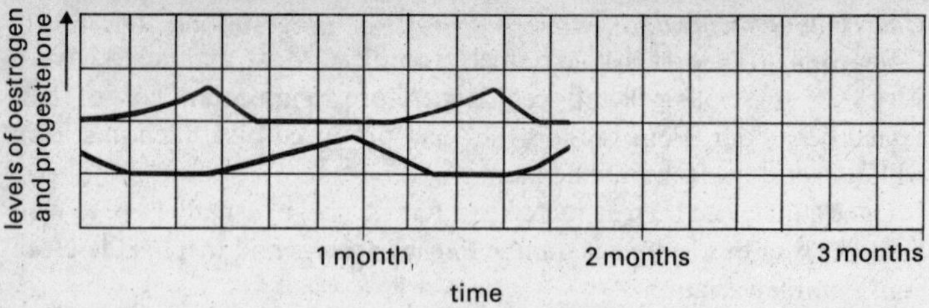
levels of oestrogen and progesterone
1 month
2 months
3 months
time

(a) (i) Mark with an X on the graph the line that represents oestrogen. **(1 mark)**

(ii) Mark with an O on the graph a probable point of ovulation. **(1 mark)**

(iii) Mark with a vertical line the most likely point on the graph when menstruation would begin. **(1 mark)**

(iv) Complete the graph to show the levels of the two hormones if pregnancy occurs. **(2 marks)**

(b) What is the function of the corpus luteum during pregnancy?

________________________________________

________________________________________

**(2 marks)**

(c) Name *two* other hormones concerned with reproduction in mammals and in each case state *one* function.

(i) name ________________________________

function ________________________________

(ii) name ________________________________

function ________________________________

**(4 marks)**

**(Total 11 marks)**

[London, Jan. 1983, Paper 1]

**Comments:**

(a) (i), (ii), (iii) and (iv). See p. 356 Fig. 9.28. It can be seen from the figure that the peak for oestrogen concentration occurs in the first half of the month, while the peak for progesterone concentration occurs in the latter part of the month.

(b) See p. 357.

(c) (i) and (ii). See p. 350 and p. 355.

**Question:**

The diagram below is of a mammalian ovary.

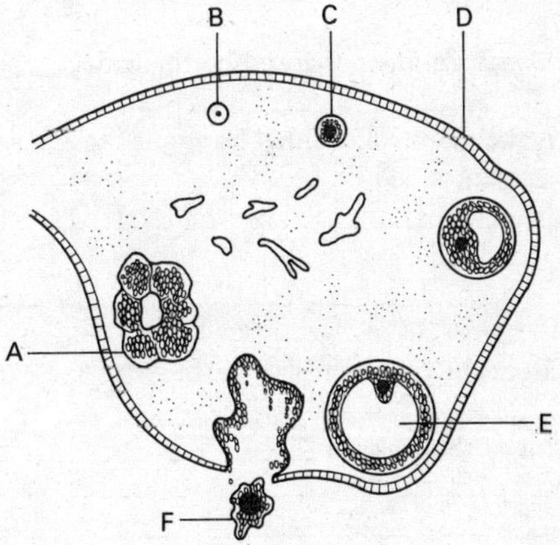

B
C
D
A
E
F


(a) Which of the following structures does the letter A indicate? Underline the correct answer.
   (i) interstitial cells
   (ii) corpus luteum
   (iii) primary follicle
   (iv) secondary oocyte
   (v) germinal epithelium **(1 mark)**

(b) Which of the following is the correct sequence in the development of the labelled structures? Underline the correct answer.
   (i) A F E D C B
   (ii) E F B C D A
   (iii) C B D A F E
   (iv) D B C E F A
   (v) D A B C E F **(1 mark)**

(c) For each of the following, state whether it is haploid or diploid.

(i) secondary oocyte ______________________

(ii) primary oocyte ______________________

(iii) germinal epithelium ______________________

(iv) oogonium ______________________

**(4 marks)**

(d) (i) Name *one* hormone produced by the ovary ______________

(ii) What is the main role of this hormone?

______________________

______________________

**(2 marks)**

(e) What part does the placenta play in the

(i) nutrition of the embryo ______________________

______________________

______________________

______________________

**(3 marks)**

(ii) protection of the embryo ______________________

______________________

______________________

______________________

**(3 marks)**

**(Total 17 marks)**

[London, July 1981, Paper 1]

**Comments:**

(a) See Fig. 9.27.

(b) In this type of question it is often helpful to briefly name each structure on scrap paper (see Fig. 9.27) and then collate them in the correct order (see p. 354). However, a much quicker way to answer multiple-choice questions of this type is to look for obvious clues and operate a process of elimination. For example, the corpus luteum is the last structure to be formed, so the answer must be (ii) or (iv). This means the first structure to be formed is either E (fluid cavity) or D (germinal epithelium). The ovaries are present at birth and, although undeveloped, they contain the germinal epithelium. No fluid cavities are present at birth, therefore the germinal epithelium is the first structure to be formed and the answer is (iv).

(c) Scc Fig. 9.26.

(d) See p. 355.

(e) (i) and (ii). See p. 361. Note that protection of the embryo involves protection from disease, as well as physical protection.

## *Growth and development*

Growth is a permanent increase in size undergone by an organism due to cell division, assimilation and cell expansion. Development may be considered as an increase in complexity. Both environment and heredity control the pattern and the rate of growth and development.

Growth can be measured by estimating the increase in:

(a) a linear dimension such as height (this does not take growth in all directions into account);

(b) volume (difficult to measure in irregular organisms);

(c) total fresh weight (may involve inaccuracies due to temporary fluctuations, e.g. increase in water content after drinking);

(d) dry weight (involves killing the organisms, thus a large number of similar organisms are required).

A common inaccuracy in the above methods is that growth may be **allometric**, i.e. different parts of the body growing at different rates (see Fig. 9.31). One example of this is the brain in man, which grows at a much greater rate than other parts of the body just before birth and in the early years of development.

The **absolute growth rate** is the amount of growth of an organism per unit time. This value may be obtained from a growth curve (Fig. 9.32).

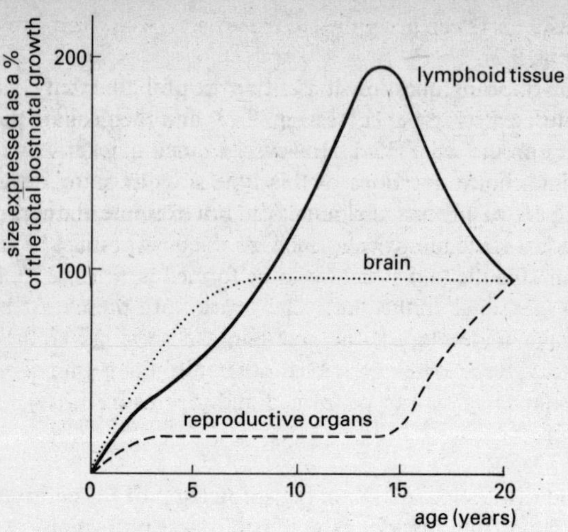
size expressed as a % of the total postnatal growth
200
100
lymphoid tissue
brain
reproductive organs
0
5
10
15
20
age (years)

*Fig. 9.31* Examples of allometric growth in man

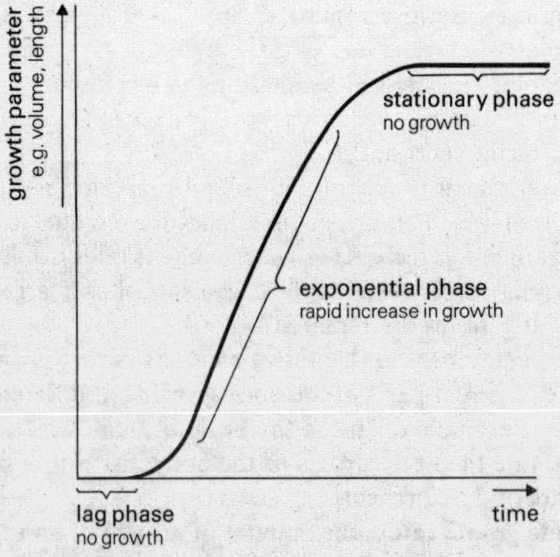
growth parameter e.g. volume, length
stationary phase
no growth
exponential phase
rapid increase in growth
lag phase
no growth
time

*Fig. 9.32* General growth curve (sigmoid curve)

This type of curve can be applied to the growth of an organ, an individual or a population.

A more meaningful expression of growth would be that of the **percentage growth rate** (Fig. 9.33). This gives an idea of the amount of growth in relation to the size of the organism.

Growth in most organisms follows the smooth pattern illustrated in Fig. 9.32. However, in arthropods the growth is intermittent because of the necessity of shedding the hard cuticle by ecdysis before further growth can occur (Fig. 9.34).

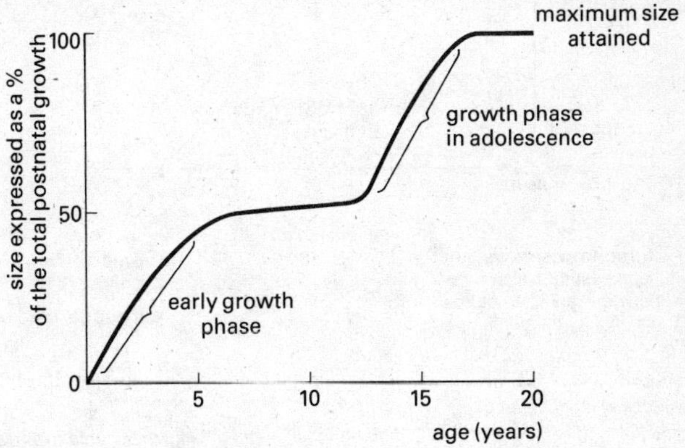
maximum size attained
growth phase in adolescence
early growth phase
size expressed as a % of the total postnatal growth
100
50
0
5
10
15
20
age (years)

*Fig. 9.33* Percentage growth rate in man

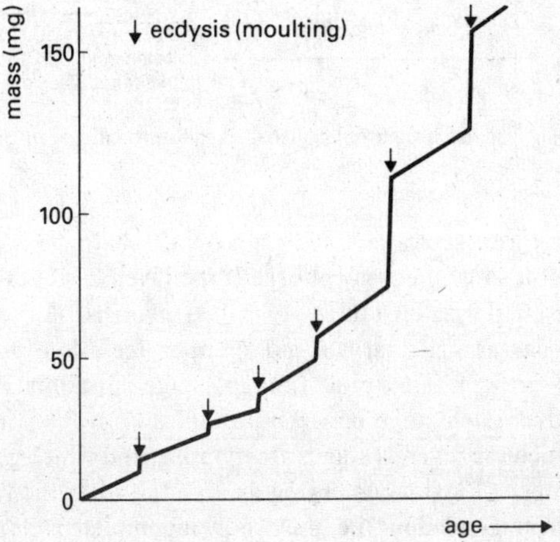
ecdysis (moulting)
mass (mg)
150
100
50
0
age

*Fig. 9.34* General growth curve of an arthropod, showing intermittent growth

### *Metamorphosis*

Metamorphosis is the change in form of an organism from the juvenile to the adult stage. The stimulus for the onset of metamorphosis is usually a change in the environments such as a change in temperature.

In insects these changes are detected by sense organs and relayed to the brain. Neuro-secretory cells in the brain produce secretions which affect the corpora cardiaca and corpora allata which lie directly behind the brain. These, and the prothoracic glands (in the thorax), constitute the endocrine system. The control of metamorphosis in insects is summarized in Fig. 9.35.

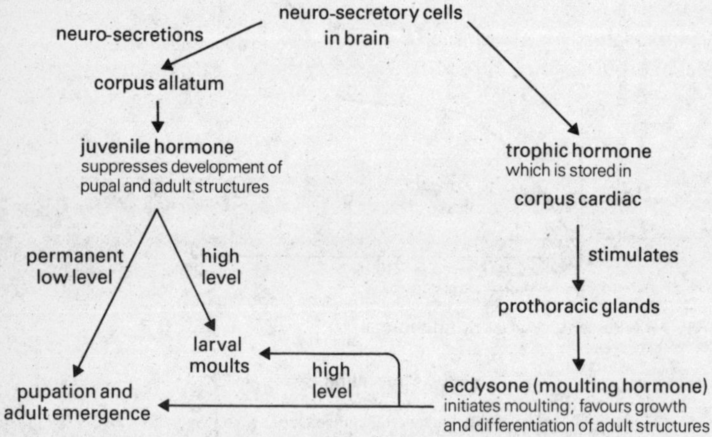
neuro-secretory cells
in brain
neuro-secretions
corpus allatum
juvenile hormone
suppresses development of
pupal and adult structures
trophic hormone
which is stored in
corpus cardiac
stimulates
prothoracic glands
permanent
low level
high
level
larval
moults
high
level
pupation and
adult emergence
ecdysone (moulting hormone)
initiates moulting; favours growth
and differentiation of adult structures

*Fig. 9.35* Summary of the hormonal control of metamorphosis in insects

### Metamorphosis in insects

All insects exhibit some metamorphosis. If the juvenile stages are similar in appearance to the adults they are called **nymphs**, if not, they are referred to as **larvae**. The larvae and nymphs feed continuously and undergo rapid growth. The adult (imago) stage is mainly locomotory and reproductive. Each stage between moults is known as an **instar**.

Insects in which the juvenile stages are nymphs, and which go gradually through a number of instars emerging as an adult after the final moult, are said to be **hemimetabolous**, i.e. they show incomplete metamorphosis. This group of insects is also classified as Exopterygota, as the wings, when present, develop from external buds. Examples are locusts, aphids and cockroaches.

Insects with larval stages are **holometabolous**, i.e. showing complete metamorphosis. They are also known as the Endopterygota, as the wings develop from internal buds. Examples include butterflies.

The advantage of holometabolous metamorphosis is that the larva and adult have a different mode of life and therefore exploit different habitats. This reduces competition and enhances their survival rate should there be a disturbance in one or other habitat.

In the pupal stage the larva metamorphoses into the adult either by

(a) differential growth of larval structures, or

(b) breakdown of larval structures and regrowth from imaginal buds.

### Metamorphosis in amphibians

Metamorphosis is an important feature in the life cycle of anurans such as frogs and toads. The hormonal control of events is summarized in Fig. 9.36.

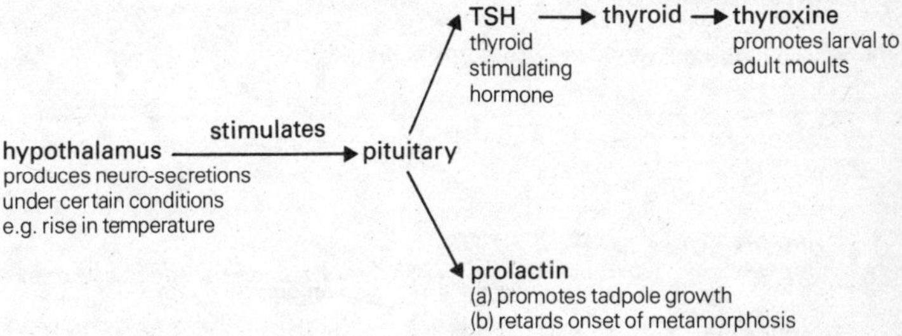
TSH
thyroid stimulating hormone
thyroid
thyroxine
promotes larval to adult moults
stimulates
hypothalamus
produces neuro-secretions under certain conditions e.g. rise in temperature
pituitary
prolactin
(a) promotes tadpole growth
(b) retards onset of metamorphosis

*Fig. 9.36* Summary of the hormonal control of metamorphosis in amphibia

## *Plant growth and development*

Cell division occurs throughout the embryo, but becomes restricted to certain areas called **meristems** in the growing plant.

Active cell division in the meristems occurs throughout the plant's life. Primary (apical) meristematic tissue is found at the shoot and root apices, and produces primary tissues and an increase in length (Figs 9.37 and 9.38). Secondary (lateral) meristems are located parallel to the organ in which they occur (e.g. vascular and cork cambium), and result in the production of secondary tissues and an increase in girth (secondary thickening) (Fig. 9.39).

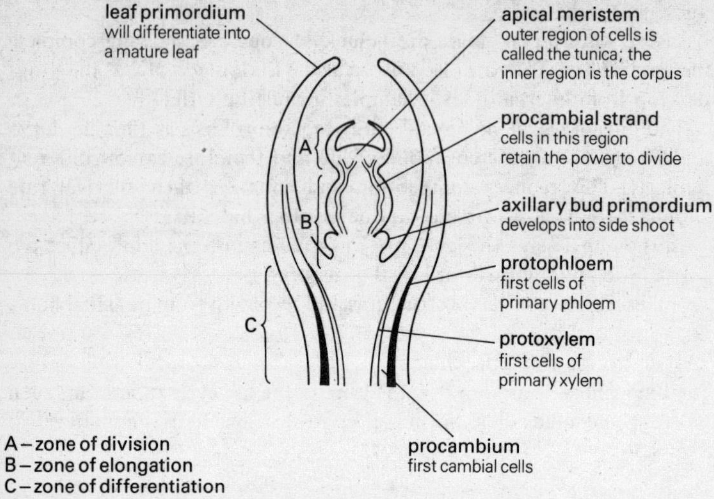
leaf primordium
will differentiate into a mature leaf
apical meristem
outer region of cells is called the tunica; the inner region is the corpus
procambial strand
cells in this region retain the power to divide
axillary bud primordium
develops into side shoot
protophloem
first cells of primary phloem
protoxylem
first cells of primary xylem
procambium
first cambial cells
A
B
C
A – zone of division
B – zone of elongation
C – zone of differentiation

*Fig. 9.37* Shoot apex of a dicotyledonous plant

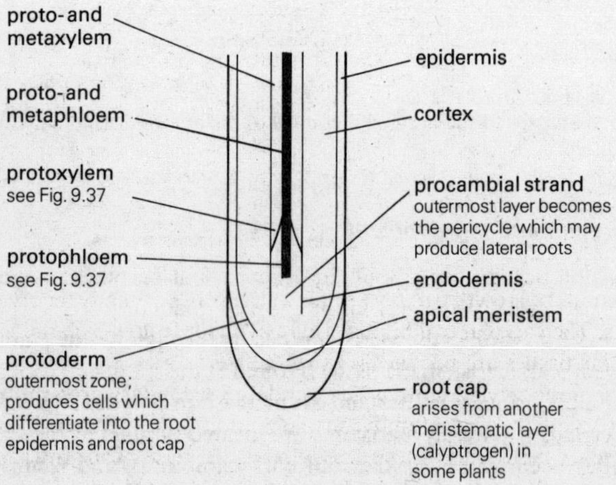
proto- and metaxylem
proto- and metaphloem
protoxylem
see Fig. 9.37
protophloem
see Fig. 9.37
protoderm
outermost zone; produces cells which differentiate into the root epidermis and root cap
epidermis
cortex
procambial strand
outermost layer becomes the pericycle which may produce lateral roots
endodermis
apical meristem
root cap
arises from another meristematic layer (calyptrogen) in some plants

*Fig. 9.38* Root apex of a dicotyledonous plant

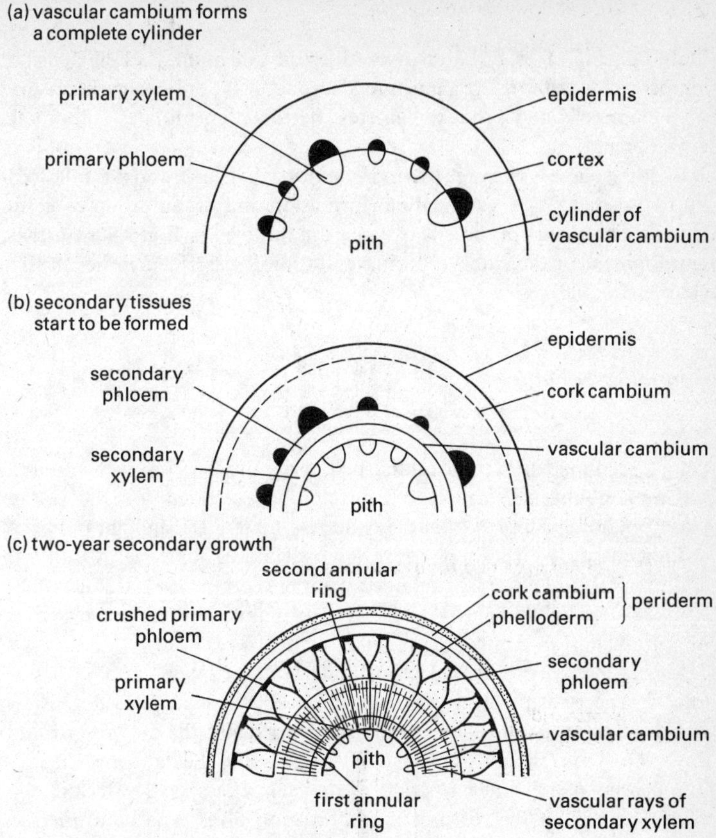
(a) vascular cambium forms a complete cylinder
primary xylem
primary phloem
epidermis
cortex
cylinder of vascular cambium
pith
(b) secondary tissues start to be formed
epidermis
secondary phloem
cork cambium
secondary xylem
vascular cambium
pith
(c) two-year secondary growth
second annular ring
crushed primary phloem
cork cambium
phelloderm
periderm
primary xylem
secondary phloem
vascular cambium
pith
first annular ring
vascular rays of secondary xylem

*Fig. 9.39* Stages in the secondary growth of a dicotyledonous stem (shown for half the stem)

Secondary growth can also occur in the roots of many dicotyledonous plants. The vascular cambium forms a cylinder from which the secondary vascular tissues are produced, as in the stem.

Few monocotyledonous species undergo secondary growth. However, members of the grass family do have additional meristems, known as **intercalary meristems**. These are found at the base of the internodes and remain meristematic. This means that grass shoots can rapidly regenerate after treatment such as cutting or grazing.

### *Animal growth and development*

Development takes place all over the body in animals. Cell division almost ceases after the organism reaches maturity, only being necessary to replace cells and produce gametes. Fertilization initiates embryonic development.

The first stage is **cleavage** (period of mitotic division), and it is followed by the second stage, **gastrulation** (formation and organization of germ layers). The events of these two stages are outlined in Fig. 9.40. Further development of the embryo during gestation is described earlier in this chapter (p. 360).

### *Control of growth*

#### Plants

Once a seedling has become established, using the food reserves stored in the seed, continued growth and development depends on the young plant obtaining supplies of energy and raw materials. Sunlight provides radiant energy, which can be converted to chemical bond energy (p. 125), and minerals are generally obtained from the soil (p. 195). Climate (e.g. temperature, light intensity and water availability) therefore plays an important part in controlling plant growth.

However, environmental factors alone cannot explain certain physiological aspects of plant growth, e.g. the exact sequence of cell division and differentiation at the apices of roots and stems, the growth of roots downwards into the soil and of stems upwards into the light, and the fact that certain plants enter a period of dormancy at specific times of the year. There must therefore be a combination of external and internal factors controlling the complex stages in the growth and development of the plant.

*External factors*

1. LIGHT: Light influences a variety of developmental processes. Light is perceived by **phytochrome**, a photochemical substance (see p. 299). Phytochrome is involved in germination, stem elongation, leaf expansion, growth of side shoots and flowering. Phytochrome is thought to act through the presence of hormones.
2. TEMPERATURE: The effects of temperature are particularly evident in flowering. In some cases growth will only take place if the seeds have been subjected to a period of cold (vernalization).

(a)

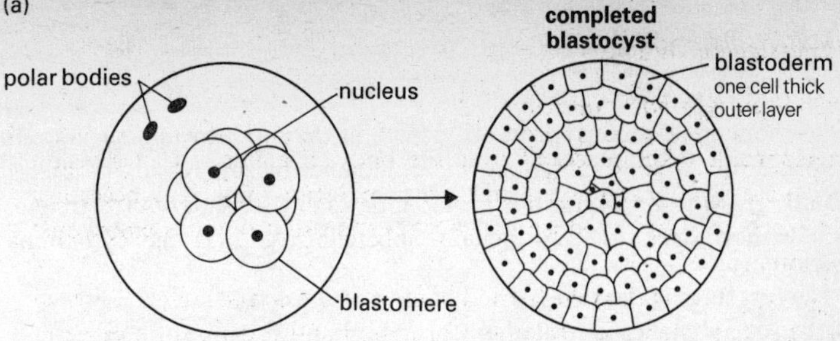

completed blastocyst
polar bodies
nucleus
blastomere
blastoderm
one cell thick
outer layer


The zygote divides mitotically to give many cells known as blastomeres

The mass of blastomeres gives rise to the blastocyst which has a hollow centre – the blastocoel. A solid ball of cells is formed in the mammal

(b)

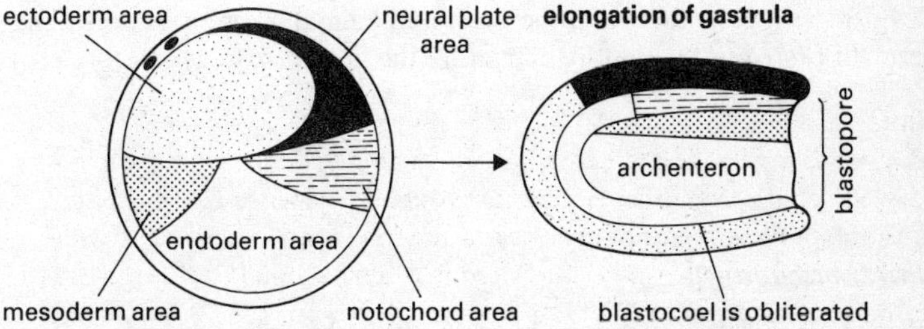

ectoderm area
neural plate area
elongation of gastrula
endoderm area
archenteron
blastopore
mesoderm area
notochord area
blastocoel is obliterated


The blastoderm has definite regions (presumptive areas) which will give rise to the ectoderm, endoderm, mesoderm, neural plate and notochord

The hollow gastrula is formed by movement of presumptive areas and invagination of cells of the vegetal pole. The gastrula then elongates

(c)

**TS of gastrula**

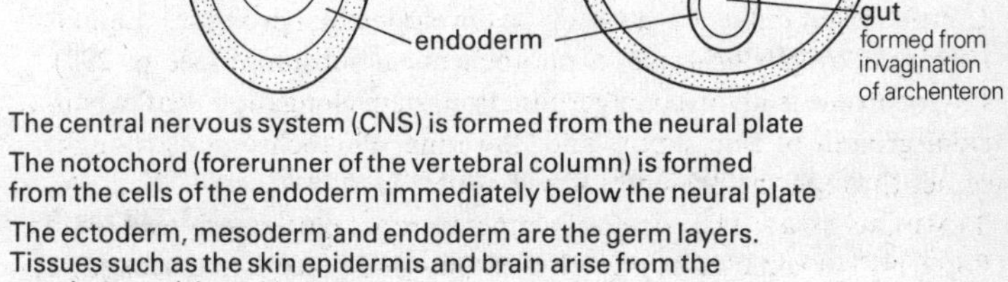

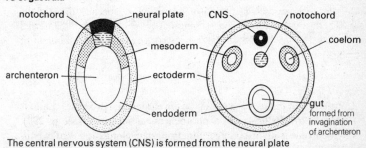

notochord
neural plate
CNS
notochord
coelom
mesoderm
archenteron
ectoderm
endoderm
gut
formed from invagination of archenteron


The central nervous system (CNS) is formed from the neural plate

The notochord (forerunner of the vertebral column) is formed from the cells of the endoderm immediately below the neural plate

The ectoderm, mesoderm and endoderm are the germ layers. Tissues such as the skin epidermis and brain arise from the ectoderm, and the epithelium of the intestine from the endoderm.

Organs such as muscles arise from the mesoderm

*Fig. 9.40* (a) Cleavage and (b) gastrulation in *Amphioxus* (a primitive chordate)

*Internal factors*

Hormones (e.g. auxins) promote growth of the shoot by influencing cell elongation. Auxins maintain apical dominance by suppression of lateral buds, growth of adventitious roots, initiation of secondary growth, etc. Other hormones involved include gibberellins (p. 291) and cytokinins (p. 292).

### Animals

Growth and development in animals is also controlled by hormones. Examples include pituitary growth hormone in mammals (p. 278) and moulting and juvenile hormones in insects (p. 370).

Evidence suggests that both the plant and animal hormones controlling growth exert their action by activating the appropriate genes.

## Further reading

R. A. L. Batt, *Influence in Animal Growth and Development*, Studies in Biology No. 116 (Arnold, 1980)

W. H. Freeman and B. Bracegirdle, *An Atlas of Embryology*, 3rd edition (Heinemann, 1978)

A. R. Gemmell, *Developmental Plant Anatomy*, Studies in Biology No. 15 (Arnold 1969)

D. R. Newth, *Animal Growth and Development*, Studies in Biology No. 24 (Arnold, 1970)

D. H. Northcote, *Differentiation in Higher Plants*, Oxford/Carolina Biology Reader No. 44 (Packard, 1974)

## Related questions

**Question:**

(a) What do you understand by 'growth' in living organisms?

**(4 marks)**

(b) The following graph illustrates the pattern of growth in living organisms.

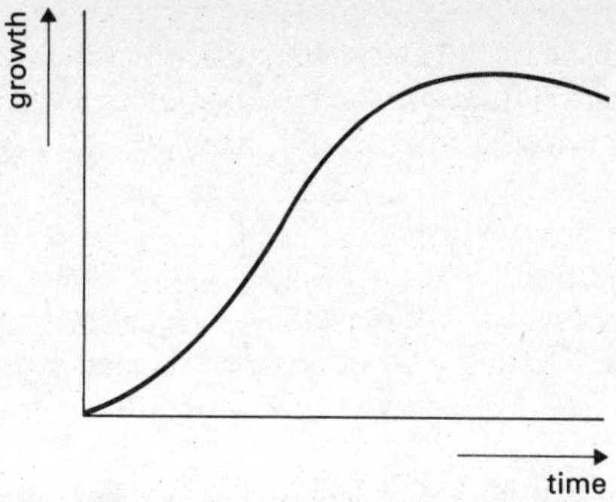
growth
time

Interpret this graph in terms of the growth of
(i) a mammal
(ii) an herbaceous perennial plant **(10 marks)**

(c) Discuss the importance of meristems in flowering plants. **(6 marks)**

[London, June 1984, Paper 2]

**Comments:**

(a) See p. 367. For four marks a full definition giving some indication of the difference in growth in plants and animals is required. For example, you should mention that growth is restricted to specialized regions called meristems in plants, whereas in animals growth occurs over the whole body, giving a more compact form.

(b) See Fig. 9.32. This general growth curve can be applied to a population or an individual.

(i) In a mammal it is likely that the growth is being measured in terms of mass. An increase in mass ceases at maturity.

(ii) The shape of the graph indicates that the growth of one organ (e.g. a leaf) is being estimated, although this usually reflects the growth of the whole plant. This is an *actual growth curve* rather than an indication of the rate of growth.

(c) See p. 371. Remember meristems may be lateral and intercalary as well as apical.

**Question:**

The following diagram represents a longitudinal section through the tip of the root of a dicotyledon.

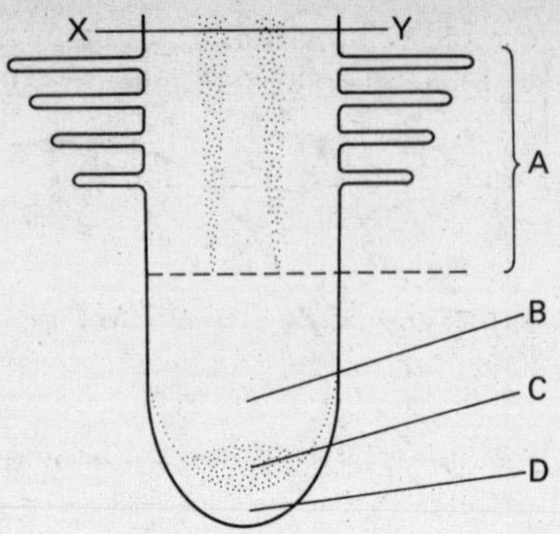
X
Y
A
B
C
D

(a) Name the regions labelled A to D. **(4 marks)**

(b) Make a labelled plan to show the distribution of tissues in a transverse section through the region X–Y.

(c) Identify a region (A, B, C or D) in which the following types of cell might be found.
 (i) A small cell, with thin cellulose walls, dense cytoplasm, no vacuole and a large nucleus.
 (ii) A peripheral cell, with a large vacuole and a long extension at one side in which is situated the nucleus.
 (iii) An elongated cell, several times longer than broad, with no living contents, but spiral bands of lignin in the wall.

**(3 marks)**

(d) State *one* function of each of the cells described in (c).

**(3 marks)**
**(Total 10 marks)**

**Comments:**

(a) See Figure 9.38.

(b) Note that the question states the *root* is *dicotyledonous*. The region X–Y does not have root hairs and the tissues are fully differentiated (see Fig. 5.13). Note: Omit root hairs in your tissue plan!

(c) This section is testing your knowledge of *detailed* plant cell structure. The keywords are:
 (i) *thin* (i.e. primary) cellulose cell walls, *no* vacuole, *large* nucleus (indicating rapidly dividing cells) – Region C.
 (ii) *peripheral cell, long extension* (i.e. root hair) – Region A.
 (iii) *elongated* cell, *no living* contents, bands of *lignin* (i.e. xylem tissue) – Region A.

(d) (i) Undergo rapid cell division resulting in growth.
(ii) Root hair is site of water and mineral salt uptake – choose one of these.
(iii) Choose water or mineral salt uptake.

**Question:**

(a) Explain the terms 'allometric growth' and 'metamorphosis' and how these phenomena are related to the growth of an insect? **(7 marks)**

(b) How does metamorphosis differ in hemimetabolous and holometabolous insects? **(5 marks)**

(c) Outline the endocrine control of metamorphosis. **(8 marks)**

**(Total 20 marks)**

[In the style of J M B]

**Comments:**

(a) The definitions of 'allometric growth' and 'metamorphosis' are outlined on pp. 367 and 370. When relating these terms to the growth of insects remember the intermittent growth pattern shown by insects (Fig. 9.34).

(b) To obtain the full five marks given, full explanations should be provided (see p. 370) with named examples.

(c) See Fig. 9.35.

# 10. Cell division and genetics

### *Cell division*

If growth or repair of tissues is to occur, new cells must be made. Generation of cells occurs by division of existing cells (mitosis) to produce a number of 'daughter' cells which can also undergo mitosis. Mitosis occurs in all somatic cells of all organisms. Another type of cell division is required to produce gametes. This is called meiosis, and it involves a reduction in the number of chromosomes in the daughter cells. The resulting cells (gametes) are said to be haploid since they contain only half the normal number of chromosomes. When two gametes fuse at fertilization, they produce a zygote, and the diploid number is restored.

### *Chromosomes*

Chromosomes are rod-like structures found in the nuclei of all living cells. Each species has its own characteristic number of chromosomes (man: 46, rat: 42) which are present in pairs, called homologous pairs (man, therefore, has 23 pairs).

Each chromosome is composed of two chromatids, joined together by the centromere. Centromeres are not always in the centre of the chromosome, but they will be in the same place for homologous pairs.

Corresponding genes on homologous chromosomes code for the same characteristics (see Fig. 10.1). At fertilization, one of each homologous pair is obtained from the mother and one from the father.

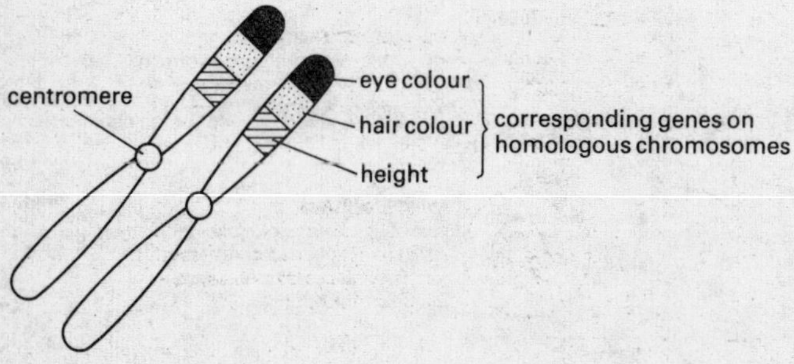
centromere
eye colour
hair colour
height
corresponding genes on homologous chromosomes

*Fig. 10.1* Homologous chromosomes

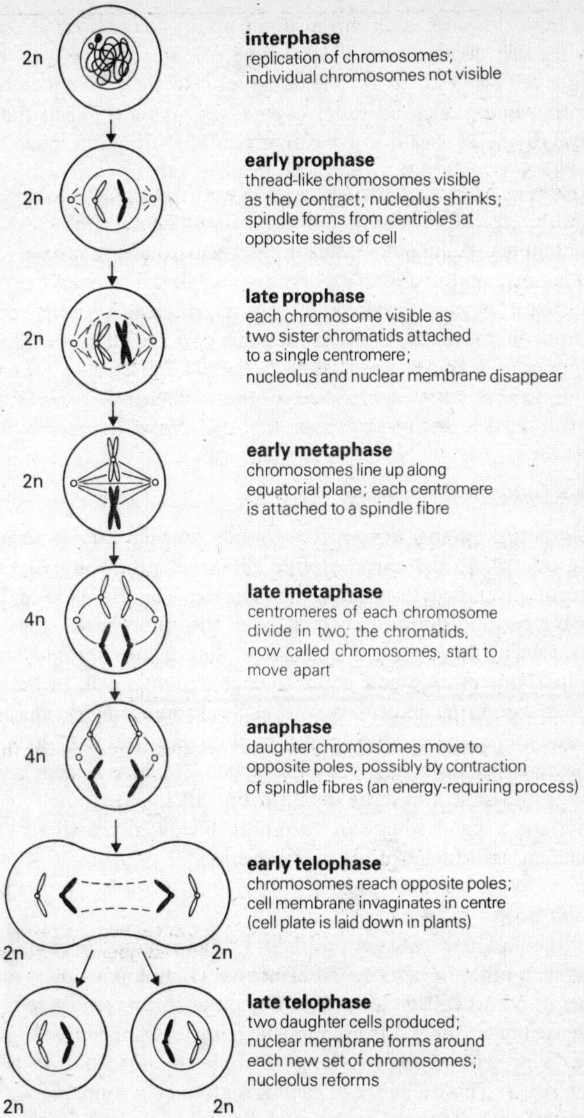
2n
interphase
replication of chromosomes;
individual chromosomes not visible
2n
early prophase
thread-like chromosomes visible
as they contract; nucleolus shrinks;
spindle forms from centrioles at
opposite sides of cell
2n
late prophase
each chromosome visible as
two sister chromatids attached
to a single centromere;
nucleolus and nuclear membrane disappear
2n
early metaphase
chromosomes line up along
equatorial plane; each centromere
is attached to a spindle fibre
4n
late metaphase
centromeres of each chromosome
divide in two; the chromatids,
now called chromosomes, start to
move apart
4n
anaphase
daughter chromosomes move to
opposite poles, possibly by contraction
of spindle fibres (an energy-requiring process)
early telophase
chromosomes reach opposite poles;
cell membrane invaginates in centre
(cell plate is laid down in plants)
2n
2n
late telophase
two daughter cells produced;
nuclear membrane forms around
each new set of chromosomes;
nucleolus reforms
2n
2n

*Fig. 10.2* Mitosis

### *Mitosis*

Before mitosis occurs, each chromosome makes an exact replica of itself. When the cell divides, one of each type of chromosome goes to each daughter cell (see Fig. 10.2). The daughter cells then have identical sets of chromosomes, each an exact copy of the parent. When the cell is ready to divide, it is said to be in interphase. During interphase:

1. The DNA replicates to produce an identical copy of each chromosome. These are present as two sets of chromatids, attached to a single centromere.
2. Many of the organelles are also duplicated to provide enough supplies for each daughter cell.
3. The cell builds up energy reserves in the form of ATP.

### *Meiosis (nuclear division)*

Meiosis occurs in the reproductive organs during gamete formation. During interphase the chromosomes replicate, producing two sets of chromatids, attached to a single centromere. This is followed by two successive meiotic divisions, which have the same basic stages as in mitosis. During the first meiotic division, homologous chromosomes are segregated, one of each pair going to each daughter cell. In the second meiotic division, the centromeres of each chromosome divide and the chromatids separate, producing four haploid gametes. Each gamete has one chromosome from each homologous pair. Meiosis is summarized in Fig. 10.3, and shown in more detail in Fig. 10.4.

Meiosis is a good source of variation, owing to crossing over and independent assortment of genes (see below).

#### Crossing over

During the diplotene stage of prophase I, homologous chromosomes lie next to each other in pairs called bivalents. Homologous pairs are held together at points called chiasmata. When the chromosomes separate, a small length of chromatid from opposite pairs is swapped (see Fig. 10.5). The genes present on the two lengths of chromatid code for the same characteristics. This exchange of genetic material is a source of variation, and ensures that the genes of the offspring can never be identical to the parent.

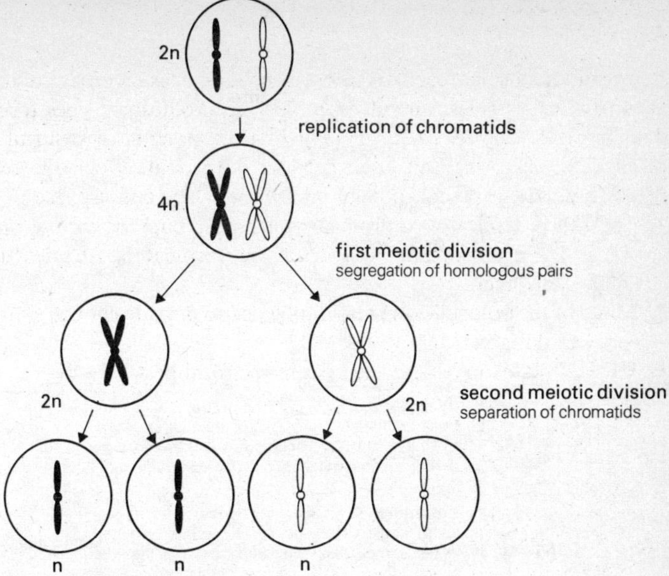
2n
replication of chromatids
4n
first meiotic division
segregation of homologous pairs
2n
2n
second meiotic division
separation of chromatids
n
n
n

*Fig. 10.3* Meiosis: a summary

## Independent assortment of genes

During metaphase I of meiosis, homologous pairs lie on the equator. The daughter cells obtain only one chromosome from each homologous pair, but which one they get is a random process. This is referred to as independent assortment of chromosomes and is an important source of variation. It ensures that no two gametes will be alike.

### *Differences between mitosis and meiosis*

See Table 10.1

## *Further reading*

B. John and K. R. Lewis, *The Meiotic Mechanism*, Oxford/Carolina Biology Reader No. 65 (Packard, 1973)

B. John and K. R. Lewis, *Somatic Cell Division*, Oxford/Carolina Biology Reader No. 26, 2nd edition (Packard, 1981)

R. Kemp, *Cell Division and Heredity*, Studies in Biology No. 21 (Arnold, 1970)

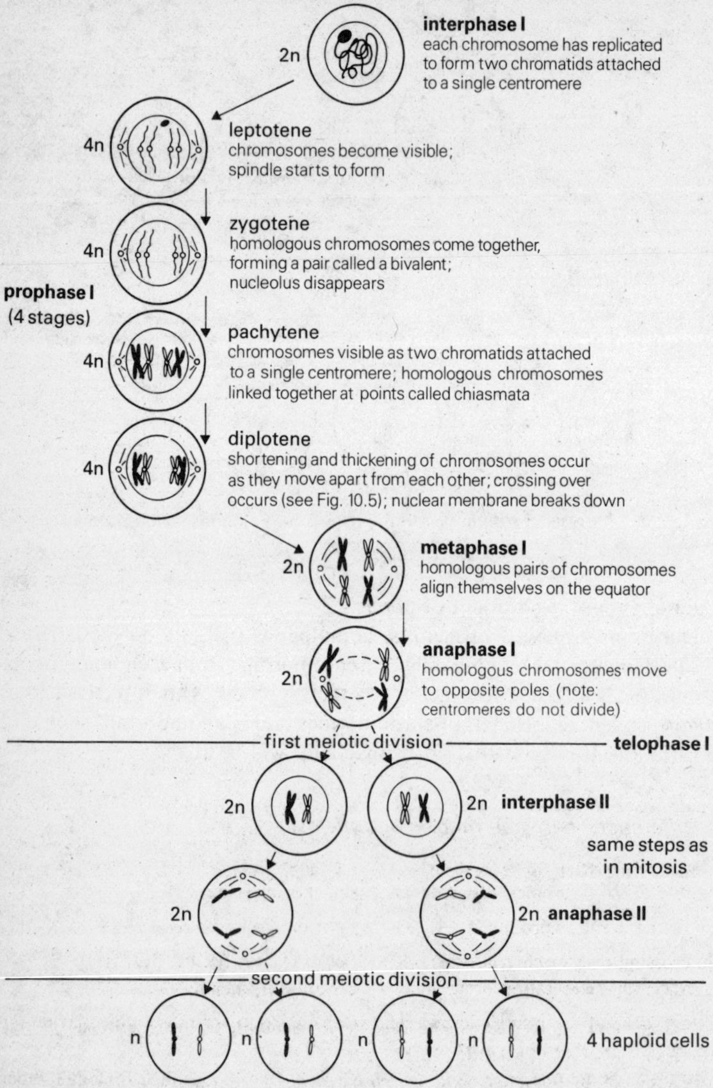
2n
interphase I
each chromosome has replicated to form two chromatids attached to a single centromere
4n
leptotene
chromosomes become visible; spindle starts to form
4n
zygotene
homologous chromosomes come together, forming a pair called a bivalent; nucleolus disappears
prophase I
(4 stages)
4n
pachytene
chromosomes visible as two chromatids attached to a single centromere; homologous chromosomes linked together at points called chiasmata
4n
diplotene
shortening and thickening of chromosomes occur as they move apart from each other; crossing over occurs (see Fig. 10.5); nuclear membrane breaks down
2n
metaphase I
homologous pairs of chromosomes align themselves on the equator
2n
anaphase I
homologous chromosomes move to opposite poles (note: centromeres do not divide)
first meiotic division
telophase I
2n
2n
interphase II
same steps as in mitosis
2n
2n
anaphase II
second meiotic division
n
n
n
n
4 haploid cells

*Fig. 10.4* Meiosis

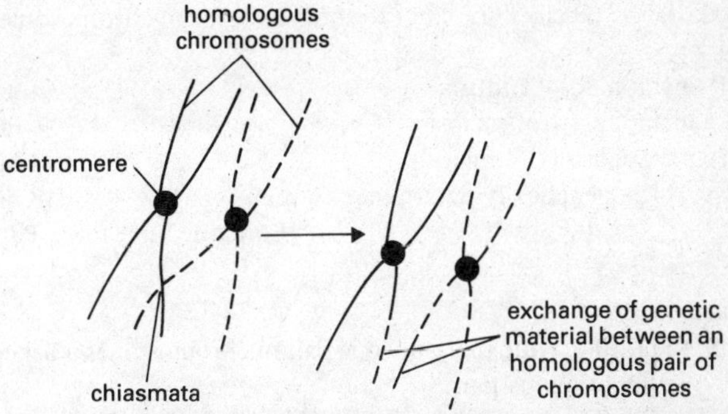
homologous chromosomes
centromere
chiasmata
exchange of genetic material between an homologous pair of chromosomes

*Fig. 10.5* Exchange of genetic material between homologous chromosomes

*Table 10.1.* Differences between mitosis and meiosis

| *Mitosis* | *Meiosis* |
|---|---|
| One division of chromosomes | Two divisions of chromosomes |
| Daughter cells identical to parent cell | Daughter cells not identical to parent cell |
| Daughter cells contain the same number of chromosomes as parent cell | Daughter cells contain half the chromosome number of parent cell |
| Two daughter cells produced | Four daughter cells produced |
| No crossing over or chromosome variation unless mutation occurs | Crossing over occurs, producing variation in chromosomes |
| Chromosomes form a single line at the equator | Chromosomes form a double line at the equator |
| No pairing of homologous chromosomes | Homologous chromosomes arrange themselves in pairs |

## Related questions

*Notes:* Before attempting any questions on cell division, you should clearly understand the differences between mitosis and meiosis. Marks cannot be given if you describe the wrong process.

**Question:**

(a) Make large, labelled drawings to show one pair of chromosomes in a cell at
  (i) metaphase of mitosis **(4 marks)**
  (ii) metaphase I of meiosis **(4 marks)**
  (iii) metaphase II of meiosis **(4 marks)**

(b) How is sex genetically determined in man? **(8 marks)**

[London, June 1981, Paper 2]

**Comments:**

(a) (i) See Fig. 10.2. Note that only one pair of chromosomes is asked for, i.e. one homologous pair.
(ii) and (iii) See Fig. 10.4. You should include evidence to show that crossing over has occurred, i.e. exchange of genetic material between homologous pairs.

(b) See p. 390. Note that the question only asks for sex inheritance in man, not other animals.

**Question:**

With the aid of annotated diagrams give an illustrated account of the process of mitosis. In what types of cell and organism does it occur and what is its significance? How do nuclear and cell division differ between plant and animal cells and how do you account for the differences?

**Comments:**

For an illustrated account of mitosis see p. 381. Mitosis occurs in the somatic cells of all organisms. The significance of mitosis is that daughter cells are produced which are identical to the parent's cells. Mitosis also forms the basis of asexual reproduction.

The final part of the question is perhaps best answered in the form of a table. Note that you are not only asked to state the differences between cell division in animals and plants, but are also asked to account for them, i.e. give reasons for the differences.

Differences between plant and animal cell division

| *Plants* | *Animals* |
|---|---|
| Each new plant cell has to have a new cell wall. A middle lamella is formed across the equator and cell wall material gradually built up around it | Animal cells do not possess cell walls, and therefore no cell wall is laid down during cell division |
| During nuclear division, spindle fibres do not originate from a centriole | Spindle fibres originate from the centrioles |

## Genetics

Genetics is the study of heredity. It was originated by the experiments of an Austrian monk called Gregor Mendel (1882–1884).

Mendel worked on the garden pea (*Pisum sativum*), using plants which had been pure-bred for several generations. First he studied the inheritance of one characteristic (monohybrid inheritance), and later he studied the inheritance of two characteristics (dihybrid inheritance).

To understand Mendel's work, it is necessary to know the following terms:

**Gene, allele, factor** – a length of a chromosome responsible for determination of particular characteristics.

**Genotype** – the type of genes present in an organism.

**Phenotype** – the actual appearance or state of an organism, expressed as a result of the genotype. The phenotype may also be affected by the environment.

**$F_1$** – the first filial or first generation.

**$F_2$** – the second generation, formed by inbreeding the $F_1$ generation.

**Dominant characteristic** – a characteristic which shows itself in the heterozygous condition. It is usually expressed as an upper-case letter, e.g. T (tall).

**Recessive characteristic** – a characteristic which does not show in the heterozygous condition. Usually represented by a lower-case letter, e.g. t (short).

**Homozygous** – two identical genes on corresponding homologous chromosomes, e.g. TT or tt.

**Heterozygous** – non-identical genes on corresponding homologous chromosomes, e.g. Tt.
**Gene pool** – the number and types of genes available in a population.

### *Mendel's experiments*

#### Monohybrid inheritance

Mendel crossed a pure-bred tall plant with a pure-bred short plant. He did this by using artificial pollination. The offspring from this cross ($F_1$) were all tall. The $F_1$ were inbred to produce the second generation ($F_2$). The numbers of tall and short plants in the $F_2$ generation were counted and found to give a ratio of 3 tall : 1 short plant. This can be represented diagrammatically:

*Parents:* phenotype tall × short
genotype TT tt

*Gametes:* T T t t

*Offspring ($F_1$):* genotype

| | T | T |
|---|---|---|
| t | Tt | Tt |
| t | Tt | Tt |

phenotype All tall

Inbreed $F_1$ generation

*$F_1$ parents:* phenotype tall × tall
genotype Tt Tt

*Gametes:* T t T t

*Offspring ($F_2$):* genotype

| | T | t |
|---|---|---|
| T | TT | Tt |
| t | Tt | tt |

phenotype 3 tall : 1 small

The 3:1 ratio was called the monohybrid ratio. From this experiment, Mendel formulated his first law of inheritance:

THE LAW OF SEGREGATION: An organism's characteristics are determined by internal factors (genes) which occur in pairs. Only one of a pair can be represented in the gametes.

*Test cross [backcross]*

An organism showing a dominant characteristic, e.g. the tall plant in the example above, could be homozygous (TT) or heterozygous (Tt). To determine the genotype, the organism is crossed with one showing the corresponding recessive characteristic.

| | | | |
|---|---|---|---|
| *Parents:* | phenotype | test plant (tall) × short plant | |
| | genotype | Tt | tt |
| *Gametes:* | | T t | t t |

*Offspring:* genotype

| | T | t |
|---|---|---|
| t | Tt | tt |
| t | Tt | tt |

phenotype 2 tall : 2 short

A ratio of 2 dominant : 2 recessive shows that the test plant was heterozygous.

| | | | |
|---|---|---|---|
| *Parents:* | phenotype | test plant (tall) × short plant | |
| | genotype | TT | tt |
| *Gametes:* | | T T | t t |

*Offspring:* genotype

| | T | T |
|---|---|---|
| t | Tt | Tt |
| t | Tt | Tt |

phenotype All tall

If the offspring are all tall, the test plant must have been homozygous.

### Dihybrid inheritance

This is the inheritance of two pairs of characteristics. For example, peas may have the following features:
yellow (dominant) or green (recessive)
round (dominant) or wrinkled (recessive)

Let yellow = Y, green = y, round = R, and wrinkled = r.

*Parents:* phenotype pure-bred yellow, round × pure-bred green, wrinkled

genotype YYRR yyrr

*Gametes:* YR YR yr yr

*Offspring* $(F_1)$*:* genotype

| | YR | YR |
|---|---|---|
| yr | YyRr | YyRr |
| yr | YyRr | YyRr |

phenotype All round and yellow (heterozygous)

If the $F_1$ generation are then inbred to obtain the $F_2$ generation:

$F_1$ *Parents:* genotype YyRr × YyRr

*Offspring* $(F_2)$*:* genotype

| | YR | Yr | yR | yr |
|---|---|---|---|---|
| YR | YYRR | YYRr | YyRR | YyRr |
| Yr | YYRr | YYrr | YyRr | Yyrr |
| yR | YyRR | YyRr | yyRR | yyRr |
| yr | YyRr | Yyrr | yyRr | yyrr |

phenotype 9 yellow, round; 3 yellow, wrinkled;
3 green, round; 1 green, wrinkled

You may come across this dihybrid ratio quite often; it is therefore useful to remember it.

From this experiment Mendel derived his second law of inheritance, the Law of Independent Assortment, which states: If a pair of alleles are on separate chromosomes they will combine randomly with another pair.

### *Sex inheritance*

In most animals the development of male or female characteristics is determined by the presence of sex chromosomes. Individuals which have chromosomes coding for male characteristics become male and those with female sex chromosomes become female. In humans, a pair of chromosomes determines sex. Females contain two X chromosomes, whereas males have an X chromosome and a Y chromosome. All female gametes (eggs) contain an X chromosome but male gametes (sperm) contain either an X or a Y chromosome. This results in there being roughly 50 per cent males and 50 per cent females in the population.

| | | | |
|---|---|---|---|
| *Parents:* | phenotype | male × | female |
| | genotype | XY | XX |
| *Gametes:* | | X Y | X X |
| *Offspring:* | genotype | | |

| | X | Y |
|---|---|---|
| X | XX | XY |
| X | XX | XY |

phenotype 50% male : 50% female

In *Drosophila*, sex inheritance is similar to that in humans, i.e. females = XX, males = XY. However, the chromosomes are not actually X- and Y-shaped, they are merely different shapes.

In birds and some species of moths the female is the heterogametic sex and the males are homogametic, e.g. females = XY, males = XX.

In some other species (e.g. grasshoppers) 'maleness' is defined by the presence of a single X chromosome while 'femaleness' is represented by the diploid set XX.

## Linkage

Linkage is said to occur when two genes are present on the same chromosome. The characteristics which these genes code for will always be inherited together as a single unit. Such genes will not show independent assortment and their inheritance pattern is different from those described above.

For example, suppose the genes for eye colour and hair colour are linked on the same chromosome.

Let G = green eyes (dominant) and g = brown eyes (recessive) and B = black hair (dominant) and b = blonde hair (recessive)

| | | | |
|---|---|---|---|
| *Parents:* | phenotype | green eyes, black hair × | brown eyes, blonde hair |
| | genotype | GGBB | ggbb |
| *Gametes:* | | GB | gb |
| *Offspring ($F_1$):* | genotype | GgBb | |
| | phenotype | All green eyes, black hair | |

If the $F_1$ are then inbred to obtain $F_2$

| | | |
|---|---|---|
| | | X Y    X X |
| *$F_1$ parents:* | genotype | GgBb × GgBb |
| *Offspring $F_2$* | genotype | |

| | GB | gb |
|---|---|---|
| GB | GGBB | GgBb |
| gb | GgBb | ggbb |

phenotype  3 green eyes, black hair: 1 brown eyes, blonde hair

Since GB and gb are inherited as single units, a 3:1 ratio is obtained rather than a 9:3:3:1 ratio as expected in the ratio of a dihybrid cross.

### Sex linkage

The sex chromosomes also contain genes which code for non-sexual characteristics. Genes which are linked to the sex chromosomes may therefore result in males or females inheriting particular 'linked' characteristics. Colour-blindness, haemophilia and muscular dystrophy are genes which are linked in this way.

Males are more likely to have these afflictions than females, and this is explained as follows:

The Y chromosome is much shorter than the X chromosome. As a result, the X chromosome will contain more genes than the Y chromosome, and these 'extra' genes will not be able to pair with corresponding genes as in a normal homologous pair.

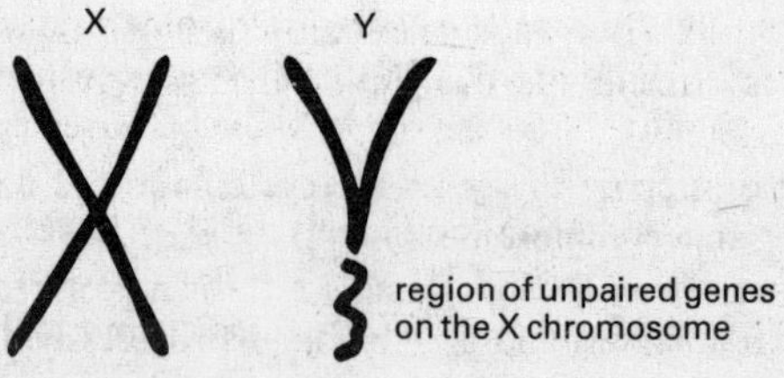
X
Y
region of unpaired genes on the X chromosome

It is this unpaired region of the X chromosome which contains the genes for colour-blindness, haemophilia and muscular dystrophy.

The results of this unpaired X chromosome can be shown in the inheritance of colour-blindness.

Let C = normal colour vision (dominant) and c = colour-blindness (recessive). Therefore,

$X^CX^C$ = normal female
$X^CX^c$ = normal female (carrier)
$X^cX^c$ = colour-blind female
$X^CY$ = normal male
$X^cY$ = colour-blind male

| | | |
|---|---|---|
| *Parents:* | phenotype | normal male × carrier female |
| | genotype | $X^CY$     $X^CX^c$ |
| *Gametes:* | | $X^C$ $Y$     $X^C$ $X^c$ |
| *Offspring:* | genotype | |

| | $X^C$ | $Y$ |
|---|---|---|
| $X^C$ | $X^CX^C$ | $X^CY$ |
| $X^c$ | $X^CX^c$ | $X^cY$ |

phenotype 1 normal female : 1 carrier female : 1 normal male : 1 colour-blind male

The recessive gene for colour-blindness must be present in a double dose $X^cX^c$ (i.e. homogametic), if it is to show in the female. However, if only a single $X^c$ is present in the male, he will be colour-blind.

*Sex-linked lethal genes*

Sometimes genes are found on the X chromosome which are lethal. This means that if a single recessive lethal gene is present on the X chromosome of a male, it will die before birth. Females are less likely to be affected since they are capable of being heterozygous.

In the fruit-fly, *Drosophila melanogaster*, some strains possess a lethal gene l on the X chromosome. This greatly reduces the number of male offspring since those of the genotype $X^l$ die before emergence as adults, as shown below.

Let L = normal condition (dominant) and l = lethal gene (recessive)

| | | | | | |
|---|---|---|---|---|---|
| *Parents:* | phenotype | female carrier × normal male | | | |
| | genotype | $X^LX^l$ | | $X^LY$ | |
| *Gametes:* | | $X^L$ $X^l$ | | $X^L$ $Y$ | |
| *Offspring:* | genotype | $X^LX^L$ | $X^LY$ | $X^LX^l$ | $X^lY$ non-viable |

phenotype 1 normal female : 1 carrier female : 1 normal male

### Genetic results of crossing over

Experiments showing the inheritance of linked genes often give odd results in the form of a small percentage of unexpected offspring.

For example, the genes AB and ab are linked:

A
a
B
b

Normally, A and B are inherited as a single unit AB, and similarly for ab. However, during prophase I of meiosis crossing over occurs (see p. 382), where linked genes may swap sites on homologous chromosomes.

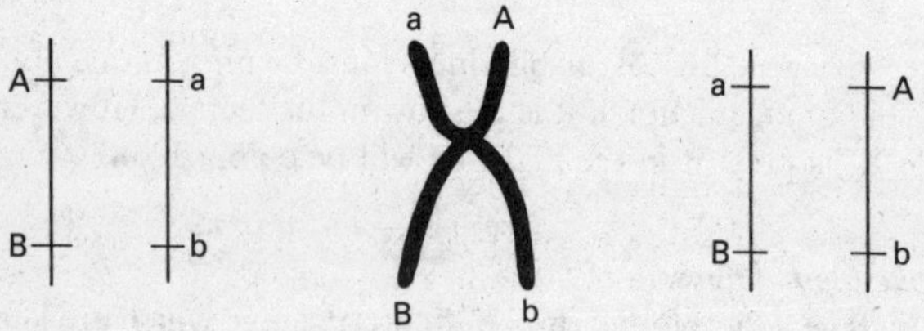
A
a
B
b
a
A
B
b
a
A
B
b

This results in gametes which contain recombinant chromosomes.

In the following cross, all the offspring would be expected to show the dominant features A and B, since the two genes are linked.

*Parents:* AABB × aabb

*Gametes:* AB ab

*Offspring:* AaBb

If crossing over has occurred, there will be some offspring with the genotypes Aabb, aaBb. These can be spotted, since they will only display one dominant feature, A or B.

Crossing over only occurs in about 25 per cent of meioses. Genes which are present on the ends of chromosomes are more likely to undergo crossing over than those in the middle, so it is possible to deduce the position of some genes on the chromosome. This is called chromosome mapping. Each gene on a chromosome can be given a cross-over value (COV).

$$\text{COV} = \frac{\text{Number of recombinant offspring}}{\text{Total number of offspring}} \times 100$$

### *Incomplete dominance*

Sometimes genes are neither dominant nor recessive, and the heterozygous condition shows characteristics which are intermediate between the two.

For example, in snapdragons (*Antirrhinums*)
R = red and r = white

Homozygous RR = red

Homozygous rr = white

Heterozygous Rr = pink

### *Inheritance of blood groups*

Sometimes there are more than two alleles controlling a characteristic. For example, the ABO blood group (see p. 170) is controlled by three alleles.
A = production of antigen A on red blood cells
B = production of antigen B on red blood cells
O = no antigen production

Each individual can only have two of the three types, hence the following combinations are possible:

| *Blood group* | *Genotype* |
|---|---|
| A | AA or AO |
| B | BB or BO |
| AB | AB |
| O | OO |

## *Further reading*

J. C. Bowman, *An Introduction to Animal Breeding*, Studies in Biology No. 46, 2nd edition (Arnold, 1984)
C. A. Clarke, *Human Genetics and Medicine*, Studies in Biology No. 20, 2nd edition (Arnold, 1978)
D. Harrison, *Problems in Genetics* (Addison Wesley, 1970)
R. Kemp, *The Cell and Heredity*, Studies in Biology No. 21 (Arnold, 1970)
W. J. C. Lawrence, *Plant Breeding*, Studies in Biology No. 12 (Arnold, 1971)

## Related questions

### *General hints for answering genetics questions*

Many students find difficulty in answering questions on genetics. By following a few basic rules this difficulty can be greatly reduced.

1. Before using any symbols in a genetics answer it is important to say what they represent. Often the symbols are given, if not then suitable letters must be chosen. Usually an upper-case letter is used to represent the dominant characteristic and a lower-case letter to represent the recessive characteristic.

   For example, a question might state that 'If a black guinea pig is mated with a white guinea pig all the offspring are black'. From this information we can see that black coat colour is dominant to white coat colour. The symbols chosen could therefore be as follows:

   Let B = black coat colour (dominant);
   Let b = white coat colour (recessive)

2. Many genetics questions can be solved by drawing a basic outline plan as below. Drawing this plan will often help to give a structure on which to base your answer.

   *Parents:* phenotype
   genotype

   *Gametes:*

   *Offspring* $(F_1)$*:* genotype
   phenotype

   Ratio of phenotypes

   To obtain $F_2$, inbreed $F_1$

3. It is often helpful to write down all the information given in the question together with that which can be deduced from it. By doing this you may find you have sometimes solved the question already. This approach is used in the comments on the first question below.

**Question:**
In humans, a gene responsible for clotting blood is carried on the X chromosome. People who carry only the recessive gene bleed easily and are called haemophiliacs. The diagram below shows the occurrence of haemophiliacs in a certain family.

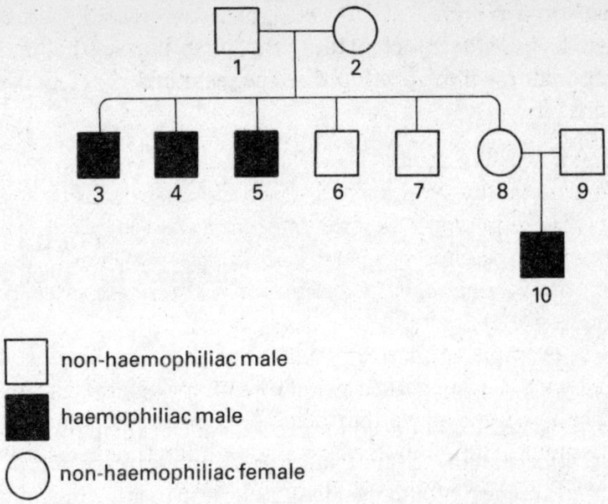
1
2
3
4
5
6
7
8
9
10
non-haemophiliac male
haemophiliac male
non-haemophiliac female

Indicate below the *genotype* for each individual numbered in the diagram.
**(10 marks)**

[London, July 1981, Paper 2 (part question)]

**Comments:**

See p. 392.

This type of question tests your ability to make logical deductions from scientific data. You may find it helpful to write down that which is immediately obvious. For example, all the females will have the genotype XX and all the males have XY.

The genes for haemophilia can then be added to the appropriate individuals. Let C = normal clotting (dominant) and c = haemophilia (recessive).

All haemophiliac males must have a c allele on their single X chromosome, hence these can be written as $X^cY$. The non-haemophiliac males must have the genotype $X^CY$. This only leaves the two females (2 and 8). Since both females give rise to haemophiliac offspring they must contain a recessive gene c on one of their X chromosomes. As they are both non-haemophiliacs, the other X chromosome must contain the normal gene C, hence they are both $X^CX^c$.

**Question:**

Give genetic explanations for each of the following.

(a) Red–green colour-blindness is more common in human males than females. **(4 marks)**

(b) When a red-flowered *Antirrhinum* plant is crossed with a white-flowered *Antirrhinum* plant and the offspring self-pollinated, the $F_2$ generation will be produced in the ratio of 1 red:2 pink:1 white coloured flowers. **(4 marks)**

(c) In a dihybrid cross one would normally expect a 9:3:3:1 ratio in the $F_2$ generation. Under certain circumstances a 3:1 ratio is obtained from this cross. **(6 marks)**

**(Total 14 marks)**

[London, Jan. 1982, Paper 1]

**Comments:**

(a) See p. 392.

(b) See p. 395.

(c) See p. 391. You do not need to give a detailed explanation of linkage and its effects on inheritance patterns. A brief explanation of linkage and the absence of independent assortment affecting inheritance ratios should be sufficient.

**Question:**

(a) Distinguish between the terms (i) phenotype and (ii) genotype. **(2 marks)**

(b) If two heterozygous black guinea pigs are mated, what is the probability of their producing (i) a homozygous recessive (white) offspring and (ii) a homozygous black offspring? **(4 marks)**

(c) (i) In cats, a gene B is responsible for black fur colour and an allele L is responsible for yellow fur. These genes show incomplete dominance and the hybrid BL is tortoiseshell. The genes are also sex-linked.

Complete the table below, to show the gametes and possible genotypes in the parents, $F_1$ and $F_2$ generations, if a black female is mated with a yellow male.

| | Black female | Yellow male |
|---|---|---|
| Parents: | | |
| Gametes: | | |
| $F_1$ generation: | | |
| Gametes: | | |
| $F_2$ generation: | | |

**(7 marks)**

(ii) To what extent are the male and female kittens produced distinguishable by their coat colour? **(4 marks)**

**(Total 17 marks)**

[London, Jan. 1983, Paper 1]

**Comments:**

(a) (i) and (ii) See p. 387.

(b) The first priority in this question is to allocate symbols to the different characteristics. Therefore, let B = black coat colour (dominant) and b = white coat colour (recessive).

Secondly, the basic diagram can be drawn:

*Parents:* phenotype black coat × black coat
genotype Bb Bb

*Gametes:* B b B b

*Offspring:* genotype

| | B | b |
|---|---|---|
| B | BB | Bb |
| b | Bb | bb |

phenotypes 1 black homozygous:
2 black heterozygous:
1 white homozygous

You are now in a position to answer the question. The probability of a homozygous recessive (white) offspring is one in every four (i.e. 1/4). The probability of a homozygous black offspring is also 1/4. Note that the other offspring are black homozygous.

(c) See p. 395 and p. 392. Symbols for coat colour are given in the question; however there is the added feature that they are sex-linked. As there is incomplete dominance both parents must be homozygous for coat colour, otherwise they would be tortoiseshell. Therefore the genotypes of the parents must be:

black female $X^BX^B$

yellow male $X^LX^L$

From these you should then be able to complete the remainder of the table.

**Question:**

In humans, the gene causing colour-blindness is carried on the X chromosome. A colour-blind boy has parents with normal colour vision.

(a) What is the genotype of (i) the mother, (ii) the father? **(2 marks)**
(b) If the boy's brother, who has normal colour vision, marries a girl who is heterozygous for colour vision, what would be the possible phenotypes and genotypes of their children? **(4 marks)**
(c) Explain, with a suitable diagram, how it might be possible for a colour-blind girl to be produced. **(4 marks)**

**(Total 10 marks)**

[London, June 1982, Paper 1]

**Comments:**

As symbols are not given you should first define them, i.e. let C = normal vision (dominant) and c = colour-blindness (recessive). See p. 392.

(a) The mother has normal colour vision but has also given rise to a colour-blind son. Since she contributes an X chromosome to the son she must be a carrier for colour-blindness. The genotype of the mother is therefore $X^CX^c$. The father has only one gene for colour-blindness, linked to the single X chromosome. Since he has normal colour vision this gene must be C. The genotype of the father is therefore $X^CY$.

(b) Remember that the gene for colour-blindness is sex-linked to the X chromosome of the male. The genotype of the brother who has normal colour vision must be $X^CY$ and his heterozygous wife must be $X^CX^c$. Using this information you should be able to work out the possible genotypes and phenotypes of the offspring. You may find it easier to use the space provided for rough work in the back of the answer book to draw a rough diagram to work out the various phenotypes and genotypes of the children. However, the final answer should be given in prose form, and using symbols for the genotypes consistent with those in (a).

(c) A good way to answer a question like this is to start by drawing the basic diagram outline (p. 393). Since the gene for colour-blindness is recessive, a colour-blind girl must be homozygous for the condition, i.e. she must have obtained a recessive gene from each parent. The genotype of the father must therefore be $X^cY$. The genotype of the mother could be $X^cX^c$ (colour-blind, homozygous) or $X^CX^c$ (carrier, heterozygous) since she only has to donate one recessive gene.

It is probably sufficient for only one basic diagram to be filled in, using either of the possible genotypes for the mother.

**Question:**

Sex-linked genes are carried on sex chromosomes, usually on the non-homologous regions of the X chromosome. The non-homologous regions of the X and Y chromosomes of a mammal are labelled on the diagram below.

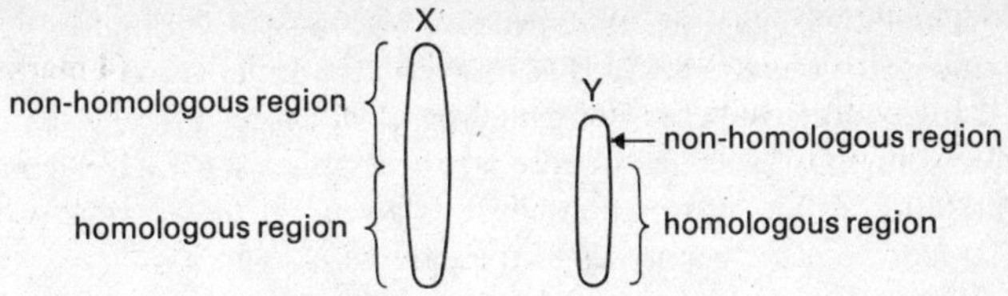
X
Y
non-homologous region
non-homologous region
homologous region
homologous region

(a) A man with a recessive sex-linked gene for red–green colour-blindness marries a woman who has normal vision but is carrying a recessive gene for red–green colour-blindness.

By means of diagrams explain the possible phenotypes of their offspring. **(6 marks)**

(b) The ability to taste phenylthiourea (PTU) is controlled by a dominant gene. Non-tasting is controlled by a recessive gene. These alleles are not sex-linked.

Two parents who are both tasters and have normal colour vision, have a colour-blind non-tasting son. By means of labelled diagrams, explain the genotypes of the parents and the possible phenotypes of any other sons they might have. **(7 marks)**

(c) (i) Sex-linked genes may be carried on the non-homologous portion of the Y chromosome. One example of such a gene was a mutation which led to a skin condition in which surface spines were found ('porcupine' condition). Explain the extent to which this 'porcupine' condition would be evident in the offspring and in future generations of a man in which the mutation first appeared. **(4 marks)**

(ii) What conclusions can be drawn about the dominant or recessive nature of the 'porcupine' gene? Explain your answer. **(2 marks)**

(d) By means of labelled diagrams showing the arrangement of the bases in a deoxyribose nucleic acid (DNA) molecule, indicate how *three* different types of gene mutation occur. **(6 marks)**

**(Total 25 marks)**

[AEB, Nov. 1980, Paper 2]

**Comments:**

(a) You should start by defining your symbols and working out the genotypes, and then you should be able to draw a basic outline plan (see p. 393).

Let C = normal vision (dominant) and c = colour-blind (recessive).

The father has a recessive gene on his single X chromosome; his genotype is therefore $X^cY$. The mother has normal vision but carries a single recessive gene. Her genotype is therefore $X^CX^c$.

(b) As with most genetics questions, the emphasis here is on interpretation of the information which is given.

To work out the genotypes of the parents:

Let P = tasters (dominant) and p = non-tasters (recessive).

Since the son is a non-taster, he must have obtained a recessive gene p from each parent. However, the parents are both tasters and must therefore be heterozygous for the condition (Pp). The son is also colour-blind. The genes for colour-blindness are sex-linked to the X chromosome. Since the son obtained an X chromosome from his mother and a Y chromosome from his father, the mother must be a carrier for colour-blindness.

Therefore the genotypes of the parents are:

mother Pp $X^CX^c$
father Pp $X^CY$

To show the possible offspring once again it advisable to follow the basic outline diagram (see p. 390). Note that the $F_2$ is not required. The diagram will follow that of a normal dihybrid cross (see p. 389) since $X^C$ and $X^c$ are treated as single genes.

(c) If the mutation occurs on the Y chromosome, any offspring arising from a gamete containing that mutation will show the 'porcupine' condition. In order to form a zygote, mitosis occurs and every cell would contain mutant Y chromosomes, all replicas of the original Y mutation. Consequently, any gametes formed by this offspring would be similarly affected, and all future male offspring would show the condition. Female offspring would not be affected since they never possess a Y chromosome.

(d) See p. 406.

**Question:**

The human family pedigree given below shows the inheritance of the nail-patella syndrome and the inheritance of blood groups A and O. People with nail-patella syndrome have skeletal deformities such as underdeveloped knee caps and abnormal fingernails.

(i) The allele producing the syndrome is extremely rare. State whether this allele is likely to be dominant or recessive.

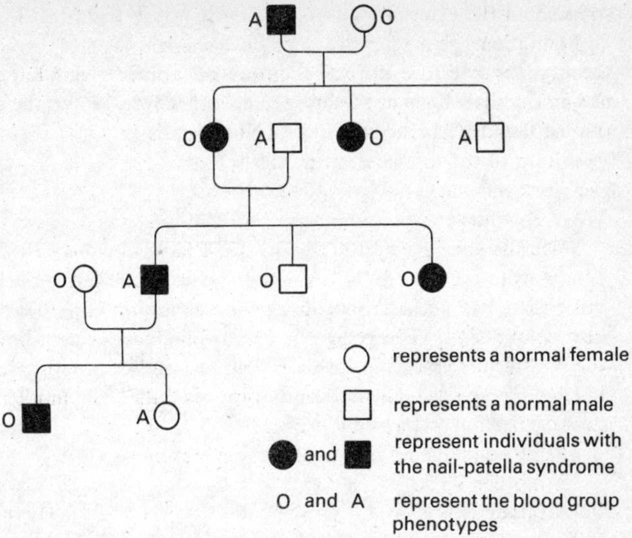
A
O
O
A
O
A
O
A
O
O
O
A
represents a normal female
represents a normal male
and
represent individuals with the nail-patella syndrome
O and A
represent the blood group phenotypes

(ii) With the aid of diagrams and appropriate symbols, explain your answer to (i).

[AEB, June 1981, Paper 1 (part question)]

**Comments:**

This is a question which tests your ability to interpret scientific data. You must be able to think clearly about the information which is given and make logical deductions from it.

(a) (i) If the gene is recessive, the condition would only occur in the offspring if they received a gene for the condition from each parent. Since the allele is extremely rare, it is unlikely that all three external parents would possess it. The allele must therefore be dominant.

(ii) This type of question requires careful planning if you are to answer it concisely. It is often useful to write a rough answer-plan on a piece of scrap paper. Even though the males and females are represented as squares and circles respectively, you should not assume there is a sex-linked inheritance, since there is not, and time could be wasted trying to find it.

Let N = nail-patella syndrome (dominant) and let n = normal condition (recessive).

Since the allele producing the syndrome (N) is extremely rare, it can be assumed that the external parents (i.e. those not in the direct family tree) all have genotype nn.

In the first generation a normal is produced, which suggests that it obtained an (n) allele from each parent. The father (who shows the condition) must therefore be heterozygous (Nn).

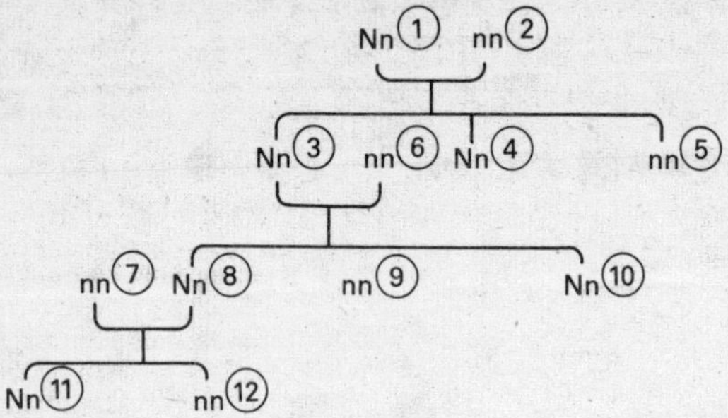
Nn 1
nn 2
Nn 3
nn 6
Nn 4
nn 5
nn 7
Nn 8
nn 9
Nn 10
Nn 11
nn 12

The external parents, 2, 6 and 7 must be nn, since N is rare. Therefore for 3, 4, 8, 10 and 11 to be produced, the allele N must be dominant.

This diagram can also be used to assess the relationship between the occurrence of nail-patella syndrome and blood group.

Individuals with blood group O have the genotype OO and those with blood group A have the genotype AO or AA. In the diagram given, all individuals with group A must have the genotype AO since they all either give rise to group O offspring or have a parent with blood group O.

By correlating the diagram above with that of blood group, it can be shown that the allele causing the syndrome (N) is linked to the blood group (O) allele.

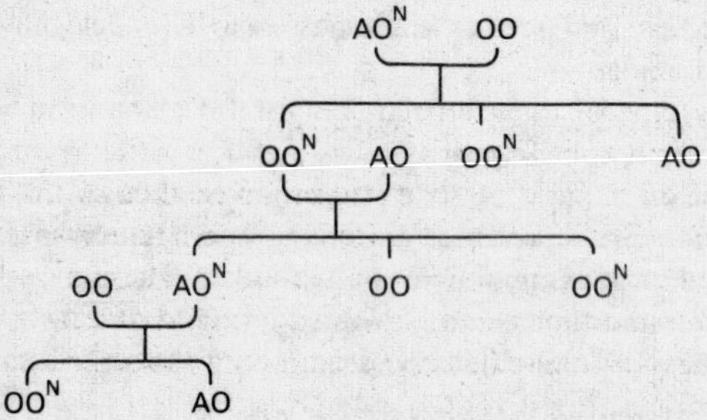
AO^N
OO
OO^N
AO
OO^N
AO
OO
AO^N
OO
OO^N
OO^N
AO

## DNA and protein synthesis

Chromosomes are responsible for the growth and development of cells. They do this by controlling protein synthesis. Each chromosome is composed of two chromatids, joined together at a point called the centromere. Each chromatid is composed of a double strand of DNA (deoxyribonucleic acid), which is coiled to form a structure known as the double helix.

A gene is a length of DNA which controls the production of a particular protein. Many genes control cellular reactions by controlling the production of enzymes (which are of course proteins).

### *Deoxyribonucleic acid (DNA)*

#### The structure of DNA

DNA is composed of structures called nucleotides, which are linked together in chains. Each nucleotide is composed of a deoxyribose sugar, a phosphate group and a nitrogen-containing base (Fig. 10.6). There are four types of bases: adenines, guanines, thymines and cytosines (Fig. 10.7).

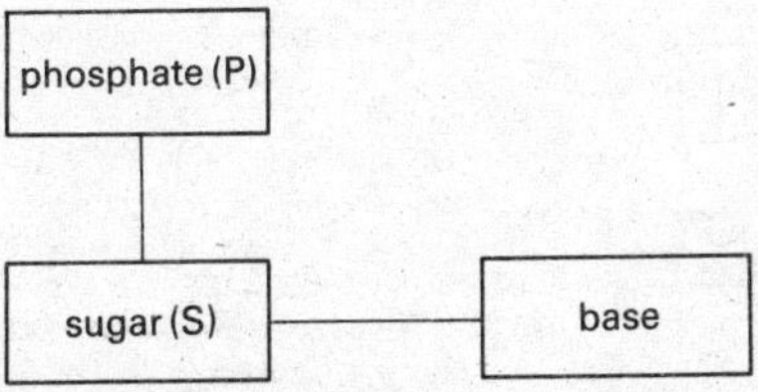
phosphate (P)
sugar (S)
base

*Fig. 10.6* The basic structure of a nucleotide

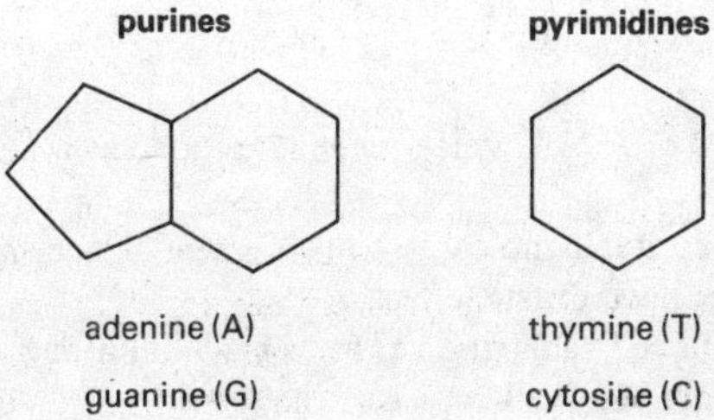
purines
pyrimidines
adenine (A)
guanine (G)
thymine (T)
cytosine (C)

*Fig. 10.7* Basic shapes of the bases in DNA

Each sugar molecule is linked to the phosphate group of the next nucleotide. Two such strands of DNA are held together by hydrogen bonds between pairs of the bases. Pairing of the bases is specific: adenine always pairs with thymine, cytosine always pairs with guanine. A pair must consist of a purine and a pyrimidine base; two purines would make a 'rung of the ladder' too large, and two pyrimidines would make the 'rung' too short. The whole structure is called a double strand of DNA (Fig. 10.8), and is subsequently coiled to form a structure known as the double helix (Fig. 10.9).

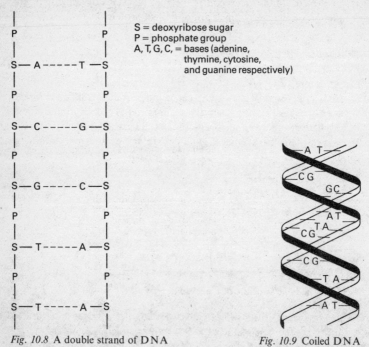

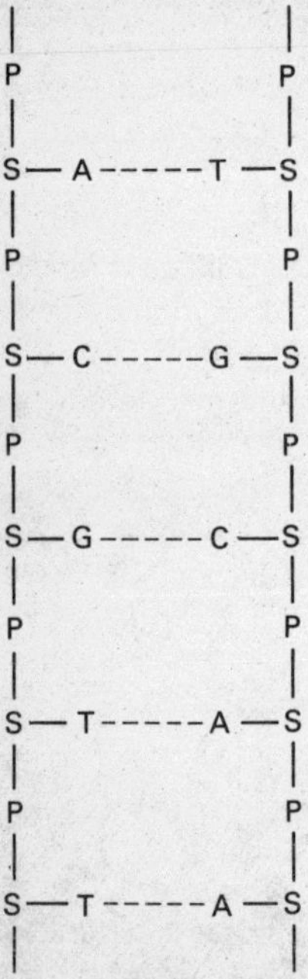
P P
S— A - - - - - T —S
P P
S—C - - - - - G —S
P P
S—G - - - - - C —S
P P
S—T - - - - - A —S
P P
S—T - - - - - A —S
S = deoxyribose sugar
P = phosphate group
A, T, G, C, = bases (adenine, thymine, cytosine, and guanine respectively)

*Fig. 10.8* A double strand of DNA

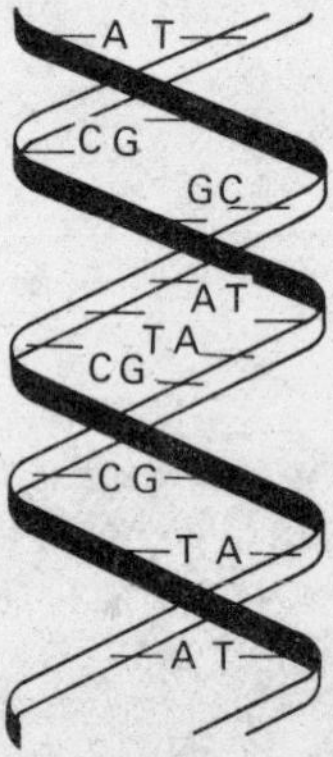
A T
C G
GC
AT
TA
CG
C G
T A
A T

*Fig. 10.9* Coiled DNA

The properties of DNA which make it suitable as a genetic material are:

1. DNA is a very stable molecule. This is essential since any changes in structure may have drastic effects.
2. It is capable of self-replication. This is essential if new cells are to be made which are identical copies of the parent.

3. Its system of coding using bases enables it to code for different proteins.

### Replication of DNA

Replication of DNA occurs during interphase of mitosis. This has been shown by feeding cells with labelled thymine. The radioactive thymine is incorporated into the new strands of DNA which are produced during interphase. If a cell is treated with a substance called colchicine, replication of DNA occurs, but subsequent division of the cell is prevented. A cell treated in this way can be seen to contain twice the normal number of chromosomes (Fig. 10.10).

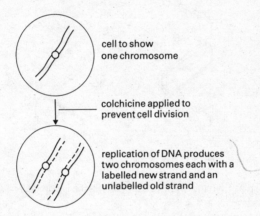

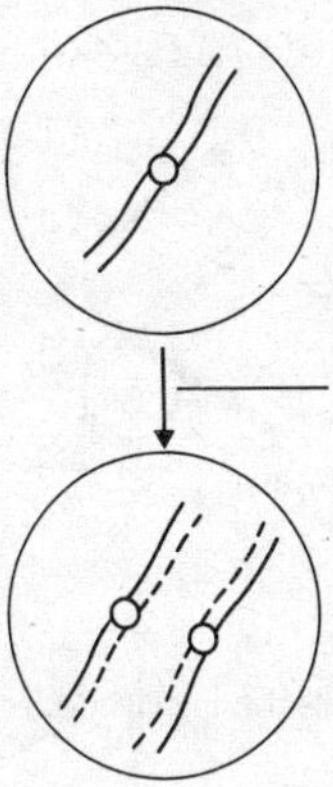
cell to show
one chromosome
colchicine applied to
prevent cell division
replication of DNA produces
two chromosomes each with a
labelled new strand and an
unlabelled old strand

*Fig. 10.10* An experiment to show replication of DNA

This experiment also shows that the daughter chromosomes each contain a labelled new strand of DNA and an unlabelled old strand of DNA. This is a more stable method of replication than one where one chromosome contained all the original DNA and the other had all the newly synthesized DNA. The method of producing daughter chromosomes, each with a new strand and an old strand, is called semi-conservative replication.

The process of replication is as follows (Fig. 10.11):

1. The two strands of DNA uncoil and separate by breaking the hydrogen bonds which hold them together.
2. Each strand then builds up a complementary strand on itself. Adenine

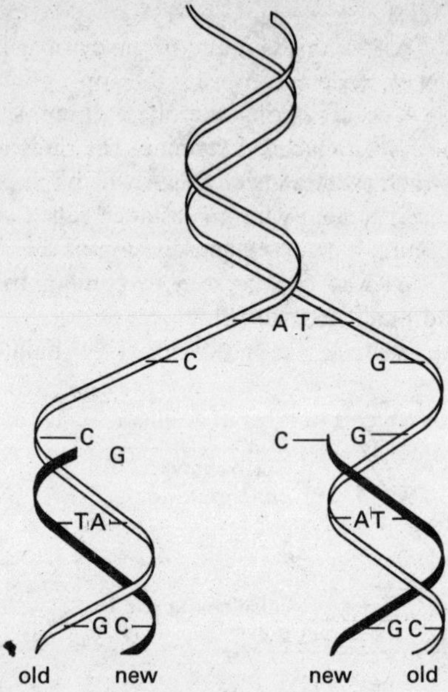
A T
C
G
C
G
C
G
TA
AT
G C
G C
old
new
new
old

*Fig. 10.11* Replication of DNA

is copied as thymine and vice versa. Cytosine is copied as guanine and vice versa.

3. The components of the new complementary strands are assembled using the enzyme DNA polymerase.

### *Ribonucleic acid (RNA)*

For protein synthesis, RNA as well as DNA is required.

#### The structure of RNA

RNA is identical to DNA apart from three changes:

1. The base uracil replaces thymine.
2. The sugar is a ribose instead of a deoxyribose sugar.
3. RNA is usually single stranded, in contrast to DNA which is double stranded.

There are three types of RNA:

mRNA (messenger RNA) – this is made as a complementary copy of a strand of DNA.

tRNA (transfer RNA) – this is found in the cytoplasm. Its function is to read the genetic code and transfer the appropriate amino acids to the ribosome.

rRNA (ribosomal RNA) – this is found in the ribosomes. Its function remains relatively unknown.

## *Protein synthesis*

This involves two main steps:

1. Transcription, in which a strand of mRNA is built using DNA as a template.
2. Translation, in which a number of amino acids are assembled together to form a protein in accordance with the code on mRNA.

### Transcription (Fig. 10.12)

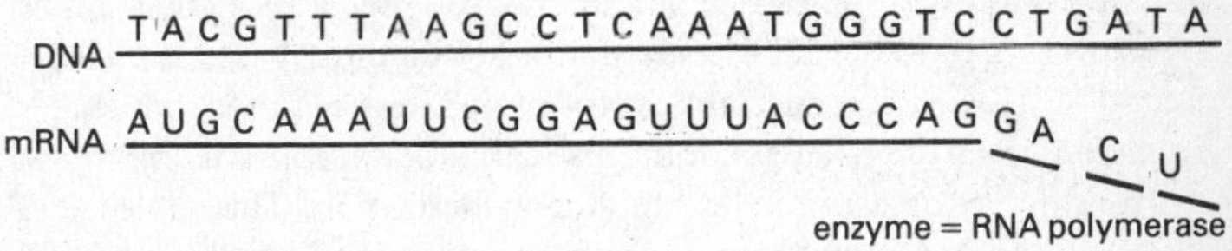
DNA
T A C G T T T A A G C C T C A A A T G G G T C C T G A T A
mRNA
A U G C A A A U U C G G A G U U U A C C C A G G A
C
U
enzyme = RNA polymerase

*Fig. 10.12* Transcription of DNA

(a) The double-stranded DNA molecule unwinds and separates by breaking the hydrogen bonds which bond it together.

(b) Two strands of DNA are then present. One is used as a template on which a new strand of mRNA is built; the other is non-functional (called the nonsense strand).

(c) The mRNA strand is built up as a complementary copy of the DNA strand. That means that cytosine is copied as guanine and vice versa. Thymine is copied as adenine, but since RNA does not contain thymine, adenine is copied as uracil. (The whole process is similiar to that of making a photographic print from a negative, where black becomes white, and white becomes black.) All the components of the new RNA strand – ribose sugars, phosphate and bases – are assembled using the enzyme RNA polymerase.

(d) When transcription has finished, the two DNA strands re-coil to form a double helix. The new strand of mRNA moves out of the nucleus to a ribosome. At this stage, the RNA strand contains a number of bases in a particular sequence. These will act as a code for the production of a protein.

## Translation

The term translation refers to all the steps in which the sequence of bases on the mRNA is used as a code to build up a linear chain of amino acids. The chain of amino acids may form a protein which has enzymatic or other cellular properties. Translation occurs at the ribosomes, which resemble microscopic protein-producing factories. The ribosomes are composed of two sub-units, a smaller part called the 30s particle and a larger portion called the 50s particle.

(a) The strand of mRNA attaches to the 30s portion of the ribosome. A number of initiation factors, including a special type of tRNA called initiator tRNA, ensure that the mRNA is aligned in the correct place for translation to begin.

(b) Three successive bases on the mRNA code for a particular amino acid. This is the genetic code, and a set of three bases is called a codon. However, a special adaptor molecule is required, which can not only read the genetic code but also carry the appropriate amino acid from the cytoplasm to the site of polymerization. This molecule is tRNA. tRNA attaches to a specific amino acid and is then available to bind to the mRNA if the corresponding codon is in the ribosome position. Similarly, the adjacent codons are then read in sequence, and the appropriate amino acids linked together by peptide bonds.

(c) When the mRNA molecule has moved a sufficient distance down the ribosome, the ribosome binding site on the mRNA becomes free again. This means that another ribosome can attach itself to the mRNA and produce a duplicate copy of the protein. There may be several ribosomes attached to a strand of mRNA, all working their way along the strand to produce several copies of the protein. The whole structure at this stage is called a polysome.

(d) At the end of the mRNA molecule is a termination codon which signals for termination of protein synthesis. At this point the polypeptide chain is released.

(e) Many post-translational modifications may then occur, e.g. coiling and production of disulphide bridges which give the protein its correct shape.

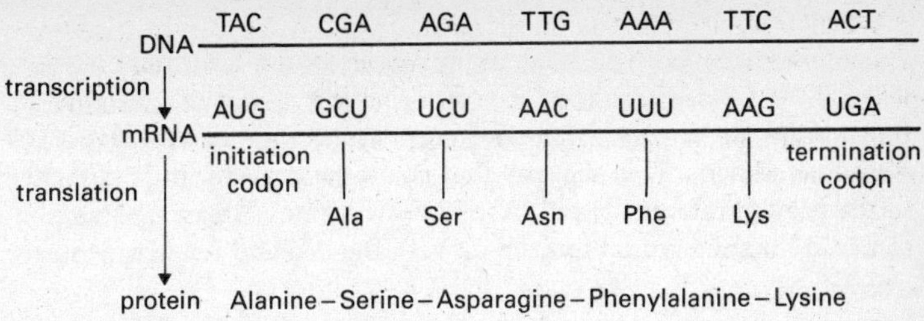
DNA
TAC CGA AGA TTG AAA TTC ACT
transcription
AUG GCU UCU AAC UUU AAG UGA
mRNA
initiation codon
termination codon
translation
Ala
Ser
Asn
Phe
Lys
protein
Alanine – Serine – Asparagine – Phenylalanine – Lysine

*Fig. 10.13* Transcription and translation

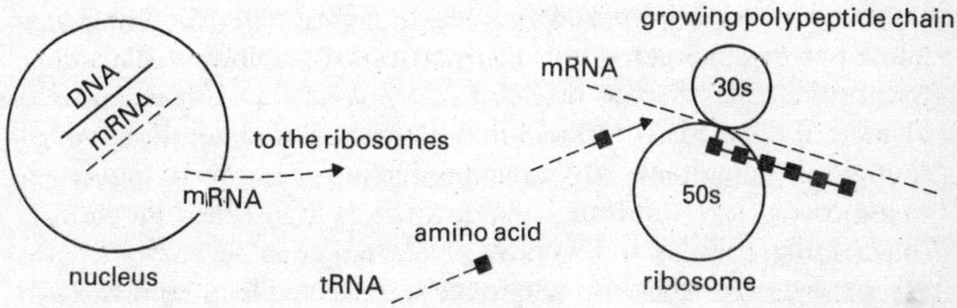
DNA
mRNA
to the ribosomes
mRNA
nucleus
amino acid
tRNA
growing polypeptide chain
mRNA
30s
50s
ribosome

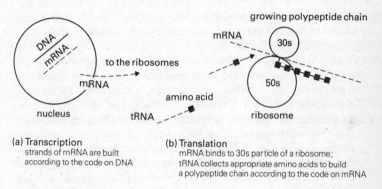

(a) Transcription
strands of mRNA are built according to the code on DNA

(b) Translation
mRNA binds to 30s particle of a ribosome; tRNA collects appropriate amino acids to build a polypeptide chain according to the code on mRNA

*Fig. 10.14* Protein synthesis

Protein synthesis, which is summarized in Figs 10.13 and 10.14, is remarkably similar in different organisms. For ease of experimentation, most work has been carried out on bacteria and bacteriophages. The genetic code, however, appears to be universal.

## Control of protein synthesis

If a cell is to function efficiently it must regulate its protein synthesis. For example, there is no need for a cell to produce large quantities of enzymes which are not required. Similarly, structural proteins such as those in hair (collagen) are only produced by specific cells. There must be some method of 'switching' genes on and off and also of regulating the amount of protein made from each mRNA strand.

*Ribosome concentration*

It is known that bacteria, such as *E. coli*, grown in a nutrient medium with all the factors required for growth, have a high ribosome content. By contrast, those grown in a poor nutrient medium tend to have a low ribosome content. This suggests that ribosome concentration is related to the growth rate of the cell. As the growth rate increases, extra ribosomes are manufactured to keep up with the demand for new proteins.

*Switching on and off of genes*

Most research in this area has dealt with bacterial systems, particularly those concerned with nutrition in *E. coli*.

In order for *E. coli* to utilize the sugar lactose, an enzyme β-galactosidase is required. β-galactosidase splits the lactose molecule into glucose and galactose, which can subsequently be used in respiration. Cells which are grown in the absence of lactose do not produce β-galactosidase. However, if lactose is introduced into the growth-medium the enzyme is produced. In this situation, enzyme production is said to be induced by the presence of the substrate lactose, which is itself called the inducer. Enzymes under this type of control are called inducible enzymes.

Normally, production of the enzyme is prevented by a repressor substance. The repressor substance is a protein, produced by a regulatory gene. Repressors prevent production of enzymes by binding to DNA and preventing transcription of the gene which codes for a particular enzyme. The repressor binds to a portion of the DNA molecule called an operator. This is usually at the beginning of the appropriate gene, and therefore when a repressor is present initiation of transcription is impossible (see Fig. 10.15).

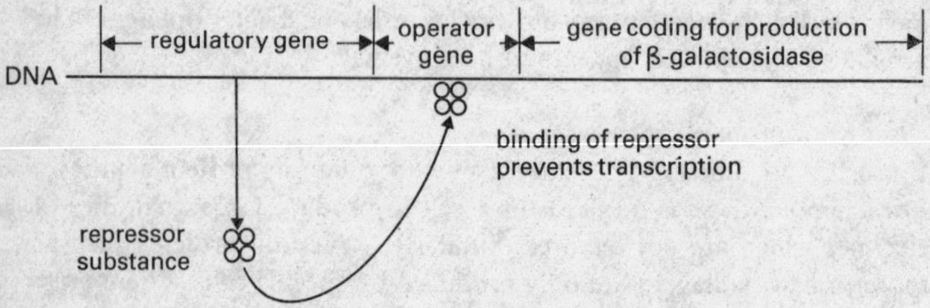
regulatory gene
operator gene
gene coding for production of β-galactosidase
DNA
binding of repressor prevents transcription
repressor substance

*Fig. 10.15* Prevention of transcription by a repressor molecule

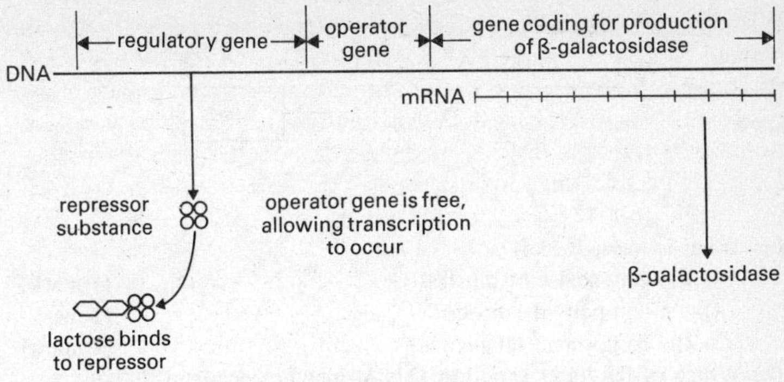
regulatory gene
operator gene
gene coding for production of β-galactosidase
DNA
mRNA
repressor substance
operator gene is free, allowing transcription to occur
β-galactosidase
lactose binds to repressor

*Fig. 10.16* Production of β-galactosidase in the presence of lactose

However, if lactose is added to the growth-medium the enzyme β-galactosidase is produced. This is because lactose attaches itself to the repressor molecule, preventing it from binding to the operator gene. Transcription is then possible and the enzyme is produced (Fig. 10.16).

The genes involved in regulation of β-galactosidase production are collectively known as the lac operon.

## Further reading

R. H. Burdon, *RNA Biosynthesis*, Outline Studies in Biology (Chapman & Hall, 1976)

B. F. C. Clark, *The Genetic Code*, Studies in Biology No. 83 (Arnold, 1977)

R. Jackson, *Protein Biosynthesis*, Oxford/Carolina Biology Reader No. 86 (Packard, 1978)

A. E. Smith, *Protein Biosynthesis* (Chapman & Hall, 1976)

A. A. Travers, *Transcription of DNA*, Oxford/Carolina Biology Reader No. 75, 2nd edition (Packard, 1978)

J. D. Watson, *The Double Helix* (Weidenfeld & Nicolson, 1976; Penguin, 1970)

## Related questions

**Question:**

The following diagram represents the basic chemical unit from which the nucleic acids DNA and RNA are formed.

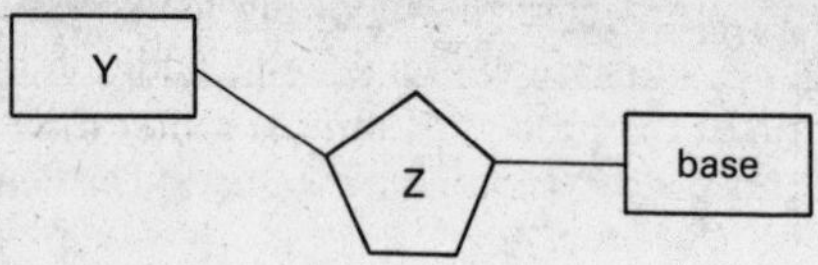
Y
Z
base

(a) What is the name of:
   (i) the chemical unit illustrated: **(1 mark)**
   (ii) the component labelled Y; **(1 mark)**
   (iii) the component labelled Z? **(1 mark)**

(b) Which of the bases found in DNA does not occur in RNA? **(1 mark)**

(c) If adenine is one of the bases on the code chain of a molecule of DNA what will be:
   (i) the base paired with it in the DNA; **(1 mark)**
   (ii) the base in messenger ribonucleic acid which is paired with it; **(1 mark)**
   (iii) the base in transfer ribonucleic acid which pairs with the answer given in (b)? **(1 mark)**

[Oxford, June 1981, Paper 1]

**Comments:**
See pp. 405 – 410.

**Question:**

(a) In the DNA molecule there are four major bases, two purines and two pyrimidines. These are ________________________ **(4 marks)**

(b) Name the sugar in (i) DNA, (ii) RNA. **(2 marks)**

(c) What is a nucleotide? **(2 marks)**

(d) What are the possible base pairings of the four bases? **(2 marks)**

(e) One of the bases in DNA is not represented in RNA. Name the base not represented and the base that replaces it. **(2 marks)**

(f) Name three types of RNA involved in protein synthesis. **(3 marks)**

**(Total 15 marks)**

[London, June 1981, Paper 2]

**Comments:**
See pp. 405 – 409.

**Question:**
Using any of the terms from the following list complete the diagram which illustrates the sequence of events in the addition of an amino acid to a peptide chain in the process of protein synthesis:

amino acid; anti-codon; centriole; chromatin; histamine; mitochondrion; mRNA; RNA; tRNA. **(2 marks)**

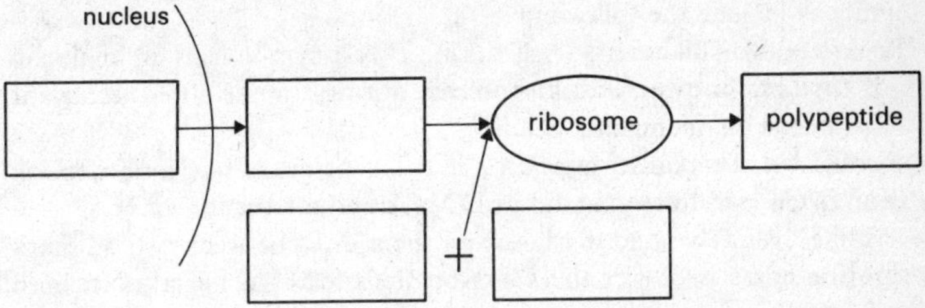
nucleus
ribosome
polypeptide
+

[Oxford, June 1982, Paper 1 (part question)]

**Comments:**
See Fig. 10.14, 'Protein synthesis'. Note that only four of the given words are required to complete the diagram. You should not panic if there are words you have not seen before. For all questions of this type it is advisable to start by filling in the most obvious answers. This will not only narrow down the choice of answers left but it will also put the question more into context and perhaps make it easier to answer parts of the question which were at first unclear.

## *Mutation*

A mutation is a change in a gene or a chromosome which often affects the individual in some way. Mutations are the basis of natural selection and evolution. If a mutation is advantageous it will increase the survival rate of the individual and become incorporated into the species. If it is disadvantageous, or even lethal, the individual will have a low survival rate and the mutation will die out.

Many mutations are caused by mistakes in cell division. If a mutation occurs during meiosis, the gametes and hence the offspring will be affected. Other mutations are caused by environmental factors called mutagenic agents, or mutagens. These mutagens include ionizing radiations such as X-rays, ultraviolet rays, radioactivity and chemicals.

### Chemical mutagens

Hundreds of chemicals have been shown to produce mutagenic activity in various organisms.

Most mutagenic chemicals act by altering the structure of nucleotides. This causes subsequent problems in replication of DNA (during meiosis and mitosis) and in transcription of DNA. If production of a vital protein is affected the mutation can be lethal. Examples of chemical mutagens include the following:

$^5$Bromouracil. This inserts itself during DNA synthesis as an analogue of thymine but introduces problems during transcription because it can pair with adenine or guanine.

Nitrous acid. This causes alteration in the structure of nucleotides which can often lead to inactivation of DNA and a lethal effect.

Acridine dyes. These act by inserting themselves between two adjacent purine bases on a strand of DNA. This leads to mistakes in both replication and transcription of the mutated strand.

## *Types of mutations*

There are two types of mutation: chromosome mutations and gene mutations.

### Chromosome mutations

These include changes in chromosome number and in chromosome structure.

#### *Variation in chromosome number*

During meiosis homologous chromosomes are normally segregated into separate cells, so that each gamete contains only one of each pair. However, sometimes a pair of chromosomes fail to separate and both enter the same gamete. This results in half the gametes containing an extra chromosome and the other half being one short, a condition known as non-disjunction. Down's syndrome (mongolism) is caused by the presence of an extra chromosome in the cells. Several sex abnormalities are also a result of non-disjunction.

1. Klinefelter's syndrome (XXY) is caused by failure of the XX chromosomes to separate during oogenesis in the mother. Individuals are outwardly male but also have some female characteristics.
2. Turner's syndrome (X−) arises when the female gamete contains no X chromosomes. Individuals are sterile females.

3. XYY syndrome occurs when the male gamete contains two Y chromosomes. It is thought that this condition is linked with criminal behaviour since maximum-security prisons contain a high proportion of XYY males.

Polyploidy occurs when an individual contains more than two full sets of chromosomes (2n). Polyploid individuals are created when a full set of chromosomes enters a single gamete during meiosis. This produces some gametes with no chromosomes at all and some which are diploid. If a diploid gamete fuses with a normal haploid gamete the resulting zygote is triploid (3n). If the diploid gamete fuses with another diploid gamete a tetraploid individual results (4n).

Polyploidy is rare in animals but common in plants. Polyploid plants are often hardier, more resistant to disease and produce a larger endosperm than normal plants; their disadvantage is that they are less fertile owing to their inability to produce viable gametes.

Polyploidy can be induced artificially into cells by application of the substance colchicine. This allows chromosome replication but prevents cell division, resulting in cells with twice the normal number of chromosomes. This method is often used to introduce polyploidy into crop plants, thereby increasing the yield of starch in the endosperm. For example, hexaploid varieties (6n) of wheat are common.

A haploid (or monoploid) individual contains only one set of chromosomes (n). Many fungi and algae exist as haploids throughout the majority of their life cycles. Haploids also occur in some diploid species of insects and mites as a result of parthenogenesis (development of a gamete into an individual in the absence of fertilization) of the male gametes. However, most haploids which arise accidentally are abnormal. They do not normally reach the adult stage and are sterile owing to their inability to produce gametes.

*Alteration in chromosome structure*

1. ADDITIONS AND DELETIONS: These occur because of mistakes in crossing over. A chromosome may contain an extra length of DNA or, conversely, may have a piece missing.

| A B C F G H I J K L M | A B C D E <u>D E</u> F G H I J K L M |
|---|---|
| two genes missing | two extra genes |

Additions and deletions may also occur because of mistakes in DNA replication or the presence of chemical mutagens.

2. INVERSION: This occurs when a chromosome breaks in two and rejoins in an inverted position.

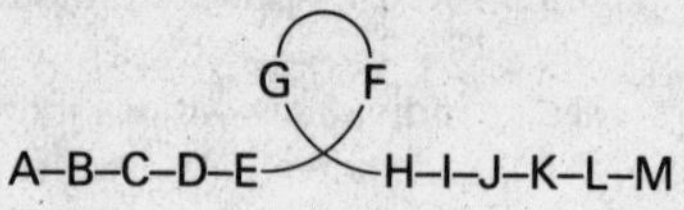
G F
A–B–C–D–E
H–I–J–K–L–M

3. TRANSLOCATION: This is when crossing over (exchange of genetic material) occurs between non-homologous pairs of chromosomes.

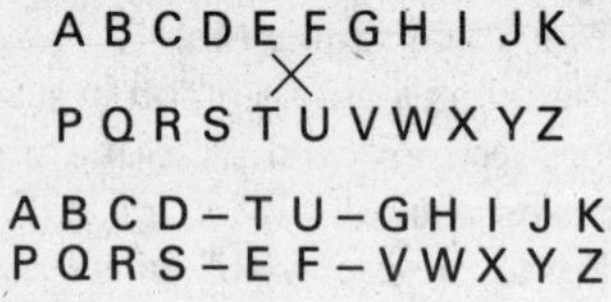
A B C D E F G H I J K
P Q R S T U V W X Y Z
A B C D – T U – G H I J K
P Q R S – E F – V W X Y Z

## Gene mutations

These are chemical changes in individual genes such as those caused by chemical mutagens. They cannot be detected microscopically. A change in one or two bases on a chromosome will not only affect the production of one amino acid, it can affect the coding for all subsequent amino acids. This can have drastic effects if the protein in question is an essential one.

*Non-sense and mis-sense mutations*

If a codon undergoes a mutation, it will no longer code for the same amino acid. If the mutation causes the codon to become a termination codon (i.e. one signalling the end of transcription) it is called a non-sense mutation. If, on the other hand, the mutation causes the codon to code for a different amino acid it is called a mis-sense mutation (see Fig. 10.17).

An addition or deletion of one or more bases will affect the coding of all subsequent codons, since a codon is read as three consecutive bases. Mis-sense mutations lead to the production of incorrect proteins which can often have drastic effects. An example is sickle-cell anaemia which is due to mutant haemoglobin; the result of a single mutant gene.

*Inversions and translocations*

These types of mutations can also occur among bases within a single gene (see Fig. 10.18).

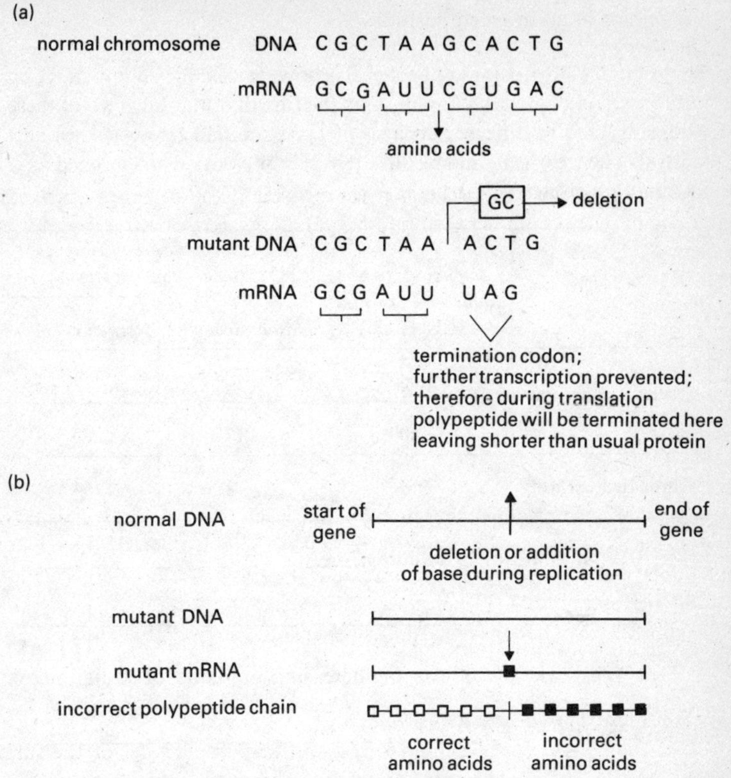
(a)
normal chromosome
DNA C G C T A A G C A C T G
mRNA G C G A U U C G U G A C
amino acids
GC
deletion
mutant DNA C G C T A A A C T G
mRNA G C G A U U U A G
termination codon;
further transcription prevented;
therefore during translation
polypeptide will be terminated here
leaving shorter than usual protein
(b)
normal DNA
start of gene
end of gene
deletion or addition
of base during replication
mutant DNA
mutant mRNA
incorrect polypeptide chain
correct
amino acids
incorrect
amino acids

*Fig. 10.17* (a) Non-sense and (b) mis-sense mutations

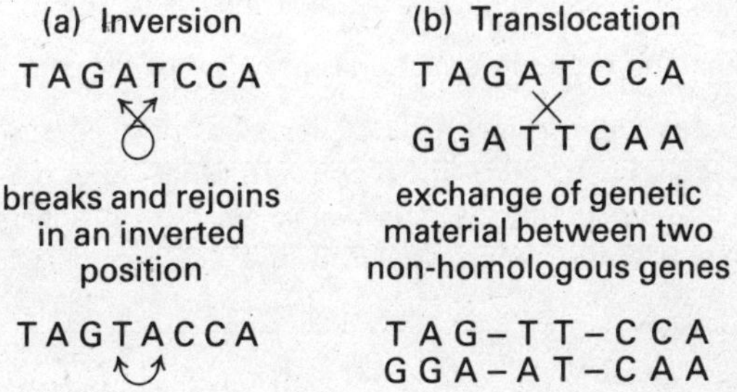
(a) Inversion
TAGATCCA
breaks and rejoins
in an inverted
position
TAGTACCA
(b) Translocation
T A G A T C C A
G G A T T C A A
exchange of genetic
material between two
non-homologous genes
T A G – T T – C C A
G G A – A T – C A A

*Fig. 10.18* Inversions and translocations

## *Related questions*

**Question:**
Three similar suspensions of bacterial cells were used for an investigation into the effect of ionizing radiation on the rate of mutation. Two of these were subjected to different dosages of radiation and one was kept as a control. The treatment and results after planting out on an enriched agar medium are shown in the table.

| | *Amount of ionizing radiation in roentgen (r) units* | *Average numbers of colonies on each agar plate* | |
|---|---|---|---|
| | | *Mutant colonies* | *Normal colonies* |
| Treated suspensions | 1,500 | 7 | 48 |
| | 2,500 | 14 | 60 |
| Untreated control | nil | 2 | 64 |

(a) (i) What is meant by *mutation*? ______________________________

______________________________

**(1 mark)**

(ii) What are the effects of increasing amounts of radiation on bacterial cells? ______________________________

______________________________

______________________________

**(1 mark)**

(iii) What important information is provided by the control group?

______________________________

______________________________

______________________________

**(2 marks)**

(b) State *two* agents other than ionizing radiation which induce mutations.

(i) ____________________________

(ii) ____________________________

**(2 marks)**

(c) Give two reasons why micro-organisms such as bacteria are frequently used in the study of mutation.

(i) ____________________________

____________________________

(ii) ____________________________

____________________________

**(2 marks)**

(d) Why is mutation considered to be an important factor in the evolution of new species? ____________________________

____________________________

**(1 mark)**

[Oxford, June 1982, Paper 1]

**Comments:**

(a) (i) See p. 415.

(ii) and (iii) These questions test your ability to interpret experimental data. From the table it can be seen that increasing the radiation dosage also increases the number of mutant colonies.

The control group shows the number of mutants arising in the absence of radiation.

(b) See p. 416.

(c) (i) Bacteria are often used to study mutations since they have a rapid lifecycle and therefore experimental results can often be observed in 24 hours.

(ii) Bacteria are also relatively simple organisms enabling mutations to be recognized easily.

(d) See p. 415.

**Question:**

Explain what is meant by each of the following:

(a) Chromosome variation **(4 marks)**
(b) Haploidy **(4 marks)**
(c) Gene pool **(4 marks)**
(d) Mutation **(4 marks)**
(e) Codon **(4 marks)**

[London, June 1982, Paper 1]

**Comments:**

This type of question requires a short, concise account for each of the topics listed. A common mistake is to write too much on one topic, leaving insufficient time to finish the rest of the question. You should remember that there are only 4 marks for each part of the question, so only the most relevant facts should be included. It is important to avoid the temptation to write down everything you know about a subject as this will not gain extra marks.

(a) A simple description of how variation in chromosome number arises is required (see p. 416). Problems arising from such variations could be mentioned, e.g. sex abnormalities, Down's syndrome, etc, but detailed explanations are not required.
(b) See p. 380.
(c) See p. 445.
(d) See p. 415. You should condense the information given in the text. Only a brief explanation of mutation is required, including what mutations are, what causes them, their effect on evolution and the two main types of mutations.
(e) See p. 410. This question is probably best answered using annotated diagrams.

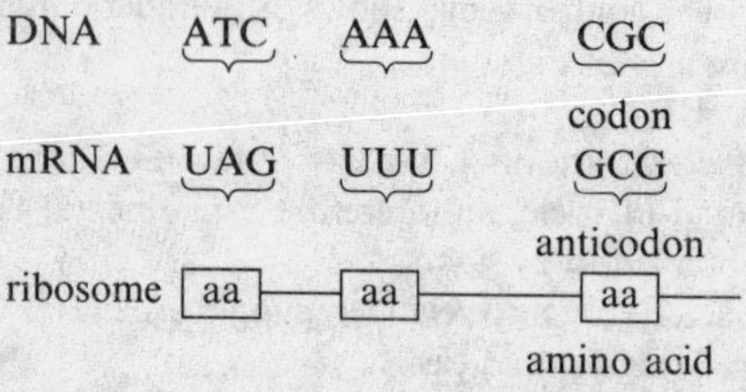
DNA
ATC
AAA
CGC
codon
mRNA
UAG
UUU
GCG
anticodon
ribosome
aa
aa
aa
amino acid

Three consecutive bases on DNA are called a codon. During transcription mRNA is produced and the codons are copied as anticodons. Each base on the DNA codes for its 'opposite' base in the anticodon:

A ⟶ U

T ⟶ A

C ⟶ G

G ⟶ C

At the ribosomes each anticodon codes for a particular amino acid and these are linked together to form a polypeptide chain.

# 11. Evolution

## *Development of the evolutionary theory*

There is enormous diversity in the organisms alive today.

Linnaeus (1707–1778) and his contemporaries attributed this wide diversity to special creation, i.e. there are as many species of organism today as were formed by the 'Creator'.

Some biologists, such as Buffon (1707–1788), did consider the possibility of a gradual development or evolution of all species from one or a few ancestors. Buffon recognized vestigial structures in animals and their importance.

Jean Baptiste de Monet Lamarck (1744–1829) made the first major effort to explain the origin of species on an evolutionary basis. He proposed the gradual development of species from similar ancestors on the basis of four principles:

1. All organisms tend to increase in size.
2. New organs arise because of new needs.
3. Use of an organ results in further development of the organ, while disuse results in degeneration.
4. These changes in an individual are inherited by its progeny (i.e. inheritance of required characteristics).

His Law of Use and Disuse could not be wholly proven.

Charles Darwin (1809–1882) was more successful in developing a reasonable hypothesis on the mechanism of evolution. He also assembled a great mass of data for the actual occurrence of evolution. His hypothesis can be summarized in five points:

1. All species tend to reproduce in numbers greatly in excess of those which can possibly survive, i.e. a species tends to increase its numbers exponentially.
2. However, the actual size of a population remains fairly consistent, indicating a high death rate.
3. This proposes a struggle for existence in which the majority of individuals die.
4. The members of the population vary in many respects. Variation is one of the most universal characteristics of organisms. Some of the variations will give individuals an advantage in the struggle for survival.

5. This results in natural selection of those organisms best fitted to their environment. In each generation relatively more of these will survive and produce offspring which will inherit the characteristics of their parents. Thus species are gradually modified and become better adapted to their environment.

Points 1 and 4 are observed facts, as is point 2 over a long period of time although great fluctuations can occur. Point 3 logically explains 1 and 2, and point 5 is a logical result of points 1 to 4.

Opposition to Darwinism comes from three areas:

1. Lamarckists – they accepted evolution but could not accept natural selection as its cause.
2. Theory of Cataclysm – species are fixed and do not evolve from similar ancestors. The followers of this theory account for fossils by extinction of the species in a disaster.
3. Creationist Theory – biblical explanation.

Darwin's evidence was drawn from domestication, geographical distribution, taxonomy, comparative anatomy, comparative embryology and palaeontology. We can now add evidence from comparative physiology and biochemistry and genetics.

## *Summary of the evidence for evolution*

### Domestication

Darwin noted that animals and plants selectively bred by man had produced well-defined strains. Examples include the various dog breeds, pigeons specially bred for racing, and fruit and vegetables bred for taste, hardiness, etc.

This artificial selection is based on the same principles as natural selection except that it is vastly quicker and the features selected may not be of survival value.

### Taxonomy

It is possible to group organisms into taxonomic groups from phyla to species on the basis of similar characters. Classification is possible since the species present today are descended from a few simpler forms. If each species *was* a result of special creation their relationships would be difficult to determine.

## Embryology

Ernst Haeckel (1834–1919) advanced the 'Theory of Recapitulation'. This proposed that during an organism's development it passes through embryological stages which represent the adult stages of its evolutionary ancestors. For example, a four-week human embryo has five pairs of branchial grooves corresponding to the gill clefts of fishes.

The closer the organisms are taxonomically, the greater the proportion of embryological stages they have in common.

## Comparative physiology

There is considerable uniformity of cell structure and function in living organisms, and these would appear to indicate common descent.

Comparison of proteins can provide evidence of relationships between organisms. For example, the closer two species are phylogenetically, the more alike their blood proteins are liable to be. Illustrating this, serum immunized against human blood gives an agglutination of 64 per cent with gorilla blood, 42 per cent with orang-utan blood, 29 per cent with baboon blood and 10 per cent with ox blood.

Differences in the sequence of amino acids on haemoglobins and cytochromes can be used to estimate the time of divergence of related organisms from a common ancestor.

## Geographical distribution

Areas of the earth with almost identical climates often have different fauna. For example, Africa and South America have similar climates but Africa has lions, elephants, zebra, giraffes, etc. and South America, panthers, jaguars, llama, opossums, etc. Australasia contains primarily marsupials and monotremes whereas in Asia placental mammals predominate. Also, penguins are found in Antarctica, and polar bears in the Arctic.

These observations may be explained by the following:

1. The southern hemisphere has several large land masses showing divergent evolutions owing to geographical isolation.
2. The northern hemisphere land masses are more accessible to the spread of new species, the barriers being climatic.
3. The mammals arose in the northern hemisphere and then migrated in three major directions – South America, Africa, Australia.
4. In isolation, groups of animals evolved along different paths and were prevented from interbreeding. This eventually led to the formation of new species. Thus, adaptive radiation has occurred independently in each of the continents.

### Palaeontology

Most fossils are found in sedimentary rock. Each layer can be dated by its relative position in the layers of rock, and by radioactive dating methods.

Fossils show that organic evolution was a gradual process spanning the last 3,000 million years and that evolutionary changes were not linear but a branching process of descent from a common ancestor.

Evolutionary theories are also supported by specimens which appear to form a transition between two groups. For example, *Archaeopteryx* was a bird-like animal with teeth and it provides a link between birds and their reptile ancestors.

Fossil evidence is most convincing when fossils from one locality found in successive layers of rock exhibit a gradual change.

### Comparative anatomy

On comparing the anatomy of one vertebrate with that of another many similarities are apparent. When two structures are similar in two different species they are said to be homologous, i.e. they have the same origin in a common ancestor but variations have arisen because of different needs. This divergent evolution results in adaptive radiation.

A good example is the pentadactyl limb which is common in many mammals. It is developed for digging in the mole, swimming in the whale, flying in the bat, running in the horse, and so on.

Analogous structures have the same functions but different origins. For example, the wings of an insect and a bird are functionally similar but structurally very different. This is an example of convergent evolution, i.e. the structures have adapted to a common function.

Vestigial is the term applied to reduced structures such as the reduced bones in the horse's limb, the caecum, appendix and coccyx in man, and the stomata on the petals of flowering plants. These are taken as evidence of descent with modification.

## *Neo-Darwinism*

The mechanics of evolution are now explained on the basis of mutation and selection, the predominant theory being called the neo-Darwinian theory.

Inheritable variation is continually arising in all species by means of mutation: both gene and chromosomal mutations. Sexual reproduction also produces further variability. These variations are then tested by natural selection. All of the conditions under which an organism lives act as selective agencies which permit the better adapted individuals to survive and reproduce.

## *Examples of natural selection*

### Sickle-cell anaemia

This is an inheritable disease which is due to a mutation of a recessive gene (h) on an autosome. It results in the incorporation of an incorrect amino acid at one point in the protein chains of the haemoglobin.

The red blood cells of both heterozygotes (Hh) and homozygotes (hh) develop a sickle shape in conditions of low oxygen tension. Heterozygotes have the sickle-cell trait and experience above-average breathlessness during exercise or at high altitudes. Recessive homozygotes suffer sickle-cell anaemia. This severe anaemia causes death, usually before puberty.

New sickle-cell genes arise spontaneously so they will always be present in the population, but a percentage of them should be eliminated at each generation. However, in certain East African and Asian populations the sickle-cell gene has a high frequency with 4 per cent of all children being born with sickle-cell anaemia. There is also a higher frequency of sickle-cell trait in the population.

The reason for this is that individuals with sickle-cell trait have a *selective advantage* because they have a higher resistance to certain malarial diseases compared to normal (HH) individuals. Thus the heterozygous sickle-cell trait individuals are naturally selected and are able to survive and reproduce, and the frequency of the sickle-cell gene (h) *increases* in the gene pool.

### Industrial melanism

The peppered moth, *Biston betularia*, is found in two distinct forms – the black, melanic form and the light, peppered natural form.

In 1848, 99 per cent of the moth population of Manchester was of the light form and 1 per cent was the melanic form. Fifty years later 99 per cent of the moth population was melanic and only 1 per cent was light. Over this period the level of air pollution had increased, covering the tree trunks and other vertical surfaces with a dark, sooty grime. The light form of the moth, resting on tree trunks, etc. during the day, was easily visible to bird predators. The melanic form of the moth was not so easily seen, and was therefore more likely to survive and breed, thus increasing the frequency of the melanic genes in the population.

In the later part of the nineteenth century, the rest of Britain received the melanic forms. This was due to migration from Manchester as well as natural selection in other cities.

Since then, anti-pollution measures have cut down the amount of air pollution in the cities and industrial areas. The lighter forms, which all along were better adapted to the lichen-covered tree trunks of country areas, have thus been able to recolonize.

**Polymorphism.** This is a term used to describe distinctly different inheritable forms within one species. Other examples are the sickle-cell anaemia trait and normal haemoglobin; red/green colour-blindness and normal vision and the four human blood groups.

### Resistance to antibiotics, insecticides, poisons, etc.

Bacteria develop a resistance to antibiotics, insects to insecticides and rats to poisons such as warfarin. This resistance arises by the natural selection of resistant mutants, i.e. individuals resistant to the use of the specific substances. This resistance can be selected for in the laboratory.

Staphylococcal resistance appeared soon after penicillin became widely used in hospitals. Certain staphylococci are now resistant to all major antibiotics, often having a triple resistance to penicillin, tetracycline and streptomycin.

Also, in a relatively short time, the widespread use of insecticides has resulted in many strains of completely resistant insects. For example, in some parts of the world *Musca domestica* (the house-fly) has developed resistance to all 'safe' insecticides except pyrethrum compounds. In some instances the mutant genes, via enzyme induction, cause the breakdown of the insecticide.

Similarly, the extensive use of warfarin, which interferes with blood clotting mechanisms, has selected for resistant strains of rat. The resistance is due to a single mutant gene. Individuals homozygous for this gene are weaker than normal rats.

Further examples of selective pressure on mutants include the occurrence of myxomatosis-resistant rabbits and metal-tolerant plants (e.g. zinc- and lead-tolerant grass species which colonize chemical-waste dumping areas).

## *Species and speciation*

There is no single definition of a **species**, but the following features generally apply.

1. Members of a species are similar in appearance; thus a species is the smallest taxonomic group usually used.
2. Members of a species are generally distinctly different from members of other species, with no intermediate forms. However, some species are polymorphic (see p. 429) and the offspring can differ considerably from the parent and each other.
3. Members of a species are capable of interbreeding and producing fertile offspring. If hybrids are produced with a member of another species their offspring are usually sterile (e.g. a horse and a donkey produce a sterile mule). However, this cannot apply to organisms such as bacteria where sexual reproduction is not well developed.

**Speciation** is the process by which a new species is formed by the splitting of a line of descent into two or more new lines. Speciation depends on many complex factors but reproductive isolation is essential to prevent exchange of genes between populations. A combination between isolation and migration results in speciation. Some of the main isolating mechanisms are listed below.

### 1. Pre-zygotic reproductive isolating mechanisms

These prevent the fusion of gametes occurring.

(a) ECOLOGICAL ISOLATION: Organisms occupy different habitats so they never meet to mate except for a few migrants. This type of isolation is present in virtually all natural populations.
(b) GEOGRAPHICAL ISOLATION: Various geographical barriers, e.g. seas, rivers, mountains and deserts, may prevent meeting and mating.
(c) ETHOLOGICAL ISOLATION: Organisms may share the same habitat but have different migratory patterns and breeding grounds. Examples include the herring gull and lesser black-backed gull.
(d) SEASONAL ISOLATION: The organisms may have incompatible breeding seasons.

### 2. Post-zygotic reproductive isolating mechanisms

These prevent the successful development of the result of fertilization.

(a) The zygote may fail to develop.
(b) The offspring may not reach reproductive maturity.
(c) The offspring may be sterile.

A certain amount of genetic exchange is necessary to introduce new and possibly advantageous variations.

### *The Hardy–Weinberg equation*

When considering an allele (A) (recessive allele a), a randomly breeding population will comprise homozygous dominant (AA), homozygous recessive (aa), and heterozygous (Aa) individuals. The proportion of individuals of each kind in the population will depend on the frequency of the alleles, i.e. A and a, in the gene pool. If the frequency of gametes with gene A is 'p' and the frequency of gametes with gene a is 'q', the proportion of the *genotypes* in the population can be determined:

Gametes

| | A (p) | a (q) |
|---|---|---|
| A (p) | AA ($p^2$) | Aa (pq) |
| a (q) | Aa (pq) | aa ($q^2$) |

From the ratios of the genotypes as calculated in the table above it follows that

AA + 2Aa + aa = 100% or 1.0

therefore $p^2 + 2pq + q^2 = 1.0$ (this is the **Hardy–Weinberg equation**)
thus $(p + q)^2 = 1.0$ and therefore $p + q = 1.0$

The relative proportions of the three genotypes in subsequent generations remain constant provided:

1. matings are random,
2. there are no selection pressures,
3. there is no migration into or out of the population,
4. there are no mutations.

#### An example – tongue rolling

The ability in man to roll the tongue longitudinally into a U-shape is due to the dominant allele (R). If 85 per cent of the population can roll their tongues (the remaining 15 per cent cannot) the Hardy–Weinberg equation can be used to calculate the percentage of the population that are homozygous and heterozygous tongue rollers.

Tongue rollers can be homozygous dominant (RR) or heterozygous (Rr). Non-rollers must be homozygous recessive (rr). Using the Hardy–

Weinberg equation:
Frequency of RR = $p^2$
Frequency of Rr = $2pq$
Frequency of rr = $q^2$
The 15 per cent who are non-rollers must be rr.

Thus $q^2 = 0.15$

$q = \sqrt{0.15} = 0.39$

As $p + q = 1.0$

$p = 1.0 - q$

$\therefore p = 1.0 - 0.39 = 0.61$

So $2pq = 2 \times 0.61 \times 0.39$

$= 0.48$

Expressing these results as the percentage of individuals in the population:

RR = $p^2$ = 37 per cent
Rr = $2pq$ = 48 per cent
rr = $q^2$ = 15 per cent

The frequencies of the genotypes will remain the same in subsequent generations provided all the conditions outlined previously are met. In terms of evolutionary importance, the changes in genotype frequency that occur if the genes mutate or the environment changes favouring a particular genotype are the most important.

## Further reading

R. J. Berry, *Neo-Darwinism*, Studies in Biology No. 144 (Arnold, 1982)
K. J. R. Edwards, *Evolution in Modern Biology*, Studies in Biology No. 87 (Arnold, 1977)
J. Maynard Smith, *The Theory of Evolution*, 3rd edition (Pelican, 1975)

## Related questions

**Question:**

(a) The sequence of changes in the structure of the limbs and teeth in the horse is illustrated opposite.
Give explanations for the changes in
(i) limb structure and size
(ii) tooth structure

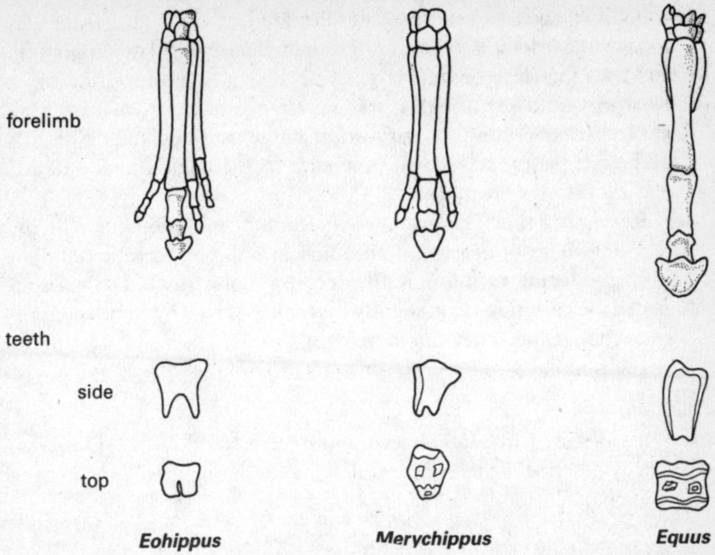
forelimb
teeth
side
top
Eohippus
Merychippus
Equus

(b) How would Darwin account for the development of *Equus*, the modern horse, from *Eohippus*.

**Comments:**

(a) To answer this question a knowledge of the changes that occurred in the environment during the time is necessary. This gives information on the terrain the horse encountered and the type of food material that was available. At the time of *Eohippus*, marshes were prevalent with an abundance of plant material. *Eohippus* probably fed on soft vegetation and fruit which its small, smooth teeth could cope with. Its four splayed-out toes on the forelimbs (three on the hindlimbs) gave stability on the marshy ground.

The climatic changes caused a gradual drying out of the terrain, producing drier grasslands with little foliage. The lack of shelter in the sparse foliage left the descendants of *Eohippus* open to predation. These descendants, e.g. *Merychippus*, needed to be able to observe the predators and escape quickly. Thus the bones in the limbs increased in length, resulting in a much taller animal with greater speed. Eventually the number of toes was reduced and then (in *Equus*) they were replaced by a hoof which is more suitable in dry conditions such as prairies. The diet gradually changed from soft foliage to harder grass. This requires more mechanical manipulation, and thus the teeth became larger with strong ridges for grinding.

(b) Darwin would explain this gradual change in terms of variation, natural selection and the survival of the fittest. You should discuss each of these processes with reference to the adaptations outlined above.

Remember that Darwin knew nothing of mutations, nor of the rearrangement of genes and chromosomes during meiotic cell divisions producing variation in the ancestral horse stock. Darwin suggested the variations (e.g. slightly longer legs) arose by some spontaneous change, but knew no more detail.

**Question:**

(a) What is meant by 'organic evolution'? **(3 marks)**

(b) Briefly describe the use of the following for dating fossils and in each case comment on its reliability.
 (i) evidence from sedimentary rocks
 (ii) radioactive decay **(4 marks)**

(c) State three structural changes seen in the series of horse fossils which can be used as evidence for the evolution of this group. **(3 marks)**

(d) Briefly describe how each of the following can be used to provide evidence for evolution.
 (i) homologous organs
 (ii) development of vertebrate embryos
 (iii) industrial melanism **(9 marks)**

**Comments:**

This type of question requires short answers, in most cases just one line.

(a) Organic evolution refers to the way complex organisms have developed from simpler ancestors over a period of time.

(b) See p. 427.

(i) Often sedimentary rocks are in strata, the oldest at the bottom and the most recently formed at the top. An indication of the course of evolution can be obtained by comparing the sorts of fossils in the strata and knowing the approximate age of each stratum.

(ii) Radioactive decay of unstable isotopes can be used to give a much more accurate estimate of the age of a fossil. The unstable isotopes decay by releasing $\alpha$ and $\beta$ particles until they become more

stable:
uranium$^{238}$ $\rightarrow$ lead$^{206}$
carbon$^{14}$ $\rightarrow$ carbon$^{12}$

The half-life of an isotope is the time taken for half of a given amount of an unstable isotope to break down into a stable form. The half-lives of many isotopes are known and thus the age of a fossil can be estimated by measuring the ratio of unstable to stable isotopes in it. The ratios of several isotopes can be measured at the same time thus cross-checking the dating.

(c) See the comments on the previous question.

(d) (i) See p. 427. A good example is the pentadactyl limb.
(ii) See p. 426.
(iii) See p. 428.

# 12. Ecology

## *Food chains and webs*

### *Food chains*

The sequence of events by which a plant is eaten by an animal and that animal is itself eaten by another animal, and so on, is called a food chain. In all environments, examples of the following linear food chain can be found:

plants → herbivores → carnivores

Plants obtain their food from photosynthesis, the energy to do so being obtained from the sun. Plants are consumed by herbivores, which in turn may be eaten by carnivores. Table 12.1 gives some examples.

*Table 12.1.* Linear food chains

| | *Freshwater habitat* | *Marine habitat* | *Terrestrial habitat* |
|---|---|---|---|
| Plants | microscopic plants (e.g. diatoms) | diatoms | grass |
| | ↓ | ↓ | ↓ |
| Herbivores | tadpoles | copepods | deer |
| | ↓ | ↓ | ↓ |
| Carnivores | water scorpion | herring | lions |

A food chain is a simple, linear series. If the plants were to die out, the herbivores, and consequently the carnivores, would be reduced in number. However, this is only true if the herbivores have no alternative plant source. This does sometimes happen. For example, there is concern about the fate of the giant panda in China, which feeds exclusively on bamboo shoots. Since all the bamboo plants in an area tend to flower and die in synchronization (and only flower relatively rarely), it is quite possible that the pandas would starve and become extinct should this occur.

However, a single food chain is usually only a small part of a more complex interaction called a food web.

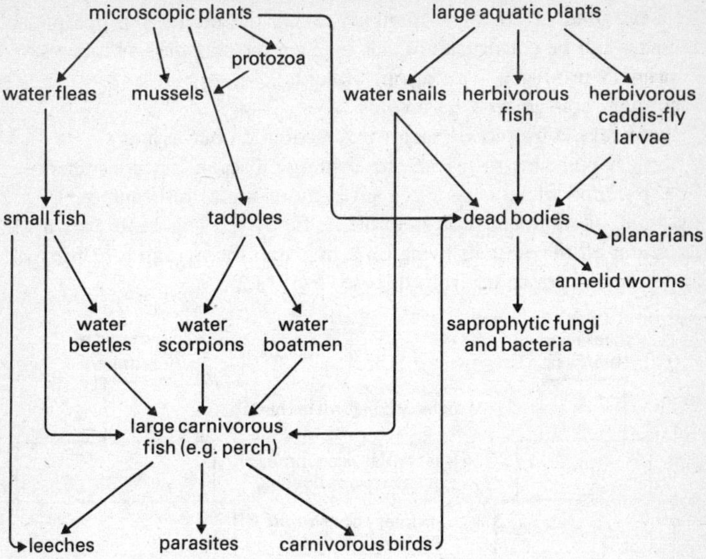
microscopic plants
large aquatic plants
protozoa
water fleas
mussels
water snails
herbivorous fish
herbivorous caddis-fly larvae
small fish
tadpoles
dead bodies
planarians
annelid worms
water beetles
water scorpions
water boatmen
saprophytic fungi and bacteria
large carnivorous fish (e.g. perch)
leeches
parasites
carnivorous birds

*Fig. 12.1* Food web for a typical freshwater pond

## *Food webs*

A food web can be shown in a diagram which illustrates the nutritional relationships between organisms in an ecosystem (e.g. Fig. 12.1).

Energy is passed from one stage of a food web to the next in the form of chemical energy in food. However, the estimated transfer of energy when one organism is consumed by another is less than 20 per cent. In other words only 20 per cent of the energy contained in a food source is converted to stored energy in the consumer. This means that the number of individuals at each level of the food web is restricted. The total amount of living matter at a particular level of the food web is called the **biomass**. On ascending the levels of a food web, the number of individuals on successive levels decreases. For example, there may be billions of microscopic plants in a small pond, but relatively few large carnivorous fish.

### *Ecological pyramids*

The numbers of individuals at each level of a food web can be represented by a pyramid of numbers. Similarly, using the biomass, a pyramid of biomass can be constructed. Each level can be classified as follows:

primary producers – autotrophs (plants)
primary consumers – herbivores
secondary consumers – carnivores feeding on herbivores
tertiary consumers – carnivores feeding on secondary consumers

A pyramid of biomass often gives more useful information than a pyramid of numbers. For example, a food web can be drawn up to represent all the animals living on a tree, and the pyramids of numbers and biomass drawn up from this (see Fig. 12.2).

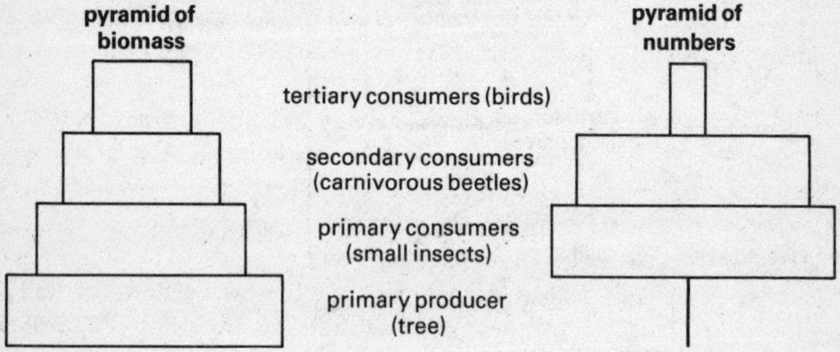
pyramid of biomass
pyramid of numbers
tertiary consumers (birds)
secondary consumers (carnivorous beetles)
primary consumers (small insects)
primary producer (tree)

*Fig. 12.2* Pyramids of biomass and numbers

The pyramid of biomass gives an idea of the amount of photosynthesizing tissue present, whereas the pyramid of numbers simply shows the relative numbers of organisms in the ecosystem. There is no distinction made for size; the primary producer in Fig. 12.2 could be anything from a small bush to a huge tree.

The types of pyramids already described are all upright pyramids. Inverted pyramids are used to represent parasitic food webs (see Fig. 12.3).

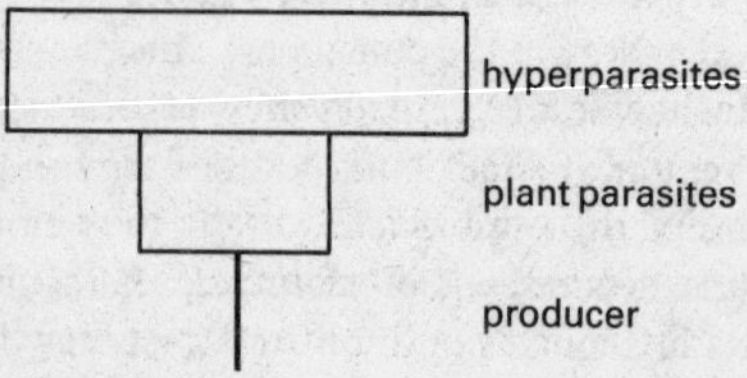
hyperparasites
plant parasites
producer

*Fig. 12.3* An inverted pyramid

### Food-chain efficiency

The percentage efficiency with which a food supply is exploited by a predator population can be found using the formula

$$\text{Food-chain efficiency} = \frac{\text{kilojoules of prey consumed by predator}}{\text{kilojoules of food consumed by prey}} \times 100$$

## *Recycling of matter*

### *The nitrogen cycle*

Nitrogen is used to make the amino group ($NH_2$), which is found in all amino acids and proteins. It is therefore an essential component of living tissues.

Nitrogen is present in the atmosphere as free nitrogen gas ($N_2$). It is made available to plants by processes involving lightning, nitrogen fixation, ammonification and nitrification. Plants absorb nitrogen from the soil in the form of ammonium ions ($NH_4^+$) or as nitrate ions ($NO_3^-$). Animals obtain nitrogen by consuming plant material. When plants and animals die, their tissues decompose and the nitrogenous matter is returned to the soil. Nitrogen is also returned to the soil in the form of urea, which is present in urine, and in the form of artificial fertilizers.

Nitrogen is returned to the atmosphere by the process of denitrification. In this way, there is a continuous cycling of nitrogen between the atmosphere, the soil and living organisms (Fig. 12.4).

### Processes occurring in the nitrogen cycle

1. LIGHTNING: This is an electronic discharge resulting in the combination of atmospheric nitrogen and oxygen to give nitrites and nitrates which are washed into the soil by rain water.
2. NITROGEN FIXATION: This is the conversion of atmospheric nitrogen into proteins. There are two types of nitrogen-fixing organisms:
   (a) Free-living bacteria, e.g. *Azobacter* and *Clostridium*, and blue–green algae, e.g. *Nostoc*.
   (b) Bacteria which live symbiotically in the roots of leguminous plants (peas, beans, clover), e.g. *Rhizobium*.
3. AMMONIFICATION: This is the breakdown of proteins and amino acids found in decaying organic matter to produce ammonium ions

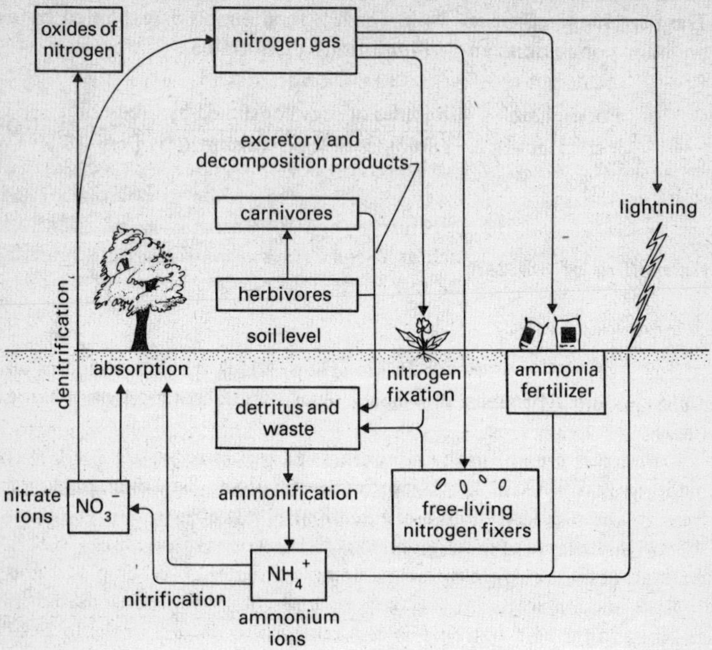
oxides of nitrogen
nitrogen gas
excretory and decomposition products
carnivores
herbivores
lightning
soil level
denitrification
absorption
nitrogen fixation
ammonia fertilizer
detritus and waste
ammonification
nitrate ions
$NO_3^-$
free-living nitrogen fixers
$NH_4^+$
nitrification
ammonium ions

*Fig. 12.4* The nitrogen cycle

($NH_4^+$). A wide range of saprophytic bacteria and fungi decompose substrates in this way.

4. NITRIFICATION: This is the conversion of ammonium ions to nitrate ions which can readily be used by plants. It occurs in two main stages:
   (a) Conversion of ammonium ions to nitrites. Ammonia combines with carbon dioxide in the soil to form ammonium carbonate ($(NH_4)_2CO_3$). The ammonium carbonate is then converted to nitrous acid ($HNO_2$) by bacteria (e.g. *Nitrosomonas* and *Nitrococcus*) as in the following reaction:

   $$(NH_4)_2CO_3 + 3O_2 \rightarrow 2HNO_2 + CO_2 + 3H_2O + \text{energy}$$

   The nitrous acid reacts with metal ions in the soil (e.g. $Mg^{2+}$, $Ca^{2+}$, $K^+$) to form nitrites (e.g. calcium nitrite $Ca(NO_2)_2$).

(*b*) Conversion of nitrites to nitrates, for example by the bacterium Nitrobacter:

$$2Ca(NO_2)_2 + 2O_2 \rightarrow 2Ca(NO_3)_2 + \text{energy}$$
calcium nitrite calcium nitrate

5. DENITRIFICATION: This is the breakdown of nitrogen compounds to produce nitrogen. The bacteria which carry out the process usually live in conditions of oxygen shortage. In order to generate oxygen they reduce nitrates to nitrites and subsequently to nitrogen. Denitrifying bacteria such as *Pseudomonas denitrificans* thus have the effect of depriving the soil of essential nitrates.

### *The carbon cycle (Fig. 12.5)*

The amount of carbon dioxide in the atmosphere is balanced by the processes which remove it (photosynthesis), and those which add to it (respiration, combustion). As a result of these processes, the level of carbon dioxide in the atmosphere is maintained at approximately 0.04 per cent, although increased industrialization is having the effect of increasing this value (see Table 12.2).

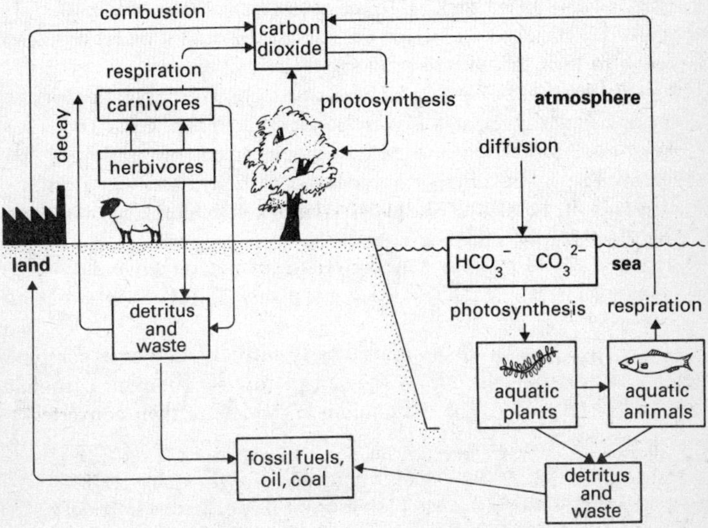

combustion
carbon dioxide
respiration
carnivores
photosynthesis
atmosphere
decay
herbivores
diffusion
land
$HCO_3^-$ $CO_3^{2-}$
sea
photosynthesis
respiration
detritus and waste
aquatic plants
aquatic animals
fossil fuels, oil, coal
detritus and waste


*Fig. 12.5* The carbon cycle

### *The oxygen cycle*

The amount of oxygen in the atmosphere is controlled by the process of photosynthesis, which produces oxygen, and respiration and combustion which both remove oxygen. The level of oxygen in the atmosphere is approximately 20 per cent. Scientists are predicting that if the present scale of rain forest destruction is maintained there could be a drastic effect on atmospheric oxygen levels.

## Symbiosis

Symbiosis is an association between two organisms from which both partners benefit. Three examples are given below.

1. Some species of the hermit crab (*Pagurus*) have the sea-anemone *Adamsia palliata* attached to their shells. The mouth and tentacles of the anemone are close to those of the crab. Hence, the anemone gains food and transport while the crab gains protection from the anemone's stinging cells.
2. Many herbivores (e.g. cows and horses) have bacteria in their stomachs which secrete the enzyme cellulase that is used in digestion. This association is beneficial to the bacteria since they obtain food. It is also beneficial to the herbivores, since they cannot digest cellulose owing to their inability to produce the correct enzyme.
3. The green hydra, *Chlorohydra viridissima*, contains large numbers of the unicellular green alga *Chlorella* in its endodermal cells. The algae gain food, protection and carbon dioxide from respiration in the hydra. The hydra obtains oxygen and carbohydrates from photosynthesis in the algae. The hydra is also well camouflaged amongst the water plants, since the algae make it appear green.

## Further reading

J. R. Etherington, *Plant Physiological Ecology*, Studies in Biology No. 98 (Arnold, 1978)

J. Phillipson, *Ecological Energetics*, Studies in Biology No. 1 (Arnold, 1977)

J. Postgate, *Nitrogen Fixation*, Studies in Biology No. 92 (Arnold, 1978)

M. J. Samways, *Biological Control of Pests and Weeds*, Studies in Biology No. 132 (Arnold 1981).

G. D. Scott, *Plant Symbiosis*, Studies in Biology No. 16 (Arnold, 1969)

### Related questions

**Question:**

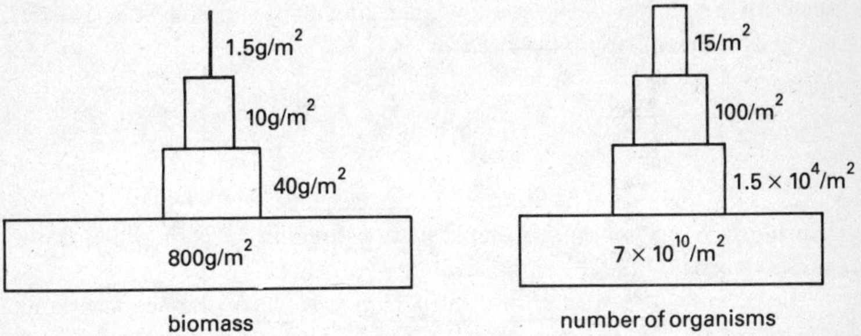
1.5g/m²
10g/m²
40g/m²
800g/m²
biomass
15/m²
100/m²
1.5 × 10⁴/m²
7 × 10¹⁰/m²
number of organisms

The above figures represent pyramids of biomass and number of organisms in the same ecosystem, each of which is not drawn to scale.

(a) Explain why the relationships between the various trophic levels are different when comparing the two figures.

(b) What further kind of pyramid could be constructed to give additional information about the four trophic levels?

(c) Why are there seldom more than four trophic levels in each pyramid?

[AEB, Nov. 1980, Paper 1]

**Comments:**

See p. 438.

(a) The first figure gives an indication of biomass only, and not numbers of individuals. For example, the producer may be an individual plant such as a tree, or many plants such as grass. The second diagram gives no indication of biomass at the various trophic levels.

(b) An indication of energy flow through the trophic levels could be illustrated in an energy pyramid. The amount of energy is given in kilojoules at each trophic level.

(c) Energy is lost between each trophic level, and therefore less energy is available at the next level to support living biomass. This energy loss is so great that the ecosystem cannot support more than four trophic levels.

**Question:**

(a) Complete the diagram below, which shows some processes and substances involved in the nitrogen cycle, by putting the correct word(s) in boxes A–C.

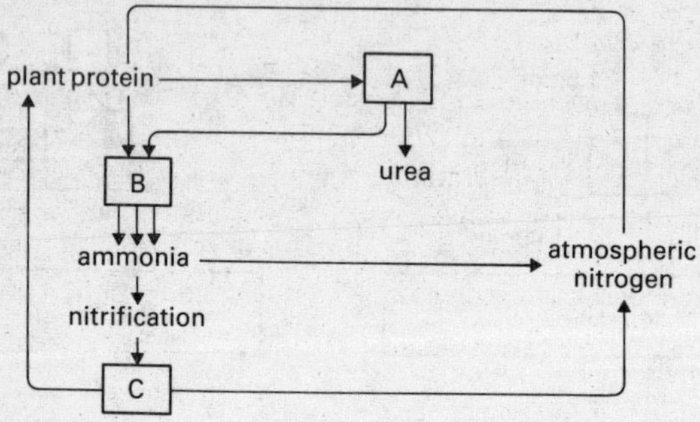
plant protein
A
urea
B
ammonia
atmospheric nitrogen
nitrification
C

(b) Name a bacterium which effects nitrification.

(c) Suggest (i) how nitrifying bacteria benefit from nitrification; (ii) why waterlogged soils are unfavourable to nitrifying bacteria.

[Oxford, June 1979, Paper 1A]

**Comments:**

(a) A – a suitable answer would be animal protein. Urea is the product of protein metabolism in animals only.
B – plant and animal protein and urea are linked to ammonia via B, thus a suitable answer for B would be decomposition.
C – C is utilized by plants and produced by the process of nitrification. Thus a suitable answer would be nitrate ions.

(b) See p. 439.

(c) (i) Nitrifying bacteria are chemosynthetic and derive chemical energy from nitrification.
(ii) Nitrifying bacteria are aerobic, and the anaerobic conditions which would be produced by waterlogging are unfavourable for the oxidation process involved in nitrification.

## *Population ecology*

The term *population*, in ecology, is used to describe all the members of the same species occupying a given area at the same time, e.g. oak trees in a wood, plantains in a lawn, mice in a wood. Members of a population generally interbreed (unless they only breed asexually, which is rare) and so each population represents a pool of genes. A population is an important ecological and evolutionary unit.

### *Population fluctuations*

The numbers of a population depend on the rates of birth, death, immigration and emigration. When considering an isolated population of one species in which migration is minimal, a population growth pattern emerges. There is an initial phase of exponential growth, particularly in a new, active population. This rapid growth continues in some populations, where density of individuals is not restricting, until it is checked by:

(i) the environment no longer being able to support the population,
(ii) an adverse climatic change, or
(iii) migrations.

In other populations the increasing density of the population *smoothly* slows up the rate of growth. This results in an S-shaped (sigmoid) curve (Fig. 12.6). This type of population growth usually establishes stable populations with minor fluctuations from year to year. In natural populations there may be examples of three- to four-year cycles (Fig. 12.7). However, there would be a likely time-lag of a year in the response to a change in the environment by the organisms; this is because the restrictions of the environment do not operate instantaneously. In species which have only one breeding season per year, this lag is inevitable.

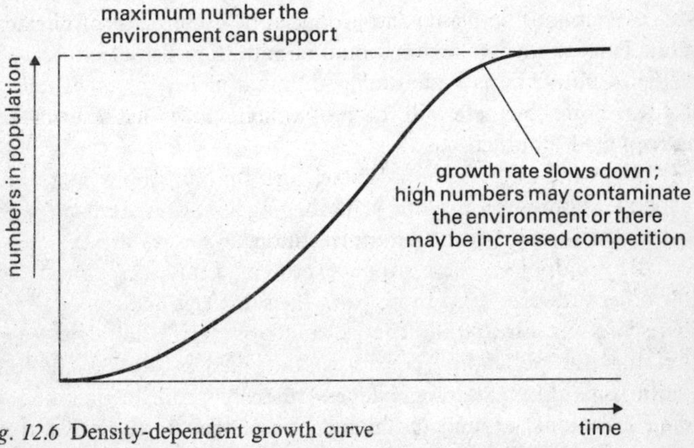
maximum number the
environment can support
numbers in population
growth rate slows down;
high numbers may contaminate
the environment or there
may be increased competition
time

*Fig. 12.6* Density-dependent growth curve

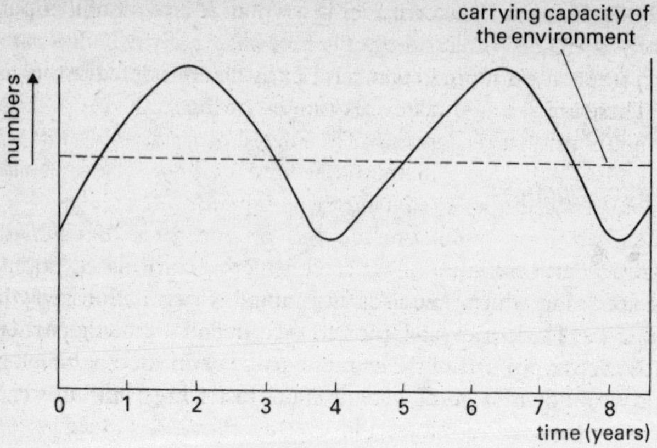
carrying capacity of
the environment
numbers
0
1
2
3
4
5
6
7
8
time (years)

*Fig. 12.7* Fluctuations in population numbers in a four-year cycle

### *Competition*

Competition occurs when the demands on resources exceed the supply, and it makes the individuals or populations involved less successful. In a woodland, plants compete for light and nutrients and animals compete for food and shelter. If the population consists of only a few scattered individuals, competition will not be a factor of ecological importance.

Obviously, competitive interactions affect the niche of an organism. The niche can be defined as the total relationship of the organism with its environment, i.e. the physical conditions (climatic, edaphic) and the nutritional relationships (producers, consumers, decomposers, parasites) (p. 437). Factors such as hibernation and migration will also affect the niche. Most populations exploit many different niches for each stage of their lives. Some of these will, of course, overlap with those already being exploited by others.

#### Intraspecific competition

This is competition between members of the same species. An example is provided by tadpoles. These produce proteinaceous secretions which inhibit other tadpoles, even those from the same egg-mass.

There is often intraspecific competition over territorial rights. This ensures that the population density is controlled before lack of food takes its toll. Mammals (e.g. badgers) usually produce pheromones (scented secretions) around the boundaries of their territory, or there may be ritual fighting. The territorial behaviour of birds usually involves singing or hooting.

Intraspecific competition in plants is clearly demonstrated in the desert shrubs. These are very uniformly distributed owing to the production of leaf or root hormones by some species. These hormones inhibit development of other individuals in the immediate vicinity. This mechanism keeps plants spaced apart, reducing the competition for water.

### Interspecific competition

Interspecific competition becomes important where there are two or more closely related species adapted to the same or similar niche. If the competition is severe, one of the species may be eliminated completely or forced into another niche or geographical location. Alternatively, the species may share the resources and live together at a reduced density, eventually reaching an equilibrium.

One example of interspecific competition involves two species of barnacles on the Scottish shoreline – *Chthamalus* and *Balanus*. *Chthamalus* occupies a band near the upper part of the intertidal zone, while the larger *Balanus* inhabits a wide band below the *Chthamalus* population. The larvae of both species settle over a wider range than that occupied by the adult population; however, the larvae of *Chthamalus* are crushed or buried by *Balanus*. Thus the lower limit of *Chthamalus* is determined by the upper limit of growth by *Balanus*, which is less well adapted to the prolonged exposure of the upper part of the intertidal zone.

Interspecific competition is important in nature, but less important where climate, productivity, etc. are strongly limiting. It regulates the ecological separation of closely related species and the density of the population where species are able to coexist.

## *Predation*

Predators are secondary and tertiary consumers through which the energy flow is relatively small. They regulate the primary consumers. A small number of predators can have a marked effect on the size of specific prey populations. However, more often, a predator may only be a minor factor in determining the size and growth rate of a prey population.

The predator/prey relationship between two species depends on:

1. The degree of vulnerability of the prey to the predator, as well as the relative density levels and the energy flow from prey to predator.
2. The length of association between the predator and prey. Extreme

predator/prey interactions happen most frequently when the interaction is of recent origin or where there has been a recent disturbance in the ecosystem by man or climatic change.

Predators are obviously not beneficial to the individuals they kill, but they may be beneficial to the prey population as a whole. One example of this is certain species of deer which are strongly regulated by predators. When the natural deer predators (wolves, puma, etc.) were exterminated man found it difficult to maintain a constant deer population through hunting. There was a period of overhunting which wiped out the deer population from large areas. This was followed by a period of hunting restriction and reintroduction, and the deer became abundant again. However, this resulted in overgrazing and death by starvation in winter. Thus some predation is necessary and beneficial in a population that has adapted to it.

Much of what has been said about predation is true for parasitism (p. 154). A population of parasites, whether they are bacteria, protozoans, fungi or other species, can be either strongly limiting or relatively unimportant to a particular host population. However, parasites generally have higher reproductive rates and exhibit greater 'host' specificity than do most predators.

### *Succession*

The organisms in a community (i.e. a collection of organisms living together) often create conditions unsuitable for themselves. Other species will arrive which find these conditions more favourable, and so the species composition in that place changes. A whole series of changes can occur before the composition of the community stabilizes, i.e. a climax community is established. Woodland is the climax community for most of the soils in the British Isles. Grasslands are the climax community in the prairies. The intermediate communities before the establishment of the climax community are known as seres.

A peat bog provides a good example of the stages in plant succession. A bog is composed of open water, plus various mosses, sedges and grasses (which form tussocks) and heather. The mosses invade the open water forming small mounds. Sedges and grasses can then grow on the moss. This results in large tussocks, on which heather can grow. This is followed by a phase in which the tussock sinks, the heather dies and there is a return to open water. Therefore, at any one place one species is constantly being replaced by another, but the whole community keeps its species proportions constant.

## Study of an ecosystem

The study of a selected ecosystem, aquatic or terrestrial, should be undertaken as field-work, which is an essential part of all A-level courses.

There are certain points to which you should pay particular attention when attempting an essay on the subject. The information from the field-work project should be loosely divided into the following areas for revision:
(a) the objectives of your study
(b) the methods you used
(c) the observations you made – with illustrations if relevant
(d) the results obtained – with comments on their presentation
Always have an idea of what further work would be useful. Also pay attention to the need for statistical testing to ensure that the results you obtained were significant and not due to factors such as sampling error or bias.

## *Soil as an ecosystem*

Soil is a mixture of organic matter and mineral particles. It is the habitat for decomposers, detritus feeders and carnivores as well as the roots of green plants. Many of the stages in the cycling of matter take place in the soil.

### Soil composition and characteristics

*1. Mineral particles*
These include gravel, sand, silt, clay and mineral salts. They result from the weathering of rocks. The physical condition of a soil partly depends on its mineral components.

*2. Soil water*
Soil water forms a film around the soil particles. It contains soluble organic and inorganic mineral salts. Water moves up through the soil by capillarity. Hygroscopic water is chemically combined with clay particles and organic matter, and is therefore not available for plant use.

The water content of a soil sample can be estimated by:
(a) Allowing a weighed soil sample to dry to a constant weight in an oven at 110 °C.
(b) Reweighing the sample.

(c) Calculating the percentage of water in soil, i.e.

$$\frac{\text{loss in weight}}{\text{original fresh weight}} \times 100$$

The main reason for fluctuation of this value is rainfall differences.

*3. Soil air*

The air in the pore spaces between soil particles is continuous with the earth's atmosphere, and gaseous exchange occurs between the two. However, in the lower soil horizons the soil air has less oxygen and more carbon dioxide than atmospheric air. Waterlogged and marsh soils have no soil air.

*4. Soil pH*

Alkaline soils are usually chalky or limestone soils. Poorly drained, peaty and marshy soils are acid. Organisms often prefer a certain pH. For example, conifers grow in acid soils, whereas snails prefer an alkaline chalky soil.

Soil pH can be estimated by:

(a) Mixing a sample of soil with distilled water and barium sulphate and allowing it to settle for at least 15 minutes.
(b) Adding universal indicator paper. The colour obtained can then be compared with the pH value colour chart.

*5. Organic matter*

Organic matter in soils is in the form of humus (i.e. decomposing plant and animal remains). The decomposition is brought about by saprophytic micro-organisms. Humus is a colloidal organic material which has water absorbing properties and retains water by hygroscopic action. It improves sandy soils by its adhesive properties. Clay soil particles cling to the humus fibres.

The organic content of a soil can be estimated by:

(a) Oven-drying the soil sample (to drive off soil water) and putting a weighed sample in an evaporating basin.
(b) Heating strongly over a Bunsen burner. This oxidizes all the carbon-containing material.
(c) Weighing the cooled sample.
(d) Calculating the percentage of organic matter in the soil, i.e.

$$\frac{\text{loss in weight}}{\text{weight of original dry sample}} \times 100$$

*6. Soil drainage*

The water-holding capacity and drainage of a soil depends on the mineral content, air spaces and organic content.

Soil drainage can be compared as follows:

1. Equal volumes of the soil samples to be compared should be placed in filter-funnels containing a small plug of glass wool. The funnels are placed above measuring cylinders.
2. An equal quantity of water is poured into each funnel. The volume of water draining into the cylinders is noted. The amount which drains in a given time is an indication of the soil drainage and water-holding capacity.

Sandy soil exhibits rapid drainage, leaving the soil prone to drying out and erosion. Clay soil shows slow drainage, making it sticky and likely to drain in cakes.

### Soil organisms

Bacteria are the most common soil microbes (with approximately $1 \times 10^9$ per gram of soil). They may be photosynthetic and therefore act as producers, or chemosynthetic, such as the nitrifying bacteria which are important in the recycling of nitrogen. The decomposers are heterotrophic bacteria which feed saprophyticaly on a wide range of organic matter in detritus.

Fungi are abundant in acid soils, and are heterotrophic. They are particularly important in decomposing woody detritus.

Soil animals are conveniently grouped according to size:

1. MICROFAUNA: These are microscopic animals. All groups of Protozoa are common in most soils. The majority are primary consumers, feeding on the plentiful supply of soil bacteria.
2. MESOFAUNA: These animals are under 10 mm long. The most abundant are the nematodes. They may be detritus feeders or primary consumers. They frequently live in the roots of plants and act as vectors of viral diseases. The mesofauna also includes some of the many arthropods found in soils. Examples include springtails (wingless insects) which are detritus feeders, predatory spiders, which live on insect larvae, etc. near the surface of the soil, and mites (the most abundant) which may be detritus feeders, herbivores, carnivores or parasites.
3. MACROFAUNA: These are animals larger than 10 mm. Many are insects or insect larvae. They may be predators (e.g. ground beetles which prey on mites), primary consumers (e.g. leather jackets (crane-fly larvae) which feed on plant roots), or detritus feeders (e.g. woodlice).

Other soil macrofauna includes molluscs such as slugs and snails, which live off plant material, and annelids. The most common annelid is the earthworm, and there are 25 species in Britain. They are detritus feeders, feeding on partly decayed leaves which they drag into their burrows. This behaviour helps to mix the mineral particles of the soil with organic matter. Their burrows and movements help to aerate and drain the soil, and their excreta is rich in ammonia which improves soil fertility.

## Further reading


J. Cloudsley-Thompson, *Microecology*, Studies in Biology No. 6 (Arnold, 1967)

M. J. Delany, *The Ecology of Small Mammals*, Studies in Biology No. 51 (Arnold, 1974)

P. J. Edwards and S. D. Wratten, *Ecology of Insect–Plant Interactions*, Studies in Biology No. 121 (Arnold, 1980)

M. P. Hassell, *The Dynamics of Competition and Predation*, Studies in Biology No. 72 (Arnold, 1976)

R. M. Jackson and F. G. Raw, *Life in the Soil*, Studies in Biology No. 2 (Arnold, 1966)

J. Phillipson, *Ecological Energetics*, Studies in Biology No. 1 (Arnold, 1966)

M. E. Solomon, *Population Dynamics*, Studies in Biology No. 18, 2nd edition (Arnold, 1976)


## Related questions

**Question:**

(a) Explain what is meant by an ecosystem. **(5 marks)**

(b) Using named examples explain in detail the following:
  (i) habitat
  (ii) energy flow through an ecosystem
  (iii) ecological niche **(15 marks)**

[in the style of the London Board]

**Comments:**

It is essential to be able to clearly define, with examples, an ecosystem and all its components.

(a) An ecosystem can be considered as an area comprising a community of organisms interacting with each other in the biotic (living) environment and with the abiotic (non-living) environment. However, there is a minimum definition; 5 marks requires examples and a fuller account of the biotic and abiotic factors.

Examples of ecosystems range from the very small, e.g. a pool, to a large moorland. Biotic factors include feeding interrelationships, i.e. parasitism, predator–prey relations, symbiosis, etc. Abiotic factors can be divided into physical (temperature, light, substrate type), chemical (oxygen, pH, minerals), edaphic (factors related to soil type).

(b) Remember to use specific examples, and give *detailed* explanations.

(i) The term habitat means the place within the ecosystem where an organism lives, e.g. leaf-litter (fungi), crevice in a rotting log (woodlouse), sea-shore (*Carcinus* or shore crab). Obviously a habitat can be exploited by more than one individual or species.

(ii) See p. 437.

(iii) See p. 446. Remember a niche is a description of the role of an organism in the ecosystem.

**Question:**

A suspension of *Saccharomyces* (yeast) cells was added to a dilute sucrose solution at 25 °C. The mixture was gently agitated for 16 days and 10 cm³ (ml) samples were withdrawn each day and the number of organisms counted. On the fifth day a small quantity of a culture of the ciliate *Paramecium* was added. The results of the experiments are shown below.

| | *No. of organisms in 10 cm³ (ml) samples* | | | *No. of organisms in 10 cm³ (ml) samples* | |
|---|---|---|---|---|---|
| *Days* | *Yeast* | *Paramecium* | *Days* | *Yeast* | *Paramecium* |
| 1 | 20 | | 9 | 222 | 72 |
| 2 | 84 | | 10 | 218 | 138 |
| 3 | 224 | | 11 | 120 | 162 |
| 4 | 264 | | 12 | 84 | 96 |
| 5 | 266 | 30 | 13 | 180 | 54 |
| 6 | 224 | 150 | 14 | 178 | 90 |
| 7 | 114 | 168 | 15 | 120 | 144 |
| 8 | 154 | 76 | 16 | 60 | 120 |

(a) Plot a graph to show the number of organisms of *Saccharomyces* (yeast) and *Paramecium* in the sample during the period of the experiment. **(6 marks)**

(b) State *two* factors that might be responsible for the difference in population growth of the *Saccharomyces* (yeast) between days 2 and 3, and days 4 and 5. **(4 marks)**

(c) Outline the likely causes of the changes in the *Paramecium* population between (i) days 5 and 6 and (ii) days 7 and 8. **(4 marks)**

(d) Outline a likely cause of the change in the *Saccharomyces* (yeast) population between days 7 and 8. **(2 marks)**

**(Total 16 marks)**

[London, Jan. 1982, Paper 1]

**Comments:**

(a) Graph to show the number of organisms/10 cm³ sample during the period of the experiment.

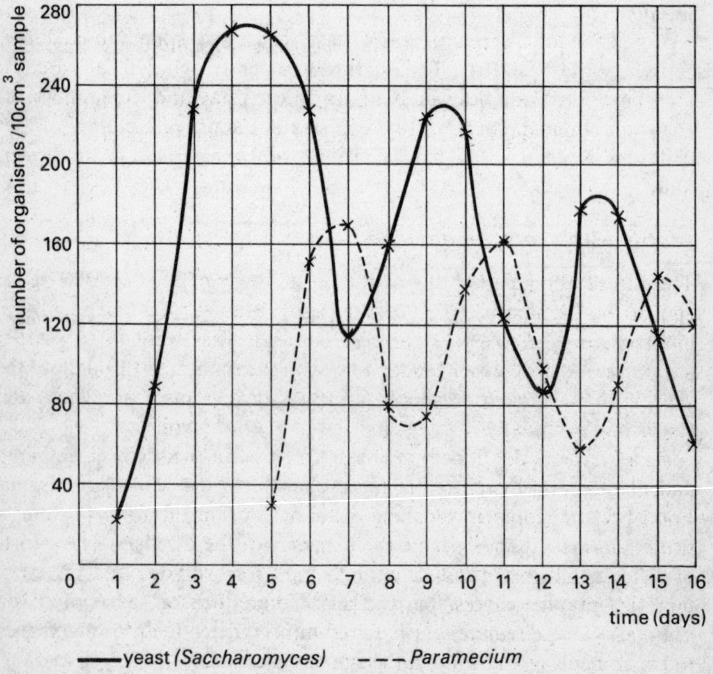
number of organisms /10cm³ sample
280
240
200
160
120
80
40
0
1 2 3 4 5 6 7 8 9 10 11 12 13 14 15 16
time (days)
yeast (Saccharomyces)
Paramecium

Maximum marks are easily attainable when plotting a graph of the data provided. As the numbers of yeast and *Paramecium* are fairly close, one $y$-axis scale can be used. The graph must be given a title, the axes labelled and the two curves made distinct in some way.

(b) Although there is an increase in the yeast population in both cases, there is obviously a more substantial increase from day 2 to 3. Remember that in the early stages of the experiment there is a plentiful supply of food (i.e. sucrose), whereas by day 4 there is a large population of yeast competing for a decreased food source. In addition, there would be a buildup of toxic waste. The mixture was agitated during the experiment indicating oxygen is available; however, if it should become limiting yeast is able to respire anaerobically.

(c) The form of the graph is typical of a predator–prey relationship. The *Paramecium* feeds on *Saccharomyces*. The answers to this section are based on this relationship.

(i) Between days 5 and 6 the *Paramecium* population increases fivefold owing to the abundant food source, i.e. large population of yeast.

(ii) Between days 7 and 8 there is a decrease in *Paramecium* numbers as the sudden decrease in the *Saccharomyces* numbers drastically reduces the food supply.

(d) During days 7 and 8 there is a dramatic decrease in the prey population, allowing the yeast to multiply in substantial numbers.

### *Man's effect on the environment*

The end of nomadic hunting as the normal way of life occurred at the end of the Pleistocene (25,000 years ago). Man turned to agricultural methods for a stable food source. Hunting was confined to smaller game, such as deer, which tended to stay in the same area throughout the year. A more stable food supply led to the development of villages and towns and eventually to cities and the industrial revolution.

As agriculture developed, man started to select the seeds he gathered and planted and therefore produced changes in the wild plant strains. Food became stored in silos and granaries and in the form of domesticated animals. Land became the property of the dwellers. The efforts of a few could then produce enough food for everyone and the communities became diversified and lived more densely associated (an average of 2 square miles are required to provide enough for one family to eat in hunting and food-gathering communities).

When families became sedentary more young survived and there was also a decrease in the mortality rate. About 25,000 years ago there were approximately 3 million people, 10,000 years ago about 5 million, and about 6,000 years ago the human population had increased enormously to more than 86 million. In 1974 there were approximately 4,000 million people on earth and the population is still increasing rapidly. However, growth is not increasing at a uniform rate in all parts of the world. For example, in Asia and Africa population doubling times range from 20 to 36 years, whereas in Britain it is nearer 200 years.

Overpopulation is one of the reasons why at least half the human population is undernourished. Another reason for lack of food is that a significant number of people eat foods high on the food chain, with livestock being fed on crops which could directly provide humans with protein.

To overcome these problems, in addition to stabilizing population numbers, e.g. by birth control programmes, new food sources and production methods must be investigated. These might include:

1. Growth of algae in large quantities as animal fodder.
2. Growth of micro-organisms, e.g. bacteria and yeasts (possibly on simple hydrocarbons) to provide protein as a source of food for domestic animals and humans.
3. Large-scale desalination of water to irrigate deserts for crop production.
4. Large-scale fish-farming to prevent exploitation of natural fish stocks.

### *Pollution*

All living organisms produce metabolic wastes which are discarded into the air, water and land. When man was nomadic, he left his excreta at various sites where it was broken down and recycled by living organisms. However, in densely populated cities sewage disposal is a major problem with waste often being discarded into rivers or the sea.

The pollution problem due to man's increasing numbers is also intensified by present-day technology which produces many waste products. The main types of pollution are:

1. Atmospheric pollution which is mainly due to the burning of fossil fuels.
2. Radioactive pollution; a consequence of using nuclear energy as a fuel and a weapon.

3. Pesticides, which are a pollutant resulting from man's attempt to increase crop yield to meet the human population's food demands.
4. Heavy metal pollution. This is largely a result of modern technology, e.g. lead in petrol and solder, mercury resulting from refining of ores, etc.

Some of the most common pollutants are outlined in Tables 12.2 to 12.5.

## Further reading

R. Arvill, *Man and Environment*, 3rd edition (Penguin, 1973)
K. Mellanby, *The Biology of Pollution*, Studies in Biology No. 38, 2nd edition (Arnold, 1980)
I. F. Spellerberg, *Ecological Evaluation for Conservation*, Studies in Biology No. 133 (Arnold, 1980)

## Related questions

**Question:**
Write a brief essay on the influence which man has on natural habitats. **(25 marks)**

[Southern Universities Joint Board, June 1979, Paper 2]

**Comments:**
The key words in this essay are 'influence' and 'natural habitats'. Influence encompasses both good *and* bad effects. 'Natural habitats' indicates that all aspects of the environment must be considered, i.e. aquatic, terrestrial and atmospheric environments.

An introduction should include an account of the development of a settled way of life leading to improvements in agriculture, an increase in population, and ultimately to technological advances. You could then explain how these trends lead to an increase in pollution through the use of pesticides and because of the by-products resulting from industrial processes (e.g. heavy metals, toxic gases, etc.) (see Tables 12.2–12.5). You could also mention that the increase in population numbers has led to an increased need for land to produce food, thus resulting in large-scale deforestation.

The essay should be balanced with an account of the methods man is using to conserve natural habitats. (See suggested essay plan on p. 464.)

*Table 12.2.* Pollution of the atmosphere

| *Pollutant* | *Source* | *Effect* |
| --- | --- | --- |
| Carbon dioxide | Burning of fuels | (i) May stimulate *extra* photosynthesis. However, this may only be a small increase since other factors, such as mineral availability and light, have a limiting effect on photosynthesis.<br>(ii) The 'greenhouse effect'. Increased concentration of carbon dioxide in the atmosphere has the effect of reducing the amount of heat which escapes into outer space. Ecologists have predicted that if carbon dioxide levels continue to increase, drastic events, such as melting of the polar ice-caps and subsequent flooding of land, could occur. |
| Sulphur dioxide | Burning of fuels and melting of ores | (i) Acid rain. Thirty million tonnes of sulphur dioxide are released into the atmosphere every year in Western Europe alone. The gas is carried towards Scandinavia in the prevailing winds, and there it combines with rain water to produce sulphuric acid as 'acid rain'. Acid rain is responsible for the death of large areas of coniferous forests in affected areas, and for the production of 'dead lakes' – lakes where the water is too acid for any animals or plants to live. |

| | | |
|---|---|---|
| | | (ii) Human health. Sulphur dioxide appears to slow down ciliary activity in the respiratory tract, leading to diseases such as bronchitis, pneumonia and heart failure. |
| Carbon monoxide | Incomplete combustion of fuels, cigarette smoke | Haemoglobin has a higher affinity for carbon monoxide than for oxygen. It combines with carbon monoxide to form the stable compound carboxyhaemoglobin, and this reduces the ability of the blood to supply oxygen to respiring tissues. |
| Nitrogen oxides (nitric oxide and nitrogen dioxide) | Car exhaust fumes | These substances play an important role in the formation of photochemical smog. In hot weather, nitrogen oxides become trapped in the layer of air just above the road surface, causing a severe reduction in visibility. Peroxyacyl nitrates in the smog cause lung and eye irritation, as well as damage to vegetation. |
| Particulate matter (smoke, soot, ash) | Burning of fuels and refining of ores | Cause smog and build-up of black soot on buildings. Also cause lung diseases. |

*Table 12.3*. Pollution by radiation

| *Pollutant* | *Source* | *Effect* |
|---|---|---|
| Electromagnetic waves (gamma rays) and particles (e.g. alpha and beta rays) | Natural radiation from rocks. Use and testing of nuclear bombs. Effluent from nuclear power-stations. For example in the 1960s there was an increase in the level of $^{90}Sr$ in milk due to testing of nuclear weapons by the USA and USSR. After the nuclear test-ban treaty, levels returned to normal. Accidents at nuclear power-stations may also result in large-scale contamination of the environment. The main risk is failure of the cooling system, e.g. the accidents at Windscale (now Sellafield) in Cumbria (1957), Three Mile Island, USA (1979) and Chernobyl, USSR (1986). Spent reactor cores, which are still radioactive, are presently dumped at sea or in underground containers. | (i) Radiation causes gene mutations which in turn will code for abnormal proteins and be passed on to future generations via the gametes. Chromosomes may become fragmented and cease to function properly.<br>(ii) People affected by very high doses of radiation, e.g. those at the nuclear bomb explosions in Hiroshima and Nagasaki, suffered dreadful effects including tumours, brain damage, leukaemia, fever, haemorrhages, vomiting and diarrhoea. |

| | | |
|---|---|---|
| Heat | Power-stations release heated effluents from their cooling systems | Eutrophication of rivers and lakes into which heated effluent pours. This occurs as follows. Excessive growth of phytoplankton (because of the increased heat) produces algal blooms. Some algae produce toxins which kill fish. When the algae die, the amount of dead organic matter in the water is increased, and hence the amount of oxygen consumed by the bacteria which break it down is also increased. This causes a reduction in the amount of oxygen available for other plant and animal life, which subsequently decrease in numbers. In the worst cases, rivers and lakes can be reduced to lifeless pools of anaerobic sludge. |

*Table 12.4.* Pollution by pesticides

| *Pollutant* | *Source* | *Effect* |
|---|---|---|
| Herbicides | In the manufacture of trinitrophenol derivatives, which are used in herbicides, a lethal chemical, dioxin, is produced. | Spontaneous abortion, haemorrhages, flooding of the lungs due to membrane irritation, blindness. The disaster at the Bhopal herbicide factory in India (1985) was due to leakage of such chemicals. Also the accident at Seveso in Italy (1978) caused hundreds of abortions. Dioxin is so lethal that ½ gram can kill 3,000 people. |
| | 'Agent Orange' (50% 2,4,5-trinitrophenol) is a potent herbicide. Eleven million gallons were sprayed on to Vietnamese forests during the 1970s. | Survivors have given birth to children with very serious malformations. |
| Fungicides | Main pollution due to mercury and copper components. See Table 12.5. | |
| Insecticides | Pyrethrum, nicotine and organophosphate insecticides are all biodegradable and pose no pollution hazard if used properly.<br>Organochlorine insecticides, e.g., DDT, persist for many years in the environment. Other examples include aldrin, dieldrin, heptachlor and lindane.<br>Widespread use of organochlorines in the hope of reducing the number of insect-borne diseases has been halted. Its failure was due to the occurrence of resistant insect species. Such species have multiplied and brought populations to record levels. | Organochlorine insecticides are very stable substances which persist in tissues for long periods of time. Therefore, high levels can accumulate. Experiments have shown that organochlorine insecticides cause birds to lay eggs with thin shells which are more likely to be broken during incubation and by predators. The reduction in numbers of flesh-eating birds, such as the peregrine falcon, is thought to be due to consumption of DDT along food chains.<br>In Canada the use of DDT had to be severely restricted because of the large numbers of wild animals which were being killed. |

*Table 12.5*. Pollution by heavy metals

| *Pollutant* | *Source* | *Effect* |
|---|---|---|
| Lead | Car exhaust fumes (lead is added to petrol to make it burn more efficiently). Disused lead mines (lead is washed from the mines into tributaries which feed main water supplies). Lead tanks and pipes used to supply drinking water in old houses. Lead solder used to seal canned food. Vegetables grown in polluted soils with high lead concentrations. | Inhaled or ingested lead is absorbed into the bones, liver and kidneys. It is thought to affect the mental development of children in urban areas. |
| Mercury | Burning of fuels and refining of ores.<br>Production of vinyl plastics and paper involves release of mercury pollutants which are often discharged into rivers. Mercury accumulates in the mud at the bottom of rivers and lakes where it is converted into methyl mercury by bacteria. This compound is highly toxic and is absorbed by aquatic organisms which may be part of a food web involving man.<br>Mercuric sprays are used to control fungal diseases of seeds and plants. Mercury in the soil enters plant roots and eventually reaches the fruits and leaves. | Absorbed into liver, kidney and bones. The devastating effects of mercury poisoning were evident in the 1950s in Minemata Bay, Japan. Hundreds of people were either killed or suffered severely owing to ingestion of mercury-infested shellfish. The shellfish were polluted by the mercuric discharge from a vinyl plastics factory. Symptoms included total paralysis and loss of all sensation. Children were born with cerebral palsy and mental retardation. |
| Copper | Copper-plating works, disused copper mines.<br>Fungicides containing copper. | Aquatic plants and fish killed. |
| Zinc | Zinc mines | Fish killed by relatively low levels (less than 1 p.p.m.) |
| Cadmium | Drainage water from zinc mines contains cadmium.<br>Smelting-works produce effluent which is used to flood paddy fields in Japan. | Inhaled in the lungs, it concentrates in the kidneys, causing renal failure and high blood pressure. Minerals withdrawn from bones causing severe pain. |

**Suggested essay plan:**

(a) The natural environment is a stable system provided it is not interferred with. An example of the ways in which the natural balance can be disturbed is shown by eutrophication of lakes through the use of fertilizers on neighbouring land or through phosphates being present in detergent-rich runoff. Lake Erie in Canada is now eutrophic with only a few pollution-tolerant species of flora and fauna.

(b) Increasing use of land for agriculture owing to the population explosion, i.e. deforestation, land overgrazed by domesticated animals leading to soil erosion.

(c) Introduction of crops not normally found in the habitat and their affects on the food webs in that area.

(d) Use of pesticides to increase crop yield. Their adverse effects (see Table 12.4). These should be related to soil, air and water.

(e) Vigorous hunting of animals for food, clothing, etc., thus disrupting the natural fauna and flora of the habitat.

(f) Pollution owing to use of machinery in food and energy production.

(g) Man's attempt to conserve the environment, e.g. replanting forests, conservation areas for fauna and flora, use of biological control of pests, as by introduction of myxomatosis virus in rabbits in Australia, more efficient food sources, e.g. fish farming, which do not destroy natural ecosystem.

Remember always to use a variety of *specific* examples. For every point made at least one example should be given.

# 13. Classification

There are two main purposes of classification:

1. Convenience – it is obviously practical to have a system by which any living organism can be identified according to its place in the relevant animal or plant kingdom.
2. To show relationships between living organisms. Our modern-day method of classification aims to group animals and plants according to their evolutionary development. This is more useful than earlier systems – like that of Aristotle, for example – which grouped together organisms with superficial characteristics (all worm-like organisms, or all four-legged creatures).

The basic building blocks of classification are species. A species is a group of individuals which have many characteristics in common and differ from all other forms in one or more ways. The individuals of a species are usually derived from a common ancestry. They can breed with each other to form viable offspring, but generally cannot breed successfully with the members of another species.

Living organisms are initially assigned to one of two main kingdoms: plants or animals. Each kingdom is subdivided as shown.

| | | |
|---|---|---|
| Kingdom | Plantae | Animalia |
| Phylum | Spermatophyta | Chordata |
| Class | Angiospermae | Mammalia |
| Order | Ranales | Primates |
| Family | Ranunculacea | Hominidae |
| Genus | *Ranunculus* | *Homo* |
| Species | *repens* | *sapiens* |

### *The main phyla*

Some unicellular flagellates can be either autotrophic or heterotrophic, depending on external conditions. This makes the distinction between unicellular algae and protozoans rather artificial. Some taxonomists argue that they should be grouped into a separate kingdom called the Protista.

Bacteria, due to their prokaryotic nature, are often classified in a separate kingdom together with the blue–green algae.

Viruses also pose a problem for taxonomists as they cannot be classified as either plants or animals. Some authorities would not even consider them to be living at all. Some viruses (e.g. potato spindle virus) are composed of a single strand of DNA with no outer protein coat. The limits of what is considered to be a living organism are most definitely stretched in such an example.

### *The plant kingdom*

| | |
|---|---|
| Algae: | single-celled or simple multicellular plants (Table 13.1) |
| Fungi: | simple plants without chlorophyll (Table 13.2) |
| Bryophyta: | green plants with simple leaves (Table 13.3) |
| Pteridophyta: | green plants with stems, roots and leaves but no flowers (Table 13.4) |
| Spermatophyta: | seed plants with flowers or cones (Table 13.5) |

### *The animal kingdom*

| | |
|---|---|
| Protozoa: | unicells (Table 13.6) |
| Coelenterata: | jellyfish and corals (Table 13.7) |
| Platyhelminthes: | flat-worms (Table 13.8) |
| Nematoda: | round-worms (Table 13.9) |
| Annelida: | segmented worms (Table 13.10) |
| Arthropoda: | joint-limbed animals with hard exoskeleton (Table 13.11) |
| Mollusca: | soft-bodied animals with shells (Table 13.12) |
| Echinodermata: | spiny-skinned, pentaradiate animals (Table 13.13) |
| Chordata: | possess a notochord at some stage in their life history (Table 13.14) |

## *Classification within the phyla*

*Table 13.1.* Classification of algae

**Phylum: Algae**

General features: The plant body is a thallus, i.e. not differentiated into leaves, roots or stems
Found in aquatic or moist areas
Size ranges from microscopic varieties to those which are many metres in length
All are autotrophic and contain chlorophyll
Additional pigmentation makes many of them coloured and forms a basis for their classification

| *Main classes* | *Distinguishing features* | *Examples* |
|---|---|---|
| Cyanophyta (blue–green algae) | Single cells or simple filaments and colonies encased in a gelatinous envelope. Ubiquitous distribution. | *Nostoc* |
| Rhodophyta (red algae) | Feather-like in shape, and red in colour owing to presence of carotenes and water-soluble phycobilins. Found on the coasts of rocky oceans. | *Polysiphonia* |
| Phaeophyta (brown algae and seaweeds) | Multicellular: size ranges from microscopic varieties to the giant kelps which are over 10 m in length. Brown colour is due to a brown pigment called fucoxanthin. Food is stored as a carbohydrate called laminarin. Usually found along coastlines. | *Laminaria* |
| Chlorophyta (green algae) | Unicellular and filamentous forms. Contain chlorophylls a and b and carotenes. Store food as starch. Common in fresh water. | *Spirogyra, Chlamydomonas, Ulothrix* |

*Table 13.2.* Classification of fungi

**Phylum: Fungi**

General features: Do not contain chlorophyll
- Saprophytic, parasitic or symbiotic
- Composed of hyphae which are grouped into a mycelium
- Coenocytic hyphae, i.e. are not composed of true cells but septa may be present along their length
- Cell walls are composed of chitin, hemicellulose, lipid and protein
- Classification mainly on reproductive structures

| *Main classes* | *Distinguishing features* | *Examples* |
|---|---|---|
| Phycomycetes (lower fungi) | Aseptate, vegetative mycelium. Asexual reproduction by means of sporangia or zoospores. Sexual reproduction by means of zygospores or oospores. | *Mucor* (bread mould), *Phytophthera* (potato blight), *Saprolegnia* (water mould) |
| Ascomycetes | Septate hyphae. Asexual reproduction by budding or production of conidia. Sexual reproduction by formation of ascospores. | *Saccharomyces* (yeast), *Claviceps* (ergot), *Penicillium*, *Neurospora*, *Monilinia* (brown rot fungus) |
| Basidio-mycetes | Septate hyphae often arranged into characteristic structures, e.g. mushrooms and toadstools, puff-balls. Sexual reproduction by means of basidiospores. | *Ustilago* (smut fungus), *Agaricus* (e.g. cultivated mushroom), *Amanita phalloides* (death cap) |

*Table 13.3.* Classification of bryophytes

**Phylum: Bryophyta**

General features: No filamentous forms – all bryophytes (except one stage in mosses) have flat, parenchymatous structures

Sexual reproduction by means of gametangia – multicellular structures surrounded by a layer of sterile cells.

Alternation of generations occurs with haploid gametophyte and diploid sporophyte

| *Main classes* | *Distinguishing features* | *Examples* |
|---|---|---|
| Hepaticae (liverworts) | Flat, ribbon-like thalli | *Riccia, Marchantia* |
| Musci (mosses) | Larger and more conspicuous than Hepaticae. Gametophyte has two structures – a filamentous protonema and small upright stems bearing spirally arranged leaves with rhizoids at the base. The sporophyte stage is composed of small shoots, each with a foot, seta and sporangium. | *Funaria, Polytrichum* |

*Table 13.4.* Classification of pteridophytes

**Phylum: Pteridophyta**

General features: Alternation of generations

Sporophyte is dominant stage and gametophyte often reduced to a small prothallus

Sporophyte has roots, stems, leaves and a simple vascular system

| *Main classes* | *Distinguishing features* | *Examples* |
|---|---|---|
| Lycopodiales (club mosses) | Upright stems possessing small, spirally arranged leaves. Sporophyte bears spores which are grouped on the tips of upright branches to form cones or strobili. | *Selaginella*<br>*Lycopodium* |
| Equisitales (horsetails) | Whorls of leaves arranged on upright stems with cones or strobili at the tips. Stem epidermis contains silica. | *Equisetum* |

*Table 13.4.* contd.

| *Main classes* | *Distinguishing features* | *Examples* |
|---|---|---|
| Filicales (true ferns) | Sporophyte has frond-like leaves with sporangia on the undersurface. Underground rhizomes present. Vascular tissue arranged into one or more vascular strands, phloem contains sieve elements but no companion cells. | *Dryopteris*, *Polypodium*, *Phyllitis* |

*Table 13.5.* Classification of spermatophytes

**Phylum: Spermatophyta (seed plants)**

General features: All vascular plants
Produce seeds
Heterosporous: male spore is pollen grain, female spore is embryo sac
Gametophyte is very reduced

| *Main classes* | *Distinguishing features* | *Examples* |
|---|---|---|
| Gymnospermae (naked seeds) | Seeds not enclosed in a fruit (i.e. seeds not surrounded by ovary). Mostly conifers (have cones instead of flowers). Leaves needle-shaped and evergreen. Vascular system composed of tracheids. | *Pinus* (pine)<br>*Larix* (larch)<br>*Sequoia* (redwood)<br>*Picea* (spruce)<br>*Pseudotsuga* (Douglas firs) |
| Angiospermae (flowering plants) | Seeds enclosed in some kind of fruit (i.e. the seeds are surrounded by an ovary). Produce flowers. Vascular system composed of vessels. | |

*Table 13.5.* contd

| *Main classes* | *Distinguishing features* | *Examples* |
|---|---|---|
| Subgroup: Monocotyledons | One cotyledon or seed leaf. Leaves show parallel venation. Flower parts in groups of three or multiples of three. Stem contains scattered vascular bundles. No cambium or secondary thickening. | Graminae (grasses): *Asparagus, Zea mays* (corn), Bamboo, Rice<br>Irises: *Freesia, Crocus, Gladiolus,*<br>Orchids |
| Subgroup: Dicotyledons | Two cotyledons or seed leaves. Leaves contain a network of veins. Flower parts in groups of four or five. Vascular system composed of cylindrically shaped vascular bundles. Cambium and secondary thickening present. | Magnoliaceae: Magnolia<br>Ranunculaceae: Buttercup<br>Cruciferae: Cabbage<br>Cauliflower<br>Solanaceae: Tomato<br>Potato<br>Peppers<br>Aubergine<br>Salicaceae: Willow<br>Poplar<br>Labiatae: Mint<br>Thyme<br>Sage<br>Rosaceae: Rose<br>Plum<br>Peach<br>Cucurbitae (gourds): Melon<br>Cucumber<br>Pumpkin<br>Leguminosae (pods): Pea<br>Bean<br>Peanut<br>Clover<br>Compositae: Chrysanthemum<br>Sunflower<br>Artichokes |

*Table 13.6.* Classification of protozoa

| | |
|---|---|
| **Phylum: Protozoa** | |
| General features: | Unicellular, microscopic |
| Locomotion: | Pseudopodia, flagella or cilia |
| Nutrition: | Holozoic, holophytic or saprophytic |
| Reproduction: | Asexual (budding, binary fission) |
| | Sexual (gamete formation, conjugation) |
| Excretion: | Direct diffusion to environment |
| Nervous system: | Non-existent |
| Circulatory system: | Non-existent (food and gases enter by direct diffusion) |

| *Main classes* | *Distinguishing features* | *Examples* |
|---|---|---|
| Sarcodina (Rhizopoda)* | Amoeba-like, pseudopodia | *Amoeba* |
| Mastigophora | Flagella | *Euglena* |
| Sporozoa | Spore formers – parasitic | *Plasmodium* (malaria) |
| Ciliata | Cilia | *Paramecium* |

* Two orders of the Sarcodina, the Radiolaria and the Foraminifera, possess hard outer shells. Many of these have fossilized beneath the sea, forming calcium carbonate based rocks – chalk and limestone. Subsequent changes in sea-level have exposed such rocks in which millions of these tiny fossils can still be observed.

*Table 13.7.* Classification of coelenterata

| | |
|---|---|
| **Phylum: Coelenterata** | |
| General features: | Lowest animals with definite tissues<br>Radially symmetrical: body consists of two layers of cells surrounding a tube-like gut<br>Life cycle involves two stages: an attached polyp stage and a free-living, umbrella-shaped, medusoid stage<br>Mostly marine |
| Locomotion: | Primitive skeleton containing lime and horn, with muscle fibres in the body wall |
| Nutrition: | Food is moved into the mouth by tentacles. The sac-like digestive cavity has no anus |
| Reproduction: | Alternation of generations: asexual budding occurs in the polyp stage, sexual reproduction involves gamete formation in simple gonads of the medusoid stage |
| Excretion: | By simple diffusion to the environment |
| Nervous system: | Nematocysts: stinging cells present in the body wall<br>Statocysts: granules which help in orientation |
| Circulatory system: | Non-existent |

| *Main classes* | *Distinguishing features* | *Examples* |
|---|---|---|
| Hydrozoa | Polyp and medusoid forms | *Hydra*, *Obelia*, *Physalia* |
| Scyphozoa | Mainly medusoid forms | *Aurelia* (jellyfish) |
| Anthozoa | All polyps commonly form reefs consisting of millions of tiny polyps | *Heliopora* (blue coral of Indo-Pacific), *Corallium* (red coral), *Oribicella* (reef-building coral from West Indies) |

*Table 13.8.* Classification of platyhelminthes

**Phylum: Platyhelminthes (flat-worms)**

| | |
|---|---|
| General features: | Soft, flat bodies with definite anterior and posterior ends. Bilaterally symmetrical. Body wall consists of three layers of cells with muscular tissue between them. No true segmentation |
| Locomotion: | Cestoids and Tremotoda have no locomotory organs, only hooks and suckers. Turbellaria have cilia |
| Nutrition: | Cestoida: no digestive system, food enters body by diffusion. Trematoda and Turbellaria: incomplete digestive system with a mouth but no anus |
| Reproduction: | Individuals are monoecious, containing reproductive apparatus for both sexes. Internal fertilization produces eggs which either develop directly into the adult, or may pass through many larval stages |
| Excretion: | Excretion is through flame cells which are connected to excretory ducts |
| Nervous system: | Consists of a pair of anterior ganglia or a nerve ring, connected to longitudinal nerve cords |
| Circulatory system: | Non-existent |

| *Main classes* | *Distinguishing features* | *Examples* |
|---|---|---|
| Turbellaria | Free-living flat-worms. Paired 'eyes' in head. Move by means of cilia | *Planaria* |
| Trematoda | Parasitic flat-worms | *Fasciola hepatica* (liver fluke of sheep) |
| Cestoida | Parasitic. No mouth or gut. Consists of 'segments' (proglottids) linked together No sense organs | *Taenia* (pork tape-worm) |

*Table 13.9.* Classification of nematodes

| | |
|---|---|
| **Phylum: Nematoda (round-worms)** | |
| General features: | Cylindrically shaped, bilaterally symmetrical, unsegmented. Covered in white cuticle |
| Locomotion: | Move by muscular contractions (longitudinal muscles only; no circular muscles) |
| Nutrition: | Complete digestive tract linking mouth to anus |
| Reproduction: | Separate sexes, sexual reproduction involving internal fertilization |
| Excretion: | Excretory canal empties into small excretory pore near the mouth |
| Nervous system: | Nerve ring around the oesophagus connects to six anterior and six posterior nerve cords |
| Circulatory system: | Non-existent |

| *Main class* | *Examples* |
|---|---|
| Nematoda | *Ascaris* (hookworm – a parasite of man's intestines)<br>*Wuchereria bancrotti* (a filarial worm responsible for elephantiasis) |

*Table 13.10*. Classification of annelids

| | |
|---|---|
| **Phylum: Annelida (segmented worms)** | |
| General features: | Bilaterally symmetrical. Body wall composed of three layers, segmented, and covered in a thin layer of collagen |
| Locomotion: | Contraction of muscles in body wall (longitudinal and circular muscles)<br>Also use of bristles called chaetae |
| Nutrition: | Complete digestive tract extending full length of body |
| Reproduction: | Some are monoecious; others have separate sexes and eggs develop into larval stage |
| Excretion: | One pair of nephridia per segment remove wastes from coelom and bloodstream directly to exterior |
| Nervous system: | A pair of cerebral ganglia connect to mid-ventral nerve chord which extends the full length of the body and has a ganglion and pairs of lateral nerves going to each segment. Sensory cells are also present, enabling perception of touch, taste and light |
| Circulatory system: | A closed circulatory system consisting of longitudinal blood vessels with branches to each segment. Blood plasma contains dissolved haemoglobin and free amoebocytes |

| *Main classes* | *Distinguishing features* | *Examples* |
|---|---|---|
| Oligochaeta | Few chaetae, reduced head, hermaphrodite | *Lumbricus terrestris* (earthworm) |
| Polychaeta (sandworms, tubeworms) | Many chaetae, have larval stage | *Sabella* (fanworm), *Nereis* (ragworm), *Arenicola* (lugworm) |
| Hirudinea (leeches) | Ectoparasites (have suckers) | *Hirudo medicinalis* (European medicinal leech) |

*Table 13.11.* Classification of arthropods

| | |
|---|---|
| **Phylum: Arthropoda (joint-footed animals)** | |
| General features: | Bilaterally symmetrical<br>Body wall has three main layers<br>Segmented bodies divided into three main regions – head, thorax and abdomen<br>Body is covered in a hardened exoskeleton containing chitin |
| Locomotion: | By means of jointed legs containing opposed sets of muscles |
| Nutrition: | Complete digestive tract, anterior mouth, posterior anus<br>Mouth parts may be adapted for either chewing or sucking |
| Reproduction: | Separate male and female sexes<br>Internal fertilization produces eggs which usually go through one or more larval stages before metamorphosis into the adult form |
| Excretion: | By means of coxal or green glands, or by means of Malpighian tubules joined to the gut. |
| Nervous system: | A pair of dorsal ganglia near the mouth, attached to a pair of ventral nerve chords with ganglia and lateral nerves going to each segment |
| Circulatory system: | Open circulatory system; heart supplies arteries with blood. Blood from the arteries passes into the body spaces (haemocoel) to supply nutrients to tissues and organs |
| Respiratory system: | By tracheae, gills or diffusion through the body surface |

| *Main classes* | *Distinguishing features* | *Examples* |
|---|---|---|
| Crustacea | Two pairs of antennae. Gills. | *Cambarus* (crayfish), *Daphnia* (water-flea), *Balanus* (barnacle), *Peneaus* (prawn) |
| Insecta | One pair of antennae. Three pairs of jointed legs.<br>Tracheae.<br>Two pairs of wings | Odonata: Dragonflies<br>Ephemeroptera: Mayflies<br>Orthoptera: Grasshoppers, crickets, locusts, cockroaches<br>Dermaptera: Earwigs<br>Plecoptera: Stoneflies<br>Isoptera: Termites<br>Anoplura: Lice<br>Hemiptera: Bugs<br>Corixidae: Waterboatmen, water-scorpions<br>Homoptera: Aphids, cicadas<br>Trichoptera: Caddis flies |

*Table 13.11.* contd.

| *Main classes* | *Distinguishing features* | *Examples* |
|---|---|---|
| | | Lepidoptera: Moths, butterflies<br>Diptera: Mosquitos, house-flies, *Drosophila*<br>Siphonaptera: Fleas<br>Coleoptera: Beetles, weevils<br>Hymenoptera: Wasps, ants, bees |
| Arachnida | No antennae or mandibles. Four pairs of jointed legs. One pair of chelicerae. One pair of pedipalps. Book lungs for respiration. | Spiders |
| Chilopoda | Flat body. 15–20 pairs of legs. Poisonous claws. | Centipedes |
| Diplopoda | Cylindrical body. Up to 200 pairs of short legs. | Millipedes |

*Table 13.12.* Classification of molluscs

| | |
|---|---|
| **Phylum: Mollusca** | |
| General features: | Bilaterally symmetrical<br>Unsegmented body wall has three layers<br>Epithelium is ciliated with mucous glands<br>Body usually enclosed in a shell |
| Locomotion: | By means of a ventral muscular foot – adapted for crawling, burrowing, etc. |
| Nutrition: | Full digestive tract with mouth and anus<br>Mouth has radula containing minute chitinous teeth<br>Digestive and salivary glands often present |
| Reproduction: | Separate male and female sexes<br>Gonads present<br>Internal or external fertilization |
| Excretion: | By means of nephridia (kidneys). |
| Nervous system: | Three pairs of ganglia, interlinked by nerves throughout the body<br>Have sense organs for touch, smell, taste and sight |
| Circulatory system: | Dorsal heart with one or two atria and one ventricle. Aorta and other vessels |
| Respiratory system: | Gills, or 'lungs' in mantle |

| *Main classes* | *Distinguishing features* | *Examples* |
|---|---|---|
| Gastropoda | Asymmetrical due to torsion. Body enclosed in spiral shell. Feed by radula. | *Buccinum* (whelk), *Haliotis* (limpet), *Helix* (snail) |
| Bivalvia | Symmetrical, soft body enclosed in a rigid shell of two parts. Filter-feeders. | *Anodonta* (clams), *Mytilus* (mussel), *Ostrea* (oyster) |

*Table 13.13.* Classification of echinoderms

| | |
|---|---|
| **Phylum: Echinodermata (spiny skins)** | |
| General features: | Radially symmetrical, often five-armed in adult stage<br>Body wall has three layers – all ciliated<br>No head or segmentation<br>Movable endoskeleton consists of plates with spiny surface |
| Locomotion: | Tube feet |
| Nutrition: | Complete digestive tract usually present |
| Reproduction: | Separate sexes<br>External fertilization produces eggs which develop into free-swimming larvae<br>Larvae metamorphose into adults |
| Excretion: | By outgrowths from the skin (called papullae) |
| Nervous system: | Circumoral ring and radial nerves |
| Circulatory system: | Radial circulatory system<br>Coelom ciliated and contains free amoebocytes |
| Respiratory system: | Gills and tube feet |

| *Main class* | *Distinguishing features* | *Examples* |
|---|---|---|
| Asteroidea | Central disc with five radial arms. | *Asterias* (starfish) |
| Echinoidea | Rounded bodies covered in bristles or spines. | *Arbacia* (sea-urchin) |

*Table 13.14.* Classification of chordates

**Phylum: Chordata**

| | |
|---|---|
| General features: | Bilaterally symmetrical<br>Three-layered body wall, segmented<br>Have three features which distinguish them from other animals: (i) a single, tubular dorsal nerve chord; (ii) gill slits in the pharynx; (iii) notochord. These features are always present in the embryo, but may disappear in the adult |
| Locomotion: | Usually by means of a supporting skeleton and muscle action |
| Nutrition: | Complete digestive tract |
| Reproduction: | Separate sexes<br>Fertilization internal or external depending on species |
| Excretion: | Usually well-developed nephridia |
| Nervous system: | Well-developed system with brain and many-branching lateral nerves |
| Circulatory system: | Dorsal heart with blood vessels containing blood |
| Respiratory system: | Gills, lungs |

**Sub-phylum: Craniata (vertebrates)**

| | |
|---|---|
| General features: | Notochord develops into vertebral column in adult. Cranium encloses brain |

| *Main classes* | *Distinguishing features* | *Examples* |
|---|---|---|
| Chondrichthyes (cartilaginous fishes) | Cartilaginous skeleton. No operculum or swim bladder. | *Odontaspididae ferox* (ragged-tooth shark), *Scyliorhinus* (dogfish) |
| Osteichthyes (bony fishes) | Bony skeleton and scales. Operculum and swim bladder. | *Clupea* (herring), *Perca* (perch), *Anguillidae* (eels) |
| Amphibia | Live partly in water and partly on land; therefore many adaptations to terrestrial life:<br>Moist glandular skin,<br>Limbs for walking and swimming,<br>Bony skeleton, | *Rana* (frog), *Xenopus* (clawed toad), *Triturus* (newt), *Salamandra* (salamander) |

*Table 13.14.* contd.

| *Main classes* | *Distinguishing features* | *Examples* |
|---|---|---|
| | Nostrils connected to mouth cavity, and valves which exclude water, Respiration by gills, lungs and skin. | *Rana* (frog), *Xenopus* (clawed toad), *Triturus* (newt), *Salamandra* (salamander) |
| Reptilia | Adapted for life on land: Dry, scaly skin to reduce moisture loss, Respiration by lungs, Internal fertilization, Large eggs with much yolk and tough leathery or limy shells. | *Chelonia* (turtles), *Testudo* (tortoise), *Lacerta* (lizard), *Naja naja* (Indian cobra), *Crocodylus* (crocodile) |
| Aves (birds) | Body covered with feathers. Limbs modified to form wings. Endothermic. Respiration by lungs. Beaks. High metabolic rate. | *Nyctea scadiaca* (snowy owl), *Picidae* (woodpecker), *Hirundo rustica* (song swallow) |
| Mammalia | Covered in hair or fur. Endothermic. Mammary glands to suckle the young. Respiration by lungs. Diaphragm separates lungs and heart from abdominal cavity. | *Rattus* (rat), *Homo sapiens* (man), *Ursus maritimus* (polar bear), *Delphinus delphis* (dolphin), *Canis lupus* (wolf), *Callorhinus ursinus* (northern fur seal), *Leo* (lion) |

## *Further reading*

H. Belcher and E. Swale, *A Beginner's Guide to Freshwater Algae* (Natural Environment Research Council, Institute of Terrestrial Ecology, HMSO, 1976)
H. E. Goto, *Animal Taxonomy*, Studies in Biology No. 143 (Arnold, 1982)
V. H. Heywood, *Plant Taxonomy*, Studies in Biology No. 5 (Arnold, 1976)
R. W. Horne, *The Structure and Function of Viruses*, Studies in Biology No. 95 (Arnold, 1978)
E. J. Marson, *Water Animal Identification Keys*, School Natural Science Society, Publication No. 8 (1974)
Reader's Digest Association, *Classification of the Animal Kingdom: An Illustrated Guide* (Hodder & Stoughton, 1972)
M. Robinson and J. Wiggins, *Animal Types – Invertebrates* (Hutchinson, 1971)
M. Robinson and J. Wiggins, *Animal Types – Vertebrates* (Hutchinson, 1973)
T. Savory, *Animal Taxonomy* (Heinemann, 1970)

## *Related questions*

**Question:**

(a) Each of the following lists of characteristics refers to a different organism. Identify the classificatory group to which each organism belongs, e.g. Mammalia.
   (i) Radially symmetrical, diploblastic.
   (ii) Acoelomate, triploblastic, flame cells present.
   (iii) Coelomate, bilaterally symmetrical, chitinous cuticle present.
   (iv) Scales, lungs and teeth present.
   (v) Scales, bone and gills present.
   (vi) Multicellular thallus, brown pigment (fucoxanthin) present.
   (vii) Sporophyte and gametophyte generations existing as independent autotrophs.
   (viii) Vessels present in vascular tissue, seed producing.
(b) State the principal difference between diploblastic and triploblastic organization.
(c) Briefly describe the formation of coelomic cavities during embryonic development.

[AEB, June 1981]

**Comments:**

(a) See pp. 467–482.
(b) Diploblastic organisms have two layers of cells in the body wall, whereas triploblastic organisms have three layers.
(c) See p. 360.

**Question:**
The diagrams below are of two invertebrates. Examine the diagrams carefully and then complete the table.

diagram 1

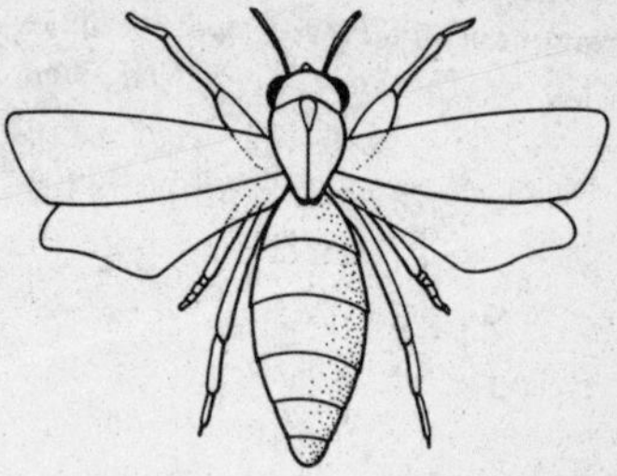

diagram 2

| | *Diagram 1* | *Diagram 2* |
|---|---|---|
| Name the phylum to which each organism belongs | | |
| For each phylum give *three* characteristic features not present in the other phylum. At least *three* of the *six* features must be evident on the diagrams. | 1 | 1 |
| | 2 | 2 |
| | 3 | 3 |

[In the style of AEB]

**Comments:**
See p. 477 and p. 479. Note that the features listed must be exclusive to that phylum and at least *three* of them visible on the diagrams.

**Question:**
(a) Give *three* reasons why a frog and a mammal are classified in the same phylum. **(3 marks)**
(b) Give *three* ways in which a frog and a lizard differ structurally from each other. **(3 marks)**

**(c)** State *three* features of birds that have contributed to the success of this group. **(3 marks)**

**(Total 9 marks)**

[London, June 1982, Paper 1]

**Comments:**

(a) See p. 481.

(b) See pp. 481–482. You should be able to deduce three structural differences between amphibians and reptiles.

(c) See p. 482. You should note that you are asked for features which have contributed to the success of the group, i.e. features which give them advantages over other groups.

# Index

Note: figures and tables, where separate from the main entry, are shown in **bold**